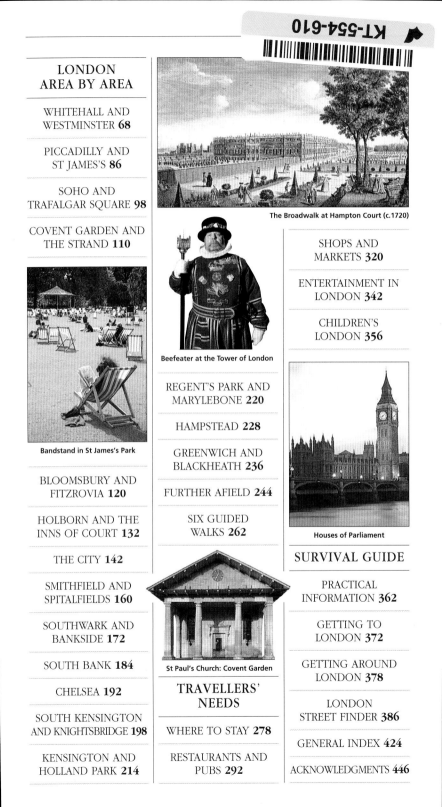

LONDON AREA BY AREA

The Broadwalk at Hampton Court (c.1720)

Bandstand in St James's Park

Beefeater at the Tower of London

St Paul's Church: Covent Garden

TRAVELLERS' NEEDS

Houses of Parliament

SURVIVAL GUIDE

HOW TO USE THIS GUIDE

This Eyewitness Travel Guide helps you get the most from your stay in London with the minimum of practical difficulty. The opening section, *Introducing London*, locates the city geographically, sets modern London in its historical context and describes the regular highlights of the London year. *London at a Glance* is an overview of the city's specialities. *London Area by Area* takes you round the city's areas of interest.

It describes all the main sights with maps, photographs and detailed illustrations. In addition, six planned walking routes take you to parts of London you might otherwise miss.

Well-researched tips on where to stay, eat, shop, and on entertainments are in *Travellers' Needs*. *Children's London* lists highlights for young visitors, and *Survival Guide* tells you how to do anything from posting a letter to using the Underground.

LONDON AREA BY AREA

The city has been divided into 16 sightseeing areas, each with its own section in the guide. Each section opens with a portrait of the area, summing up its character and history and listing all the sights to be covered. Sights are numbered and clearly located on an *Area Map*. After this comes a large-scale *Street-by-Street Map* focusing on the most interesting part of the area. Finding your way about the area section is made simple by the numbering system. This refers to the order in which sights are described on the pages that complete the section.

1 The Area Map
For easy reference, the sights in each area are numbered and located on an Area Map. *To help the visitor, the map also shows Underground and mainline stations.*

2 The Street-by-Street Map
This gives a bird's-eye view of the heart of each sight-seeing area. The most important buildings are picked out in stronger colour, to help you spot them as you walk around.

Photographs of facades and distinctive details of buildings help you to locate the sights.

A locator map shows you where you are in relation to surrounding areas. The area of the *Street-by-Street Map* is shown in red.

Colour-coding on each page makes the area easy to find in the book.

Sights at a Glance lists the sights in the area by category: Historic Streets and Buildings, Churches, Museums and Galleries, Monuments, Parks and Gardens.

The area covered in greater detail on the *Street-by-Street Map* is shaded red.

A suggested route for a walk takes in the most attractive and interesting streets in the area.

Numbered circles pinpoint all the listed sights on the area map. St Margaret's Church, for example, is **6**

Travel tips help you reach the area quickly by public transport.

St Margaret's Church is shown on this map as well.

Stars indicate the sights that no visitor should miss.

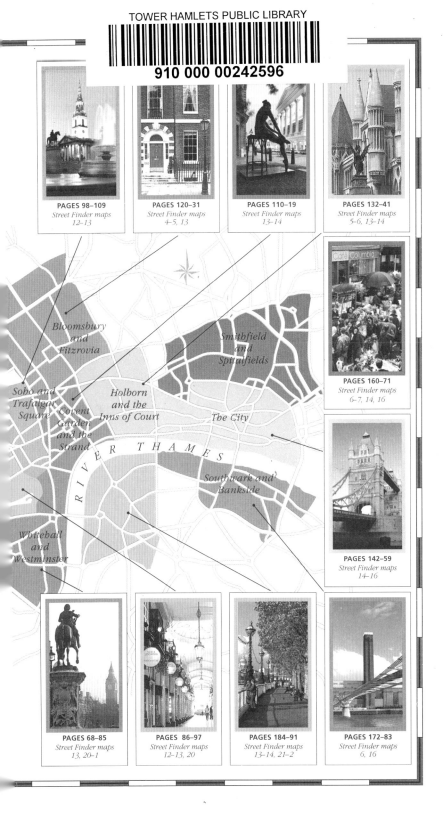

PAGES 98–109
*Street Finder maps
12–13*

PAGES 120–31
*Street Finder maps
4–5, 13*

PAGES 110–19
*Street Finder maps
13–14*

PAGES 132–41
*Street Finder maps
5–6, 13–14*

PAGES 160–71
*Street Finder maps
6–7, 14, 16*

PAGES 142–59
*Street Finder maps
14–16*

Bloomsbury
and
Fitzrovia

Smithfield
and
Spitalfields

Soho and
Trafalgar
Square

Holborn
and the
Inns of Court

The City

Covent
Garden
and the
Strand

RIVER THAMES

Southwark and
Bankside

Whitehall
and
Westminster

PAGES 68–85
*Street Finder maps
13, 20–1*

PAGES 86–97
*Street Finder maps
12–13, 20*

PAGES 184–91
*Street Finder maps
13–14, 21–2*

PAGES 172–83
*Street Finder maps
6, 16*

Before you book your London hotel, check out the **London HotelMap™** at LondonTown.com

Visually compare best hotel rates and availability

London's hotels all on one map

See real customer feedback on all hotels

View entertainment, including ticket prices and availability

Hotel Price Guarantee: "Find it cheaper, get £ 100"

www.londontown.com/hotels

EYEWITNESS TRAVEL

LONDON

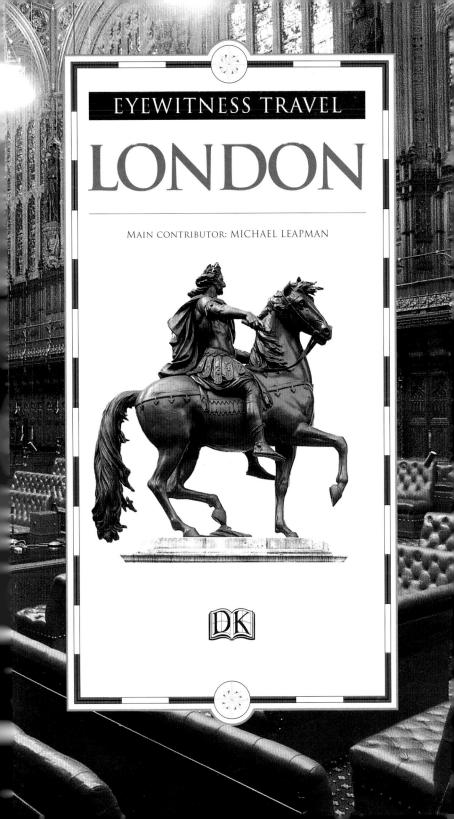

EYEWITNESS TRAVEL

LONDON

MAIN CONTRIBUTOR: MICHAEL LEAPMAN

DK

LONDON, NEW YORK,
MELBOURNE, MUNICH AND DELHI
www.dk.com

PROJECT EDITOR Jane Shaw

ART EDITOR Sally Ann Hibbard

EDITOR Tom Fraser

DESIGNERS Pippa Hurst, Robyn Tomlinson

DESIGN ASSISTANT Clare Sullivan

CONTRIBUTORS
Christopher Pick, Lindsay Hunt

PHOTOGRAPHERS
Max Alexander, Philip Enticknap,
John Heseltine, Stephen Oliver

ILLUSTRATORS
Brian Delf, Trevor Hill, Robbie Polley

This book was produced with the assistance
of Websters International Publishers.

Reproduced by Colourscan (Singapore)
Printed and bound by South China Printing Co. Ltd., China.

First published in Great Britain in 1993
by Dorling Kindersley Limited
80 Strand, London WC2R 0RL

Reprinted with revisions 1994, 1995, 1996, 1997, 1999, 2000 (twice), 2001,
2002, 2003, 2004, 2005, 2006, 2007, 2008, 2009, 2010, 2011 (001)

Copyright 1993, 2011 © Dorling Kindersley Limited, London
A Penguin Company

ISBN 978-1-40535-840-8

Front cover main image: The London Eye

MIX
Paper from
responsible sources
FSC

◁ Interior of the House of Lords in Westminster

CONTENTS

Portrait of Sir Walter Raleigh (1585)

INTRODUCING LONDON

Bedford Square doorway (1775)

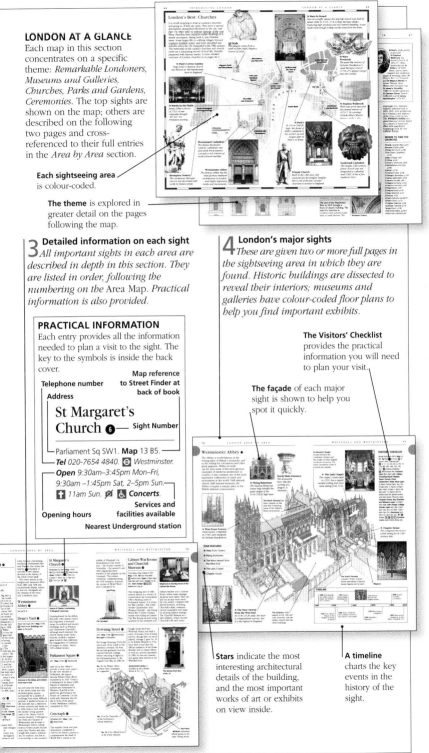

LONDON AT A GLANCE

Each map in this section
concentrates on a specific
theme: *Remarkable Londoners,
Museums and Galleries,
Churches, Parks and Gardens,
Ceremonies.* The top sights are
shown on the map; others are
described on the following
two pages and cross-
referenced to their full entries
in the *Area by Area* section.

Each sightseeing area
is colour-coded.

The theme is explored in
greater detail on the pages
following the map.

3 Detailed information on each sight

*All important sights in each area are
described in depth in this section. They
are listed in order, following the
numbering on the* Area Map. *Practical
information is also provided.*

PRACTICAL INFORMATION

Each entry provides all the information
needed to plan a visit to the sight. The
key to the symbols is inside the back
cover.

Telephone number

Address

**Map reference
to Street Finder at
back of book**

St Margaret's
Church ⑥ — Sight Number

Parliament Sq SW1. **Map** 13 B5.
Tel 020-7654 4840. ⊖ *Westminster.*
Open 9:30am–3:45pm Mon–Fri,
9:30am –1:45pm Sat, 2–5pm Sun.
🕇 11am Sun. 🚫 & *Concerts.*

Opening hours

**Services and
facilities available**

Nearest Underground station

4 London's major sights

*These are given two or more full pages in
the sightseeing area in which they are
found. Historic buildings are dissected to
reveal their interiors; museums and
galleries have colour-coded floor plans to
help you find important exhibits.*

The Visitors' Checklist
provides the practical
information you will need
to plan your visit.

The façade of each major
sight is shown to help you
spot it quickly.

Stars indicate the most
interesting architectural
details of the building,
and the most important
works of art or exhibits
on view inside.

A timeline
charts the key
events in the
history of the
sight.

INTRODUCING
LONDON

FOUR GREAT DAYS IN LONDON

For things to see and do, visitors to London are spoiled for choice. Whether here for a short stay or just wanting a flavour of this great city, you need to make the most of your time. So here are ideas for four days of sightseeing and fun. You'll

Chinatown dragon

find suggestions on what to see, how to get about and where to eat. Each of these four itineraries follows a theme and sights are reachable using public transport. Prices include travel, food and admission. Family prices are for two adults and two children.

Café at the National Portrait Gallery with a view of Trafalgar Square

HISTORY AND CULTURE

- **Art at the National Gallery**
- **Coffee with a view**
- **Houses of Parliament**
- **Buckingham Palace**

TWO ADULTS allow at least £140

Morning

Start the day by 10am in **Trafalgar Square** *(see p102).* This is when the **National Gallery** *(see p104)* opens. Give yourself an hour and a half. The gallery is free, but visitors are encouraged to make a donation. After, go for a coffee at the Portrait Restaurant on the top floor of the neighbouring **National Portrait Gallery** *(see p102),* which has a great view over Trafalgar Square and Nelson's column. Set off down Whitehall to Parliament Square, a 15-minute walk that may be extended by the passing distractions of Horse Guard's Parade, **Banqueting House** *(see p80)* and **Downing Street** *(see p75).* See the **Houses of Parliament** *(see pp72–3)* before visiting the next highlight, the

fabulous **Westminster Abbey** *(see pp76–7).* There are a number of inexpensive lunch spots around St James's Park tube station, such as Fuller's Ale and Pie House, 33 Tothill Street. Or go to the more pricey but attractive Inn the Park (must book; 020 7451 9999) by the lake in **St James's Park** *(see p93).*

Afternoon

On the far side of St James's Park is **Buckingham Palace** *(see p94–5).* The Queen's Gallery has changing exhibitions and you can buy regal souvenirs in its shop. For tea, head up past St James's Palace to Piccadilly. You may not feel you can afford a £70 tea for two at the Palm Court at the **Ritz** *(see p91)* but there are several cafés and patisseries nearby, such as Richoux at 172 Piccadilly. For the best evening entertainment, get tickets for a West End play or show. These should be booked in advance *(see p343),* although last-minute tickets are sometimes on sale at the theatre box offices.

SHOPPING IN STYLE

- **St James's – shopping with history**
- **Old Bond Street for style**
- **Browse in trendy Covent Garden and the Piazza**

TWO ADULTS allow at least £55

Morning

Start in Piccadilly and **St James's Street,** *(see pp88–9),* home of suppliers to royalty and historic fashion leaders: John Lobb, the bootmaker is at No. 9 and Lock the hatter at 6. Turn right into Jermyn Street for high-class men's tailors such as Turnbull & Asser and New Lingwood, outfitters to Eton College. Floris the perfumer at 89 was founded in 1730 and the cheese shop Paxton & Whitfield at 93 has been here since 1740. Walk through Piccadilly Arcade to **Fortnum & Mason** *(see p313),* where the Fountain Tea Room can provide refreshment before

Historic shopping mall at the Burlington Arcade, Piccadilly

The Queen's House, Greenwich

buying souvenirs. Stop in at **The Royal Academy** *(see p90)* and the **Burlington Arcade** *(see p91)*, before heading up **Old** and **New Bond** streets *(see p322)*, the smartest shopping address in town, with art galleries, antiques and designer shops. Try South Molton Street for women's fashion and Oxford Street for **Selfridge's** massive department store *(see p321)*.

Afternoon
Head to **Covent Garden** *(see p114)*. Take a look around **London's Transport Museum** *(see p114)*, then wander the Piazza and streets to the north; Floral Street is renowned for high fashion. Check out alternative lifestyles in **Neal's Yard** *(see p115)*. Stop for tea in Paul Bakery and Café at 29 Bedford Street.

THE GREAT OUTDOORS

- **Sail to the Cutty Sark**
- **Ponds and a memorial in the Palace gardens**
- **Tea at Kensington Palace**

TWO ADULTS allow at least £100

Morning
Take a one-hour boat trip from Westminster Millennium Pier to **Greenwich** *(see pp238–43)*. A morning is easily passed at this UNESCO World Heritage Site. There's the Maritime Museum, Royal Observatory, Queen's House, and Cutty Sark. Have a snack

lunch overlooking the river at the historic **Trafalgar Tavern** *(see p242)*.

Afternoon
Return by boat and head to **Kensington Gardens** *(see p210)*. Admire the boats on the Round Pond, and see what's on at the **Serpentine Gallery** *(see p210)*. To the east is the Princess Diana Memorial Fountain. By the Long Water is the delightful statue of Peter Pan. Visit **Kensington Palace** *(see p210)*, Princess Diana's former home. Have tea in the Palace's Orangery Tea Room.

A FAMILY FUN DAY

- **Take the kids to the Tower**
- **Messing about in boats**
- **Enjoy the undersea world**
- **Hit Chinatown**

FAMILY OF 4 allow at least £300.

Predators at the London Aquarium

Morning
Head to the **Tower of London** *(see pp154-7)*, London's top visitor attraction and an

established family favourite. Book tickets to avoid the queue. The fascinating castle and Crown Jewels will take at least a couple of hours to explore. For lunch, head across Tower Bridge to **St Katherine's Dock** *(see p158)* where, among an eclectic collection of boats, there are several attractive places to eat, including the Dickens Inn for snacks or a full meal.

Afternoon
The **London Eye** is a thrilling trip above the city on the South Bank *(see p189*; phone bookings can be made on 0870 5000 600).

Nearby there is plenty of other entertainment, especially in **County Hall** *(see p188)*, which was the seat of London's local government for more than 60 years. This leisure complex has the Sea Life London Aquarium. Younger people will enjoy the video games and simulators, bowling alley and bumper cars in the Namco Station. Afterwards, take the tube to **Chinatown** *(see p108)*, situated in and around Gerrard Street, which with its many superb restaurants, colourful shops and vibrant streetlife, is always lively and interesting. Go for an early Chinese supper of *dim sum*, or small dishes. If the kids are still up for entertainment, end the day at a film in one of the many luxurious cinemas in and around Leicester Square.

The gracious sweep of the Diana Memorial Fountain, Hyde Park

Putting London on the Map

London, the capital of the United
Kingdom, is a city of over seven million
people covering 620 sq miles (1,606 sq
km) of southeast England. It is built on
the River Thames and is at the centre of
the UK road and rail networks. From
London visitors can easily reach the
country's other main tourist attractions.

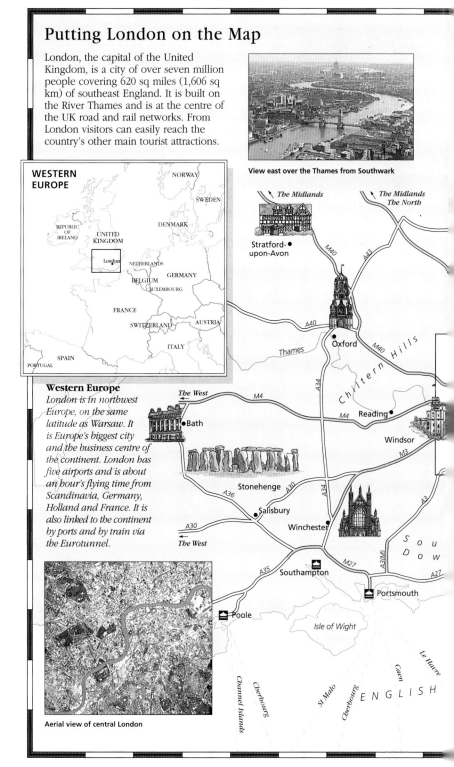

View east over the Thames from Southwark

WESTERN EUROPE

NORWAY

SWEDEN

DENMARK

REPUBLIC OF IRELAND   UNITED KINGDOM

London   NETHERLANDS

GERMANY

BELGIUM

LUXEMBOURG

FRANCE

SWITZERLAND   AUSTRIA

ITALY

SPAIN

PORTUGAL

Western Europe
*London is in northwest
Europe, on the same
latitude as Warsaw. It
is Europe's biggest city
and the business centre of
the continent. London has
five airports and is about
an hour's flying time from
Scandinavia, Germany,
Holland and France. It is
also linked to the continent
by ports and by train via
the Eurotunnel.*

The Midlands   *The Midlands
The North*

Stratford-
upon-Avon

M40   A43

A40

Thames

Oxford   M40   Chiltern Hills

The West   M4

Bath   M4   Reading

Windsor

M3

Stonehenge   A30   A34   A3

A36

Salisbury

A30   Winchester   S o u
D o w

The West

A35   Southampton   M27   A3(M)   A27

Poole   Portsmouth

Isle of Wight

Le Havre

Caen

Channel Islands   Cherbourg   St Malo   Cherbourg   E N G L I S H

Aerial view of central London

Greater London

London has gradually swallowed up many of the towns and villages that once surrounded it. Now it is an urban sprawl bounded by the M25 ring road. Details of important sights outside central London but within the M25 are on pages 244–61.

GREATER LONDON

Watford
Enfield
Barnet
Edgware
Finchley
Walthamstow
Ruislip
see next page
Barking
Uxbridge
Dagenham
Ealing
London City
Heathrow
Greenwich
Richmond
Dartford
Wandsworth
Bexley
Staines
Dulwich
Wimbledon
Beckenham
Kingston
Upon-
Thames
Bromley
Orpington
Epsom

0 kilometres   10

0 miles   5

The North
The Midlands
Cambridge

Luton
Stansted

Felixstowe
Harwich

Hook of Holland
(Hoek van Holland)

London City

Heathrow

M25
A127
Southend-on-Sea
Sheerness

North   Downs
Canterbury
Ramsgate

Gatwick
Folkestone   Dover
Dunkirk
Calais

Channel Tunnel
Boulogne
Calais

Tunbridge
Wells

Strait of Dover

Brighton   Newhaven

Boulogne

FRANCE

Le Havre

Dieppe

CHANNEL

KEY

	Greater London
	Ferry port
	Airport
	Motorway
	Major road (A-road)

0 kilometres   25

0 miles   15

Central London

Most of the sights described in this book lie within 14 areas of central London, plus two outlying districts of Hampstead and Greenwich. Each area has its own chapter. If time is short, you may decide to restrict yourself to the five areas that contain most of London's famous sights: Whitehall and Westminster, The City, Bloomsbury and Fitzrovia, Soho and Trafalgar Square, and South Kensington.

Tower of London
For much of its 900-year history the Tower was an object of fear. Its bloody past and the Crown Jewels make it a major attraction (see pp154–7).

National Gallery
This gallery has over 2,300 paintings, and the collection is particularly strong on Dutch, early Renaissance Italian and 17th-century Spanish painting (see pp104–7).

Natural History Museum
Life on earth and the earth itself are vividly explored at the museum, through a combination of interactive techniques and traditional displays (see pp208–9).

KEY

▢	Major sight
⊖	Underground Station
⇄	Railway Station
⊟	River Boat Pier
ℹ	Tourist information

0 kilometres 1

0 miles 0.5

Buckingham Palace
The office and home of the monarchy, the palace is also used for state occasions. The State Rooms open to the public in the summer (see pp94–5).

Museum of London
This museum, on the edge of the Barbican complex in the City, provides a lively account of London life from prehistoric times to the present day (see pp166–7).

Houses of Parliament
The Palace of Westminster has been the seat of the two Houses of Parliament, called the Lords and the Commons, since 1512 (see pp72–3).

TIIE IIISTORY OF LONDON

In 55 BC, Julius Caesar's Roman army invaded England, landed in Kent, and marched north-west until it reached the broad River Thames at what is now Southwark. There were a few tribesmen living on the opposite bank but no major settlement. However, by the time of the second Roman invasion 88 years later, a small port and mercantile community had been established here. The Romans bridged the river and built their administrative headquarters on the north bank, calling it Londinium – a version of its old Celtic name.

The dragon: the City of London's symbol

LONDON AS CAPITAL

London was soon the largest city in England and, by the time of the Norman Conquest in 1066, it was the obvious choice for national capital.

Settlement slowly spread beyond the original walled city, which was virtually wiped out by the Great Fire of 1666. The post-Fire rebuilding formed the basis of the area we know today as the City but, by the 18th century, London enveloped the

settlements around it. These included the royal city of Westminster which had long been London's religious and political center. The explosive growth of commerce and industry during the 18th and 19th centuries made London the biggest and wealthiest city in the world, creating a prosperous middle class who built the fine houses that still grace parts of the capital. The prospect of riches also lured millions of the dispossessed from the countryside and from abroad. They crowded into insanitary dwellings, many just east of the City, where docks provided employment.

By the end of the 19th century, 4.5 million people lived in inner London and another 4 million in its immediate vicinity. Bombing in World War II devastated many central areas and led to substantial rebuilding in the second half of the 20th century, when the docks and other Victorian industries disappeared.

The following pages illustrate London's history by giving snapshots of significant periods in its evolution.

A map of 1580 showing the City of London and, near the lower left corner, the City of Westminster

◁ A 15th-century manuscript showing the Tower of London with London Bridge in the background

Roman London

1st-century Roman coin

When the Romans invaded Britain in the 1st century AD, they already controlled vast areas of the Mediterranean, but fierce opposition from local tribes (such as Queen Boudicca's Iceni) made Britain difficult to control. The Romans persevered however, and had consolidated their power by the end of the century. Londinium, with its port, developed into a capital city; by the 3rd century, there were some 50,000 people living here. But, as the Roman Empire crumbled in the 5th century, the garrison pulled out, leaving the city to the Saxons.

EXTENT OF THE CITY

☐ *125 AD*   ☐ *Today*

Public Baths
Bathing was an important part of Roman life. This pocket-sized personal hygiene kit (including a nail pick) and bronze pouring dish date from the 1st century.

Site of present-day Museum of London

Roman fort

Site of present-day St Paul's

Basilica

Forum

LONDINIUM
Roman London was an important centre on the site of the present-day City (see pp142–159). On the Thames, it was in a good position to trade with the rest of the Empire.

Temple of Mithras
Mithras protected the good from evil. This 2nd-century head was in his temple.

Forum and Basilica
About 200 m (600 ft) from London Bridge was the forum (the chief market and meeting place) and the basilica (the town hall and court of justice).

TIMELINE

55 BC Julius Caesar invades Britain	**200** City wall built	**410** Roman troops begin to leave
AD 61 Boudicca attacks		
100	**200**	**300** **400** **50**
AD 43 Claudius establishes Roman London and builds the first bridge		

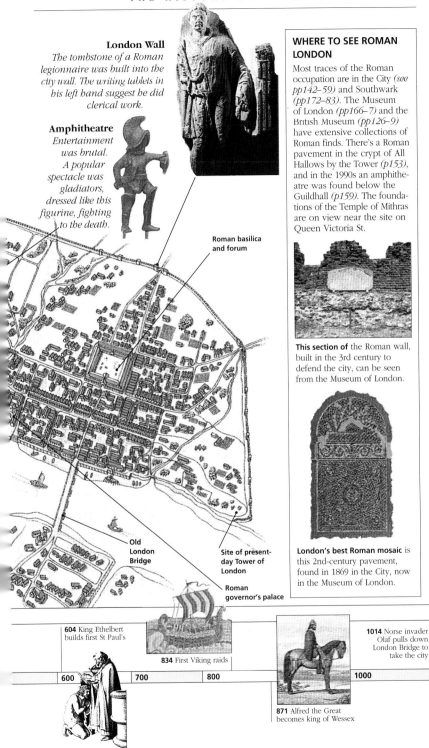

London Wall
The tombstone of a Roman legionnaire was built into the city wall. The writing tablets in his left hand suggest he did clerical work.

Amphitheatre
Entertainment was brutal. A popular spectacle was gladiators, dressed like this figurine, fighting to the death.

Roman basilica and forum

Old London Bridge

Site of present-day Tower of London

Roman governor's palace

WHERE TO SEE ROMAN LONDON

Most traces of the Roman occupation are in the City (see pp142–59) and Southwark (pp172–83). The Museum of London (pp166–7) and the British Museum (pp126–9) have extensive collections of Roman finds. There's a Roman pavement in the crypt of All Hallows by the Tower (p153), and in the 1990s an amphitheatre was found below the Guildhall (p159). The foundations of the Temple of Mithras are on view near the site on Queen Victoria St.

This section of the Roman wall, built in the 3rd century to defend the city, can be seen from the Museum of London.

London's best Roman mosaic is this 2nd-century pavement, found in 1869 in the City, now in the Museum of London.

604 King Ethelbert builds first St Paul's

834 First Viking raids

1014 Norse invader Olaf pulls down London Bridge to take the city

600   700   800   1000

871 Alfred the Great becomes king of Wessex

Medieval London

The historic division between London's centres of commerce (the City) and government (Westminster) started in the mid-11th century when Edward the Confessor established his court and sited his abbey *(see pp76–9)* at Westminster. Meanwhile, in the City, tradesmen set up their own institutions and guilds, and London appointed its first mayor. Disease was rife and the population never rose much above its Roman peak of 50,000. The Black Death (1348) reduced the population by half.

EXTENT OF THE CITY

◼ *1200*   ☐ *Today*

LONDON BRIDGE
The first stone bridge was built in 1209 and lasted 600 years. It was the only bridge across the Thames in London until Westminster Bridge (1750).

The Chapel of St Thomas, erected the year the bridge was completed, was one of its first buildings.

Iron railings

St Thomas à Becket
As Archbishop of Canterbury he was murdered in 1170, at the prompting of Henry II with whom he was quarrelling. Thomas was made a saint and pilgrims visited his Canterbury shrine.

Houses and shops projected over both sides of the bridge. Shopkeepers made their own merchandise on the premises and lived above their shops. Apprentices did the selling.

Dick Whittington
The 15th-century trader was thrice mayor of London (see p39).

The piers were made from wooden stakes rammed into the river bed and filled with rubble.

Stag Hunting
Such sports were the chief recreation of wealthy landowners.

The arches ranged from 4.5 m (15 ft) to 10 m (35 ft) in width.

TIMELINE

1042 Edward the Confessor becomes king	**1086** Domesday Book, England's first survey, published	**1191** Henry Fitzalwin becomes London's first mayor	**1215** King John's Magna Carta gives City more powers

1050	1100	1150	1200	1250

1066 William I crowned in Abbey

1065 Westminster Abbey completed

1176 Work starts on the first stone London Bridge

1240 First parliament sits at Westminster

Chivalry

Medieval knights were idealized for their courage and honour. Edward Burne-Jones (1833–98) painted George, patron saint of England, rescuing a maiden from this dragon.

Geoffrey Chaucer
The poet and customs controller (see p39), is best remembered for his Canterbury Tales *which creates a rich picture of 14th-century England.*

WHERE TO SEE MEDIEVAL LONDON

There were only a few survivors of the Great Fire of 1666 (*see pp24–5*) – the Tower (*pp154–7*), Westminster Hall (*p72*) and Westminster Abbey (*pp76–9*), and a few churches (*p46*). The Museum of London (*pp166–7*) has artifacts, while Tate Britain (*pp82–5*) and the National Gallery (*pp104–7*) have paintings. Manuscripts, including the Domesday Book, are found at the British Library (*p125*).

The Tower of London was started in 1078 and became one of the few centres of royal power in the largely self-governing City.

A 14th-century rose window is all that remains of Winchester Palace near the Clink on Bankside (*see p182*).

Plan of the Bridge
The bridge had 19 arches to span the river making it, for many years, the longest stone bridge in England.

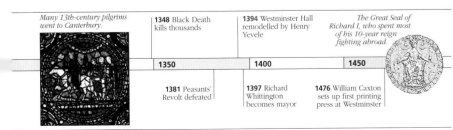

Many 13th-century pilgrims went to Canterbury.

1348 Black Death kills thousands

1394 Westminster Hall remodelled by Henry Yevele

The Great Seal of Richard I, who spent most of his 10-year reign fighting abroad.

1350   **1400**   **1450**

1381 Peasants' Revolt defeated

1397 Richard Whittington becomes mayor

1476 William Caxton sets up first printing press at Westminster

Elizabethan London

In the 16th century the monarchy was stronger than ever before. The Tudors established peace throughout England, allowing art and commerce to flourish. This renaissance reached its zenith under Elizabeth I as explorers opened up the New World, and English theatre, the nation's most lasting contribution to world culture, was born.

Curtain

SHAKESPEARE'S GLOBE
Elizabethan theatres were built of wood and only half covered, so plays had to be cancelled in bad weather.

EXTENT OF THE CITY
▨ 1561   ☐ Today

A balcony on the stage was part of the scenery.

The apron stage had a trap door for special effects.

Death at the Stake
The Tudors dealt harshly with social and religious dissent. Here Bishops Latimer and Ridley die for so-called heresy in 1555, when Elizabeth's sister, Mary I, was queen. Traitors could expect to be hung, drawn and quartered.

In the pit, below the level of the stage, commoners stood to watch the play.

Hunting and Hawking
Popular 16th-century pastimes are shown on this cushion cover.

TIMELINE

1536 Henry VIII's second wife, Anne Boleyn, executed

1535 Sir Thomas More executed for treason

1553 Edward dies, succeeded by his sister Mary I

1530

1550

Rat catchers, and other pest controllers, could not prevent epidemics of plague.

1534 Henry VIII breaks with the Roman Catholic church

1547 Henry dies, succeeded by his son Edward VI

The galleries were for rich theatre-goers who could watch from the comfort of seats.

Elizabeth I
The "Virgin Queen" sat for this portrait to celebrate victory over the Spanish in 1588.

Tilting Spurs
The aim of this highs-peed sport, popular among noblemen, was to knock opponents off their horses.

Steps allowed tiered seating.

Astronomical Clock
Made in 1540 at Hampton Court, it shows the sun moving round the earth.

Audience entrance

WHERE TO SEE ELIZABETHAN LONDON

The Great Fire of 1666 wiped out the City. Fortunately, Middle Temple Hall (*see p139*), Staple Inn (*p141*) and the Lady Chapel inside Westminster Abbey (*pp76–9*) were beyond its reach. The Museum of London (*pp166–7*), Victoria and Albert (*pp202–5*), and Geffrye Museums (*p248*) have fine furniture and artefacts. Further afield are Hampton Court (*pp254–7*) and Sutton House (*p248*).

Elizabeth I watched *Twelfth Night* by Shakespeare under the hammerbeam roof of Middle Temple Hall in 1603.

The Parr Pot, now in the Museum of London, was made by Venetian craftsmen in London in 1547.

63 Plague weeps Europe

1570 Francis Drake makes first voyage to the West Indies

1584 Walter Raleigh's first attempt to colonize America

1588 Drake defeats Spanish Armada

1591 First play by Shakespeare produced

| 1560 | 1570 | 1580 | 1590 |

1558 Mary I's death makes Elizabeth queen

Gloves made from imported silk and velvet

1603 Elizabeth dies, James I accedes

Restoration London

Civil War had broken out in 1642 when the mercantile class demanded that some of the monarch's power be passed to Parliament. The subsequent Commonwealth was dominated by Puritans under Oliver Cromwell. The Puritans outlawed simple pleasures, such as dancing and theatre, so it was small wonder that the restoration of the monarchy under Charles II in 1660 was greeted with rejoicing and the release of pent-up creative energies. The period was, however, also marked with two major tragedies: the Plague (1665) and the Great Fire (1666).

EXTENT OF THE CITY
▪ 1680   ☐ Today

St Paul's was destroyed in the fire that raged as far west as Fetter Lane *(map 14 E1).*

London Bridge itself survived, but many of the buildings on it were burned down.

Oliver Cromwell
He led the Parliamentarian army and was Lord Protector of the Realm from 1653 until his death in 1658. At the Restoration, his body was dug up and hung from the gallows at Tyburn, near Hyde Park (see p207).

Charles I's Death
The king was beheaded for tyranny on a freezing day (30 January 1649) outside Banqueting House (see p80).

Charles I
His belief in the Divine Right of Kings angered Parliament and was one of the causes of civil war.

TIMELINE

1623 Shakespeare's First Folio published

1625 James I dies, succeeded by his son Charles I

1642 Civil war starts when Parliament defies king

1620   1640   1650

Feathered helmet worn by Royalist cavaliers.

1605 Guy Fawkes leads failed attempt to blow up the King and Parliament

1649 Charles I executed, Commonwealth established

Newton's Telescope
*Physicist and astronomer
Sir Isaac Newton
(1642–1727) dis-
covered the law
of gravity.*

Samuel Pepys
*His exuberant diaries
tell us much about
courtly life of the time.*

**The Tower of
London** was
just out of the
fire's reach.

THE GREAT FIRE OF 1666
*An unidentified Dutch artist painted this view of the fire
that burned for 5 days, destroying 13,000 houses.*

The Plague
*During 1665, carts
collected the dead
and took them to
communal graves
outside the city.*

WHERE TO SEE
RESTORATION LONDON
Wren's churches and his
St Paul's Cathedral *(see p47
and pp148–51)* are, with
Inigo Jones's Banqueting
House *(p80)*, London's most
famous 17th-century build-
ings. Other fine examples are
Lincoln's Inn *(p136)* and
Cloth Fair *(p165)*. The Museum
of London *(pp166–7)* has a
period interior. The British
Museum *(pp126–9)* and the
V&A *(pp202–205)* have
numerous pottery, silver and
textile collections.

Ham House *(p252)* was built in
1610 but much enlarged later in
the century. It has the finest
interior of its time in England.

Peter Paul Rubens painted the
ceiling in 1636 for Inigo
Jones's Banqueting House
(p80). This is one of its panels.

1664–5 Plague kills
100,000

1666 Great Fire

1685 Charles II dies,
Catholic James II
becomes
king

1692 First
insurance market
opens at Lloyd's

1660   **1670**   **1690**

1660 Monarchy
restored under
Charles II

*A barber's bowl
made by London
potters in 1681.*

1688 James ousted in
favour of Protestant
William of Orange

1694 First Bank of England set up by
William Paterson

Georgian London

The foundation of the Bank of England in 1694 spurred the growth of London and, by the time George I came to the throne in 1714, it had become an important financial and commercial centre. Aristocrats with West End estates began laying out elegant squares and terraces to house newly-rich merchants. Architects such as the Adam brothers, John Soane and John Nash developed stylish medium-scale housing. They drew inspiration from the great European capitals, as did English painters, sculptors, composers and craftsmen.

**George I
(reigned
1714–27)**

EXTENT OF THE CITY

▨ 1810   ☐ Today

Manchester Square was laid out in 1776–8.

Portman Square was on the town's outskirts when it was started in 1764.

Great Cumberland Place
Built in 1790, it was named after a royal duke and military commander.

Grosvenor Square
Few of the original houses remain on one of the oldest and largest Mayfair squares (1720).

Docks
Purpose-built docks handled the growth in world trade.

TIMELINE

1714 George I becomes king

1727 George II becomes king

1759 Kew Gardens established

1768 Royal Academy of Art established

| 1720 | | 1740 | | 1760 | | 177 |

1717 Hanover Square built, start of West End development

1729 John Wesley (1703–91) founds the Methodist Church

1760 George III becomes king

John Nash
Stylish Nash shaped 18th-century London with variations on Classical themes, such as this archway in Cumberland Terrace, near Regent's Park.

GEORGIAN LONDON

The layout of much of London's West End has remained very similar to how it was in 1828, when this map was published.

WHERE TO SEE GEORGIAN LONDON

The portico of the Theatre Royal Haymarket *(see pp344–5)* gives a taste of the style of fashionable London in the 1820s. In Pall Mall *(p92)* Charles Barry's Reform and Travellers' Clubs are equally evocative. Most West End squares have some Georgian buildings, while Fournier Street *(p170)* has good small-scale domestic architecture. The Victoria and Albert Museum (V&A, *pp202–5*) has silver, as do the London Silver Vaults *(p141)*, where it is for sale. Hogarth's pictures, at Tate Britain *(pp82–5)* and Sir John Soane's Museum *(pp136–7)*, show the social conditions.

This English long-case clock (1725), made of oak and pine with Chinese designs, is in the V&A.

Captain Cook
This Yorkshire-born explorer discovered Australia during a voyage round the world in 1768–71.

Berkeley Square
Built in the 1730s and 1740s in the grounds of the former Berkeley House, several characteristic original houses remain on its west side.

Ironwork
Crafts flourished. This ornate railing is on Manchester Square.

Signatories of the American Declaration of Independence

1776 Britain loses American colonies with Declaration of Independence

1802 Stock Exchange formally established

1811 George III goes mad, his son George is made Regent

1820 George III dies, Prince Regent becomes George IV

1830 George IV dies, brother William IV is king

1829 London's first horse bus

1800 **1810** **1820** **1830**

Victorian London

Much of London today is Victorian. Until the early 19th century, the capital had been confined to the original Roman city, plus Westminster and Mayfair to the west, ringed by fields and villages such as Brompton, Islington and Battersea. From the 1820s these green spaces filled rapidly with terraces of houses for the growing numbers attracted to London by industrialization. Rapid expansion brought challenges to the city. The first cholera epidemic broke out in 1832, and in 1858 came the Great Stink, when the smell from the Thames became so bad that Parliament had to go into recess. But Joseph Bazalgette's sewerage system (1875), involving banking both sides of the Thames, eased the problem.

Queen Victoria in her coronation year (1838)

EXTENT OF THE CITY

☐ *1900*   ☐ *Today*

The building was 560 m (1,850 ft) long and 33 m (110 ft) high.

Nearly 14,000 exhibitors came from all over the world, bringing more than 100,000 exhibits.

Pantomime
The traditional family Christmas entertainment – still popular today (see p344) – started in the 19th century.

Soldiers marched and jumped on the floor to test its strength before the exhibition opened.

Massive elm trees growing in Hyde Park were left standing and the exhibition was erected around them.

The Crystal Fountain was 8 m (27 ft) high.

Carpets and stained glass were hung from the galleries.

TIMELINE

1837 Victoria becomes queen

1851 Great Exhibition | *Season ticket for Great Exhibition*

A Wedgwood plate in typically florid Victorian style

1861 Prince Albert dies

1860

1836 First London rail terminus opens at London Bridge

1840 Rowland Hill introduces the Penny Post

1863 Metropolitan Railway, world's first underground system, is opened

1870 First Peabody Buildings, to house the poor, built in Blackfriars Road

Railways
By 1900 fast trains, such as this Scotch Express, were crossing the country.

WHERE TO SEE VICTORIAN LONDON

Grandiose buildings best reflect the spirit of the age, notably the rail termini, the Kensington Museums *(see pp198–213)* and the Royal Albert Hall *(p207)*. Leighton House *(p218)* has a well-preserved interior. Pottery and fabrics are in the Victoria and Albert Museum, and London's Transport Museum *(p114)* has buses, trams and trains.

Telegraph
Newly invented communications technology, like this telegraph from 1840, made business expansion easier.

Crystal Palace
Between May and October 1851, six million people visited Joseph Paxton's superb feat of engineering. In 1852 it was dismantled and reassembled in south London where it remained until destroyed by fire in 1936.

The Victorian Gothic style suited buildings like the Public Record Office in Chancery Lane.

THE GREAT EXHIBITION OF 1851
The exhibition, held in the Crystal Palace in Hyde Park, celebrated industry, technology and the expanding British Empire.

Formal Dress
Under Victoria, elaborate men's attire was replaced by more restrained evening wear.

A special box for carrying top hats

1889 London County Council (LCC) established

1891 First LCC public housing built, in Shoreditch

1899 First motor buses introduced

1901 Queen Victoria dies, Edward VII accedes

1880   **1890**   **1900**

1890 First electric Underground line, from Bank to Stockwell, opens

Commemorative fan for the Boer War, which ended in 1903

London Between the World Wars

The society that emerged from World War I grasped eagerly at the innovations of early 20th-century London – the motor car, the telephone, commuter transport. The cinema brought transatlantic culture, especially jazz and swing music. Victorian social restraints were discarded as people flocked to dance in restaurants, clubs and dance halls. Many left the crowded inner city for new suburban estates. Then came the 1930s global Depression, whose effects had barely worn off when World War II began.

Art Deco china by Clarice Cliff

EXTENT OF THE CITY

▨ *1938*   ☐ *Today*

Formal evening wear, including hats for both sexes, was still compulsory when going to smart West End night spots.

Commuting
London's new outer suburbs were made popular by the under-ground railway. In the north was "Metroland", named after the Metro-politan line which penetrated Hertfordshire.

High Fashion
The sleek flowing new styles contrasted with the fussy elaboration of the Victorians and Edwardians. This tea gown is from the 1920s.

A LONDON STREET SCENE
Maurice Greiflenhagen's painting (1926) captures the bustle of London after dark.

TIMELINE

Medals, like this from 1914, were struck during the campaign for women's votes.

1921 North Circular Road links northern suburbs

1922 First BBC national radio broadcast

1910

1920

1910
George V succeeds Edward VII

Cavalry was still used in the Middle Eastern battles of World War I (1914–18).

Early Cinema
London-born Charlie Chaplin (1889–1977), seen here in City Lights, was a popular star of both silent and talking pictures.

Seven new theatres were built in central London from 1924 to 1931.

George VI
Oswald Birley painted this portrait of the king who became a model for wartime resistance and unity.

Early motor buses had open tops, like the old horse-drawn buses.

Throughout the period newspaper circulations increased massively. In 1930 *The Daily Herald* sold 2 million copies a day.

Communications
The radio provided home entertainment and information. This is a 1933 model.

WORLD WAR II AND THE BLITZ
World War II saw large-scale civilian bombing for the first time, bringing the horror of war to Londoners' doorsteps. Thousands were killed in their homes. Many people took refuge in Underground stations and children were evacuated to the safety of the country.

WOMEN OF BRITAIN
COME INTO THE FACTORIES

As in World War I, women were recruited for factory work formerly done by men who were away fighting.

Bombing raids in 1940 and 1941 (the Blitz) caused devastation all over the city.

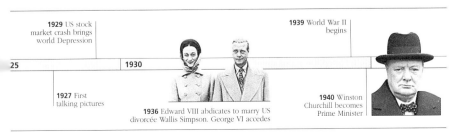

1929 US stock market crash brings world Depression

25

1930

1927 First talking pictures

1936 Edward VIII abdicates to marry US divorcée Wallis Simpson. George VI accedes

1939 World War II begins

1940 Winston Churchill becomes Prime Minister

Postwar London

Much of London was flattened by World War II bombs. Afterwards, the chance for imaginative rebuilding was missed – some badly designed postwar developments are already being razed. But, by the 1960s, London was such a dynamic world leader in fashion and popular music that *Time* magazine dubbed it "swinging London". Skyscrapers sprang up, but some stayed empty as 1980s boom gave way to 1990s recession.

EXTENT OF THE CITY

▨ *1959*	☐ *Today*

The Beatles
The Liverpool pop group, pictured in 1965, had rocketed to stardom two years earlier with songs of appealing freshness and directness. The group symbolized carefree 1960s London.

Margaret Thatcher
Britain's first woman Prime Minister (1979–90) promoted the market-led policies that fuelled the 1980s boom.

Festival of Britain
After wartime, the city's morale was lifted by the Festival, marking the 1851 Great Exhibition's centenary (see pp28–9).

The Royal Festival Hall (1951) was the Festival's centrepiece and is still a landmark (*see p188*).

Telecom Tower (1964), at 189 m (620 ft) high, dominates the Fitzrovia skyline.

The Lloyd's Building (1986) is Richard Rogers' Post-Modernist emblem (*see p159*).

TIMELINE

1948 Olympic Games held in London	**1952** George VI dies; his daughter Elizabeth II accedes	*Minis became a symbol of the 1960s; small and manoeuvrable, they typified the go-as-you-please mood of the decade.*					
1945	**1950**	**1955**	**1960**	**1965**	**1970**	**1975**	**198**
1951 Festival of Britain	**1954** Food rationing, introduced during World War II, abolished		**1963** National Theatre founded at the Old Vic		**1977** Queen's Silver Jubilee; work starts on Jubilee line underground	**1982** Last of the London docks closes
1945 End of World War II			**1971** New London Bridge built			

Docklands Light Railway
In the 1980s, new, driverless trains started to transport people to the developing Docklands.

POST-MODERN ARCHITECTURE

Since the 1980s architects have reacted against the stark shapes of the Modernists. Landmarks like the "Gherkin" by David Foster now dominate the skyline and architects like Richard Rogers emphasize structural features in their designs. Others, Terry Farrell for example, adopt a more playful approach using pastiches of Classical features such as columns.

Canada Tower (1991) is London's tallest building. It was designed by César Pelli *(see p249).*

Charing Cross (1991) has Terry Farrell's glasshouse on top of the Victorian station *(see p119).*

YOUTH CULTURE

With their new mobility and spending power, young people began to influence the development of British popular culture in the years after World War II. Music, fashion and design were increasingly geared to their rapidly changing tastes.

Punks were a phenomenon of the 1970s and 1980s. Their clothes, music, hair and habits were designed to shock.

The Prince of Wales
As heir to the throne, he is outspokenly critical of much of London's modern architecture. He prefers more traditional styles.

1984 Thames Barrier completed	1986 Greater London Council abolished	*Vivienne Westwood's clothes won prizes in the 1980s and 1990s.*	2000 Ken Livingstone becomes London's first directly elected mayor	*The observation wheel, the London Eye, was raised during the spring of 2000.*

1985	1990	1995	2000	2005	2010	2015	2020

1985 Ethiopian famine leads to Live Aid relief campaign	1992 Canary Wharf development opens	1997 Princess Diana's funeral procession brings London to a halt	2005 London shaken by bombs on the public transport system	2012 London is set to host the Olympic games

Kings and Queens in London

London has been the royal capital of England since 1066, when William the Conqueror began a tradition of holding coronations in Westminster Abbey. Since then, successive kings and queens have left their mark on London and many of the places described in this book have royal associations: Henry VIII hunted at Richmond, Charles I was executed on Whitehall and the young Queen Victoria rode on Queensway. Royalty is also celebrated in many of London's traditional ceremonies – for more details on these turn to pages 52–5.

1413–22 Henry V

1509–47 Henry VIII

1399–1413 Henry IV

1485–1509 Henry VII

1553–8 Mary I

1066–87 William the Conqueror

1087–1100 William II

1100–35 Henry I

1135–54 Stephen

1327–77 Edward III

1483–5 Richard III

1050	1100	1150	1200	1250	1300	1350	1400	1450	1500	1550
NORMAN		PLANTAGENET					LANCASTER	YORK	TUDOR	
1050	1100	1150	1200	1250	1300	1350	1400	1450	1500	1550

1154–89 Henry II

1189–99 Richard I

1199–1216 John

1216–72 Henry III

1307–27 Edward II

1272–1307 Edward I

1461–70 and 1471–83 Edward IV

1422–61 and 1470–1 Henry VI

1547–53 Edward VI

1377–99 Richard II

Matthew Paris's 13th-century chronicle showing Kings Richard I, Henry II, John and Henry III.

1483 Edward V

1685–8 James II

1689–1702 William and Mary

1702–14 Anne

1714–27 George I

1660–85 Charles II

1603–25 James I

1936 Edward VIII

1837–1901 Victoria

1901–10 Edward VII

1727–60 George II

1952– Elizabeth II

1600	1650	1700	1750	1800	1850	1900	1950	2000	2050
STUART		HANOVER				WINDSOR			
1600	1650	1700	1750	1800	1850	1900	1950	2000	2050

1830–37 William IV

1649–60 The Commonwealth, established by Oliver Cromwell

1936–52 George VI shown on the George Medal

1820–30 George IV

1910–36 George V

1625–49 Charles I

1558–1603 Elizabeth I

1760–1820 George III

LONDON AT A GLANCE

There are nearly 300 places of interest described in the Area by Area section of this book. These range from the magnificent National Gallery *(see pp104–7)* to gruesome Old St Thomas' Operating Theatre *(p176)*, and from ancient Charterhouse *(p164)* to modern Canary Wharf *(p249)*. To help you make the most of your stay, the following 18 pages are a time-saving guide to the best London has to offer. Museums and galleries, churches, and parks and gardens each have a section, and there are guides to remarkable Londoners and ceremonies in London. Each sight mentioned is cross-referenced to its own full entry. Below are the ten top tourist attractions to start you off.

LONDON'S TOP TEN TOURIST ATTRACTIONS

St. Paul's
See pp148–51.

Hampton Court
See pp254–7.

Changing of the Guard
Buckingham Palace, see pp94–5.

British Museum
See pp126–9.

National Gallery
See pp104–7.

Westminster Abbey
See pp76–9.

Madame Tussaud's
See p224.

Victoria and Albert Museum
See pp202–5.

Houses of Parliament
See pp72–3.

Tower of London
See pp154–7.

Remarkable Londoners

London has always been a gathering place for the most prominent and influential people of their times. Some of these figures have come to London from other parts of Britain or from countries further afield; others have been Londoners, born and bred. All of them have left their mark on London, by designing great and lasting buildings, establishing institutions and traditions, and by writing about or painting the city they knew. Most of them have also had an influence on their times that spread out from London to the rest of the world.

Caricature of the Duke of Wellington

Venus Venticordia by Dante Gabriel Rossetti

ARCHITECTS AND ENGINEERS

John Nash's Theatre Royal Haymarket (1821)

A number of people who built London still have works standing. Inigo Jones (1573–1652), London-born, was the father of English Renaissance architecture. He was also a landscape painter and a stage designer. Jones lived and worked at Great Scotland Yard, Whitehall, then the residence of the royal architect – the post in which he was later succeeded by Sir Christopher Wren (1632–1723).

Wren's successors as the prime architects of London were his protégé Nicholas Hawksmoor (1661–1736) and James Gibbs (1682–1754). Succeeding generations each produced architects who were to stamp their genius on the city: in the 18th century the brothers Robert (1728–92) and James Adam (1730–94), then John Nash (1752–1835), Sir Charles Barry (1795–1860), Decimus Burton (1800–81), and the Victorians Alfred Waterhouse (1830–1905),

Norman Shaw (1831–1912), and Sir George Gilbert Scott (1811–78). The engineer Sir Joseph Bazalgette (1819–91) built London's sewer system and the Thames Embankment.

ARTISTS

Painters in London, as elsewhere, often lived in enclaves, for mutual support and because they shared common priorities. During the 18th century, artists clustered around the court at St James's

to be near their patrons. Thus both William Hogarth (1697–1764) and Sir Joshua Reynolds (1723–92) lived and worked in Leicester Square, while Thomas Gainsborough (1727–88) lived in Pall Mall. (Hogarth's Chiswick house was his place in the country.) Later, Cheyne Walk in Chelsea, with its river views, became popular with artists, including the masters J M W Turner (1775–1851), James McNeill Whistler (1834–1903), Dante Gabriel Rossetti (1828–82), Philip Wilson Steer, (1860–1942) and the sculptor

HISTORIC LONDON HOMES

Dickens Museum

Four writers' homes that have been recreated are those of the romantic poet **John Keats** (1795–1821); the historian **Thomas Carlyle** (1795–1881); the lexicographer **Dr. Samuel Johnson** (1709–84); and the prolific and popular novelist **Charles Dickens** (1812–70). The house that the architect **Sir John Soane** (1753–1837) designed for himself remains largely as it was when he died, as does the house where the psychiatrist **Sigmund Freud** (1856–1939) settled after fleeing from the Nazis before World War II.

Apsley House, on Hyde Park Corner, was the residence of the **Duke of Wellington** (1769–1852), hero of the Battle of Waterloo. The life and music of Baroque composer **George Frideric Handel** (1685–1759) are on show at his former home in Mayfair. Finally, the rooms of Sir Arthur Conan Doyle's fictional detective **Sherlock Holmes** have been created in Baker Street.

Carlyle's House

PLAQUES

All over London the former homes of well-known figures are marked by plaques. Look out for these, especially in Chelsea, Kensington, and Mayfair, and see how many names you recognize.

No. 3 Sussex Square, Kensington

No. 27b Canonbury Square, Islington

No. 56 Oakley Street, Chelsea

Sir Jacob Epstein (1880–1959). Augustus John (1879–1961) and John Singer Sargent (1856–1925) had studios in Tite Street. John Constable (1776–1837) is best known as a Suffolk painter but lived for a while at Hampstead, from where he painted many fine views of the heath.

WRITERS

Geoffrey Chaucer (c.1345–1400), author of *The Canterbury Tales*, was born in Upper Thames Street, the son of an innkeeper. Both the playwrights William Shakespeare (1564–1616) and Christopher Marlowe (1564–93) were associated with the theaters in Southwark, and may have lived nearby.

The poets John Donne (1572–1631) and John Milton (1608–74) were both born in Bread Street in the City. Donne, after a profligate youth, became Dean of St Paul's. The diarist Samuel Pepys (1633–1703) was born off Fleet Street.

The young novelist Jane Austen (1775–1817) lived briefly off Sloane Street, near the Cadogan Hotel, where the flamboyant Oscar Wilde (1854–1900) was arrested in 1895 for homosexuality. Playwright George Bernard Shaw (1856–1950) lived at No. 29 Fitzroy Square in Bloomsbury. Later the same house was home to Virginia Woolf (1882–1941) and

George Bernard Shaw

became a meeting place for the Bloomsbury Group of writers and artists, which included Vanessa Bell, John Maynard Keynes, E M Forster, Roger Fry, and Duncan Grant.

LEADERS

In legend, a penniless boy named Dick Whittington came to London with his cat seeking streets paved with gold, and later became Lord Mayor. In fact, Richard Whittington (1360?–1423), Lord Mayor three times between 1397 and 1420 and one of London's most celebrated early politicians, was the son of a noble. Sir Thomas More (1478–1535), a Chelsea resident, was Henry VIII's chancellor until they quarreled over the king's break with the Catholic church and Henry ordered More's execution. More was canonized in 1935. Sir Thomas Gresham (1519?–79) founded the Royal Exchange. Sir Robert Peel (1788–1850) started the London police force, who were known as "bobbies" after him.

ACTORS

Nell Gwynne (1650–87) won more fame as King Charles II's mistress than as an actress. However, she did appear on stage at Drury Lane Theatre; she also sold oranges there. The Shakespearean actor Edmund Kean (1789–1833) and the great tragic actress

Sarah Siddons (1755–1831) were more distinguished players at Drury Lane. So were Henry Irving (1838–1905) and Ellen Terry (1847–1928), whose stage partnership lasted 24 years. Charlie Chaplin (1889–1977), born in Kennington, had a poverty-stricken childhood in the slums of London.

In the 20th century, a school of fine actors blossomed at the Old Vic, including Sir John Gielgud (1904–2001), Sir Ralph Richardson (1902–83), Dame Peggy Ashcroft (1907–91), and Laurence (later Lord) Olivier (1907–89), who was appointed the first director of the National Theatre.

Laurence Olivier

WHERE TO FIND HISTORIC LONDON HOMES

London's Best: Museums and Galleries

London's museums are filled with an astonishing diversity of treasures from all over the world. This map highlights 15 of the city's most important galleries and museums whose exhibits cater to most interests. Some of these collections started from the legacies of 18th- and 19th-century explorers, traders and collectors. Others specialize in one aspect of art, history, science or technology. A more detailed overview of London's museums and galleries is on pages 42–3.

British Museum
This Anglo-Saxon helmet is part of a massive collection of antiquities.

Wallace Collection
Frans Hals's Laughing Cavalier *is a star attraction in this museum of art, furniture, armour and* objets d'art.

Royal Academy of Arts
Major international art exhibitions are held here, and the renowned Summer Exhibition, when works are on sale, takes place every year.

Regent's Park and Marylebone

Kensington and Holland Park

South Kensington and Knightsbridge

Piccadilly and St James

Science Museum
Newcomen's steam engine of 1712 is just one of many exhibits that cater for both novice and expert.

Chelsea

Natural History Museum
All of life is here, with vivid displays on everything from dinosaurs (like this Triceratops skull) to butterflies.

0 kilometres   1

0 miles   0.5

Victoria and Albert
It is the world's largest museum of decorative arts. This Indian vase is 18th century.

National Portrait Gallery
Important British figures are documented in paintings and photographs. This is Vivien Leigh, by Angus McBean (1954).

National Gallery
The world-famous paintings in its collection are mainly European and date from the 15th to the 19th centuries.

Museum of London
London's history is told through fascinating objects such as this 15th-century reliquary.

Tower of London
The Crown Jewels and a vast collection of arms and armour are here. This armour was worn by a 14th-century Italian knight.

Bloomsbury and Fitzrovia

Smithfield and Spitalfields

Holborn and the Inns of Court

The City

Design Museum
The changing exhibitions here showcase all aspects of design from household prototypes to high fashion garments.

Soho and Trafalgar Square

Covent Garden and the Strand

Southwark and Bankside

South Bank

Whitehall and Westminster

Tate Modern
Works of the 20th century, such as Dali's Lobster Telephone, *are celebrated here.*

Tate Britain
Formerly the Tate Gallery, this museum showcases an outstanding collection of British art covering the 16th century to the present.

Imperial War Museum
It uses displays, film and special effects to recreate 20th-century battles. This is one of the earliest tanks.

Courtauld Gallery
Well-known works, such as Manet's Bar at the Folies-Bergère, *line its galleries.*

Exploring Museums and Galleries

London boasts an astonishingly rich and diverse collection of museums. The city's position for centuries at the hub of worldwide trade has been partly responsible for this extraordinarily rich cultural heritage. Britain's rule of a far-flung empire has also played its part. The world-renowned collections are impressive, but find time for the city's range of smaller museums, which are often more peaceful than their grander counterparts. Brimming with character, they cover every imaginable theme from buses and toys to electricity and water power.

Geffrye Museum: Art Nouveau Room

ANTIQUITIES AND ARCHAEOLOGY

Some of the most celebrated artifacts of ancient Asia, Egypt, Greece and Rome are housed in the **British Museums's** fine collection. Other antiquities, including books, manuscripts, paintings, busts and gems, are displayed in **Sir John Soane's Museum**, which is one of the most idiosyncratic to be found in London.

The **Museum of London** contains much of archaeological interest from all periods of the city's history.

FURNITURE AND INTERIORS

The Museum of London recreates typical domestic and commercial interiors from the Roman period right up to the present day. The **Victoria and Albert Museum** (or V&A) contains complete rooms rescued from now vanished buildings, plus a magnificent collection of furniture ranging from the 16th century to work by contemporary designers.

Eclectic collection at Sir John Soane's Museum

On a more modest scale, the **Geffrye Museum** consists of fully-furnished period rooms dating from 1600 to the 1990s. Writers' houses, such as the **Freud Museum**, give insights into the furniture of specific periods, while the **Linley Sambourne House** offers visitors a perfectly preserved example of a late Victorian interior.

COSTUME AND JEWELLERY

The **V&A's** vast collections include English and European clothes of the last 400 years, and some stunning jewellery from China, India and Japan. The priceless Crown Jewels, at the **Tower of London**, should not be missed. Here you can also see the world's largest cut diamond, Cullinan I, set in the Sovereign's Sceptre. **Kensington Palace's** Court Dress Collection opens a window on Court uniforms and protocol from about 1750. The **British Museum** displays ancient Aztec, Mayan and African costume.

CRAFTS AND DESIGN

Once again, the **Victoria and Albert Museum** (V&A) is the essential first port of call; its collections in these fields remain unrivalled. The **William Morris Gallery** shows every aspect of the 19th-century designer's work within the Arts and Crafts movement. The **Design Museum** focuses on modern design including products and fashion, while the **Crafts Council Gallery** displays (and sometimes sells) contemporary British craftwork.

MILITARY ARTIFACTS

The **National Army Museum** uses vivid models and displays to narrate the history of the British Army from the reign of Henry VII to the present. The crack regiments of Foot Guards, who are the elite of the British Army, are the main focus of the **Guards Museum**. The **Tower of London** holds part of the

Design Museum display of chairs

national collection of arms and armour; the **Wallace Collection** also has a large and impressive display. The **Imperial War Museum** has recreations of World War I trenches and the 1940 Blitz. The **Florence Nightingale Museum** illustrates the hardships of 19th-century warfare.

TOYS AND CHILDHOOD

Teddy bears, toy soldiers and dolls' houses are some of the toys that can be seen in **Pollock's Toy Museum**. The collection includes Eric, "the oldest known teddy-bear". The **V&A Museum of Childhood** and the **Museum of London** are a little more formal, but still fun, and illustrate aspects of the social history of childhood with the former offering some interesting children's activities.

SCIENCE AND NATURAL HISTORY

Computers, electricity, space exploration, industrial processes and transport can all be studied at the **Science Museum**. Transport enthusiasts are also catered for at **London's Transport Museum**. There are other specialized museums such as the **Faraday Museum** concerning the development of electricity, and the **Kew Bridge Steam Museum**, focusing on water power. The **National Maritime Museum** and the **Royal Observatory** in Greenwich chart both maritime history and the creation of GMT, by which the world still sets its clocks.

Samson and Delilah (1620) by Van Dyck at the Dulwich Picture Gallery

The **Natural History Museum** mixes displays of animal and bird life with ecological exhibits. The **Museum of Garden History** is devoted to the favourite British pastime.

Imperial War Museum

VISUAL ARTS

The particular strengths of the **National Gallery** are early Renaissance Italian and 17th-century Spanish painting and a wonderful collection of Dutch masters. **Tate Britain** specializes in British paintings spanning all periods, while **Tate Modern** has displays of international modern art from 1900 to the present day. The **V&A** is strong on European art from 1500–1900 and British art of 1700–1900. The **Royal Academy** and **The Hayward** specialize in major

Stone Dancer (1913) by Gaudier-Brzeska at Tate Britain

temporary exhibitions. The **Courtauld Institute of Art Gallery** contains Impressionist and Post-Impressionist works, while the **Wallace Collection** has 17th-century Dutch and 18th-century French paintings. The **Dulwich Picture Gallery** includes works by Rembrandt, Rubens, Poussin and Gains-borough, while **Kenwood House** is home to paintings by Reynolds, Gainsborough and Rubens in fine Adam interiors. The **Saatchi Gallery** is devoted to contemporary, mainly British, art.

WHERE TO FIND THE COLLECTIONS

London's Best: Churches

It is worth stopping to look at London's churches
and going in, if they are open. They have a special
atmosphere unmatched elsewhere in the city, and
they can often yield an intimate glimpse of the past.
Many churches have replaced earlier buildings in a
steady succession, dating back to pre-Christian
times. Some began life in outlying villages beyond
London's fortified centre, and were absorbed into
suburbs when the city expanded in the 18th century.
The memorials in the capital's churches and churchyards are a fascinating record of local life, liberally
peppered with famous names. A more detailed
overview of London churches is on pages 46–7.

All Souls
*This plaque comes from a
tomb in John Nash's Regency
church of 1824.*

St Paul's Covent Garden
*Inigo Jones's Classical church
was known as "the handsomest
barn in England".*

*Bloomsbury
and Fitzrovia*

*Regent's Park
and Marylebone*

*Soho and
Trafalgar
Square*

*Piccadilly
and St James's*

St Martin-in-the-Fields
*James Gibbs's church
of 1722–6 was
originally thought
"too gay" for
Protestant worship.*

*South Kensington
and Knightsbridge*

0 kilometres   1

0 miles   0.5

*Whitehall a
Westminste*

Westminster Cathedral
*The Italian-Byzantine
Catholic cathedral's red-
and-white brick exterior
conceals a rich interior of
multicoloured marbles.*

Westminster Abbey
*The famous abbey has the
most glorious medieval
architecture in London,
and highly impressive
tombs and monuments.*

Brompton Oratory
*This sumptuous Baroque
church was decorated with
works by Italian artists.*

St Mary-le-Strand
Now on a traffic island, this ship-like church was built by James Gibbs in 1714–17 to a lively Baroque design. Featuring high windows and rich interior detailing, it was made solid enough to keep out the noise from the street.

St Mary Woolnoth
The jewel-like interior of Nicholas Hawksmoor's small Baroque church (1716–27) appears larger than the outside.

Smithfield and Spitalfields

Holborn and the Inns of Court

Covent Garden and the Strand

The City

RIVER THAMES

South Bank

Southwark and Bankside

St Stephen Walbrook
Wren was at his best with this domed interior of 1672–7. Its carvings include Henry Moore's austere modern altar.

St Paul's
At 110 m (360 ft) high, the dome of Wren's cathedral is the world's second largest after St Peter's in Rome.

Southwark Cathedral
This largely 13th-century priory church was not designated a cathedral until 1905. It has a fine medieval choir.

Temple Church
Built in the 12th and 13th centuries for the Knights Templar, this is one of the few circular churches to survive in England.

Exploring Churches

The church spires that puncture London's skyline span nearly a thousand years of the city's history. They form an index to many of the events that have shaped the city – the Norman Conquest (1066); the Great Fire of London (1666); the great restoration, led by Wren, that followed it; the Regency period; the confidence of the Victorian era; and the devastation of World War II. Each has had its effect on the churches, many designed by the most influential architects of their times.

St Paul's, Covent Garden

MEDIEVAL CHURCHES

The most famous old church to survive the Great Fire of 1666 is the superb 13th-century **Westminster Abbey**, the church of the Coronation, with its tombs of British monarchs and heroes. Less well known are the well-hidden Norman church of **St Bartholomew-the-Great**, London's oldest church, (1123), the circular **Temple Church** founded in 1160 by the Knights Templar and **Southwark Cathedral**, set amid Victorian railway lines and warehouses. **Chelsea Old Church** is a charming village church near the river.

CHURCHES BY JONES

Inigo Jones (1573–1652) was Shakespeare's contemporary, and his works were almost as revolutionary as the great dramatist's. Jones's Classical churches of the 1620s and 1630s shocked a public used to conservative Gothic finery. By far the best-known is **St Paul's Church** of the 1630s, the centrepiece of Jones's Italian-style piazza in Covent Garden. **Queen's Chapel, St James's** was built in 1623 for Queen Henrietta Maria, the Catholic wife of Charles I. It was the first Classical church in England and has a magnificent interior but is, unfortunately, usually closed to the public.

CHURCHES BY HAWKSMOOR

Nicholas Hawksmoor (1661–1736) was Wren's most talented pupil, and his churches are among the finest

Spires
Look out for London's richly decorated church steeples. Here are four of the city's most distinctive to get you started.

St Martin-in-the-Fields, by James Gibbs, is in a prominent position grandly overlooking Trafalgar Square.

Clock dating from 1758

St Mary-le-Bow, by Christopher Wren, has a copper dragon weathervane on top of its fine steeple.

Graceful bow arches

St Bride's has Wren's tallest steeple. Originally 234 ft (71m) high, 8 ft (2.5 m) were lost in a thunderstorm in 1764.

Four octagonal tiers

St George's Bloomsbury, by Nicholas Hawksmoor, is topped by George I in a Roman toga.

Steeple rising in steps

Baroque buildings to be found in Britain.

St George's, Bloomsbury (1716–31) has an unusual centralized plan and a pyramid steeple topped by a statue of King George I. **St Mary Woolnoth** is a tiny jewel of 1716–27, and further east **Christ Church, Spitalfields** is a Baroque tour-de-force of 1714–29, now being restored.

Among Hawksmoor's East End churches are the stunning **St Anne's, Limehouse** and **St Alfege**, of 1714–17, which is across the river in Greenwich. The tower on this temple-like church was added later by John James in 1730.

St Anne's, Limehouse

CHURCHES BY GIBBS

James Gibbs (1682–1754) was more conservative than his Baroque contemporaries such as Hawksmoor, and he also kept his distance from the Neo-Classical trend so popular after 1720. His idiosyncratic London churches were enormously influential. **St Mary-le-Strand** (1714–17) is an island church which appears to be sailing down the Strand. The radical design of **St Martin-in-the-Fields** (1722–6) predates its setting, Trafalgar Square, by a hundred years.

REGENCY CHURCHES

The end of the Napoleonic Wars in 1815 brought a flurry of church building. The need for churches in London's new suburbs fused with a Greek Revival. The

CHRISTOPHER WREN

Sir Christopher Wren (1632–1723) was leader among the many architects who helped restore London after the Great Fire of London. He devised a new city plan, replacing the narrow streets with wide avenues radiating from piazzas. His plan was rejected, but he was commissioned to build 52 new churches; 31 have survived various threats of demolition and the bombs of World War II, although six are shells. Wren's great masterpiece is the massive

St Paul's, while nearby is splendid **St Stephen Walbrook**, his domed church of 1672–77. Other landmarks are **St Bride's**, off Fleet Street, said to have inspired the traditional shape of wedding cakes, **St Mary-le-Bow** in Cheapside and **St Magnus Martyr** in Lower Thames Street. Wren's own favourite was **St James's, Piccadilly** (1683–4). Smaller gems are **St Clement Danes**, Strand (1680–82) and **St James, Garlickhythe** (1674–87).

results may lack the exuberance of Hawksmoor, but they have an austere elegance of their own. **All Souls, Langham Place** (1822–4), at the north end of Regent Street, was built by the Prince Regent's favourite, John Nash, who was ridiculed at the time for its unusual combination of design styles. Also worth visiting is **St Pancras**, Greek Revival church of 1819–22, which is typical of the period.

VICTORIAN CHURCHES

London has some of the finest 19th-century churches in Europe. Grand and colourful, their riotous decoration is in marked contrast to the chaste Neo-Classicism of the preceding Regency era. Perhaps the best of the capital's late Victorian churches is **Westminster Cathedral**, a

stunningly rich, Italianate Catholic cathedral built in 1895–1903, with architecture by J F Bentley and *Stations of the Cross* reliefs by Eric Gill. **Brompton Oratory** is a grand Baroque revival, based on a church in Rome and filled with magnificent furnishings from all over Catholic Europe.

WHERE TO FIND THE CHURCHES

Brompton Oratory

London's Best: Parks and Gardens

Since medieval times London has had large expanses of green. Some of these, such as Hampstead Heath, were originally common land, where small-holders could graze their animals. Others, such as Richmond Park and Holland Park, were royal hunting grounds or the gardens of large houses; several still have formal features dating from those times. Today you can cross much of central London by walking from St James's Park in the east to Kensington Gardens in the west. Purpose-built parks, like Battersea, and botanical gardens, like Kew, appeared later.

Hampstead Heath
This breezy, open space is located in the midst of north London. Nearby Parliament Hill offers views of St Paul's, the City and the West End.

Kensington Gardens
This plaque is from the Italian Garden, one of the features of this elegant park.

Holland Park
The former grounds of one of London's grandest homes are now its most romantic park.

Kew Gardens
The world's premier botanic garden is a must for anyone with an interest in plants, exotic or mundane.

Richmond Park
The biggest Royal Park in London remains largely unspoiled, with deer and magnificent river views.

0 kilometres 1

0 miles 0.5

Regent's Park
In this civilized Park, surrounded by fine Regency buildings, you can stroll around the rose garden, visit the open-air theatre, or simply sit and admire the view.

Greenwich Park
Its focal point is the National Maritime Museum, well worth a visit for its architecture as well as its exhibits. There are also fine views.

Hyde Park
The Serpentine is one of the highlights of a park which also boasts restaurants, an art gallery and Speakers' Corner.

Regent's Park and Marylebone

Bloomsbury and Fitzrovia

Holborn and the Inns of Court

Smithfield and Spitalfields

Soho and Trafalgar Square

The City

Piccadilly

South Bank

Southwark and Bankside

RIVER THAMES

Whitehall and Westminster

Greenwich and Blackheath

Green Park
Its leafy paths are favoured by early-morning joggers from the Mayfair hotels.

St James's Park
People come here to feed the ducks, or watch the pelicans. A band plays throughout the summer.

Battersea Park
Visitors can hire a rowing boat for the best view of the Victorian landscaping around the lake.

Exploring Parks and Gardens

London has one of the the world's greenest city centres, full of tree-filled squares and grassy parks. From the intimacy of the Chelsea Physic Garden to the wild, open spaces of Hampstead Heath, every London park has its own charm and character. For those looking for a specific outdoor attraction – such as sports, wildlife or flowers – here are some of the most interesting London parks.

Camilla japonica

Embankment Gardens

FLOWER GARDENS

The British are famed for their gardens and love of flowers and this is reflected in several of London's parks. Really keen gardeners will find all they ever wanted to know at **Kew Gardens** and the **Chelsea Physic Garden**, which is especially strong on herbs. Closer to the centre of town, **St James's Park** boasts some spectacular flower beds, filled with bulbs and bedding plants, which are changed every season. **Hyde Park** sports a magnificent show of daffodils and crocuses in the spring and London's best rose garden is Queen Mary's in

Regent's Park. Kensington Gardens' flower walk has an exemplary English mixed border, and there is also a delightful small 17th-century garden at the **Museum of Garden History**.

Battersea Park also has a charming flower garden, and indoor gardeners should head to the **Barbican Centre**'s well-stocked conservatory.

FORMAL GARDENS

The most spectacular formal garden is at **Hampton Court**, which has a network of gardens from different periods, starting with Tudor. The gardens at **Chiswick**

House remain dotted with their 18th-century statuary and pavilions. Other restored gardens include 17th-century **Ham House**, and **Osterley Park**, whose 18th-century layout was retraced through the art of dowsing. **Fenton House** has a really fine walled garden; **Kenwood** is less formal, with its woodland area. **The Hill** is great in summer. The sunken garden at **Kensington Palace** has a formal layout and **Holland Park** has flowers around its statues.

RESTFUL CORNERS

London's squares are cool, shady retreats but, sadly, many are reserved for key-holders, usually residents of the surrounding houses. Of those open to all, **Russell Square** is the largest and most secluded. **Berkeley Square** is open but barren. **Green Park**, with its shady trees and deck chairs, offers a cool picnic spot right in central London. The Inns of Court provide some really pleasant havens: **Gray's Inn** gardens, **Middle Temple**

Sunken garden at Kensington Palace

GREEN LONDON

In Greater London there are 1,700 parks covering a total of 67 sq miles (174 sq km). This land is home to some 2,000 types of plant and 100 bird species that breed in the trees. Trees help the city to breathe, manufacturing oxygen from the polluted air. Here are some of the species you are most likely to see in London.

The London plane, now the most common tree in London, grows along many streets.

The English oak grows all over Europe. The Royal Navy used to build ships from it.

gardens and **Lincoln's Inn Fields**. **Soho Square**, which is surrounded by streets, is more urban and animated.

MUSIC IN SUMMER

Stretching out on the grass or in a deck chair to listen to a band is a British tradition. Military and other bands give regular concerts throughout the summer at **St James's** and **Regent's Parks** and also at **Parliament Hill Fields**. The concert schedule will usually be found posted up close to the bandstand in the park.

Open-air festivals of classical music are held in the summer in several parks (see p349).

WILDLIFE

There is a large and well-fed collection of ducks and other water birds, even including a few pelicans, in **St James's Park**. Duck lovers will also appreciate **Regent's, Hyde** and **Battersea Parks**, as well as **Hampstead Heath**. Deer roam in **Richmond** and **Greenwich Parks**. For a wide variety of captive animals, **London Zoo** is in **Regent's Park** and there are aviaries or aquariums at several parks and gardens, including **Kew Gardens** and **Syon House**.

Geese in St James's Park

HISTORIC CEMETERIES

In the late 1830s a ring of private cemeteries was established around London to ease the pressure on the monstrously overcrowded and unhealthy burial grounds of the inner city. Today some of these (notably **Highgate Cemetery** and Kensal Green – Harrow Road W10) are worth visiting for their air of repose and their Victorian monuments. **Bunhill Fields** is earlier; it was first used during the plague of 1665.

Kensal Green cemetery

Boating pond at Regent's Park

SPORTS

Cycling is not universally encouraged in London's parks, and footpaths tend to be too bumpy to allow much rollerskating. However, most parks have tennis courts, which normally have to be reserved in advance with the attendant. Rowing boats may be hired at **Hyde**, **Regent's** and **Battersea Parks**, among others. Athletics tracks are at both Battersea Park and also **Parliament Hill**. The public may swim at the ponds on **Hampstead Heath** and in the Serpentine in Hyde Park. Hampstead Heath is also ideal kite-flying territory.

WHERE TO FIND THE PARKS

The common beech has a close relation, the copper beech, with reddish purple leaves.

The horse chestnut's hard round fruits are used by children for a game called conkers.

London's Best: Ceremonies

Much of London's rich inheritance of tradition and ceremony centres on royalty. Faithfully enacted today, some of these ceremonies date back to the Middle Ages, when the ruling monarch had absolute power and had to be protected from opponents. This map shows the venues for some of the most important ceremonies in London. For more details on these and other ceremonies please turn to pages 54–5; information on all sorts of events taking place in London throughout the year can be found on pages 56–9.

St James's Palace and Buckingham Palace
Members of the Queen's Life Guard stand at the gates of these two palaces.

Bloomsbury and Fitzrovia

Soho and Trafalgar Square

South Kensington and Knightsbridge

Piccadilly and St James's

Hyde Park
Royal Salutes are fired by guns of the King's Troop Royal Horse Artillery on royal anniversaries and ceremonial occasions.

Whitehall and Westminster

Chelsea

Chelsea Hospital
In 1651 Charles II hid from parliamentary forces in an oak tree. On Oak Apple Day, Chelsea Pensioners decorate his statue with oak leaves and branches.

Horse Guards
At Trooping the Colour, the most elaborate of London's royal ceremonies, the Queen salutes as a battalion of Foot Guards parades its colours before her.

The City and Embankment
At the Lord Mayor's Show, pikemen and musketeers escort the newly elected Lord Mayor through the City in a gold state coach.

Holborn and the Inns of Court

Covent Garden and the Strand

The City

The Cenotaph
On Remembrance Sunday the Queen pays homage to the nation's war dead.

R I V E R   T H A M E S

South Bank

Southwark and Bankside

0 kilometres 1

0 miles 0.5

Tower of London
In the nightly Ceremony of the Keys, a Yeoman Warder locks the gates. A military escort ensures the keys are not stolen.

Houses of Parliament
Each autumn the Queen goes to Parliament in the Irish State Coach to open the new parliamentary session.

Attending London's Ceremonies

Royalty and commerce provide the two principal sources of London's rich calendar of ceremonial events. Quaint and old-fashioned these events may be, but what may seem arcane ritual has real historical meaning – many of the capital's ceremonies originated in the Middle Ages.

ROYAL CEREMONIES

Although the Queen's role is now largely symbolic, the Guard at Buckingham Palace still patrols the palace grounds. The impressive ceremony of the **Changing of the Guard** – dazzling uniforms, shouted commands, military music – consists of the Old Guard, which forms up in the palace forecourt, going off duty and handing over to the New Guard. The Guard consists of three officers and 40 men when the Queen is in residence, but only three officers and 31 men when she is away. The ceremony takes place in front of the palace. In another changeover ceremony, the Queen's Life Guards travel daily from Hyde Park Barracks to Horse Guards' Parade.

One of the Queen's Life Guards

The **Ceremony of the Keys** at the Tower of London is one of the capital's most timeless ceremonies. After each of the Tower gates has been locked, the last post is sounded by a trumpeter before the keys are secured in the Queen's House.

The Tower of London and Hyde Park are also the scene of **Royal Salutes** which take place on birthdays and other occasions throughout the year. At such times 41 rounds are fired in Hyde Park at noon, and 62 rounds at the Tower at 1pm. The spectacle in Hyde Park is a stirring one as 71 horses and six 13-pounder cannons swirl into place and the roar of the guns begins.

The combination of pageantry, colour, and music makes the annual **Trooping the Colour** the high point of London's ceremonial year. The Queen takes the Royal Salute, and after her troops have marched past, she leads them to Buckingham Palace where a second march past takes place. The best place to watch this spectacle is from the Horse Guards Parade side of St James's Park.

Bands of the Household Cavalry and the Foot Guards stage the ceremony of **Beating the Retreat** at Horse

A Queen's Guard in winter

Guards Parade. This takes place three or four evenings a week in the fortnight leading up to Trooping the Colour.

The spectacular **State Opening of Parliament**, when the Queen opens the annual parliamentary session in the House of Lords – usually in November – is not open to the general public, although it is now televised. The huge royal procession, which moves from Buckingham Palace to Westminster, is, however, a magnificent sight, with the Queen traveling in the highly ornate Irish State Coach drawn by four horses.

MILITARY CEREMONIES

The Cenotaph in Whitehall is the setting for a ceremony held on **Remembrance Sunday**, to give thanks to those who died fighting in any conflict from World War I onwards.

National **Navy Day** is commemorated by a parade down the Mall, followed by a service held at Nelson's Column in Trafalgar Square.

Royal salute, Tower of London

Trooping the Colour

Silent Change ceremony at Guildhall for the new Lord Mayor

CEREMONIES IN THE CITY

November is the focus of the City of London's ceremonial year. At the **Silent Change** in Guildhall, the outgoing Lord Mayor hands over symbols of office to the new Mayor in a virtually wordless ceremony. The following day sees the rumbustious **Lord Mayor's Show**. Accompanying the Lord Mayor in his gold state coach a procession of bands, decorated floats, and military detachments makes its way through the City from Guildhall past the Mansion House to the Law Courts, and back again along the Embankment.

Lord Mayor's chain of office

Many of the ceremonies that take place in the City are linked to the activities of the Livery Companies *(see p152)*. These include the Worshipful Companies of **Vintners' and Distillers'** annual celebration of the wine harvest and the Stationers' **Cakes and Ale Sermon**, held in St Paul's. Cakes and ale are provided according to the will of a 17th-century stationer.

NAME-DAY CEREMONIES

Every 21 May **King Henry VI**, who was murdered in the Tower of London in 1471, is still remembered by the members of his two famous foundations, Eton College and King's College, Cambridge,

who meet for a ceremony at the Wakefield Tower where he was killed. **Oak Apple Day** commemorates King Charles II's lucky escape from the Parliamentary forces of Oliver Cromwell in 1651. The King managed to conceal himself in a hollow oak tree, and today Chelsea Pensioners honor his memory by decorating his statue at Chelsea Royal Hospital with oak leaves and branches. On 18 December, the lexicographer **Dr Johnson** is commemorated in an annual service held at Westminster Abbey.

INFORMAL CEREMONIES

Each July, six guildsmen from the Company of Watermen compete for the prize in **Doggett's Coat and Badge Race**. In autumn, the **Pearly Kings and Queens**, representatives of east London's traders, meet at St Martin-in-the-Fields. In March children are given oranges and lemons at the **Oranges and Lemons service** at St Clement Danes church. In February, clowns take part in a service for **Joseph Grimaldi** (1779–1837) at the Holy Trinity Church in Dalston, E8.

Pearly Queen

WHERE TO FIND THE CEREMONIES

Beating the Retreat
Horse Guards *p80*, date arranged during first two weeks of June.

Cakes and Ale Sermon
St Paul's *pp148–51*, Ash Wed

Ceremony of the Keys
Tower of London *pp154–7*, 9:30pm daily. Tickets from the Tower, but book well in advance.

Changing of the Guard
Buckingham Palace *pp94–5*, Apr–Jul: 11:30am daily; Aug–Mar: alternate days. Horse Guards, Whitehall *p80*, 11am Mon–Sat, 10am Sun. For details call the London Tourist Board Information Line on 0906 866 3344.

Doggett's Coat and Badge Race
From London Bridge to Cadogan Pier, Chelsea *pp192–7*, July.

Dr Johnson Memorial
Westminster Abbey *pp76–9*, 18 Dec.

Joseph Grimaldi Memorial
Holy Trinity Church, Dalston E8, 7 Feb.

King Henry VI Memorial
Wakefield Tower, Tower of London *pp154–7*, 21 May.

Lord Mayor's Show
The City *pp143–53*, second Sat Nov.

Navy Day
Trafalgar Sq *p102*, 21 Oct.

Oak Apple Day
Royal Hospital *p197*, Thu after 29 May.

Oranges and Lemons Service
St Clement Danes *p138*, March.

Pearly Kings and Queens Harvest Festival
St Martin-in-the-Fields *p102*, autumn.

Remembrance Sunday
Cenotaph *p74*, Sun nearest 11 Nov.

Royal Salutes
Hyde Park *p211*, royal anniversaries and other state occasions.

Silent Change
Guildhall *p159*, second Fri Nov.

State Opening of Parliament
Houses of Parliament *pp72–3*, Oct–Nov. Procession from Buckingham Palace to Westminster.

Trooping the Colour
Horse Guards *p80*, 2nd Sat Jun (rehearsals on previous two Sats). Tickets from Household Division, Horse Guards.

Vintners' and Distillers' Wine Harvest
St Olave's Church, Hart St EC3, second Tue Oct.

LONDON THROUGH THE YEAR

Springtime in London carries an almost tangible air of a city waking up to longer days and outdoor pursuits. The cheerful yellow of daffodils studs the parks, and less hardy Londoners turn out for their first jog of the year to find themselves puffing in the wake of serious runners training for the Marathon. As spring turns into summer, the royal parks reach their full glory, and in Kensington Gardens nannies gather to chat under venerable chestnut trees. As autumn takes hold, these same trees are ablaze with red and gold, and Londoners' thoughts turn to afternoons in museums, followed by tea in a café. The year closes with Guy Fawkes and Christmas shopping. The official visitor organization, Visit London, www.visitlondon.com *(p362)*, and the listings magazines *(p342)* have details of seasonal events.

SPRING

The weather during the spring months may be raw, and an umbrella is a necessary precaution. Druids celebrate the Spring Equinox in a subdued ceremony on Tower Hill. Painters compete to have their works accepted by the Royal Academy. Footballers close their season in May with the FA Cup Final, while cricketers don their sweaters to begin theirs. Oxford and Cambridge Universities row their annual boat race along the Thames, and Marathon runners pound the streets.

Runners in the London Marathon passing Tower Bridge

MARCH

Chelsea Antiques Fair *(2nd week, also Sep)*, Chelsea Old Town Hall, King's Rd SW3.
Ideal Home Exhibition *(17 days from mid-Mar)*, Earl's Court, Warwick Rd SW5. It is a long-established show with the latest in domestic gadgetry and state-of-the-art technology.
Oranges and Lemons Service, St Clement Danes *(p55)*. Service for school-children; each child is given an orange and a lemon.
Oxford and Cambridge boat race *(late Mar or early Apr)*, Putney to Mortlake *(p355)*.
Spring Equinox celebration *(21 Mar)*, Tower Hill EC3. Historic pagan ceremony with modern-day druids.

EASTER

Good Fri and following Mon are public holidays.
Easter parades, Battersea Park *(p251)*.

Kite flying, Blackheath *(p243)*.
Easter Kite Festival Hampstead Heath *(p234)*.
Easter procession and hymns *(Easter Mon)*, Westminster Abbey *(pp76–9)*. One of London's most evocative religious celebrations.
International Model Railway Exhibition *(Easter weekend)*, Royal Horticultural Hall, Vincent Sq SW1. Of real interest to everyone.

A London park in the spring

APRIL

London Harness Horse Parade *(early Apr)*, Battersea Park *(p251)*.
Queen's Birthday gun salutes *(21 Apr)*, Hyde Park, Tower of London *(p54)*.
London Marathon *(Sun in Apr or May)*, champions and novices run from Greenwich to Westminster *(p355)*.

MAY

First and last Mon are public holidays.
FA Cup Final, football season's climax *(p354)*.
Henry VI Memorial *(p55)*.
Beating the Bounds *(Ascension Day)*, throughout the City. Young boys from the City parish beat buildings that mark the parish boundaries.
Oak Apple Day, at the Royal Hospital, Chelsea *(p55)*.
Funfairs *(late May public hol weekend)*, various commons.
Chelsea Flower Show *(late May)*, Royal Hospital, Chelsea.
Beating the Retreat *(p54)*.

AVERAGE DAILY HOURS OF SUNSHINE

Hours
10
8
6
4
2
0

Jan Feb Mar Apr May Jun Jul Aug Sep Oct Nov Dec

Sunshine Chart
London's longest and hottest days fall between May and August. In the height of summer, daylight hours can extend from well before 5am to after 9pm. Daytime is much shorter in the winter, but London can be stunning in the winter sunshine.

SUMMER

London's summer season is packed full of indoor and outdoor events. The weather is very unreliable, even at the height of summer, but unless you are notably unlucky there should be enough fine days to sample what is on offer.

The selection includes many traditional events, such as the Wimbledon tennis championships and the cricket test matches at Lord's and the Oval. Well out of view from the general public and prying photographers, the Queen holds garden parties for favoured subjects in the splendid grounds of Buckingham Palace. The summer public holiday is also marked with funfairs in some of London's parks.

JUNE

Coronation Day gun salutes *(2 Jun),* Hyde Park and Tower of London *(p54).*
International Ceramics Fair, Park Lane Hotel, Park Lane W1.
Fine Art and Antiques fair, Olympia, Olympia Way W14.
Trooping the Colour, Horse Guards Parade *(p54).*
Duke of Edinburgh's Birthday gun salutes *(10 Jun),* Hyde Park and Tower of London *(p54).*
Covent Garden Flower Festival *(mid-Jun),* Covent Garden WC2 *(pp111–119).* Floral installations, street performers and fashion shows. Free entry to all.
Wimbledon Lawn Tennis Championships *(two weeks in late Jun; (p354).*
Cricket test match, Lord's Cricket Ground *(p354).*

Revellers at Notting Hill Carnival

Open-air theatre season *(throughout the summer),* Regent's Park and Holland Park. Shakespeare, Shaw and others offer the perfect opportunity for a picnic *(p344).*
Open-air concerts, Kenwood, Hampstead Heath, Crystal Palace, Marble Hill, St James's Park *(p349).*
Summer festivals *(late Jun),* Spitalfields and Primrose Hill. Contact Visit London *(p362)* or see the listings magazines *(p342)* for times and venues of all these events and see July, below.
City of London Festival *(late Jun–mid-July),* various City venues *(p143).* Arts and music festival with concerts taking place in some of London's most beautiful historic churches.

JULY

Summer festivals Greenwich and Docklands, Regent's Park, Richmond and Soho.
Sales. Price reductions across

London's shops *(p321).*
Doggett's Coat and Badge Race *(p55).*
Hampton Court Flower Show, Hampton Court Palace *(pp254–7).*
Capital Radio Jazz Festival, Royal Festival Hall *(p188).*
Henry Wood Promenade Concerts *(late Jul–Sep),* Royal Albert Hall *(p207).*
Royal Academy Summer Exhibition *(Jun–Aug),* Piccadilly *(p90).*

AUGUST

Last Monday in August is a public holiday.
Notting Hill Carnival *(late Aug holiday weekend).* An internationally famous and well attended Caribbean carnival organized by the area's various ethnic communities *(p219).*
Funfairs *(Aug holiday).* These tend to run throughout London's parks during the summer months.

Regimental band, St James's Park

AVERAGE MONTHLY RAINFALL

MM | Inches
64
48
32
16
0

Jan Feb Mar Apr May Jun Jul Aug Sep Oct Nov Dec

2.5
2
1.5
1
0.5
0

Rainfall Chart
London's average monthly rainfall remains much the same throughout the year. July and August, the capital's warmest months, are also two of its wettest. Rain is less likely in spring, but visitors should be prepared for a shower at any time of year.

AUTUMN

There is a sense of purpose about London in autumn. The build-up to the busiest shopping season, the start of the academic year, and the new parliamentary session, opened by the Queen, inject some life into the colder months. The cricket season ends in mid-September, while food-lovers may be interested in the spectacular displays of fresh fish that are laid out in the vestry of St Mary-at-Hill, celebrating the harvest of this island nation.

Memories of a more turbulent opening of Parliament are revived on 5 November. Bonfires and fireworks accross the country commemorate the failed conspiracy, led by Guy Fawkes in 1605, to blow up the Palace of Westminster. A few days later, the dead of any conflict, from World War I onwards, are honoured at a ceremony held in Whitehall.

Pearly Kings gathering for the harvest festival at St Martin-in-the-Fields

SEPTEMBER

Mayor Thames Festival, *(mid-Sep).* Entertainment by and on the river between Westminster Bridge and Southwark Cathedral.
Great River Race, Thames.
Last Night of the Proms *(mid-Sep),* Royal Albert Hall *(p207).* Rousing classical hits.
Spitalfields Show *(mid-Sep),* Old Spitalfields Market *(p170).*

OCTOBER

Pearly Harvest Festival *(first Sun)*, St Martin-in-the-Fields.
Punch and Judy Festival Covent Garden WC2. Celebration of puppet duo.
Harvest of the Sea *(second Sun),* St Mary-at-Hill Church *(p152).*
Horse of the Year Show Wembley Arena *(p353).*
Vintners' and Distillers' Wine Harvest *(p55).*
Navy Day *(p54).*

NOVEMBER

State Opening of Parliament *(p54).*
Guy Fawkes Night *(5 Nov).* Listings magazines give details of firework displays *(p342).*
Remembrance Day Service *(p54).*
Silent Change *(p55).*
Lord Mayor's Show *(p55).*
London to Brighton veteran car rally *(first Sun).*
Christmas lights *(late Nov– 6 Jan).* The West End *(p323),* especially Regent's Street, lights up for the festive season.

London-to-Brighton veteran car run

Autumn colours in a London park

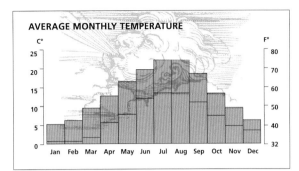

AVERAGE MONTHLY TEMPERATURE

Temperature Chart
The chart shows the average minimum and maximum temperatures for each month. Top temperatures averaging 22° C (75° F) belie London's reputation for year-round chilliness, although November through to February can be icy.

WINTER

Some of the most striking images of London are drawn from winter: paintings of frost fairs in the 17th and 18th centuries, when the River Thames froze over completely; and Claude Monet's views of the river and its bridges.

For centuries thick "pea-souper" fogs were an inevitable part of winter, until the Clean Air Act of 1956 barred coal-burning in open grates.

Christmas trees and lights twinkle everywhere – from the West End shopping streets to construction sites. The scent of roasting chestnuts pervades as street pedlars sell them from glowing mobile braziers.

Seasonal menus feature roast turkey, mince pies and rich, dark Christmas pudding. Traditional fare in theatres includes colourful family pantomimes (where the customary cross-dressing between the sexes baffles many visitors – *p344*) and popular ballets such as *Swan Lake* or *The Nutcracker*.

Skaters use the open-air rink at the Broadgate Centre in the City, and at Somerset House *(see p117)*. It is rarely safe to use the parks' frozen lakes.

PUBLIC HOLIDAYS

New Year's Day (1 Jan); **Good Friday; Easter Monday; May Day** (first Monday in May); **Whit Monday** (last Monday in May); **August Bank Holiday** (last Monday in Aug); **Christmas Day and Boxing Day** (25–26 Dec).

Winter in Kensington Gardens

DECEMBER

Oxford v Cambridge rugby union match Twickenham *(p355)*.
International Showjumping Championships *(late Dec)*, Olympia. Equestrian competition featuring the cream of riders from around the world.

CHRISTMAS, NEW YEAR

25–26 Dec and **1 Jan** are public hols. There is no train service on Christmas Day.

Carol services *(leading up to Christmas)*, Trafalgar Square *(p102)*, St Paul's *(pp148–51)*, Westminster Abbey *(pp76–9)* and many other churches.
Turkey auction *(24 Dec)*, Smithfield Market *(p164)*.
Christmas Day swim Serpentine, Hyde Park *(p211)*.
New Year's Eve celebrations *(31 Dec)*, Trafalgar Square, St Paul's.

JANUARY

Sales *(p321)*.
New Year's Day Parade starts at Parliament Sq *(p74)*.
International Boat Show, Earl's Court, Warwick Rd SW5.
International Mime Festival *(mid Jan–early Feb)*, various venues.
Charles I Commemoration *(last Sun)*, procession from St James's Palace *(p91)* to Banqueting House *(p80)*.
Chinese New Year *(late Jan–mid-Feb)*, Chinatown *(p108)* and Soho *(p109)*.

FEBRUARY

Queen's Accession gun salutes *(6 Feb)*, 41-gun salute Hyde Park; 62-gun salute Tower of London *(p54)*.
Pancake races *(Shrove Tue)*, Lincoln's Inn Fields *(p137)* and Covent Garden *(p112)*.

Christmas illuminations in Trafalgar Square

A RIVER VIEW OF LONDON

Cruising down the Thames is one of the most interesting ways to experience London. As the country's main commercial artery from the Roman invasion to well into the 1950s, the river is packed with historical references, including the reconstruction of the Elizabethan Globe Theatre, royal palaces and parks, numerous storied bridges and decommissioned power stations. Now the river is the city's foremost leisure amenity, with the banks accessible via the Thames Path, numerous riverside pubs and commuters as well as tourists sailing the river. Passenger boat services cover about 50 kilometres (30 miles) of the Thames, from Hampton Court in the west to the Thames Barrier in the east. The most popular and best served section runs through the heart of the city from Westminster to Tower Bridge. Often accompanied by interesting and witty commentary, a cruise along this fascinating stretch of the Thames should not be missed.

Decoration on Chelsea Bridge

View west from Shad Thames, with Tower Bridge

Kew Bridge
Kew Pier
Kew Rail Bridge
Chiswick Bridge
Barnes Rail Bridge
Twickenham Bridge
Richmond St Helena Pier
Twickenham Rail Bridge
Richmond Bridge
Richmond Landing Stage

Hammersmith Bridge
Putney Bridge
Putney Rail Bridge
Wandsworth Bridge
Battersea Bridge
Cadogan Pier
Chelsea Bridge
Chelsea Harbour Pier
Albert Bridge
Grosvenor Rail Bridge
Vauxhall Bridge
Lambeth Bridge
Millbank Millennium Pier

Teddington Foot Bridge

Kingston
Kingston Turks Pier
Kingston Bridge
Kingston Town End Pier
Hampton Bridge
Hampton Court Pier

0 kilometres   4

0 miles   2

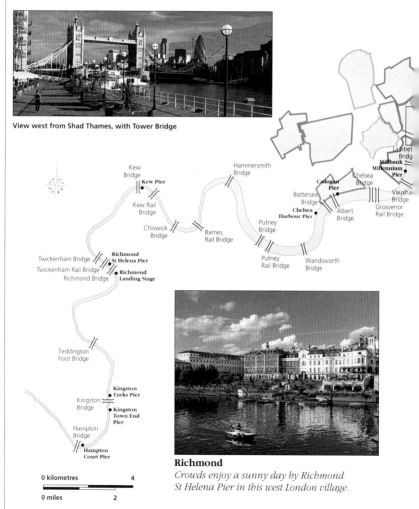

Richmond
Crowds enjoy a sunny day by Richmond St Helena Pier in this west London village.

The Thames Barrier
Completed in 1982, the world's largest moveable flood barrier protects London from rising water levels. The massive steel gates have been raised over 60 times.

Riverside pubs
Beautifully preserved pubs, such as the Prospect of Whitby in Wapping, hug the river's banks.

Rotherhithe Tunnel
Blackwall Tunnel
Canary Wharf Pier
Thames Barrier
Hilton Docklands
Nelson Dock Pier
Thames
Greenland Pier
Masthouse Terrace
Barrier Gardens Pier
See pp64–5
See pp62–3
Greenwich Foot Tunnel
Greenwich Pier

CRUISE OPERATORS

Bateaux London/ Catamaran Cruisers
Tel 020-7695 1800.
www.bateauxlondon.com

Campion Launches
Tel 020-8305 0300.

City Cruises
Tel 020-7740 0400.
www.citycruises.com

Crown River Cruises
Tel 020-7936 2033.
www.crownriver.com

Thames Clippers
Tel 0870-781 5049.
www.thamesclippers.com

Thames Executive Charters
Tel 01342-820600.
www.thamesexecutive charters.com

Thames River Services
Tel 020-7930 4097.
www.thamesriverservices. co.uk

Turks Launches
Tel 020-8546 2434.
www.turks.co.uk

Westminster Passenger Service Association (Upriver) Ltd
Tel 020-7930 2062 or *020-7930 4721.*
www.wpsa.co.uk

CRUISE HIGHLIGHTS

Most regular services run from April through September, with some routes having winter schedules. During the summer, sailing times are frequent from Westminster and Embankment to Greenwich, with a boat arriving between every half hour and every hour. Commuter river services link Canary Wharf and Chelsea Harbour with some of the city's main termini. Numerous operators cover a variety of routes and a River Thames Boat Service Guide is available at tube stations. Most operators give a third off the ticket price to Travelcard holders *(see p378)*.

GREENWICH *(see pp236–43)*
Blessed with frequent service, accessing this area steeped in shipping lore by boat gives a day trip a fitting nautical spin.
Operators: Bateaux London/ Catamaran Cruisers, City Cruises, Thames River Services.
Piers: Westminster, Waterloo, Embankment, Bankside, Tower.
Duration: 1 hr (Westminster).

THAMES BARRIER *(see p249)*
Sail between the nine massive piers that raise the steel gates. Cruises to the barrier also pass the O2 Arena, formerly the Millennium Dome.
Operator: Thames River Services.
Piers: Westminster, Greenwich.
Duration: 30 min (Greenwich).

KEW *(see pp260–61)*
A cruise to Kew leaves the city behind after passing the Battersea Power Station and sailing through Hammersmith.
Operator: WPSA (upriver only).
Piers: Westminster.
Duration: 1.5 hrs (Westminster).

HAMPTON COURT *(see pp254–7)* Arrive at Hampton Court in regal style, but be aware that the round trip from Westminster can take up to eight hours. Consider sailing from one of the piers upriver.
Operator: WPSA (upriver only), Turks Launches.
Piers: Kew, all Richmond and Kingston piers.
Duration: 2 hrs (Kew).

Westminster Bridge to Blackfriars Bridge

Until World War II, this stretch of the Thames marked the division between rich and poor London. On the north bank were the offices, shops, luxury hotels and apartments of Whitehall and the Strand, the Inns of Court and the newspaper district. To the south were smoky factories and slum dwellings. After the war, the Festival of Britain in 1951 started the revival of the South Bank *(see pp184–91)*, which now has some of the capital's most interesting modern buildings.

Savoy Hotel
This hotel is on the site of a medieval palace (p116).

Somerset House, built in 1786, houses an art gallery *(p117)*.

Shell Mex House
Once offices for the oil company, they were built in 1931 on the site of the vast Cecil Hotel.

Cleopatra's Needle was made in ancient Egypt and given to London in 1819 *(p118)*.

Embankment Gardens is the site of many open-air concerts held in the bandstand during the summer months *(p118)*.

Charing Cross

Savoy Pier

Waterloo Bridge

Festival Pier

Embankment

Embankment Pier

The **South Bank** was the site of the 1951 Festival of Britain and is London's most important arts complex. It is dominated by the Royal Festival Hall, the National Theatre and The Hayward *(pp184–91)*.

Hungerford Railway Bridge and Golden Jubilee Footbridges

Waterloo Millennium Pier

Jubilee Gardens

The London Eye offers breathtaking views over London *(p189)*.

Charing Cross
The rail terminus is encased in a Post-Modernist office complex with many shops (p119).

The Banqueting House is one of Inigo Jones's finest works, built as part of Whitehall Palace *(p80)*.

The Ministry of Defence is a bulky white fortress completed in the 1950s.

Westminster Pier

Westminster

Westminster Bridge

County Hall
This is now home to the state-of-the-art London Aquarium and its 350 species of fish.

St Paul's
Christopher Wren's masterwork, finished in 1708, formerly dominated the London skyline (pp148–51).

Temple and the Inns of Court
These historic buildings have been the offices of lawyers and barristers for over 500 years (pp136–9).

Blackfriars

Blackfriars
Millennium
Pier

Blackfriars
Bridge

Millennium
Bridge

Tate Modern
is located in the old Bankside power station (pp178–81).

Gabriel's Wharf
A lively craft market operates where once there were warehouses *(p191).*

Doggett's Coat and Badge
The modern pub here is named after a river race in which boatmen compete for this huge badge.

Blackfriars Bridge
The logo of a former railway company adorns the bridge.

OXO Tower
The windows were designed to spell the brand name of a popular meat extract.

KEY

 Underground station

Railway station

River boat boarding point

St Paul's
The cathedral dominates views from the South Bank.

Southwark Bridge to St Katharine's Dock

For centuries the stretch just east of London Bridge was the busiest part of the Thames, with ships of all sizes jostling for position to unload at the wharves on both banks. Then, in the 19th century, the construction of the docks to the east eased congestion. Today most landmarks on this section hark back to that commercial past.

Old Billingsgate
Note the flying fish weather vanes on what was London's main fish market (p152).

Fishmongers' Hall
The hall (1834) of this ancient City guild dominates the view north from London Bridge (p152).

A Custom House has been here since 1272. This version dates from 1825.

Monument
The Great Fire of 1666 started near this spot (p152).

Cannon Street

Monument

Bankside Pier

Southwark Bridge

Cannon Street Railway Bridge

London Bridge

London Bridge City Pier

London Bridge

The Globe Theatre
This replica Elizabethan theater was built to recreate the experience of the way Shakespeare's plays were first performed (p177).

St Olave's House
A fine Art Deco building shows its best face to the river.

Hay's Galleria
Once a wharf for unloading food, it has been covered to house shops and restaurants.

Southwark Cathedral
Parts of this building date from the 12th century. It contains memorials to Shakespeare (p176).

Southwark Wharves
Now there are walkways with river views where ships used to dock.

Tower Bridge
It still opens to let tall ships pass, but not as often as it did when cargo vessels came through (p153).

Tower of London
Look out for Traitors' Gate, where prisoners would be taken into the Tower by boat (pp154–7).

St Katharine's Dock
The former dock is now a lively attraction for visitors. Its yacht marina is a highlight (p158).

Tower Millennium Pier

Tower Bridge

St Katharine's Pier

A stunning new building, City Hall, houses the Mayor and the governing offices.

Victorian warehouses on Butlers Wharf have been converted into apartments.

HMS Belfast
This World War II cruiser has been a museum since 1971 (p183).

Design Museum
Opened in 1989, this ship-like building is a shining example of Docklands' renaissance (p183).

Colourful procession of a Guards band ▷

LONDON AREA BY AREA

WHITEHALL AND WESTMINSTER

Whitehall and Westminster have been at the centre of political and religious power in England for a thousand years. King Canute, who ruled at the beginning of the 11th century, was the first monarch to have a palace on what was then an island in the swampy meeting point of the Thames and its vanished tributary, the Tyburn. Canute built his palace beside the church that, some 50 years later, Edward the Confessor would enlarge into England's greatest abbey, giving the area its name (a minster is an abbey church). Over the following centuries the offices of state were established in the vicinity. All this is still reflected in Whitehall's heroic statues and massive government buildings. But, to its north, Trafalgar Square marks the start of the West End entertainment district.

Horse Guard on Whitehall

SIGHTS AT A GLANCE

Historic Streets and Buildings
Houses of Parliament pp72–3 ❶
Big Ben ❷
Jewel Tower ❸
Dean's Yard ❺
Parliament Square ❼
Downing Street ❾
Cabinet War Rooms and Churchill Museum ❿
Banqueting House ⓫
Horse Guards Parade ⓬
Queen Anne's Gate ⓮
St James's Park Station ⓰
Blewcoat School ⓱

Churches, Abbeys, and Cathedrals
Westminster Abbey pp76–9 ❹
St Margaret's Church ❻
Westminster Cathedral ⓲
St John's, Smith Square ⓳

Museums and Galleries
Guards' Museum ⓯
Tate Britain pp82–5 ⓴

Theatres
Trafalgar Studios ⓭

Monuments
Cenotaph ❽

GETTING THERE
Rail services and the Victoria, Jubilee, District, and Circle lines all serve the area. Bus numbers 3, 11, 12, 24, 29, 53, 77, 77A, 88, 109, 159, 170, and 184 go to Whitehall; 2, 2B, 16, 25, 36A, 38, 39, 52, 52A, 73, 76, 135, 507, and 510 serve Victoria.

KEY
▢ Street by Street map
Ⓔ Underground station
➷ Railway station

SEE ALSO
• *Street Finder,* maps 13, 20, 21
• *Where to Stay* pp278–91
• *Restaurants, Pubs* pp292–319

◁ **Looking down Whitehall towards Big Ben**

Street-by-Street: Whitehall and Westminster

Compared with many capital cities, London has little monumental architecture designed to overawe with pomp. Here, at the historic seat both of the government and of the established church, it most closely approaches the broad, stately avenues of Paris, Rome and Madrid. On weekdays the streets are crowded with members of the civil service, as most of their work is based in this area. At weekends, however, it is popular with tourists visiting some of London's most famous sights.

Earl Haig, the British World War I chief, was sculpted by Alfred Hardiman in 1936.

Downing Street
British Prime Ministers have lived here since 1732 **9**

Central Hall is a florid example of the Beaux Arts style, built in 1911 as a Methodist meeting hall. In 1946 the first General Assembly of the United Nations was held here.

★ **Cabinet War Rooms and Churchill Museum**
The War Rooms were Winston Churchill's World War II headquarters **10**

★ **Westminster Abbey**
The Abbey is London's oldest and most important church **4**

The Sanctuary was a medieval safe place for those escaping the law.

Richard I's Statue, by Carlo Marochetti (1860), depicts the 12th-century *Coeur de Lion* (Lionheart).

Dean's Yard
Westminster School was founded here in 1540 **5**

Jewel Tower
Kings once stored their most valuable possessions here **3**

The Burghers of Calais is a cast of Auguste Rodin's original in Paris.

★ Horse Guards
A mounted guard is ceremonially changed here twice a day **12**

To Trafalgar Square

Dover House, a stately mansion dating from 1787, now houses the Scottish Office.

LOCATOR MAP
See Central London Map pp14–15

★ Banqueting House
Inigo Jones designed this elegant building, which has a Rubens ceiling, in 1622 **11**

Cenotaph
Edwin Lutyens's war memorial dates from 1920 **8**

Richmond House
is William Whitfield's prize-winning 1980s building for the Department of Health.

The Treasury
is where the nation's finances are administered.

Norman Shaw Buildings,
the Victorian site of New Scotland Yard, the Metropolitan Police headquarters.

Westminster Pier
is a starting point for river excursions.

Westminster station

Boudicca,
the British queen who resisted the Romans, was portrayed by Thomas Thornycroft in the 1850s.

★ Houses of Parliament and Big Ben
These were designed by Barry in 1834 when the Palace of Westminster burned down **1** **2**

Parliament Square
Statues of famous statesmen, such as Benjamin Disraeli, Sir Winston Churchill and Nelson Mandela, stand here **7**

St Margaret's Church
Society weddings often take place here, in Parliament's church **6**

STAR SIGHTS

★ Westminster Abbey

★ Houses of Parliament and Big Ben

★ Banqueting House

★ Cabinet War Rooms and Churchill Museum

★ Horse Guards

KEY

- - - Suggested route

0 metres 100

0 yards 100

Houses of Parliament ❶

Since 1512 the Palace of
Westminster has been the
seat of the two Houses of
Parliament, called the
Lords and the Commons.
The Commons is made up
of elected Members of
Parliament (MPs) of
different political parties;
the party with the most
MPs forms the Govern-
ment, and its leader
becomes Prime Minister.
MPs from other parties
make up the Opposition.
Commons' debates can
become heated and are
impartially chaired by an
MP designated as Speaker.
The Government formu-
lates legislation which
is first debated in both
Houses before
becoming law.

The mock-Gothic building was
designed by Victorian
architect Sir Charles Barry.
Victoria Tower, on the left,
contains 1.5 million Acts of
Parliament passed since 1497.

★ Commons' Chamber
*The room is upholstered in
green. The Government sits on
the left, the Opposition on the
right, and the Speaker presides
from a chair between them.*

Big Ben
*The vast bell was hung
in 1858 and chimes on
the hour; four smaller
ones ring on the quarter
hours (see p74).*

Members' entrance

STAR FEATURES

★ Westminster Hall

★ Lords' Chamber

★ Commons' Chamber

★ Westminster Hall
*The only surviving part
of the original Palace
of Westminster, it
dates from 1097; its
hammerbeam roof is
14th century.*

Central Lobby
People who come to meet their MP wait here under a ceiling of rich mosaics.

Peers are members of the House of Lords – many receive their titles for services to their country. This is their lobby.

Royal Gallery
The Queen passes through here at the State Opening. It is lined with peers' desks.

St Stephen's entrance

Cromwell Green entrance

★ **Lords' Chamber**
At the State Opening of Parliament (see pp54–5) the Queen delivers a speech from the throne of the House of Lords, which outlines the Government's plans.

TIMELINE

1042 Work starts on first palace for Edward the Confessor	**1547** St Stephen's chapel becomes first Chamber of the House of Commons	**1642** Charles I tries to arrest five MPs but is forced to withdraw by the Speaker	**1941** Chamber of House of Commons destroyed by World War II bomb	

1000	1200	1400	1600	1800	2000

1087–1100 Westminster Hall built

1512 After a fire, palace stops being a royal residence

The Mace: symbol of royal authority in the Commons

1605 Guy Fawkes and others try to blow up the king and Houses of Parliament

1834 Palace destroyed by fire; only Westminster Hall and the Jewel Tower survive

1870 Present building completed

Houses of Parliament ❶

See pp72–3.

Big Ben ❷

Bridge St SW1. **Map** 13 C5.
🚇 *Westminster.*
Not open *to the public.*

To be pedantic, Big Ben is
not the name of the world-
famous four-faced clock in
the 106-m (320-ft) tower that
rises above the Houses of
Parliament, but of the
resonant 14-tonne bell
on which the hours are
struck. It was named
after Sir Benjamin Hall,
Chief Commissioner of
Works when the bell
was hung in 1858.
Cast at White-
chapel, it was the
second giant bell
made for the clock,
the first having
become cracked
during a test
ringing. (The
present bell also has
a slight crack.) The
clock is the largest
in Britain, its four
dials 7.5 m (23 ft) in
diameter and the
minute hand 4.25 m (14 ft)
long, made in hollow copper
for lightness. It has kept exact
time for the nation more or
less continuously since it was
first set in motion in May
1859. The deep chimes have
become a symbol of Britain
all over the world and are
broadcast daily on BBC radio.

Jewel Tower ❸

Abingdon St SW1. **Map** 13 B5.
Tel *020-7222 2219.* 🚇 *Westminster.*
Open *Apr–Oct: 10am–5pm;*
Nov–Mar: 10am–4pm daily. **Closed**
24–26 Dec, 1 Jan. **Adm charge.** 📷
🚹 *ground floor only.* 🚻
www.english-heritage.org.uk

This and Westminster Hall
(see p72) are the only vestiges
of the old Palace of
Westminster. The tower was
built in 1365 as a stronghold
for Edward III's treasure and
today houses a fascinating
exhibition, *Parliament Past
and Present,* that relates the
history of Parliament. It
includes a display devoted
to the history of the Jewel
Tower itself.
The tower served as the
weights and measures office
from 1869 until 1938 and
another small display relates
to that era. Alongside are
the remains of the moat
and a medieval quay.

Westminster Abbey ❹

See pp76–9.

Dean's Yard ❺

Broad Sanctuary SW1. **Map** 13 B5.
🚇 *Westminster.* **Buildings not**
open *to the public.*

**Entrance to the Abbey and cloisters
from Dean's Yard**

An arch near the west door
of the Abbey leads into this
secluded grassy square,
surrounded by a jumble of
buildings from many different
periods. A medieval house on
the east side has a distinctive
dormer window and backs on
to Little Dean's Yard, where
the monks' living quarters
used to be. Dean's Yard is
private property. It belongs to
the Dean and Chapter of
Westminster and is close to
Westminster School, whose
famous former pupils include
poet John Dryden and playwright Ben Jonson. Scholars
are, by tradition, the first to
acknowledge a new monarch.

St Margaret's Church ❻

Parliament Sq SW1. **Map** 13 B5.
Tel *020-7654 4840.* 🚇 *Westminster.*
Open *9.30am–3.30pm Mon–Fri,*
9.30am–1.30pm Sat, 2–5pm Sun. 🚹
11am Sun. 📷 🚹 *by arrangement.*

**Statue of Charles I overlooking
St Margaret's doorway**

Overshadowed by the Abbey,
this late-15th-century church
has long been a favoured
venue for political and society
weddings, such as Winston
and Clementine Churchill's.
Although much restored, the
church retains some Tudor
features, notably a stained-
glass window commemorat-
ing the marriage of King
Henry VIII and his first wife,
Catherine of Aragon.

Parliament Square ❼

SW1. **Map** 13 B5. 🚇 *Westminster.*

Laid out in the 1840s to
provide a more open aspect
for the new Houses of
Parliament, the square
became Britain's first official
roundabout in 1926. Today it
is hemmed in by heavy traffic.
Statues of statesmen and
soldiers are dominated by
Winston Churchill in his
greatcoat, glowering at the
House of Commons. On the
north side Abraham Lincoln
sits in front of the mock-
Gothic Middlesex Guildhall,
completed in 1913.

Cenotaph ❽

Whitehall SW1. **Map** 13 B4.
🚇 *Westminster.*

This suitably bleak and pale
monument, completed in
1920 by Sir Edwin Lutyens to
commemorate the dead of
World War I, stands in the

middle of Whitehall. On Remembrance Day every year – the Sunday nearest 11 November – the monarch and other dignitaries place wreaths of red poppies on the Cenotaph. This solemn ceremony, commemorating the 1918 armistice, honours the victims of World Wars I and II *(see pp54–5)*.

The Cenotaph

Churchill Museum and Cabinet War Rooms ⑩

Clive Steps, King Charles St SW1. **Map** 13 B5. *Tel* 020-7930 6961. Ⓔ *Westminster.* **Open** *9.30am–6pm daily (last adm:5pm).* **Closed** *24–26 Dec.* **Adm charge.** Ⓔ ▢ ▢ **www**.iwm.org.uk/cabinet

This intriguing slice of 20th-century history is a warren of rooms below the Government Office Building north of Parliament Square. It is where the War Cabinet – first under Neville Chamberlain, then Winston Churchill – met during World War II when German bombs were falling on London. The War Rooms include living quarters for key ministers and military leaders and a Cabinet Room, where many strategic decisions were taken. They are laid out as they were when the war ended, complete with period furniture, including Churchill's desk, communications equipment and maps for plotting military strategy. The Churchill Museum is a multimedia exhibit recording Churchill's life and career.

Telephones in the Map Room of the Cabinet War Rooms

Downing Street ⑨

SW1. **Map** 13 B4. Ⓔ *Westminster.* **Not open** to the public.

Sir George Downing (1623–84) spent part of his youth in the American colonies. He was the second graduate from the nascent Harvard College before returning to fight for the Parliamentarians in the English Civil War. In 1680 he bought some land near Whitehall Palace and built a street of houses. Four of these survive, though they are much altered. George II gave No. 10 to Sir Robert Walpole in 1732. Since then it has been the official residence of the Prime Minister and contains offices as well as a private apartment. In 1989, for security reasons, iron gates were erected at the Whitehall end.

The famous front door of No. 10

No. 12, the Whips' Office, is where Party campaigns are organized.

Government policy is decided in the Cabinet Room at No. 10.

No. 11 is the Chancellor of the Exchequer's official residence.

No. 10 is the official home of the Prime Minister.

The Prime Minister entertains official guests in the State Dining Room.

Westminster Abbey ❹

The Abbey is world-famous as the
resting-place of Britain's monarchs, and
as the setting for coronations and other
great pageants. Within its walls
can be seen some of the most glorious
examples of medieval architecture in
London. It also contains one of the most
impressive collections of tombs and
monuments in the world. Half national
church, half national museum, the
Abbey occupies a unique place in the
British national consciousness.

★ Flying Buttresses
*The massive flying but-
tresses help transfer the
great weight of the
31-m (102-ft) high nave.*

North/Main Entrance
*The stonework
here, like this
carving of a
dragon, is
Victorian.*

The North Transept has
three chapels on the
east side containing
some of the Abbey's
finest monuments.

★ West Front Towers
*These towers, completed
in 1745, were designed
by Nicholas Hawksmoor.*

STAR FEATURES

★ West Front Towers

★ Flying Buttresses

★ The Nave viewed from
   the West End

★ The Lady Chapel

★ Chapter House

**★ The Nave viewed
from the West End**
*At 10 m (35 ft) wide, the nave
is comparatively narrow, but
it is the highest in England.*

The Cloisters, built
mainly in the 13th and
14th centuries, link the
Abbey church with the
other buildings.

St Edward's Chapel
houses Edward the
Confessor's shrine and
the tombs of other English
medieval monarchs. The
royal Coronation Chair is
located just outside.

★ **The Lady Chapel**
*The chapel, consecrated
in 1519, has a superb
vaulted ceiling and choir
stalls dating from 1512.*

VISITORS' CHECKLIST

Broad Sanctuary SW1. **Map 13
B5. *Tel* 020-7222 5152.** 🚇 *St
James's Park, Westminster.*
🚌 *3, 11, 12, 24, 29, 53, 70,
77, 77a, 88, 109, 148, 159, 170,
211.* 🚆 *Victoria, Waterloo.* ⛴
Westminster Pier. **Cloisters open**
8am–6pm daily. **Abbey, including Royal Chapels, Poets' Corner, Quire, Statesmen's Aisle,
Nave open** 9:30am–4:30pm
Mon, Tue, Thu, Fri (last adm:
3:30pm), 9:30am–7pm (last adm:
6pm) Wed, 9:30am–2:30pm Sat
(last adm: 1:30pm). NB: the abbey
is sometimes closed for special
events. **Chapter House, Pyx
Chamber and Museum open**
10:30am–4pm Mon–Sat. **Adm
charge. College Garden open**
Apr–Sep: 10am–6pm Tue–Thu;
Oct–Mar: 10am–4pm Tue–Thu.
Evensong 5pm Mon–Fri, 3pm
Sat, Sun. 🚫 ♿ limited. 📷 🎧
💻 🎵 **Concerts.** www.west-
minster-abbey.org

★ **Chapter House**
*This octagonal structure is
worth seeing for its 13th-
century tiles.*

The South Transept
contains "Poets' Corner",
where memorials to famous
literary figures can be seen.

Museum

TIMELINE

1050 New Benedic-tine abbey church begun by Edward the Confessor	**1376** Henry Yevele begins rebuilding the nave	*13th-century tile from the Chapter House*		**1838** Queen Victoria's coronation

1000	1200	1400	1600	1800	2000

1245 New church begun to the designs of Henry of Reyns	**1269** Body of Edward the Confessor moved to new shrine in the Abbey	**1745** West towers completed	**1953** Most recent coronation in the Abbey: Elizabeth II's
		1540 Monastery dissolved	

A Guided Tour of Westminster Abbey

The abbey's interior presents an exceptionally diverse
array of architectural and sculptural styles. These range
from the austere French Gothic of the nave to the
stunning complexity of Henry VII's Tudor chapel and
the riotous invention of the later 18th-century
monuments. Many British monarchs were buried here;
some of their tombs are deliberately plain, while others
are lavishly decorated. At the same time, there are
monuments to a number of Britain's greatest public
figures – ranging from politicians to poets – crowded
into the aisles and transepts.

HISTORICAL PLAN OF THE ABBEY

The first Abbey church was established as early as the 10th
century, when St Dunstan brought a group
of Benedictine monks to the area. The
present structure dates largely from the
13th century; the new, French-influenced
design was begun in 1245 at the behest of
Henry III. Because of its
unique role as the royal
coronation church, the Abbey
survived Henry VIII's mid-
16th-century
onslaught on Britain's
monastic buildings.

KEY

☐ Built between 1055–1350

▦ Added from 1350–1420

☐ Built between 1500–1512

☐ Towers completed 1745

☐ Restored after 1850

② Nightingale Memorial
*The North Transept chapels
contain some of the
Abbey's finest monuments
– this one, by Roubiliac,
is for Lady Elizabeth
Nightingale (1761).*

Main entrance

① The Nave
*The nave is 10.5 m
(35 ft) wide and 31 m
(102 ft) high. It took
150 years to build.*

The Choir houses a
gilded 1840s screen,
which contains
remnants of the 13th-
century original.

The Jericho Parlour,
added in the early
16th century, contains
some fine panelling. It
is closed to the public.

**The Jerusalem
Chamber**
has a 17th-century
fireplace, fine tapes-
tries and an interesting
painted ceiling. It is
closed to the public.

The Deanery, home
of the Dean of
Westminster, was once the
monastic abbot's house.
It is closed to the public.

⑧ Grave of the Unknown Warrior
*The body of an unknown soldier was
brought from the battlefields of World
War I and buried here in 1920. His grave
commemorates all who have lost their
lives in war.*

CORONATION

The abbey has been the fittingly sumptuous setting for all royal coronations since 1066. The last occupant of the Coronation Chair was the present monarch, Elizabeth II. She was crowned in 1953 in the first televised coronation.

The Chapel of St John the Baptist is full of tombs dating from the 14th to the 19th centuries.

St Faith Chapel contains works of art that date back to the 13th century.

The Pyx Chamber's gaunt columns date from the 11th century. This is where the coinage was tested in medieval times.

Dean's Yard entrance

KEY

- - - Tour route

③ **Coronation Chair**
Constructed in 1301, this is the chair on which monarchs have been crowned since 1308.

④ **Tomb of Elizabeth I**
Inside Henry VII's Chapel you will find Elizabeth I's (reigned 1558–1603) huge tomb. It also houses the body of her sister, "Bloody" Mary I.

⑤ **Henry VII Chapel**
The undersides of the choir stalls, dating from 1512, are beautifully carved with exotic and fantastic creatures.

⑥ **St Edward's Chapel**
The shrine of the Saxon king Edward the Confessor and the tombs of many medieval monarchs are here.

⑦ **Poets' Corner**
Take time to explore the memorials to countless literary giants, such as Shakespeare and Dickens, which are gathered here.

Banqueting House ⓫

Whitehall SW1. **Map** 13 B4. **Tel** 0844-482 7777 or 020-3166 6151 (possible closures – call ahead). Charing Cross, Embankment, Westminster. **Open** 10am–5pm Mon–Sat (last adm 4:30pm). **Closed** Sun, public hols, 24 Dec–1 Jan; for functions (phone first). **Adm charge.** www.hrp.org.uk

This delightful building is of great architectural importance. It was the first in central London to embody the Classical Palladian style that designer Inigo Jones brought back from his travels in Italy. Completed in 1622, its disciplined stone facade marked a startling change from the Elizabethans' fussy turrets and unrestrained external decoration. It was the sole survivor of the fire that destroyed most of the old Whitehall Palace in 1698.

The ceiling paintings by Rubens, a complex allegory on the exaltation of James I, were commissioned by his son, Charles I, in 1630. This blatant glorification of royalty was despised by Oliver Cromwell and the Parliamentarians, who executed King Charles I on a scaffold outside Banqueting House in 1649. Ironically, Charles II celebrated his restoration to the throne here 11 years later. The building is used for official functions.

Mounted sentries stationed outside Horse Guards Parade

Horse Guards Parade ⓬

Whitehall SW1. **Map** 13 B4. **Tel** 0906-201 5151. Westminster, Charing Cross, Embankment. **Open** 8am–6pm daily. **Changing the Guard** 11am Mon–Sat, 10am Sun. **Dismounting Ceremony** 4pm daily. Times for both are subject to change (phone for details). **Trooping the Colour** see **Ceremonial London** pp52–5.

Once Henry VIII's tiltyard (tournament ground), nowadays the Changing of the Guard takes place here every morning. The elegant buildings, completed in 1755, were designed by William Kent. On the left is the Old Treasury, also by Kent, and Dover House, completed in 1758 and now used as the Scottish Office.

Nearby is a trace of the "real tennis" court where Henry VIII is said to have played the ancient precursor of modern lawn tennis. On the opposite side, the view is dominated by the ivy-covered Citadel. This is a bomb-proof structure that was erected in 1940 beside the Admiralty. During World War II it was used as a communications headquarters by the Navy.

Trafalgar Studios ⓭

Whitehall SW1. **Map** 13 B3. **Tel** 0844-871 7632. Charing Cross. **Open** for performances only. See **Entertainment** pp344–5.

Detail of a Whitehall Theatre box

Formerly the Whitehall Theatre and built in 1930, the plain white front seems to emulate the Cenotaph (see p74) at the other end of the street but, inside, the theatre boasts fine Art Deco detailing. The studios comprise two intimate spaces.

Queen Anne's Gate ⓮

SW1. **Map** 13 A5. St James's Park.

The spacious terraced houses at the west end of this well-preserved enclave date from 1704 and are notable for the ornate canopies over their front doors. At the other end are houses built some 70 years later, sporting blue plaques that record former residents, such as Lord Palmerston, the Victorian Prime Minister. Until recently, the British Secret Service, MI5, was allegedly based in this unlikely spot. A small statue of Queen Anne stands in front of the wall separating Nos. 13 and 15. To the west, situated at the corner of Petty France, Sir Basil Spence's Home Office building (1976)

Panels from the Rubens ceiling, Banqueting House

is an architectural incongruity. Cockpit Steps, leading down to Birdcage Walk, mark the site of a 17th-century venue for the popular, yet blood-thirsty, sport of cockfighting.

Guards Museum **⑮**

Birdcage Walk SW1. **Map** 13 A5. **Tel** 020-7414 3428. ⊖ *St James's Park.* **Open** *10am–4pm daily (last adm: 3.30pm).* **Closed** *Christmas, ceremonies.* **Adm charge** *(free for under-16s).* ⌖ ♿ ⧠ **www**.theguardsmuseum.com

Entered from Birdcage Walk, the museum is under the parade ground of Wellington Barracks, headquarters of the five Guards regiments. A must for military buffs, the museum uses tableaux and dioramas to illustrate various battles in which the Guards have taken part, from the English Civil War (1642–8) to the present. Weapons and row after row of colourful uniforms are on display, as well as a fascinating collection of models.

St James's Park Station **⑯**

55 Broadway SW1. **Map** 13 A5. ⊖ *St James's Park.*

Epstein sculpture outside St James's Park Station

The station is built into Broadway House, Charles Holden's 1929 headquarters for London Transport. It is notable for its sculptures by Jacob Epstein and reliefs by Henry Moore and Eric Gill.

Blewcoat School **⑰**

23 Caxton St SW1. **Map** 13 A5. **Tel** 020-7222 2877. ⊖ *St James's Park.* **Open** *10am–5.30pm Mon–Fri (and 10am–4pm Sat, 7 Nov–19 Dec).* ⧠

Statue of a Blewcoat pupil above the Caxton Street entrance

A red-brick gem hemmed in by the office towers of Victoria Street, it was built in 1709 as a charity school to teach pupils how to "read, write, cast accounts and the catechism". It remained as a school until 1939, then became an army store during World War II and was bought by the National Trust in 1954. The beautifully proportioned interior now serves as a National Trust gift shop.

Westminster Cathedral **⑱**

Ashley Place SW1. **Map** 20 F1. **Tel** 020-7798 9055. ⊖ *Victoria.* **Open** *7am–7pm Mon–Fri, 8am–7pm Sat & Sun.* **Adm charge** *for bell tower lift (Apr–Nov: 9am–5pm daily, Dec–Mar: 9am–5pm Thu–Sun).* ⧠ *5.30pm Mon–Fri, 10.30am Sat & Sun, sung Mass.* ♿ ⧠ ⧠ **www**.westminstercathedral.org.uk

One of London's rare Byzantine buildings, it was designed by John Francis Bentley for the Catholic diocese and completed in 1903 on the site of a former prison. Its 87-m (285-ft) high, red-brick tower, with horizontal stripes of white stone, stands out on the skyline in sharp contrast to the Abbey nearby. A restful piazza on the north side provides a good view of the cathedral from Victoria Street. The rich interior deco-ration, with marble of varying colours and intricate mosaics, makes the domes above the nave seem incongruous. They were left bare because the project ran out of money.

Eric Gill's dramatic reliefs of the 14 Stations of the Cross, created during World War I, adorn the pier of the nave, which is the widest in Britain. The organ is one of the finest in Europe, and there are often free recitals on Sunday afternoons at 4.45pm.

St John's, Smith Square **⑲**

Smith Sq SW1. **Map** 21 B1. **Tel** 020-7222 1061. ⊖ *Westminster. Box office open 10am–5pm Mon–Fri. Not open to public except for concerts.* ⌖ ♿ *phone first.* ⧠ **www**.sjss.org.uk

Baroque interior of St John's, Smith Square

Described by artist and art historian Sir Hugh Casson as one of the masterpieces of English Baroque architecture, Thomas Archer's plump church, with its turrets at each corner, looks as if it is trying to burst from the confines of the square, and rather over-powers the pleasing 18th-century houses on its north side. Today it is principally a concert hall. It has an accident-prone history: com-pleted in 1728, it was burned down in 1742, struck by light-ning in 1773 and destroyed by a World War II bomb in 1941. There is a reasonably priced basement restaurant that is open daily for lunch and on concert evenings.

Tate Britain **⑳**

See pp82–5.

Tate Britain ⑳

Tate Britain displays the world's largest collection of British art from the 16th to the 21st century. The international modern art once housed here is now held at Tate Modern *(see pp178–81)*. In the Clore Galleries are works from the magnificent Turner Bequest, left to the nation by the great landscape artist J M W Turner in 1851. The Clore Galleries have their own entrance, giving direct access to the Turner Collection and allowing a full appreciation of Sir James Stirling's Post-Modernist design for the building.

Loan exhibitions covering aspects of British art are installed here and on the lower floor.

Main floor

Lower floor

Manton entrance

The Saltonstall Family *(c.1637)*
David Des Granges's life-size family portrait includes the dead first Lady Saltonstall as the second shows off her new baby.

★ Ophelia *(1851–2)*
Taken from Shakespeare's play Hamlet, *the scene of the drowning of Ophelia by Pre-Raphaelite John Everett Millais is one of the most famous – and popular – paintings at Tate Britain.*

GALLERY GUIDE
The permanent collection occupies three quarters of the main floor. Starting in the northwest corner, the displays follow a broad chronological sweep from the early 16th century to the present. Each room explores a contemporary or historical theme or is devoted to a major artist. The remainder of the gallery space is used for major loan exhibitions. Due to refurbishment, some rooms may be closed to the public.

KEY TO FLOORPLAN

- ☐ 1500–1900
- ☐ 1900–1960
- ☐ 1960 to present
- ☐ Art Now
- ☐ Duveen Sculpture Gallery
- ☐ Clore Galleries
- ☐ Loan Exhibitions
- ☐ Non-exhibition space

Carnation, Lily, Lily, Rose *(1885–6)*
John Singer Sargent (1856–1925) moved to Britain from Paris in 1885 and adopted some of the Impressionist techniques established by his personal friend, Claude Monet. The title of this work is taken from a popular song of the time.

THE ART OF GOOD FOOD

The lower floor of Tate Britain boasts a café and an espresso bar, as well as a restaurant. Celebrated murals by Rex Whistler adorn the walls of the restaurant, telling the tale of the mythical inhabitants of Epicuriana and their expedition in search of rare foods. The extensive wine list has won awards. Open for lunch and afternoon tea.

Entrance to Clore Galleries

Rotunda

Millbank entrance

Stairs to lower floor

The Lady of Shalott *(1888)*
J W Waterhouse's work reflects the Pre-Raphaelite fascination with Arthurian myth.

★ **Peace – Burial at Sea** *(1842)*
This is J M W Turner's tribute to his friend and rival David Wilkie. It was painted in 1842, the year after Wilkie died at sea.

★ **Three Studies for Figures at the Base of a Crucifixion**
(c.1944, detail)
Francis Bacon's famous triptych encapsulates an anguished vision of human existence. When first displayed, its savagery deeply shocked audiences.

STAR PAINTINGS

★ Peace – Burial at Sea by Turner

★ Ophelia by John Everett Millais

★ Three Studies for Figures at the Base of a Crucifixion by Francis Bacon

Exploring Tate Britain

Tate Britain draws its displays from the massive Tate Collection. The variety of works on show, combined with a rigorous programme of loan exhibitions and career retrospectives of British artists results in a selection to suit all tastes – from Elizabethan portraiture to cutting-edge installation. The displays are changed frequently to explore many different aspects of the history and art of Britain from 1500 to the present day.

The Cholmondeley Ladies (c. 1600–10), British School

1500–1800

This group of galleries covers a period of dramatic change in British history, from the Tudors and Stuarts through to the age of Thomas Gainsborough. "Hogarth" includes important works by one of Britain's greatest painters, known for his biting satire on the lifestyle and beliefs of his contemporaries. By contrast, "The Grand Manner" shows dramatic large-scale paintings in an idealised style by artists such as Benjamin West and Joshua Reynolds, the head of the newly established Royal Academy. Landscape painting lies at the heart of the revolution in British painting during

the nineteenth century, and "British Landscape" shows how images of the countryside changed ideas not only about art, but about what it means to be British. The last room in this section is devoted to a series of changing displays about the poet and artist William Blake.

Satan Smiting Job with Sore Boils (c.1826) by William Blake

1800–1900

The end of the eighteenth century and the first half of the nineteenth saw dramatic expansion and change in the arts in Britain. New themes began to emerge, and artists started working on a much larger scale as they competed with each other for attention on the walls of public exhibitions. "Romantic Painting in Britain" includes monumental canvases by John Martin, Thomas Lawrence and William Etty, as well as celebrated works by David Wilkie. This is followed by a series of three rooms that tell the story of Victorian art. Storytelling was at the heart of the Victorians' belief in the power of art to convey moral messages, and "Victorian Paintings of Modern Life" includes such important works as Augustus Egg's series *Past and Present*. "Pre-Raphaelites and Painters of the Ideal" brings together work by perhaps the most popular group of artists at Tate Britain: it includes John Everett Millais's *Ophelia*, William Holman Hunt's *Awakening Conscience* and several paintings by Dante Gabriel Rossetti. The last in this sequence of three rooms, "Victorian Spectacle", is a dramatic display of painting and sculpture from the late Victorian period, including John Singer Sargent's haunting evocation of young girls in a garden at twilight *Carnation, Lily, Lily, Rose*.

TURNER AT THE CLORE GALLERIES

The Turner Bequest comprises some 300 oil paintings and about 20,000 watercolours and drawings received by the nation from the great landscape painter J M W Turner after his death in 1851. Turner's will had specified that a gallery be built to house his pictures and this was finally done in 1987 with the opening of the Clore Galleries. Most of the oil paintings are on view in the main galleries, while the watercolours are the subject of changing displays.

Shipping at the Mouth of the Thames (c. 1806–7)

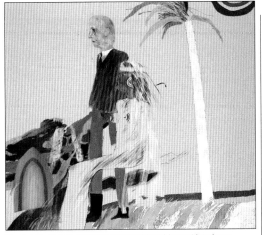

The First Marriage (A Marriage of Styles I) **(1962) by David Hockney**

1900–1960

The modern section of the gallery begins with the early twentieth century. "Modern Figures" looks at artists' fascination with modern cities: cosmopolitan, noisy places with crowded streets, continually changing architecture and fast, mechanized transport, as well as new places of entertainment. It

Recumbent Figure **(1938) by Henry Moore**

includes Jacob Epstein's *Torso in Metal from "The Rock Drill"*, a machine-like robot, visored and menacing, that became a symbol of the new age, as well as the work of Wyndham Lewis and his Vorticist group, who saw the artist at the still centre of the vortex of modern life.

Work by celebrated British sculptors, such as Barbara Hepworth and Henry Moore, can also be seen in this section. Paintings by two of the most famous, and disturbing, modern British artists are also on display here: Francis Bacon, whose *Three Studies for Figures at the Base of a Crucifixion* (c. 1944) depicts three mutant organisms in agony, confined in an apparently hostile and godless world; and Lucian Freud, whose expressive nudes are on display.

1960 TO PRESENT

From the 1960s, Tate's funding for the purchase of works began to increase substantially, while artistic activity continued to pick up speed, encouraged by public funding. As a result, the Tate Collection is particularly rich on this time period, which means that the frequent rotation of displays is necessary.

There is, however, one room devoted to "Pop", one of the liveliest developments of British art in the 1960s, which focuses in particular on the beginnings of the movement through iconic works by artists such as Sir Peter Blake, Richard Hamilton, the early work of David Hockney, and Gerald Laing, deriving his inspiration for *Skydiver VI* (1964) from mass produced images of the 1960s.

A revolt against this movement took place at the end of the 1960s, with the emergence of Conceptual artists such as Gilbert & George, known as the Living Sculptures, and Richard Long, who created a whole new approach to landscape painting by importing the land itself into the gallery.

Conceptual art in turn was rejected at the start of the 1980s by the School of London painters, including Howard Hodgkin, Frank Auerbach and R B Kitaj, while Tony Cragg, Richard Deacon and Antony Gormley pioneered a new kind of sculpture.

The 1990s saw a new surge in British art. Most recent British movements are well represented at Tate Britain. These include the work of the so-called Young British Artists (YBAs), who include Damien Hirst, perhaps the most notorious, as well as the controversial installations and photographic work of Tracey Emin and Sarah Lucas, exhibiting as both a collective and individually. Many contemporary British artists, including Tacita Dean, Douglas Gordon, Sam Taylor-Wood, Steve McQueen and Jane and Louise Wilson, use film and video as their medium – a major development of recent times and the subject of a number of special displays at Tate Britain.

The frequently changing displays at Tate Britain include wider surveys as well as rooms devoted to single artists, and feature important works newly acquired by Tate. Art Now reflects current developments in contemporary British art and is devoted to new work by the latest up-and-coming artists.

Skydiver VI **(1964) by Gerald Laing**

PICCADILLY AND ST JAMES'S

Piccadilly is the main artery of the West End. Once called Portugal Street, it acquired its present name from the ruffs, or pickadills, worn by 17th-century dandies. St James's still bears traces of the 18th century, when it surrounded the royal residences, and denizens of the court and society shopped and disported

Buckingham Palace decorative lock

themselves here. Two shops in St James's Street – James Lock the hatter and Berry Bros. & Rudd vintners – recall that era. Fortnum and Mason, on Piccadilly, has served high-quality food for nearly 300 years. Mayfair to the north is still the most fashionable address in London, while Piccadilly Circus marks the start of Soho.

SIGHTS AT A GLANCE

Historic Streets and Buildings
Piccadilly Circus ❶
Albany ❸
Burlington Arcade ❺
Ritz Hotel ❻
Spencer House ❼
St James's Palace ❽
St James's Square ❾
Royal Opera Arcade ❿
Pall Mall ⓫
The Mall ⓮
Marlborough House ⓯
Clarence House ⓱
Lancaster House ⓲
Buckingham Palace pp94–5 ⓳
Royal Mews ㉑
Wellington Arch ㉒
Shepherd Market ㉔

Museums and Galleries
Royal Academy of Arts ❹
Institute of Contemporary Arts ⓬
The Queen's Gallery ⓴
Royal Mews ㉑
Apsley House ㉓
Faraday Museum ㉖

Churches
St James's Church ❷
Queen's Chapel ⓰

Parks and Gardens
St James's Park ⓭
Green Park ㉕

KEY

▦	Street-by-Street map
Ⓔ	Underground station
🚆	Railway station

SEE ALSO

- *Street Finder*, maps 12, 13
- *Where to Stay* pp278–291
- *Restaurants, Pubs* pp292–319

GETTING THERE
The Piccadilly line serves Hyde Park Corner, Piccadilly Circus, and Green Park – also served by the Jubilee and Victoria lines. The Bakerloo and Northern lines serve Charing Cross. The area is served by buses 6, 9, 15, 23, 139.

0 metres   500
0 yards   500

◁ **Piccadilly Arcade with its many fine shops**

Street-by-Street: Piccadilly and St James's

As soon as Henry VIII built St James's Palace in the 1530s, the area around it became the centre of fashionable London, and it has remained so ever since. The most influential people in the land strut importantly along its historic streets as they press on with the vital business of lunching in their clubs, discussing matters of pith and moment and brandishing their gold cards in the capital's most exclusive stores, or paying a visit to one of the many art galleries.

Albany
This has been one of London's smartest addresses since it opened in 1803 ❸

★ **Royal Academy of Arts**
Sir Joshua Reynolds founded the Academy in 1768. Now it mounts large popular exhibitions ❹

★ **Burlington Arcade**
Uniformed beadles discourage unruly behaviour in this 19th-century mall ❺

Fortnum and Mason
was founded in 1707 by one of Queen Anne's footmen *(see p321).*

The Ritz Hotel
Named after César Ritz, and opened in 1906, it still lives up to his name ❻

Spencer House
An ancestor of Princess Diana built this house in 1766 ❼

St James's Palace
This Tudor palace is still the Court's official headquarters ❽

To The Mall

Jermyn Street is one of London's most elegant streets, lined with shops for style-conscious men *(see p324).*

Piccadilly station

★ Piccadilly Circus
The crowds and dazzling neon lights make Piccadilly Circus the West End's focal point **1**

LOCATOR MAP
See Central London Map pp14–15

★ St James's Church
The organ in Christopher Wren's favourite church was brought here from Whitehall Palace in 1691 **2**

Pall Mall
Its famous clubs provide a haven for businessmen (and a few women) **11**

St James's Square
William III's statue dominates the square **9**

King Street is lined with art galleries, including Christie's, St James's.

STAR SIGHTS

★ Burlington Arcade

★ Royal Academy

★ St James's Church

★ Piccadilly Circus

KEY

– – – Suggested route

0 metres	100
0 yards	100

Piccadilly Circus ❶

W1. **Map** 13 A3. ⊖ *Piccadilly Circus*

Alfred Gilbert's statue of Eros

For years people have congregated beneath the symbolic figure of Eros, originally intended as an angel of mercy but renamed after the Greek god of love. Poised delicately with his bow, Eros has become almost a trade mark for the capital. It was erected in 1892 as a memorial to the Earl of Shaftesbury, the Victorian philanthropist. Part of Nash's master plan for Regent Street, Piccadilly Circus has been considerably altered over the years and consists for the most part of shopping malls. One of them can be found behind the façade of the London Pavilion (1885), once a popular music hall. The circus has London's gaudiest array of neon advertising signs marking the entrance to the city's lively entertainment district with cinemas, theatres, night clubs, restaurants and pubs.

St James's Church ❷

197 Piccadilly W1. **Map** 13 A3. **Tel** *020-7734 4511.* ⊖ *Piccadilly Circus.* **Open** *8am–6:30pm daily.* **Craft market** *9am–6pm Wed–Sat,* **antiques market** *9am–6pm Tue.* ⓐ *access from Jermyn St.* ▢ **Concerts, talks, events.** **www**.st-james-piccadilly.org

Among the many churches Wren designed *(see p47),* this is said to be one of his favourites. It has been altered

over the years and was half-wrecked by a bomb in 1940, but it maintains its essential features from 1684 – the tall, arched windows, thin spire (a 1966 fibreglass replica of the original) and a light, dignified interior. The ornate screen behind the altar is one of the finest works of the 17th-century master carver Grinling Gibbons, who also made the exquisite marble font, with a scene depicting Adam and Eve standing by the Tree of Life. Artist and poet William Blake and Prime Minister Pitt the Elder were both baptized here. More of Gibbons's carvings can be seen above the grandiose organ, made for Whitehall Palace chapel but installed here in 1691. Today the church has a full calendar of events, and houses a popular café.

Albany ❸

Albany Court Yard, Piccadilly W1. **Map** 12 F3. ⊖ *Green Park, Piccadilly Circus.* **Closed** *to the public.*

These desirable and discreet bachelor apartments, half hidden through an entrance off Piccadilly, were built in 1803 by Henry Holland. Notable residents have included the poet Lord Byron, novelist Graham Greene, two Prime Ministers (William Gladstone and Edward Heath) and the actor Terence Stamp. Married men were admitted in 1878 but could not bring their wives to live with them until 1919. Women are now allowed to live here in their own right.

Byron lived in The Albany

Royal Academy of Arts ❹

Burlington House, Piccadilly W1. **Map** 12 F3. **Tel** *020-7300 8000.* ⊖ *Piccadilly Circus, Green Park.* **Open** *10am–6pm Sun–Thu, 10am–10pm Fri & Sat.* **Closed** *Good Fri, 24–25 Dec.* **Adm charge** *some exhibitions.* ▢ ⓐ ▢ ▢ ▢ ▢ **www**.royalacademy.org.uk

Michelangelo's Madonnna and Child

The courtyard in front of Burlington House, one of the West End's few surviving mansions from the early 18th century, is often crammed with people waiting to get into one of the prestigious visiting art exhibitions on show at the Royal Academy (founded 1768). The famous annual summer exhibition, which has now been held for over 200 years, comprises around 1,200 new works by both established and unknown artists. Any artist, established or unknown, may submit work.

The airy Sackler Galleries (1991), designed by Norman Foster, show visiting exhibitions. There are permanent items in the sculpture promenade outside the galleries, notably a Michelangelo relief of the Madonna and Child (1505). The exceptional permanent collection (not all on display) includes one work by each current and former Academician; the highlights are displayed in the Madejski Rooms. Two shops adjacent to the gallery exits sell merchandise inspired by the current exhibitions, as well as a great range of art books.

Burlington Arcade **5**

Piccadilly W1. **Map** 12 F3. 🚇 *Green Park, Piccadilly Circus. See **Shops and Markets** p328.*

This is one of four 19th-century arcades of small shops which sell traditional British luxuries. (The Princes and Piccadilly Arcades are on the south side of Piccadilly, while the Royal Opera Arcade is off Pall Mall.) It was built for Lord Cavendish in 1819 to stop rubbish being thrown into his garden. The arcade is still patrolled by beadles who make sure an atmosphere of refinement is maintained. They have authority to eject anyone who sings, whistles, runs or opens an umbrella; those powers are infrequently invoked now, perhaps because the dictates of commerce take precedence over those of decorum.

Ritz Hotel **6**

Piccadilly W1. **Map** 12 F3. **Tel** *020-7493 8181.* 🚇 *Green Park.* **Open** *to non-residents for tea or restaurant (book ahead).* 🚻 *(See p287.)* **www**.theritzlondon.com

Cesar Ritz, the famed Swiss hotelier who inspired the adjective "ritzy", had virtually retired by the time this hotel was built and named after him in 1906. The colonnaded frontal aspect of the imposing château-style building was meant to suggest Paris, where the very grandest and most fashionable hotels were to be

The exquisite Palm Room of Spencer House

found around the turn of the century. It maintains its Edwardian air of opulence and is a popular stop, among those who are suitably dressed (no jeans or trainers; jacket and tie for men), for afternoon tea, with daily servings in the Palm Court at 11.30am, 1.30, 3.30 and 5.30pm. Champagne tea is served at 7.30pm.

Spencer House **7**

27 St James's Pl SW1. **Map** 12 F4. **Tel** *020-7514 1958.* 🚇 *Green Park.* **Open** *10:30am–5:45pm Sun (last adm: 4:45pm). Garden open one Sunday in June 2pm–5pm.* **Closed** *Jan & Aug.* **Adm charge. Children** *not under 10.* 🚫 🚻 📷 *compulsory.* **www**.spencerhouse.co.uk

This Palladian palace, built in 1766 for the first Earl Spencer, an ancestor of the late Princess of Wales, has been completely restored to its 18th-century splendour (thanks to an £18

million renovation project). It contains some wonderful paintings and contemporary furniture; one of the highlights is the beautifully decorated Painted Room. The house is open to the public for guided tours, receptions and meetings.

St James's Tudor gatehouse

St James's Palace **8**

Pall Mall SW1. **Map** 12 F4. 🚇 *Green Park.* **Not open** *to the public.*

Built by Henry VIII in the late 1530s on the site of a former leper hospital, it was a primary royal residence only briefly, mainly during the reign of Elizabeth I and during the late 17th and early 18th centuries. In 1952 Queen Elizabeth II made her first speech as queen here, and foreign ambassadors are still officially accredited to the Court of St James's. Its northern gatehouse, seen from St James's Street, is one of London's most evocative Tudor landmarks. Behind it the palace buildings are now occupied by privileged Crown servants.

Afternoon tea served in the opulent Palm Court of the Ritz

Royal Opera Arcade

St James's Square ⑨

SW1. **Map** 13 A3. 🚇 *Green Park, Piccadilly Circus.*

One of London's earliest squares, it was laid out in the 1670s and lined by exclusive houses for those whose business made it vital for them to live near St James's Palace. Many of the buildings date from the 18th and 19th centuries and have had many illustrious residents. During World War II Generals Eisenhower and de Gaulle both had headquarters here.

   Today No. 10 on the north side is Chatham House (1736), home of the Royal Institute for International Affairs and, in the northwest corner, can be found the London Library (1896), a private lending library founded in 1841 by historian Thomas Carlyle *(see p196)* and others. The lovely gardens in the middle contain an equestrian statue of William III, here since 1808.

Royal Opera Arcade ⑩

SW1. **Map** 13 A3. 🚇 *Piccadilly Circus.*

London's first shopping arcade was designed by John Nash and completed in 1818, behind the Haymarket Opera House (now called Her Majesty's Theatre). It beat the Burlington Arcade *(see p91)* by a year or so. The traditional shops that once used to be based here have since moved

on: Farlows, selling shooting and fishing equipment, and the famous Hunter's green Wellington boots, are now nearby, at No. 9 Pall Mall.

Pall Mall ⑪

SW1. **Map** 13 A4. 🚇 *Charing Cross, Green Park, Piccadilly Circus.*

The Duke of Wellington (1842): a frequent visitor to Pall Mall

This dignified street is named from the game of palle-maille – a cross between croquet and golf – which was played here in the 17th century. For more than 150 years Pall Mall has been at the heart of London's clubland. Here, exclusive gentlemen's clubs were formed to provide members with a refuge from their womenfolk.

   The clubhouses now amount to a text book of the most fashionable architects of the era. From the east end, on the left is the colonnaded entrance to No. 116, Nash's United Services Club (1827). This was the favourite club of the Duke of Wellington and

now houses the Institute of Directors. Facing it, on the other side of Waterloo Place, is the Athenaeum (No. 107), designed three years later by Decimus Burton, and long the power house of the British establishment. Next door are two clubs by Sir Charles Barry, architect of the Houses of Parliament *(see pp72–3)*; the Travellers' is at No. 106 and the Reform at No. 104. The clubs' stately interiors are well preserved but only members and their guests are admitted.

Institute of Contemporary Arts ⑫

The Mall SW1. **Map** 13 B3. *Tel 020-7930 3647.* 🚇 *Charing Cross, Piccadilly Circus.* **Open** *noon–11pm Mon–Wed, noon–1am Thu–Sat, noon–9pm Sun. (Exhibition space closes 7pm, 9pm Thu, bookshop 9pm.)* **Closed** *24–26, 31 Dec, 1 Jan, public hols.* **Adm charge.** ♿ *(cinema and lower gallery) phone first.* 📷 🍴 🛍 *Concerts, theatre, dance, lectures, films, exhibitions. See Entertainment pp350–51.* **www**.ica.org.uk

The Institute (ICA) was established in 1947 in an effort to offer British artists some of the facilities which were available to artists at The Museum of Modern Art in New York. Originally on Dover Street, it has been situated in John Nash's Classical Carlton House Terrace (1833) since 1968. With its entrance on The Mall, this extensive warren contains a cinema, auditorium, bookshop, art gallery, bar and restaurant. It also offers plays, concerts and lectures. Non-members pay a charge.

Institute of Contemporary Arts, Carlton House Terrace

St James's Park ⓭

SW1. **Map** 13 A4. **Tel** 020-7298 2000 🚇 St James's Park. **Open** dawn to dusk daily. 🍴 **Open** daily. 🎵 **Concerts** twice daily on summer weekends in good weather. **Bird collection.** www.royalparks.org.uk

In summer office workers sunbathe between the dazzling flower beds of this, the capital's most ornamental park. In winter overcoated civil servants discuss affairs of state as they stroll by the lake and eye its ducks, geese and pelicans. Originally a marsh, the park was drained by Henry VIII and incorporated into his hunting grounds. Later Charles II redesigned it for pedestrian pleasures, with an aviary along its southern edge (hence Birdcage Walk, the street where the aviary was). It is still a popular place to take the air, with an appealing view of Whitehall rooftops. In the summer there are concerts on the bandstand.

The Mall ⓮

SW1. **Map** 13 A4. 🚇 Charing Cross, Green Park, Piccadilly Circus.

This broad triumphal approach to Buckingham Palace was created by Aston Webb when he redesigned the front of the palace and the Victoria Monument in 1911 (see picture p96). It follows the course of the old path at the edge of St James's Park, laid out in the reign of Charles II when it became London's most fashionable promenade. On the flagpoles down both sides of The Mall fly national flags of foreign heads of state during official visits.

Marlborough House ⓯

Pall Mall SW1. **Map** 13 A4. **Tel** 020-7747 6491. 🚇 St James's Park, Green Park. **Open** 3rd Sat in Sep only (phone for details). 📷 by appt Mon–Fri.

Marlborough House was designed by Christopher Wren (see p47) for the Duchess of Marlborough, and finished in 1711. It was substantially enlarged in the 19th century and used by members of the Royal Family. From 1863 until he became Edward VII in 1901, it was the home of the Prince and Princess of Wales and the social centre of London. An Art Nouveau memorial in the Marlborough Road wall of the house commemorates Edward's queen, Alexandra. The building now houses the Commonwealth Secretariat.

Queen's Chapel ⓰

Marlborough Rd SW1. **Map** 13 A4. **Tel** 020-7930 4832. 🚇 Green Park. **Open** Easter–July: 8:30–11:30am Sun, Saints' Days.

This exquisite work of the architect Inigo Jones was built for Charles I's French wife, Henrietta Maria, in 1627, and was the first Classical church in England. It was initially

Queen's Chapel

intended to be part of St James's Palace but is now separated from it by Marlborough Gate. George III married his queen, Charlotte of Mecklenburg-Strelitz (who was to bear him 15 children), here in 1761. The interior of the chapel, with its wonderful Annibale Carracci altarpiece and glorious 17th-century fittings is open to both regular worshippers and visitors during the spring and early summer.

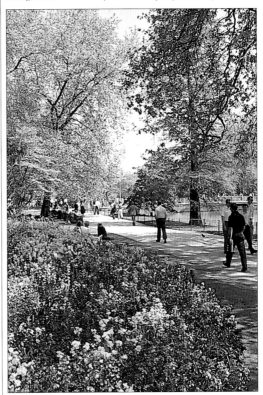

Early summer in St James's Park

Buckingham Palace ⑲

Buckingham Palace is both office and home to the British monarchy. It is also used for ceremonial state occasions such as banquets for visiting heads of state. About 300 people work at the palace, including officers of the Royal Household and domestic staff.

John Nash converted the original Buckingham House into a palace for George IV (reigned 1820–30). Both he and his brother, William IV (reigned 1830–37), died before work was completed, and Queen Victoria was the first monarch to live at the palace. The present east front, facing The Mall, was added to Nash's conversion in 1913. The State Rooms are now open to the public in summer.

Music Room
State guests are presented and royal christenings take place in this room, which boasts a beautiful, original parquet floor by Nash.

The State Dining Room is where meals that are less formal than state banquets are held.

State Ballroom
The Edwardian French-style ballroom is used for state banquets and investitures.

Blue Drawing Room
Imitation onyx columns, created by John Nash, decorate this room.

Court post office

The Queen's Gallery
Artworks from the Queen's Collection (see p96), such as Canaletto's Rome: The Pantheon, *are often on display.*

Changing of the Guard
During the summer the palace guard is changed regularly in a colourful and musical military ceremony (see pp52–5).

The White Drawing Room is where the Royal Family assemble before passing into the State Dining Room or Ball Room.

The garden is a haven for wildlife and is overlooked by most of the lavishly decorated state rooms at the back of the palace.

VISITORS' CHECKLIST

SW1. **Map** 12 F5. **Tel** 020-7766 7300. ⊖ St James's Park, Victoria. 🚌 2B, 11, 16, 24, 25, 36, 38, 52, 73, 135, C1. 🚆 Victoria. **State rooms open** end-Jul–end-Sep: 9.30am–5:30pm daily. **Adm charge.** 📷 www.royalcollection.org.uk **Changing of the Guard:** May–Jul: 11.30am daily; Aug–Apr: alternate days. Tickets free, book at **www.royal.gov.uk**

The Throne Room is illuminated by seven magnificent chandeliers.

The Green Drawing Room is the first of the state rooms entered by guests at royal functions.

Queen's Audience Chamber
This is one of the Queen's 12 private rooms on the first floor of the palace.

The Royal Standard flies when the Queen is in residence.

WHO LIVES IN BUCKINGHAM PALACE?

The palace is the London residence of the Queen and her husband, the Duke of Edinburgh. Prince Edward also has an apartment here, as do Princess Anne and the Duke of York. About 50 domestic staff have rooms in the palace. There are more staff homes situated in the Royal Mews *(see p96)*.

View over The Mall
Traditionally, the Royal Family waves to crowds from the balcony.

Clarence House ⓱

Stable Yard SW1. **Map** 12 F4.
Tel 020-7766 7303. 🄴 Green Park,
St James's Park. **Open** 31 Jul–1 Sep:
10am-4pm (further dates may be
added). 🄰 🄰 🄰 mandatory.
www.royalcollection.org.uk

Designed by John Nash for
William IV in 1827, this is
Prince Charles's London home.
Once a year, the public can
visit the opulent ground floor.

Lancaster House ⓲

Stable Yard SW1. **Map** 12 F4.
🄴 Green Park, St James's Park.
Not open to the public.

Lancaster House

This royal residence was
built for the Duke of York
by Benjamin Wyatt, architect
of Apsley House, in 1825. In
1848 Chopin played here for
Queen Victoria, Prince Albert
and the Duke of Wellington.
It is now a conference centre.

Buckingham Palace ⓳

See pp94–5.

The Queen's Gallery ⓴

Buckingham Palace Rd SW1.
Map 12 F5. **Tel** 020-7766 7301.
🄴 St James's Park, Victoria. **Open**
10am–5.30pm daily (27 Jul–29 Sep:
9:30am–5:30pm). **Closed** dates vary;
call or check website. **Adm charge.**
🄰 **www**.royalcollection.org.uk

The Queen possesses one of
the finest and most valuable art
collections in the world, rich
in the work of Old Masters,
including Vermeer and Leonardo. In 2002 the galleries were
expanded in the most extensive addition to Buckingham
Palace in 150 years, resulting in
three and a half times more
display space and an impressive new entrance gallery with
a striking columned portico.
    Among the gallery's seven
rooms, one is dedicated to a
permanent display of some of
the royal collection's masterpieces. Changing exhibitions
call on an array of works, from
fine art to jewels, porcelain,
furniture and manuscripts.

Fabergé egg, The Queen's Gallery

Royal Mews ㉑

Buckingham Palace Rd SW1. **Map**
12 E5. **Tel** 020-7766 7302. 🄴 St
James's Park, Victoria. **Open** end
Mar–Oct: 11am–4pm Sat–Thu (27
Jul–29 Sep: closure at short notice (phone first).
Adm charge. 🄰 🄰 🄰
www.royalcollection.org.uk

Although open for only
a few hours each day,
the Mews is worth
catching for all lovers of
horses and of royal
pomp. The stables
and coach houses,
designed by Nash in
1825, accommodate
the horses and coaches
used by the Royal
Family on state
occasions. The star
exhibit is the gold
state coach, built
for George III in
1761, with fine panels
by Giovanni Cipriani.
Among the other
vehicles are

the Irish state coach, bought
by Queen Victoria for the
State Opening of Parliament;
the open-topped royal landau; and the glass coach which
was used for royal weddings
and for transporting foreign
ambassadors. The elaborate
horses' harnesses are also on
display, and so are some of
the fine animals that wear
them. The Mews
has an exhibition
that explains
its history and
current workings.
Visitors may see carriages
being prepared for use or
limousines in action. A
new guided route
around the mews
includes a chance to
view the 18th-century
riding school where
the horses are put
through their paces.
There is also a shop
here selling royal
souvenirs, open
daily from 9.30am
until 5pm.

The Victoria Monument outside Buckingham Palace

Wellington Arch ②

SW1. **Map** 12 D4. **Tel** 020-7930 2726. ⊖ Hyde Park Corner. **Open** Apr–Oct: 10am–5pm Wed–Sun & bank hols; Nov–Mar: 10am–4pm Wed–Sun. **Closed** 24–26 Dec, 1 Jan. **Adm charge** joint ticket with Apsley House available ♿ limited 🚻 **www**.english-heritage.org.uk

After nearly a century of debate about what to do with the patch of land in front of Apsley House, Wellington Arch, designed by Decimus Burton, was erected in 1828. The sculpture, by Adrian Jones, was added in 1912. Before it was installed Jones seated three people for dinner in the body of one of the horses.

The public now has access to exhibitions in the inner rooms of the arch. A viewing platform beneath the sculpture has great views over London.

Wellington Arch

Apsley House ②

Hyde Park Corner W1. **Map** 12 D4. **Tel** 020-7499 5676. ⊖ Hyde Park Corner. **Open** Apr–Oct: 11am–5pm Wed–Sun & bank hols; Nov–Mar: 11am–4pm Wed–Sun & bank hols. **Closed** 24–26 Dec, 1 Jan. **Adm charge** joint ticket with Wellington Arch available. 📷 📹 📹 pre-booked only. **www**.english-heritage.org.uk

Apsley House, on the south-east corner of Hyde Park, was completed by Robert Adam for Baron Apsley in 1778. Fifty years later it was enlarged and altered by the architect Benjamin Dean Wyatt, to provide a grand home for the Duke of Wellington. His dual career as soldier and politician brought him victory against Napoleon at Waterloo (1815), and two terms as prime minister (1828–30, 1834).

Interior of Apsley House

Against a sumptuous background of silk hangings and gilt decoration hangs the duke's art collection. Paintings by Goya, Velázquez, Brueghel and Rubens stand alongside displays of porcelain, silver and furniture. The duke's memorabilia include swords and medals, but are dominated by Canova's colossal statue of Napoleon, who was Wellington's arch-enemy.

Shepherd Market ②

W1. **Map** 12 E4. ⊖ Green Park.

This attractive and bijou pedestrianized enclave of small shops, restaurants, and outdoor cafés, between Piccadilly and Curzon Street, was named after Edward Shepherd, who built it in the middle of the 18th century. During the 17th century the annual 15-day May Fair (from which the name of the area is derived) took place on this site, and today Shepherd Market is still very much the centre of Mayfair.

Green Park ②

SW1. **Map** 12 E4. **Tel** 020-7930 1793. ⊖ Green Park, Hyde Park Corner. **Open** all day, year-round. **www**.royalparks.org.uk

Once part of Henry VIII's hunting ground, it was, like St James's Park, adapted for public use by Charles II in the 1660s and is a natural, undulating landscape of grass and trees (with a good spring show of daffodils). It was a favourite site for duels during the 18th century; in 1771 the poet Alfieri was wounded here by his mistress's husband, Viscount Ligonier, but then rushed back to the Haymarket Theatre in time to catch the last act of a play. Today the park is popular with guests staying at the Mayfair hotels as a place to jog.

Faraday Museum ②

The Royal Institution, 21 Albemarle St W1. **Map** 12 F3. **Tel** 020-7409 2992. ⊖ Green Park. **Open** 9am–9pm Mon–Fri. **Closed** 24 Dec–3 Jan. 📷 🍴 🚻 📹 phone first. **Lectures**. **www**.rigb.org

Michael Faraday was a 19th-century pioneer of the uses of electricity. The collections in the Michael Faraday Museum include some of his scientific apparatus and personal effects, as well as the work of other great scientists across the lower three floors.

Michael Faraday

SOHO AND TRAFALGAR SQUARE

Soho has been renowned for pleasures of the table, the flesh and the intellect ever since it was first developed in the late 17th century. For its first century the area was one of London's most fashionable, and Soho residents of the time have gone down in history for their extravagant parties.

During the later part of the 20th century, Soho consolidated its reputation as a centre for entertainment. With a

Clock on Liberty department store

cosmopolitan mix of people, visitors here enjoy the many pleasant bars, restaurants and cafés – popular with everyone from tourists to locals, office workers and London's gay community.

Soho is one of London's most multi-cultural districts. The first immigrants were 18th-century Huguenots from France *(see Christ Church, Spitalfields p170)*. Soho is also famous as a Chinatown; Gerrard Street is lined with Chinese restaurants.

SIGHTS AT A GLANCE

Historic Streets and Buildings
Trafalgar Square ❶
Admiralty Arch ❷
Leicester Square ❻
Shaftesbury Avenue ❽
Chinatown ❾
Charing Cross Road ❿
Soho Square ⓬
Carnaby Street ⓮

Shops and Markets
Berwick Street Market ⓭
Liberty ⓯

Churches
St Martin-in-the-Fields ❹

Museums and Galleries
National Gallery pp104–7 ❸
National Portrait Gallery ❺
Photographers' Gallery ⓰

Theatres
Palace Theatre ⓫
Theatre Royal Haymarket ❼

GETTING THERE
This area is served by the Central, Piccadilly, Bakerloo, Victoria and Northern lines. Many buses pass through Trafalgar Square and Piccadilly Circus. Rail services run from Charing Cross.

KEY
Street-by-Street map
Underground station
Railway station

0 metres 500
0 yards 500

SEE ALSO

◁ St Martin-in-the-Fields and Trafalgar Square

Street-by-Street: Trafalgar Square

This area buzzes both day and night with crowds enjoying the numerous restaurants, cinemas and nightclubs. Broad avenues lined with regal office buildings converge at Trafalgar Square. Some of the roads that ring the square have now been pedestrianized, making this already popular meeting place far more accessible.

To Tottenham Court Road station

Charing Cross Road
The shops here are a feast for booklovers ⑩

Shaftesbury Avenue
Theatreland's main artery is lined with announcements for current shows ⑧

★ Chinatown
An area of Chinese restaurants and shops, this is home to many Chinese-speaking people ⑨

The Blue Posts pub stands on the site of a pick-up point for sedan chairs in the 18th century.

The Trocadero's neon and laser beam decorations attract a youthful crowd to the floors of games, cafés, shops and cinemas.

Leicester Square
Film pioneer Charlie Chaplin stands in the traffic-free square ⑥

STAR SIGHTS

★ National Gallery

★ National Portrait Gallery

★ St Martin-in-the-Fields

★ Chinatown

★ Trafalgar Square

KEY

– – – Suggested route

0 metres   100

0 yards   100

Theatre Royal Haymarket
It is graced by a John Nash portico ⑦

Notre Dame, once a theatre, was converted into a church in 1855. The Jean Cocteau murals inside date from 1960.

The Hippodrome, a former night-club, was once a variety theatre and is now a cabaret venue.

BLOOMSBURY & FITZROVIA

HOLBORN & THE INNS OF COURT

SOHO & TRAFALGAR SQUARE

COVENT GARDEN & THE STRAND

PICCADILLY & ST JAMES'S

WHITEHALL & WESTMINSTER

SOUTH BANK

Thames

LOCATOR MAP
See Central London Map pp14–15

Cecil Court is lined with shops selling old books and prints.

★ **St Martin-in-the-Fields**
James Gibbs's masterpiece set the US "colonial" style ④

★ **National Portrait Gallery**
Portraits of prominent Britons from Tudor times to the present-day adorn the walls here ⑤

Leicester Square station

DUNCANNON ST

Charing Cross station

STRAND

★ **National Gallery**
The national collection of art is housed in these buildings ③

NORTHUMBERLAND AVE

TRAFALGAR SQUARE

CHARING CROSS

COCKSPUR STREET

MALL MALL EAST

Nelson's Column

Admiralty Arch
The entrance to the Mall was designed in 1911 ②

★ **Trafalgar Square**
Millions of tourists come here to admire the statues and the fountains ①

Trafalgar Square ❶

WC2. **Map** 13 B3.
🚇 Charing Cross.

London's main venue for rallies and outdoor public meetings was conceived by John Nash and was mostly constructed during the 1830s. The 50-m (165-ft) column commemorates Admiral Lord Nelson, Britain's most famous sea lord, who died heroically at the Battle of Trafalgar against Napoleon in 1805. It dates from 1842; 14 stonemasons held a dinner on its flat top before the statue of Nelson was finally installed. Edwin Landseer's four lions were added to guard its base 25 years later. The north side of the square is now taken up by the National Gallery and its annexe (see pp104–7), with Canada House on the west side, and South Africa House on the east. The restored Grand Buildings on the south side, with their fine arcade, were built in 1880 as the Grand Hotel. The square was partially pedestrianized in 2003, with other refurbishments including an enlarged central staircase descending from the National Gallery.

Nelson's statue over-looking the square

Admiralty Arch ❷

The Mall SW1. **Map** 13 B3.
🚇 Charing Cross.

Designed in 1911, this triple archway was part of Aston Webb's scheme to rebuild The Mall as a grand processional route honouring Queen Victoria. The arch effectively seals the eastern end of The Mall, although traffic passes through the smaller side gates, and separates courtly London from the hurly-burly of Trafalgar Square. The central gate is opened only for royal processions, making a fine setting for the coaches and horses trotting through.

Filming *Howard's End* at Admiralty Arch

National Gallery ❸

See pp104–7.

St Martin-in-the-Fields ❹

Trafalgar Sq WC2. **Map** 13 B3. *Tel* 020-7766 1100. 🚇 Charing Cross. **Open** 8am–6.30pm daily. ✝ 8am, 10am, noon, 5pm, 6.30pm Sun (phone for other days). ♿ 🔊 📖 🎧 *London Brass Rubbing Centre Tel* 020-7766 1122. **Open** 10am–7pm Mon–Wed, 10am–9pm Thu-Sat, 11:30am–6pm Sun (last brass rubbing entry 1 hr before close). **Concerts** see **Entertainment** pp348–9. **www**.stmartin-in-the-fields.org

There has been a church on this site since the 13th century. Many famous people were buried here, including Charles II's mistress, Nell Gwynne, and the painters William Hogarth and Joshua Reynolds. The present church was designed by James Gibbs and completed in 1726. In architectural terms it was one of the most influential ever built; it was much copied in the United States, where it became a model for the Colonial style of church-building. An unusual feature of St Martin's spacious interior is the royal box at gallery level on the left of the altar.

From 1914 until 1927 the crypt was used as a shelter for homeless soldiers and down-and-outs; during World War II it was an air-raid shelter. Today it helps the homeless by providing a lunchtime soup kitchen for them. It also has a café in the crypt, and a religious bookshop as well as the London Brass Rubbing Centre. Lunchtime and evening concerts are held in the church and in the café.

National Portrait Gallery ❺

2 St Martin's Place WC2. **Map** 13 B3. *Tel* 020-7312 2463. 🚇 Leicester Sq, Charing Cross. **Open** 10am–6pm Sat-Wed, 10am–9pm Thu–Fri. **Closed** 24–26 Dec. 🚫 ♿ Orange St entrance. 🔊 🍴 📖 🎧 **Lectures**. **www**.npg.org.uk

Too often ignored in favour of the National Gallery next door, this fascinating museum recounts Britain's development through portraits of its main characters, giving faces to names which are familiar from the history books. There are pictures of kings, queens, poets, musicians, artists,

William Shakespeare portrait on display in the Ondaatje Wing

thinkers, heroes and villains from all periods since the late 14th century. The oldest works, on the fourth floor, include a Hans Holbein cartoon of Henry VIII and paintings of several of his six wives.

The National Portrait Gallery's millennium development project, the Ondaatje Wing, opened in May 2000, allowing it 50 per cent more exhibition and public space. It includes a Tudor Gallery, displaying some of the earliest and most important paintings, including one of Shakespeare (by John Taylor in 1651), and the Ditchley portrait of Elizabeth I. A balcony provides an extra display area for portraits from the 1960s to the 1990s.

The gallery has a rooftop restaurant, and the spacious lecture theatre in the basement which is also used for drama and film events.

The gallery also houses temporary exhibitions and has an excellent shop selling books on art and literature, as well as an extensive range of cards, prints and posters featuring pictures from the main collection.

Leicester Square **6**

WC2. **Map** *13 B2.* 🚇 *Leicester Sq, Piccadilly Circus.*

It is hard to imagine that this, the perpetually animated heart of the West End entertainment district, was once a fashionable place to live. Laid out in 1670 south of Leicester House, a long-gone royal residence, the square's occupants included the scientist Isaac Newton and the artists Joshua Reynolds and William Hogarth. Reynolds made his fortune painting high society in his elegant salon at No. 46. Hogarth's house, in the south-east corner, became the Hôtel de la Sablionère in 1801, probably the area's first public restaurant.

In Victorian times several of London's most popular music halls were established here, including the Empire (today

the cinema on the same site perpetuates the name) and the Alhambra, replaced in 1937 by the Art Deco Odeon. A useful booth selling cut-price theatre tickets *(see p344)* sits in the square. There is also a statue of Charlie Chaplin (by John Doubleday), which was unveiled in 1981. The Shakespeare fountain dates from an earlier renovation in 1874.

Theatre Royal Haymarket **7**

Haymarket SW1. **Map** *13 A3.* **Tel** *0845-481 1870.* 🚇 *Piccadilly Circus.* **Open** *performances and guided tours (phone to check).* ♿ **www**.trh.co.uk

The fine frontage of this theatre, with its portico of six Corinthian columns, dates from 1821, when John Nash designed it as part of his plan for a stately route from Carlton House to Regent's Park. The interior is equally grand.

Shaftesbury Avenue **8**

W1. **Map** *13 A2.* 🚇 *Piccadilly Circus, Leicester Sq.*

The main artery of London's theatreland, Shaftesbury Avenue has six theatres and two cinemas, all on its north side. This street was cut through an area of terrible slums between 1877 and 1886 in order to improve communications across the city's busy West End; it follows the route of a much earlier highway. It is named after the Earl of Shaftesbury (1801–85), whose attempts to improve housing conditions had helped some of the local poor. (The Earl is also commemorated by the Eros statue in Piccadilly Circus – *see p90.*) The Lyric Theatre, which was designed by C J Phipps, has been open for almost the same length of time as the avenue.

London's West End: the façade of the Gielgud Theatre

National Gallery ❸

Trafalgar Square façade

The National Gallery has flourished since its inception in the early 19th century. In 1824 the House of Commons was persuaded to buy 38 major paintings, including works by Raphael and Rubens, and these became the start of a national collection. Contributions by rich benefactors have today resulted in a collection of some 2,000 Western European paintings. The main gallery building was designed in Greek Revival style by William Wilkins and built in 1833–8. To its left lies the Sainsbury Wing, financed by the grocery family and completed in 1991.

Doge Leonardo Loredan *(1501–2) Giovanni Bellini portrays this Venetian head of state as a serene father figure.*

Education Centre entrance ♿

Stairs to lower floor ♿ 🚹

Link to main building

Stairs to lower floors

Stairs and lift to lower galleries

GALLERY GUIDE

Most of the collection is housed on one floor divided into four wings. The paintings hang chronologically, with the earliest works (1250–1500) in the Sainsbury Wing. The North, West and East Wings cover 1500–1600, 1600–1700 and 1700–1900. Lesser paintings of all periods are on the lower floor.

★ **The Baptism of Christ** *Piero della Francesca painted this tranquil masterpiece (1450s) of early Renaissance perspective for a church in his native Umbria.*

Entrance Sainsbury Wing ♿

★ The Rokeby Venus
*(1647–51) Diego Velázquez
painted it to match a lost
Venetian nude.*

★ The Hay Wain *(1821)
John Constable brilliantly
caught the effect of distance
and the changing light
and shadow of a typically
English cloudy summer
day in this famous classic.*

VISITORS' CHECKLIST

Trafalgar Sq WC2. **Map** 13 B3.
Tel 020-7747 2885. ⊖ Charing
Cross, Leicester Sq, Piccadilly
Circus. 🚌 3, 6, 9, 11, 12, 13,
15, 23, 24, 29, 53, 88, 91, 139,
159, 176, 453.
🚆 Charing Cross. **Open** 10am–
6pm daily (9pm Fri). **Closed** 24–
26 Dec, 1 Jan. 🚫 ♿ Sainsbury
Wing and Getty entrances. 📷
🏠 🖥 🍴 🎫 ⬆ 📖 Sainsbury
Wing & temporary exhibitions.
**Lectures, film presentations,
exhibitions, special events.**
www.nationalgallery.org.uk

Central
Hall

33
32
34
37
35
36
41
39 38
43 42
45 44
46
2 1

Getty
entrance ♿

Trafalgar
Square entrance

At the Theatre *(1876–7)
Renoir was one of the
greatest painters of the
Impressionist movement.
The theatre was a
popular subject among
artists of the time.*

**★ The Leonardo
Cartoon** *(c.1500)
The genius of Leonardo da
Vinci glows through this chalk
drawing of the Virgin and
Child with St Anne and
St John the Baptist.*

KEY TO FLOORPLAN

☐	13th- to 15th-century
▨	16th-century
☐	17th-century
☐	18th- to early 20th-century
▨	Special exhibitions
☐	Non-exhibition space

★ The Ambassadors
*The strange shape in
the foreground of this
Hans Holbein portrait
(1533) is an anamor-
phic or distorted skull,
a symbol of mortality.*

STAR PAINTINGS

★ The Baptism of Christ
 by Piero della
 Francesca

★ The Leonardo Cartoon
 by Leonardo da Vinci

★ The Rokeby Venus by
 Diego Velázquez

★ The Ambassadors
 by Hans Holbein

★ The Hay Wain by John
 Constable

Exploring the National Gallery

The National Gallery has over 2,300 paintings, most kept on permanent display. The collection ranges from early works by Cimabue, in the 13th century, to 19th-century Impressionists, but its particular strengths are in Dutch, early Renaissance Italian and 17th-century Spanish painting. The bulk of the British collections are housed in Tate Britain *(see pp82–5)* while Tate Modern specializes in international modern art *(pp178–81).*

The Adoration of The Kings (1564) by Pieter Brueghel the Elder

EARLY RENAISSANCE (1250–1500): ITALIAN AND NORTHERN PAINTING

Three lustrous panels from the *Maestà*, Duccio's great altarpiece in Siena cathedral, are among the earliest paintings here. Other Italian works of the period include his outstanding *Madonna*.

The fine *Wilton Diptych* portraying England's Richard II is probably by a French artist. It displays the lyrical elegance of the International Gothic style that swept Europe.

Italian masters of this style include Pisanello and Gentile da Fabriano, whose *Madonna* often hangs beside another, by Masaccio – both date from 1426. Also shown are works by Masaccio's pupil, Fra Filippo Lippi, as well as Botticelli and Uccello. Umbrian paintings include Piero della Francesca's *Nativity* and *Baptism*, and an excellent collection of Mantegna, Bellini and other works from the Venetian and Ferrarese schools. Antonello da Messina's *St Jerome in his Study* has been mistaken for a van Eyck; it is not hard to see why, when you compare it with van Eyck's *Arnolfini Portrait*. Important

Netherlandish pictures, including some by Rogier van der Weyden and his followers, are also here, in the Sainsbury Wing.

HIGH RENAISSANCE (1500–1600): ITALIAN, NETHERLANDISH AND GERMAN PAINTING

Christ Mocked (1490–1500) by Hieronymus Bosch

Sebastiano del Piombo's *The Raising of Lazarus* was painted, with Michelangelo's assistance, to rival Raphael's great *Transfiguration*, which hangs in the Vatican in Rome.

These and other well-known names of the High (or Late) Renaissance are extremely well represented, often with massive works. Look out for Parmigianino's *Madonna and Child with Saints*, Leonardo da Vinci's charcoal cartoon of the *Virgin and Child* (a full-sized drawing used for copying as a painting), and his second version of the *Virgin of the Rocks*. There are also tender and amusing works by Piero di Cosimo, and several Titians, including *Bacchus and Ariadne* – which the public found too bright and garish when it was first cleaned by the gallery in the 1840s.

The Netherlandish and German collections are weaker. Even so, they include *The Ambassadors*, a fine double portrait by Holbein; and Altdorfer's superb *Christ Taking Leave of his Mother*, bought by the gallery in 1980. There is also an Hieronymus Bosch of *Christ Mocked* (sometimes known as *The Crowning with Thorns*), and an excellent Brueghel, *The Adoration of the Kings.*

The Annunciation (c. late 1450s) by Fra Filippo Lippi

THE SAINSBURY WING

Plans for the Sainsbury Wing, opened in 1991, provoked a storm of dissent. An incensed Prince Charles dubbed an early design "a monstrous carbuncle on the face of a much-loved friend". The final building, by Venturi, has drawn criticism from other quarters for being a derivative compromise.

This is where major changing exhibitions are held. It also houses the Micro Gallery, a computerized database of the Collection.

DUTCH, ITALIAN, FRENCH AND SPANISH PAINTING (1600–1700)

The superb Dutch collection gives two entire rooms to Rembrandt. There are also works by Vermeer, Van Dyck (among them his equestrian portrait of King Charles I) and Rubens (including the popular *Chapeau de Paille*).

From Italy, the works of Carracci and Caravaggio are strongly represented, and Salvatore Rosa has a glowering self-portrait.

French works on show include a magnificent portrait of Cardinal Richelieu by Philippe de Champaigne. Claude's seascape, *The Embarkation of the Queen of Sheba*, hangs beside Turner's rival painting *Dido Building Carthage*, as Turner himself had instructed.

The Spanish school has works by Murillo, Velázquez, Zurbarán and others.

Young Woman Standing at a Virginal (1670) by Jan Vermeer

The Scale of Love (1715–18) by Jean-Antoine Watteau

VENETIAN, FRENCH AND ENGLISH PAINTING (1700–1800)

One of the gallery's most famous 18th-century works is Canaletto's *The Stone-Mason's Yard*. Other Venetians here are Longhi and Tiepolo.

The French collection includes Rococo masters such as Chardin, Watteau and Boucher, as well as landscapists and portraitists.

Gainsborough's early work *Mr and Mrs Andrews* and *The Morning Walk* are favourites with visitors; his rival, Sir Joshua Reynolds, is represented by some of his most Classical work and by more informal portraits.

ENGLISH, FRENCH AND GERMAN PAINTING (1800–1900)

The great age of 19th-century landscape painting is amply represented here, with fine works by Constable and Turner, including Constable's *The Hay-Wain* and Turner's *The Fighting Temeraire*, as well as works by the French artists Corot and Daubigny.

Of Romantic art, there is Géricault's vivid work, *Horse Frightened by Lightning*, and several interesting paintings by Delacroix. In contrast, the society portrait of *Mme Moitessier* by Ingres, though still Romantic, is more restrained and Classical.

Impressionists and other French avant-garde artists are well represented. Among the highlights are *Waterlilies* by Monet, Renoir's *At the Theatre*, Van Gogh's *Sunflowers*, not to mention Rousseau's *Tropical Storm with Tiger*. In Seurat's *Bathers at Asnières* he did not originally use the pointillist technique he was later to invent, but subsequently reworked areas of the picture using dots of colour.

At the Theatre (1876–7) by Pierre-Auguste Renoir

Chinatown �ⓐ

Streets around Gerrard St W1.
Map 13 A2. 🔲 *Leicester Sq,
Piccadilly Circus.*

There has been a Chinese
community in London since the
19th century. Originally it was
concentrated around the East
End docks at Limehouse,
where the opium dens of
Victorian melodrama were
sited. As the number of
immigrants increased in the
1950s, many moved into Soho
where they created an ever-
expanding Chinatown. It
contains scores of restaurants,
and mysterious aroma-filled
shops selling oriental produce.
Three Chinese arches straddle
Gerrard Street, where a vibrant,
colourful street festival, held in
late January, celebrates Chinese
New Year *(see p59).*

Charing Cross Road 🔟

WC2. **Map** 13 B2. 🔲 *Leicester Sq.
See **Shops and Markets** pp318–19.*

**Antiquarian books from the
shops on Charing Cross Road**

The road is a mecca for book-
lovers, with a row of second-
hand bookshops south of
Cambridge Circus and, north of
these, a clutch of shops that,
between them, should be able
to supply just about any recent
volume. Visit the giants: huge
Foyle's and busy Waterstones;
and the smaller, specialist
shops: try Francis Edwards
(see p330) for travel and art
and Sportspages for sports.
Sadly, rent rises have put this
unique mix under threat. At
the junction with New Oxford
Street rises the 1960s tower,
Centrepoint. It lay empty for
ten years after it was built,
its owners finding this more
profitable than renting it out.

At the Palace Theatre in 1898

Palace Theatre 🕚

Shaftesbury Ave W1. **Map** 13 B2. **Tel
Box office** *0844-755 0016.* 🔲
Leicester Sq. **Open** *for performances
only. See **Entertainment** pp344–5.*
www.palace-theatre.co.uk

Most West End theatres are
disappointingly unassertive.
This one, which dominates
the west side of Cambridge
Circus, is a splendid
exception, with its sparkling
terracotta exterior and
opulent furnishings.
Completed as an opera house
in 1891, it became a music
hall the following year. The
ballerina Anna Pavlova made
her London debut here in
1910. Now the theatre, owned
by Andrew Lloyd Webber
whose own musicals are all
over London, stages hit shows
such as *Spamalot.*

Soho Square 🔢

W1. **Map** 13 A1. 🔲 *Tottenham
Court Rd.*

Soon after it was laid out in
1681 this Square enjoyed a
brief reign as the most
fashionable address in London.
Originally it was called King
Square, after Charles II, whose
statue was erected in the
middle. The square went out
of fashion by the late 18th
century and is now surrounded by bland office buildings.
The mock-Tudor garden shed
in the centre was added much
later in Victorian times.

Berwick Street Market 🔢

W1. **Map** 13 A1. 🔲 *Piccadilly
Circus.* **Open** *9am–6pm Mon–Sat.
See **Shops and Markets** p324.*

There has been a market here
since the 1840s. Berwick
Street trader Jack Smith
introduced grapefruit to
London in 1890. Today this is
the West End's best street
market, at its cheeriest and
most crowded during the
lunch hour. The freshest and
least expensive produce for
miles around is to be had
here. There are also some
interesting shops, including
Borovick's, which sells
extraordinary fabrics, and a
growing number of cafés and
restaurants. At its southern
end the street narrows into an
alley on which Raymond's
Revue Bar (the comparatively
respectable face of Soho
sleaze) has presented its
festival of erotica since 1958.

Some of London's cheapest produce at Berwick Street Market

Carnaby Street ⓮

W1. **Map** 12 F2. 🚇 *Oxford Circus.*

During the 1960s this street was so much the hub of swinging London that the Oxford English Dictionary recognized the term "Carnaby Street" as meaning "fashionable clothing for young people". Today fashion shops can be found on nearby streets such as Kingly Court and Fouberts Place.

Liberty ⓯

Regent St W1. **Map** 12 F2. 🚇 *Oxford Circus. See **Shops and Markets** p313.* www.liberty.co.uk

Arthur Lasenby Liberty opened his first shop, selling oriental silks, on Regent Street in 1875. Among his first customers were the artists Ruskin and Rossetti. Soon Liberty prints and designs, by artists such as William Morris, epitomized the Arts and Crafts movement of the late 19th and early 20th centuries. They are still fashionable today.

Liberty's mock-Tudor façade

The present mock-Tudor building with its country-house feel dates from 1925, and was built specifically to house the store.

Today the shop maintains its strong links with crafts of all kinds, including potters, jewellers and furniture designers.

Photographers' Gallery ⓰

16-18 Ramillies St W1. **Map** 12 F1. 🚇 *Oxford Circus. **Closed** until late 2011. Check website for details.* 🏛 www.photonet.org.uk

Dedicated to photography, this gallery exhibits work from new artists as well as more renowned artists. The gallery is closed for renovation, but the café and shop remain open.

The Heart of Soho

Old Compton Street is Soho's High Street. Its shops and restaurants reflect the variety of people who have lived in the area over the centuries. These include many great artists, writers and musicians.

Maison Bertaux is known for producing delicious croissants and coffee and wonderful cakes as good as those found in Paris.

Ronnie Scott's opened in 1959, and nearly all the big names of jazz have played here *(see pp351–3)*.

Bar Italia is a coffee shop situated under the room where John Logie Baird first demonstrated television in 1926. As a child, Mozart stayed next door with his family in 1764 and 1765.

The Coach and Horses pub has been a centre of bohemian Soho since the 1950s and is still popular.

Algerian Coffee Stores is one of Soho's oldest shops. Delicious aromas of the world's coffees fill the shop.

Patisserie Valerie is a Hungarian-owned café serving delicious pastries *(see pp312–15)*.

St Anne's Church Tower is all that remains after a bomb destroyed the church in 1940.

The French House was frequented by Maurice Chevalier and General de Gaulle.

The Palace Theatre has hosted many successful musicals.

COVENT GARDEN AND THE STRAND

The open-air cafés, street entertainers, stylish shops, and markets make this area a magnet for visitors. At its centre is the Piazza, site of a wholesale market until 1974. Since then, the Georgian and Victorian buildings here and in the surrounding streets have been converted into one of the city's liveliest districts. In medieval times the area was occupied by a convent garden that supplied Westminster Abbey with produce. Then in the 1630s, Inigo Jones laid out the Piazza as London's first square, with its west side dominated by his St Paul's Church. The Piazza was commissioned as a residential development by the Earl of Bedford, owner of one of the mansions that lined the Strand. Before the Embankment was built, the Strand ran along the river.

Dried flowers from the Piazza

SIGHTS AT A GLANCE

Historic Streets and Buildings
The Piazza and Central Market **1**
Neal Street and Neal's Yard **7**
Savoy Hotel **12**
Somerset House **14**
Roman Bath **16**
Bush House **17**
Adelphi **20**
Charing Cross **21**

Museums and Galleries
London's Transport Museum **3**

Churches
St Paul's Church **2**
Savoy Chapel **13**
St Mary-le-Strand **15**

Monuments and Statues
Seven Dials **9**
Cleopatra's Needle **18**

Famous Theaters
Theatre Royal Drury Lane **5**
Royal Opera House **6**
Adelphi Theatre **11**
The London Coliseum **22**
Wyndham's Theatre **10**

Parks and Gardens
Victoria Embankment Gardens **19**

Historic Pubs and Shopping Arcades
Lamb and Flag **4**
Thomas Neal's **8**

```
0 metres        500
0 yards         500
```

GETTING THERE
Covent Garden, Leicester Square, and Charing Cross Underground stations are all nearby. There are frequent buses: 9, 11, 15, and 30 to the Strand or 14, 19, 22b, 24, 29, 38, and 176 to Shaftesbury Avenue. Charing Cross rail station is a short walk.

SEE ALSO
• *Street Finder*, maps 13, 14
• *Where to Stay* pp278–291
• *Restaurants, Pubs* pp292–319

KEY

▨	Street-by-Street map
⊖	Underground station
⊟	Railway station

◁ Enzo Piazotta's statue *The Young Dancer* (1988), opposite the Royal Opera House

Street-by-Street: Covent Garden

Once an area of decaying streets and
warehouses, Covent Garden came alive
only after dark when the fruit and
vegetable market traders went
about their business. Now it
is completely revitalized.
Day and night, visitors,
residents and street-
entertainers of every
vocation throng the
Piazza, much as
they would have
done several
centuries ago.

★ **Neal Street
and Neal's Yard**
*Shops line this
traffic-free area* ❼

Thomas Neal's
*This airy
complex is full
of designer
shops and
cafés* ❽

Covent Garden
station

Seven Dials
*A replica of a
17th-century
monument
marks the
crossroads* ❾

Ching Court
is a Post-
Modernist
courtyard
by architect
Terry Farrell.

St Martin's Theatre
is home to the world's
longest running play:
The Mousetrap.

Stanfords,
established in 1852,
is the largest map and
guide retailer in the
world (*see pp326–7*).

Lamb and Flag
*Parts of this pub, one of
London's oldest, date
from 1623* ❹

**The Garrick
Club** is London's
literary club.

New Row
is lined with
little shops
and cafés.

Goodwin's Court
was inhabited by a
colony of tailors in the
18th century.

Rules
is frequented by the rich
and famous for its
typically English food.

★ **The Piazza and Central Market**
Performers of all kinds – jugglers, clowns, acrobats and musicians – entertain the crowds in the square ❶

LOCATOR MAP
See Central London Map pp14–15

Royal Opera House
Most of the world's greatest singers and dancers have appeared on its stage ❻

Bow Street Police Station
housed London's first police force, the Bow Street Runners, in the 18th century. It closed in 1992.

★ **Theatre Royal Drury Lane**
A theatre has stood on this site since 1663, making it London's oldest theatre. The present theatre was built in 1812. It is owned by composer Andrew Lloyd Webber and stages popular musicals ❺

Boswells, now a coffee house, is where Dr Johnson first met his biographer, Boswell.

STAR SIGHTS

★ The Piazza and Central Market

★ St Paul's Church

★ London's Transport Museum

★ Theatre Royal

★ Neal Street and Neal's Yard

Jubilee Market
sells clothes and bric-à-brac.

★ **London's Transport Museum**
The history of the city's tube and buses is brought to life in this museum ❸

★ **St Paul's Church**
Despite appearances, Inigo Jones's church faces away from the Piazza – the entrance is through the churchyard ❷

KEY

– – – Suggested route

0 metres   100

0 yards   100

The Piazza and Central Market ❶

Covent Garden WC2. **Map** 13 C2.
🚇 *Covent Garden.* 🚼 *but cobbled streets.* **Street performers** *10am–dusk daily. See **Shops and Markets** p333.*

The 17th-century architect Inigo Jones originally planned this area to be an elegant residential square, modelled on the piazza at Livorno, northern Italy. Today the buildings on and around the Piazza are almost entirely Victorian. The covered central market was designed by Charles Fowler in 1833 for fruit and vegetable whole-salers, the glass and iron roof anticipating the giant rail termini built later in the century – for instance, St Pancras *(see p130)* and Waterloo *(see p191)*. It now makes a magnificent shell for an array of small shops selling designer clothes, books, arts, crafts, decorative items and antiques, all surrounded by bustling market stalls that continue south in the neighbouring Jubilee Hall, which was built in 1903.

The colonnade Bedford Chambers, on the north side, give a hint of Inigo Jones's plan, although even they are not original: they were rebuilt and partially modified in 1879.

Street entertainment is a well-loved and now expected tradition of the area; in 1662, diarist Samuel Pepys wrote of watching a Punch and Judy show under the portico of St Paul's Church.

West entrance to St Paul's

St Paul's Church ❷

Bedford St WC2. **Map** 13 C2. **Tel** *020-7836 5221.* 🚇 *Covent Garden.* **Open** *8:30am–4:30pm Mon–Fri, 9am–1pm Sun.* ✝ *11am Sun, 2nd Sun of the month 4pm evensong.* 🚼

Inigo Jones built this church (completed in 1633) with the altar at the west end, so as to allow his grand portico, with its two square and two round columns, to face east into the Piazza. Clerics objected to this unorthodox arrangement, and the altar was moved to its conventional position at the east end. Jones went ahead with his original exterior design. Thus the church is entered from the west, and the east portico is a fake door, used now as an impromptu stage for street entertainers. In 1795 the interior was destroyed by fire but was rebuilt in Jones's airy, uncomplicated style. Today the church is all that is left of Jones's original plan for the Piazza. St Paul's has long been called "The Actors' Church" and plaques commem-orate distinguished men and women of the theatre. A 17th-century carving by Grinling Gibbons, on the west screen, is a memorial to the architect.

Punch and Judy performer

London's Transport Museum ❸

The Piazza WC2. **Map** 13 C2. **Tel** *020-7379 6344.* 🚇 *Covent Garden.* **Open** *10am–6pm Sat–Thu, 11am–6pm Fri (last adm: 5:15pm).* **Adm charge.** 📷 🖥 🎁 🚼 🍽 *book ahead.* **www**.ltmuseum.co.uk

London's Transport Museum

You do not have to be a train spotter or a collector of bus numbers to enjoy this museum. The intriguing collection is housed in the picturesque Victorian Flower Market, which was built in 1872, and features public transport from the past and present.

The history of London's transport is in essence a social history of the capital. Bus, tram and underground route patterns first reflected the city's growth and then promoted it: the northern and western suburbs began to develop only after their tube connections were built. The museum houses a fine collection of 20th-century commercial art. London's bus and train companies have been, and still are, prolific patrons of contemporary artists, and copies of some of the finest posters on display can be bought at the well-stocked museum shop. They include the innovative Art Deco designs of E McKnight Kauffer, as well as work by renowned artists of the 1930s, such as Graham Sutherland and Paul Nash.

This museum is excellent for children. There are plenty of hands-on exhibits, and these include the opportunity for children to put themselves in the driver's seat of a London bus, or a train from the underground system.

A mid-18th-century view of the Piazza

Lamb and Flag ④

33 Rose St WC2. **Map** 13 B2.
Tel 020-7497 9504.
🚇 Covent Garden, Leicester Sq.
Open 11am–11pm Mon–Sat,
noon–10:30pm Sun.
See **Restaurants and Pubs** p317.

There has been an inn here
since the 16th century, making the Lamb and Flag the
oldest tavern in Covent
Garden. Tucked away next to
a narrow alleyway linking
Garrick Street with Floral
Street, the cramped bars are
still largely unmodernized.
A plaque concerns satirist
John Dryden, attacked in the
alley outside in 1679. He was
set upon by hooligans sent
by Charles II to uphold the
honour of the Duchess of
Portsmouth, one of his
mistresses. Dyden had
lampooned her in some of his
verse. The upstairs bar is also
named after Dryden.
 The pub is popular with both
city centre workers and in-
the-know tourists, who spill
out into the courtyard.

Theatre Royal
Drury Lane ⑤

Catherine St WC2. **Map** 13 C2. **Tel**
0844-412 2955. 🚇 Covent Garden,
Holborn. **Open** for performances and
guided tours (phone to check). **Adm
charge**. See **Entertainment** p344.
www.theatreroyaldrurylane.co.uk

The first theatre on this
site was built in 1663 as
one of only two venues
in London where drama
could legally be staged.
Nell Gwynne acted here.
Three of the theatres
built here since then
burned down, including
one designed by Sir
Christopher Wren (see
p47). The present one,
by Benjamin Wyatt, was
completed in 1812 and
has one of the city's
largest auditoriums. In
the 1800s it was famous
for pantomimes – now it
stages block-buster
musicals. It is called the
Theatre Royal Drury Lane
even though its entrance
is on Catherine Street.

The glass Floral Hall, part of the Royal Opera House

Royal Opera
House ⑥

Covent Garden WC2. **Map** 13 C2.
Tel 020-7304 4000. 🚇 Covent
Garden. **Open** for performances and
guided tours (phone to check). See
Entertainment p348. 🔢
www.roh.org.uk

Built in 1732, the first theatre
on this site staged more spo-
ken drama than music drama,
although many of Handel's
operas and oratorios were
premiered here. Like its
neighbour the Theatre Royal
Drury Lane, the building
proved prone to fire and was
destroyed in 1808 and again
in 1856. The present opera
house was designed in 1858
by E M Barry. John Flaxman's
portico frieze, depicting trage-
dy and comedy, survived
from the previous build-
ing of 1809.
    The Opera House has
had both high and low
points during its history.
In 1892, the first British
performance of Wagner's
Ring was conducted
here by Gustav Mahler.
Later, during World
War I, the building was
used as a storehouse
by the government.
Today, it is home to the
Royal Opera and Royal
Ballet Companies – the
best tickets can cost
over £100. An extensive
renovation project, com-
pleted in 1999, added
a second auditorium,
along with rehearsal

rooms for the Royal Opera
and Royal Ballet companies.
Backstage tours are available,
and once a month visitors
can watch the Royal Ballet
attending its daily class.

Neal Street and
Neal's Yard ⑦

Covent Garden WC2. **Map** 13 B1.
🚇 Covent Garden. See **Shops and
Markets** pp322–3.

A specialist shop on Neal Street

In this attractive street,
former warehouses from the
19th century can be identified
by the hoisting mechanisms
high on their exterior walls.
The buildings have been
converted into shops, art galleries and restaurants. Off
Neal Street in Short's Gardens
is Neal's Yard Dairy, one of
London's best cheese shops,
which also sells delicious
breads. Brainchild of the late
Nicholas Saunders, it, and
Neal's Yard itself, remain an
oasis of alternative values
amid the growing commer-
cialism of the area.

Entrance to Thomas Neal's

Thomas Neal's ❽

Earlham St WC2. **Map** 13 B2.
🚇 *Covent Garden, Leicester Sq.*
Open *10am–7pm Mon–Sat, noon–6pm Sun.* ♿ *ground floor only.*

Opened in the early 1990s in an old converted banana warehouse, this upscale shopping complex offers an interesting range of shops, selling designer clothes and cosmetics, jewellery and accessories, antique clothing and lace. When it is time for a break from shopping, there is a café and restaurant on the lower floor. The Donmar Warehouse theatre *(see p346)* is also part of the complex, staging must-see productions such as *The Blue Room*.

Seven Dials ❾

Monmouth St WC2. **Map** 13 B2.
🚇 *Covent Garden, Leicester Sq.*

The pillar at this junction of seven streets incorporates six sundials (the central spike acted as a seventh). It was installed in 1989 and is a copy of a 17th-century monument. The original was removed in the 19th century because it had become a notorious meeting place for criminals who operated in an area that had become one of London's most infamous slums.

Today Seven Dials is a vibrant shopping and dining area. Its streets and alleyways are known for their one-off shops, funky boutiques, holistic medicine shops, restaurants and bars.

Wyndham's Theatre ❿

Charing Cross Rd, WC2. **Map** 13 B2. *Tel* 0844-482 5138. 🚇 *Leicester Square.* **Open** *for performances only.* www.wyndhams-theatre.com
See *Entertainment pp344–5.*

The Wyndham's Theatre opened its doors in 1899 and takes its name from Charles Wyndham (1837–1919) – lauded as one of the greatest actors of his day. Designed by the architect William Sprague, the Wyndham was the first of seven theatres he completed that year. It boasts a Portland stone exterior and a turquoise, cream and gold interior decorated in Louis XVI style, with a ceiling painted in the style of Boucher.

Many greats in British theatre have graced the stage since Wyndham himself: Vanessa Redgrave, Sir Alec Guinness and Sir John Gielgud among them. More recent talents to have appeared are Dame Judi Dench in *Madame de Sade* and Jude Law as Hamlet.

Adelphi Theatre ⓫

Strand WC2. **Map** 13 C3.
Tel 0844-412 4651. 🚇 *Charing Cross, Embankment.*
Open *for performances only.*
www.adelphitheatre.co.uk
See *Entertainment pp344–5.*

There has been a theatre on this site since 1806, when the Sans Pareil Theatre opened here. It was set up by John Scott, a wealthy tradesman, who was helping to launch his daughter on the stage. After several refurbishments and name changes, the current Adelphi Theatre was remodelled in 1930 in Art Deco style by Ernest Schaufelburg. His modernist "straight-line" design resulted in a building without curves. Note the highly distinctive lettering on the frontage, and the well-kept lobby and auditorium, with their stylized motifs.

Although threatened by demolition in the 1960s, the Adelphi survived and now stages popular musicals such as *Joseph and the Amazing Technicolor Dreamcoat.*

Savoy Hotel ⓬

Strand WC2. **Map** 13 C2. *Tel* 020-7836 4343. 🚇 *Charing Cross, Embankment.* See *Where to Stay p290.* www.fairmont.com/savoy

Pioneer of en suite bathrooms and electric lighting, the grand Savoy was built in 1889 on the site of the medieval Savoy Palace. A £100 million lavish refurbishment took place in 2008–2010, incorporating both the original Edwardian and the later Art Deco style. The forecourt is the only street in Britain where traffic drives on the right. Attached to the hotel are the Savoy Theatre built for D'Oyly Carte opera, famed for performing the operas of Gilbert and Sullivan; and Simpson's-in-the-Strand English restaurant *(see p308).*

Front entrance to the Savoy Hotel

Savoy Chapel ⓭

Strand WC2. **Map** 13 C2. *Tel* 020-7836 7221. 🚇 *Charing Cross, Embankment.* **Open** *11.30am–3.30pm Tue–Fri.* **Closed** *Aug–Sep.* 🕆 *11am Sun.* 🚫 📷 *phone to book.*

The first Savoy Chapel was founded in the 16th century as the chapel for the hospital set up by Henry VII on the site of the old Savoy Palace. Parts of the outside walls date from 1512, but most of the present building dates from the mid-19th century. In 1890 it was London's first church to be electrically lit. It became the chapel of the Royal Victorian Order in 1937, and is now a private chapel of the Queen. Nearby on Savoy Hill were the first studios of the BBC.

Somerset House ⓮

Strand WC2. **Map** 14 D2.
Tel 020-7845 4600 🚇 *Temple*
Open *10am–6pm daily (last adm to galleries: 5:30pm).* **Closed** *1 Jan, 24–26 Dec.* **Ice rink** *open two months in winter.* **Adm charge.** 🖥
Courtauld Institute of Art Gallery
Adm charge 🖥 📷 ♿
Embankment Galleries
Adm charge ♿ **Admiralty**
Restaurant Tel *020-7845 4646 for reservations.*
www.somersethouse.org.uk

This elegant Georgian building was the creation of Sir William Chambers. It was erected in the 1770s after the first Somerset House, a Renaissance palace built for the Duke of Somerset in the mid-16th century, was pulled down following years of neglect. The replacement was the first major building to be designed for use as government offices and has served to house the Navy Board (note that the classical grandeur of the Seamen's Waiting Hall and Nelson's Staircase are not to be missed), a succession of Royal Societies and, for a substantial amount of time, the Inland Revenue.

Today it is home to the Courtauld Institute of Art Gallery. The courtyard of Somerset House was closed to the public for nearly a century, but on the Inland Revenue's departure in 1997 it was cleared, as part of a £48-million restoration scheme. This created an attractive piazza with a 55-jet fountain. Films and concerts are often staged here in the summer, and for a few weeks in winter, there is an enchanting ice rink. From the courtyard visitors can stroll through the South Building, where the highly regarded Admiralty Restaurant overlooks the Thames, on to a riverside terrace that includes an open-air summer café and a restaurant, with pedestrian access to Waterloo Bridge and the South Bank's theatres and other attractions.

Fountains at Somerset House

Located in Somerset House, but famous in its own right, is the small but spectacular **Courtauld Institute of Art Gallery**. Its exquisite collection of paintings has been displayed here since 1990 and owes its existence to the bequest of textile magnate and philanthropist Samuel Courtauld. On display are works by Botticelli, Brueghel, Bellini and Rubens (including one of his early masterpieces *The Descent from the Cross*), but it is the Courtauld's collection of Impressionist and Post-Impressionist paintings that draws the most attention. As well as works by Monet, Gauguin, Pissarro, Renoir and Modigliani, visitors can gaze captivated on Manet's *A Bar at the Folies-Bergères*, Van Gogh's *Self-Portrait with Bandaged Ear*, Cézanne's *The Card Players* and some evocative studies of dancers by Degas. In addition to its permanent collection, the Courtauld Institute now hosts a series of world-class temporary exhibitions that take place throughout the year.

A modern riverside gallery was launched within Somerset House in 2008. The **Embankment Galleries** occupy 750 square metres of exhibition space on the two lower floors of the south wing. The changing exhibition programme covers a broad range of contemporary arts, including photography, design, fashion and architecture.

Van Gogh's *Self-Portrait with Bandaged Ear* (1889) at the Courtauld

St Mary-le-Strand ⓯

Strand WC2. **Map** 14 D2. **Tel** 020-7836 3126. 🚇 Temple. **Open** 11am–4pm Mon–Fri, 10am–3pm Sun. ✝ 11am Sun, 1.05pm Tue & Thu. 🔲 🔲
www.stmarylestrand.org

Now beached on a road island at the east end of the Strand, this pleasing church was consecrated in 1724. It was the first public building by James Gibbs, who designed St-Martin-in-the-Fields *(see p102)*. Gibbs was influenced by Christopher Wren, but the exuberant external decorative detail here was inspired by the Baroque churches of Rome, where Gibbs studied. Its multi-arched tower is layered like a wedding cake, and culminates in a cupola and lantern. St-Mary-le-Strand is now the official church of the Women's Royal Naval Service.

St-Mary-le-Strand

Roman Bath ⓰

5 Strand Lane WC2. **Map** 14 D2. **Tel** 020-8232 5050. 🚇 Temple, Embankment, Charing Cross. **Open** Apr–Sep: 1–5pm most Wed; phone to book. ♿ via Temple Pl.

This little bath and its surround may be seen from a full-length window on Surrey Street, by pressing a light switch on the outside wall. It is almost certainly not Roman, for there is no other evidence

Bush House from Kingsway

of Roman habitation in the immediate area. It is more likely to have been part of Arundel House, one of several palaces which stood on the Strand from Tudor times until the 17th century, when they were demolished for new building. In the 19th century the bath was open to the public for cold plunges, believed to be healthy.

Bush House ⓱

Aldwych WC2. **Map** 14 D2. 🚇 Temple, Holborn. **Not open** to the public.

Situated at the centre of the Aldwych crescent, this Neo-Classical building was first designed as manufacturers' showrooms by an American, Irving T Bush, and completed in 1935. It appears especially imposing when viewed from Kingsway, its dramatic north entrance graced with various statues symbolizing Anglo-American relations. Since 1940 it has been used as radio studios, and is the head-quarters of the BBC World Service, which is due to be relocated to West London within a few years.

Cleopatra's Needle ⓲

Embankment WC2. **Map** 13 C3. 🚇 Embankment, Charing Cross.

Erected in Heliopolis in about 1500 BC, this incongruous pink granite monument is much older than London itself. Its inscriptions celebrate

the deeds of the pharaohs of ancient Egypt. It was presented to Britain by the then Viceroy of Egypt, Mohammed Ali, in 1819 and erected in 1878, shortly after the Embankment was built. It has a twin in New York's Central Park, behind the Metropolitan Museum of Art. The bronze sphinxes, added in 1882, are not Egyptian.

In its base is a Victorian time capsule of artifacts of the day, such as the day's newspapers, a rail timetable and photographs of 12 contemporary beauties.

Victoria Embankment Gardens ⓳

WC2. **Map** 13 C3. 🚇 Embankment, Charing Cross. **Open** 7.30am–dusk daily. ♿ 🔲

This narrow sliver of a public park, created when the Embankment was built, boasts well-maintained flower beds, a clutch of statues of British worthies (including the Scottish poet Robert Burns) and, in summer, a season of concerts. Its main historical feature is the water gate at its northwest corner, which was built as a triumphal entry to the Thames for the Duke of Buckingham in 1626. It is a relic of York House, which used to stand on this site and was the home first of the Archbishops of York and then of the Duke. It is still in its original position and although the water used to lap against it, because of the Thames's Embankment the gate is now a good 100 m (330 ft) from the river's edge.

Victoria Embankment Gardens

The shopping and office block above Charing Cross

Adelphi ⑳

Strand WC2. **Map** 13 C3. **Tel** 020-7451 6845. ⊖ *Embankment, Charing Cross.* **Not open** to the public.

John Adam Street, Adelphi

Adelphi is a pun on *adelphoi*, the Greek word for brothers – this area was once an elegant riverside residential development designed in 1772 by brothers Robert and John Adam. The name now refers to the Art Deco office block, its entrance adorned with N A Trent's heroic reliefs of workers at toil, which in 1938 replaced the Adams' much admired Palladian-style apartment complex. That destruction is now viewed as one of the worst acts of 20th-century official vandalism. A number of the Adams' surrounding buildings survive, notably No. 8, the ornate Royal Society for the encouragement of Arts, Manufactures & Commerce just opposite (open first Sunday of the month, 10am–12.30pm, not January). In the same exuberant idiom are Nos. 1–4 Robert Street, where Robert Adam lived for a time, and No. 7 Adam Street.

Charing Cross ㉑

Strand WC2. **Map** 13 C3. ⊖ *Charing Cross, Embankment.*

The name derives from the last of the 12 crosses erected by Edward I to mark the funeral route in 1290 of his wife, Eleanor of Castile, from Nottinghamshire to Westminster Abbey. Today a 19th-century replica stands in the forecourt of Charing Cross station. Both the cross and the Charing Cross Hotel, built into the station frontage, were designed in 1863 by E M Barry, architect of the Royal Opera House *(see p115)*.

Above the station platforms has risen an assertive shopping centre and office block, completed in 1991. Designed by Terry Farrell it resembles a giant ocean liner, with portholes looking on to Villiers Street. The building is best seen from the river, where it dominates its neighbours. The railway arches at the rear of the station have been modernized as a suite of small shops and cafés, as well as a venue for the Players Theatre, the last repository of Victorian music hall entertainment.

The London Coliseum ㉒

St Martin's Lane WC2. **Map** 13 B3. **Tel** 0871-911 0200. ⊖ *Leicester Sq, Charing Cross.* **Open** performances ♿ ▢ ▾ **Lectures**. See **Entertainment** *pp348–9*. **www**.eno.org

London's largest theatre and one of its most elaborate, this flamboyant building, topped with a large globe, was designed in 1904 by Frank Matcham and was equipped with London's first revolving stage. It was also the first theatre in Europe to have lifts. A former variety house, today it is the home of the English National Opera, and well worth visiting, if only for the Edwardian interior with its gilded cherubs and heavy purple curtains. In 2003, the original glass roof was restored, providing dramatic views over Trafalgar Square.

London Coliseum

BLOOMSBURY AND FITZROVIA

Since the beginning of the 20th century, Bloomsbury and Fitzrovia have been synonymous with literature, art and learning. The

Carving in Russell Square

Bloomsbury Group of writers and artists were active from the early 1900s until the 1930s; the name Fitzrovia was invented by writers such as Dylan

Thomas who drank in the Fitzroy Tavern. Bloomsbury still boasts the University of London, the British Museum and many fine Georgian squares. But it is now also noted for its Charlotte Street restaurants and the furniture and competitively priced electrical shops lining Tottenham Court Road.

SIGHTS AT A GLANCE

Historic Streets and Buildings
Bloomsbury Square **2**
Russell Square **4**
Queen Square **5**
British Library **8**
St Pancras International **9**
Woburn Walk **11**
Fitzroy Square **13**
Charlotte Street **15**

Museums
British Museum pp126–9 **1**
Charles Dickens Museum **6**

Foundling Museum **7**
Wellcome Collection **12**
Pollock's Toy Museum **16**

Churches
St George's, Bloomsbury **3**
St Pancras Parish Church **10**

Pubs
Fitzroy Tavern **14**

SEE ALSO

• *Street Finder,* maps 4, 5, 6, 13
• *Where to Stay* pp278–291
• *Restaurants, Pubs* pp292–319

KEY

▦	Street-by-Street map
⊖	Underground station
⇄	Railway station

GETTING THERE
This area is served by the Circle, Northern, Piccadilly, Victoria and Central lines. Useful buses include Nos. 8, 25, 30, 73 and 98. Major railway stations are at Euston, St Pancras and King's Cross.

0 metres   500
0 yards   500

◁ **A grand Georgian house in Bedford Square**

Street-by-Street: Bloomsbury

The British Museum dominates Bloomsbury. Its earnestly intellectual atmosphere spills over into the surrounding streets, and to its north lies the main campus of London University. The area has been home to writers and artists, and is a traditional centre of the book trade. Most of the publishers have left, but there are still many bookshops around.

The Senate House (1932) is the administrative headquarters of the University of London. It holds a priceless library.

Bedford Square is one of London's most complete Georgian squares. Its uniform doorways are fringed in artificial stone.

★ British Museum
Designed in the mid-19th century, it is extremely popular and attracts some five million visitors a year ❶

STAR SIGHTS

★ British Museum

★ Russell Square

KEY

— — — Suggested route

0 metres   100

0 yards   100

Museum Street is lined with small cafés and shops selling old books, prints and antiques.

Pizza Express occupies a charming and little-altered Victorian dairy.

The Duke of Bedford's statue commemorates the fifth duke, Francis Russell (1765–1805). An avid farmer, he is shown with sheep and a plough.

LOCATOR MAP
See Central London Map pp14–15

★ Russell Square
It was once part of the Duke of Bedford's estate, and is now a shady retreat on a hot day **❹**

Bloomsbury Square
Laid out in 1661, it is graced by a statue of statesman Charles James Fox (1749–1806) **❷**

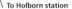

To Holborn station

St George's, Bloomsbury
The tower on this typically flamboyant Hawksmoor church is modelled on the tomb of King Mausolus **❸**

Sicilian Avenue is a small and unexpected pedestrian precinct from 1905, where colonnades evoke Roman architecture.

British Museum ❶

See pp126–9.

Bloomsbury Square ❷

WC1. **Map** 5 C5. ⊖ *Holborn.*

This is the oldest of the Bloomsbury squares. It was laid out in 1661 by the Earl of Southampton, who owned the land. None of the original buildings survives and its shaded garden is encircled by a busy one-way traffic system. (Unusually for central London, you can nearly always find a space in the car park under the square.)

The square has had many famous residents; a plaque commemorates members of the literary and artistic Bloomsbury Group, who lived in the area during the early years of the last century. The group included novelist Virginia Woolf, biographer Lytton Strachey, and artists Vanessa Bell, Duncan Grant and Dora Carrington. Look out for their individual plaques throughout the area.

A plaque commemorating famous Bloomsbury residents

St George's, Bloomsbury ❸

Bloomsbury Way WC1. **Map** 13 B1. **Tel** 020-7242 1979. ⊖ *Holborn, Tottenham Court Rd, Russell Sq.* **Open** 1–4pm daily (times may vary – call to check). 🕐 1:10pm Wed & Fri, 10:30am Sun. **Recitals**. ♿ www. stgeorgesbloomsbury.org.uk

A slightly eccentric church, St George's was designed by Nicholas Hawksmoor, Wren's pupil, and completed in 1730.

The flamboyant Russell Hotel on Russell Square

It was built as a place of worship for the prosperous residents of newly-developed, fashionable Bloomsbury. The layered tower, modelled on the tomb of King Mausolus (the original mausoleum in Turkey) and topped by a statue of George I, was for a long time an object of derision – the king was thought to be presented too heroically. In 1913, the funeral of Emily Davison, the suffragette who threw herself under King George V's horse, was held here.

Russell Square ❹

WC1. **Map** 5 B5. ⊖ *Russell Sq.* 🕐 7:30am–10pm daily.

One of London's largest squares, Russell Square is a lively place, with a fountain, café and traffic roaring around its perimeter. The east side boasts perhaps the best of the Victorian grand hotels to survive in the capital. Charles Doll's Russell Hotel, which was opened in 1900, is a wondrous confection of red terracotta,

with colonnaded balconies and prancing cherubs beneath the main columns. The exuberance is continued in the lobby, faced with marble of many colours.

Poet T S Eliot worked at the west corner of the square, from 1925 until 1965, in what were the offices of publishers Faber and Faber.

Queen Square ❺

WC1. **Map** 5 C5. ⊖ *Russell Sq.*

In spite of being named after Queen Anne, this square contains a statue of Queen Charlotte. Her husband, George III, stayed at the house of a doctor here when he became ill with the hereditary disease that drove him mad before his death in 1820. Originally, the north side of the square was left open so that inhabitants had a clear view of Hampstead and Highgate. Today the square is almost completely surrounded by hospital buildings, with early Georgian houses on the west side.

Queen Charlotte's statue in Queen Square

Charles Dickens Museum ❻

48 Doughty St WC1. **Map** 6 D1. **Tel** 020-7405 2127. 🚇 *Chancery Lane, Russell Sq.* **Open** *10am–5pm daily (last adm 4:30pm).* **Adm charge**. ♿ *ground floor.* 🚫 📷
www.dickensmuseum.com

The novelist Charles Dickens lived in this early 19th-century terraced house for three of his most productive years (from 1837 to 1839). The popular works *Oliver Twist* and *Nicholas Nickleby* were entirely written here, and *Pickwick Papers* was finished. Although Dickens had many London homes throughout his lifetime, this is the only one to have survived. In 1923 it was acquired by the Dickens Fellowship and it is now a well-conceived museum with some of the principal rooms laid out exactly as they were in Dickens's time. Others have been adapted to display a varied collection of articles associated with him. The exhibits include papers, portraits and pieces of furniture taken from his other homes as well as first editions of many of his best-known works. The most moving mementos are of Mary Hogarth, the author's sister-in-law, who died, aged 17, a month after the family moved here.

Nautical publisher's trade sign, Dickens Museum

Foundling Museum ❼

40 Brunswick Square WC1. **Map** 5 C4. **Tel** 020-7841 3600. 🚇 *Russell Square.* ⏰ *10am–5pm Tue–Sat, 11am–5pm Sun.* **Adm charge**. 🚫 📷 *book ahead.* 📷 📷 **Coram's Fields** *Guilford St WC1.* ⏰ *9am–dusk.* **www**.foundlingmuseum.org.uk

In 1722, Captain Thomas Coram, a retired sailor and ship-builder recently returned from the Americas, vowed to establish a refuge for abandoned children. Horrified by

Portrait of Captain Coram (1740) by William Hogarth

the poverty on London streets, Coram was determined to alter the fate of the city's foundlings by housing, educating and placing them in private homes. Assisted by his friend, the artist William Hogarth, Coram worked tirelessly to raise funds for the refuge. Finally in 1739, after much petitioning of George II, he was granted a Royal Charter to establish a Foundling Hospital. Hogarth donated numerous paintings to the hospital and other artists followed suit, effectively creating the first art gallery in Britain. The wealthy were encouraged to view the works of art and the children at the hospital, in the hope that they would contribute to the charity. The original hospital located at the end of Lambs Conduit Street was demolished in the 1920s, but the interiors of two of the 18th-century rooms were saved and relocated to 40 Brunswick Square, the current location of the museum. On the ground floor, the story of the thousands of children who were cared for in the Foundling Hospital since its establishment is told. The nationally important collection of 18th-century paintings, sculpture, furniture and interiors is displayed on the first floor.

Adjacent to the museum, with its entrance on Guilford Street, is **Coram's Fields**, a favourite central London playground with lots of space. It's highly popular with children and a convenient pace-changer for families visiting the museums. Dogs are not allowed, and all adults must be accompanied by children.

British Library ❽

96 Euston Rd NW1. **Map** 5 B3. **Tel** 0843-208 1144. 🚇 *King's Cross St Pancras.* **Open** *9:30am–6pm Mon–Fri (8pm Tue), 9:30am–5pm Sat, 11am–5pm Sun.* **Regular events.** ♿ 🚫 📷 📷 📷 **www**.bl.uk

London's most important building from the late 20th century houses the national collection of books, manuscripts and maps, as well as the British Library Sound Archive. Designed in red brick by Sir Colin St John Wilson, it opened in 1997 after nearly 20 years under construction, involving controversial cost over-runs, but is now widely admired.

A copy of nearly every printed book in the United Kingdom is held here – more than 16 million – and can be consulted by those with a reader's ticket. There are also exhibition galleries open to everyone. Visitors may view some of the Library's most precious items, including the Lindisfarne Gospels, with the Turning the Pages system which shows each page on a monitor. Other volumes include a Gutenberg Bible and Shakespeare's First Folio. Running through six floors is a spectacular glass tower holding George III's library.

Page from the Lindisfarne Gospels

British Museum

The oldest public museum in
the world, the British Museum
was established in 1753 to
house the collections of the
physician Sir Hans Sloane
(1660–1753), who also helped
create the Chelsea Physic
Garden *(see p197)*. Sloane's

The innovatively designed Great Court

artefacts have been added to by
gifts and purchases from all over the world, and the museum
now contains innumerable items stretching from the present
day to prehistory. Robert Smirke designed the main
part of the building (1823–50), but the architectural
highlight is Norman Foster's Great Court, with the
world-famous Reading Room at its centre.

Upper floor

94
90
91
67
95
66
63
62
57
61   58
59
73
72

★ **Egyptian Mummies**
*The ancient Egyptians preserved
their dead in expectation of an
afterlife. Animals that were
believed to have sacred powers
were also often mummified. This
cat comes from Abydos on the
Nile and dates from about 30 BC.*

**Montague Place
entrance**

34

**Main
floor**

33
26
24
35

Numerous large-scale
sculptures are featured
in the Concourse Gallery
of the Great Court.

**Lower
floor**

25

KEY TO FLOORPLAN

- ☐ Asian collection
- ▨ Enlightenment
- ☐ Coins and medals
- ▨ Greek and Roman collection
- ☐ Egyptian collection
- ▨ Middle Eastern collection
- ☐ Europe collection
- ☐ Temporary exhibitions
- ▨ Non-exhibition space
- ▨ Africa, Oceania and the Americas

21
20   9
19   22   4
78   77   8
17
18   16   10
7
**Lower
floor**
15

★ **Parthenon Sculptures**
*These reliefs were brought to
England by Lord Elgin from the
Parthenon in Athens. The
British government purchased
them from him in 1816.*

**Ground
floor**

11

★ Lindow Man
The skin on this 2,000-year-old human body was preserved by the acids of a peat bog in Cheshire. He was probably killed in an elaborate ritual.

Two grand staircases wrap around the Reading Room and link to the upper floors via a bridge.

Upper floor

★ Sutton Hoo Treasure
Remarkably preserved, the 7th-century ship burial includes this striking helmet.

Reading Room

The Great Court

Paul Hamlyn Library

Main entrance

VISITORS' CHECKLIST

Great Russell St WC1. **Map** 5 B5.
Tel 020-7323 8000. ⊖
Tottenham Court Rd, Holborn,
Russell Sq. 🚌 7, 8, 10, 14, 19,
24, 25, 29, 30, 38, 55, 68, 73,
134, 188. 🚆 Euston, King's
Cross. **Open** 10am 5.30pm daily
(selected galleries until 8.30pm
Thu, Fri). **Closed** 1 Jan, Good Fri,
24–26 Dec. 🎟 ♿ 📷 📱 🍴
📖 📱 *Lectures, film presentations, exhibitions, events.*
www.thebritishmuseum.ac.uk

Portland Vase
It was made in Italy or Egypt shortly before the birth of Christ. In 1845 a visitor smashed it into 200 pieces, since then it has been reassembled.

GALLERY GUIDE
The Greek and Roman and Ancient Near Eastern collections are found on all three levels of the museum, predominantly on the west side. The African collection is located on the lower floor, while Asian exhibits are found on the main and upper floors on the north side of the Museum. The Americas collection is located in the northeast corner of the main floor. Egyptian artifacts are found west of the Great Court and on the upper floors.

STAR EXHIBITS

★ Parthenon Sculptures

★ Lindow Man

★ Egyptian Mummies

★ Sutton Hoo Treasure

Exploring the British Museum's Collections

The Museum's immense hoard of treasure spans two million years of history and culture. The 94 galleries, which stretch 2.5 miles (4 km), cover civilisations from ancient Egypt and Assyria to modern Japan.

Ornamental detail from a Sumerian Queen's lyre

PREHISTORIC AND ROMAN BRITAIN

1st-century BC bronze helmet dredged up from the Thames

Relics of prehistoric Britain are on display in six separate galleries. The most impressive items include the gold "Mold Cape", a ceremonial bronze-age cape found in Wales; an antlered headdress worn by hunter-gatherers some 9000 years ago; and "Lindow Man", a 1st-century AD sacrificial victim who lay preserved in a bog until 1984. Some superb Celtic metalwork is also on show, alongside the silver Mildenhall Treasure and other Roman pieces. The Hinton St. Mary mosaic (4th century AD) features a roundel containing the earliest known British depiction of Christ.

EUROPE

The spectacular Sutton Hoo ship treasure, the burial hoard of a 7th-century Anglo-Saxon king, is on display in Room 41. This superb find, made in 1939, revolutionized our understanding of Anglo-Saxon life and ritual. The artifacts include a helmet and shield, Celtic hanging bowls, the remains of a lyre, and gold and garnet jewellery.

Adjacent galleries contain a collection of clocks, watches and scientific instruments. Some exquisite timepieces are on view, including a 400-year-old clock from Prague,

designed as a model galleon; in its day it pitched, played music, and even fired a cannon. Also nearby are the famous 12th-century Lewis chessmen, and a gallery housing Baron Ferdinand Rothschild's (1839–98) remarkably varied treasures.

The museum's modern collection includes some Wedgwood pottery, glassware, and a series of Russian revolutionary plates.

Gilded brass late-16th-century ship clock from Prague

ANCIENT NEAR EAST

There are numerous galleries devoted to the Western Asian collections, covering 7,000 years of history. The most famous items are the 7th-century BC Assyrian reliefs from King Ashurbanipal's palace at Nineveh, but of equal interest are two large human-headed bulls from 7th-century BC Khorsabad, and an inscribed Black Obelisk of Assyrian King Shalmaneser III. The upper floors contain pieces from ancient Sumeria, part of the Oxus Treasure (which lay buried for over 2,000 years), and the museum's collection of clay

cuneiform tablets. The earliest of these are inscribed with the oldest known pictographs (c.3300 BC). Also of interest is a skull discovered in Jericho in the 1950s; augmented with shells and lime plaster, the skull belonged to a hunter who lived in the area some 7,000 years ago.

EGYPT

In Room 4 are Egyptian sculptures. These include a fine red granite head of a king, thought to depict Amenophis III, and a colossal statue of King Rameses II. Also on show is the Rosetta Stone, used by Jean-François Champollion (1790–1832) as a primer for deciphering Egyptian hieroglyphs. An extraordinary array of mummies, jewellery and Coptic art can also be found upstairs. The various instruments that were used by embalmers to preserve bodies before entombment are all displayed. Room 61 houses paintings from the lost tomb-chapel of Nebamun.

Part of a colossal granite statue of Rameses II, the 13th-century BC Egyptian monarch

GREECE AND ROME

The Greek and Roman collections include the museum's most famous treasure, the Parthenon sculptures. These 5th century BC reliefs were once part of a marble frieze that decorated the Parthenon, Athena's temple on the Acropolis in Athens. Much of it was ruined in battle in 1687, and most of what survived was removed between 1801 and 1804 by the British diplomat Lord Elgin, and sold to the British nation. Other highlights include the Nereid Monument

Ancient Greek vase illustrating the mythical hero Hercules's fight with a bull

and sculptures and friezes from the Mausoleum at Halicarnassus. The beautiful 1st-century BC cameo-glass Portland Vase is located in the Roman Empire section.

ASIA

The Chinese collection boasts fine porcelain and ancient Shang bronzes (c.1500–1050 BC). Particularly impressive are the ceremonial ancient Chinese bronze vessels, with their enigmatic animal-head shapes.

The fine Chinese ceramics range from delicate tea bowls to a model pond, which is almost a thousand years old. In the Sir Percival David gallery the Chinese ceramics date from the 10th to early 20th centuries.

Adjacent to these is one of the finest collections of Asian religious sculpture outside India. A major highlight is an assortment of sculpted reliefs, which once covered the walls of the Buddhist temple at Amaravati, and which recount stories from the life of the Buddha. A Korean section contains some gigantic works of Buddhist art.

The museum's collection of Islamic art, including a

Statue of the Hindu god Shiva as Nataraja, or Lord of the Dance (11th century AD)

jade terrapin found in a water tank, can be found in Room 34. Rooms 92 to 94 house the Japanese galleries, with a Classical teahouse in Room 92.

AFRICA

An interesting collection of African sculptures, textiles and graphic art can also be found in Room 25 on the lower floor of the museum. Famous bronzes from the Kingdom of Benin stand alongside modern African prints, paintings, drawings and colourful fabrics.

THE GREAT COURT AND THE READING ROOM

Surrounding the Reading Room of the former British Library, the £100-million Great Court opened to coincide with the new millennium. Designed by Sir Norman Foster, the Court is covered by a wide-span, lightweight roof, creating London's first indoor public square. The Reading Room has been restored to its original design, so visitors can sample the atmosphere which Karl Marx, Mahatma Gandhi and George Bernard Shaw found

so agreeable. From the outside, however, it is scarcely recognizable; it is housed in a multi-level construction which partly supports the roof, and which also contains a Centre for Education, temporary exhibition galleries, bookshops, cafés and restaurants. Part of the Reading Room also serves as a study suite where those wishing to learn more about the Museum's collections have access to information.

Fine lattice roof of glass and steel

Restored decoration

The massive former Midland Grand Hotel above St Pancras Station

St Pancras International ❾

Euston Rd NW1. **Map** 5 B2.
Tel 020-7843 7688 🚇 King's Cross,
St Pancras. **Open** 5am–11pm daily.
See **Getting to London** pp372–3.
www.stpancras.com

St Pancras – the London terminal for Eurostar services to continental Europe – is easily the most spectacular of the three rail termini along Euston Road, thanks to the extravagant frontage, in red-brick gingerbread Gothic, of the former Midland Grand Hotel, opened in 1874 as one of the most sumptuous hotels of its time. By 1935 it was too expensive to run and became office space. Threatened with demolition in the 1960s, the poet John Betjeman

Figures on St Pancras Church

campaigned to save it (there is a statue of him on the upper level). Abandoned in the early 1980s and left empty for 20 years, it is now being lavishly restored as a 5-star hotel, plus apartments and penthouses.

St Pancras Parish Church ❿

Euston Rd NW1. **Map** 5 B3. **Tel** 020-7388 1461. 🚇 Euston. **Open** Mon–Fri (phone to check). ✝ 8am, 10am Sun. ♿ **Recitals** 1.15pm Mon–Thu, evensong 6pm Sun. **www.** stpancraschurch.org

This is a stately Greek revival church of 1822 designed by William Inwood and his son Henry, both great enthusiasts for Athenian architecture. The design is based on the Erectheum on the Acropolis in Athens, and even the wooden pulpit stands on miniature Ionic columns of its own. The long, galleried interior has a dramatic severity appropriate to the church's style. The female figures on the northern outer wall were originally taller than they are now; a chunk had to be taken out of the middle of each to make them fit under the roof they were meant to be supporting.
    The maze of corridors and alcoves in the church's crypt are sometimes the setting for art exhibitions.

Woburn Walk ⓫

WC1. **Map** 5 B4. 🚇 Euston,
Euston Sq.

A well-restored street of bow-fronted shops, it was designed by Thomas Cubitt in 1822. The high pavement on the east side was to protect shop fronts from the mud thrown up by carriages. The poet W B Yeats lived at No. 5 from 1895 until 1919.

Wellcome Collection ⓬

183 Euston Rd NW1. **Map** 5 A4.
Tel 020-7611 2222. 🚇 Euston,
King's Cross, Warren St. **Open**
10am–6pm Tue–Sat (to 10pm Thu),
11am–6pm Sun, noon–6pm public
hols. **Closed** 24–26 Dec. ♿ ▢ ▢
www.wellcomecollection.org

Sir Henry Wellcome was a pharmacist, entrepreneur and collector. His passionate interest in medicine and its history, as well as ethnography and archaeology, led him to gather more than one million objects from around the world. Wellcome Collection is a £30-million public venue used to house his vast collection as well as explore the connections between medicine, art and the human condition through events and exhibitions.
    Exhibits range from the bizarre to the beautiful, the ancient to the futuristic. More than 900 objects are on permanent display, including a used guillotine blade and Napoleon's toothbrush. Contemporary works include a DNA sequencing robot and a sculpture exploring HIV by Mark Quinn. The Wellcome library, on the upper floors, is the world's largest devoted to the history of medicine.

Fitzroy Square ⓭

W1. **Map** 4 F4. 🚇 Warren St,
Great Portland St.

Designed by Robert Adam in 1794, the square's south and east sides survive in their original form, in dignified

Portland stone. Blue plaques record the homes of many artists, writers and statesmen: George Bernard Shaw and Virginia Woolf both lived at No. 29 – although not at the same time. Shaw gave money to the artist Roger Fry to establish the Omega workshop at No. 33 in 1913. Here young artists were paid a fixed wage to produce Post-Impressionist furniture, pottery, carpets and paintings for sale to the public.

No. 29 Fitzroy Square

Fitzroy Tavern ⑭

16 Charlotte St W1. **Map** 4 F5. **Tel** 020-7580 3714. 🚇 Tottenham Court Rd, Goodge St. **Open** 11am–11pm Mon–Sat, noon–10:30pm Sun. ♿ See **Pubs** pp316–19.

This traditional pub was a meeting place between World Wars I and II for a group of writers and artists who dubbed the area around Fitzroy Square and Charlotte Street "Fitzrovia". A basement "Writers and Artists Bar" contains pictures of former customers, including the writers Dylan Thomas and George Orwell, and the artist Augustus John.

Charlotte Street ⑮

W1. **Map** 5 A5. 🚇 Goodge St.

As the upper classes moved west from Bloomsbury in the early 19th century, a flood of artists and European immigrants moved in, turning the area into a northern appendage to Soho (see pp98–109). The artist John Constable lived and worked for many years at No. 76. Some of the new residents established small workshops

to service the clothing shops on Oxford Street and the furniture stores on Tottenham Court Road. Others set up reasonably-priced restaurants. The street still boasts a great variety of eating places. It is overshadowed from the north by the 189-m (620-ft) Telecom Tower, built in 1964 as a vast TV, radio and telecommunications aerial (see p32).

Telecom Tower

Pollock's Toy Museum ⑯

1 Scala St W1. **Map** 5 A5. **Tel** 020-7636 3452. 🚇 Goodge St, Warren St, Tottenham Court Rd. **Open** 10am–5pm Mon–Sat. **Adm charge.** 🅿 www.pollockstoymuseum.com

Benjamin Pollock was a renowned maker of toy theatres in the late 19th and early 20th centuries – the novelist Robert Louis Stevenson was an enthusiastic customer. The museum opened in Monmouth Street in Covent Garden in 1956 and relocated to these premises in 1969. The final room is devoted to stages and puppets from Pollock's theatres, together with a reconstruction of his workshop. This is a child-sized museum created in two largely unaltered 18th-century houses. The small rooms have been filled with a fascinating assortment of historic toys from all over the world. There are dolls, puppets, trains, cars, construction sets, a fine rocking horse and a splendid collection of mainly Victorian doll's houses. Parents should beware – the exit leads you through a very tempting toyshop.

Pearly king and queen dolls from Pollock's Toy Museum

HOLBORN & THE INNS OF COURT

This area is traditionally home to the legal and journalistic professions. The law is still here, in the Royal Courts of Justice and the Inns of Court, but most national newspapers left Fleet Street in the 1980s. Several buildings here predate the Great Fire of 1666 (see pp24–5). These include the

Royal crest at Lincoln's Inn

superb façade of Staple Inn, Prince Henry's Room, and the interior of Middle Temple Hall. Holborn used to be one of the capital's main shopping districts. Times have changed the face of the area, but the jewellery and diamond dealers of Hatton Garden are still here, as are the London Silver Vaults.

SIGHTS AT A GLANCE

Historic Buildings, Sights and Streets
Lincoln's Inn ❷
Old Curiosity Shop ❹
Law Society ❺
Royal Courts of Justice ❼
Fleet Street ❾
Prince Henry's Room ❿
Temple ⓫
Dr Johnson's House ⓮
Holborn Viaduct ⓰
Hatton Garden ⓲
Staple Inn ⓳
Gray's Inn ㉑

Museums and Galleries
Sir John Soane's Museum ❶

Churches
St Clement Danes ❻
St Bride's ⓬
St Andrew, Holborn ⓯
St Etheldreda's Chapel ⓱

Monuments
Temple Bar Memorial ❽

Parks and Gardens
Lincoln's Inn Fields ❸

Pubs
Ye Olde Cheshire Cheese ⓭

Shops
London Silver Vaults ⓴

KEY

▢	Street-by-Street map
⊖	Underground station
≋	Railway station

GETTING THERE

This area is served by the Circle, Central, District, Metropolitan and Piccadilly lines. Buses 17, 18, 45, 46, 171, 243 and 259 are among many in the area, and trains run from a number of mainline stations inside or close to the area.

SEE ALSO

- *Street Finder, maps* 6, 13, 14
- *Where to Stay* pp278–91
- *Restaurants, Pubs* pp292–319

◁ The Royal Courts of Justice on the Strand

Street-by-Street: Lincoln's Inn

This is calm, dignified, legal London, packed with history and interest. Lincoln's Inn, adjoining one of the city's first residential squares, has buildings dating from the late 15th century. Dark-suited lawyers carry bundles of briefs between their offices here and the Neo-Gothic Law Courts. Nearby is the Temple, another historic legal district with a famous 13th-century round church.

★ Sir John Soane's Museum
The Georgian architect made this his London home and left it, with his collection, to the nation ❶

To Kingsway

LINCOLN'S INN FIELDS

LINCOLN'S INN FIELDS

★ Lincoln's Inn Fields
The mock-Tudor archway, leading to Lincoln's Inn and built in 1845, overlooks the Fields ❸

Old Curiosity Shop
This is a rare 17th-century, pre-Great Fire building which is now a shop ❹

PORTSMOUTH ST

PORTUGAL STREET

CAREY

The Royal College of Surgeons was designed in 1836 by Sir Charles Barry. Inside there are laboratories for research and teaching as well as a museum of anatomical specimens.

STAR SIGHTS

- ★ Sir John Soane's Museum
- ★ Temple
- ★ Lincoln's Inn Fields
- ★ Lincoln's Inn

KEY

– – – Suggested route

0 metres	100
0 yards	100

Twinings has been selling tea from here since 1706. The doorway dates from 1787 when the shop was called the Golden Lion.

The Gladstone Statue was erected in 1905 to commemorate William Gladstone, the Victorian statesman who was Prime Minister four times.

★ **Lincoln's Inn**
The Court of Chancery sat here, in Old Hall, from 1835 until 1858. Sir John Taylor Coleridge, nephew of the poet, was a well-known judge of the time **2**

LOCATOR MAP
See Central London Map pp14–15

Royal Courts of Justice
The country's main court for civil cases and appeals was built in 1882. It is made out of 35 million bricks faced with Portland stone **7**

Law Society
Look for the gold lions on the railings of this superb building **5**

Fleet Street
For two centuries this was the centre of the national press. Today the newspaper offices are gone **9**

El Vino is a venerable wine bar, where journalists still mingle with lawyers.

Prince Henry's Room
There is an authentic 17th-century room in this former gatehouse **10**

St Clement Danes
Designed by Wren (1679), it is the Royal Air Force church **6**

Temple Bar Memorial
A dragon marks where the City of London meets Westminster **8**

★ **Temple**
It was built for the Knights Templar in the 13th century, but today lawyers stroll here **11**

Wigged barristers on their way to their offices in Lincoln's Inn

Lincoln's Inn ❷

WC2. **Map** 14 D1. **Tel** 020-7405 1393. ⊖ Holborn, Chancery Lane. **Grounds open** 7am–7pm Mon–Fri. **Chapel open** 12–2.30pm Mon–Fri. **Hall** not open to the public. ♿ www.lincolnsinn.org.uk

Some of the buildings in Lincoln's Inn, the best-preserved of London's Inns of Court, go back to the late 15th century. The coat of arms above the arch of the Chancery Lane gatehouse is Henry VIII's, and the heavy oak door is of the same vintage. Shakespeare's contemporary, Ben Jonson, is believed to have laid some of the bricks of Lincoln's Inn during the reign of Elizabeth I. The chapel is early 17th-century Gothic. Women were not allowed to be buried here until 1839, when the grieving Lord Brougham petitioned to have the rule changed so that his beloved daughter could be interred in the chapel, to wait for him to join her.

Lincoln's Inn has its share of famous alumni. Oliver Cromwell and John Donne,

Sir John Soane's Museum ❶

13 Lincoln's Inn Fields WC2. **Map** 14 D1. **Tel** 020-7405 2107. ⊖ Holborn. **Open** 10am–5pm Tue–Sat, 6–9pm first Tue of month. **Closed** Sun, Mon, bank hols & Christmas Eve. ♿ limited – phone first. 📷 Sat 2.30pm; groups book ahead. 🎧 www.soane.org

One of the most surprising museums in London, this house was left to the nation by Sir John Soane in 1837, with a far-sighted stipulation that nothing at all should be changed. One of Britain's leading 19th-century architects, responsible for designing the Bank of England, Soane was the son of a bricklayer. After prudently marrying the niece of a wealthy builder, whose fortune he inherited, he bought and reconstructed No. 12 Lincoln's Inn Fields. In 1813 he and his wife moved into No. 13 and later, in 1824, he rebuilt No. 14, extending his museum into the rear of

this building. Today, the collections are much as Soane left them – an eclectic gathering of beautiful, peculiar and often instructional objects.

The building itself abounds with architectural surprises and illusions. In the main ground floor room, with its deep red and green colouring, cunningly placed mirrors play tricks with light and space. The picture gallery is lined with layers of folding panels to increase its capacity. The panels open out to reveal galleried extensions to the room itself. Among other works here are many of Soane's own exotic designs, including those for Pitzhanger Manor (see p258) and the Bank of England (see p147). Here also is William Hogarth's Rake's Progress series.

In the centre of the low-ceilinged basement an atrium stretches up to the roof. A glass dome lights galleries, on every floor, that are laden with Classical statuary.

A glass dome allows light into the basement.

A vast sarcophagus (1300 BC) stands on the floor of the basement.

the 17th-century poet, were both students here, as was William Penn, founder of the US state of Pennsylvania.

Lincoln's Inn Fields ❸

WC2. **Map** 14 D1. 🚇 *Holborn*. **Open** *dawn–dusk daily*. **Public tennis courts.**

This used to be a public execution site. Under the Tudors and the Stuarts, many religious martyrs, and those suspected of treachery to the Crown, perished here.

When the developer William Newton wanted to build here in the 1640s, students at Lincoln's Inn and other residents made him undertake that the land in the centre would remain a public area forever. Thanks to this early protest, lawyers today play tennis here throughout the summer, or read their briefs in the fresh air. For some years it has also been the site of an evening soup kitchen for some of London's homeless.

Old Curiosity Shop sign

Old Curiosity Shop ❹

13–14 Portsmouth St WC2. **Map** 14 D1. 🚇 *Holborn*.

Whether it is or is not the original for Charles Dickens's novel of the same name, this is a genuine 17th-century building and almost certainly the oldest shop in central London. With its overhanging first floor, it gives a rare impression of a London streetscape from before the Great Fire of 1666.

The Old Curiosity Shop maintains its retailing tradition, and currently operates as a shoe shop. A preservation order guarantees the long-term future of the building.

Law Society ❺

113 Chancery Lane WC2. **Map** 14 E1. **Tel** *020-7242 1222*. 🚇 *Chancery Lane*. **Not open** to the public.

The headquarters of the solicitors' professional body is, architecturally, one of the most interesting buildings in the legal quarter. The main part, dominated by four Ionic columns, was completed in 1832. More significant is the northern extension, an early work of Charles Holden, an Arts and Crafts enthusiast who later made his name as a designer of London Underground stations. In his window arches the four seated figures depict truth, justice, liberty and mercy.

The building is on the corner of Carey Street, the site of the bankruptcy court whose name, corrupted to "Queer Street", entered the language to describe a state of destitution.

Every wall is covered, and every room filled, with artifacts from Soane's massive collection.

In the picture gallery, panels covered with paintings unfold to reveal more works of art behind them.

The Monk's Parlour is full of grotesque, Gothic casts.

St Clement Danes ❻

Strand WC2. **Map** 14 D2. **Tel** 020-7242 8282. ⊖ *Temple.* **Open** *9am–4pm daily.* **Closed** *noon 25 Dec–27 Dec, public hols.* ✝ *12.30am Wed & Fri, 11am Sun.* ♿ *See* **Ceremonial London** *p55.*

Christopher Wren designed this wonderful church in 1680. Its name derives from anearlier church built here by the descendants of Danish invaders whom Alfred the Great had allowed to remain in London in the 9th century. From the 17th to 19th centuries many people were buried here, and their restplates are now in the crypt. The chain now hanging on the crypt wall was probably used to secure coffin lids against body snatchers who stole fresh corpses and sold them to the teaching hospitals.

St Clement Danes sits proudly isolated on a traffic island. It is now the Royal Air Force (RAF) church, and the interior

Clock at the Victorian law courts

is dominated by RAF symbols, memorials and monuments. Outside, to the east, is a statue (1910) of Dr Johnson *(see p140)*, who often came to services here. The church bells ring to the tune of the English nursery rhyme "Oranges and Lemons" at 9am, noon, 3pm and 6pm Mon–Sat, and there is an annual oranges and lemons service in March.

Royal Courts of Justice (the Law Courts) ❼

Strand WC2. **Map** 14 D2. **Tel** 020-7947 6000. ⊖ *Holborn, Temple, Chancery Lane.* **Open** *9am–4:30pm Mon–Fri.* **Closed** *public hols.* ♿ 🖥 🖱 **www**.hmcourts-service.gov.uk

Knots of demonstrators and television cameras can often be seen outside this sprawling and fanciful Victorian Gothic building, waiting for the result of a contentious case. These are the nation's main civil courts, dealing with such matters as divorce, libel, civil liability and appeals. Criminals are dealt with at the Old Bailey *(see p147)*, ten minutes' walk to the east. The public are admitted to all the court rooms and a list tells you which case is being heard in which court. The massive Gothic building was completed in 1882. It is said to contain 1,000 rooms and 5.6 km (3.5 miles) of corridors.

Temple Bar Memorial ❽

Fleet St EC4. **Map** 14 D2. ⊖ *Holborn, Temple, Chancery Lane.*

The monument in the middle of Fleet Street, outside the Law Courts, dates from 1880 and marks the entrance to the City of London. On state occasions it is a long-standing tradition for the monarch to have to pause here and ask permission of the Lord Mayor to enter. Temple Bar, a huge archway designed by Wren, used to stand here. You can see what it used to look like from one of the four reliefs that surround the base of the present monument.

Fleet Street ❾

EC4. **Map** 14 E1. ⊖ *Temple, Blackfriars, St Paul's.*

England's first printing press was set up here in the late 15th century by William Caxton's assistant, and Fleet

The dragon, symbol of the City, at the entrance to the City at Temple Bar

William Capon's engraving of Fleet Street in 1799

Street has been a centre of London's publishing industry ever since. Playwrights Shakespeare and Ben Jonson were patrons of the old Mitre tavern, now No. 37 Fleet Street. In 1702 the first newspaper, *The Daily Courant*, was issued from Fleet Street – conveniently placed for the City and Westminster which were the main sources of news. Later the street became synonymous with the Press.

The printing presses underneath the newspaper offices were abandoned in 1987, when new technology made it easy to produce papers away from the centre of town in areas such as Wapping and the Docklands. Today the newspapers have left their Fleet Street offices and only the agencies, Reuters and the Press Association, remain.

El Vino wine bar, at the western end opposite Fetter Lane, is a traditional haunt of journalists and lawyers.

Effigies in Temple Church

Prince Henry's Room ⑩

17 Fleet St EC4. **Map** 14 E1.
🚇 *Temple, Chancery Lane.*
Closed *to the public – check website for further information.* 📷
www.cityoflondon.gov.uk

Built in 1610 as part of a Fleet Street tavern, this gets its name from the Prince of Wales's coat of arms and the initials PH in the centre of the ceiling. They were probably put there to mark the investiture as Prince of Wales of Henry, James I's eldest son who died before he became king.

The fine half-timbered front, alongside the gateway to Inner Temple, is original and so is some of the room's oak panelling. It contains an exhibition about the diarist Samuel Pepys.

Temple ⑪

Inner Temple, King's Bench Walk EC4. **Map** 14 E2. **Tel** 020-7797 8250. 🚇 *Temple.* **Open** *12:30pm–3pm Mon–Fri (grounds only).* ♿
Middle Temple Hall, Middle Temple Lane EC4. **Tel** 020-7427 4800. **Open** *10am–11:30, 3–4pm Mon–Fri.*
Closed *at short notice for functions.*
♿ 📷 *book ahead.* 🚇 **Temple Church Tel** 020-7353 8559. **Open** *Wed–Fri; call for times & services.*
www.templechurch.com

This embraces two of the four Inns of Court, the Middle Temple and the Inner Temple. (The other two are Lincoln's and Gray's Inns, *pp136, 141*.) The name derives from the

Knights Templar, a chivalrous order which used to protect pilgrims to the Holy Land. The order was based here until it was suppressed by the Crown because its power was viewed as a threat. Initiations probably took place in the crypt of Temple Church and there are 13th-century effigies of Knights Templar in the nave.

Among some other ancient buildings is the Middle Temple Hall. Its fine Elizabethan interior survives – Shakespeare's *Twelfth Night* was performed here in 1601. Behind Temple, peaceful lawns stretch lazily down towards the Embankment.

St Bride's ⑫

Fleet St EC4. **Map** 14 F2. **Tel** 020-7427 0133. 🚇 *Blackfriars.* **Open** *8am–6:30pm Mon–Fri, 10am–1pm & 5–7:30pm Sun.* **Closed** *public hols.*
♿ 🕑 *11am & 6:30pm Sun.* 📷
Concerts *Check website for details.*
www.stbrides.com

St Bride's, church of the Press

St Bride's is one of Wren's best-loved churches. Its position just off Fleet Street has made it the traditional venue for memorial services to departed journalists. Wall plaques commemorate Fleet Street journalists and printers.

The marvellous octagonal layered spire has been the model for tiered wedding cakes since shortly after it was added in 1703. Bombed in 1940, the interior was faithfully restored after World War II. The fascinating crypt contains remnants of earlier churches on the site, and a section of Roman pavement.

Ye Olde Cheshire Cheese ⑬

145 Fleet St EC4. **Map** 14 E1.
Tel 020-7353 6170. ⊖ Blackfriars.
Open 11am–11pm Mon–Fri, noon–
11pm Sat, noon–7pm Sun. See **Pubs**
pp316–19.

There has been an inn here
for centuries; parts of this
building date back to 1667,
when the Cheshire Cheese
was rebuilt after the Great
Fire. The diarist Samuel Pepys
often drank here in the 17th
century, but it was Dr Samuel
Johnson's association with
"the Cheese" that made it
a place of pilgrimage for
19th-century literati. These
included novelists Mark
Twain and Charles Dickens.
   This is one of the few
pubs to have kept the 18th-
century arrangement of
small rooms with fireplaces,
tables and benches, instead
of knocking them into
larger bars.

Dr Johnson's House ⑭

17 Gough Sq EC4. **Map** 14 E1. **Tel**
020-7353 3745. ⊖ Blackfriars,
Chancery Lane, Temple. **Open** May–
Sep: 11am–5:30pm Mon–Sat; Oct–
Apr: 11am–5pm Mon–Sat. **Closed**
public hols. **Adm charge.** ◙ small
charge. ▮ book ahead. ▯
www.drjohnsonshouse.org

Dr Samuel Johnson was an
18th-century scholar famous
for the many witty (and often
contentious) remarks that his
biographer, James Boswell,

Schoolgirl figure mounted on the
façade of St Andrew church

recorded and published.
Johnson lived here from 1748
to 1759. He compiled the first
definitive English dictionary
(1755) in the attic, where six
scribes and assistants stood all
day at high desks.
   The house, built before 1700,
is furnished with 18th-century
pieces and a small collection
of exhibits relating to Johnson
and the times in which he
lived. These include a tea set
belonging to his friend Mrs
Thrale and pictures of Johnson
and his contemporaries. It
also houses a selection of
replica Georgian costumes for
children to try on.

St Andrew, Holborn ⑮

5 St Andrew St EC4. **Map** 14 E1. **Tel**
020-7583 7394. ⊖ Chancery Lane.
Open 8:30am–5pm Mon–Fri. ◙ ▯
⛪ **www**.standrewholborn.org.uk

The medieval church here
survived the Great Fire of
1666. In 1686 Christopher
Wren was, however, asked to
redesign it, and the lower part
of the tower is virtually all that
remains of the earlier church.
One of Wren's most spacious
churches, it was gutted during
World War II but faithfully
restored as the church of the
London trade guilds. Benjamin
Disraeli, the Jewish-born Prime
Minister, was baptized here in
1817, at the age of 12. In the
19th century a charity school
was attached to the church.

Holborn Viaduct ⑯

EC1. **Map** 14 F1. ⊖ Farringdon,
St Paul's, Chancery Lane.

Civic symbol on Holborn Viaduct

This piece of Victorian
ironwork was erected in the
1860s as part of a much-
needed traffic scheme. It is
best seen from Farringdon
Street which is linked to the
bridge by a staircase. Climb
up and see the statues of City
heroes and bronze images of
Commerce, Agriculture,
Science and Fine Arts.

St Etheldreda's Chapel ⑰

14 Ely Place EC1. **Map** 6 E5.
Tel 020-7405 1061. ⊖ Farringdon.
Open 8am–7pm daily. ◙ ▯ ▭
noon–2pm. **www**.stetheldreda.com

This is a rare 13th-century
survivor, the chapel and crypt
of Ely House, where the
Bishops of Ely lived until the

Reconstructed interior of Dr Johnson's house

Reformation Then it was acquired by an Elizabethan courtier, Sir Christopher Hatton, whose descendants demolished the house but kept the chapel and turned it into a Protestant church. It passed through various hands and, in 1874, reverted to the Catholic faith.

Hatton Garden ⑱

EC1. **Map** 6 E5. 🚇 Chancery Lane, Farringdon.

Built on land that used to be the garden of Hatton House, this is London's diamond and jewellery district. Gems ranging from the priceless to the mundane are traded from scores of small shops with sparkling window displays, and even from the pavements. One of the city's few remaining pawnbrokers is here – look for its traditional sign of three brass balls above the door.

Staple Inn ⑲

Holborn WC1. **Map** 14 E1. 🚇 Chancery Lane. **Courtyard open** 9am–5pm Mon–Fri. 🏠

This building was once the wool staple, where wool was weighed and taxed. The frontage overlooks Holborn and is the only real example of Elizabethan half-timbering left in central London. Although now much restored, it would still be recognizable by someone who had known it in 1586, when it was built. The shops at street level have the feel of the 19th century, and there are some 18th-century buildings in the courtyard.

London Silver Vaults ⑳

53–64 Chancery Lane WC2. **Map** 14 D1. 🚇 Chancery Lane, Holborn.

These silver vaults originate from the Chancery Lane Safe Deposit Company, established in 1885. After descending a

Staple Inn, a survivor from 1586

staircase you pass through formidable steel security doors and reach a nest of underground shops sparkling with antique and modern silverware. London silver makers have been renowned for centuries, reaching their peak in the Georgian era. The best examples sell for many thousands of pounds but most shops also offer modest pieces at realistic prices.

Coffee pot (1716): Silver Vaults

Gray's Inn ㉑

Gray's Inn Rd WC1. **Map** 6 D5. **Tel** 020-7458 7800. 🚇 Chancery Lane, Holborn. **Grounds open** noon–2.30pm Mon–Fri. 🔲 ask first. 🚻 🔲

This ancient legal centre and law school goes back to the 14th century. Like many of the buildings in this area, it was badly damaged by World War II bombs but much of it has been rebuilt. At least one of Shakespeare's plays (*A Comedy of Errors*) was first performed in Gray's Inn hall in 1594. The hall's 16th-century interior screen still survives.

More recently, the young Charles Dickens was employed as a clerk here in 1827–8. Today the garden, once a convenient site for staging duels, is open to lunchtime strollers for part of the year, and typifies the cloistered calm of the four Inns of Court. The buildings may be visited only by prior arrangement.

THE CITY

ondon's financial district is built on the site of the original Roman settlement. Its full title is the City of London, but it is usually referred to as the City. Most traces of the early City were obliterated by the Great Fire of 1666 and World War II *(see pp24–5 and 33)*. Today glossy modern offices stand among a plethora of banks, with marbled halls and stately pillars. It is the con-

Traditional bank sign on Lombard Street

trast between dour, warren-like Victorian buildings and shiny new ones that gives the City its distinctive character. Though it hums with activity in business hours, few people have lived here since the 19th century, when it was one of London's main residential centres. Today only the churches, many of them by Christopher Wren *(see p47)*, are a reminder of those past times.

SIGHTS AT A GLANCE

Historic Streets and Buildings
Mansion House **1**
Royal Exchange **3**
Old Bailey **7**
Apothecaries' Hall **8**
Fishmongers' Hall **9**
Tower of London pp154–7 **16**
Tower Bridge **17**
Stock Exchange **19**
Lloyd's of London **23**

Museums and Galleries
Bank of England Museum **4**
Guildhall Art Gallery **24**

Historic Markets
Old Billingsgate **12**
Leadenhall Market **22**

Monuments
Monument **11**

Churches and Cathedrals
St Stephen Walbrook **2**
St Mary-le-Bow **5**
St Paul's Cathedral pp148–51 **6**
St Magnus the Martyr **10**
St Mary-at-Hill **13**
St Margaret Pattens **14**
All Hallows by the Tower **15**
St Helen's Bishopsgate **20**
St Katharine Cree **21**

Docks
St Katharine's Dock **18**

SEE ALSO

• **Street Finder**, maps 14, 15, 16

• **Where to Stay** pp278–291

• **Restaurants, Pubs** pp292–319

GETTING THERE
The City is served by the DLR and the Circle, Central, District, Northern, Metropolitan, Hammersmith and City and Waterloo and City lines, and numerous bus routes. There are many mainline railway stations.

KEY

	Street-by-Street map
⊖	Underground station
≈	Railway station

0 metres 500
0 yards 500

◁ **Tower Bridge, a combined bascule and suspension bridge completed in 1894**

Street-by-Street: The City

This is the business centre of London, home to vast financial institutions such as the Stock Exchange and the Bank of England. But in contrast to these 19th- and 20th-century buildings are the older survivors. A walk through the City is in part a pilgrimage through the architectural visions of Christopher Wren, England's most sublime and probably most prolific architect. After the Great Fire of 1666 he supervised the rebuilding of 52 churches within the area, and enough survive to testify to his genius.

St Mary-le-Bow
Anyone born within earshot of the bells of this Wren church (the historic Bow Bells) is said to be a true Londoner or Cockney ❺

★ St Paul's
Wren's masterpiece still dominates the City skyline ❻

St Paul's station

Mansion House station

The College of Arms received its royal charter in 1484 from Richard III. Still active today, it assesses who has a legitimate claim to a British family coat of arms.

St Nicholas Cole Abbey was the first church Wren built in the City (in 1677). Like many others, it had to be restored after World War II bomb damage.

St James Garlickhythe contains unusual sword rests and hat stands, beneath Wren's elegant spire of 1717.

STAR SIGHTS

- ★ St Paul's
- ★ St Stephen Walbrook
- ★ Bank of England Museum

KEY

--- — Suggested route

0 metres   100

0 yards   100

Skinners' Hall is the Italianate 18th-century guild hall for the leather trade.

Mansion House
The official home of the City of London's Lord Mayor contains a small prison ❶

★ Bank of England Museum
The intriguing story of England's financial system is vividly displayed here ❹

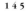

LOCATOR MAP
See Central London Map pp14–15

SMITHFIELD & SPITALFIELDS

THE CITY

Thames

SOUTHWARK & BANKSIDE

KING ST
IRONMONGER LANE
OLD JEWRY
PRINCE'S STREET
THREADNEEDLE STREET
CORNHILL
Bank station
LOMBARD ST
STREET
WALBROOK
KING WILLIAM STREET
ST SWITHIN'S
CANNON STREET

Royal Exchange
Since its foundation in Tudor times, this has been at the heart of London's commerce ❸

Lombard Street
is named after Italian bankers who settled here from Lombardy in the 13th century. It is still a banking centre.

St Mary Abchurch owes its unusually spacious feel to Wren's large dome. The altar carving is by Grinling Gibbons.

★ St Stephen Walbrook
Experimenting for St Paul's, Wren created its unique dome. The interior contains original features, such as this font ❷

St Mary Woolnoth is a characteristically powerful work by Wren's pupil, Nicholas Hawksmoor.

Mansion House ❶

Walbrook EC4. **Map** 15 B2 **Tel** 020-7626 2500. 🚇 Bank, Mansion House. **Open** to group tours only by appt or 2pm Tue on first-come-first-served basis. **www**.cityoflondon.gov.uk

The official residence of the Lord Mayor, it was completed in 1753 to the design of George Dance the Elder, whose work is now in John Soane's Museum (see pp136–7). The Palladian front with its six Corinthian columns is one of the most familiar City landmarks. The state rooms have a dignity appropriate to the office of mayor, one of the most spectacular being the 27-m (90-ft) Egyptian Hall.

Formerly located here, and now in the Museum of London (see pp166–7), were 11 holding cells, a reminder of the building's other function as a magistrate's court; the Mayor is chief magistrate of the City during his year of office. Emmeline Pankhurst, who campaigned for women's suffrage in the early 20th century, was once held here.

Egyptian Hall in Mansion House

St Stephen Walbrook ❷

39 Walbrook EC4. **Map** 15 B2. **Tel** 020-7626 9000. 🚇 Bank, Cannon St. **Open** 10am–4pm Mon–Fri. 🕇 12.45pm Thu, sung Mass. 🎹 **Organ recitals** Fri.

The Lord Mayor's parish church was built by Christopher Wren in 1672–9. Architectural writers consider it to be the finest of his City churches (see p47). The deep, coffered dome, with its ornate plasterwork, was a forerunner of St Paul's. St Stephen's airy columned interior comes as a surprise after its plain exterior. The font cover and pulpit canopy are decorated with exquisite carved figures that contrast strongly with the stark simplicity of Henry Moore's massive white stone altar (1987).

However, perhaps the most moving monument of all is a telephone in a glass box. This is a tribute to Rector Chad Varah who, in 1953, founded the Samaritans, a voluntarily staffed telephone help-line for people in emotional need. *The Martyrdom of St Stephen*, which hangs on the north wall, is by American painter Benjamin West, who became a Royal Academician (see p90) in 1768.

The spire was added in 1717.

The dome makes this small church light and airy.

Wren's original altar and screen are still here.

Wren's pulpit has a delicate canopy.

Henry Moore's polished stone altar was added in 1987.

Royal Exchange **3**

EC3. **Map** 15 C2. **Tel** 020-7623 0444. ☻ Bank. **Not open** to the public.

Sir Thomas Gresham, the Elizabethan merchant and courtier, founded the Royal Exchange in 1565 as a centre for commerce of all kinds. The original building was centred on a vast courtyard where merchants and tradesmen did business. Queen Elizabeth I gave it its Royal title and it is still one of the sites from which new kings and queens are announced. Dating from 1844, this is the third splendid building on the site since Gresham's.

Britain's first public lavatories were built in the forecourt here in 1855. Exclusively for male use, they symbolized the era's unenlightened attitudes.

Bank of England Museum **4**

Bartholomew Lane EC2. **Map** 15 B1. **Tel** 020-7601 5545. ☻ Bank. **Open** 10am–5pm Mon–Fri, Lord Mayor's Show (p55). **Closed** public hols. ♿ phone first. ☻ ☻ **Films, lectures.** www.bankofengland. co.uk/education/museum

The Duke of Wellington (1884) opposite the Bank of England

The Bank of England was set up in 1694 to raise money for foreign wars. It grew to become Britain's central bank, and also issues currency notes. Sir John Soane *(see pp136–7)* was the architect of the 1788 bank building on this site, but only the exterior wall of his design has survived. The rest was destroyed in the 1920s and 1930s when the Bank was enlarged. There is now a

The façade of William Tite's Royal Exchange of 1844

reconstruction of Soane's stock office of 1793.

Glittering gold bars, silver plated decoration and a Roman mosaic floor, discovered during the rebuilding, are among the items on display. The museum illustrates the work of the Bank and the financial system. The gift shop sells paperweights which are made out of used banknotes.

St Mary-le-Bow **5**

(Bow Church) Cheapside EC2. **Map** 15 A2. **Tel** 020-7248 5139. ☻ St Paul's, Mansion Hse. **Open** 7am–6pm Mon– Wed, 7am–6:30pm Thu, 7am–4pm Fri. ☩ 7:30am Tue, 1pm Wed & Fri, 6pm Thu. ☻ www.stmarylebow.co.uk

The church takes its name from the bow arches in the Norman crypt. When Wren rebuilt the church (in 1670– 80) after the Great Fire, he continued this architectural pattern through the graceful arches on the steeple. The weathervane, dating from 1674, is an enormous dragon.

The church was bombed in 1941 leaving only the steeple and two outer walls standing. It was restored in 1956–62 when the bells were recast and rehung. Bow bells are important to Londoners: traditionally only those born within their sound can claim to be true Cockneys.

St Paul's **6**

See pp148–51.

Old Bailey **7**

EC4. **Map** 14 F1. **Tel** 020-7248 3277. ☻ St Paul's. **Open** 10am–1pm, 2–5pm Mon–Fri (but opening hours vary from court to court). **Closed** Christmas, New Year, Easter, public hols. ♿ www.cityoflondon.gov.uk

Old Bailey's rooftop Justice

This short street has a long association with crime and punishment. The new Central Criminal Courts opened here in 1907 on the site of the notorious and malodorous Newgate prison (on special days in the legal calendar judges still carry small posies to court as a reminder of those times). Across the road, the Magpie and Stump served "execution breakfasts" until 1868, when mass public hangings outside the prison gates were stopped.

Today, when the courts are in session, they are open to members of the public.

St Paul's Cathedral ❻

Following the Great Fire of London in 1666, the medieval cathedral of St Paul's was left in ruins. The authorities turned to Christopher Wren to rebuild it, but his ideas met with considerable resistance from the conservative Dean and Chapter. Wren's 1672 Great Model plan was not at all popular with them, and so a watered-down plan was finally agreed in 1675. Wren's determination paid off though, as can be witnessed from the grandeur of the present cathedral.

Stone urn outside the South Transept

★ The Dome
At 110 m (360 ft) high, the dome at St Paul's is the second biggest in the world after St Peter's in Rome, as spectacular from inside as outside.

The balustrade along the top was added in 1718 against Wren's wishes.

The pediment carvings, dating from 1706, show the Conversion of St Paul.

★ The West Front and Towers
The towers were not on Wren's original plan – he added them in 1707, when he was 75 years old. Both were designed to have clocks.

Flying buttresses support the nave walls and the dome.

STAR SIGHTS

★ West Front and Towers

★ Dome

★ Whispering Gallery

The West Portico comprises two tiers of columns rather than the single colonnade that Wren intended.

The West Porch, approached from Ludgate Hill, is the main entrance to St Paul's.

Queen Anne's Statue
An 1886 copy of Francis Bird's 1712 original now stands on the forecourt.

The lantern weighs a massive 850 tonnes.

The golden gallery lies at the highest point of the dome.

The brick cone located inside the outer dome supports the heavy lantern

The oculus is an opening through which the lantern can be seen.

The stone gallery offers a splendid view over London.

Upper screen wall masks the flying buttresses.

VISITORS' CHECKLIST

Ludgate Hill EC4. **Map** 15 A2
Tel 020-7236 4128. ⊖ St Paul's,
Mansion House. ▦ 6, 8, 11, 15,
22, 23, 25, 76. ⊟ City Thameslink **Cathedral open** 8:30am–
4pm Mon–Sat **Galleries open**
9:30am–4:15pm. **Crypt &
ambulatory open** 9:15am–
4:15pm **Closed** for sightseeing
on Sun **Adm charge.** ⬆11am
Sun. ⌀ ▣ ▣ ▣ ▣ ▣ ⬇
Concerts. www.stpauls.co.uk

★ **Whispering Gallery**
*The unusual acoustics here cause
whispers to echo around the dome.*

**The North and South
Transepts** cross the
nave in a medieval
style that contrasts
with Wren's original
plan *(see p150).*

South Porch
*Wren took the idea of
a semi-circular porch
from a Baroque
church in Rome.*

TIMELINE

Detail on Tijou gate (see p151)

604 Bishop Mellitus built the first St Paul's. It burned down in 1087				**1666** St Paul's reduced to a burnt ruin after the Great Fire	**1708** Wren's son Christopher lays the last stone on the lantern		**2011** Extensive restorations finished	
600	800	1000	1200	1400	1600	1800	2000	
	1087 Bishop Maurice began Old St Paul's: a Norman cathedral of stone			**1675** Foundation stone of Wren's design laid	**1940–1** Slight bomb damage to the cathedral	**1981** Prince Charles marries Lady Diana Spencer		

A Guided Tour of St Paul's

The visitor to St Paul's will be immediately impressed by its cool, beautifully ordered and extremely spacious interior. The nave, transepts and choir are arranged in the shape of a cross, as in a medieval cathedral, but Wren's Classical vision shines through this conservative floor plan, forced on him by the cathedral authorities. Aided by some of the finest craftsmen of his day, he created an interior of grand majesty and Baroque splendour, a worthy setting for the many great ceremonial events that have taken place here. These include the funeral of Winston Churchill in 1965 and the wedding of Prince Charles and Lady Diana Spencer in 1981.

The mosaics on the choir ceiling were completed in the 1890s by William Richmond.

① The Nave
Take in the full glory of the massive arches and the succession of saucer domes that open out into a huge space below the main dome.

② The North Aisle
As you walk along the North Aisle, look above: the aisles are vaulted with small domes mimicking those of the nave ceiling.

⑨ South Aisle
From here the brave can ascend the 259 steps to the Whispering Gallery and test the acoustics.

Entrance to Whispering Gallery

Main entrances

⑧ Florence Nightingale's Tomb
Famous for her pioneering work in nursing standards, Florence Nightingale was the first woman to receive the Order of Merit.

The Geometrical Staircase is a spiral of 92 stone steps giving access to the cathedral library.

⑦ Wren's Tomb
Wren's burial place is marked by a slab. The inscription states: "Reader, if you seek a monument, look around you."

KEY

— — — Tour route

③ The Crossing
The climax of Wren's interior is this great open space. The vast dome is decorated with monochrome frescoes by Sir James Thornhill, the leading architectural painter of Wren's time.

Entrance to crypt

④ The Choir
Jean Tijou, a Huguenot refugee, created much of the cathedral's fine wrought ironwork, such as these screens in the choir aisles.

John Donne's memorial, from 1631, was the only monument to survive the Great Fire of 1666 intact. The poet posed for it in his lifetime.

⑤ The High Altar
The canopy over the altar was replaced after World War II. It is based on Wren's original Baroque drawings.

Grinling Gibbons's work can be found on the choir stalls, with typically intricate carvings of cherubs, fruits and garlands.

T E Lawrence, or Lawrence of Arabia, the British World War I hero who earned his nickname by fighting alongside Arab tribes in their resistance to Turkish rule in 1915, is commemorated by this bust in the crypt.

⑥ The Crypt
The tombs of famous figures and such popular heroes as Lord Nelson, can be seen in the crypt.

Apothecaries' Hall **8**

Blackfriars Lane EC4. **Map** 14 F2. **Tel** *020-7236 1180.* ⊖ *Blackfriars.* **Courtyard open** *9am–5pm Mon–Fri.* **Closed** *public hols, end Aug.* **Phone Hall** *for appt to visit (groups only).* ⬧

Apothecaries' Hall, rebuilt in 1670

London has had livery companies, or guilds, to protect and regulate specific trades since early medieval times. The Apothecaries' Society was founded in 1617 for those who prepared, prescribed or sold drugs. It has some surprising alumni, including Oliver Cromwell and the poet John Keats. Now nearly all the members are physicians or surgeons.

Fishmongers' Hall **9**

London Bridge EC4. **Map** 15 B3. **Tel** *020-7626 3531.* ⊖ *Monument.* **Not open** *to the public. Limited tours by appt only.* **www**.fishhall.co.uk

This is one of the oldest livery companies, established in 1272. Lord Mayor Walworth, a member of the Fishmongers' Company, killed Wat Tyler, leader of the Peasants' Revolt, in 1381 *(see p162).* Today it still fulfils its original role; all the fish sold in the City must be inspected by Company officials.

St Magnus the Martyr **10**

Lower Thames St EC3. **Map** 15 C3. **Tel** *020-7626 4481.* ⊖ *Monument.* **Open** *10am–4pm Tue–Fri, 10am–1pm Sun.* ♦ *11am Sun.* ⬧ **www**.stmagnusmartyr.org.uk

There has been a church here for over 1,000 years. Its patron saint, St Magnus, Earl of the Orkney Islands and a renowned Norwegian Christian leader, was brutally murdered in 1116.

When Christopher Wren built this church in 1671–6, it was at the foot of old London Bridge, until 1738 the only bridge across the River Thames in London. Anyone going south from the city would have passed under Wren's magnificent arched porch spanning the flagstones leading to the old bridge.

Highlights of St Magnus the Martyr include the carved musical instruments that decorate the organ case. Wren's pulpit, with its slender supporting stem, was restored in 1924.

Monument **11**

Monument St EC3. **Map** 15 C2. **Tel** *020-7626 2717.* ⊖ *Monument.* **Open** *9:30am–5:30pm daily.* **Closed** *1 Jan, 24–26 Dec.* **Adm charge.** ⬧ **www**.themonument.info

The column, designed by Christopher Wren to commemorate the Great Fire of London which devastated the original walled city in September 1666, is the tallest isolated stone column in the world. It is 62 m (205 ft) high and is said to be 62 m west of where the fire started in Pudding Lane. It was sited on the direct approach to old London Bridge, which was a few steps downstream from the present one. Reliefs around the column's base

The altar of St Magnus the Martyr

show Charles II restoring the city. The 311 steps to the top lead to a viewing platform. In 1842 this was enclosed with railings after a suicide. The views are spectacular.

Old Billingsgate **12**

Lower Thames St EC3. **Map** 15 C3. ⊖ *Monument.* **Not open** *to the public.*

Fish weathervane at Billingsgate

London's main fish market was based here for 900 years, on one of the city's earliest quays. During the 19th and early 20th centuries 400 tonnes of fish were sold here every day, much of it delivered by boat. It was London's noisiest market, renowned, even in Shakespeare's day, for foul language. In 1982 the market moved from this building (1877) to the Isle of Dogs.

St Mary-at-Hill **13**

Lovat Lane EC3. **Map** 15 C2. **Tel** *020-7626 4184.* ⊖ *Monument.* **Concerts. Open** *11am–4pm Mon–Fri.* ♦ *1pm Wed, 1:05pm Thu.*

The interior and east end of St Mary-at-Hill were Wren's first church designs (1670–76). The Greek cross design was a prototype for his St Paul's proposals. Ironically, the delicate plasterwork and rich 17th-century fittings, which had survived both the Victorian mania for refurbishment and the bombs of World War II, were lost in a fire in

1988. The building was then restored to its original appearance, only to be damaged again by an IRA bomb in 1992.

St Margaret Pattens ⓮

Rood Lane and Eastcheap EC3.
Map 15 C2. **Tel** 020-7623 6630
🚇 Monument. **Open** 10:30am–4pm Mon–Thu, 7:30am–4pm Fri. **Closed** Christmas week. ✝ 1.15pm Thu, 11am Sun. ♿

Wren's church of 1684–7 was named after a type of overshoe made near here. Its rendered brickwork and Portland stone contrast with the Georgian stucco shopfront in the forecourt. The interior retains 17th-century canopied pews and an ornate font.

All Hallows by the Tower ⓯

Byward St EC3. **Map** 16 D3. **Tel** 020-7481 2928. 🚇 Tower Hill. **Open** 8am–6pm Mon–Fri, 10am–5pm Sat & Sun. **Closed** 26 Dec–2 Jan. ✝ 11am Sun. ♿ 🔼 🚻 🅿 **Adm charge** undercroft museum.
www.allhallowsbythetower.org.uk

The first church on this site was Saxon. The arch in the southwest corner, which contains Roman tiles, dates from that period, as do some crosses in the crypt. There is a Roman pavement in the crypt. William Penn, founder of Pennsylvania, was baptized here in 1644. Most of the interior has been altered, but a limewood font cover, carved by Grinling Gibbons in 1682, survives. John

Roman tile from All Hallows

Quincy Adams married here in 1797 before he was US president. Samuel Pepys watched the Great Fire from the church tower. There are a small museum, brass rubbing centre, concerts and a bookstall.

Tower of London ⓰

See pp154–7.

Tower Bridge ⓱

SE1. **Map** 16 D3. **Tel** 020-7403 3761. 🚇 Tower Hill. **The Tower Bridge Exhibition Open** Apr–Sep: 10am–6.30pm daily; Oct–Mar: 9.30am–6pm daily (open from noon on Jan 1). **Closed** 24, 25 & 26 Dec. **Adm charge.** 📷 🔼 ♿ 🅿
www.towerbridge.org.uk

Completed in 1894, this flamboyant piece of Victorian engineering quickly became a symbol of London. Its pinnacled towers and linking catwalk support the mechanism for raising the roadway when big ships have to pass through, or for special and historic occasions.

The bridge now houses The Tower Bridge Exhibition, with interactive displays bringing the bridge's history to life, river views from the catwalk and a close-up look at the steam engine which powered the lifting machinery until 1976, when the system was electrified.

The walkways, which are now open to the public, afford stunning views along the river.

When raised, the bridge is 40 m (135 ft) high and 60 m (200 ft) wide. In its heyday it was opened five times a day.

There are nearly 300 stairs to the top of the towers.

The Victorian winding machinery was powered by steam until 1976.

Tower of London 🔞

For much of its 900-year history the Tower was an object of fear. Those who had committed treason or threatened the throne were held within its dank walls. A lucky few lived in comparative comfort, but the majority had to put up with appalling conditions. Many did not get out alive, and some were tortured before meeting violent deaths on nearby Tower Hill.

★ **The White Tower**
When it was finished, c.1097, it was the tallest building in London – 30 m (90 ft) high.

★ **The Jewel House** is where the magnificent Crown Jewels are housed *(see p156).*

"Beefeaters"
Thirty-five Yeoman Warders guard the Tower and live here.

Beauchamp Tower
Many high-ranking prisoners were held here, often with their own retinues of servants.

STAR BUILDINGS

★ White Tower

★ Jewel House

★ Chapel of St. John

★ Traitors' Gate

Tower Green was where the aristocratic prisoners were executed, away from the ghoulish crowds on Tower Hill. But only seven people died here – including two of Henry VIII's six wives – hundreds had to undergo public executions on Tower Hill.

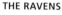

Main entrance

THE RAVENS

The Tower's most celebrated residents are a small colony of ravens. It is not known when they first settled here, but there is a legend that should they desert the Tower, the kingdom will fall. In fact the birds have part of their wings clipped on one side, making flight impossible. The Ravenmaster, one of the Yeoman Warders, looks after the birds.

A memorial in the moat commemorates some of the ravens who have died at the Tower since the 1950s.

Queen's House
This is the official residence of the Tower's governor.

★ **Chapel of St John**
Stone for this austerely beautiful Romanesque chapel was brought from France.

Wakefield Tower, part of the Medieval Palace, has been carefully refurbished to match its original appearance in the 13th century.

The Bloody Tower
is associated with the legend of the two princes and other deaths *(see p157)*.

Medieval Palace
This was created by Henry III in 1220. It was enlarged by his son, Edward I, who added Traitors' Gate.

★ **Traitors' Gate**
Prisoners, many on their way to die, entered the Tower by boat here.

TIMELINE

1078 White Tower started	**1536** Anne Boleyn executed		**1810–15** Mint moves from the Tower and arms stop being manufactured here		
	1483 Princes probably murdered in the Tower	**1553–4** Lady Jane Grey held and executed			

1050	1250	1450	1650	1850	1950

			1671 "Colonel Blood" tries to steal Crown Jewels	**1834** Menagerie moves out of Tower	
1066 William I erects a temporary castle					
	1534–5 Thomas More imprisoned and executed	**1603–16** Walter Raleigh imprisoned in Tower		**1941** Rudolf Hess is the last prisoner held in Queen's House	

Inside the Tower

The Tower has been a tourist attraction since the reign of Charles II (1660–85), when both the Crown Jewels and the collection of armour were first shown to the public. They remain powerful reminders of royal might and wealth.

The Orb, symbolizing the power and Empire of Christ the Redeemer

THE CROWN JEWELS

The Crown Jewels comprise the regalia of crowns, sceptres, orbs and swords used at coronations and other state occasions. They are impossible to price but their worth is irrelevant beside their enormous significance in the historical and religious life of the kingdom. Most of the Crown Jewels date from 1661, when a new set was made for the coronation of Charles II; Parliament had destroyed the previous crowns and sceptres after the execution of Charles I in 1649. Only a few pieces survived, hidden by the clergy of Westminster Abbey until the Restoration.

The Coronation Ceremony
Many elements in this solemn and mystical ceremony date from the days of Edward the Confessor. The king or queen proceeds to Westminster Abbey, accompanied by objects of the regalia, including the State Sword which represents the monarch's own sword. He or she is then anointed with holy oil, to signify divine approval, and invested with ornaments and royal robes. Each of the jewels represents

an aspect of the monarch's role as head of the state and church. The climax comes when St Edward's Crown is placed on the sovereign's head; there is a cry of "God Save the King" (or Queen), the trumpets sound, and guns at the Tower are fired. The last coronation was Elizabeth II's in 1953.

The Imperial State Crown, containing more than 2,800 diamonds, 273 pearls as well as other gems

The crowns
There are 10 crowns on display at the Tower. Many of these have not been worn for years, but the Imperial State Crown is in frequent use. The Queen wears it at the Opening of Parliament *(see p73)*. The crown was made in 1937 for George VI, and is similar to the one made for Queen Victoria. The sapphire set in the cross is said to have been worn in a ring by Edward the Confessor (ruled 1042–66).

The most recent crown is not at the Tower, however. It was made for Prince Charles's investiture as Prince of Wales at Caernarvon Castle in north Wales in 1969, and is kept at the Museum of Wales in Cardiff. The Queen Mother's

crown was made for the coronation of her husband, George VI, in 1937. It is the only one to be made out of platinum – all the other crowns on display at the Tower are made of gold.

Other regalia
Apart from the crowns, there are other pieces of the Crown Jewels that are essential to coronations. Among these are three Swords of Justice, symbolizing mercy, spiritual and temporal justice. The orb is a hollow gold sphere encrusted with jewels and weighing about 1.3 kg (3 lbs). The Sceptre with the Cross contains the biggest cut diamond in the world, the 530-carat First Star of Africa. The rough stone it comes from weighed 3,106 carats.

The Sovereign's Ring, sometimes referred to as "the wedding ring of England"

Plate Collection
The Jewel House also holds a collection of elaborate gold and silver plate. The Maundy Dish is still used on Maundy Thursday when the monarch distributes money to selected old people. The Exeter Salt (a very grand salt cellar from the days when salt was a valuable commodity) was given by the citizens of Exeter, in west England, to Charles II; during the 1640s' Civil War Exeter was a Royalist stronghold.

The hilt and solid-gold scabbard of the jewelled State Sword, one of the most valuable swords in the world

The Sceptre with the Cross (1660), rebuilt in 1910 after Edward VII was presented with the First Star of Africa diamond

THE WHITE TOWER

This is the oldest surviving building in the Tower of London, begun by William I in c.1070 and completed before 1100. For centuries it served as an armoury, and much of the national collection of arms and armour was held here. In the 1990s many exhibits moved to the Royal Armouries' other museums in Leeds or Portsmouth, but some of the most historic items, especially those connected with the Tower, have remained. The extra space allows the exhibits to be displayed more effectively, and highlights architectural features of the building itself.

The Royal Castle and Armour Gallery

These two chambers on the first floor were the main ceremonial rooms of the original Norman castle. The first one, to the east, is the smaller, probably an antechamber to the Banqueting Hall beyond, and contains exhibits setting out the history of the White Tower. It adjoins St John's Chapel, a rare surviving early Norman chapel virtually intact, a powerfully solid interior with little ornamentation. Originally the two main rooms were twice their present height; a pitched roof was removed in 1490 to allow extra floors to be built on top. Suits of armour from Tudor and Stuart times are here, including three made for Henry VIII, one covering his horse as well. A suit made in Holland for Charles I is decorated in gold leaf.

Japanese armour presented to James I in 1613

The Ordnance Gallery

This and the temporary exhibition gallery next door were chambers created in 1490 when the roof was raised. They were used chiefly for storage and in 1603 a new floor was installed to allow gunpowder to be kept here: by 1667 some 10,000 barrels of it were stored in the Tower. Among the displays are gilt panels and ornament from the barge of the Master of the Ordnance built in 1700.

The Small Armoury and Crypt

The westerly room on the ground floor may originally have been a living area, and has traces of the oldest fireplaces known in England. Pistols, muskets, swords, pikes and bayonets are

mounted on the walls and panels in elaborate symmetrical patterns based on displays in the Tower armouries in the 18th and 19th centuries. They were shown in the Grand Storehouse until it burned down in 1841. A collection of weapons taken from the men who planned to assassinate William III in 1696 is on show, and next door is a wooden block made in 1747 for the execution of Lord Lovat – the last public beheading in England. The crypt now houses a shop.

The Line of Kings

The Line of Kings, ten life-size carvings of prominent English Monarchs, wearing armour and seated on horseback, originated in Tudor times, when eight such figures adorned the royal palace at Greenwich. Two more had been added by the time they first appeared in the Tower in 1660, celebrating the Restoration of Charles II. In 1688, 17 new horses and heads were commissioned, some from the great carver Grinling Gibbons (the third from the left is reputed to be his work).

Henry VIII's armour (1540)

The yacht haven of the restored St Katharine's Dock

St Katharine's Dock ⑱

E1. **Map** 16 E3. *Tel 020-7488 0555.*
🚇 *Tower Hill.* ♿ 🍴 🛒 🏠
www.skdocks.co.uk

This most central of all London's docks was designed by Thomas Telford and opened in 1828 on the site of St Katharine's hospital. Commodities as diverse as tea, marble and live turtles (turtle soup was a Victorian delicacy) were unloaded here.

During the 19th and early 20th centuries the docks flourished, but by the mid-20th century cargo ships were delivering their wares in massive containers. The old docks became too small and new ones had to be built downstream. St Katharine's closed in 1968.

St Katharine's is now one of London's most successful developments, with its commercial, residential and entertainment facilities, including a hotel and a yacht haven. Old warehouse

St Helen's Bishopsgate

buildings have shops and restaurants on their ground floors, and offices above.

On the north side of the dock is LIFFE Commodity Products, trading in commodities such as coffee, sugar and oil. There is no public gallery but, if you ask at the door, you may be able to look down from the glass-walled reception area on to the frenzied trading floors. The dock is worth wandering through after visiting Tower or Tower Bridge *(see pp154–7 and p153).*

Stock Exchange ⑲

Paternoster Sq EC4. **Map** 15 A1.
🚇 *Bank, Farringdon.* **Not open** to the public.

The first Stock Exchange was established in Threadneedle Street in 1773 by a group of stockbrokers who previously met and did business in nearby City coffee houses. By the 19th century the rules of exchange were laid down, and for a hundred years London's was the biggest stock exchange in the world. Nevertheless, the rise of the American and Japanese economies during the 20th century gradually challenged London's dominance.

In 1986 the deregulation of the UK market, known as the "Big Bang", resulted in the computerization of trades, making the trade floor redundant and setting London's financial markets on a course of rapid growth. Today London has reclaimed its position as the market of choice for companies around the world wishing to raise capital.

St Helen's Bishopsgate ⑳

Great St Helen's EC3. **Map** 15 C1.
Tel 020-7283 2231. 🚇 *Liverpool St, Bank.* **Open** *9:30am–5pm Mon–Fri.*
✝ *1pm Tue & Thu, 10:30am, 6pm Sun.* 📷 ♿
www.st-helens.org.uk

The curious appearance of this 13th-century church is due to its origins as two places of worship: one a parish church, the other the chapel of a long-gone nunnery next door. (The medieval nuns of St Helen's were notorious for their "secular kissing".)

Among its monuments is the tomb of Sir Thomas Gresham, who founded the Royal Exchange *(see p147).*

St Katharine Cree ㉑

86 Leadenhall St EC3. **Map** 16 D1.
Tel 020-7283 5733. 🚇 *Aldgate, Tower Hill.* **Open** *10:30am–4pm Mon–Fri.* ✝ *1:10pm Wed.*
www.london.anglican.org

The organ at St Katharine Cree

A rare pre-Wren 17th-century church with a medieval tower, this was one of only eight churches in the City to survive the fire of 1666. Some of the elaborate plasterwork on and beneath the high ceiling of the nave portrays the coats of arms of the guilds, with which the church has special links. The 17th-century organ, supported on magnificent carved wooden columns, was played by both Purcell and Handel.

Leadenhall Market ㉒

Whittington Ave EC3. **Map** 15 C2.
🚇 *Bank, Monument.* **Open**
7am–4pm Mon–Fri. See **Shops
and Markets** *pp332–41.* **www.**
leadenhallmarket.co.uk

There has been a food market
here, on the site of the Roman
forum *(see pp18–19)*, since the
Middle Ages. Its name comes
from a lead-roofed mansion
that stood nearby in the 14th
century. The ornate, Victorian
covered shopping precinct of
today was designed in 1881 by
Sir Horace Jones, the architect
of Billingsgate fish market *(see
p152)*. Essentially a food market, offering traditional game,
poultry, fish, and meat, Leadenhall also has a number of
independent shops, which
offer all kinds of fare from
chocolates to wine. The area is
busiest during breakfast and
lunch hours, and is best seen at
Christmas when all the stores
are decorated. Next door is the
Lloyd's of London building.

Lloyd's of London ㉓

1 Lime St EC3. **Map** 15 C2. **Tel** *020-
7327 1000.* 🚇 *Bank, Monument,
Liverpool St, Aldgate.* **Not open** *to
the public.* **www.**lloyds.com

Lloyd's was founded in the
late 17th century and takes its
name from the coffee house
where underwriters and
shipowners used to meet to
arrange marine insurance
contracts. Lloyd's soon
became the world's main
insurers, issuing policies on
everything from oil tankers
to Betty Grable's legs.
　The present building, by
Richard Rogers, dates from
1986 and is one of the most
interesting modern buildings
in London *(see p32)*. Its
exaggerated stainless steel
external piping and high-tech
ducts echo Rogers' forceful
Pompidou Centre in Paris.
Lloyd's is a far more elegant
building and particularly worth
seeing floodlit at night. Nearby
is 30 St Mary Axe, otherwise
known as "the Gherkin", one
of the most recognisable landmarks on the London skyline.

Leadenhall Market in 1881

Guildhall Art Gallery ㉔

Guildhall Yard EC2. **Map** 15 B1. **Tel**
020-7332 3700. 🚇 *St Paul's.* **Open**
*10am–5pm Mon–Sat, noon–4pm
Sun (last adm: 30 mins prior).* **Closed**
1 Jan, 25 & 26 Dec. **Adm charge.** ⬚
♿ 🎧 **Guildhall** *Gresham St EC2.*
Tel *020-7606 3030.* **Open** *phone to
check.* **www.**cityoflondon.gov.uk

The Guildhall Art Gallery was
built in 1885 to house the art
collection of the Corporation
of London, but was destroyed

in World War II. The present
gallery houses the studio
collection of 20th-century
artist Sir Matthew Smith,
portraits from the 16th
century to the present day, a
gallery of 18th-century works,
including John Singleton
Copley's *Defeat of the Floating Batteries at Gibraltar*, and
numerous Victorian works.
　In 1988, the foundations of
a Roman amphitheatre were
discovered beneath the gallery.
Built in 70 AD and capable of
holding about 6000 spectators,
the arena would have featured
animal hunts, executions and
gladitorial combat. Access to
the atmospheric ruins is included with gallery admission.
　The adjacent Guildhall itself
has been the administrative
centre of the City for at least
800 years. For centuries the
hall was used for trials and
many people were condemned
to death here, including
Henry Garnet, one of the Gunpowder Plot conspirators *(see
p24)*. Today, a few days after
the Lord Mayor's parade *(see
pp54–5)*, the Prime Minister
addresses a banquet here.

Richard Rogers' Lloyd's building illuminated at night

SMITHFIELD AND SPITALFIELDS

The areas just north of the City walls have always been a refuge for those who did not want to come under its jurisdiction, or were not welcome there. These included Huguenots in the 17th century and, in later times, other immigrants from Europe and then Bengal. They founded small industries and brought with them their restaurants and places of worship. The name Spitalfields comes from the

Stone dragon in Smithfield Market

medieval priory of St Mary Spital. Middlesex Street became known as Petticoat Lane in the 16th century, for its clothing stalls; it is still the hub of a popular Sunday morning street market that spreads as far east as Brick Lane, today lined with aromatic Bengali food shops. London's meat market is at Smithfield, and nearby is the Barbican, a late 20th-century residential and arts complex.

SIGHTS AT A GLANCE

Historic Streets and Buildings
Charterhouse ❹
Cloth Fair ❺
Barbican ❼
Whitbread's Brewery ❾
Wesley's Chapel–Leysian
   Mission ⓫
Broadgate Centre ⓬
Petticoat Lane ⓭
Fournier Street ⓱
Spitalfields Centre Museum of
   Immigration & Diversity ⓳
Brick Lane ⓴
Dennis Severs House ㉑

Museums and Galleries
Museum of London
   pp166–7 ❸
Whitechapel Gallery ⓮

Churches and Mosques
St Botolph, Aldersgate ❷
St Bartholomew-
   the-Great ❻
St Giles, Cripplegate ❽
Christ Church, Spitalfields ⓰
London Jamme Masjid ⓲

Cemeteries
Bunhill Fields ❿

Markets
Smithfield Market ❶
Old Spitalfields Market ⓯
Columbia Road Market ㉒

GETTING THERE
This area is served by the Northern, Hammersmith and City, Central and Circle Underground lines and by rail. The Nos. 8, 15 and many other buses run close by.

SEE ALSO
• *Street Finder,* maps 6, 7, 8, 15, 16
• *Where to Stay* pp278–91
• *Restaurants, Pubs* pp292–319

KEY
■ Street-by-Street map
🔵 Underground station
🚉 Railway Station

◁ **Columbia Road flower and plant market**

Street-by-Street: Smithfield

This area is among the most historic in London. It contains one of the capital's oldest churches, some rare Jacobean houses, vestiges of the Roman wall (near the Museum of London) and central London's only surviving wholesale food market.

Smithfield's long history is also bloody. In 1381 the rebel peasant leader, Wat Tyler, was killed here by an ally of Richard II as he presented the king with demands for lower taxes. Later, in the reign of Mary I (1553–8), scores of Protestant religious martyrs were burned at the stake here.

The Fat Boy: the Great Fire ended here

The Fox and Anchor pub is open from 7am for hearty breakfasts, washed down with ale by the market traders of Smithfield.

★ Smithfield Market
A contemporary print shows Horace Jones's stately building for the meat market when it was completed in 1867 ❶

Fat Boy

The Saracen's Head, an historic inn, stood on this site until the 1860s when it was demolished to make way for Holborn Viaduct *(see p140)*.

St Bartholomew-the-Less has a 15th-century tower and vestry. Its links to the hospital are shown by this early 20th-century stained glass of a nurse; a gift of the Worshipful Company of Glaziers.

St Bartholomew's Hospital has stood on this site since 1123. Some of the existing buildings date from 1759.

KEY

‒ ‒ ‒ Suggested route

0 metres   100
0 yards   100

Charterhouse
The square contains the remnants of a medieval monastery and a school where John Wesley (see p168) studied **4**

Barbican station

★ Barbican
World War II bombs flattened this immense site, which was rebuilt as a housing development in the 1960s. It contains the famous Barbican Centre **7**

LOCATOR MAP
See Central London Map pp14–15

BEECH STREET

ALDERSGATE STREET

Cloth Fair
Two of its houses are survivors of the 1666 Great Fire **5**

St Bartholomew-the-Great
It has the best-preserved medieval interior of any London church **6**

LONDON WALL

★ Museum of London
The city's history is told vividly through fascinating and colourful exhibits **3**

Christ Church tower is all that remains of one of Wren's most splendid churches (1704).

To St Paul's station

STAR SIGHTS

★ Museum of London

★ Barbican

★ Smithfield Market

Smithfield Market, now officially known as London Central Markets

the nearby Post Office head-quarters. In the late 19th century, the Victorian artist G F Watts dedicated one of the walls to a quirky collection of plaques that commemorate acts of bravery and self-sacrifice by ordinary people. Some of these plaques are still here and can be viewed. There are three St Botolph churches in the City; the other two can be found at Aldgate and in Bishopsgate.

Museum of London ❸

See pp166–7.

Charterhouse ❹

Charterhouse Sq EC1. **Map** 6 F5. **Tel** *020-7251 5002.* ⊖ *Barbican.* **Open** *for* 🔲 *only; book well ahead Apr–Aug: Wed pm.*

The Tudor gateway on the north side of the square leads to the site of a former Carthusian monastery which was dissolved under Henry VIII. In 1611 the buildings were converted into a hospital for poor pensioners, and a charity school – called Charterhouse – whose pupils included John Wesley *(see p168)*, writer William Thackeray and Robert Baden-Powell, founder of the Boy Scouts. In 1872 the school, which is now a top boarding school, relocated to Godalming in Surrey. Part of the original site was subsequently taken over by St Bartholomew's Hospital medical school. Some of the old buildings survived. These include the chapel and part of the cloisters. Today Charterhouse is still home to over 40 pensioners, supported by the charitable foundation.

Charterhouse: stone carving

Smithfield Market ❶

Charterhouse St EC1. **Map** 6 F5. ⊖ *Farringdon, Barbican.* **Open** *3–9am Mon–Fri.* **www**.smithfieldmarket.com

Animals have been traded here since the 12th century, but the site was granted its first official charter in 1400. In 1648 it was officially established as a cattle market and live cattle contin-ued to be sold here until the mid-19th century. It now confines itself to wholesale trading in dead meat and poultry. It was originally sited in Smithfield outside the city walls, London's main location for public executions. Although moved to its present location in Charterhouse Street in the 1850s and called the London Central Meat Market, the original name stuck. The old buildings are by Horace Jones, the Victorian architect, but there are 20th-century addi-tions. Some pubs in the area keep market hours and, from dawn, serve hearty breakfasts. After much-needed moderni-sation, the market is now one of the best equipped meat markets in the world.

St Botolph, Aldersgate ❷

Aldersgate St EC1. **Map** 15 A1. **Tel** *020-7606 0684.* ⊖ *St Paul's, Barbican, Moorgate.* 🕇 *1pm Tue–Thu.* ♿

A modest late Georgian exterior (completed in the late 18th century) conceals a flamboyant, well-preserved interior which has a finely decorated plaster ceiling, a rich brown wooden organ case and galleries, as well as an oak pulpit resting on a carved palm tree. The original box pews have been kept in the galleries rather than in the body of the church. Some of the memorials come from a 14th-century church that originally existed on the site.

The former church-yard alongside was converted in 1880 into a relaxing green space known as Postman's Park, because it was used by workers from

Cloth Fair ❺

EC1. **Map** 6 F5. 🌐 *Barbican.*

This pretty street is named after the notoriously rowdy Bartholomew Fair, which was the main cloth fair in medieval and Elizabethan England, held annually at Smithfield until 1855. Nos. 41 and 42 are fine 17th-century houses and have distinctive two-storeyed wooden bay windows, although their ground floors have since been modernized. The former poet laureate John Betjeman, who died in 1984, lived in No. 43 for most of his life. It has now been turned into a wine bar named after him.

17th-century houses: Cloth Fair

St Bartholomew-the-Great ❻

West Smithfield EC1. **Map** 6 F5. **Tel** 020-7606 5171. 🌐 *Barbican.* **Open** 8:30am–5pm (4pm in winter) Mon–Fri, 10:30am–4pm Sat, 8:30am–8pm Sun. 🔔 9am, 11am, 6.30pm Sun. **Adm charge** ♿ 📷 by appt. 📷 **Concerts.** www.greatstbarts.com

One of London's oldest churches was founded in 1123 by the monk Rahere, whose tomb is inside. He was Henry I's courtier and had a dream in which St Bartholomew saved him from a winged monster.

The 13th-century arch used to be the door to the church until the nave of that earlier building was pulled down when Henry VIII dissolved the priory. Today the arch leads from West Smithfield to the burial ground – the gatehouse above it is from a later period. The present building retains the crossing and chancel of the original, with its round arches and other fine Norman detailing. There are also some fine Tudor monuments. The painter William Hogarth was baptized here in 1697.

Parts of the church have been used for secular purposes. In 1725 US statesman Benjamin Franklin worked for a printer in the Lady Chapel. The church also featured in the films *Four Weddings and a Funeral*, *Shakespeare in Love* and *The Other Boleyn Girl*.

Barbican ❼

Silk St EC2. **Map** 7 A5. **Tel** 020-7638 8891. 📠 *020-7638 4141.* 🌐 *Barbican, Moorgate.* **Barbican Centre open** 9am–11pm Mon–Sat, noon–11pm Sun, public hols. 📷 📖 🍴 🔔 📷 ♿ induction loop. See **Entertainment** pp342–53. **www**.barbican.org.uk

An ambitious piece of 1960s city planning, this residential, commercial and arts complex was begun in 1962 on a site devastated by World War II bombs, and not completed for nearly 20 years. Residential tower blocks surround the Barbican Centre, the arts complex, which also includes an ornamental lake and fountains.

The old city wall turned a corner here and substantial remains are still clearly visible (particularly so from the Museum of London – *see* pp166–7). The word barbican

St Bartholomew's gatehouse

means a defensive tower over a gate – perhaps the architects were trying to live up to the name when they designed this self-sufficient community with formidable defences against the outside world. Obscure entrances and raised walkways remove pedestrians from the cramped bustle of the City, but, in spite of the signposts, and yellow lines on the pavement, the complex can be difficult to navigate.

As well as two theatres and a concert hall, the Barbican Centre has two cinemas, two galleries, an excellent library with children's and music sections, and a surprising conservatory. The Guildhall School of Music and Drama is also located in the Barbican.

The well-stocked conservatory at the Barbican Centre

Museum of London ❸

Opened in 1976 on the edge of the Barbican, this museum provides a lively account of London life from prehistoric times to the present day. Reconstructed interiors and street scenes are alternated with displays of original domestic artifacts and items found in the museum's archaeological digs. The museum underwent a huge redevelopment in its lower galleries in 2009, which opened up 25 per cent more gallery space.

★ **Marble Head of Serapis**
This statue of the Egyptian god of the underworld (2nd–3rd century) was discovered in the temple of Mithras (see p144).

Stairs to Galleries of Modern London

London's Burning experience

Main entrance

Leather Shoes
These remarkably well-preserved shoes (13th and 14th centuries) illustrate changing fashion in Medieval London.

Boy's Leather Jerkin
This practical sleeveless jacket (c.1560), decorated with punched hearts and stars, would have been worn over a doublet for extra warmth.

Flint Hand Axe
Thousands of these cutting tools (c.350,000–120,000 BC) have been found in the gravels beneath modern London.

GALLERY GUIDE
The galleries are laid out chronologically, starting on the entrance level with prehistory. Visitors can walk through Roman and medieval London galleries to the War, Plague and Fire gallery, which includes a special display on the Great Fire. On the lower level, they can learn about London from 1666 to the present day, and see the Lord Mayor of London's spectacular State Coach.

STAR EXHIBITS

★ Marble Head of Serapis

★ Lord Mayor's Coach

KEY

- ☐ London before London
- ☐ Roman London
- ☐ Great Fire of London
- ☐ Medieval London
- ☐ 1550s–1660s: War, Plague and Fire
- ☐ 1670s–1850s: Later London
- ☐ Victorian Walk
- ☐ Sackler Hall
- ☐ 1850s–1940s: People's City
- ☐ 1950s–Today: World City
- ☐ Inspiring London
- ☐ Linbury Gallery
- ☐ City Gallery

Tobacconist
The Victorian Walk uses several original shop fronts and objects to recreate the atmosphere of late 19th-century London.

VISITORS' CHECKLIST

London Wall EC2. **Map** 15 A1.
Tel 020-7001 9844. 🌐
Barbican, St Paul's, Moorgate.
🚌 4, 8, 25, 56, 100, 172, 242,
521. 🚆 City Thameslink,
Moorgate. **Open** 10am–6pm
daily. **Closed** 24–26 Dec.
♿ Induction loops fitted.
📷 🎬 **Lectures, film
presentations.**
www.museumoflondon.org.uk

**The Galleries of
Modern London**
re-tell the story of
Londoners from 1666
to the present day.

**Motor Goggles and
Licence**
*Goggles like these (c.1912)
were necessary to drive
open-top cars on Lon-
don's dusty roads.*

Selfridges Lift
*These bronze and cast iron
Brandt Edgar lifts were
installed in 1928.*

Beatles Dress
*Made in 1964,
this cotton dress
is printed with the
Beatles' heads
alongside a
guitar that
features their
signatures.*

★ **Lord Mayor's Coach**
*Finely carved and painted, this gilded
coach (c.1757) is paraded once a year
during the Lord Mayor's Show (see p55).*

St Giles, Cripplegate ❽

Fore St EC2. **Map** 7 A5. **Tel** 020-7638 1997. ⊖ Barbican, Moorgate. **Open** 11am–4pm Mon–Fri. 🚹 Sun: 8am, 10am, 6pm Easter–Sep, 4pm Oct–Easter Sun (family service 11.30am 1st Sun of month). 📷 2–4.40pm Tue. ♿ **www**.stgilescripplegate.co.uk

Completed in 1550, this church survived the ravages of the Great Fire in 1666, but was so badly damaged by a World War II bomb that only the tower survived. St Giles was refurbished during the 1950s to serve as the parish church of the Barbican, and now stands awkwardly amidst the stark modernity of the Barbican.

Oliver Cromwell married Elizabeth Bourchier here in 1620 and the poet John Milton was buried here in 1674. Well-preserved remains of London's Roman and medieval walls can be seen to the south.

Whitbread's Brewery ❾

Chiswell St EC1. **Map** 7 B5. ⊖ Barbican, Moorgate. **Not open** to public.

In 1736, when he was aged just 16, Samuel Whitbread became an apprentice brewer in Bedford. By the time of his death in 1796, his Chiswell Street brewery (which he had bought in 1750) was brewing

Blake's gravestone at Bunhill Fields

909,200 litres (200,000 gal) a year. The building has not been used as a brewery since 1976 when it was converted into rooms hired out for private functions – they are no longer open to the public. The Porter Tun room, which is now used as a banqueting suite, boasts the largest timber post roof in Europe, and has a huge span of 18 m (60 ft).

The street's 18th-century buildings are well-preserved examples of their period, and are worth a look from the outside. A plaque on one commemorates a visit to the brewery in 1787 by George III and Queen Charlotte.

Bunhill Fields ❿

City Rd EC1. **Map** 7 B4. **Tel** 020-7374 4127. ⊖ Old St. **Open** Apr–Sep: 7.30am–7pm or dusk (Oct–Mar: 7.30am–4pm) Mon–Fri, 9.30am–4pm Sat, Sun. **Closed** 1 Jan, 25 & 26 Dec. ♿ phone first. **www**.cityoflondon. gov.uk/openspaces

This spot was first designated a cemetery after the Great Plague of 1665 (see p25), when it was enclosed by a brick wall and gates. Twenty years later it was allocated to Non-conformists, who were banned from being

buried in churchyards because of their refusal to use the Church of England prayer book. The cemetery is situated on the edge of the City, and shaded by large plane trees. There are monuments to the well-known writers Daniel Defoe, John Bunyan and William Blake, as well as to members of the Cromwell family. John Milton wrote his epic poem *Paradise Lost* while he lived in Bunhill Row, located on the west side of the cemetery. The website has further information on the burial records of Bunhill Fields.

Wesley's Chapel-Leysian Mission ⓫

49 City Rd EC1. **Map** 7 B4. **Tel** 020-7253 2262. ⊖ Old St. **Open** 10am–4pm Mon–Sat, 12.30–1.45pm Sun. **Closed** between Christmas & New Year, public & bank hols (except Good Friday). ♿ not house. 🚹 9.45am (not 1st Sun of month), 11am Sun, 12.45pm Thu. 📷 groups book ahead. 🖥 **www**.wesleychapel.org.uk

Wesley's Chapel

John Wesley, the founder of the Methodist church, laid the chapel's foundation stone in 1777. He preached here until his death in 1791, and is buried behind the chapel. Next door is the house where he lived, and today some of his furniture, books and other assorted possessions can be seen on display there.

The chapel, adorned in a spartan style, in accordance with Wesley's austere religious principles, has columns made from ships' masts. Beneath it is a small museum that explores the history of the Methodist church. Baroness Thatcher, the first British woman Prime Minister, in office from 1979 to 1990, was married in the chapel.

St Giles, Cripplegate

Broadgate Centre ⓬

Exchange Sq EC2. **Map** 7 C5. **Tel** 020-7505 4068 (ice arena; see pp354–5). 🚇 Liverpool St. 🍴 🖥 🚻 ♿

Broadgate Centre skating rink

Situated around Liverpool Street station, the terminus for trains to eastern England, this is one of the most successful recent (1985–91) shop and office developments. Each of the squares has its own distinctive character. Broadgate Arena emulates New York's Rockefeller Center, doubling as a skating rink until the end of March (depending on the weather) and a venue for entertainment in summer.

Among the many sculptures in the complex are George Segal's *Rush Hour Group*, and Barry Flanagan's *Leaping Hare on Crescent and Bell*. Don't miss the spectacular view of Liverpool Street station and its glass-roofed train shed, seen from Exchange Square to the north.

Petticoat Lane ⓭

Middlesex St E1. **Map** 16 D1. 🚇 Aldgate East, Aldgate, Liverpool St. **Open** 10am–2:30pm Mon–Fri, 9am–2pm Sun. See **Shops and Markets** pp332–41.

In Queen Victoria's prudish reign the name of this street, long famous for its market, was changed to the respectable but colourless Middlesex Street. That is still its official designation, but the old name, derived from its many years as a centre of the clothing trade,

has stuck, and is now applied to the market held every Sunday morning in this and the surrounding streets. Numerous attempts were made to stop the market, but it was allowed by Act of Parliament in 1936. A great variety of goods is sold but there is still a bias towards clothing, especially leather coats. The atmosphere is noisy and cheerful, with Cockney stall-holders making use of their wit to attract custom. There are scores of snack bars, and many of these sell traditional Jewish food such as salt beef sandwiches and bagels with smoked salmon.

Whitechapel Art Gallery ⓮

Whitechapel High St E1. **Map** 16 E1. **Tel** 020-7522 7888. 🚇 Aldgate East, Aldgate. **Open** 11am–6pm Tue–Sun, (to 9pm Thu & 11pm Fri). **Closed** 1 Jan, 25 & 26 Dec. **Occasional adm charge** for exhibitions. ♿ 🛍 🖥 🎤 **Wide range of talks & events.** www.whitechapel.org

A striking Art Nouveau façade by C Harrison Townsend fronts this light, airy gallery, founded

Entrance to Whitechapel Gallery

in 1901 and expanded in the 1980s and again in 2007–9. Situated close to Brick Lane and the area's burgeoning art scene, this independent gallery was founded with the aim of bringing great art to the people of East London. Today it enjoys an excellent international reputation for high-quality shows of major contemporary artists. In the 1950s and 1960s the likes of Jackson Pollock, Robert Rauschenberg, Anthony Caro and John Hoyland all displayed their work here. In 1970 David Hockney's first exhibition was held here.

The gallery has a well-stocked arts bookshop and a café, serving a range of appetizing and healthy wholefoods in a relaxed atmosphere.

Bustling Petticoat Lane Market

18th-century Fournier Street

Old Spitalfields Market ⓯

Commercial St E1. **Map** 8 E5.
🚇 *Liverpool St.* **Open** *10am–4pm
Thu–Fri, 9am–5pm Sun. See **Shops
and Markets** pp332–41.*

One of the oldest markets in
London, Spitalfields started
life as a produce market in
1682. Today good quality
food, including organic fruit
and vegetables, breads and
preserves, can still be
purchased here. Although
open during the week it is
on Sundays that hundreds
of people throng the market
in search of vintage clothing,
bric-a-brac, crafts and especially innovative fashion by
young designers.

Christ Church, Spitalfields ⓰

Commercial St E1. **Map** 8 E5. **Tel**
020-7377 6793. 🚇 *Liverpool St.*
Open *11am–4pm Tue, 1–4pm Sun
during services.* ✝ *10.30am Sun.*
Concerts ♿ 🎫 *book ahead.*
www.spitalfieldsvenue.org

The finest of Nicholas Hawksmoor's six London churches,
Christ Church was commis-
sioned by parliament in the
Fifty New Churches Act of
1711, aimed at combating the
threat of Non-conformism. It
was intended to make a powerful statement in an area fast
becoming a Huguenot stronghold. (The Protestant Huguenots had fled from persecution
in Catholic France and came
to Spitalfields to work in the
local silkweaving industry).

Completed in 1729, the building was mauled by alterations
in the 1850s. By 1960 it was
derelict, narrowly escaping
demolition. In 1976 the Friends
of Christ Church Spitalfields
was formed to restore the
building to its former glory –
a goal finally achieved in 2004.

Christ Church still domi-
nates the surrounding streets.
The impression of size and
strength created by its portico
and spire is continued inside
by the high ceiling, the sturdy
wooden canopy over the
west door, and the gallery.

Fournier Street ⓱

E1. **Map** 8 E5. 🚇 *Aldgate East,
Liverpool Street.*

The 18th-century houses on
the north side of this street
have attics with broad windows that were designed to
give maximum light to the
silkweaving French Huguenot
community who lived here.
Even now, the textile trade
lives on, in this and nearby
streets, still dependent on
immigrant labour. Today it is
Bengalis who toil at sewing
machines in workrooms that
are as cramped as they were
when the Huguenots used
them. Working conditions are
improving, however, and
many of the sweatshops have
been converted into show-
rooms for companies which
now have modern factories
away from the town centre.

Christ Church, Spitalfields

Bengali sweet factory: Brick Lane

London Jamme Masjid ⓲

Brick Lane E1. **Map** 8 E5. 🚇
Liverpool St, Aldgate East.

Muslims now worship here,
in a building whose life story
as a religious site reflects the
fascinating history of immigration in the area. Built in
1743 as a Huguenot chapel, it
was a synagogue in the 19th
century, a Methodist chapel in
the early 20th century, and is
now a mosque.

Spitalfields Centre Museum of Immigration & Diversity ⓳

19 Princelet St E1. **Map** 8 E5.
Tel *020-7247 5352.* 🚇 *Liverpool St.*
Open *some days & by appt (phone to
check).* **www.**19princeletstreet.org.uk

A little Victorian synagogue
hidden behind a 1719 Huguenot silk merchant's house with
exhibitions celebrating the
Jewish and other peoples
who arrived as immigrants
and settled in London's East
End. This historic gem is under
constant threat of closure due
to lack of funding.

Brick Lane ⓴

E1. **Map** 8 E5. 🚇 *Liverpool St,
Aldgate East, Shoreditch.* **Market
open** *dawn–noon Sun. See **Shops
and Markets** pp332–41.*

Once a lane running through
brickfields, this is now the
busy centre of London's

The grand bedroom of Dennis Severs House

Bengali district. Its shops and houses, some dating from the 18th century, have seen waves of immigrants of many nationalities, and most now sell food, spices, silks and sarees. The first Bengalis to live here were sailors who came in the 19th century. In those days it was a predominantly Jewish quarter, and a few Jewish shops remain, including a 24-hour bagel shop at No. 159.

On Sundays a large market is held here and in the surrounding streets, complementing Petticoat Lane (see p169). At the northern end of Brick Lane is the former Black Eagle Brewery, a medley of 18th- and 19th-century industrial architecture, now reflected in, and set off by, a sympathetic mirror-glassed extension.

Dennis Severs House ㉑

18 Folgate St E1. **Map** 8 D5.
Tel 020-7247 4013. ⊖ Liverpool St.
Open noon–4pm Sun; 6–9pm Mon (book ahead); noon–2pm 1st & 3rd Mon of month; for further dates see website. Private and group bookings welcome. **Adm charge**.
www.dennissevershouse.co.uk

At No. 18 Folgate Street, built in 1724, the late designer and performer Dennis Severs recreated a historical interior that takes you on a journey from the 17th to the 19th centuries. It offers what he called "an adventure of the imagination … a visit to a time-mode rather than … merely a look at a house". The rooms are like a series of *tableaux vivants*, as if the

**18th-century portrait:
Dennis Severs House**

occupants had simply left for a moment. There is broken bread on the plates, wine in the glasses, fruit in the bowl; the candles flicker and horses' hooves clatter on the cobbles outside. This highly theatrical experience is far removed from more usual museum recreations and is not suitable for the under-12s. Praised by many, including artist David Hockney, it is truly unique. The house's motto is "you either see it or you don't". Around the corner on Elder Street are two of London's earliest surviving terraces, where many of the Georgian red-brick houses have been carefully restored.

Columbia Road Market ㉒

Columbia Rd E2. **Map** 8 D3.
⊖ Liverpool St, Old St, Bethnal Green. **Open** 8am–3pm Sun.
See **Shops and Markets** pp332–41.

A visit to this flower and plant market is one of the most delightful things to do on a Sunday morning in London, whether you want to take advantage of the exotic species on offer there or not. Set in a well-preserved street of small Victorian shops, it is a lively, sweet-smelling and colourful event. Apart from the stalls, there are several shops selling, among other things, home-made bread and farmhouse cheeses, antiques and interesting objects, many of them flower-related. There is also a Spanish delicatessen and an excellent snack bar that sells bagels and welcome mugs of hot chocolate on chilly winter mornings.

Columbia Road flower market

SOUTHWARK AND BANKSIDE

Southwark once offered an escape route from the City, where many forms of entertainment were banned. Borough High Street was lined with taverns: the medieval courtyards that still run off it mark where they stood. The George survives as the only galleried London inn. Among the illicit pleasures that thrived here were brothels that occupied houses by the river, as well as theatres and bear and cock

Shakespeare window, Southwark Cathedral

pits, which were established in the late 16th century. Shakespeare's company was based at the Globe Theatre, which has now been rebuilt close to its original site. Today the south bank of the river has undergone extensive renovation. Southwark's riverside attractions range from the Design Museum and Tate Modern, next to the Millennium Bridge, to historic pubs, Borough Market and Southwark Cathedral.

SIGHTS AT A GLANCE

Historic Streets and Areas
Hop Exchange ❷
The Old Operating Theatre ❺
Cardinal's Wharf ❼
Bermondsey ❸

Museums and Galleries
Shakespeare's Globe ❻
Bankside Gallery ❽
Tate Modern ❾
Vinopolis ⓫
Clink Prison Museum ⓬

London Dungeon ⓮
Design Museum ⓯

Cathedrals
Southwark Cathedral ❶

Pubs
George Inn ❹
The Anchor ❿

Markets
Borough Market ❸

Historic Ships
HMS Belfast ⓰

| 0 metres | 500 |
| 0 yards | 500 |

GETTING THERE
The Northern line runs a regular Underground service to this area. Nearly every train from Charing Cross or Cannon Street stops at London Bridge and the Jubilee line offers connections from east and west London.

SEE ALSO

• *Street Finder*, maps 14, 15, 16

• *Where to Stay* pp278–91

• *Restaurants, Pubs* pp292–319

KEY

🛈 Tourist information

▢ Street-by-Street map

⊖ Underground station

⇄ Railway station

◁ **The Millennium Bridge located opposite Tate Modern**

Street-by-Street: Southwark

From medieval times until the 18th century, Southwark was a venue for the pursuit of illicit pleasures. Located south of the Thames, it was out of the jurisdiction of the City authorities. The 18th and 19th centuries brought docks, warehouses and factories. Now Southwark is once again one of London's most exciting boroughs, with the arrival of Tate Modern, a regenerated Borough Market and the stunning recreation of Shakespeare's Globe Theatre.

Southwark Bridge was opened in 1912 to replace a bridge of 1819.

Millennium Bridge

BLACKFRIARS BRIDGE

HOLLAND STREET

SUMNER STREET

PARK STREET

EMERSON STREET

SOUTHWARK BRIDGE ROAD

★ **Tate Modern**
The former Bankside Power Station is now a powerhouse of contemporary art, its spectacular open spaces showing off exhibits to perfection ❾

★ **Shakespeare's Globe**
This brilliant recreation of an Elizabethan theatre has open-air performances in the summer months and an exhibition open all year round ❻

STAR SIGHTS

★ Southwark Cathedral

★ Tate Modern

★ Shakespeare's Globe

0 metres   100

0 yards   100

KEY

 Suggested route

Southwark Quayside

LOCATOR MAP
See Central London Map pp14–15

The Anchor
For centuries it has been a favourite riverside pub with fine views **10**

Vinopolis
This attraction is a city of wine on the banks of the river **11**

Clink Prison Museum
This museum, on the site of the notorious old prison, looks back at Southwark's colourful past **12**

Fourteenth-century rose window

Replica of Sir Francis Drake's *Golden Hinde*

★ Southwark Cathedral
Despite major alterations, it still contains medieval elements **1**

London Bridge, in its various forms, was the only river crossing in London from Roman times until 1750. The present bridge, completed in 1972, replaced the one of 1831 now in the US.

Borough Market
There has been a market on or near this site since 1276. Now it is a flourishing fine food market **3**

The War Memorial, commemorating soldiers who fell in World War I, was erected in 1924 on Borough High Street where it has become a powerful landmark.

George Inn
This is London's only surviving traditional, galleried inn **4**

Southwark Cathedral ❶

Montague Close SE1. **Map** 15 B3. **Tel** 020-7367 6700. London Bridge. **Open** 8am–6pm daily. daily (phone to check). **Concerts**. www.southwark.anglican.org/cathedral

This church did not become a cathedral until 1905. However, some parts of it date back to the 12th century, when the building was attached to a priory, and many of its medieval features remain. The memorials are fascinating, including a late 13th-century wooden effigy of a knight. John Harvard, who went on to found Harvard University, was baptized here in 1607 and there is a chapel named after him.

In 2000 the cathedral was restored in a multi-million pound restoration programme including the addition of new buildings, which house a shop and a refectory. The exterior has been landscaped to create a herb garden and an attractive Millennium Courtyard that leads to the riverside.

Shakespeare Window in Cathedral

Hop Exchange ❷

Southwark St SE1. **Map** 15 B4. London Bridge. **Not open** to the public.

Southwark, with its easy access to Kent where hops are grown, was a natural venue for brewing beer and trading hops. In 1866 this building was constructed as the centre of that trade. Now

The George Inn, now owned by the National Trust

offices, it retains its original pediment complete with carved scenes showing the hop harvest, and iron gates with a hop motif.

Borough Market ❸

8 Southwark St SE1. **Map** 15 B4. London Bridge. **Retail market open** 11am–5pm Thu, noon–6pm Fri, 8am–5pm Sat.

Borough Market was until recently an exclusively wholesale fruit and vegetable market, which had its origins in medieval times, and moved to its current atmospheric position beneath the railway tracks in 1756. A popular fine food market, it sells gourmet foods from Britain and Europe, as well as quality fruit and vegetables, and organic meat, fish and dairy produce.

George Inn ❹

77 Borough High St SE1. **Map** 15 B4. **Tel** 020-7407 2056. London Bridge, Borough. **Open** 11am–11pm Mon–Sat, noon–10:30pm Sun. See **Restaurants and Pubs** pp316–19.

Dating from the 17th century, this building is the only example of a traditional galleried coaching inn left in London and is mentioned by Dickens in *Little Dorrit*. It was rebuilt after the Southwark fire of 1676 in a style that dates back to the Middle Ages.

Originally there would have been three wings around a courtyard where plays were staged in the 17th century. In 1889 the north and east wings were demolished, so there is only one wing remaining.

The inn, now owned by the National Trust, is still a restaurant. Perfect on a cold wet day, the pub has a well-worn, comfortable atmosphere. In the summer, the yard fills with picnic tables and patrons are occasionally entertained by actors and morris dancers.

The Old Operating Theatre ❺

9a St Thomas St SE1. **Map** 15 B4. **Tel** 020-7188 2679. London Bridge. **Open** 10:30am–5pm daily. **Closed** 15 Dec–5 Jan. **Adm charge**. www.thegarret.org.uk

Guy's & St Thomas' Hospital, one of the oldest in Britain, stood here from its foundation in the 12th century until it was moved west in 1862. At this time nearly all of its buildings were demolished in order to make way for the railway. The women's operating

19th-century surgical tools

theatre (The Old Operating Theatre Museum and Herb Garret) survived only because it was located away from the main buildings, in a garret over the hospital church. The UK's oldest operating theatre, it dates back to 1822, lay, bricked up and forgotten, until the 1950s. It has now been fitted out just as it would have been in the early 19th century, before the discovery of either anaesthetics or antiseptics. The display shows how patients were blindfolded, gagged and bound to the wooden operating table, while a box of sawdust underneath was used to catch the blood.

Shakespeare's Henry IV (performed at the Globe Theatre around 1600)

Shakespeare's Globe ❻

New Globe Walk SE1. **Map** 15 A3. **Tel** 020-7902 1500. **Tel** box office 020-7401 9919. ⊖ *Southwark, London Bridge.* **Exhibition Open** *May–Sep:* 9am–5pm; *Oct–Apr:* 10am–5pm daily. **Adm charge**. 📷 every 30 mins. (Rose Theatre tours for groups of 15 or more by appt only.) **Performances** Apr–early Oct. 🔌 📺 🍴 🏠 www.shakespeares-globe.org

Built on the banks of the Thames, Shakespeare's Globe is an impressive recon-struction of the Elizabethan theatre where many of his plays were first performed. The wooden, circular struc-ture is open in the middle, leaving some of the audience exposed to the elements. Those holding seat tickets have a roof over their heads. The performances operate only in summer, and seeing a play here is a thrilling experi-ence, with top-quality acting. There is an informative tour for visitors, and groups may book to see the foundations of the nearby Rose Theatre. Beneath the theatre, and open all year round, is Shakespeare's Globe Exhibition, which brings his work and times to life.

Cardinal's Wharf ❼

SE1. **Map** 15 A3. ⊖ *London Bridge.*

A small group of 17th-century houses still survives here in the shadow of Tate Modern art gallery *(see pp178–81).* A plaque com-memorates Christopher Wren's stay here while St Paul's Cathedral *(see pp148–51)* was being built. He would have had a partic-ularly fine view of the works. It is thought that the wharf got its name from Cardinal Wolsey who was Bishop of Winchester in 1529.

Bankside Gallery ❽

48 Hopton St SE1. **Map** 14 F3. **Tel** 020-7928 7521. ⊖ *Blackfriars, Southwark.* **Open** 11am–6pm daily. **Closed** 24–26 Dec, 1 Jan. 🔌 🏠 **Lectures**. www.banksidegallery.com

This modern riverside gallery is the headquarters of two historic British societies, namely the Royal Watercolour Society and the Royal Society of Painter-Printmakers. The members of these societies

View from the Founders' Arms

are elected by their peers in a tradition that dates back over 200 years. Their work embraces both established and experimental practices. The gallery's permanent collection is not on show here but there are constantly changing temporary displays of contemporary water colours and original artists' prints. The exhibitions feature the work of both societies and many of the pieces on display are for sale. There is also a superb specialist art shop that sells both books and materials.

There is an unparalleled view of St Paul's Cathedral from the nearby pub, the Founders' Arms – built on the site of the foundry where the cathedral's bells were cast. South of here, on Hopton Street, is a series of almshouses which date from 1752.

Row of 17th-century houses on Cardinal's Wharf

Tate Modern ⑨

Looming over the southern bank of the Thames, Tate Modern occupies the converted Bankside power station, a dynamic space for one of the world's premier collections of contemporary art. Up until 2000, the Tate collection was shown at three galleries: Tate St Ives, Tate Liverpool and the Tate Gallery, now Tate Britain (see pp82–85). When Tate Modern joined this family of galleries, space was made for an ever-expanding collection of contemporary art. Tate Modern continually re-hangs its collection, so works and exhibitions may change from those described here.

★ **Fish (1926)**
Constantin Brancusi attempted to portray the "spirit" of a fish in this abstract work constructed from bronze, metal and wood.

Whaam! *(1963)*
Roy Lichtenstein took inspiration from commercial art sources such as comics for many of his works, of which Whaam! *is one of his most famous.*

Quattro Stagioni *(1993–4)*
Cy Twombly's four paintings depict the changes of light and colour over the seasons.

KEY TO FLOORPLAN

☐	Turbine Hall
▦	Material Gestures
☐	Poetry and Dream
▦	Energy and Process
▰	States of Flux
▨	Temporary exhibition space
☐	Non-exhibition space

Level 7

Level 6

Level 5

Level 4

Level 3

Level 2

& entrance

Level 1

North entrance

West entrance

★ The Snail (1953)
One of Henri Matisse's final works, The Snail was also one of his largest. It is a cutout, a medium Matisse focused on during his later years where pieces of gouache-painted paper are arranged to form a composition.

The **"light beam"**, a two-storey glass box, allows light to filter into the upper galleries.

A balcony gives great views of St Paul's Cathedral (pp148–51) across the river.

Soft Drainpipe – Blue (Cool) Version (1967)
An advert for drainpipes was the inspiration for this sculpture by Pop artist Claes Oldenburg. Like many of his pieces, Soft Drainpipe uses pliable material to represent hard surfaces, and thus renders a familiar object strange.

GALLERY GUIDE
The main west entrance opens into the expansive, sloped Turbine Hall. From here, a flight of stairs leads to the café and foyer of level 2, or an escalator whisks visitors straight up to gallery level 3. Temporary exhibitions are on level 4, while level 5 is again devoted to galleries. Level 6 is members' access only, but a superb restaurant and spectacular city views can be found on level 7.

★ Spatial Concept "Waiting" (1960)
Cut canvases became a feature of Lucio Fontana's work from 1959, serving to draw the viewer almost inside the work.

The Turbine Hall
The massive scale of this space – it covers 3,300 sq m (35,520 sq ft) – presents an unusual challenge for the artists who install pieces here.

STAR EXHIBITS
★ Fish by Brancusi

★ The Snail by Matisse

★ Spatial Concept "Waiting" by Fontana

Exploring Tate Modern

Tate Modern's displays are arranged into four thematic wings, each of which revolves around a large central room that focuses on a key period of modern art: Cubism, Futurism and Vorticism; Surrealism; Post-war painting and sculpture; and Minimalism. Around these focal points, smaller, regularly changing displays explore how each movement reflects earlier artistic practice or influenced subsequent developments.

After Lunch (1975) by Patrick Caulfield

MATERIAL GESTURES

The Material Gestures wing is centred around a room committed to painting and sculpture from the 1940s and 1950s which demonstrates how new forms of abstraction and expressive figuration arrived in America and Europe in the aftermath of the Second World War.

The pieces that occupy the surrounding rooms seek to relate the innovative artists of this post-war period to their predecessors, whilst also illustrating how their ideas have influenced modern artists and inspired the further development of art.

Pieces by the British artist Anish Kapoor and the American Barnett Newman are brought together as an introduction to the wing. A frequent feature of Newman's paintings is a vertical line representative of a column of light. Kapoor has adapted this concept to real space in *Ishi's Light* (2003), a sculptural installation in which a column of light is generated at the centre of the piece.

Subsequent rooms in the wing focus on Mark Rothko, Expressionism, Picasso and Matisse, and the resurgence of painting since the 1990s. However, the most visually arresting room in Material Gestures is perhaps that which brings together works by Claude Monet with pieces by Jackson Pollock, Mark Rothko and Joan Mitchell. The correlation between Monet's later semi-abstract works and those of the Abstract Expressionists is clear to see.

POETRY AND DREAM

The central concept of Poetry and Dream is the process by which modern and contemporary art develops out of what has gone before, whilst also fuelling our understanding of these past movements. Poetry and Dream illustrates this primary concept using the key artists of the Surrealist movement, including Salvador Dalí, René Magritte and Pablo Picasso. After identifying key Surrealist themes, techniques and principles, the wing invites visitors to examine works by more modern figures such as Cindy Sherman, Louise Bourgeois and Francis Bacon and illustrates how these artists invoke the legacy of their Surrealist predecessors. Further rooms focus on the use of film as a Surrealist medium, Cy Twombly, Joseph Beuys, Susan Hiller and her installation piece *From the Freud Museum* (1991-6), and the survival of Realism alongside the burgeoning Surrealist movement using works by André Derain, Max Beckman and Diego Rivera.

ENERGY AND PROCESS

"Artists' interest in transformation and natural forces" is the concept behind this sequence of 11 rooms. Room 1 contrasts the work of painter Kasimir Malevich, a pioneer of the early-20th-century avant-garde, and

BANKSIDE POWER STATION

This forbidding fortress was designed in 1947 by Sir Giles Gilbert Scott, the architect of Battersea Power Station, Waterloo Bridge and London's famous red telephone boxes. The power station is of a steel-framed brick skin construction, comprising over 4.2 million bricks. The Turbine Hall was designed to accommodate huge oil-burning generators and three vast oil tanks are still in situ, buried under the ground just south of the building. The tanks are to be employed in a future stage of Tate Modern development. The power station itself was converted by Swiss architects Herzog and de Meuron who designed the two-storey glass box, or lightbeam, which runs the length of the building. This serves to flood the upper galleries with light and also provides wonderful views of London.

The façade, chimney, and lightbeam of Tate Modern

Summertime: Number 9A (1948) by Jackson Pollock

contemporary sculptor Richard Serra, known for his sheet-metal assemblages. Non-traditional approaches to canvas are explored in room 2. Sculptures made from everyday materials are featured in room 3, whereas photography is the focus in room 4, with work from Ana Mendieta. More sculpture follows in room 5 with work by the Italian sculptor Marisa Merz, who applies craft techniques to industrial materials. Room 6 brings together three representatives of the Arte Povera school – Boetti, Fabro and Pistoletto. Magdalena Abakanowicz's striking, sculptural textiles are found in room 7. Room 8 documents artistic "interventions" in the natural landscape and room 9 highlights a video installation by Brazilian artist Lucia Nogueira. In Room 10 you can view an early video art piece – Juan Downey's *Video Trans Americas*. Finally, room 11 has an installation by artists Peter Fischli and David Weiss, whose work re-creates cheap, mass-produced objects.

Unique Forms of Continuity in Space (1913) by Umberto Boccioni

STATES OF FLUX

The States of Flux wing focuses on the ways artists have developed new visual languages to represent the complexity and dynamism of life. The opening room presents a dramatic pairing of works from the first and second halves of the 20th century: Umberto Boccioni's striding figure *Unique Forms of Continuity in Space*, a Futurist vision of speed, strength and mechanization, alongside Pop artist Roy Lichtenstein's comic-book scene of aerial combat *Whaam!*.

The large central space is devoted to early 20th-century avant-garde. Cubism is represented with major works by figures such as Picasso, Braque, Gris, Lipchitz and Leger. There are also examples of the Italian Futurist movement and the short-lived British response, Vorticism, with works by Wyndham Lewis, David Bomberg and

Jacob Epstein. An adjoining display, After Impressionism, looks at the very different work of artists working in the same period, with stunning canvases by Matisse, Munch, Vuillard and Bonnard. Other rooms explore the Fluxus movement and how the innovations of this period influenced experimental film, photography and design, sometimes with a more pointed political agenda. Displays of collage and Pop Art feature works by Andy Warhol, Jasper Johns and Claes Oldenburg.

Maman (2000) by Louise Bourgeois

SPECIAL EXHIBITIONS

To complement its permanent collection, Tate Modern presents a programme of exhibitions including three large shows a year (retrospectives of modern masters or surveys of important movements). Smaller-scale projects are dotted around, and occasionally outside, the gallery. Once a year Tate Modern challenges an artist to create a work capable of occupying the vast Turbine Hall. Louise Bourgeois was the first artist to install here, with works that included her sculpture *Maman*. Recently, Olafur Eliasson's *The Weather Project* lit the Turbine Hall with a giant glowing sun.

The Bath (1925) by Pierre Bonnard

The Anchor ❿

34 Park St SE1. **Map** 15 A3.
Tel 020-7407 1577. 🚇 London
Bridge. **Open** 11am–11pm Mon–
Wed, 11am–midnight Thu–Sat,
noon–10:30pm Sun. 🚻 🍴

This is one of London's most
famous riverside pubs. It
dates from after the Southwark
fire of 1676, which devastated
the area *(see pp24–5)*. The
present building is 18th-
century, but traces of much
earlier hostelries have been
found beneath it. The inn was
once connected with a
brewery across the road that
belonged to Henry Thrale, a
close friend of Dr Johnson
(see p140). When Thrale died
in 1781, Johnson went to the
brewery sale and encouraged
the bidders with a phrase that
has passed into the English
language: "The potential of
growing rich beyond the
dreams of avarice."

Pub sign at the Anchor Inn

Vinopolis ⓫

1 Bank End SE1. **Map** 15 B3. **Tel**
020-7940 3000. 🚇 London Bridge.
Open noon–10pm Thu–Sat, noon–
6pm Sun (bank hols: phone to check);
last adm: 2.5 hrs before close. **Closed**
25 & 26 Dec, 1 Jan. Adm charge. 🚻
🍴 📷 📷 📷 www.vinopolis.co.uk

Vinopolis is a unique attraction
devoted to the enjoyment of
wine. Its blend of interactive
fun and educational exhibits
has made it a popular
destination for anyone who
wishes to know more about
making and drinking wine.
Set within cavernous Victorian
railway arches, Vinopolis
explores the history of the

grape from earliest
times and illuminates
the process of wine-
making from planting
the vines through to
labelling the bottles.
"Tasting stations" pro-
vide an opportunity
to savour the subject
matter along the way.
A selection of choice
vintages can be pur-
chased from the wine
warehouse after the
tour, while the shop
has a vast assortment
of wine-related
merchandise. Cantina
Vinopolis offers good
food, great service,
and, unsurprisingly,
high-quality wines.

Clink Prison Museum ⓬

1 Clink St SE1. **Map** 15 B3. **Tel** 020-
7403 0900. 🚇 London Bridge. **Open**
Jul–Sep: 10am–9pm daily; Oct–Jun:
10am–6pm Mon–Fri, 10am–7:30pm
Sat & Sun. **Closed** 25 Dec. **Adm
charge**. 📷 📷 📷 for groups (phone
first). www.clink.co.uk

Now a macabre museum, the
prison that was once located
here first opened in the 12th
century. It was owned by
successive Bishops of
Winchester, who lived in the
adjoining palace just east of
the museum, of which all that
now remains is a lovely rose
window. During the 15th
century, the prison became
known as the "Clink", and
finally closed in 1780.
    The museum illustrates the
history of the prison. Tales of
the inmates are told, including
those of the numerous
prostitutes, debtors and priests

Antiques stall at Bermondsey Market

that were incarcerated
here. Hands-on displays of
instruments of torture leave
little to the imagination and
are not for the faint-hearted.

Bermondsey ⓭

SE1. **Map** 15 C5. 🚇 London
Bridge, Borough. **Market
Open** 4am–1pm Fri, starts closing
noon. **Fashion and Textile
Museum** 83 Bermondsey St SE1.
Tel 020-7407 8664. **Open** 11am–
6pm Wed–Sun. **Adm charge**. 🚻
📷 on request. 📷 📷 www.
ftmlondon.org

Bermondsey's winding streets
still hold traces of its historic
past in the form of medieval,
18th-century and Victorian
buildings. Today it is famous
for its antique market. Each
Friday at dawn, seriously
committed antiques dealers
trade their latest acquisitions
at Bermondsey. There are
occasional press reports about
long-lost masterpieces changing hands here for a song,
and optimists are welcome to
try their luck and test their
judgment. However, trading
starts at the crack of dawn,
and the best bargains tend to
go before most people are
even awake.
    The Fashion and Textile
Museum in Bermondsey
Street re-opened in 2008
and now combines an
education, exhibition and
visitor centre for contemporary
fashion, textiles and jewellery.
A shop sells products by up-
and-coming designers.

**Replica of Civil
War trooper's helmet
made in the Clink**

London Dungeon **14**

Tooley St SE1. **Map** 15 C3. **Tel** *020 7403 7221.* **Station** *London Bridge.* **Open** *daily Jul–Aug: 9:30am–6:30pm; Sep–Oct 10am–5:30pm; Nov–Apr: 10:30am–5pm; Apr–Jun: 10am–5:30pm (times may vary slightly so call or check website).* **Closed** *25 Dec.* **Adm charge.** **access** **photo** **film** **www**.thedungeons.com

In effect a much-expanded version of the chamber of horrors at Madame Tussaud's *(see p224)*, this is a great hit with children. It illustrates the most bloodthirsty events in British history, with live actors and special effects. It is played strictly for terror, and screams abound with experiences such as Gruesome Goings-on, which includes live actors, a ride and shows; the Great Plague; the Torture Chamber; and Jack the Ripper.

Eduardo Paolozzi sculpture outside the Design Museum

Design Museum **15**

Butlers Wharf, Shad Thames SE1. **Map** 16 E4. **Tel** *020-7940 8783.* **Station** *Tower Hill, London Bridge.* **Open** *10am–5:45pm daily (last adm: 5:15pm).* **Closed** *25 & 26 Dec.* **Adm charge.** **restaurant** **Blueprint Café** *020-7378 7031 (booking advised).* **photo** **film** **shop** **access** **www**.designmuseum.org

This museum was the first in the world to be devoted solely to modern and contemporary design when it was founded in 1989. A frequently changing programme of exhibitions explores landmarks in modern design history and the most exciting innovations in contemporary design set against the context of social, cultural, economic

Spooky London Dungeon logo, an indication of the gruesome displays

and technological changes. The Design Museum embraces every area of design, from furniture and fashion, to household products, cars, graphics, websites and architecture in exhibitions and new design commissions. Each spring the museum hosts Designer of the Year, a national design prize, with an exhibition at which the public can vote for the winner.

The museum is arranged over three floors, with major exhibitions on the first floor. There is a choice of smaller displays on the second, which also houses an Interaction Space, where visitors can play vintage video games and learn about the designers featured in the museum in the Design at the Design Museum online research archive. The shop and café are on the ground floor. On the first floor is the **Blueprint Café** restaurant, which has stunning views of the Thames.

HMS Belfast **16**

Morgan's Lane, Tooley St SE1. **Map** 16 D3. **Tel** *020-7940 6300.* **Station** *London Bridge, Tower Hill.* **Open** *Mar–Oct: 10am–6pm daily; Nov–Feb: 10am–5pm daily (last adm: 1 hour before closing).* **Closed** *24–26 Dec.* **Adm charge.** **access** limited. **photo** **film** **www**.iwm.org.uk

Originally launched in 1938 to serve in World War II, HMS *Belfast* was instrumental in the destruction of the German battle cruiser, *Scharnhorst*, in the battle of North Cape, and also played an important role in the Normandy Landings.

After the war, the battle cruiser, designed for offensive action and for supporting amphibious operations, was sent to work for the United Nations in Korea. The ship remained in service with the British navy until 1965.

Since 1971, the cruiser has been used as a floating naval museum. Part of it has been recreated to show what the ship was like in 1943, when it participated in sinking the German battle cruiser. Other displays portray life on board during World War II and there are also exhibits relating to the history of the Royal Navy.

As well as being a great family day out, it is also possible for children to take part in educational activity weekends on board the ship.

The now familiar sight of the naval gunship HMS *Belfast* on the Thames

SOUTH BANK

Following the Festival of Britain in 1951, the Southbank Centre grew up around the newly erected Royal Festival Hall. The architecture has been criticized over the years, especially the chunky concrete building that houses The Hayward, but now appears to be valued as an important part of London's river frontage. The area functions well, and is crowded with culture-seekers most evenings and afternoons. As well as the National Theatre and the Old Vic theatre, concert halls, and galleries, the South Bank has the BFI Southbank and London's most striking cinema, the BFI IMAX *(see p347)*. In keeping with Festival of Britain tradition, the South Bank was a focal point for the new millennium, with the raising of the world's highest observation wheel, the London Eye.

SIGHTS AT A GLANCE

Historic Streets and Buildings
Lambeth Palace ⑧
Gabriel's Wharf ⑪
Waterloo Station ⑫

Museums and Galleries
The Hayward ②
Florence Nightingale Museum ⑥
Museum of Garden History ⑦
Imperial War Museum ⑨

Attractions
County Hall ④
The London Eye ⑤

Theatres and Concert Halls
Royal National Theatre ①
Royal Festival Hall ③
The Old Vic ⑩

0 metres 500
0 yards 500

GETTING THERE
The Northern, Bakerloo, and Jubilee lines pass through Waterloo station, which is also a major rail terminus. The Riverside 1 (RV1) bus service links the South Bank with Covent Garden, Bankside, and the Tower, and runs every 10 minutes from 6am to midnight.

SEE ALSO
- *Street Finder,* maps 13, 14, 22
- *Where to Stay* pp278–291
- *Restaurants, Pubs* pp292–319

KEY
- Street by Street map
- Underground station
- Railway station

◁ **Riverside walk on the South Bank**

Street-by-Street: Southbank Centre

Originally this was an area of wharves and factories which was much damaged by bombing during World War II. It was chosen as the site of the 1951 Festival of Britain *(see p32)*, celebrating the centenary of the Great Exhibition *(see pp28–9)*. The Royal Festival Hall is the only building from 1951 to remain, but since then London's main arts centre has been created around it, including the national showplaces for theatre, music and film, and a major art gallery.

Memorial to the International Brigade of the Spanish Civil War

To the Strand

★ National Theatre
Its three auditoriums offer a choice of plays ranging from the classics to the sharpest modern writing **❶**

BFI Southbank, previously the National Film Theatre, was established in 1953 to show historic films *(see p347)*.

Festival Pier

The Queen Elizabeth Hall stages more intimate concerts than the Festival Hall. The adjoining Purcell Room is for chamber music *(see pp348–9)*.

Hayward Gallery
The concrete interior of this venue for important exhibitions is well suited to many modern works **❷**

★ Royal Festival Hall
The London Philharmonic is one of many world-class orchestras to perform here in the focal point of the Southbank Centre **❸**

Hungerford Bridge was built in 1864 to carry both trains and pedestrians to Charing Cross. It now includes two foot-bridges, the Golden Jubilee Bridges.

STAR SIGHTS

★ The London Eye

★ Royal National Theatre

★ Royal Festival Hall

KEY

– – – Suggested route

0 metres   100

0 yards   100

★ The London Eye
The world's tallest cantilevered observation wheel offers passengers a unique view of London **❺**

Waterloo Bridge was completed in 1945 to Sir Giles Gilbert Scott's design. It replaced Rennie's bridge of 1817.

LOCATOR MAP
See Central London Map pp14–15

SOHO & TRAFALGAR SQUARE

COVENT GARDEN & THE STRAND

HOLBORN & THE INNS OF COURT

PICCADILLY & ST JAMES'S

Thames

SOUTH BANK

WHITEHALL & WESTMINSTER

The Struggle is My Life is a bronze of Nelson Mandela, the South African leader. Made by Ian Walters, it was unveiled here in 1985.

THE STRUGGLE IS MY LIFE
NELSON MANDELA

The Shell Building, head-quarters of the international oil company, was completed in 1963. Its architectural merit is still hotly debated.

CONCERT HALL APPROACH

Southbank Centre

County Hall
This is now home to the Sea Life London Aquarium, the London Film Museum, hotels and restaurants. **4**

BELVEDERE ROAD

CHICHELEY STREET

WESTMINSTER BRIDGE ROAD

Jubilee Gardens were laid out in 1977 to celebrate the Silver Jubilee of Queen Elizabeth II.

To Westminster station

UPPER GROUND

The façade of the Hayward Gallery

London following World War II. It has stood the test of time so well that many of the capital's major arts institutions have gathered round it. Festival Riverside on level 1 opened in 2004, with restaurants and retail, community and visitors facilities. Phase II of the redevelopment began in 2005 and was completed in 2007. The stage has hosted renowned musicians, including the cellist Jacqueline du Pré and the conductor Georg Solti. The organ was installed in 1954. There are cafés and book stalls on the lower floors.

National Theatre ❶

South Bank SE1. **Map** 14 D3.
📋 020-7452 3000. 🚇 Waterloo.
Open 9:30am–10:45pm Mon–Sat.
Closed 24, 25 Dec, Good Fri, bank hols. 🚫 during performances. 🎭
🖥 🚻 ♿ 🎵 **Concerts** at 6pm, **exhibitions**. See **Entertainment** p344. **www**.nationaltheatre.org.uk

Even if you don't want to see a play, this well-appointed complex is worth a visit. Sir Denys Lasdun's building was opened in 1976 after 200 years of debate about whether there should be a national theatre and where it should be sited. The company was formed in 1963, under Laurence (later Lord) Olivier, Britain's leading 20th-century actor. The largest of the three theatres is named after him; the others are the Cottesloe and the Lyttleton. There are sometimes free evening concerts in the foyer.

Festival of Britain: symbol of 1951

The Hayward ❷

South Bank SE1. **Map** 14 D3.
Tel 0844-875 0073. 🚇 Waterloo.
Open 10am–6pm daily (to 10pm Fri). **Closed** 1 Jan, 24–26 Dec, between exhibitions. **Adm charge.**
♿ 🖥 🚻 **www**.southbank centre.co.uk

The Hayward is one of London's main venues for large art exhibitions. Its slabby grey concrete exterior is too starkly modern for some tastes, but it is also considered by many as an icon of 1960s "Brutalist" architecture. The foyer by Dan Graham, completed in 2003, shows a selection of cartoons and artists' videos.
Hayward exhibitions cover classical and contemporary art, but the work of British contemporary artists is particularly well represented.

Royal Festival Hall ❸

South Bank SE1. **Map** 14 D4.
Tel 0844-875 0073. 🚇 Waterloo.
Open 10am–11pm daily. **Closed** 25 Dec. 🚫 during performances.
🎭 🖥 🚻 ♿ **Pre-concert talks, exhibitions, free concerts.** See **Entertainment** p346.
www.southbankcentre.co.uk

This was the only structure in the 1951 Festival of Britain (see p32) designed for permanence. Sir Robert Matthew and Sir Leslie Martin's concert hall was the first major public building in

County Hall ❹

Westminster Bridge Rd SE1.
Map 13 C4. **Aquarium Tel** 020-7967 8000. 🚇 Waterloo. **Open** 10am–6pm daily. **Closed** 25 Dec. **Adm charge.** ♿ 🖥 🚻 **www**.londonaquarium.co.uk

Shark in a scenic tank at the London Aquarium

Once the home of London's elected government, this imposing building now houses a leisure complex. The Sea Life London Aquarium, the London Film Museum and *Namco Station*, a computer games hall, occupy the space alongside two hotels, several restaurants and a health club.
The Aquarium is home to hundreds of aquatic species from all over the world, including stingrays, turtles and sea scorpions. Special features include a 25-m (82-ft) glass tunnel walkway through a tropical ocean environment, and, for the brave, a Shark Walk across a suspended glass platform.

The London Eye ➎

The Merlin Entertainments London Eye is a 135-m (443-ft) high observation wheel. Erected in 2000 as part of London's millennium celebrations, it immediately became one of the city's most recognizable landmarks, notable not only for its size, but for its circularity amid the block-shaped buildings flanking it. Thirty-two capsules, each holding up to 25 people, take a gentle 30-minute round trip. On a clear day, the Eye affords a unique 40-km (25-mile) view which sweeps over the capital in all directions and on to the countryside and hills beyond.

VISITORS' CHECKLIST

Jubilee Gardens SE1. **Map** 14 D4. *Tel 0870 5000 600 (info and 24-hour advance booking – strongly recommended).* 🚇 *Waterloo, Westminster.* 🚌 *11, 24, 211.* **Open** *daily Oct–Apr: 10am–8pm; May–Jun, Sep: 10am–9pm; Jul–Aug: 10am–9:30pm.* **Closed** *25 Dec and early Jan for maintenance.* **Adm charge**. *Pick up tickets at County Hall (adjacent to Eye) at least 30 mins before boarding time. Fast-track tickets are also available.* 🎫 📷 ♿ www.londoneye.com

The glass capsules are mounted on the outside of the rim, allowing unobstructed 360-degree views.

80 spokes made from 6 km (3.7 miles) of cable hold the structure in tension, strengthening the wheel.

Houses of Parliament
Seventeen minutes into the flight, the spectacular aerial view of Westminster should not be missed.

Two cables, 60 metres (197 feet) in length, support the entire structure from concrete bases in Jubilee Gardens.

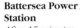

Battersea Power Station
After 15 minutes, the distinctive white smokestacks of this old power station are visible.

The wheel rim was floated down the Thames in sections and then assembled on site.

Buckingham Palace
Ten minutes into the journey, the Queen's official residence glides into view.

The Eye turns continuously and moves slowly enough that the capsules are boarded here while moving. The wheel is halted for those requiring assistance.

Florence Nightingale Museum ❻

2 Lambeth Palace Rd SE1. **Map** 14
D5. **Tel** 020-7620 0374. ⊖
Waterloo, Westminster. **Open**
10am–5pm daily (last adm 4.30pm).
Closed 25 Dec (and some other
dates; call to check). **Adm charge.**
🚫 📷 ♿ **Videos, lectures.**
www.florence-nightingale.co.uk

This determined woman
captured the nation's
imagination as the "Lady of
the Lamp", who nursed the
wounded soldiers of the
Crimea War (1853–6). She
also founded Britain's first
school of nursing at old St
Thomas' Hospital in 1860.
Obscurely sited near the
entrance to the new St
Thomas' Hospital, the
museum is worth finding.
It gives a fascinating
account of Nightingale's
career through displays
of original documents
and personal memorabilia.
They illustrate her
life and the develop-
ments she pioneered
in health care, until
her death in 1910,
aged 90.

Florence Nightingale

Museum of Garden History ❼

Lambeth Palace Rd SE1. **Map** 21 C1.
Tel 020-7401 8865. ⊖ Waterloo,
Lambeth North, Westminster. **Open**
10:30am–5pm Sun–Fri, 10:30am–
4pm Sat. **Closed** 1st Mon of month;
22 Dec–1 Jan. ♿ 📷 **Library by**
appt, lectures, filmshows. www.
museumgardenhistory.org

The world's first museum of
garden history is housed in
the restored church of St Mary
of Lambeth Palace. In the
grounds are the tombs of John
Tradescant, father and son
who, as well as being gardeners to Charles I and Charles II,
were also adventurous plant
hunters and collectors of curiosities. The tomb of William
Bligh of *The Bounty* can also
be seen here.
The Museum of Garden His-
tory consists of a history of

gardening in Britain, illustrated by a selection of historic
garden tools, artifacts and
curiosities. It also runs a programme of exhibitions, events,
lectures and eductional activities. There is a shop with a
stock of garden-related items
for freshly inspired gardeners.

Lambeth Palace ❽

SE1. **Map** 21 C1. ⊖ Lambeth
North, Westminster, Waterloo,
Vauxhall. **Not open** to the public.

This palace has housed Archbishops of Canterbury since
the 13th century and today
remains the Archbishop of
Canterbury's official London
residence. The chapel and its
undercroft contain elements
from the 13th century, but a
large part of the rest of
the building is far more
recent. It has been
frequently restored,
most recently by
Edward Blore in 1828.
The Tudor gatehouse,
however, dates from
1485 and is one of
London's most
pleasing and
familiar riverside
landmarks.
Until the first
Westminster Bridge
was built, the horse ferry that
operated between here and
Millbank was a principal river
crossing. The revenues from it
went to the Archbishop, who
received compensation for loss
of business when the bridge
opened in 1750.

The Tudor gatehouse

Imperial War Museum ❾

Lambeth Rd SE1. **Map** 22 E1. 🅵
020-7416 5000. ⊖ Lambeth North,
Elephant & Castle. **Open** 10am–6pm
daily. **Closed** 24–26 Dec. 📷 ♿ 🍴
📺 📷 **Filmshows, lectures.**
www.iwm.org.uk

In spite of the two colossal
guns that point up the drive
from the main entrance, this
museum is not just concerned
with the engines of modern
warfare. Massive tanks, artillery, bombs and aircraft are on
show, yet some of the most
fascinating exhibits in the
museum relate more to the
impact on the lives of people
at home than to the business
of fighting. There are displays
about food rationing, air raid
precautions, censorship and
morale-boosting.
The arts are well represented,
with extracts from wartime
films, radio programmes and
literature, plus many
hundreds of photographs,
paintings by Graham

The machinery of war through the ages

Sutherland and Paul Nash, and sculpture by Jacob Epstein. Henry Moore did some evocative drawings of life during the Blitz of 1940, when many Londoners slept in Underground stations in order to protect themselves from falling bombs. There is also a library with a fascinating archive. The Holocaust exhibition is a major permanent display, using historical material and original artifacts to tell its story.

The museum is housed in part of what used to be the Bethlehem Royal Hospital for the Insane ("Bedlam"), built in 1811. In the 19th century, visitors would come for the afternoon to enjoy the antics of the patients. The hospital moved out to new premises in Surrey in 1930, leaving this vast building empty. Its two large, flanking wings were pulled down and this central block converted into the museum which moved here from its former South Kensington site in 1936.

The Old Vic's façade from 1816

The Old Vic ⓾

Waterloo Rd SE1. **Map** 14 E5.
Tel 0844-871 7628. ⊖ *Waterloo.*
Open for performances only. & ⚑
⚑ See **Entertainment** pp344–5.
www.oldvictheatre.com

This splendid building dates back to 1818, when it was opened as the Royal Coburg Theatre. In 1833 the name was changed to the Royal Victoria, in honour of the future queen. Shortly after this the theatre became a centre for "music hall", the immensely popular Victorian entertainment which included singers,

The memorial to the dead of World War I at Waterloo Station

comedians and other acts. In 1912 Lillian Baylis became manager and from 1914 to 1923 she staged all of Shakespeare's plays here. In the 1960s the National Theatre *(see p188)* was founded and based at this site.

In 1997, Sally Greene, with the director Stephen Daldry and others, set up a charitable trust to secure the theatre's future. The Trust set up The Old Vic Theatre Company as a resident company in 2003, with Kevin Spacey as Artistic Director. There are cheap seats for younger people and pantomimes at Christmas.

Gabriel's Wharf ⓫

56 Upper Ground SE1. **Map** 14 E3.
⊖ *Waterloo. See **Shops and Markets** pp332–41.*

This pleasant enclave of boutiques, craft shops and cafés was the product of a long and stormy debate over the future of what was once an industrial riverside area. Residents of Waterloo strongly opposed various schemes for office developments before a community association was able to acquire the site in 1984 and build co-operative housing around the wharf.

Adjoining the market is a small garden and a riverside walkway with marvellous views to the north of the City. The OXO Tower to the east, built in 1928 surreptitiously to advertise a meat extract by means of its window shapes, is now the setting for a fine restaurant *(see p302).*

Waterloo Station ⓬

York Rd SE1. **Map** 14 D4.
Tel 08457 484950. ⊖ *Waterloo.*
See **Getting to London** p372.

The terminus for trains to southwest England, Waterloo station was originally built in 1848 but completely remodelled in the early 20th century, with the addition of a grand formal entrance on the northeast corner. Today the spacious concourse, lined with shops, cafés and bars, makes it one of the most practical of the London rail terminals.

Towards the end of the 20th century the station was enlarged again to serve as London's first Channel Tunnel rail link to Europe. In autumn 2007, the Eurostar terminal moved from Waterloo station to its present home at St Pancras International.

The area around Waterloo has a great community feel and it is worth passing down Lower Marsh with its shops, eateries and street market.

Illusionistic painting on the buildings around Gabriel's Wharf

CHELSEA

The showy young shoppers who paraded along the King's Road from the 1960s until the 1980s have more or less gone, along with Chelsea's reputation for extreme behaviour established by the bohemian

Cow's head outside the Old Dairy on Old Church Street

Cheyne Walk. The historian Thomas Carlyle and the essayist Leigh Hunt arrived in the 1830s and began a literary tradition continued by writers such as the poet Swinburne. Yet Chelsea has always had a raffish

Chelsea Set of writers and artists in the 19th century. Formerly a riverside village, Chelsea became fashionable in Tudor times. Henry VIII liked it so much that he built a small palace (long vanished) here. Artists, including Turner, Whistler and Rossetti, were attracted by the river views from

element, too: in the 18th century the pleasure gardens were noted for beautiful courtesans and the Chelsea Arts Club has had riotous balls for nearly a century. Chelsea is too expensive for most artists now, but the artistic connection is maintained by many galleries and antique shops.

SIGHTS AT A GLANCE

Historic Streets and Buildings
King's Road ❶
Carlyle's House ❷
Cheyne Walk ❺
Royal Hospital ❽
Sloane Square ❿

Museums
National Army Museum ❼
Saatchi Gallery ❾

Churches
Chelsea Old Church ❸

Gardens
Roper's Garden ❹
Chelsea Physic Garden ❻

GETTING THERE
The District and Circle Underground lines serve Sloane Square; the Piccadilly line passes just outside this area, through South Kensington. Buses 11, 19 and 22 all stop on the King's Road.

SEE ALSO

- **Street Finder,** maps 19, 20

- **Where to Stay** pp278–91

- **Restaurants, Pubs** pp292–319

- **Chelsea and Battersea Walk** pp266–7

KEY

Street-by-Street map

Underground station

0 metres   500
0 yards   500

◁ **Picturesque Chelsea residences in a cul-de-sac off the King's Road**

Street-by-Street: Chelsea

Once a peaceful riverside village, Chelsea has been fashionable since Tudor times when Sir Thomas More, Henry VIII's Lord Chancellor, lived here. Artists, including Turner, Whistler and Rossetti, were attracted by the views from Cheyne Walk, before a busy main road disturbed its peace. Chelsea's artistic connection is maintained by its galleries and antique shops, while enclaves of 18th-century houses preserve its old village atmosphere.

The Old Dairy, at 46 Old Church Street, was built in 1796, when cows still grazed in the surrounding fields. The tiling is original.

King's Road
In the 1960s and 1970s it was the boutique-lined centre of fashionable London, and is still a main shopping street ❶

To King's Road

Carlyle's House
The historian and philosopher lived here from 1834 until his death in 1882 ❷

Chelsea Old Church
Although severely damaged during World War II, it still holds some fine Tudor monuments ❸

Roper's Garden
It includes a sculpture by Jacob Epstein who had a studio here ❹

Thomas More, sculpted in 1969 by L Cubitt Bevis, gazes calmly across the river near where he lived.

STAR SIGHTS

★ Chelsea Physic Garden

KEY

- - - Suggested route

| 0 metres | 100 |
| 0 yards | 100 |

To Sloane Square station

Chelsea Old Town Hall was built in the late 19th century and now hosts exhibitions and antique fairs.

LOCATOR MAP
See Central London Map pp14–15

SOUTH KENSINGTON & KNIGHTSBRIDGE

Brompton

Belgravia

CHELSEA

Thames

Battersea

★ **Chelsea Physic Garden**
The statue is of Sir Hans Sloane, benefactor of this historic herb garden **6**

CHELSEA MANOR STREET

FLOOD STREET

HENE ST

OAKLEY GNS

ST LOO AVENUE

CHEYNE GARDENS

ROYAL HOSPITAL RD

Cadogan Pier

Albert Bridge, completed in 1873, is the most elegant of the Thames Bridges, especially at night when it is illuminated by hundreds of light bulbs.

Boy and Dolphin, the vigorous sculpture (1975) by David Wynne, enlivens the Albert Bridge junction.

Cheyne Walk
Once favoured by artists, it boasts some of London's finest houses and has had many famous residents. Look out for the plaques **5**

The Pheasantry, King's Road

King's Road **❶**

SW3 and SW10. **Map** 19 B3.
🚇 *Sloane Square. See **Shops and Markets** pp332–41.*

This is Chelsea's central artery, with its wealth of small fashion shops packed with young people looking for designer fashions. The mini-skirt revolution of the 1960s began here and so have many subsequent style trends, perhaps the most famous of them being punk.

Look out for the Pheasantry at No. 152, with its columns and statuary. It was built in 1881 as the shop-front of a furniture maker's premises but now conceals a modern restaurant. Antique-lovers will find three warrens of stalls on the south side of the King's Road: Antiquarius at No. 137, the Chenil Galleries at Nos. 181–3 and the Chelsea Antiques Market at No. 253.

Carlyle's House **❷**

24 Cheyne Row SW3. **Map** 19 B4.
Tel *020-7352 7087.* 🚇 *Sloane Sq, South Kensington.* **Open** *Mar–Oct: 2–5pm Wed–Fri, 11am– 5pm Sat, Sun & public hols (last adm: 4:30pm).* **Adm charge.** 📷 📋 *tours 11am– 12:30pm Wed–Fri (by appt).* **www.** nationaltrust.org.uk/carlyleshouse

The historian and founder of the London Library *(see St James's Square p92)*, Thomas Carlyle moved into this mod-est 18th-century house in 1834, and wrote many of his best-known books here, nota-bly *The French Revolution* and *Frederick the Great*. His pres-ence made Chelsea more fash-ionable and the house became a mecca for some great literary figures. The novelists Charles Dickens and William Thack-eray, poet Alfred Lord Tennys-on and naturalist Charles Darwin were all regular visi-tors here. The house has been restored and looks as it did during Carlyle's lifetime.

Chelsea Old Church **❸**

64 Cheyne Walk SW3. **Map** 19 A4.
Tel *020-7795 1019.* 🚇 *Sloane Sq, South Kensington.* **Open** *2–4pm, Tue–Thu.* ♿ 📷 *by appt.* 🔔 *8am, 10am, 11am, 12:15pm, 6pm Sun.*
www.chelseaoldchurch.org.uk

Chelsea Old Church in 1860

Rebuilt after World War II, this square-towered building does not look old from the outside. However, early prints confirm that it is a careful replica of the medieval church that was largely destroyed by World War II bombs.

The glory of this church is its Tudor monuments. One to Sir Thomas More, who built a chapel here in 1528, contains an inscription he wrote (in Latin), asking to be buried next to his wife. Among other monuments is a chapel to Sir Thomas Lawrence, who was an Elizabethan merchant, and a 17th-century memorial to Lady Jane Cheyne, after whose husband Cheyne Walk was named. Outside the church is a statue in memory of Sir Thomas More, "statesman, scholar, saint", gazing piously across the river.

Roper's Garden **❹**

Cheyne Walk SW3. **Map** 19 A4.
🚇 *Sloane Square, South Kensington.*

This is a small park outside Chelsea Old Church. It is named after Margaret Roper, Thomas More's daughter, and her husband William, who wrote More's biography. The sculptor Jacob Epstein worked at a studio on the site between 1909 and 1914, and there is a stone carving by him commemorating the fact. The park also contains a figure of a nude woman by Gilbert Carter.

Cheyne Walk **❺**

SW3. **Map** 19 B4. 🚇 *Sloane Square, South Kensington.*

Until Chelsea Embankment was constructed in 1874, Cheyne Walk was a pleasant riverside promenade. Now it overlooks a busy road that has destroyed much of its charm. Many of the 18th-century houses remain, though, bristling with blue plaques celebrating some of the famous people who have lived in them. Most were writers and artists, including J M W Turner who lived incognito at No. 119, George Eliot who died at No. 4 and a clutch of writers (Henry James, T S Eliot and Ian Fleming) in Carlyle Mansions.

Thomas More on Cheyne Walk

Chelsea Physic Garden 6

66 Royal Hospital Road SW3. **Map** 19
C4. **Tel** 020-7352 5646. 🚇 *Sloane
Square.* **Open** *Mar–Oct: noon–5pm
Wed, Thu & Fri, noon–6pm Sun (Jul &
Aug: to 10pm Wed – last adm 8:30pm);
noon–5pm Mon–Fri during Chelsea
Flower Show in May, see p56.* **Adm
charge.** 🚻 🖥 🏠 **Gardening school.**
www.chelseaphysicgarden.co.uk

Established by the Society
of Apothecaries in 1673 to
study plants for medicinal
use, this garden was saved
from closure in 1722 by a gift
from Sir Hans Sloane, whose
statue adorns it. Many new
varieties have been nurtured
in its glasshouses, including
cotton sent to the plantations
of the southern United States.
Visitors can see ancient trees
and one of Britain's first rock
gardens, installed in 1772.

Chelsea Physic Garden in autumn

National Army Museum 7

Royal Hospital Rd SW3. **Map**
19 C4. **Tel** 020-7730 0717.
🚇 *Sloane Square.* **Open**
*10am–5:30pm daily; see
website for celebrity speaker
programme.* **Closed** *1 Jan,
24–26 Dec.* & 🖥 🏠 www.
national-army-museum.ac.uk

A lively account of
the history of British
land forces from
1485 to the present
can be found here. Tableaux,
dioramas, archive film and
interactive displays illustrate
major engagements and give
a taste of life behind the lines.
There are fine paintings of battle scenes and portraits of soldiers. The shop sells a range
of books and model soldiers.

Royal Hospital 8

Royal Hospital Rd SW3. **Map** 20 D3.
Tel 020-7881 5200. 🚇 *Sloane Sq.*
Open *10am–noon, 2–4pm
Mon–Sat, 2–4pm Sun.* **Closed** *Sun
Oct–Mar, public hols, functions
(check first).* & *limited.* 🏠
www.chelsea-pensioners.co.uk

This graceful complex was
commissioned by Charles II

from Christopher Wren in
1682 as a retirement home for
old or wounded soldiers, who
have been known as Chelsea
Pensioners ever since. The
hospital opened ten years later
and is still home to about 330
retired soldiers, whose
distinctive uniforms of
scarlet coats and tricorne
hats date from the 17th
century. Flanking the
northern entrance are
Wren's two main public
rooms: the chapel,
notable for its
wonderful simplicity,
and the panelled Great
Hall, still used as the
dining room. A small
museum explains the
history of the
Pensioners.
A statue of
Charles II by
Grinling Gibbons is to be
found on the terrace outside,
and there is a fine view of the
remains of Battersea Power
Station across the river.

**A Chelsea Pensioner
in uniform**

Saatchi Gallery 9

Duke of York's HQ, King's Road
Chelsea **Map** 19 C3. **Tel** 020-7823
2363. 🚇 *Sloane Square.* **Open** *10am–
6pm daily.* **Closed** *for private events.*
🏠 🖥 www.saatchi-gallery.co.uk

The Saatchi Gallery is famous
for presenting the best in
contemporary art and has
seen an astonishing rise in
interest since it opened over
twenty years ago. The gallery
now receives over 600,000
visitors each year. Many of

the featured artists are
unknown when first exhibited
at the gallery but often rise to
fame as a result. Relocated
from its original site on the
South Bank, the Saatchi
Gallery's present home at
the Duke of York's HQ offers
an ideal environment in
which to view contemporary
art. Admire pieces by established names such as Tracy
Emin and Jenny Saville while
also keeping an eye open for
up-and-coming new talent.

Sloane Square 10

SW1. **Map** 20 D2. 🚇 *Sloane Square.*

Sloane Square fountain

This pleasant small square
(rectangle to be precise) has a
paved centre with a flower
stall and fountain depicting
Venus. Laid out in the late
18th century, it was named
after Sir Hans Sloane, the
wealthy physician and
collector who bought the
manor of Chelsea in 1712.
Opposite Peter Jones, the
1936 department store on
the square's west side, is the
Royal Court Theatre, which
for over a century has
fostered new drama.

SOUTH KENSINGTON AND KNIGHTSBRIDGE

Bristling with embassies and consulates, South Kensington and Knightsbridge are among London's most desirable, and expensive, areas. The proximity of Kensington Palace, a royal residence, means they have remained fairly unchanged.

The prestigious shops of Knightsbridge serve their wealthy residents. With Hyde Park to the north, and museums that celebrated Victorian learning at its heart, visitors to this part of London can expect to find a unique combination of the serene and the grandiose.

SIGHTS AT A GLANCE

Historic Streets and Buildings
Royal College of Music ❺
Royal College of Art ❼
Kensington Palace ❿
Speakers' Corner ⓭

Churches
Brompton Oratory ❹

Museums and Galleries
Natural History Museum pp208–9 ❶
Science Museum pp212–13 ❷
Victoria and Albert Museum pp202–5 ❸

Serpentine Gallery ❾

Parks and Gardens
Kensington Gardens ⓫
Hyde Park ⓬

Monuments
Albert Memorial ❽
Marble Arch ⓮

Concert Halls
Royal Albert Hall ❻

Shops
Harrods ⓯

Statue of Peter Pan in Kensington Gardens

GETTING THERE
South Kensington tube station is on the Piccadilly, Circle, and District lines; only the Piccadilly line passes through Knightsbridge station. The No. 14 bus runs from Piccadilly Circus to South Kensington, via Green Park and Knightsbridge.

SEE ALSO
• *Street Finder*, maps 10, 11, 19
• *Where to Stay* pp278–91
• *Restaurants, Pubs* pp292–319

KEY
▨ Street by Street map
⊖ Underground station

◁ The Albert Memorial, opposite the Royal Albert Hall

Street-by-Street: South Kensington

A clutch of museums and colleges
provide this area with its dignified
character. The Great Exhibition of 1851
in Hyde Park was so successful that in
the following years smaller exhibitions
were held here, just to its south. By the
end of the 19th century some of these
had become permanent museums,
housed in grandiose buildings
celebrating Victorian self-confidence.

Royal College of Art
*David Hockney and Peter
Blake are among the great
artists who trained here* ❼

**The Royal College
of Organists** was
decorated by F W
Moody in 1876.

★ Royal Albert Hall
*Opened in 1870, the Hall
was partly funded
by selling seats on
a 999-year
lease* ❻

Royal College of Music
*Historic musical instruments, like this
harpsichord (1531), are
exhibited here* ❺

**★ Natural
History Museum**
*The dinosaur exhibits
are one of the museum's
most popular attractions* ❶

**★ Science
Museum**
*Visitors here can
experiment with
the interactive
displays* ❷

The Albert Hall Mansions, built by Norman Shaw in 1879, started a fashion for red brick.

Albert Memorial
This memorial was built to commemorate Queen Victoria's consort **8**

LOCATOR MAP
See Central London Map pp14–15

KEY

– – – Suggested route

0 metres	100
0 yards	100

The Royal Geographical Society was founded in 1830. Scottish missionary and explorer David Livingstone (1813–73) was a member.

Imperial College, part of London University, is one of the country's leading scientific institutions.

★ Victoria and Albert Museum
A range of objects and a stunning photo gallery illustrate the nation's history of design and decoration **3**

Brompton Oratory
The Oratory was built during the 19th-century Catholic revival **4**

Brompton Square, begun in 1821, established this as a fashionable residential area.

Holy Trinity church dates from the 19th century and is located in a calm backwater among cottages.

STAR SIGHTS

★ Victoria and Albert Museum

★ Natural History Museum

★ Science Museum

★ Royal Albert Hall

To Knightsbridge station

Victoria and Albert Museum ❽

The Glass Gallery

The Victoria and Albert Museum (the V&A) contains one of the world's widest collections of art and design, ranging from early Christian devotional objects to cutting-edge furniture design. Originally founded in 1852 as the Museum of Manufactures to inspire design students, it was renamed by Queen Victoria in 1899 in memory of Prince Albert. The museum is undergoing a dramatic redisplay of some of its collection, including work on a number of galleries and the Sackler Education Centre. To find out if a particular gallery is open, call the bookings office on 020-7942 2211.

British Galleries (1760–1900)
This charming sweet box (1770) is one of many pieces on display that were crafted in the workshops of Britain.

Silver Galleries
Radiant pieces such as the Burgess Cup (Britain, 1863) fill these stunning galleries.

★ British Galleries (1500–1760)
Displays of evocative objects, such as this writing desk from King Henry VIII's court, illustrate Britain's fascinating history.

★ Fashion Gallery
In this gallery, European clothing from the mid-1500s to the present day is displayed, such as these famous Manolo Blahnik shoes.

Exhibition Road entrance

KEY TO FLOORPLAN

▨	Level 0
☐	Level 1
☐	Level 2
▨	Level 3
☐	Level 4
▨	Level 6
▨	Henry Cole Wing
☐	Non-exhibition space

GALLERY GUIDE
The V&A has a 7-mile (11-km) layout spread over six levels, and the museum incorporates approximately 150 different galleries. The main floor, level 1, houses the China, Japan and South Asia Galleries, as well as the Fashion Gallery and the Cast Courts. The British Galleries are on levels 2 and 4. Level 3 contains the 20th Century Galleries and displays of silver, ironwork, paintings and works of 20th-century design. The glass display is also on level 4. The Ceramics Galleries are on level 6. The Henry Cole Wing houses the Sackler Education Centre, RIBA Architecture Study Rooms and the Prints and Drawings Study Rooms.

★ Architecture Gallery
This features highlights from the world-class collection of drawings, models, photographs and architectural fragments from the V&A and RIBA collections.

VISITORS' CHECKLIST

Cromwell Rd SW7. **Map** 19 A1.
Tel 020-7942 2000.
South Kensington.
14, 74, 414, C1.
Open 10am–5.45pm daily
(10am–10pm Fri).
Closed 24–26 Dec.
Lectures, presentations,
tours, exhibitions, events.
www.vam.ac.uk

★ Medieval and Renaissance Galleries
The stunning Burghley Nef (France, 1527) is one of the many treasures in rooms 62–64.

China Gallery
This magnificent ancestor portrait is among the many exquisite pieces on show in this gallery.

Islamic Middle East Gallery
On display are fantastic objects representing the finest in Islamic art and design, such as this 16th-century table from the Ottoman Empire.

Aston Webb's façade (1909) is decorated with 32 sculptures of English craftsmen and designers.

Main entrance

STAR EXHIBITS

★ British Galleries

★ Fashion Gallery

★ Architecture Gallery

★ Medieval and
Renaissance Galleries

Exploring the V&A's Collections

The sheer size of the V&A means you should plan your visit carefully to avoid missing a highlight or an area of particular interest. One of the joys of the V&A, however, is stumbling across unexpected treasures. Be sure to visit the museum's original refreshment rooms off rooms 11 and 16a (one of which was designed by the then unknown William Morris), now being used once again for their original purpose as a café. The Photography gallery (room 38a) displays a changing selection of 300,000 photographs from 1856 to the present.

BRITISH GALLERIES

A sequence of grand rooms starting on level 2 and continuing on level 4 are devoted to the luxurious British Galleries. By presenting design and decorative arts from 1500 to 1900, the galleries chart Britain's rise from obscure island to "workshop of the world". The galleries present the evolution of British high design and the numerous influences, whether technological or aesthetic, absorbed from all over the world.

Beautiful textiles, furniture, costumes and household objects illustrate the tastes and lifestyles of Britain's ruling classes. Among the highlights are James II's wedding suit, the opulent State Bed from Melville House, and a number of carefully preserved period rooms, including the stunning Rococo Norfolk House Music Room. Discovery Areas give visitors

Embroidered jacket (1610) in room 56

a chance to delve even deeper into the past by sporting a Tudor ruff or viewing 3-D images through a Victorian stereoscope.

CHINA, JAPAN AND SOUTH ASIA

The Jameel Gallery of Islamic Art was opened in July 2006 and houses a significant collection of more than 400 objects including ceramics, textiles, carpets, metalwork, glass and woodwork. The exhibits date from the great days of the Islamic caliphate of the 8th and 9th centuries through to the years preceding the First World War.

Middle Eastern art from Syria, Iraq, Iran, Turkey and Egypt is found in room 42. Beautifully crafted textiles and ceramics illustrate the Islamic influence on fine and decorative arts. A dramatic arc of burnished steel fins, representing the spine of a Chinese dragon, spans

the China gallery (room 44). Covering the millennia from 3000 BC to the present, the impressive collection includes a giant Buddha's head from 700–900 AD, a huge yet elegant Ming canopied bed, and rare jade and ceramics.

Japanese art is concentrated in the Japan gallery in room 45, and is particularly notable for lacquer, Samurai armour and woodblock prints.

Gilt copper ice chest (Qing Dynasty 1700s), room 44

ARCHITECTURE GALLERY

The Architecture Gallery features highlights from the world-class collections of drawings, models, photographs and architectural fragments of the V&A and the Royal Institute of British Architects (RIBA).

The gallery explores the architecture that shapes our world through five themes. "The Art of Architecture" explores the history and ideas behind architectural styles. A superb collection of artifacts and illustrations is on display, grouped by period and spanning world cultures, including Asian, Spanish Islamic, Classical, Gothic and Modernist.

THE GREAT BED OF WARE

Made in about 1590 of oak with inlaid and painted decoration, the Great Bed of Ware measures some 3.6 by 3.6 m (12 by 12 ft) and is 2.6 m (8 ft 9 inches) high. It is the V&A's most celebrated piece of furniture. Elaborately carved and decorated, the bed is a superb example of the art of the English woodworker. Its name derives from the town of Ware in Hertfordshire, about a day's ride north of London, where it resided in a number of inns. The Great Bed's enormous size made it an early tourist attraction, and no doubt interest was boosted by Shakespeare's reference to it in *Twelfth Night*, which he wrote in 1601.

Recently redecorated and refurbished, the bed is located in room 57.

Detail of the Ardabil Carpet (c. 1539–40) from the Jameel Gallery of Islamic Art

"The Function of Buildings" looks at the way in which the design of a building is informed not only by its function but also by the demands of climate.

"Architects and Architecture" examines the team effort involved in designing a building, and how this has evolved over the centuries. A huge range of sketches, models and drawings used by architects supports the theme.

"Structures" examines the different structures needed to create different buildings, from chunky low-rise to tall buildings.

"Buildings in Context" takes a look at the construction of London's Trafalgar Square, from the original maps in 1730 to the present day, in order to explore the relation-ship that exists between a building and its surroundings.

TWENTIETH CENTURY

Since its foundation in 1852, the V&A has collected examples of contemporary art and design. Two galleries show works exclusively from the 20th century. Art and design are in rooms 70 to 74, and a 20th-century study gallery in rooms 103 to 106 shows the development of furniture design, as well as ceramics, glass, metalwork and radios. Displays include objects by C R Mackintosh, Charles and Ray Eames and Marcel Breuer.

TEXTILES AND FASHION

Covering 400 years of high fashion, the Fashion gallery in room 40 includes 18th-century courtly dress and 20th-century couturiers, such as Christian Dior and Alexander McQueen. Four huge medieval tapestries, among the museum's greatest treasures, dominate room 94 on level 3. Striking in their detail and depiction of courtly pastimes, they are known as the Devonshire Hunts, despite being made in Flanders. The extensive collection of textiles continues in rooms 95 to 101. The museum's collection of Asian and Middle Eastern carpets is justifiably renowned.

Ruby glass flagon (c. 1858–9)

METALWORK

This group of galleries is located on level 3. In the Silver Galleries, 3500 pieces from 1400 to the present day are displayed in the beautifully refurbished Victorian rooms 65 to 69. Arms and armour, European metalwork from the 1500s to the present, and Islamic brass and bronze can be found in rooms 81, 82 and 87 to 89.

The Sacred Silver and Stained Glass galleries in rooms 83 and 84 display devotional treasures. The highlight of the ironwork

galleries, which are located in rooms 113 to 114e, is the dazzling Hereford Screen designed by Sir George Gilbert Scott in 1862, and displayed at the International Exhibition of that year. The screen became the V&A's largest conservation project.

The Gilbert Collection of gold, silver, micromosaics and gold boxes, formerly housed at Somerset House, re-opened here in 2009.

GLASS AND CERAMICS

Examples of 2,000 years of glass are exhibited across galleries on level 4. These contain superb porcelain from European china factories, a stunning balustrade by glass artist Danny Lane in room 131. Displays of international contemporary glass are on display in this room as well as in room 129.

The museum holds the world's largest and most comprehensive collection of ceramics. The introductory gallery presents the history and development of ceramics across the world.

Stained glass roundel entitled Susanna and the Elders (c. 1520)

Natural History Museum ❶

See pp208–9.

Relief: Natural History Museum

Science Museum ❷

See pp212–13.

Victoria and Albert Museum ❸

See pp202–205.

Brompton Oratory ❹

Brompton Rd SW7. **Map** 19 A1.
Tel 020-7808 0900. ⊖ South
Kensington. **Open** 6am–8pm daily.
🔔 11am Sun sung Latin Mass. ♿
🕘 www.bromptonoratory.com

The Italianate Oratory is a
rich (some think a little too
rich) monument to the
English Catholic revival of the
late 19th century. The Oratory
was established by John Henry
Newman (who later became
Cardinal Newman). Father
Frederick William Faber (1814–
63) had already founded a
London community of priests
at Charing Cross. The group
had moved to Brompton, then
an outlying London district,
and this was to be its oratory.
Newman and Faber (both
Anglican converts to
Catholicism) were following
the example of St Philip Neri,
who set up a community of
secular priests living without
vows and based in cities.

The present church was
opened in 1884. Its facade
and dome were added in the
1890s, and the interior has
been progressively enriched
ever since. Herbert Gribble,
the architect, who was yet
another Catholic convert,
was only 29 when he
triumphed in the
highly prestigious
competition to design
it. Inside, all the most
eye-catching treasures
predate the church –
many of them were
transported here
from Italian churches.
Giuseppe Mazzuoli
carved the huge
marble figures of the 12
apostles for Siena
Cathedral in the
late 17th century.
The beautiful Lady
Altar was originally created in
1693 for the Dominican
church in Brescia, and the
18th-century altar in St

Wilfrid's Chapel was actually
imported from a church in
Rochefort, Belgium.

The Oratory has always
been famous for its splendid
musical tradition.

Royal College of Music ❺

Prince Consort Rd SW7. **Map** 10 F5.
Tel 020-7589 3643. ⊖ Knightsbridge, South Kensington. **Museum
of Instruments Tel** 020-7591
4346. **Open** 11:30am–4:30pm
Tue–Fri in term-time or by appointment. **Adm charge**. ♿ limited.
🕘 📷 www.rcm.ac.uk

Sir Arthur Blomfield
designed the turreted Gothic
palace, with Bavarian
overtones, that has housed
this distinguished institution
since 1894. The college was
founded in 1882 by
George Grove, who
also compiled the
famous *Dictionary
of Music*; pupils have
included English
composers Benjamin
Britten and Ralph
Vaughan Williams.
The Museum of
Musical Instruments
has limited opening
hours; if you do
manage to get
inside, you will see
instruments from
the earliest times

**17th-century viol at the
Royal College of Music**

and from many parts of the
world. Some of the exhibits
were played by such greats
as Handel and Haydn.

The sumptuous interior of Brompton Oratory

Joseph Durham's statue of Prince Albert (1858) by the Royal Albert Hall

Royal Albert Hall 6

Kensington Gore SW7. **Map** 10 F5. **Tel** 020-7589 8212. ⊖ High St Kensington, South Kensington. **Open** for performances. 🔲 🎫 Six tours daily Thu–Tue, call 020-7838 3105. ♿ 🍴 💻 See **Entertainment** pp348–9. **www**.royalalberthall.com

Designed by an engineer, Francis Fowke, and completed in 1871, this huge concert hall was modelled on Roman amphitheatres and is easier on the eye than most Victorian structures. On the red-brick exterior the only ostentation is a pretty frieze symbolizing the triumph of arts and science. In plans the building was called the Hall of Arts and Science but Queen Victoria changed it to the Royal Albert Hall, in memory of her husband, when she laid the foundation stone in 1868.

The hall is often used for Classical concerts, most famously the "Proms", but it also accommodates other large gatherings, such as tennis matches, comedy shows, rock concerts, circus shows and major business conferences.

Royal College of Art 7

Kensington Gore SW7. **Map** 10 F5. **Tel** 020-7590 4444. ⊖ High St Kensington, South Kensington. **Open** 10am–6pm Mon–Fri (phone first). ♿ 💻 🎫 **Lectures, events, film presentations, exhibitions. www**.rca.ac.uk

Sir Hugh Casson's mainly glass-fronted building (1962) is in stark contrast to the Victoriana around it. The college was founded in 1837 as a school of design and practical art for the manufacturing industries. It became noted for modern art in the 1950s and 1960s when David Hockney, Peter Blake and Eduardo Paolozzi were there.

Albert Memorial 8

South Carriage Drive, Kensington Gdns SW7. **Map** 10 F5. ⊖ High St Kensington, South Kensington.

This grandiose but dignified memorial to Queen Victoria's beloved consort was completed in 1876, 15 years after his death. Albert was a German prince and a cousin of Queen Victoria's. When he died from typhoid in 1861 he was only 41 and they had been happily married for 21 years, producing nine children. It is fitting that the monument is near the site of the 1851 Exhibition (see pp28–9), for Prince Albert was closely identified with the Exhibition itself and with the scientific advances it celebrated. The larger than life statue, by John Foley, shows him with an exhibition catalogue on his knee.

The desolate Queen chose Sir George Gilbert Scott to design the monument which stands 55 m (175 ft) high. It is loosely based on a medieval market cross – although many times more elaborate, with a black and gilded spire, multicoloured marble canopy, stones, mosaics, enamels, wrought iron and nearly 200 sculpted figures. In October 1998 the re-gilded statue was unveiled by Elizabeth II; it had not been gilded since 1915 when it was painted black to avoid attracting attention during World War I.

Victoria and Albert at the Great Exhibition opening (1851)

Natural History Museum ❶

Life on Earth and the Earth itself are vividly explained at the Natural History Museum. Combining the latest interactive techniques with traditional displays, the exhibits tackle fundamental issues, such as how human beings evolved and how we can safeguard our planet. The vast, cathedral-like museum building is a masterpiece in itself. It opened in 1881 and was designed by Alfred Waterhouse using revolutionary Victorian building techniques. It is built on an iron and steel framework concealed behind arches and columns, richly decorated with sculptures of plants and animals.

★ Mammals
The life-sized model of a blue whale dwarfs everything else in this vast gallery.

The **Darwin Centre** features an eight-storey cocoon in a glass atrium. It is home to 20 million insect and plant specimens and a research centre.

Ground floor

★ Dinosaurs
T Rex, one of the museum's impressively life-like animatronic models, lurches and roars in this hugely popular gallery. More traditional exhibits of fossilized skeletons and eggs are also on display.

GALLERY GUIDE
The museum is divided into four sections, the Blue Zone, the Green Zone, the Red Zone and the Orange Zone.

A 26-m (85-ft) skeleton of the dinosaur Diplodocus dominates the central hall in the Blue Zone – Human Biology, together with Mammals and Dinosaurs, are to the left of the hall, while Creepy Crawlies and Ecology are to the right. On the first floor are found Our Place in Evolution and The Vault.

The giant escalator in Visions of Earth leads through a stunning globe to Red Zone highlights The Power Within and Earth's Treasury.

Cromwell Road entrance

Access to basement

Creepy Crawlies
Eight out of ten animal species are arthropods – insects, crustaceans, centipedes and spiders, like this tarantula.

KEY TO FLOORPLAN
- Blue Zone
- Green Zone
- Red Zone
- Orange Zone

The Vault

The Vault contains a dazzling collection of the finest gems, crystals, meteorites and metals from around the world, such as this Latrobe gold nugget.

VISITORS' CHECKLIST

Cromwell Rd SW7. **Map** 19 A1.
Tel 020-7942 5000.
South Kensington. 14,
44, 70, 74, 345, 360, 449, C1.
Open 10am–5:50pm daily (to
10:30pm last Fri of month) – last
admission 5:30pm. **Closed** 24–
26 Dec.
**Lectures, workshops for
adults and children, film
presentations.**
www.nhm.ac.uk

The Power Within gallery's convincing earthquake simulator is hugely popular.

Second floor

Second floor Red Zone

The Earth's Treasury gallery glitters with thousands of gems, rocks and minerals, including some of the Earth's rarest products.

First floor Red Zone

First floor

Access to Red Zone

★ Visions of Earth

Specimens are recessed into the etched slate walls of this beautiful gallery. Access to the rest of the Red Zone is via an escalator that runs through a massive model of the Earth.

Exhibition Road entrance – Earth Galleries

Birds

This traditional display, with many species in Victorian glass cases, includes a model of the legendary dodo. A flightless bird from Mauritius, it was extinct by the mid-1600s.

STAR EXHIBITS

★ Dinosaurs

★ Mammals

★ Visions of Earth

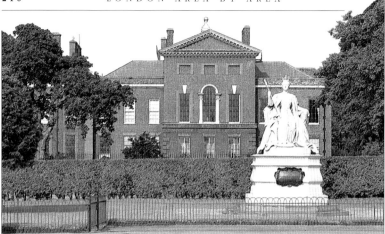

Statue of young Queen Victoria by her daughter Princess Louise outside Kensington Palace

Serpentine Gallery ❾

Kensington Gdns W2. **Map** 11 A4.
Tel 020-7402 6075. 🚇 Lancaster
Gate, South Kensington. **Open**
10am–6pm daily. **Closed** 1 Jan,
24–26, 31 Dec & between
exhibitions. **Lectures**. 🔊 📄
summer only. 🛍 art bookshop.
www.serpentinegallery.org

The Serpentine Gallery
houses temporary exhibitions
of major contemporary artists'
work. Past exhibitors include
Gilbert & George, Rachel
Whiteread and Felix Gonzal-
ez-Torres. This exciting gallery transforms its space to
suit the exhibits, sometimes
spilling out into the park.
Every summer, a temporary
pavilion is commissioned
from a major architect; this is
where you will find the café.

Kensington Palace ❿

Kensington Palace Gdns W8. **Map** 10
D4. **Tel** 0844-482 7777. 🚇 High St
Kensington, Queensway, Notting Hill
Gate. **Open** Mar–Oct: 10am–6pm
daily; Nov–Feb: 10am–5pm daily (last
adm: 1 hr earlier). **Closed** 24–26 Dec.
Adm charge. 🔊 📄 🛍 ♿
ground floor only. **Exhibitions**.
www.hrp.org.uk

Half of this spacious palace
is used as royal apartments;
the other half, which includes
the 18th- century state rooms,
is open to the public. When
William III and his wife Mary

came to the throne in 1689
they bought a mansion, dating from 1605, and commissioned Christopher Wren to
convert it into a royal palace.
He created separate suites of
rooms for the king and queen.
   Highlights include the
finely decorated state rooms.
There are no labels in these
rooms, but the free audio
guide evokes the atmosphere
of 17th- and 18th-century
court life that was once conducted here. There is also an
exhibition of court dress and
a permanent display of Princess Diana's dresses. Many of
the dresses were made
specially for her and show the
design skills and craftsman-
ship of leading British designers, such as Catherine Walker
and Bruce Oldfield.
   The palace has seen some
important royal events. In 1714
Queen Anne died here from a
fit of apoplexy brought on by
over-eating and, on 20 June
1837, Princess Victoria of
Kent was woken at 5am to
be told that her uncle
William IV had died and
she was now queen – the
start of her 64-year
reign. After the death in
1997 of Diana, Prin-
cess of Wales, the
gold gates south of
the palace became
a focal point for
mourners in their
thousands, who
turned the sur-
rounding area
into a field of
bouquets.

Kensington Gardens ⓫

W8. **Map** 10 E4. **Tel** 020-7298
2141. 🚇 Bayswater, High St
Kensington, Queensway, Lancaster
Gate. **Open** dawn–dusk daily. 📄
www.royalparks.gov.uk

The former grounds of
Kensington Palace became a
public park in 1841. A small
part of it has been dedicated
as a memorial playground to
Diana, Princess of Wales (see
p219). The gardens are full of
charm, starting with Sir George
Frampton's statue (1912) of
J M Barrie's fictional Peter Pan,
the boy who never grew up,
playing his pipes to the bronze
fairies and animals that cling
to the column below. Often
surrounded by parents, nannies
and their charges, the statue
stands near the west bank of
the Serpentine, not far from
where Harriet, wife of the
poet Percy Bysshe Shelley,
drowned herself in 1816.
   Just north of here (in Hyde
Park) are the ornamental
fountains and statues,
including Jacob Epstein's
Rima, at the lake's head.
George Frederick
Watts's statue of a
muscular horse and
rider, *Physical Energy*,
stands to the south.
Not far away is a
summer house
designed by
William Kent
in 1735, and
the Serpentine
Gallery.

**Detail of the Coalbrookdale gate,
Kensington Gardens**

The Round Pond, created in 1728 just east of the palace, is often packed with model boats navigated by children and older enthusiasts. In winter it is occasionally fit for skating. In the north, near Lancaster Gate, is a dogs' cemetery, started in 1880 by the Duke of Cambridge while mourning one of his pets.

Hyde Park ⓬

W2. **Map** 11 B3. **Tel** 020-7298 2100. ⊖ Hyde Park Corner, Knightsbridge, Lancaster Gate, Marble Arch. **Open** 5am–midnight daily. 🔲 **Sporting facilities**. www.royalparks.org.uk

Riding on Rotten Row, Hyde Park

The ancient manor of Hyde was part of the lands of Westminster Abbey seized by Henry VIII at the Dissolution of the Monasteries in 1536. It has remained a royal park ever since. Henry used it for hunting but James I opened it to the public in the early 17th century, and it became one of the city's most prized public spaces. The Serpentine, an artificial lake used for boating and bathing, was created when Caroline, George II's queen, dammed the flow of the Westbourne River in 1730.

In its time the park has been a venue for duelling, horse racing, highwaymen, demon-strations, music and parades. The 1851 Exhibition was held here in a vast glass palace *(see pp28–9)*. The aristocracy drove their carriages on the outer roads. The Princess Diana Memorial fountain is to the south of the Serpentine.

Speakers' Corner ⓭

Hyde Park W2. **Map** 11 C2. ⊖ Marble Arch.

An 1872 law made it legal to assemble an audience and address them on whatever topic you chose; since then this corner of Hyde Park has become the established venue for budding orators and a fair number of eccentrics. It is well worth spending time here on a Sunday: speakers from fringe groups and one-member political parties reveal their plans for the betterment of mankind while the assembled onlookers heckle them without mercy.

Marble Arch ⓮

Park Lane W1. **Map** 11 C2. ⊖ Marble Arch.

John Nash designed the arch in 1827 as the main entrance to Buckingham Palace. It was, however, too narrow for the grandest coaches and was moved here in 1851. Now, only senior members of the Royal Family and one of the royal artillery regiments are allowed to pass under it.

The arch stands near the site of the old Tyburn gallows (marked by a plaque), where until 1783 the city's most notorious criminals were hanged in front of crowds of bloodthirsty spectators.

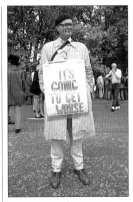

An orator at Speakers' Corner

Harrods ⓯

Knightsbridge SW1. **Map** 11 C5. **Tel** 020-7730 1234. ⊖ Knightsbridge. **Open** 10am–8pm Mon–Sat, noon–6pm Sun. 🔲 🍴 🔲 ♿ See **Shops and Markets** p321. www.harrods.com

London's most famous department store began in 1849 when Henry Charles Harrod opened a small grocery shop nearby on Brompton Road. By concentrating on good quality and impeccable service (rather than on low prices) the store was soon popular enough to expand over the surrounding area.

It used to be claimed that Harrods could supply anything from a packet of pins to an elephant – not quite true today, but the range of stock is still phenomenal.

Harrods at night, lit by 11,500 lights

Science Museum ❷

Centuries of continuing scientific and technological development lie at the heart of the
Science Museum's massive collections. The
hardware displayed is magnificent: from
steam engines to aeroengines; spacecraft
to the first mechanical computers. Equally
important is the social context of science
– what discoveries and inventions mean
for day-to-day life – and the process of
discovery itself. The high-tech Wellcome
Wing has interactive displays, an IMAX
Cinema, a SimEx simulator and galleries
devoted to new advances in science.

**★ Science and Art
of Medicine**
*A 17th-century
Italian vase for
storing snake bite
treatment is part
of this interesting
collection.*

**Science in the
18th Century**
*The original orrery, a
mechanical model of
the solar system, is one
of many beautiful
scientific instruments
in this gallery.*

Computing
Babbage's Difference
Engine No. 1 (1832), the
first automatic calculator
and a magnificent example
of precision engineering, is
a highlight of this gallery.

**Energy: Fuelling
the Future** is a new
gallery that explores
how energy powers
every aspect of
our lives.

Challenge of Materials
*Our expectations of materials
are confounded with
exhibits such as a bridge
made of glass and this
steel wedding dress.*

Stairs to
lower level

KEY TO FLOORPLAN

▦	Basement
☐	Ground floor
☐	First floor
▦	Second floor
▦	Third floor
☐	Fourth floor
☐	Fifth floor
☐	Wellcome Wing

★ The Energy Hall
*Dedicated to steam power, this gallery
includes the still-operational Harle
Syke Mill Engine (1903).*

Main entrance

★ Flight
This gallery is packed with early flying contraptions, fighter planes and aeroengines, many of them suspended as if in mid-flight.

VISITORS' CHECKLIST

Exhibition Rd SW7. **Map** 19 A1.
Tel 0870-870 4868. South
Kensington. 9, 10, 14, 49, 52,
74, 345, 350, 414, C1. **Open**
10am–6pm daily. **Closed** 24–26
Dec. **Adm charge** for some
exhibitions & IMAX cinema.
Lectures, films, workshops.
www.sciencemuseum.org.uk

Marine Engineering
The display of navigational equipment includes this ornately decorated circumferentor (1676) by the architect Joannes Macarius.

★ Wellcome Wing
The highlight of the Wellcome Wing is the "Who Am I?" exhibition, where interactive games allow visitors to explore the science of what it is to be human.

Escalator to
Imax Cinema

★ Making the Modern World
Apollo 10 took US astronauts around the moon in May 1969, and now forms part of this stunning gallery of museum highlights.

The hands-on galleries,
including The Garden, prove
very popular with children.

GALLERY GUIDE
The Science Museum is spread over seven floors, balconies and mezzanine levels. The Wellcome Wing, offering four floors of interactive technology, is at the west end of the museum and is accessible from the ground floor and third floor of the main building. Power dominates the ground floor; here too are Exploring Space and Making the Modern World. The first floor has the Challenge of Materials gallery as well as Weather and Agriculture. On the second floor is a range of such diverse galleries as shipping, mathematics and computing. The third floor includes Flight, Health Matters and Launchpad. The fourth and fifth floors (accessible by only one of the lifts) house the medical history galleries.

STAR EXHIBITS

★ Flight

★ Science and Art
of Medicine

★ Making the
Modern World

★ The Energy
Hall

★ Wellcome Wing

KENSINGTON AND HOLLAND PARK

The western and northern-perimeters of Kensington Gardens are a rich residential area and include many foreign embassies. The shops on Kensington High Street are almost as smart as those in Knightsbridge, and Kensington Church Street is a good source of quality antiques. Around Holland Park are some magnificent late Victorian houses, two of them open to the public. But as you cross into Bayswater and Notting Hill you enter a more vibrant, cosmopolitan part of London. Its stucco terraces are lined with medium-priced hotels and inexpensive restaurants. Westbourne Grove has become increasingly popular with the young, designer-clad

Tiled crest from Holland House

crowd. Whiteleys, in Queensway, is one of the many historic buildings in the area. Built in 1912 by Belcher and Joass as a fashionable department store, it was converted in the 1980s into a vibrant shopping centre. To the west, Portobello Road is a popular street market selling anything from food to antiques. Notting Hill is known for its flamboyant Caribbean carnival, which took to the streets in 1965 and has been staged every year since, on the last weekend in August *(see p57)*.

SIGHTS AT A GLANCE

Historic Streets and Buildings
Holland House **2**
Leighton House **3**
Linley Sambourne House **4**
Kensington Square **6**
Kensington Palace Gardens **7**
Queensway **9**

Parks and Gardens
Holland Park **1**
Kensington Roof Gardens **5**
The Diana, Princess of Wales Memorial Playground **8**

Markets
Portobello Road **10**

Historic Areas
Notting Hill **11**

GETTING THERE

The District, Circle and Central lines serve the area. Bus numbers C1, 9, 10, 27, 28, 31, 49, 52, 70, 73 stop on Kensington High Street; 12, 27, 28, 31, 52, 70, 94 go to Notting Hill Gate; and 7, 12, 15, 23, 27, 36, 70, 94 cross Bayswater.

KEY

▨	Street-by-Street map
Ⓔ	Underground station

0 metres 500
0 yards 500

SEE ALSO

• *Street Finder,* maps 9, 17

• *Where to Stay* pp278–91

• *Restaurants, Pubs* pp292–319

◁ **Entrance to a house in Edwardes Square, Kensington**

Street-by-Street: Kensington and Holland Park

Although now part of central London, as recently as the 1830s this was a country village of market gardens and mansions. Outstanding among these was Holland House; part of its grounds are now Holland Park. The area grew up rapidly in the mid-19th century and most of its buildings date from then – mainly expensive apartments, mansion flats and fashionable shops.

Holland House
The rambling Jacobean mansion, started in 1605 and pictured here in 1795, was largely demolished in the 1950s ❷

★ Holland Park
Parts of the old formal gardens of Holland House have been retained to grace this delightful public park ❶

The Orangery, now a restaurant has parts that date from the 1630s when it was within the grounds of Holland House.

Melbury Road is lined with large, Victorian houses. Many were built for fashionable artists of the time.

The Victorian letter box on the High Street is one of the oldest in London.

★ Leighton House
It is preserved as it was when the Victorian painter, Lord Leighton, lived here. He had a passion for Middle Eastern tiles ❸

PHILLI

ILCHESTER PLACE

MELBURY ROAD

EDWARDES SQUARE

No. 16 Phillimore Place was home to the author of the children's classic *The Wind in the Willows*, from 1901 until 1908.

KENNETH GRAHAME 1859-1932 Author of "THE WIND IN THE WILLOWS" lived here 1901-8

Church Walk leads to Church Street, which is lined with antique shops *(see p331)*.

LOCATOR MAP
See Central London Map pp14–15

Notting Hill

Shepherd's Bush

SOUTH KENSINGTON & KNIGHTSBRIDGE

KENSINGTON & HOLLAND PARK

West Kensington

Earl's Court

Kensington High Street station

Kensington Civic Centre, an assertive modern building by Sir Basil Spence, was completed in 1976.

Linley Sambourne House
Its carefully preserved late Victorian interior remains intact, complete with original furnishings and draperies ❹

Drayson Mews is one of the quaint alleys that were built behind large town houses for the stabling of horses and coaches. Today most have been converted into small houses.

Sticky Fingers, a lively café on the corner of Phillimore Gardens, is owned by Bill Wyman, former guitarist with the *Rolling Stones* rock group.

STAR SIGHTS

★ Holland Park

★ Leighton House

KEY

--- Suggested route

0 metres   100

0 yards   100

Holland Park ❶

Abbotsbury Rd W14. **Map** 9 B4.
Tel 020-7361 3003. ⊖ *Holland
Park, High St Kensington, Notting Hill
Gate.* **Open** *dawn–dusk daily (hours
are flexible depending on light).*
Closed *25 Dec.* 🚻 🎭 **Open-air
opera, theatre, dance.** **Tel** *020-
7602 7856.* **Art exhibitions** *Apr–Oct.*
See **Entertainment** *pp344–5.*

This small but delightful park,
more wooded and intimate
than the large royal parks to its
east (Hyde Park and
Kensington Gardens,
see pp206–7), was opened in
1952 on what remained of the
grounds of Holland House –
the rest had been sold off in
the late 19th century for the
construction of large houses
and terraces to the north and
west. The park still contains
some of the formal gardens,
laid out in the early 19th
century for Holland House.
There is also a Japanese
garden, created for the 1991
London Festival of Japan. The
park has an abundance of
wildlife, including peacocks.

Holland House ❷

Holland Park W8. **Map** 9 B5.
Youth Hostel Tel 020-7937 0748.
⊖ *Holland Park, High Street
Kensington.*

Original tiling in Holland House

During its heyday in the 19th
century, this was a noted
centre of social and political
intrigue. Statesmen such as
Lord Palmerston mixed here
with the likes of the poet
Byron. The remains of the
house are now used
as a youth hostel.
    The outhouses are put to
various uses: exhibitions
are held in the orangery and
the ice house (a forerunner of
the fridge), and the old Garden
Ballroom is now a restaurant.

The café in Holland Park

Leighton House ❸

12 Holland Park Rd W14. **Map** 17 B1.
Tel *020-7602 3316.* ⊖ *High St Kensington.* **Open** *11am–5:30pm Wed–
Mon.* **Closed** *1 Jan, 25 & 26 Dec.*
Adm charge 🎟 *2:30pm Wed–Thu
or by appt for groups.* 🎵 **Concerts,
exhibitions**. www.rbkc.gov.uk/
leightonhousemuseum

Built for respected Victorian
painter Lord Leighton in
1864–79, the house has been
preserved with its opulent
decoration as an extraordinary monument to Victorian
aesthetics. The highlight is the
Arab hall, added in 1879 to
house Leighton's collection of
Islamic tiles, some of which
are inscribed with pieces from
the Koran. The best paintings
include some by Edward
Burne-Jones, John Millais,
G F Watts and many works
by Leighton himself.

Linley Sambourne House ❹

18 Stafford Terrace W8. **Map** 9 C5.
Tel *020-7602 3316.* ⊖ *High St
Kensington.* **Open** *for guided tours
only, Mar–Jun: 11:15am, 1pm,
2:15pm, 3:30pm Sat & Sun; 11:15am,
2:15pm Wed; phone 020-7938 1295
to book.* **Adm charge**. 🎟 www.
rbkc.gov.uk/linleysambournehouse

The house, built in about
1870, has received a facelift,
but remains much as Linley
Sambourne decorated and
furnished it, in the Victorian
manner, with china ornaments
and heavy velvet drapes.
Sambourne was a cartoonist

for the satirical magazine
Punch and drawings cram
the walls. Some rooms have
William Morris wallpaper
(see p249).

Kensington Roof Gardens ❺

99 Kensington High Street W8
(entrance in Derry Street). **Map** 10 D5.
Tel *020-7937 7994.* **Open** *9am–5pm
daily (but call ahead, as sometimes
closed for private functions).* 🚻

A hundred feet above the
bustle of Kensington High
Street is one of London's best-
kept secrets – a 6,000 square-
metre roof garden. First
planted in the 1930s by the
owners of Derry and Toms
department store below (now
houses many different stores),
the themed gardens are a
lavish flight of fancy and

**Logo for *Punch* magazine
(1841–1992)**

feature a woodland garden, a Spanish garden (with palm trees) and a formal English garden (with a pond, live ducks and a pair of pink flamingos). Best of all, it's free to wander round, though there is no access when the gardens have been booked for events.

Kensington Square ❻

W8. **Map** 10 D5. ⊖ *High St Kensington.*

This is one of London's oldest squares. It was laid out in the 1680s, and a few early 18th-century houses still remain. (Nos. 11 and 12 are the oldest.) The renowned philosopher John Stuart Mill lived at No. 18, and the Pre-Raphaelite painter and illustrator Edward Burne-Jones at No.41.

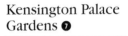

JOHN STUART MILL
1806-1873
Philosopher
Lived Here

Resident's plaque in Kensington Square

Kensington Palace Gardens ❼

W8. **Map** 10 D3. ⊖ *High St Kensington, Notting Hill Gate, Queensway.*

This private road of luxury mansions occupies the site of the former kitchen gardens of Kensington Palace *(see p210).* It changes its name half-way down; the southern part is known as Palace Green. It is open to pedestrians but closed to cars, unless they have specific business here. Most of the houses are occupied by embassies and their staff. At cocktail hour, you can watch black limousines with diplomatic number plates sweep beneath the raised barriers at each end of the road.

Queensway shop front

The Diana, Princess of Wales Memorial Playground ❽

Kensington Gardens. **Map** 10 E3. **Tel** 020-7298 2141. ⊖ *Bayswater, Queensway.* **Open** daily, Feb & Oct: 10am–4.45pm; Mar: 10am–5.45pm; Apr & Sep: 10am–6.45pm; May–Aug: 10am–7.45pm; Nov–Jan: 10am–3.45pm. **Closed** 25 Dec. 🖥 🚻

The newest of Kensington Gardens' three playgrounds was opened in 2000. Dedicated to the memory of the late Princess Diana, it is located close to the Bayswater Road, on the site of an earlier playground funded by Peter Pan's creator, J M Barrie. Diana's innovative adventure playground takes the boy who didn't want to grow up as its theme and is packed with novel ideas and activities including a beach cove with a 50-ft pirates' galleon, a tree house with walkways and ramps and a mermaid's fountain with a half-submerged slumbering crocodile (careful not to rouse him!). Though all children up to the age of 12 must be accompanied by an adult, staff are on hand to make sure the children are safe. Many features of the playground have been specially designed to be accessible to children with special needs.

Queensway ❾

W2. **Map** 10 D2. ⊖ *Queensway, Bayswater.*

One of London's most cosmopolitan streets, Queensway has the heaviest concentration of eating places outside Soho. Newsagents are abundantly stocked with foreign newspapers. At the northern end is Whiteley's shopping centre. Founded by William Whiteley, who was born in Yorkshire in 1863, it was probably the world's first department store. The present building dates from 1911.

The street is named after Queen Victoria, who rode here as a princess.

Portobello Road ❿

W11. **Map** 9 C3. ⊖ *Notting Hill Gate, Ladbroke Grove.* **Antiques market Open** 9:30am–4pm Fri, 8am–5pm Sat. *See also* **Shops and Markets** *p333.*

There has been a market here since 1837. These days the southern end consists almost exclusively of stalls that sell antiques, jewellery, souvenirs and many other collectables. The market is extremely popular with tourists and tends to be very crowded on summer weekends. However, it is well worth visiting just to experience its bustling and cheerful atmosphere even if you don't intend to buy anything. If you do decide to buy, be warned – you are unlikely to get a real bargain, since the stallholders have a sound idea of the value of what they are selling.

Antique shop on Portobello Road

Notting Hill ⓫

W11. **Map** 9 C3. ⊖ *Notting Hill Gate.*

Now the home of Europe's biggest street carnival, most of this area was farmland until the 19th century.

In the 1950s and 1960s Notting Hill became a centre for the Caribbean community, many of whom lived here when they first arrived in Britain. The carnival started in 1966 and takes over the area every August over the holiday weekend *(see p57)* when costumed parades flood through the streets.

REGENT'S PARK AND MARYLEBONE

The area south of Regent's Park, incorporating the medieval village of Marylebone, has London's highest concentration of quality Georgian housing. It was developed by Robert Harley, Earl of Oxford, as London shifted west in the 18th century. Terraces by John Nash adorn the southern edge of Regent's Park, the busiest of the Royal Parks, while to its northwest lies St John's Wood, a smart inner suburb.

GETTING THERE

Regent's Park and Baker Street are the nearest tube stations. Marylebone is served by tube and rail. Buses 13, 139 and 159 run from Trafalgar Square to near Baker Street, and numerous buses run along Oxford St, Baker St and Gloucester Pl.

| 0 metres | 500 |
| 0 yards | 500 |

SIGHTS AT A GLANCE

Historic Streets and Buildings
Harley Street **4**
Portland Place **5**
Broadcasting House **6**
Cumberland Terrace **15**

Museums and Galleries
Wallace Collection **10**
Sherlock Holmes Museum **11**

Churches and Mosques
St Marylebone Parish Church **3**
All Souls, Langham Place **7**
London Central Mosque **12**

Parks and Gardens
Regent's Park **2**

Entertainment
Madame Tussauds **1**
Wigmore Hall **9**
London Zoo **14**

Historic Hotels
Langham Hotel **8**

Historic Waterways
Regent's Canal **13**

SEE ALSO

- *Street Finder,* maps 3, 4, 12
- *Where to Stay* pp278–91
- *Restaurants, Pubs* pp292–319
- *Regent's Canal Walk* pp264–5

KEY

◻ Street-by-Street map

Ⓔ Underground station

◁ St Andrew's Place, Regent's Park

Street-by-Street: Marylebone

South of Regent's Park lies the medieval village of Marylebone (originally Maryburne, the stream by St Mary's church). Until the 18th century it was surrounded by fields, but these were built over as fashionable London drifted west. In the mid-19th century, professional people, especially doctors, used the spacious houses to receive wealthy clients.

Tiananmen Square memorial: Portland Place

The area has maintained its medical connection and its elegance. Marylebone High Street is full of interesting, high-quality food and clothes shops, bookshops and cafés.

★ Regent's Park
John Nash laid out the royal park in 1812 as a setting for classically designed villas and terraces ❷

The Royal Academy of Music, England's first music academy, was founded in 1774. The present brick building, with its own concert hall, is from 1911.

★ Madame Tussauds
The wax museum of famous people, historical and contemporary, has been in business since 1835 and remains one of London's most popular attractions. It moved to its present location in 1884 ❶

To Regent's Park

St Marylebone Parish Church
Poets Robert Browning and Elizabeth Barrett married in this church ❸

KEY

— — — Suggested route

0 metres   100

0 yards   100

Baker Street station

Park Crescent's breathtaking façades by Nash have been preserved, although the interiors were rebuilt as offices in the 1960s. The crescent seals the north end of Nash's ceremonial route from St James's to Regent's Park, via Regent Street and Portland Place.

LOCATOR MAP
See Central London Map pp14–15

The London Clinic is one of the best-known private hospitals in this medical district.

Regent's Park station

Portland Place
In the centre of this broad street stands a statue of Field Marshal Sir George Stuart White, who won the Victoria Cross for gallantry in the Afghan War of 1879 **5**

The Royal Institute of British Architects is housed in a striking Art Deco building designed by Grey Wornum in 1934.

Harley Street
Consulting rooms of eminent medical specialists have been here for more than a century **4**

STAR SIGHTS

★ Madame Tussauds

★ Regent's Park

Madame Tussauds ➊

Marylebone Rd NW1. **Map** 4 D5.
🎫 0870-400 3000. 🚇 Baker St.
Open 9.30am–5.30pm Mon–Fri,
9am–6pm Sat & Sun. **Closed** 25 Dec.
Adm charge. 📷 🖥 🚻 ♿ phone
first. **www**.madametussauds.co.uk

Madame Tussaud began her
wax-modelling career rather
morbidly, taking death masks
of many of the best-known
victims of the French Revolution. In 1835 she set up an
exhibition of her work in
Baker Street, not far from the
collection's present site.

The collection still uses
traditional wax-modelling
techniques to recreate politicians, film and television
actors, rock stars and sporting
heroes.

The main sections of the
exhibition are "Blush", where
visitors get to feel what it is
like to be at a celebrity "A-
list" party; "Premiere Night",
devoted to the giants of the
entertainment world such as

**Traditional wax-modelling at
Madame Tussauds**

Marilyn Monroe and Charlie
Chaplin; and "World Leaders",
containing a collection of
statesmen and world leaders,
writers and artists. Where else
could Lenin, Martin Luther
King, Shakespeare and Kylie
Minogue all rub shoulders?

The "Chamber of Horrors"
is the most renowned part of
Madame Tussauds and
features an interactive area
called "Scream". It includes
recreations of the most gruesome episodes in the grim

catalogue of crime and
punishment: the murderer
Dr Crippen; Vlad the impaler;
and the chill gloom of an east
London Victorian street
during Jack the Ripper's time
in the late 19th century.

The "Spirit of London" is
the finale. Visitors travel in
stylized London taxi-cabs and
participate in momentous
events of the city, from the
Great Fire of 1666 to
1960s Swinging
London.

Ticket prices also
include entry to
temporary exhibi-
tions featuring
media icons of
the moment.
There are also
educational tours
designed for
groups and
schools – check
website for
further
information.

**Waxwork of
Elizabeth II**

Tulip time at Queen Mary's Gardens in Regent's Park

Regent's Park ➋

NW1. **Map** 3 C2. **Tel** 020-7486 7905.
🚇 Regent's Park, Baker St, Great
Portland St. **Open** 5am–dusk daily.
♿ 🖥 **Open air theatre** see
Entertainment pp344–5.
Zoo see p227. **Sports facilities.**
www.royalparks.org.uk

This area of land became
enclosed as a park in 1812.
John Nash designed the
scheme and originally envis-
aged a kind of garden suburb,

dotted with 56 villas in a
variety of Classical styles, with
a pleasure palace for the
Prince Regent. In the event
only eight villas – but no
palace – were built inside the
park (three survive round the
edge of the Inner Circle).

The boating lake, which has
many varieties of water birds,
is marvellously romantic,
especially when music drifts
across from the bandstand in
the distance. Queen Mary's
Gardens are a mass of

wonderful sights and smells
in summer, when visitors
can enjoy Shakespeare
productions at the **Open Air
Theatre** nearby.

Nash's master plan for the
park continues just beyond its
northeastern edge in Park
Village East and West. These
elegant stucco buildings date
from 1828.

The park is also renowned
for its excellent sports facilities.

St Marylebone Parish Church ➌

Marylebone Rd NW1. **Map** 4 D5. **Tel**
020-7935 7315. 🚇 Regent's Park.
Open phone to check. ♿ 🚹 11am
Sun. 🖥 **www**.stmarylebone.org.uk

This is where the poets
Robert Browning and
Elizabeth Barrett were
married in 1846 after eloping
from her strict family home
on nearby Wimpole Street.
The large, stately church by
Thomas Hardwick was
consecrated in 1817 after the
former church, where Lord
Byron was christened in 1778,

had become too small. Hardwick was determined that the same should not happen to his new church – so everything is on a grand scale.

Commemorative window in St Marylebone Parish Church

Harley Street ➍

W1. **Map** 4 E5. 🔵 *Regent's Park, Oxford Circus, Bond St, Great Portland St.*

The large houses on this late 18th-century street were popular with successful doctors and specialists in the middle of the 19th century when it was a rich residential area. The doctors' practices stayed and lend the street an air of hushed order, unusual in central London. There are very few private houses or apartments here now, but William Gladstone lived at No. 73 from 1876 to 1882.

Portland Place ➎

W1. **Map** 4 E5. 🔵 *Regent's Park, Oxford Circus.*

The Adam Brothers, Robert and James, laid this street out in 1773. Only a few of the original houses remain, the best being 27 to 47 on the west side, south of Devonshire Street. John Nash added the street to his processional route from Carlton House to Regent's Park and sealed its northern end with Park Crescent.

The building of the Royal Institute of British Architects (1934) at No. 66 is adorned with symbolic statues and reliefs. Its bronze front doors depict London's buildings and the River Thames.

Broadcasting House ➏

Portland Place W1. **Map** 12 E1. 🔵 *Oxford Circus.* **Open** *Sun for guided tours only. Pre-booking essential; call 0371-901 1227.* **Adm charge.** 🚻 *No children under 12.*

Broadcasting House was built in 1931 as a suitably modern Art Deco headquarters for the brand-new medium of broadcasting. Its front, curving with the street, is dominated by Eric Gill's stylized relief of Prospero and Ariel. As the invisible spirit of the air, Shakespeare's Ariel was considered an appropriate personification of broadcasting. The character appears in two other sculptures on the western frontage, and again over the eastern entrance in "Ariel Piping to Children". Leslie French, who was playing Ariel in the Old Vic's presentation of *The Tempest* at the time, acted as Gill's model for the reliefs.

Broadcasting House is now partly occupied by management, as some radio studios moved to west London in the 1990s. Fascinating tours of Broadcasting House (and also of BBC TV Centre in White City) are available. Each tour is unique, as the itinerary depends on programming and events of the day.

Relief on the Royal Institute of British Architects on Portland Place

All Souls, Langham Place ➐

Langham Place W1. **Map** 12 F1. **Tel** *020-7580 3522.* 🔵 *Oxford Circus.* **Open** *9.30am–6pm Mon–Fri; 9am–3pm, 5:30–8:30pm Sun.* ⛪ *9.30, 11.30am, 6.30pm Sun.* 🚻 *Sun.* www.allsouls.org

John Nash designed this church in 1824. Its quirky round frontage is best seen from Regent Street. When it was first built, the spire was ridiculed as it appeared too slender and flimsy.

The only Nash church in London, it had close links with the BBC, based opposite at Broadcasting House, and ten years ago used to double as a recording studio for the daily broadcast church service.

Langham Hotel ➑

1 Portland Place W1. **Map** 12 E1. **Tel** *020-7636 1000.* 🔵 *Oxford Circus. See* **Where to Stay** *p288.* www.langhamhotels.com

This was London's grandest hotel after opening in 1865. The writers Oscar Wilde and Mark Twain, and composer Antonin Dvořák were among its many distinguished guests. It was, for a time, used by the BBC as a record library and as a venue for recording shows. It has since been restored behind its original facade and 2007 saw the opening of Artesian, a chic new bar, as well as a new restaurant, The Landau.

All Souls, Langham Place (1824)

Wigmore Hall ❾

36 Wigmore St W1. **Map** 12 E1. **Tel** 020-7935 2141. 🚇 Bond St, Oxford Cir. ♿ 🍴 🍸 See **Entertainment** p349. **www**.wigmore-hall.org.uk

This appealing little concert hall for chamber music was designed by T E Collcutt, architect of the Savoy Hotel *(see p290)*, in 1900. At first it was called Bechstein Hall because it was attached to the Bechstein piano showroom: the area used to be the heart of London's piano trade. Opposite is the Art Nouveau emporium built in 1907 as Debenham and Freebody's department store – now Debenham's on Oxford Street.

Wallace Collection ❿

Hertford House, Manchester Sq W1. **Map** 12 D1. 📞 020-7563 9500. 🚇 Bond St, Baker St. **Open** 10am– 5pm daily. **Closed** 24–26 Dec. **Lectures.** ♿ 🎥 🍴 🛗 **www**.wallacecollection.org

Late 18th-century Sèvres porcelain vase at the Wallace Collection

This is one of the world's finest private collections of art. It has remained intact since it was bequeathed to the government in 1897 with the stipulation that it should go on permanent public display with nothing added or taken away. The product of passionate collecting for four generations of the Hertford family, it is a

The Mosque on the edge of Regent's Park

must for anyone with even a passing interest in the progress of European art up to the late 19th century. In 2000 four more galleries were opened so that even more of the collection could be shown.

Among the 70 master works are Frans Hals's *The Laughing Cavalier*, Titian's *Perseus and Andromeda* and Rembrandt's *Titus*. There are superb portraits by Reynolds, Gainsborough and Romney. Other highlights include Sèvres porcelain and sculpture by Houdon and Roubiliac. The fine European and Oriental armour collection is the second largest in the UK.

Sherlock Holmes Museum ⓫

221b Baker St NW1. **Map** 3 C5. **Tel** 020-7224 3688. 🚇 Baker St. **Open** 9:30am–6pm daily. **Closed** 25 Dec. **Adm charge.** 🛗 **www**.sherlock-holmes.co.uk

Sir Arthur Conan Doyle's fictional detective lived at 221b Baker Street. This building, dating from 1815, has been converted to resemble Holmes's flat, and is furnished exactly as described in the books. Visitors are greeted by Holmes's "housekeeper" and shown to his recreated rooms on the first floor. The shop sells the novels and deerstalker hats.

London Central Mosque ⓬

146 Park Rd NW8. **Map** 3 B3. **Tel** 020-7725 2213. 🚇 Marylebone, St John's Wood, Baker St. **Open** dawn–dusk daily. ♿ 🛗 **Lectures.**

Surrounded by trees on the edge of Regent's Park, this large, golden-domed mosque was designed by Sir Frederick Gibberd and completed in 1978. Built to cater for the increasing number of Muslim residents and visitors in London, the mosque is capable of holding 1,800 worshippers. The main hall of worship is a plain square chamber with a domed roof and a magnificent carpet. Visitors must remove their shoes before entering the mosque, and women should remember to cover their heads.

Conan Doyle's Sherlock Holmes

Regent's Canal

NW1 & NW8. **Map** 3 C1. **Tel** 020-7482 2660 *(waterbus)*. 🚇 *Camden Town, St John's Wood, Warwick Ave.* **Canal towpaths open** *dawn–dusk daily. See* **Six Guided Walks** *pp264–5.*

A boat trip on Regent's Canal

John Nash was extremely enthusiastic about this waterway, opened in 1820 to link the Grand Junction Canal, which ended at Little Venice in Paddington in the west, with the London docks at Limehouse in the east. He saw it as an added attraction for his new Regent's Park, and originally wanted the canal to run through the middle of that park. He was persuaded out of that by those who thought that the bargees' bad language would offend the genteel residents of the area. Perhaps this was just as well – the steam tugs that hauled the barges were dirty and sometimes dangerous.

In 1874 a barge carrying gunpowder blew up in the cutting by London Zoo, killing the crew, destroying a bridge and terrifying the populace, and the animals. After an initial period of prosperity the canal began to be hit by increasing competition from the new railways and so gradually slipped into decline.

Today it has been revived as a leisure amenity; the towpath is paved as a pleasant walkway and short boat trips are offered between Little Venice and Camden Lock, where there is a thriving crafts market. Visitors to the zoo can use the landing stage that is situated alongside it.

London Zoo

Regent's Park NW1. **Map** 4 D2. ☎ 020-7722 3333. 🚇 *Camden Town.* **Open** *10am–5.30pm (4:30pm Nov–Mar) daily. Closed 25 Dec.* ♿ 🅿 📷 **Adm charge.** www.zsl.org

Opened in 1828, the zoo has been one of London's biggest tourist attractions ever since, and is also a major research and conservation centre. London Zoo has over 600 species of animal, from Sumatran tigers and sloth bears to Mexican red-kneed bird-eating spiders. Exhibits include the

London Zoo's aviary designed by Lord Snowdon (1964)

Web of Life which takes you through the vast range of life forms found in Earth's major habitats. There are also plenty of interactive activities.

Cumberland Terrace

NW1. **Map** 4 E2. 🚇 *Great Portland St, Regent's Park, Camden Town.*

James Thomson is credited with the detailed design of this, the longest and most elaborate of the Nash terraces around Regent's Park. Its imposing central block of raised Ionic columns is topped with a decorated triangular pediment. Completed in 1828, it was designed to be visible from the palace Nash planned for the Prince Regent (later George IV). The palace was never built because the Prince was too busy with his plans for Buckingham Palace *(see pp94–5).*

Nash's Cumberland Terrace, dating from 1828

HAMPSTEAD

ampstead has always stayed aloof from London, looking down from its site on the high ridge north of the metropolis. Today it is essentially a Georgian village. The heath separating Hampstead from Highgate reinforces its appeal, isolating it further from the hurly-burly of the modern city. A stroll around the charming village streets, followed by a tramp across the Heath, makes for one of the finest walks in London.

SIGHTS AT A GLANCE

Historic Streets and Buildings
Flask Walk and Well Walk ❶
Church Row ❺
Downshire Hill ❻
Vale of Health ❸

Museums and Galleries
Burgh House ❷
Fenton House ❹
Keats House ❼
Kenwood House ❿

Parks and Gardens
Hampstead Heath ❽
Parliament Hill ❾
The Hill Garden ❿

Pubs and Restaurants
Old Bull and Bush ❸
Spaniards Inn ⓫

GETTING THERE

Hampstead Underground station lies on the Edgware branch of the Northern line, and there is a rail service which stops at Hampstead Heath. Bus No. 24 operates a daily service from Victoria to Hampstead Heath, via Trafalgar Square and Tottenham Court Road.

SEE ALSO

• *Street Finder,* maps 1, 2

• *Where to Stay* pp278–91

• *Restaurants, Pubs* pp292–319

KEY

▨ Street-by-Street map

🚇 Underground station

◁ **View across Hampstead Heath towards Highgate**

Street-by-Street: Hampstead

Perched awkwardly on a hilltop, with its broad
heath to the north, Hampstead has kept its
villagey atmosphere and sense of being aloof from
urban pressures. This has attracted artists and
writers since Georgian times and made it one of
London's most desirable residential areas.
Its mansions and town houses are perfectly
maintained and a stroll through
Hampstead's narrow
streets is one of
London's quieter
pleasures.

Old Bull and Bush
*This pub on the edge of the Heath
was a former haunt for writers
and artists* ❸

★ **Hampstead Heath**
*A welcome retreat from the
city, its broad open spaces
include bathing ponds,
meadows and lakes* ❽

Whitestone Pond takes its
name from the old white
milestone nearby. It is 4.5
miles (7 km) from Holborn
(see pp132–41).

STAR SIGHTS

★ Burgh House

★ Hampstead Heath

★ Fenton House

★ Church Row

KEY

– – – Suggested route

0 metres   100

0 yards   100

Grove Lodge was home to
novelist John Galsworthy
(1867–1933), author of the
Forsyte Saga, for the last 15
years of his life.

Admiral's House dates from
about 1700. Built for a sea
captain, its name derives
from its external maritime
motifs. No admiral ever
actually lived in it.

★ **Fenton House**
*Summer visitors should seek
out this late 17th-century
house and its exquisite
walled garden, which are
well hidden in the jumble of
streets near the Heath* ❹

★ Burgh House
Built in 1702 but much altered since, the house contains an intriguing local history museum and a café overlooking the small garden ❷

LOCATOR MAP
See Central London Map pp14–15

The New End Theatre
produces rare but significant work. The building used to be a morgue.

No. 40 Well Walk is where artist John Constable lived while working on his many Hampstead pictures.

Flask Walk and Well Walk
An alley of charming specialist shops broadens into a residential village street ❶

Hampstead station

The Everyman Cinema has been an art cinema since 1933.

★ Church Row
The tall houses are rich in original detail. Notice the superb ironwork on what is probably London's finest Georgian street ❺

Old Bull and Bush in 1900

Flask Walk and Well Walk ❶

NW3. **Map** 1 B5. ⊖ *Hampstead.*

Flask Walk is named after the Flask pub. Here, in the 18th century, therapeutic spa water from what was then the separate village of Hampstead was put into flasks and sold to visitors or sent to London. The water, rich in iron salts, came from nearby Well Walk where a disused fountain now marks the site of the well. The Wells Tavern, almost opposite the spring, used to be a hostelry that specialized in accommodating those who engaged in the illicit liaisons for which the spa became notorious.

In later times, there have been many notable residents of Well Walk including artist John Constable (at No. 40), novelists D H Lawrence and J B Priestley and the poet John Keats, before he moved to his better-known house in what is now Keats Grove.

Site of the well on Well Walk

At the High Street end, Flask Walk is narrow and lined with old shops. Beyond the pub (note the Victorian tiled panels outside) it broadens into a row of Regency houses, one of which used to belong to the novelist Kingsley Amis.

Burgh House ❷

New End Sq NW3. **Map** 1 B4. *Tel* 020-7431 0144. ⊖ *Hampstead.* **Open** noon–5pm Wed–Sun (Sat by appt), 2–5pm public hols. **Closed** Christmas week. 🖼 ♿ 🍴 🎫 **Music recitals.** **www**.burghhouse.org.uk

The last private tenant of Burgh House was the son-in-law of the writer Rudyard Kipling, who visited here occasionally in the last years of his life until 1936. After a period under the ownership of Hampstead Borough Council, the house was let to the independent Burgh House Trust. Since 1979 the Trust has run it as the Hampstead Museum, which illustrates the history of the area and concentrates on some of its most celebrated residents.

One room is devoted to the life of John Constable, who painted an extraordinary series of studies of clouds from Hampstead Heath. The house also has sections on Lawrence, Keats, the artist Stanley Spencer and others who lived and worked in the area. There is a display about Hampstead as a spa in the 18th and 19th centuries, which is also worth a visit. Burgh House often has exhibitions by contemporary local artists.

The house itself was built in 1703 but is named after a 19th-century resident, the Reverend Allatson Burgh. It has been much altered inside, and today the marvellously carved staircase is a highlight of the interior. Also worth seeing is the music room which was reconstructed in 1920, but contains good 18th-century pine panelling from another house. In the 1720s Dr William Gibbons, chief physician to the then thriving Hampstead spa, lived here.

There is a basement café, with a terrace that overlooks the house's pretty garden.

Burgh House staircase

Old Bull and Bush ❸

North End Rd NW3. **Map** 1 A2. *Tel* 020-8905 5456. ⊖ *Golders Green.* **Open** 11am–11pm Mon–Sat, 11am–10:30pm Sun. ♿ 🍴

This pub, one of London's oldest and most famous, dates back to 1645, when it was a farmhouse. It received its licence to sell ale in 1721 and quickly became a haunt for artists and literary figures, including the famous artist William Hogarth *(see p259)* and the writer Austin Dobson. It is reputed that Hogarth planted a tree in the pub's garden. Located next to Hampstead Heath, the pub serves food at lunchtime and in the evening, and has barbecues in the summer in the garden. The interior is comfortably furnished.

Fenton House ❹

20 Hampstead Grove NW3. **Map** 1 A4. **Tel** 01494-755563. 🚇 Hampstead. **Open** end Mar–Oct: 2–5pm Wed–Fri, 11am–5pm Sat & Sun (Sat & Sun only in Nov), public hols. **Adm charge.** 👟 ground floor only. 📷 book ahead. **www**.nationaltrust.org.uk/fentonhouse

Built in 1686, this splendid William and Mary house is the oldest mansion in Hampstead. It contains two specialized exhibitions that are open to the public during the summer: the Benton-Fletcher collection of early keyboard instruments, which includes a harpsichord dating from 1612, said to have been played by Handel; and a fine collection of porcelain. The instruments are kept in full working order and are actually used for concerts held in the house. The porcelain collection was largely accumulated by Lady Binning who, in 1952, bequeathed the house and its contents to the National Trust.

Church Row ❺

NW3. **Map** 1 A5. 🚇 Hampstead.

The row is one of the most complete Georgian streets in London. Much of its original detail has survived, notably the ironwork.

At the west end is St John's, Hampstead's parish church, built in 1745. The iron gates are earlier and come from Canons Park in Edgware. Inside the church is a bust of John Keats. John Constable's grave is in the churchyard, and many Hampstead luminaries are buried in the adjoining cemetery.

Downshire Hill ❻

NW3. **Map** 1 C5. 🚇 Hampstead.

A beautiful street of mainly Regency houses, it lent its name to a group of artists, including Stanley Spencer and Mark Gertler, who would gather at No. 47 between the two World Wars. That same

house had been the meeting-place of Pre-Raphaelite artists, among them Dante Gabriel Rossetti and Edward Burne-Jones. A more recent resident, at No. 5, was the late Jim Henson, the creator of the television puppets, The Muppets.

The church on the corner (the second Hampstead church to be called St John's) was built in 1823 to serve the Hill's residents. Inside, it still has its original box pews.

Keats House ❼

Keats Grove NW3. **Map** 1 C5. 📷 020-7332 3868. 🚇 Hampstead, Belsize Park. **Open** call in the morning to book an afternoon visit. 👟 ground floor only. 🎭 **Poetry readings, talks, lectures**. **www**.cityoflondon.gov.uk/keats

Lock of Fanny Brawne's hair

Originally two semi-detached houses built in 1816, the smaller one became Keats's home in 1818 when a friend persuaded him to

St John's, Downshire Hill

move in. Keats spent two productive years here: Ode to a Nightingale, perhaps his most celebrated poem, was written under a plum tree in the garden. The Brawne family moved into the larger house a year later and Keats became engaged to their daughter, Fanny. However, the marriage never took place because Keats died of consumption in Rome before two years had passed. He was only 25 years old.

A copy of one of Keats's love letters to Fanny, the engagement ring he offered her, and a lock of her hair are among the mementos that are exhibited at the house – it was first opened to the public in 1925. Visitors are also able to see facsimiles of some of Keats's manuscripts, part of a collection that serves as an evocative and memorable tribute to his life and work.

Fenton House's 17th-century façade

View over London from Hampstead Heath

Hampstead Heath ⑧

NW3. **Map** 1 C2. **Tel** 020-7332 3322. ⊖ Belsize Park, Hampstead. **Open** 24hrs daily. **Special walks** on Sundays. 🚻 phone for disability buggies. 🎦 **Concerts, some children's activities** in summer. **Sports facilities, bathing ponds. Sports bookings Tel** 020-7332 3774.

The best time to stride across these broad 3 sq miles (8 sq km) is Sunday afternoon, when the local residents walk off their roast beef lunches, discussing the contents of the Sunday papers. Separating the hilltop villages of Hampstead and Highgate *(see p246)*, the Heath was made from the grounds of several, formerly separate, properties and embraces a variety of landscapes – woods, meadows, hills, ponds and lakes. It remains uncluttered by the haphazard buildings and statues that embellish the central London parks, and its open spaces have become increasingly precious to Londoners as the areas around it get more crowded. There are ponds for bathing and fishing and, on three holiday weekends – Easter, late spring and late summer – the southern part of the Heath is taken over by a funfair *(see pp56–9).*

Parliament Hill ⑨

NW5. **Map** 2 E4. **Tel** 020-7332 3773. ⊖ Belsize Park, Hampstead. 🚻 **Concerts, children's activities** in summer. **Sporting facilities.** 🎦

An unlikely but romantic explanation for the area's name is that it is where Guy Fawkes's fellow-plotters gathered on 5 November 1605 in the vain hope of watching the Houses of Parliament blow up after they had planted gunpowder there *(see p24)*. More probably it was a gun emplacement for the Parliamentary side during the Civil War 40 years later. The gunners would have enjoyed

Kenwood House ⑩

Hampstead Lane NW3. **Map** 1 C1. **Tel** 020-8348 1286. ⊖ Highgate, Archway. **Open** 11:30am–4pm daily. **Closed** 1 Jan, 24–26 Dec. 🚫 **Lakeside concerts** in summer. **Regular events.** 🚻 ground floor. 🎦 📷 See **Entertainment** pp348–9.**www**.english-heritage.org.uk

This is a magnificent Adam mansion, filled with Old Master paintings, including works by Vermeer, Turner and Romney (who lived in Hampstead). It is situated in landscaped grounds high on the edge of Hampstead Heath. There has been a house here since 1616 – the present one was remodelled by Robert Adam in 1764 for the Earl of Mansfield. Adam refitted existing rooms and added to the original building. Most of his work has survived, the highlight being the library. A Rembrandt self-portrait is the star attraction of the collection, and there are also works by Van Dyck, Hals and Reynolds.

The orangery is now used for occasional concerts and recitals.

a broad view across London: even today, when tall buildings intervene, it provides one of the most spectacular views over the capital. From here the dome of St Paul's is prominent. Parliament Hill is also a popular place for flying kites and sailing model boats on the boating pond.

Spaniards Inn **⓫**

Spaniards Rd NW3. **Map** 1 B1.
Tel 020-8731 6571. 🚇 Hampstead, Golders Green. **Open** 11am–11pm Mon–Fri, 10am–11pm Sat, 10am–10:30pm Sun. 🅿 See **Restaurants and Pubs** pp292–319.

The historic Spaniards Inn

Dick Turpin, the notorious 18th-century highwayman, is said to have frequented this pub. When he wasn't holding up stage-coaches on their way to and from London, he stabled his horse, Black Bess, at the Kenwood stables. The building certainly dates from Turpin's

time and, although the bar downstairs has been altered frequently, the small upstairs Turpin Bar is original. A pair of guns over the bar were reputedly taken from anti-Catholic rioters, who came to Hampstead to burn the Lord Chancellor's house at Kenwood during the Gordon Riots of 1780. The landlord detained them by offering pint after pint of free beer and, when they were drunk, disarmed them.

Among the pub's noted patrons have been the poets Shelley, Keats and Byron, the actor David Garrick and the artist Sir Joshua Reynolds.

The toll house has been restored; it juts into the road so that, in the days when tolls were levied, traffic could not race past without paying.

The Hill Garden **⓬**

North End Way NW3. **Map** 1 A2
Tel 020-8455 5183. 🚇 Hampstead, Golders Green. **Open** 9am–one hour before dusk daily.

This charming garden was created by the Edwardian soap manufacturer and patron of the arts, Lord Leverhulme. It was originally the grounds to his house, and is now part of Hampstead Heath. It boasts a pergola walkway, best seen in summer when the plants are in flower; the garden also has a beautiful formal pond.

Pergola walk at The Hill Garden

Vale of Health **⓭**

NW3. **Map** 1 B4. 🚇 Hampstead.

This area was famous as a distinctly unhealthy swamp before it was drained in 1770; until then it was known as Hatches Bottom. Its newer name may derive from people fleeing here from cholera in London at the end of the 18th century. Alternatively, the name could have been the hype of a property developer, when it was first recorded in 1801.

The poet James Henry Leigh Hunt put it on the literary map when he moved here in 1815, and played host to Coleridge, Byron Shelley and Keats.

D H Lawrence lived here briefly and Stanley Spencer painted in a room above the Vale of Health Hotel, demolished in 1964.

Adam redesigned the façade of the old building.

Adam furnished these older rooms.

Lord Mansfield, who lived here from 1754 until 1793, had his dressing room here.

The ante-room was designed at the same time as the library.

The Adam library has a spectacularly curved, painted ceiling.

GREENWICH AND BLACKHEATH

B est known as the place from which the world's time is measured, Greenwich marks the historic eastern approach to London by land and water. Home to the National Maritime Museum and the Queen's House, Greenwich remains an elegant oasis of bookshops, antique shops and markets. Blackheath lies just to the south.

SIGHTS AT A GLANCE

Historic Streets and Buildings
Queen's House **2**
Old Royal Naval College **7**
Royal Observatory Greenwich **9**
Croom's Hill **12**

Museums
National Maritime Museum **1**
Fan Museum **13**

Wernher Collection **4**

Churches
St Alfege Church **3**

Parks and Gardens
Greenwich Park **10**
Blackheath **11**

Walkway
Greenwich Foot Tunnel **6**

Pubs and Restaurants
Trafalgar Tavern **8**

Ships
Cutty Sark **5**

KEY

▨ Street-by-Street map
◉ Underground station
🚆 Railway Station

GETTING THERE
The best way is by rail from Charing Cross or London Bridge, or by the DLR. The 188 bus goes five times an hour to Greenwich from Euston. There are also numerous river boats *(pp60–65).*

SEE ALSO

◁ **View north across the Thames from Greenwich Park, overlooking Queen's House**

Street-by-Street: Greenwich

This historic town marks the eastern approach to
London and is best visited by river *(see pp60–5)*. In
Tudor times it was the site of a palace much enjoyed
by Henry VIII, near a fine hunting ground and his naval
base. The old palace is gone, leaving Inigo Jones's
exquisite Queen's House, built for James I's wife.
Museums, book and antique shops, markets, Wren's
architecture and the magnificent park make Greenwich
an enjoyable day's excursion. Greenwich has also
been awarded the status of a World Heritage Site.

Greenwich Foot Tunnel,
*leading to the Isle of Dogs,
is one of two tunnels built
solely for pedestrians* **6**

Greenwich Pier provides a
boarding point for boat
services to Westminster
and the Thames Barrier.

Cutty Sark
*Clipper ships such as this
once traded across the
oceans. The Cutty Sark is
being restored following a
fire. Her figurehead can be
seen in the visitors' centre* **5**

To Cutty
Sark DLR →

COLLEGE
APPROACH

Greenwich Market
*Selling crafts, antiques and books,
this market is popular on Sundays.*

K I N G   W I L L I A M   W A L K

GREENWICH CHURCH STREET

NELSON ROAD

STOCKWELL STREET

NEVAD
STREE

St Alfege Church
*There has been a church
here since 1012* **3**

Spread Eagle Yard
*Once a stopping point for horse-
drawn carriages. The Spread
Eagle restaurant is next to the si
of the ticket office.*

LOCATOR MAP
See Greater London Map pp12–13

★ Old Royal Naval College
Wren's stately structure was built in two halves so that the Queen's House would keep its river view ⑦

George II Statue
Sculpted by John Rysbrack in 1735, this statue depicts the king as a Roman emperor.

The Painted Hall contains 18th-century murals by Sir James Thornhill, who painted the interior of the dome at St Paul's Cathedral.

R O A D

★ Queen's House
On his return from Italy, this was the first building Inigo Jones designed in the Palladian style ②

National Maritime Museum
Real and model boats, paintings and instruments, like this 18th-century compass, illustrate naval history ①

STAR SIGHTS

★ Old Royal Naval College

★ Queen's House

KEY

– – – Suggested route

| 0 metres | 100 |
| 0 yards | 100 |

National Maritime Museum ❶

Romney Rd SE10. **Map** 23 C2.
Tel 020-8312 6565. ⓔ *Cutty
Sark DLR.* ⭧ *Greenwich.* **Open**
*10am–5pm daily (last adm: 30 mins
before close).* **Closed** *24–26 Dec.*
Adm charge *special
exhibitions.* ⏀ ♿ 🖵 📷
Lectures. **www**.nmm.ac.uk

The sea has always played
an extremely important
role in British history as a
means of both defence and
expansion, and this museum
celebrates the "island
nation's" seafaring heritage.
Exhibits tell the story of
explorers, from early
Elizabethan times through the
development of passenger
lines to the modern day.
There are sections devoted
to trade and empire, the
exploratory expeditions
of Captain Cook and Sir
Ernest Shackleton, and the
Napoleonic Wars.

One of the star exhibits is
the uniform that Lord Horatio
Nelson was wearing when he
was shot at the Battle of
Trafalgar in October 1805:
you can easily see the bullet
hole and the bloodstains.

Rather more spectacular,
however, is the royal barge
that was built for Prince
Frederick in 1732, decorated
with gilded mermaids, shells,
garlands and his Prince of
Wales's feathers on the stern.
Throughout the museum,
(built in the 19th century
as a school for sailors'
children), are scores of finely
crafted models of ships and
historic paintings.

St Alfege's altar with rails attributed to Jean Tijou

Queen's House ❷

Romney Rd SE10. **Map** 23 C2. **Tel**
020-8312 6565. ⓔ *Cutty Sark DLR.*
⭧ *Greenwich.* **Open** *10am–5pm
daily (last adm: 4.30pm). Closes early
some Fri & Sat for special events –
phone to check.* **Closed** *24–26 Dec.*
⏀ ♿ 🍴 🖵 📷 **www**.nmm.ac.uk

The house was
designed by Inigo
Jones and was com-
pleted in 1637. It was
originally meant to be
the home of Anne of
Denmark, wife of James I,
but she died while it was
still being built and it was
finished for Charles I's
queen, Henrietta Maria. She
fell in love with it and called
it her house of delights. After
the Civil War it was briefly
occupied by Henrietta as
dowager queen, but was not
much used by the royal
family after that.

The building has been
refurbished, and in 2001 the
house opened with galleries
displaying the art collection of
the National Maritime
Museum. On the ground floor
is a permanent exhibition,
Historic Greenwich, which
includes two models showing
how the house looked in
17th-century Greenwich. The
paintings on show include
early views of Greenwich and
portraits of historical figures
associated with the house,
including Inigo Jones. Visitors
can also see the spiral "tulip
staircase", which curves sinu-
ously upwards without a
central support.

St Alfege Church ❸

Greenwich Church St SE10.
Map 23 B2. **Tel** 020-8853 0687.
ⓔ *Cutty Sark DLR.* **Open** *11.30am–
4pm Sat, 12–4pm Sun.* ✟ *8am,
10am Sun.* ♿ *phone ahead.*
Concerts. **www**.st-alfege.org

This is one of Nicholas
Hawksmoor's most distinctive
and powerful designs, with its
gigantic columns and

Prince Frederick's barge at the
National Maritime Museuum

pediments topped by urns. It was completed in 1714 on the site of an older church which marked the martyrdom of St Alfege, the then Archbishop of Canterbury, killed on this spot by Danish invaders in 1012. A second church here was the site of Henry VIII's baptism in 1491 and of 16th-century composer and organist Thomas Tallis's burial in 1585. Today a stained-glass window commemorates Thomas Tallis.

Some of the carved wood inside is by Grinling Gibbons, but much of it was badly damaged by a World War II bomb and has been restored. The wrought iron of the altar and gallery rails is original, attributed to Jean Tijou.

Wernher Collection **❹**

Ranger's House, Chesterfield Walk, Greenwich Park SE10. **Map** 23 C4. **Tel** 020-8853 0035. 🚇 *Cutty Sark DLR.* 🚆 *Blackheath.* **Open** *Apr–Sep: 11am–5pm Sun.* **Closed** *20 Dec–end Feb.* **Adm charge.** 🎧 *guided tours by appt Apr–Sep: 11:30am, 2:30pm Mon–Wed.* 🚻 **www**.english-heritage.org.uk

Opal-set lizard pendant at the Wernher Collection

The Wernher Collection is located in Ranger's House (1688), an elegant building southeast of Greenwich Park *(see p243)*. It is an enchanting array of over 650 pieces accumulated by South African mine owner Sir Julius Wernher in the late 19th century. The collection is displayed in 12 rooms and includes paintings, jewellery, furniture and porcelain. Highlights include Renaissance masterworks by Hans Memling and Filippo Lippi, over 100 Renaissance jewels, and an opal-set lizard pendant jewel. Other curiosities include enamelled skulls.

The domed terminal of the Greenwich Foot Tunnel

Cutty Sark **❺**

King William Walk SE10. **Map** 23 B2. **Tel** 020-8858 2698. 🚇 *Cutty Sark DLR.* 🚆 *Greenwich Pier.* **Open** *Currently closed to the public, due to re-open in 2011; call or check website for details.* **Adm charge.** 📷 *restricted.* 🚻 **www**.cuttysark.org.uk

This majestic vessel is a survivor of the clippers that crossed the Atlantic and Pacific Oceans in the 19th century. Launched in 1869 as a tea carrier, it was something of a speed machine in its day, winning the annual clippers' race from China to London in 1871 in a time of 107 days. It made its final voyage in 1938 and was put on display here in 1957. In 2006 the Cutty Sark was closed to visitors for renovation work, which suffered a major setback in May 2007 when the ship was severely damaged by fire. It is due to re-open in 2011, fully restored.

Greenwich Foot Tunnel **❻**

Between Greenwich Pier SE10 and Isle of Dogs E14. **Map** 23 B1. 🚇 *Island Gardens, Cutty Sark DLR.* 🚆 *Greenwich Pier.* **Open** *24hrs daily.* **Lifts open** *7am–7pm Mon–Sat, 10am–5.30pm Sun.* 📷 ♿ *when lifts open.*

This 370-m (1,200-ft) long tunnel was opened in 1902 to allow south London labourers to walk to work in Millwall

Docks. Today it is worth crossing for the wonderful views, across the river, of Christopher Wren's Royal Naval College and of Inigo Jones's Queen's House.

Matching round red-brick terminals, with glass domes, mark the top of the lift shafts on either side of the river. The tunnel is about 2.5 m (9 ft) high and is lined with 200,000 tiles. Both ends of the tunnel are close to stations on the Docklands Light Railway (DLR), with trains to Canary Wharf *(see p249)*, Limehouse, East London, Tower Hill and Lewisham. Although there are security cameras, the tunnel can be eerie at night.

A late 19th-century figurehead in the Cutty Sark

Old Royal Naval College ❼

King William Walk SE10. **Map** 23 C2.
📠 *020-8269 4747.* 🚇 *Cutty Sark, Greenwich.* 🚉 *Greenwich, Maze Hill.* **Open** *10am–5pm daily.* **Grounds open** *8am–6pm daily.* **Chapel open** *10am–5pm Mon–Sat, 12:30am–5pm Sun.* 📷 ♿ 🍴 🛒 🏪
www.oldroyalnavalcollege.org

These ambitious buildings by Christopher Wren were built on the site of the old 15th-century royal palace, where Henry VIII, Mary I and Elizabeth I were born. Only the chapel, the hall and the visitors' centre are open to the public. The west front was completed by Vanbrugh.
Wren's chapel was destroyed by fire in 1779. The present Greek Revival interior, by James Stuart, is light and airy, with dainty plasterwork decorations. The Painted Hall was opulently decorated by Sir James Thornhill in the early 18th century. The ceiling paintings are supported by his illusionistic pillars and friezes. At the foot of one of his paintings, the artist himself is shown, apparently extending his hand for more money.

Trafalgar Tavern ❽

Park Row SE10. **Map** 23 C1. **Tel** *020-8858 2909.* 🚇 *Greenwich.* **Open** *noon–11pm Mon–Thu, noon–midnight Fri & Sat, noon–10:30pm Sun.* ♿ *See* **Restaurants and Pubs** *pp315–19.*

This charming panelled pub was built in 1837 and quickly became established, along

Thornhill's painting of King William III in the Hall of the Naval College

with other waterside inns in Greenwich, as a venue for "whitebait dinners". Government ministers, legal luminaries and the like would arrive from Westminster and Charing Cross by water on celebratory occasions and feast on the tiny fish. The last such meeting of government ministers was held here in 1885. Whitebait still features, when they are in season, on the menu at the pub's restaurant, although they are no longer fished from the Thames.
This was another of Charles Dickens's haunts. He drank here with one of his novels' most famous illustrators, George Cruickshank.
In 1915 the pub became an institution for old merchant seamen. It was restored in 1965 after a spell of being used as a social club for working men.

Royal Observatory Greenwich ❾

Greenwich Park SE10. **Map** 23 C3.
Tel *020-8312 6565.* 🚇 *Cutty Sark DLR.* 🚉 *Greenwich.* **Open** *10am–5pm daily (last adm: 4:30pm).* **Closed** *24–26 Dec.* **Adm charge** *for Planetarium shows (last show 4pm).* 📷 ♿ 🏪 **www**.rog.nmm.ac.uk

The meridian (0° longitude) that divides the Earth's eastern and western hemispheres passes through here, and millions of visitors have taken the opportunity of being photographed standing with a foot on either side of it. In 1884, Greenwich Mean Time became the basis of time measurement for most of the world, following an important international agreement.
The original building, Flamsteed House, was designed by Christopher Wren. Above one of the building's two turrets is a ball on a rod which has dropped at 1pm every day since 1833, so that sailors on the Thames, and makers of chronometers (navigators' clocks), could set their clocks by it. The house now contains a display of John Harrison's marine timekeepers and an intriguing exhibition about Greenwich Mean Time. Flamsteed was the first Astronomer Royal, appointed by Charles II, and

Trafalgar Tavern viewed from the Thames

this was the official government observatory from 1675 until 1948, when the lights of London became too bright and the astronomers moved to darker Sussex.

A state-of-the-art planetarium, the only one in London, opened here in 2007.

A rare 24-hour clock at the Royal Observatory Greenwich

Greenwich Park ⑩

SE10. **Map** 23 C3. **Tel** 020-8858 2608. 🄴 🚇 *Greenwich, Blackheath, Maze Hill.* **Open** *6am–dusk daily.* 🔲 🔾 **Children's shows, sports facilities. Ranger's House**, *Chesterfield Walk, Greenwich Park SE10.* **Map** 23 C4. www.english-heritage.co.uk *see also* **Wernher Collection**, *p241.*

Originally the grounds of a royal palace and still a Royal Park, Greenwich Park was enclosed in 1433 and its brick wall built in the reign of James I. Later, in the 17th century, the French royal landscape gardener André Le Nôtre, who laid out the gardens at Versailles and Fontainebleau, was invited to design one at Greenwich. The broad avenue, rising south up the hill, was part of his plan.

There are great river views from the hilltop and on a fine day, most of London can be seen.

To the southeast of the park, and on the edge of the park's rose garden, is the Ranger's House (1688), which now houses the art collection of diamond magnate Julius Wernher *(see p241).*

From here the walk to the charming village of Blackheath is flat, compared with the steep walk down to the village of Greenwich at the bottom of the hill.

Blackheath ⑪

SE3. **Map** 24 D5. 🚇 *Blackheath.*

This open heath used to be a rallying point for large groups who were entering London from the east, including Wat Tyler's band of rebels at the time of the Peasants' Revolt in 1381.

Blackheath is also the place where King James I of England (who was also King James VI of Scotland) introduced the game of golf from his native Scotland, to the then largely sceptical English.

Today the heath is well worth exploring for the stately Georgian houses and terraces that surround it. In the prettily-named Tranquil Vale to the south, there are shops selling books, prints and antiques. The heath will host the Olympic and Paralympic equestrian events in 2012.

Ranger's House in Greenwich Park

Croom's Hill ⑫

SE10. **Map** 23 C3. 🚇 *Greenwich.*

This is one of the best kept 17th- to early 19th-century streets in London. The oldest buildings are at the southern end, near Blackheath: the original Manor House of 1695; near it, No. 68, from about the same date; and No. 66 the oldest of all. Famous residents of Croom's Hill include Irish actor Daniel Day Lewis.

Fan Museum ⑬

12 Croom's Hill SE10. **Map** 23 B3. **Tel** 020-8305 1441. 🚇 *Greenwich.* **Open** *11am–5pm Tue–Sat, noon–5pm Sun.* **Closed** *1 Jan, 24–26 Dec.* **Adm charge.** 🄾 *no flash.* 🄿 *by appt.* 🄸 🔾 **Lectures, fan-making workshops** *first Sat of the month.* www.fan-museum.org

One of London's most unlikely museums – the only one of its kind in the world – opened in 1991. It owes its existence and appeal to the enthusiasm of Helene Alexander, whose personal collection of about 3,500 fans from the 17th century onwards has been augmented by donations, including several fans that were made for the stage. If there, Mrs Alexander will act as a guide.

Stage fan used in a D'Oyly Carte operetta

FURTHER AFIELD

Many of the great houses originally built as country retreats for London's high and mighty were overrun by sprawling suburbs in the Victorian era. Fortunately several have survived as museums in these now less-rustic surroundings. Most are less than an hour's journey from central London. Richmond Park and Wimbledon Common give a taste of the country, while a trip to the Thames Barrier is an adventure.

SIGHTS AT A GLANCE

Historic Streets and Buildings
Sutton House ⑪
Charlton House ⑲
Eltham Palace ⑳
Hampton Court pp254–5 ㉘
Ham House ㉙
Orleans House Gallery ㉚
Marble Hill House ㉛
Syon House ㉝
Osterley Park House ㉟
PM Gallery and House ㊱
Strand on the Green ㊳
Chiswick House ㊵
Fulham Palace ㉔

Churches
St Mary, Rotherhithe ⑬
St Anne's, Limehouse ⑭
St Mary's, Battersea ㉔

Markets
Camden Market ❷

Museums and Galleries
Lord's Cricket Ground ❶
Freud Museum ❸
The Jewish Museum ❻
St John's Gate ❼
Crafts Council Gallery ❽
Geffrye Museum ❿
Bethnal Green Museum
  of Childhood ⑫
William Morris Gallery ⑯
Horniman Museum ㉑
Dulwich Picture Gallery ㉒
Wimbledon Lawn Tennis
  Museum ㉕
Wimbledon Windmill
  Museum ㉖
Musical Museum ㉞
Kew Bridge Steam
  Museum ㊲
Hogarth's House ㊶

Parks and Gardens
Battersea Park ㉓
Richmond Park ㉗
Kew Gardens pp260–61 ㊳

Cemeteries
Highgate Cemetery ❺

Modern Architecture
Canary Wharf ⑮
The O2 Arena ⑱
Chelsea Harbour ㊸

Historic Districts
Highgate ❹
Islington ❾
Richmond ㉜

Modern Technology
Thames Barrier ⑰

All the sights in this section lie inside
the M25 motorway (see pp12–13).

0 kilometres   5

0 miles   3

KEY
Main sightseeing areas
═══ Motorway

GREATER LONDON

M25

SIGHTS OUTSIDE
THE CENTRE

◁ Riverside pub in Richmond

North of the Centre

Lord's Cricket Ground ❶

NW8. **Map** 3 A3. **Tel** 020-7616 8595 or 020-7616 8500. ⊖ St John's Wood. **Open** for guided tours and ticket-holders to matches only. **Closed** 25 Dec. **Adm charge.** ⬤ 10am, noon, 2pm daily; groups call to pre-book. 🏠 See **Entertainment** pp354–5. **www**.lords.org

The headquarters of Britain's chief summer sport contains a museum, including a stuffed sparrow killed by a cricket ball as well as the Ashes (burned wood in an urn), the object of ferocious competition between the English and Australian national teams. The museum explains the history of the game, while paintings and mementos of notable cricketers make it a place of pilgrimage for devotees of the sport.

Cricket pioneer Thomas Lord moved his ground here in 1814. The Pavilion (1890), from which women were excluded until 1999, is late Victorian. There are tours of Lord's even when there is no game being played.

The Ashes at Lord's

Camden Market ❷

NW1. ⊖ Camden Town, Chalk Farm. **Open** 10am–6pm daily.

Camden Market is really six markets located close to each other along Chalk Farm Road and Camden High Street. Packed with shoppers at the weekends, most of the shops and some of the stalls are open on weekdays. Many units are housed in restored Victorian buildings alongside Camden Lock and the canal. The first market here was a crafts market at Camden Lock, in 1975. Today all the markets sell a wide range of exciting goods, from arts and crafts and street fashion, to new age remedies and body piercing.

Sigmund Freud's famous couch

Freud Museum ❸

20 Maresfield Gdns NW3. **Tel** 020-7435 2002. ⊖ Finchley Rd. **Open** noon–5pm Wed–Sun. **Closed** 24–26 Dec. **Adm charge**. 📷 no flash. ⬤ limited. 🏠 **Events**. **www**.freud.org.uk

In 1938 Sigmund Freud, the founder of psychoanalysis, fled from Nazi persecution in Vienna to this Hampstead house. Making use of the possessions he brought with him, his family recreated the atmosphere of his Vienna consulting rooms. After Freud died in 1939 his daughter Anna (who was a pioneer of child psychoanalysis) kept the house as it was. In 1986 it was opened as a museum dedicated to Freud. The most famous item is the couch on which patients lay for analysis. A series of 1930s home movies shows cheerful moments with his dog as well as scenes of Nazi attacks on his apartment. The bookshop has a large collection of his works.

Highgate ❹

N6. ⊖ Highgate.

There has been a settlement here since at least the early Middle Ages, when an important staging post on the Great North Road from London was established with a gate to control access. Like Hampstead across the Heath (see pp234–5), it soon became fashionable for its unpolluted air, and noblemen built country houses here. It still has an exclusive feel, with a Georgian High Street and expensive houses. It was on Highgate Hill in medieval times, that Dick Whittington (a poor young lad) and his pet cat were persuaded to turn back, and try their fortune in the city, by the sound of Bow Bells. He went on to become Lord Mayor of London. A statue of a black cat marks the spot of his epiphany (see p.39).

Highgate Cemetery ❺

Swain's Lane N6. **Tel** 020-8340 1834. ⊖ Archway. **Eastern Cemetery Open** Mar–Oct: 10am–5pm Mon–Fri, 11am–5pm Sat & Sun; Nov–Feb: 10am–4pm Mon–Fri, 11am–4pm Sat & Sun. **Western Cemetery open** ⬤ only Mar–Oct: 2pm Mon–Fri, 11am–4pm Sat & Sun; Nov–Feb: 11am–3pm Sat & Sun. **Closed** 25 & 26 Dec & during funerals (phone to check). **Adm charge.** ⬤ Eastern only. **www**.highgate-cemetery.org

The western section of this high-Victorian gem opened in 1839. For many years it lay neglected, until a voluntary group, the Friends of Highgate Cemetery, stepped in to save it from further decline. They have restored the Egyptian Avenue, a street of family vaults built in a style based on ancient Egyptian tombs, and the Circle of Lebanon, more vaults in a ring, topped by a cedar tree. In the eastern section lie Karl Marx, beneath a huge black bust of his image, Herbert Spencer and novelist George Eliot (real name, Mary Anne Evans).

George Wombwell's memorial at Highgate Cemetery

**Jewish Bakers' Union banner, c.1926,
Jewish Museum, Camden**

The Jewish Museum ⑥

129–31 Albert Street, NW1. **Map** 4
E1. **Tel** 020-7284 7384. ⊖ Camden
Town. **Open** 10am–5pm Sun–Wed,
10am–9pm Thu, 10am–2pm Fri.
Closed Sat, Jewish hols, 25 & 26
Dec. **Adm charge.** ⚙ 🖥 🛍
www.jewishmuseum.org.uk

When London's Jewish Museum was founded in 1932 it
was split between two sites, in
Finchley and Camden. In 2007
the museum celebrated its
75th anniversary with the com-
mencement of works to bring
the two collections together in
a single building. Completed
in 2010, the project has created
enlarged galleries, education
facilities and hands-on displays
for children.

Celebrating Jewish life in
this country from the Middle
Ages, the museum is packed
with memorabilia. It also has
important collections of Jewish ceremonial art, including
Hanukkah lamps, a collection
of Jewish marriage rings and
some illuminated marriage
contracts. The highlight of this
collection is a 16th-century
Venetian synagogue ark.

St John's Gate ⑦

St John's Lane EC1. **Map** 6 F4.
Tel 020-7324 4005. ⊖ Farringdon.
Open 10am–5pm Mon–Sat.
Closed bank holiday weekends.
Adm donation. 📷 11am, 2.30pm
Tue, Fri, Sat. 🛍 ⚙ limited.
www.sja.org.uk/museum

The Tudor gatehouse and parts
of the 12th-century church are
all that remain of the priory of
the Knights of St John, which
flourished here for 400 years
and was the precursor of the
St John Ambulance. Over the

years, the priory buildings
have had many uses, such as
offices for Elizabeth I's Master
of the Revels, a pub, and a
coffee shop run by the artist
William Hogarth's father. A
museum of the order's history
has been renovated, with support from the Heritage Lottery
Fund, to create an exhibition
space showing hidden
parts of the gatehouse and a
learning space in the priory
church. To see the rest of the
building, join a guided tour.

The Crafts Council

Crafts Council ⑧

44a Pentonville Rd N1. **Map** 6 D2.
Tel 020-7806 2500. ⊖ Angel. **Open**
📘 **library**, phone to check for
times. **Closed** 25 Dec–1 Jan. ⚙ 🛍
Lectures. www.craftscouncil.org.uk

The Crafts Council is the
national agency for promoting
the creation and appreciation
of contemporary crafts in the
UK. It has a collection of contemporary British crafts, some
of which are loaned to touring
exhibitions, and there is a

library. They also organise
two large craft fairs – one at
the Saatchi Gallery (see *p197*)
in May and the other at
Somerset House (see *p117*)
in September/October.

Islington ⑨

N1. **Map** 6 E1. ⊖ Angel, Highbury
& Islington.

Islington was once a highly
fashionable spa, but the rich
began to move out in the late
18th century, and the area
deteriorated rapidly. During
the 20th century, writers such
as Evelyn Waugh, George
Orwell and Joe Orton lived
here. Now Islington has again
returned to fashion as one of
London's first areas to become
"gentrified", with many young
professionals buying and
refurbishing old houses.

An older relic is Canonbury
Tower, the remains of a medieval manor house converted
into apartments in the 18th
century. Writers such as
Washington Irving and Oliver
Goldsmith lived here and
today it houses the Tower
Theatre. On Islington Green
there is a statue of Sir Hugh
Myddleton, who built a canal
through Islington in 1613 to
bring water to London from
Hertfordshire; today a landscaped walk along its banks
runs between Essex Road and
Canonbury stations. There is a
market, Chapel Market close
to the Angel station (see *p340*),
antique shops at Camden Passage, and a shopping and cinema complex, the N1 Centre.

St John's Priory: today, only the gatehouse remains intact

East of the Centre

Geffrye Museum's Georgian Room

Geffrye Museum ⑩

Kingsland Rd E2. **Tel** 020-7739 9893.
🚇 Liverpool St, Old St. **Open** 10am–
5pm Tue–Sat, noon–5pm Sun & bank
hols. **Closed** 1 Jan, Good Fri, 24–26
Dec. **Garden open** Apr–Oct. 🔊 📖
🎫 🏛 **Exhibitions & events**.
www.geffrye-museum.org.uk

This delightful museum is
housed in a set of 18th-
century almshouses. They
were built in 1715 on land
bequeathed by Sir Robert
Geffrye, a 17th-century Lord
Mayor of London who made
his fortune through trade.
Inside, you take a trip
through a series of rooms,
chronologically arranged,
which have been decorated
in different period styles, each
one providing an insight into
the domestic interiors of the
urban middle classes. The
historic room settings begin
with Elizabethan (which contains magnificent panelling)
and run through various
major styles, including High
Victorian, while an attractive
extension houses more modern settings, such as an example of 1990s "loft living".
Each room contains superb
examples of British furniture
of the period. Outside, there
is a series of garden "rooms"
that show the designs and
planting schemes popular in
urban gardens between the
16th and 20th centuries.
There is a good café which
has a children's menu.

Sutton House ⑪

2–4 Homerton High St E9. **Tel** 020-
8986 2264. 🚇 Bethnal Green then
bus 253. **Open** Feb–Dec:
12.30–4.30pm Thurs–Sun. **Adm
charge**. 🔊 limited. 📞 phone first.
📖 🏛 **Regular events**.
www.nationaltrust.org.uk

One of the few London
Tudor merchants' houses to
survive in something like its
original form. Built in 1535
for Ralph Sadleir, a courtier to
Henry VIII, it was owned by
several wealthy families before
becoming a girls' school in
the 17th century. In the 18th
century the front was altered,
but the Tudor fabric remains
surprisingly intact, with much
original brickwork, large fireplaces and linenfold panelling.

V&A Museum of Childhood ⑫

Cambridge Heath Rd E2.
Tel 020-8983 5200. 🚇 Bethnal
Green. **Open** 10am–5.45pm daily
(to 9pm 1st Thu of month). **Closed**
25–26 Dec, 1 Jan. 📷 🔊 📖 🏛
Workshop, children's activities.
www.vam.ac.uk/moc

This East London branch of
the Victoria and Albert
Museum (see pp202–5) has
the largest collection of child-
hood-related objects in the
UK. Its array of toys, games,
lavish dolls' houses, model
trains, theatres and costumes
dates from the 16th century
to the present day, and is well
explained and enticingly displayed. The upper floor has
lots of fun activities, such as

Tate "Baby" house made in 1760

dressing up, a playable juke-
box and wobbly mirror. There
is an excellent shop.
   The purpose-built museum
building was originally erected on the V&A site. In 1872,
it was dismantled and reassembled here to bring the
light of learning to the East
End. The toy collection began
in the early 20th century and
became a dedicated museum
of childhood at Bethnal
Green in 1974.

St Mary, Rotherhithe ⑬

St Marychurch St SE16. 🚇
Rotherhithe. **Open** 7.30am–6pm
daily. ⛪ 9.30am, 6pm Sun.
📷 with permission. 🔊
www.stmaryrotherhithe.org

St Mary, Rotherhithe

This church was built in 1715
on the site of a medieval
church. It has nautical conno-
tations, most notably a memorial to Christopher Jones,
captain of the *Mayflower*, on
which the Pilgrim Fathers
sailed to North America. The
communion table is made
from the timbers of the
Temeraire, a warship whose
final journey to the breaker's
yard at Rotherhithe was
evocatively recorded in
Turner's painting at the
National Gallery (see pp104–7).
The church also contains a fine
example of 18th-century organ
building by John Byfield.

William Morris tapestry (1885)

St Anne's, Limehouse ⑭

Commercial Rd E14. *Tel 020-7987 1502.* 🚇 *Westferry (DLR).* **Open** *2–4pm Mon–Fri, 2.30–5pm Sat, Sun (viewing by appointment only).* 🕐 *10.30am, 6pm Sun.* 📷 📹 **Concerts, lectures.**

This is one of a group of East End churches designed by Nicholas Hawksmoor; it was completed in 1724. Its 40-m (130-ft) tower very soon became a landmark for ships using the East End docks – St Anne's still has the highest church clock in London. The church was damaged by fire in 1850 and its interior was subsequently Victorianized. It was bombed in World War II and is today in need of further restoration.

Canary Wharf ⑮

E14. 🚇 *Canary Wharf or West India Quay (DLR).* 🚹 🍴 📶 📷 *Information centre, concerts. Museum of London Docklands No. 1 Warehouse, West India Quay E14. Tel 020-7001 9844.* **Open** *10am–6pm daily.* **Closed** *1 Jan, 24–26 Dec.* **Adm charge.** 🚹 📶 📷 www. museumoflondon.org.uk/docklands

London's most ambitious commercial development opened in 1991, when the

first tenants moved into the 50-storey Canada Tower, designed by Argentine architect César Pelli. At 250 m (800 ft), it dominates the city's eastern skyline. The tower stands on what was the West India Dock, closed, like all the London docks, between the 1960s and the 1980s, when trade moved to the modern port down river at Tilbury. Today, Canary Wharf is thriving. A major shopping complex, as well as offices and restaurants, is located in and around Canada Tower. The **Museum of London Docklands**, occupying a late Georgian warehouse, tells the story of the Port of London from Roman times to the present.

William Morris Gallery ⑯

Lloyd Park, Forest Rd E17. *Tel 020-8496 4390.* 🚇 *Walthamstow Central.* **Open** *10am–5pm Wed–Sun.* **Closed** *24–26 Dec and public hols.* 🚹 *ground floor.* 📷 **Lectures.** www.walthamforest.gov.uk/wmg

The most influential designer of the Victorian era, born in 1834, lived in this imposing 18th-century house as a youth. It is now a beguiling and well-presented museum giving a full account of William Morris the artist, designer, writer, craftsman and socialist. It has choice examples of his work and that of other members of the Arts and Crafts movement that he inspired – furniture by A H Mackmurdo, tiles by William de Morgan, and paintings by members of the Pre-Raphaelite Brotherhood.

Canada Tower at Canary Wharf

Thames Barrier ⑰

Unity Way SE18. *Tel 020-8305 4188.* 🚇 *Charlton, Silvertown.* **Open** *Apr–Sep. 10.30am–4.30pm daily; Oct Mar: 11am–3.30pm.* **Closed** *25 Dec–1 Jan.* **Adm charge.** 🚹 📶 📷 **exhibition.** www.environment-agency.gov.uk

In 1236 the Thames rose so high that people rowed across Westminster Hall; London flooded again in 1663, 1928 and in 1953. Something had to be done, and in 1965 the Greater London Council invited proposals. The Thames Barrier was opened in 1984 and is 520 m (1,700 ft) across. Its 10 gates, which pivot from being flat on the river bed, swing up to 1.6 m (6 ft) above the level reached by the tide in 1953. The barrier has been raised over 100 times since 1984, and can be visited by boat in summer.

Unique structure of the O2 Arena

The O2 Arena ⑱

North Greenwich SE10. *Tel 020-8463 2000 or 0844-856 0202 (to book tickets).* 🚇 *North Greenwich/ The O2 Arena (Jubilee Line).* **Open** *10am–late.* www.theo2.co.uk

The former Millennium Dome was the focal point of Britain's celebration of the year 2000. Controversial from its earliest days, it is nonetheless a spectacular feat of engineering. Its base is ten times that of St Paul's Cathedral, and Nelson's Column could stand beneath its roof. Its canopy is made from 100,000 sq m (109,000 sq yards) of Teflon-coated spun glass-fibre, and is held by over 70 km (43 miles) of steel cable rigged to twelve 100-m (328-ft) masts.

Now London's newest concert arena, the O2 boasts an entertainment complex with bars, restaurants, a cinema, a sports arena and IndigO2, a smaller venue.

South of the Centre

A Jacobean fireplace at Charlton House

Charlton House ⓓ

Charlton Rd SE7. **Tel** 020-8856 3951.
🚊 Charlton. **Open** Main house not
open to public. Exhibition area open
8:30am–6pm Mon–Fri. **Closed** public
hols. 📷 book ahead. 🛗 limited. 🚻
9am–3pm Mon–Fri.

The house was completed in
1612 for Adam Newton, tutor
to Prince Henry. It has good
river views and is the best-
preserved Jacobean mansion
in London – well worth the
tricky journey for enthusiasts
of that period. It is now used
as a community centre and
library, but many of the original ceilings and fireplaces
survive, as does the carved
main staircase, all with an
astonishing quantity of ornament. Parts of the wood panelling, too, are original, and
the ceilings have been restored
using the original moulds. The
summer house in the grounds
was reputedly designed by
Inigo Jones, and a mulberry
tree (probably the oldest in
England) is said to have been
planted by James I in 1608 as
part of his failed attempt to
start an English silk industry.

Eltham Palace ⓔ

Court Yard SE9. **Tel** 020-8294 2548.
🚊 Eltham, then a 15-minute walk.
Open Sun–Wed. Apr–Oct:
10am–5pm; Nov–Dec & Feb–Mar:
11am–4pm. **Closed** 31 Dec–31Jan.
Adm charge. 🛗 🚻 📷
www.english-heritage.org.uk

This unique property lets
visitors relive the grand life of
two very different eras. In the
14th century, English kings
spent Christmas in a splendid
palace here. The Tudors used
it as a base for deer-hunting
but it fell to ruin after the Civil
War (1642–8). In 1935 Stephen
Courtauld, of the wealthy
textile family, restored the
Great Hall which, apart from
the bridge over the moat, was
the only part of the medieval
palace to survive. Next to it
he built a house described as
"a wonderful combination of
Hollywood glamour and Art
Deco design". It has been
superbly restored and is
open, along with the Great
Hall, the carp-filled moat and
the 1930s garden.

Horniman Museum ⓤ

100 London Rd SE23. **Tel** 020-8699
1872. 🚊 Forest Hill. **Gardens open**
7:30am–sunset Mon–Sat, 8am–
sunset Sun. **Museum open**
10:30am–5:30pm daily. **Closed** 24–26
Dec. 📷 🚻 🛗 **Events & activities**.
www.horniman.ac.uk

Frederick Horniman, the tea
merchant, had this museum
built in 1901 to house the
curios he had collected on his
travels. Extensively developed
in 2002, the museum features
a music gallery, aquarium,
world culture displays and a
history gallery. There is a
good shop with toys that
represent the popular range
of the museum's collections.

Dulwich Picture Gallery ⓥ

College Rd SE21. 📞 020-8693
5254. 🚊 West Dulwich, North
Dulwich. **Open** 10am–5pm Tue–Fri,
11am–5pm Sat, Sun & bank hol Mon.
(last adm 4:30pm). **Closed** all public
hols (except bank hol Mon & Good
Fri). **Adm charge.** 📷 📷 3pm
Sat & Sun. 🛗 🚻 📷 **www**.
dulwichpicturegallery.org.uk

England's oldest public art
gallery, it was opened in 1817
and designed by Sir John
Soane (see pp136–7). Its

Rembrandt's *Jacob II de Gheyn* at
Dulwich Picture Gallery

imaginative use of skylights made it the prototype of most art galleries built since. The gallery was originally commissioned to house the royal collection for the King of Poland. The superb collection has works by Rembrandt (his *Jacob II de Gheyn* has been stolen from here four times), Canaletto, Poussin, Watteau, Claude, Murillo and Raphael.

The building houses Soane's mausoleum to Desenfans and Bourgeois, who were the original founders of the collection.

Tennis racket and net from 1888, Wimbledon Lawn Tennis Museum

Battersea Park ㉓

Albert Bridge Rd SW11. **Map** 19 C5. *Tel* 020-8871 7530. ⊖ Sloane Sq then bus 137. ⇄ Battersea Pk. **Open** 8am–dusk daily. ♿ ⬛ **Sports facilities.** See **Six Guided Walks** pp266–7. **www**.batterseapark.org

Peace Pagoda, Battersea Park

This was the second public park created to relieve the growing urban stresses on Victorian Londoners (the first was Victoria Park in the East End). It opened in 1858 on the former Battersea Fields – a swampy area notorious for every kind of vice, centred around the Old Red House, a disreputable pub.

The new park immediately became popular, especially for its man-made boating lake, with its romantic rocks, gardens and waterfalls. Later it became a great site for the new craze of cycling.

In 1985 a peace pagoda was opened, a 35-m (100-ft) high monument built by Buddhist nuns and monks. There are also a small zoo, sports activities and an art gallery, the Pumphouse.

St Mary's, Battersea ㉔

Battersea Church Rd SW11. *Tel* 020-7222 9648. ⊖ Sloane Sq then bus 19 or 219. **Open** daily by arrangement. ⛪ 8.30am, 11am, 6.30pm Sun. 📷 ♿ **Concerts**. **www**.southwark.anglican.org

There has been a church here since at least the 10th century. The present brick building dates from 1775, but the 17th-century stained glass, commemorating Tudor monarchs, comes from the former church.

In 1782 the poet and artist William Blake was married in the church. Later J M W Turner was to paint some marvellous views of the Thames from the church tower. Benedict Arnold, who served George Washington in the American War of Independence, is buried in the crypt.

Wimbledon Lawn Tennis Museum ㉕

Church Rd SW19. *Tel* 020-8946 6131. ⊖ Southfields. **Open** 10am–5pm daily (not during championships except to ticket holders). **Closed** 24–26 Dec, 1 Jan. **Adm charge**. ♿ 📷 call for times. ⬛ 🚻 **www**.wimbledon.org/museum

Even those with only a passing interest in the sport will find plenty to enjoy at this museum. It traces tennis's development from its invention in the 1860s as a diversion for country house parties, to the sport it is today. Alongside strange 19th-century equipment are

film clips showing the great players of the past. More recent matches may be viewed in the video theatre.

Wimbledon Windmill Museum ㉖

Windmill Rd SW19. *Tel* 020-8947 2825. ⊖ ⇄ Wimbledon then 30-min walk. **Open** Apr–Oct: 2–5pm Sat, 11am–5pm Sun & pub hols (Nov–Mar: groups only, by arrangement). **Adm charge**. 📷 ⬛ 🚻 **www**. wimbledonwindmillmuseum.org.uk

The mill on Wimbledon Common was built in 1817. The building at its base was turned into cottages in 1864. Boy Scout founder Lord Baden-Powell lived in the mill house. Today the site is a museum housing model windmills.

St Mary's, Battersea

West of the Centre

Ham House

Richmond Park ㉗

Kingston Vale SW15. **Tel** 020-8948 3209. 🚇 🚊 Richmond then bus 65 or 71. **Open** daily until 30 mins before dusk. Oct–Feb: from 7.30am; Mar–Sep: from 7am. **www**.royalparks.gov.uk

Deer in Richmond Park

In 1637, Charles I built a wall 8 miles (13 km) round to enclose the royal park as a hunting ground. Today the park is a national nature reserve and deer still graze warily among the chestnuts, birches and oaks, no longer hunted but still discreetly culled. They have learned to co-exist with the thousands of human visitors who stroll here on fine weekends.

In late spring the highlight is the Isabella Plantation with its spectacular display of azaleas, while the nearby Pen Ponds are very popular with optimistic anglers. (Adam's Pond is for model boats.) The rest of the park is heath, bracken and trees (some of them hundreds of years old). Richmond Gate, in the north-west corner, was designed by the landscape gardener Capability Brown in 1798. Nearby is Henry VIII Mound,

where in 1536 the king, staying in Richmond Palace, awaited the signal that his former wife, Anne Boleyn, had been executed. The Palladian White Lodge, built in 1729, is home to the Royal Ballet School.

Hampton Court ㉘

See pp254–7.

Ham House ㉙

Ham St, Richmond. **Tel** 020-8940 1950. 🚇 🚊 Richmond then bus 65 or 371. **Open** mid-Mar–Nov: noon–4pm Sat–Wed. **Closed** 25–26 Dec, 1 Jan. **Adm charge**. 🎧 by appt. 🚻 🔲 🚼 11am–5.30pm. **Gardens open** Jan–mid-Feb: 11am–4pm Sat & Sun, mid-Feb–Oct: 11am–5pm Sat–Wed; Nov–Dec: 11am–5pm Sat & Sun. **www**.nationaltrust.org.uk

This magnificent house by the Thames was built in 1610, but

Marble Hill House

its heyday came when it was home to the Duke of Lauderdale, confidant to Charles II and Secretary of State for Scotland. His wife, the Countess of Dysart, inherited it from her father, who had been Charles I's "whipping boy" (punished for the future king's misdemeanours). From 1672 the Duke and Countess modernized the house, and it was regarded as one of Britain's finest. The garden has been restored to its 17th-century form.

On some days in summer, a foot passenger ferry runs from here to Marble Hill House and Orleans House at Twickenham.

Orleans House Gallery ㉚

Orleans Rd, Twickenham. **Tel** 020-8831 6000. 🚇 🚊 Richmond then bus 33, 90, 290, R68 or R70. **Open** Apr–Sep: 1–5.30pm Tue–Sat, 2–5.30pm Sun & bank hols; Oct–Mar: 1–4.30pm Tue–Sat, 2–4.30pm Sun & bank hols. **Closed** 24–26 Dec, 1 Jan, Good Fri. **Gardens open** 9am–dusk daily. 🚻 limited. 🔲 🚼

This gallery is located on the site of the original Orleans House, named after Louis Philippe, Duke of Orleans, who lived there from 1815 to 1817. Adjacent is the Octagon Room, designed by James Gibbs for James Johnson in 1720. The gallery opened to the public in 1972, and shows temporary exhibitions, including local history displays.

Marble Hill House ㉛

Richmond Rd, Twickenham. **Tel** 020-8892 5115. 🚇 🚊 Richmond then bus 33, 90, 290, R68 or R70. **Open** Apr–Oct: 10am–2pm Sat, 10am–5pm Sun & bank hols; prebooked guided tours at other times (phone to check). **Closed** 21 Dec–28 Feb. 🚻 restricted. 🚫 🔲 🚼 **Fireworks** at weekends. See **Entertainment** p349. **www**.english-heritage.org.uk

Built in 1729 for George II's mistress, Henrietta Howard, the house and its grounds have been open to the public since 1903. It has now been fully restored to its Georgian appearance. There are paintings by William Hogarth and a view of the river and house in 1762 by Richard Wilson, who is regarded as the father of English landscape painting. The café is especially good.

Richmond ❷

SW15. 🚇 🚃 *Richmond.*

Richmond side street

This attractive London town took its name from the palace that Henry VII built here in 1500. Many early 18th-century houses survive near the river and off Richmond Hill, notably Maids of Honour Row, which was built in 1724. The beautiful view of the river from the top of the hill has been captured by many artists, and is largely unspoiled.

Syon House ❸

London Rd, Brentford. **Tel** 020-8560 0882. 🚇 *Gunnersbury then bus 237 or 267.* **House open** *mid-Mar–Oct: 11am–5pm Wed–Thu, Sun.* **House closed** *Nov–mid-Mar.* **Gardens open** *mid-Mar–Oct: 10:30am–5pm daily; Nov–mid-Mar: 10:30am–4pm Sat & Sun.* **Closed** *25–26 Dec.* **Adm charge**. ⊘ 🚻 🅿 🍴 🛍 ♿ *gardens only.* **www**.syonpark.co.uk

The Earls and Dukes of Northumberland have lived here for 400 years – it is the only large mansion in the London area still in its hereditary ownership. The interior of the house was remodelled in 1761 by Robert Adam, and is considered to be one of his masterpieces. The five Adam rooms house original furnishings and a significant collection of Old Master paintings. The 200 acre park was landscaped by Capability Brown, and includes a 40 acre garden with more than 200 species of rare trees. The Great Conservatory inspired Joseph Paxton's designs for the Crystal Palace.

Musical Museum ❹

399 High St, Brentford. 🚻 *020-8560 8108.* 🚇 *Gunnersbury, South Ealing then bus 65, 237 or 267.* **Open** *11am–5:30pm Tue–Sun & bank hol Mondays.* **Adm charge**. 📷 ♿ 🛍 🚻 **www**.musicalmuseum.co.uk

The collection is arranged over three floors and comprises chiefly large instruments, including player (or automatic) pianos and organs, miniature and cinema pianos, and what is thought to be the only surviving self-playing Wurlitzer organ in Europe.

Drawing room: Osterley Park House

Osterley Park House ❺

Isleworth. 🚻 *020-8232 5050.* 🚇 *Osterley.* **Open** *Mar–Oct: noon–4:30pm Wed–Sun, noon–3:30pm first 3 weekends in Dec.* **Closed** *end Dec–Feb.* **Adm charge**. 🅿 **Park open** *8am–dusk daily.* **www**.nationaltrust.org.uk/osterley

Osterley is ranked among Robert Adam's finest works, and its colonnaded portico and elegant library ceiling are the proof. Much of the furniture is by Adam; the garden and temple are by William Chambers, architect of Somerset House. The garden house is by Adam.

Robert Adam's red drawing room at Syon House

Hampton Court ⑳

Cardinal Wolsey, powerful Archbishop of York to Henry VIII, began building Hampton Court in 1514. Originally it was not a royal palace, but was

Ceiling decoration from the Queen's Drawing Room

intended as Wolsey's riverside country house. Later, in 1528, in the hope of retaining royal favour, Wolsey offered it to the king. After the royal takeover, Hampton Court was twice rebuilt and extended, first by Henry himself and then, in the 1690s, by William and Mary, who employed Christopher Wren as architect.

There is a striking contrast between Wren's Classical royal apartments and the Tudor turrets, gables and chimneys elsewhere. The inspiration for the gardens as they are today comes largely from the time of William and Mary, who created a vast, formal Baroque landscape, with radiating avenues of majestic limes and many collections of exotic plants.

★ The Maze
Lose yourself in one of the garden's most popular features.

Royal tennis court

River boat pier

Main entrance

River Thames

Privy Garden

★ The Great Vine
The vine was planted in the 1760s, and, in the 19th century, produced up to 910 kg (2,000 lbs) of black grapes.

The Pond Garden
This sunken garden was once a pond to store fresh fish for Henry VIII's Court.

★ The Mantegna Gallery
Andrea Mantegna's nine canvases depicting The Triumphs of Caesar *(c.1484–1505) are housed here.*

VISITORS' CHECKLIST

Surrey KT8 9AU. 0844-482
7777. 111, 216, 411, 718.
Hampton Court.
Hampton Court pier. **Open**
Apr–Oct: 10am–6pm daily; Nov–
Mar: 10am–4.30pm daily (last
adm: 1 hour before closing).
Closed 24–26 Dec. **Adm
charge.**
www.hrp.org.uk

Broad Walk
*A contemporary print shows the
East Front and the Broad Walk
during the reign of George
II (1727–60).*

Long Water
*A man-made lake runs
parallel to the Thames,
from the Fountain Garden
across the Home Park.*

Fountain Garden
*A few of the clipped yews
here were planted in the
reign of William and Mary.*

The East Front
*The windows of the
Queen's Drawing
Room, designed by
Wren, overlook the
central avenue of the
Fountain Garden.*

STAR FEATURES

★ The Great Vine

★ The Mantegna
  Gallery

★ The Maze

Exploring the Palace

Carving on the roof of the Great Hall

As an historic royal palace, Hampton Court bears traces of many of the kings and queens of England from Henry VIII to the present day. The building itself is a harmonious blend of Tudor and English Baroque architecture. Inside, visitors can see the Great Hall, built by Henry VIII, as well as state apartments of the Tudor court. Many of the Baroque state apartments, including those above Fountain Court by Christopher Wren, are decorated with furniture, tapestries and old masters from the Royal Collection.

Tudor Chimneys
Ornate chimneys, some original, some careful restorations, adorn the roof of the Tudor palace.

Queen's Presence Chamber

Queen's Guard Chamber

★ Chapel Royal
The Tudor chapel was re-fitted by Wren except for the carved and gilded vaulted ceiling.

Haunted Gallery

★ Great Hall
The stained-glass window in the Tudor Great Hall shows Henry VIII flanked by the coats of arms of his six wives.

STAR FEATURES

★ Great Hall

★ Fountain Court

★ Clock Court

★ Chapel Royal

★ Clock Court
Anne Boleyn's Archway is at the entrance to Clock Court. The Astronomical Clock, created for Henry VIII in 1540, is also located here.

King's Great Bedchamber
William III bought the crimson bed from his Lord Chamberlain.

Wren's east façade

Queen's Gallery
This marble chimneypiece by John Nost was moved from the King's Great Bedchamber to the Queen's Gallery.

CARDINAL WOLSEY

Thomas Wolsey (c.1475–1530), simultaneously a cardinal, Archbishop of York and chancellor, was, after the king, the most powerful man in England. However, when he was unable to persuade the pope to allow Henry VIII to divorce his first wife, Catherine of Aragon, Wolsey fell from royal favour. He died while making his way to face trial for treason.

★ **Fountain Court**
The windows of state apartments are visible above the cloisters of Fountain Court.

King's Staircase
Leading to the state apartments, the King's Staircase has wall paintings by Antonio Verrio.

TIMELINE

1500	1600	1700	1800	1900

1514 Construction of palace begins

1532 Henry starts new hall

1647 Charles I imprisoned by Cromwell

1734 William Kent decorates the Queen's Staircase

1838 Public apartments first admitted to the palace

1986 State apartments partly damaged by fire

1528 Wolsey gives the palace to Henry VIII

Henry VIII painted by Hans Holbein

1689 William and Mary move to Hampton Court

c. 1727 Queen's apartments are finally completed

1773 Great Gatehouse reduced by two storeys

1992 Damaged apartments are reopened

PM Gallery and House ㊱

Mattock Lane W5. **Tel** 020-8567 1227. ⊖ Ealing Broadway. **Open** 1–5pm Tue–Fri, 11am–5pm Sat. **Closed** public hols. ⬚ ⬚ **Exhibitions.** www.ealing.gov.uk/ pmgalleryandhouse

Sir John Soane, architect of the Bank of England *(see p147)*, designed this house, Pitzhanger Manor, on the site of an earlier one. Completed in 1803, it was to become his own country residence. There are clear echoes of his elaborately constructed town house in Lincoln's Inn Fields *(see pp136–7)*, especially in the library, with its imaginative use of mirrors, in the darkly-painted breakfast room opposite and in the "monk's dining room" which is located on the basement level.

Soane retained two of the principal formal rooms: the drawing room and the dining room. These were designed in 1768 by George Dance the Younger, with whom Soane had worked before establishing his own reputation.

A sympathetic 20th-century extension has been refurbished as a gallery offering a wide range of contemporary art exhibitions and associated events. The house also contains a large exhibition of Martinware, highly decorated glazed pottery made in nearby Southall between 1877

Martinware bird at PM Gallery

and 1915 and fashionable in late Victorian times. The gardens of Pitzhanger Manor are now a pleasant public park and offer a welcome contrast to the bustle of nearby Ealing.

Kew Bridge Steam Museum ㊲

Green Dragon Lane, Brentford. **Tel** 020-8568 4757. ⊖ Kew Bridge, Gunnersbury then bus 65, 237 or 267. **Open** 11am–4pm Tue–Sun (engines operate at set times – check website for details). **Closed** Mon (except bank hols). **Adm charge.** ⬚ book ahead. ⬚ Sat & Sun. ⬚ ⬚ www.kbsm.org

The 19th-century water pumping station, near the north end of Kew Bridge, is now a museum of steam power and water in London. Its main exhibits are five giant Cornish beam engines that pumped water here from the river, to be distributed in London. The earliest engines, dating from 1820, are similar to those built to pump water out of Cornish mines. See them working at weekends and on public holidays.

Kew Gardens ㊳

See pp260–61.

City Barge: Strand on the Green

Strand on the Green ㊴

W4. ⊖ Gunnersbury then bus 237 or 267. ⊠ Kew Bridge.

This charming Thames-side walk passes some fine 18th-century houses as well as rows of more modest cottages once inhabited by fishermen. The oldest of its three pubs is the City Barge *(see pp316–19)*, parts of which date from the 15th century: the name is older and derives from the time when the Lord Mayor's barge was moored on the Thames outside.

Chiswick House ㊵

Burlington Lane W4. **Tel** 020-8995 0508. ⊖ Chiswick. **Open** Apr: 10am–5pm daily; May–Oct: 10am–5pm Sun–Wed & bank hols; Nov: pre-booked visits only. **Closed** end Dec–Mar. **Adm charge.** ⬚ phone ahead. ⬚ **Gardens Open** 7am–dusk daily. **No adm charge.** www.chgt.org.uk

Completed in 1729 to the design of its owner, the third Earl of Burlington, this is a

Chiswick House

fine example of a Palladian villa. Burlington revered both Palladio and his disciple Inigo Jones, and their statues stand outside. Built round a central octagonal room, the house is packed with references to ancient Rome and Renaissance Italy, as is the garden.

Chiswick was Burlington's country residence and this house was built as an annexe to a larger, older house (since demolished). It was designed for recreation and entertaining – Lord Hervey, Burlington's enemy, dismissed it as "too little to live in and too big to hang on a watch chain". Some of the ceiling paintings are by William Kent, who also contributed to the garden design.

The house was a private mental home from 1892 until 1928, when a long process of restoration began. The layout of the garden, now a public park, is much as Burlington designed it.

Plaque on Hogarth's House

Hogarth's House ❹

Hogarth Lane, W4. **Tel** 020-8994 6757. ⊖ Turnham Green. **Open** Apr–Oct: 1–5pm Tue–Fri, 1–6pm Sat, Sun; Nov–Dec & Feb–Mar: 1–4pm Tue–Fri, 1–5pm Sat, Sun. **Closed** Jan, Good Fri, 25 & 26 Dec. 📷 🎥 ♿ ground floor only. 🛗

When the painter William Hogarth lived here from 1749 until his death in 1764, he called it "a little country box by the Thames" and painted bucolic views from its windows – he had moved from Leicester Square *(see p103)*. Today traffic roars by along the Great West Road, on its way to and from Heathrow Airport – rush hour traffic is also notoriously bad here. In an environment as

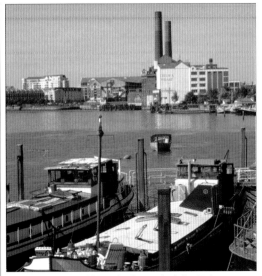

Attractive residential and leisure development in Chelsea Harbour

hostile as this, and following years of neglect and then bombing during World War II, the house has done well to survive. It has now been turned into a small museum and gallery, which is filled mostly with a collection of engraved copies of the moralistic cartoon-style pictures with which Hogarth made his name. Salutary tales, such as *The Rake's Progress* (in Sir John Soane's Museum – *see pp136–7*), *Marriage à la Mode, An Election Entertainment* and many others, can all be seen here.

Fulham Palace ❷

Bishops Ave SW6. **Tel** 020-7736 8140. ⊖ Putney Bridge. **Open** noon–4pm Mon & Tue, 11am–2pm Sat, 11.30am–3.30pm Sun. **Closed** Good Fri, 25 & 26 Dec. **Park open** daylight hours daily. ♿ 🎥 🖥 🛗 **Events, concerts, lectures.** www.fulhampalace.org

The home of the Bishops of London from the 8th century until 1973, the oldest surviving parts of Fulham Palace date from the 15th century. The palace stands in its own landscaped gardens northwest of Putney Bridge. A restoration project completed in 2007 revealed a grand, long-hidden Rococo ceiling.

Chelsea Harbour ❸

SW10. ⊖ Fulham Broadway. ♿ **Exhibitions**. 🖥 🛗

This is an impressive development of modern apartments, shops, offices, restaurants, a hotel and a marina. It is near the site of Cremorne Pleasure Gardens, which closed in 1877 after more than 40 years as a venue for dances and circuses. The centrepiece is the Belvedere, a 20-storey apartment tower with an external glass lift and pyramid roof, topped with a golden ball on a rod that rises and falls with the tide.

Eye-catching entrance to Fulham Palace dating from Tudor times

Kew Gardens 🔞

The Royal Botanic Gardens, Kew are a World Heritage Site and the most complete public gardens in the world. Their reputation was first established by Sir Joseph Banks, the British naturalist and plant hunter, who worked here in the late 18th century. In 1841 the former royal gardens were given to the nation and now display about 40,000 plants. Garden enthusiasts will want a full day to visit. Kew is also a centre for scholarly research.

HIGHLIGHTS

Spring
Cherry Walk ①
Crocus "carpet" ②
Rhizotron and Xstrata
Treetop Walkway ③

Summer
Rock Garden ④
Rose Garden ⑤

Autumn
Autumn foliage ⑥

Winter
Winter Garden ⑦
Witch Hazels ⑧

★ **Pagoda**
Britain's fascination with the Orient influenced William Chambers's pagoda, built in 1762.

STAR SIGHTS

★ Temperate House

★ Pagoda

★ Palm House

Princess Augusta
King George III's mother established the first garden on a nine-acre (3.6 ha) site here in 1759.

Queen Charlotte's Cottage

Waterlily Pond

River Thames

Lion Gate entrance

Evolution House
gives a detailed history of plant life on Earth.

★ **Temperate House**
The building dates from 1899. Delicate woody plants are arranged here according to their geographical origins.

Minka House
This minka (traditional wooden Japanese house), built around 1900, was shipped from Japan and reconstructed in the Bamboo Garden in 2001

Princess of Wales Conservatory
Encompassing ten climatic zones, this glasshouse contains cacti, giant waterlilies and orchids.

White Peaks (exhibition centre)

Azalea Garden

Brentford Gate entrance

Kew Palace

Nash Conservatory

Main gate entrance

The Orangery

Duke's Garden

Alpine House

Campanile

Temple of Bellona

Victoria Gate entrance and visitor centre

★ Palm House
Designed by Decimus Burton in the 1840s, this famous jewel of Victorian engineering houses exotic plants in tropical conditions.

SIX GUIDED WALKS

London is an excellent city for walkers. Although it is much more spread out than most European capitals, many of the main tourist attractions are fairly close to each other *(see pp14–15)*. Central London is full of parks and gardens *(see pp48–51)*, and there are also several walk routes planned by the tourist board and local history societies. These include footpaths along canals and the Thames, and the Silver Jubilee Walk. Planned in 1977 to commemorate the Queen's Silver Jubilee, the walk runs for 12 miles (19 km) between Lambeth Bridge in the west and Tower Bridge in the east; Visit London *(see p362)* has maps of the route, which is marked by silver-coloured plaques placed at intervals on the pavement.

Statue of boy and dolphin in Regent's Park

Each of the 16 areas described in the *Area-by-Area* section of this book has a short walk marked on its *Street-by-Street* map. These walks will take you past many of the most interesting sights in that area. On the following twelve pages are routes for six walks that take you through areas of London not covered in detail elsewhere. These range from the bustling, fashionable King's Road *(see pp266–7)* to the wide open spaces of riverside Richmond and Kew *(see pp268–9)*.

Several companies offer guided walks *(see below)*. Most of these have themes, such as ghosts or Shakespeare's London. Look in listings magazines *(see p342)* for details.

USEFUL NUMBERS The Original London Walks
Tel 020-7624 3978. **www**.walks.com

CHOOSING A WALK

The Six Walks
This map shows the location of the six guided walks in relation to the main sightseeing areas of London.

King's Road, Chelsea

Strand on the Green, Kew

Regent's Canal *(pp264–5)*

Mayfair *(pp270–1)*

Notting Hill *(pp274–5)*

South Bank *(pp272–3)*

Chelsea and Battersea *(pp266–7)*

Richmond and Kew *(pp268–9)*

0 kilometres 4

0 miles 2

KEY

······ Walk route

◁ Houseboats on Regent's Canal, Little Venice

A Two-Hour Walk along the Regent's Canal

Master builder John Nash wanted the Regent's Canal to pass through Regent's Park, but instead it circles north of the park. Opened in 1820, it is long defunct as a commercial waterway but is today a valuable leisure amenity. This walk starts at Little Venice and ends at Camden Lock market, diverting briefly to take in the view from Primrose Hill. For more details on the sights near the Regent's Canal, see pages 220–27.

Houseboat on the canal ③

From Little Venice to Lisson Grove

At Warwick Avenue station ① take the left-hand exit and walk straight to the traffic lights by the canal bridge at Blomfield Road. Turn right and descend to the canal through an iron gate ② opposite No. 42, marked "Lady Rose of Regent". The pretty basin with moored narrow boats is Little Venice ③. At the foot of the steps turn left to walk back beneath the blue iron bridge ④. You soon have to climb up to street level again because this stretch of the towpath is reserved for access to the

The Warwick Castle, near Warwick Avenue

barges. Cross Edgware Road and walk down Aberdeen Place. When the road turns to the left by a pub, Crockers ⑤, follow the signposted Canal Way down to the right of some modern flats. Continue your route along the canal towpath, crossing Park Road at street level. The scenery along this stretch is unremarkable, but it is not long before a splash of green to your right announces that you are now walking alongside Regent's Park ⑥.

Houseboats moored at Little Venice ③

TIPS FOR WALKERS

Starting point: Warwick Avenue Underground station.
Length: 3 miles (5 km).
Getting there: Warwick Avenue and Camden Town Underground stations are at either end of the walk. Buses 16, 16A and 98 go to Warwick Avenue; 24, 29 and 31 go to Camden Town.
Stopping-off points: Crockers, Queens and The Princess of Wales (corner of Fitzroy and Chalcot Roads) are good pubs. At the junction of Edgware Road and Aberdeen Place is Café La Ville. Camden Town has many cafés, restaurants and sandwich shops.

KEY

•••• Walk route
☆ Good viewing point
● Underground station
▆ Railway station

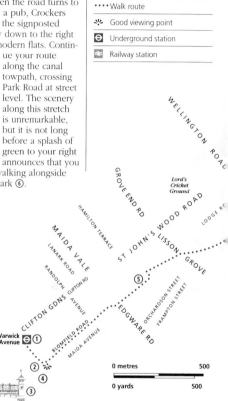

Regent's Park

Soon you see four mansions ⑦. A bridge on huge pillars marked "Coalbrookdale" ⑧ carries Avenue Road into the park. Cross the next bridge, with London Zoo ⑨ on your right, then turn left up a slope. A few steps later, take the right fork, and turn left to cross Prince Albert Road. Turn right before entering Primrose Hill through a gate ⑩ on your left.

Mansion with riverside gardens ⑦

Indoor market, Camden Lock ⑲

Primrose Lodge, Primrose Hill ⑩

Primrose Hill

From here there is a view of the zoo aviary ⑪, designed by Lord Snowdon and opened in 1965. Inside the park, keep to the left-hand path that climbs to the top of the hill. Soon you fork right to the summit, which offers a fine view of the city skyline. A viewing panel ⑫ helps identify the landmarks but it does not include the 1990 skyscraper at Canary Wharf, with its pyramid crown, on the left. Descend on the left, making for the park gate at the junction of Regent's Park Road and Primrose Hill Road.

Towards Camden

Almost opposite the gate is the Queens ⑬, a Victorian pub and, just to the left, is No. 122 Regent's Park Road ⑭. This was for 24 years the home of the communist philosopher Friedrich Engels; he was often visited there by his friend Karl Marx.

Turn right and walk down Regent's Park Road for 135 m (150 yd) then turn left up Fitzroy Road. On the right, between Nos. 41 and 39, is the entrance to Primrose Hill Studios ⑮, built in 1882. Residents have included the musician Sir Henry Wood and illustrator Arthur Rackham, famous for his fairy pictures.

Continue down Fitzroy Road past No. 23 ⑯, once home to the poet W B Yeats, then go right into Chalcot Road and left down Princess Road, past a Victorian board school ⑰. Turn right and rejoin the canal down steps across Gloucester Avenue. Turn left under the railway bridge and past the Pirate Castle ⑱, a water sports centre. Cross a hump bridge and enter Camden Lock Market ⑲ (see p332) through an arch on your left. After browsing there you can take the water bus ⑳ back to Little Venice or turn right into Chalk Farm Road and walk up to Camden Town Underground station.

Pedestrian bridge over the canal at Camden Lock ⑲

A Three-Hour Walk in Chelsea and Battersea

This delightful circular walk ambles through the grounds of the Royal Hospital and across the river to Battersea Park, with its romantic Victorian landscaping. It then returns to the narrow village streets of Chelsea and the stylish shops on the King's Road. For more details on the sights in Chelsea see pages 192–7.

Royal Hospital ③

Sloane Square to Battersea Park

From the station ①, turn left and walk down Holbein Place. The Renaissance painter's connection with Chelsea stems from his friendship with Sir Thomas More who lived nearby. Pass the cluster of good antique shops ② as you turn on to Royal Hospital Road. Enter the grounds of the Royal Hospital ③, designed by Christopher Wren, and turn left into the informal Ranelagh Gardens ④. The small pavilion by John Soane ⑤ displays a history of the gardens as a Georgian pleasure resort – it was the most fashionable meeting place for London society.

Galleon on Chelsea Bridge

Leave the gardens for fine views of the hospital and Grinling Gibbons's bronze of Charles II ⑥. The granite obelisk ⑦ commemorates the 1849 battle at Chilianwalla, in what is now Pakistan, and forms the centre-piece of the main marquee at the Chelsea Flower Show (see p56).

Charles II statue in Royal Hospital ⑥

Battersea Park

When crossing the Chelsea Bridge ⑧ (1937), look up at the four gilded galleons on top of the pillars at each end. Turn into Battersea Park ⑨ (see p251), one of London's liveliest, and follow the main path along the river to enjoy the excellent views of Chelsea. Turn left at the exotic Buddhist Peace Pagoda ⑩ to the main part of the park.

Past the bowling greens lies Henry Moore's carving of *Three Standing Figures* ⑪ (1948) and the lake, a favoured spot for wildfowl. (There are boats for hire.) Just beyond the sculpture head northwest and, after crossing the central avenue, fork right and make for the wooden gate into the rustic Old English Garden ⑫. Leave the garden by the metal gate and return to Chelsea via the Victorian Albert Bridge ⑬.

Three Standing Figures by Henry Moore ⑪

TIPS FOR WALKERS

Starting point: *Sloane Square.*
Length: *4 miles (6.5 km).*
Getting there: *Sloane Square is the nearest tube. There are frequent buses 11, 19, 22 and 349 to Sloane Square and along the King's Road.*
Royal Hospital Grounds are open only *10am–6pm Mon–Sat, 2–6pm Sun.*
Stopping-off points: *There is a café in Battersea Park, by the lake. The Eight Bells, on Cheyne Walk, is a well-known local pub. There are several other pubs, restaurants and sandwich shops to be found along the King's Road. The Chelsea Farmers' Market on Sydney Street has several cafés.*

KEY

• • •   Walk route

⚜   Good viewing point

🚇   Underground station

Old English Garden in Battersea Park ⑫

Albert Bridge ⑬

much of its original character. Where Glebe Place meets the King's Road are three pretty, early 18th-century houses ㉓. Cross Dovehouse Green opposite (it used to be a burial ground), to Chelsea Farmers' Market ㉔, an enclave of cafés and craft shops.

The King's Road
Leave the market on Sydney Street and cross into the garden of St Luke's Church ㉕, where the writer Charles Dickens was married. The walk then winds through pretty back streets until it rejoins the King's Road ㉖ *(see p196)*, which was very fashionable in the 1960s. On the left is The Pheasantry ㉗. Look down the side streets on both left and right to see the squares and terraces: Wellington Square ㉘, then Royal Avenue ㉙, intended as a triumphal way to the Royal Hospital, and Blacklands Terrace ㉚, where book-lovers will want to visit John Sandoe's shop. The Duke of York's Territorial Headquarters ㉛ (1803) on the right – now home to the Saatchi Gallery – marks the approach to Sloane Square ㉜ and the Royal Court Theatre *(see Sloane Square p197)*.

The Back Streets of Chelsea

Thomas Carlyle statue ⑮

Over the bridge is David Wynne's sculpture of a boy and dolphin ⑭ (1975). Pass the sought-after residences on Cheyne Walk and the statues of historian Thomas Carlyle ⑮, and Sir Thomas More ⑯. The area was renowned for gatherings of intellectuals. Past Chelsea Old Church ⑰ is Roper's Gardens ⑱ with

its carving by Jacob Epstein. Just beyond these is the old, medieval Crosby Hall ⑲. Justice Walk ⑳ has a nice view of two early Georgian houses – Duke's House and Monmouth House. Turn left to pass the site of the Chelsea porcelain factory ㉑, which used to make highly fashionable (and today very highly collectable) wares in the late 18th century. Glebe Place ㉒ has retained

Royal Court Theatre ㉜

A 90-Minute Walk around Richmond and Kew

This delightful riverside walk begins in historic Richmond by the remains of Henry VII's once-splendid palace and ends at Kew, Britain's premier botanic garden. For more details on the sights in Richmond and Kew, turn to pages 252–8.

The river at low tide

Richmond Green

From Richmond station ①, proceed to Oriel House ②, which is practically opposite. Take the alleyway beneath it, and turn left towards the red-brick and terracotta Richmond Theatre ③, built in 1899. The remarkable Edmund Kean, whose brief, meteoric career in the early 19th century had a lasting impact on English acting, was closely associated with the previous theatre on the site. Opposite is Richmond Green ④. Cross it diagonally and go through the entrance arch ⑤ of the old Tudor palace, which is adorned with the arms of Henry VII.

Old Palace: carving over entrance ⑤

contain remnants, much modified, of the 16th-century buildings.

Leave Old Palace Yard at the right-hand corner ⑥, following a sign "To the River", and turn left to pass the White Swan pub ⑦. At the river, go right along the towpath under the iron railway bridge and then the concrete Twickenham Bridge ⑧, completed in 1933, to reach Richmond Lock ⑨, with its cast-iron footbridge built in 1894. The Thames is tidal as far as Teddington, some 3 miles (5 km) upstream, and the lock is used to make the river continuously navigable.

Richmond Theatre ③

Richmond

Richmond owes much of its importance – as well as its name – to Henry, victor of the Wars of the Roses and the first Tudor monarch. On becoming king in 1485 he spent a lot of time at an earlier residence on this site, Sheen Palace, dating from the 12th century. The palace burned down in 1499 and Henry had it rebuilt, naming it Richmond after the town in Yorkshire where he held an earldom. In 1603 Henry's granddaughter, Elizabeth I, died here. The houses inside the archway on the left

The Riverside

Do not cross the bridge but continue along the wooded path by the river to Isleworth Ait ⑩, a large island where herons may be standing warily on the river bank. Just beyond it, on the far shore, is All Saints' Church ⑪, where the 15th-century tower has survived several rebuildings, most recently in the 1960s. Further round the inlet, Isleworth ⑫, once a small riverside village with a busy harbour, is now a dormitory for central London. Here there is river traffic to watch: barges, yachts and, in summer, the passenger boats that ply up-river to Hampton Court *(see pp254–7)*. Rowers are out at most times of year, training for races. The most prestigious occasions are the Henley Regatta in July and the Oxford v Cambridge boat race, every spring from Putney to Mortlake *(see p56)*.

Herons fish the river

KEY

• • •	Walk route
⚶	Good viewing point
Ⓔ	Underground station
🚉	Railway station

Kew

After a while the appearance of iron railings on your right marks where Old Deer Park ⑬ turns into Kew Gardens ⑭ (officially known as the Royal Botanic Gardens – *see pp260–61*). There used to be a riverside entrance for visitors arriving on foot or by water, but the gate ⑮ is now

Kew Palace in Kew Gardens ⑲

closed and the nearest entrance is to the north, near the car park.

Across the river, there are magnificent views of Syon House ⑯, seat of the Dukes of Northumberland since 1594. Part of the present house dates from the 16th century but it was largely redesigned by Robert Adam in the 1760s. You are looking at it across the garden Capability Brown laid out in the 18th century.

Just beyond are modern waterside apartments at Brentford ⑰. This was originally an industrial suburb, sited where the Grand Union Canal runs into the Thames, and its residential potential has only recently been exploited. You can pick out the tall chimney of the waterworks ⑱, now a museum dedicated to steam power. On the right, behind the Kew Gardens car park, there is soon a view of Kew Palace ⑲, now fully restored and open to the public.

Beyond the car park, leave the river by Ferry Lane on to Kew Green ⑳. Now you could spend the rest of the day in Kew Gardens or cross Kew Bridge and turn right on to Strand on the Green ㉑, a fine riverside walkway with atmospheric pubs, the oldest of them the City Barge ㉒. Head south down Kew Road if you need to get back, then turn left at Kew Gardens Road to depart from Kew Gardens Underground station (District line).

TIPS FOR WALKERS

Starting point: Richmond station, District Line.
Length: 3 miles (5 km).
Getting there: Richmond Underground or railway station. Buses 391 and R68 come here from Kew.
Stopping-off points: There are many cafés, pubs and tearooms in Richmond. The famous Maids of Honour tearoom is at Kew, as is Jasper's Bun in the Oven, a good restaurant.

Steam Museum ⑱

0 metres 500
0 yards 500

The river bank between Richmond and Kew

A Two-Hour Walk Through Mayfair to Belgravia

This walk takes you from Green Park to Hyde Park, through the hearts of Mayfair and Belgravia, two of London's most elegant Georgian residential districts. It includes a bracing stroll through Hyde Park and, if you're feeling energetic, a row on the Serpentine.

L'Artiste Musclé restaurant, Shepherd Market, Mayfair

Green Park to Berkeley Square

Exit Green Park station ① following the signs for Piccadilly North. With Green Park opposite you, turn left. Pass Devonshire House ②, a 1920s office block that replaced the 18th-century mansion designed by William Kent. Only Kent's gates survive, now at the park entrance across Piccadilly. Turn left and walk up Berkeley Sreet to Berkeley Square ③. To the south, Lansdowne House by Robert Adam has been replaced by an advertising agency ④.

Berkeley Square statue ③

TIPS FOR WALKERS

Starting point: *Green Park Underground station.*
Length: *3 miles (5 km)*
Getting there: *Green Park is on the Victoria, Jubilee and Piccadilly Underground Lines. Or take bus Nos. 9, 14, 19, 22, 25 or 38 and go to Green Park underground station entrance.*
Stopping-off points: *There are numerous pubs, cafés and eateries in the area. Dell Café on the Serpentine is open 8am–8pm.*

There are still a few splendid 18th-century houses to the west, including No. 45 ⑤, home of the soldier and governor, Lord Clive of India.

Mayfair

Keep to the south of the square and turn into Charles Street, noting the evocative lampholders at Nos. 40 and 41 ⑥. Turn left into Queen Street and cross Curzon Street to enter Shepherd Market ⑦ (*see p97*) through Curzonfield House alleyway. Turn right up a pedestrian-only street then right onto Hertford Street, passing the Curzon Cinema ⑧ on the corner of Curzon Street. Here you are almost facing Crewe House ⑨, built in 1730 by Edward Shepherd who also laid out the market.

Turn left and walk up Curzon Street, then turn right onto Chesterfield Street. A left turn at Charles Street brings you to Red Lion Yard ⑩, where a pub stands opposite one of the few weatherboarded buildings in the West End. Turn right into Hay's Mews and left up Chesterfield Hill. Cross Hill Street and South Street and head left until you reach an alley leading to the peaceful haven of Mount Street Gardens ⑪. The gardens back on to the Church of the Immaculate Conception ⑫. Cross the garden and turn left

Berkeley Square, with its ancient plane trees and Georgian houses

```
0 metres        400
0 yards         400
```

Memorial in Grosvenor Square ⑬

Official supplier to the royal family: royal coat of arms above the door

onto Mount Street; then right onto South Audley Street and left at Grosvenor Square ⑬ into Upper Grosvenor Street, passing to the left of the US Embassy. Look out for the statue of Franklin D Roosevelt. Turn right up Park

Lane and walk past houses that are the remnants of what used to be the city's most desirable residential street before the traffic got so heavy ⑭. At the end you can see Marble Arch *(see p211)*.

Hyde Park
Enter the pedestrian subway ⑮ at exit No. 6 and follow signs for Park Lane West Side, exit No. 5. You will emerge at Speakers' Corner ⑯ *(see p211)*, where on Sundays anyone can make a speech on any topic. Cross Hyde Park *(see p211)* south-

southwest, enjoying the views on all sides, and make for the boat house ⑰ on the Serpentine (an artificial lake created by Queen Caroline in 1730), where you rent a rowing boat. Turn left and follow the path to the Dell Café ⑱ for some refreshments. From there, take the stone bridge ⑲ and cross Rotten Row ⑳, where the very fashionable exercise their horses. Leave the park at Edinburgh Gate ㉑.

Speakers' Corner ⑯

eccentric structure fronted by colossal Doric columns, built in 1830. A path beside it leads to Halkin Arcade ㉔, built in the 1830s and adorned by Geoffrey Wickham's fountain built in 1971.

Belgravia
Turn left out of the arcade onto Kinnerton Street, which boasts one of London's smallest pubs, the Nag's Head ㉕. A street of pretty mews houses runs off to the left of this street at its northern end: look for Ann's Close and Kinnerton Place North. Almost opposite the latter, the street makes a sharp right turn to emerge into Wilton Place opposite St Paul's Church (1843). Turn right here and follow Wilton Crescent round to the left before turning left into Wilton Row, where there is another small pub, the Grenadier ㉖, once the officers' mess of the Guards' barracks and reputedly frequented by the Duke of Wellington. Up Old Barracks Yard to its right there are some old officers' billets and a worn stone said to have been used by the Iron Duke when mounting his horses. The alley leads to a T-junction. To finish the walk, turn right onto Grosvenor Crescent Mews, then left onto Grosvenor Crescent, which leads you to Hyde Park Corner Underground station.

The Serpentine, on a fine day ⑰

Knightsbridge
Cross Knightsbridge and, resisting the temptations of two of London's great department stores – Harvey Nichols ㉒ and Harrods ㉓ *(see p207)* on Brompton Road – head down Sloane Street to turn left at Harriet Street. At Lowndes Square turn right and leave the square on the far side, turning left into Motcomb Street. On your left is the Pantechnicon, an

KEY
• • • Walk route
🔆 Good viewing point
🔵 Underground station

Once the officers' mess, now the Grenadier pub, Belgravia ㉖

A 90-Minute Walk Along the South Bank

The Riverside Walk along the South Bank from Westminster Bridge *(see page 187)* via Bankside to Southwark Cathedral is one of the most entertaining excursions in town. From County Hall to Shakespeare's Globe, with the South Bank's well-known music, theatre and film venues, the shops and galleries of Gabriel's Wharf and the Oxo Tower, there's something for everyone. For more details on the sights in Southwark and Bankside, see pages 173–83.

Cafés and shops at Gabriel's Wharf ⑭

Westminster

Begin at Westminster station ① by the statue of Queen Boudica (or Boadicea), and walk over Westminster Bridge. Once on the south side ②, there is a fine view back over the river to the Houses of Parliament *(see pp72–3)*. The main building on this side is the former County Hall ③, now offering two hotels, several restaurants and a range of entertainment *(see p188)*. There's Dalí Universe for a glimpse of the Surreal, the Sea Life London Aquarium ④ to see the vibrant underwater world, and Namco Station, a games hall with computer games,

TIPS FOR WALKERS

Starting point: *Westminster Bridge.*
Length: *1.75 miles (2.75 km)*
Getting there: *Westminster Underground station on the District, Circle and Jubilee lines.*
Stopping off points: *All the South Bank's art centres have cafés, bars and restaurants. Also: Gourmet Pizza, Gabriel's Wharf; EAT, Riverside House (snacks and sandwiches); Anchor pub with river terrace (bars and restaurant).*

cars and pool tables. For the best city view, the London Eye ⑤ *(see p189)* is beside Jubilee Gardens ⑥, where buskers and mime artists perform. Walk past Hungerford Bridge ⑦ with its modern walkways and trains to Charing Cross Station, on the site of the former Hungerford market. Ahead is the Southbank Centre ⑧ *(see pp186–7)*, the capital's main arts showcase. Music and exhibitions fill the Royal Festival Hall ⑨ *(see p188)*, created for the Festival of Britain in 1951. Check to see what's showing at The Hayward ⑩ *(see p188)* too, just beyond, on the level above. Moving on along the

Riverside Walk, past Waterloo Bridge, you reach BFI Southbank ⑪ *(see p347)* where films are shown throughout the day. Outside its lively café, rows of tables stacked with second-hand books shelter beneath the bridge. The National Theatre ⑫ *(see p188)* also has exhibitions and musical events as well as a good bookshop, while in summer there are free outdoor performances. Several of the theatre's restaurants,

View from the Oxo Tower ⑮

cafés and bars offer outside seating overlooking the South Bank. Past the London Studios (ITV) ⑬ is Gabriel's Wharf ⑭ *(see p191)*, a pleasant diversion of art and craft shops and lively cafés.

The Oxo Tower

The next landmark you come to is the Oxo Tower ⑮, a red-

Art at The Hayward,
South Bank ⑩

Christopher Wren had a
house by Cardinal Cap
Alley in Cardinal's Wharf
㉓, where he had a good
view of it. Next door to his
house now is the exhibition
and tour centre for
Shakespeare's Globe ㉔
(see p177). A tour around
the theatre is the next best
thing to attending a
performance.

Bankside
Bankside becomes more
cramped here, as the historic
streets pass The Anchor ㉕
riverside pub and Vinopolis
㉖ to reach the Clink Prison
Museum ㉗ *(see p182)*, on

KEY

• • • Walk route

🔵 Underground station

🚆 Train station

The Anchor pub, Bankside ㉕

brick industrial building, with
contemporary designer shops
and galleries, such as gallery@.
Take the lift to the top of the
tower for an excellent, free
view of the city: the Inner
Temple and Fleet Street lie
opposite. Once down again,
the Riverside Walk passes by
Sea Containers House ⑯,
with gold trimmings (built as
a hotel, but now offices) and
Doggett's Coat and Badge
pub ⑰ *(see p63)*, then
continue under Blackfriars
Bridge ⑱, emerging by the
remaining piers and railway
emblem of a former bridge.
On the right, opposite the
Founders Arms ⑲, is the
esteemed Bankside Gallery ⑳
(see p177), which has regular
exhibitions of its members'
work and a shop. Behind it,
opposite Falcon Point Piazza
is Marcus Campbell, an

excellent art bookshop, a
stone's throw from Tate
Modern ㉑ *(see pp178–81)*,
the best free show on the
river. Drop in for a coffee if
nothing else. The Millennium
Bridge ㉒ leads over to St
Paul's *(see pp148–9)* and the
City. Its architect Sir

the site of one of London's
first lock-ups. At St Mary
Ovarie Dock, climb aboard
a replica (1973) of *Golden
Hinde* ㉘, in which the Elizabethan buccaneer Sir Francis
Drake became the second man
to circumnavigate the world.
Southwark Cathedral ㉙ *(see
p176)*, is a quiet place to end
the walk -there is a good tea
shop here. Or, if you still feel
energetic, browse around Borough Market *(see p176)* before
heading to the tube or train at
London Bridge station ㉛.

Tate Modern: a vast space for contemporary British art ㉑

A Two-Hour Walk Around Notting Hill

This walk centres around Portobello Road, the city's most famous antiques and bric-a-brac shopping area in one of the ultra-fashionable parts of London. Great for original souvenirs, the neighbourhood is fascinating at any time, though the streets are busiest on Fridays and Saturdays, when all the shops are open and the market stalls laid out *(see page 333)*. This is the heart of Notting Hill, renowned for its carnival and, in recent years, favoured as a film setting and a smart address.

Odd bric-a-brac at a market stall

Sun in Splendour pub frontage ⑤

Portobello Road

Leaving Notting Hill Gate tube station ①, follow the signs to Portobello Road *(see p219)*, taking Pembridge Road ②. Intriguing shops here include Retro Woman ③ (Nos. 20 and 32) and Retro Man ④ (No. 34) for period clothes and accessories. At the Sun in Splendour pub ⑤, turn left into Portobello Road. No. 22, among the attractively painted terraced houses on the right, was where George Orwell lived in 1927 before his writing career began ⑥. Cross Chepstow Villas ⑦ and

the serious antique shops begin. Near the Portobello Arcade ⑧, signposted with a large teapot, is Portobello Gold (Nos. 95–7), a guest house where Bill, Hillary and Chelsea Clinton dropped in for a beer and a snack in 2000. At No. 115 ⑨ is a plaque to June Aylward who

opened the first antique shop in the street. At Colville Terrace ⑩ the daily fruit and vegetable market begins. On the left is the Electric Cinema ⑪, said to be the oldest working cinema in Britain (1910),

TIPS FOR WALKERS

Starting point: *Notting Hill Gate Underground station.*
Length: *1.85 miles (3 km)*
Getting there: *Notting Hill Underground station on Central, District and Circle lines.*
Stopping-off points: *The area is known for its pubs and restaurants. Try Grove Café at 253a Portobello Road; Eve's Market Café at 222 Portobello Road; Toms at 127 Westbourne Grove (great sandwiches and snacks); Ottolernghi's Patisserie at 62 Ledbury Road (superb pastries).*

The Electric Cinema, the UK's oldest working cinema ⑪

and certainly one of the most delightful. If there is not a film showing, you can go in and try the comfortable armchair seats and sofas.

The Travel Bookshop

Turn left down Blenheim Crescent to find The Travel Bookshop ⑫, inspiration for the location of the 1999 film *Notting Hill*, in which Hugh Grant was the assistant. Books for Cooks ⑬ (No. 4) is where recipes from the latest books are prepared and sold. Head back to Portobello Road and pass the local Salvation Army centre ⑭. Amble for several blocks to Grove Café ⑮ (No. 253a) on the corner (opposite the Market Bar ⑯). If you can find a table on the

Notting Hill's Travel Bookshop ⑫

Bevington Road, right along Blagrove Road and right again into Acklam Road to bring you back to Portobello Road. Continue for several blocks, turning left on Talbot Road, where All Saints' Church ⑲ has a glassed-in shrine to Our Lady of Walsingham – an unusual feature in a Protestant church. Just beyond the red-brick Tabernacle Centre for Arts and Education ⑳, where Pink Floyd made their debut

in 1966, is My Beautiful Laundrette ㉑, named after the successful 1986 film. Turn right into Ledbury Road to find high fashion shops, and also, at its end in the still-functioning Westbourne Grove Church ㉒. As you are passing No. 62, try the pastries in Ottolenghi Patisserie ㉓ for a snack to hit the spot. Turn right into Westbourne Grove for more stylish shopping. Nicole Farhi has a shop ㉔ (No. 202) of new and second-hand clothes. Detour to Toms deli and café ㉕ at 127, which claims the best toasted sandwiches in town, and is run by Tom Conran, son of the style guru Terence Conran. The Wild at Heart flower stall on Turquoise Island ㉖ opposite, won awards for its designer, Piers Gough, in 1993. On the far side is the Oxfam thrift shop ㉗, where its bargains reflect the good taste of the locals. Head back to Portobello Road ㉘ and Notting Hill Gate tube.

Award-winning Wild at Heart flower stall ㉖

upstairs terrace, you'll have a good view of the street. All-day breakfasts are a specialty. Excitement dwindles once you pass under the Westway flyover, except on Fridays and Saturdays when Tent City ⑰ and the Golborne Road Flea Market ⑱ are fully active, and the Portuguese cafés (especially the Lisboa at 55) are bustling. From Golborne Road, turn right into

The clock tower on All Saints Church ⑲

KEY

• • • Walk route

Ⓔ Underground station

TRAVELLERS' NEEDS

WHERE TO STAY

The high cost of accommodation in London is one of the biggest drawbacks for visitors. At the top end of the market, there is no shortage of expensive pedigree hotels, such as the Savoy and the Ritz. Mid-range hotels, while there are many, tend to be slightly further out of the centre of town. Sadly, most of the budget hotels are seedy and unappealing, a problem exacerbated by rising land and property prices. However, there are ways to stay in the capital without breaking the bank. Low-cost hotel chains such as Travel Inn, Express by Holiday Inn and Ibis have

Hilton doorman

been established in many convenient locations throughout the city, offering good-quality if standardized accommodation at affordable prices. We have inspected more than 250 hotels and apartment complexes across a range of price brackets and localities and have more than 120 of the best of their kind. For further details on these, turn to the listings on pages 278–91. Self-catering apartments and private homes (see pp280–81) are available at a wide range of prices. Student halls and hostels, even a few camping sites on London's outskirts, are additional possibilities for budget travellers (see p281).

WHERE TO LOOK

The most expensive hotels tend to be in smart West End areas such as Mayfair and Belgravia. Often large and opulent, with uniformed staff, they are not always the most relaxing places to stay. For smaller, more personal, but still luxurious hotels, try South Kensington or Holland Park.

The streets off Earl's Court Road are full of hotels at the lower end of the price range. Several of the big railway stations are well served with budget hotels too. Try Ebury Street near Victoria, or Sussex

Gardens near Paddington. Close to Euston or Waterloo and in the City and Docklands, well-known hotel chains cater for travellers at a range of prices. The area immediately north of King's Cross is best avoided at night.

There are also inexpensive hotels in the suburbs, such as Ealing, Hendon, Wembley, Bromley or Harrow. From here you can get into town on public transport. Take care not to miss the last train back.

If you get stranded at an airport or have to catch a very early morning flight, consult the list on page 377.

For further information, advice and reservation services, contact **Visit London**, which publishes several annually updated booklets on accommodation in Greater London.

DISCOUNT RATES

Prices in the capital tend to stay high all year round, but there are bargains. Many hotels, especially the groups, offer reduced rates for weekends and special breaks (see p280). Others work on a more ad hoc basis, depending on how busy they are. If a hotel isn't full, it is always worth trying to negotiate a discount, especially if it is off-season. Older budget hotels may have rooms without showers or private bathrooms. These usually cost less than those with private facilities.

HIDDEN EXTRAS

Read the small print carefully. Most hotels quote room rates rather than rates per person, but not all. Service charges are usually included in the quoted price but in some cases they are added on later. Beware of high mark-ups on telephone calls. A hotel with a high room tariff may be even more expensive than at first appears, which means that the final bill can come as a shock to many visitors.

Imaginative design at One Aldwych hotel (see p289)

◁ Street entertainer and crowd in Covent Garden Piazza

The Radisson Edwardian Hampshire hotel *(see p287)*

Breakfast may not be included in room rates, though it generally is in cheaper hotels. The definition of breakfast ranges from "full English" (a hearty, traditional fry-up which will see you through the most hectic sightseeing programme), to a "Continental" cup of coffee and a roll or croissant. Buffet breakfasts with lavish spreads of fruit, muesli and yoghurt are increasingly popular with health-conscious visitors.

Tipping is expected in the more expensive hotels, but there is no need to tip staff other than porters, except perhaps a helpful concierge for arranging theatre tickets or phoning for taxis.

Single travellers are usually charged a "supplement" and end up paying about 80 per cent of the double room rate, even if they are occupying a "single" room – so don't accept anything substandard.

The elegant hallway of The Gore hotel in Kensington *(see p283)*

FACILITIES

Room sizes in London hotels at all price ranges tend to be on the small side, but the majority of hotels now provide telephones, televisions and private baths or showers in all their rooms. At the top end of the scale, hotels compete to provide the very latest sound-and-video systems, computer equipment and high-tech gadgetry. Many hotel rooms also come equipped with iPod docks. Whatever the hotel, you will be expected to vacate your room by noon on the day you leave, sometimes earlier.

HOW TO BOOK

It is always advisable to book well in advance, as room availability fluctuates and better quality hotels are in constant demand. Direct bookings can be made by letter, phone, fax, or via the Internet. This generally entails giving some kind of guarantee: either a credit card number from which a cancellation fee can be deducted, or remitting a one-night deposit (some hotels will expect more for longer stays). Don't forget that if you subsequently cancel for any reason, part or all of the room price may be charged unless the hotel can relet the accommodation. Insurance cover is advised.

Travellers can phone the Visit London Accommodation Booking Service on 0870-156 6366 (also at www.super-break.com). There is no booking fee but customers will need to give a credit card number. During high season there may be a one-night deposit to pay, but that is at the discretion of the hotel. The Booking Service will advise, of course, if there is a deposit to pay. alternatively, travellers can use a similar booking service on the London Tourist Board's website (www.visitlondon.com) or they can e-mail the service directly at admin@superbreak.com. There is no booking fee if booking online.

Tourists can also book in person at the London Visitor Centre at No. 1 Regent Street,

One of the stylish bathrooms at the Portobello Hotel *(see p283)*

and can order a brochure, "Where to Stay on a Budget", from the Visit London brochure line on 0870-240 4326.

Accommodating booking services are also available at the British Travel Centre on Regent Street. A number of non-LTB booking agencies operate from booths in the major railway stations, charging a small fee to personal callers. Unidentified touts, who hang around at railway and coach stations offering cheap accommodation to tourists, should be avoided.

BOOKING ON-LINE

On-line booking is the easiest way to book hotels, with the best prices often only available if you book via the Internet. Many hotels have their own on-line advance purchase rate while Internet travel sites and hotel wholesalers such as Expedia (www.expedia.co.uk) and Travelocity (www.travelocity.co.uk) can also offer good rates, particularly if you book a hotel and flight together. Accommodation agencies more often than not use the Internet as a cost-effective way of doing business and, in most cases, at least some of the savings are passed on to customers. Increasingly, the Internet demonstrates the fluidity of many hotel "rack rates" (i.e. the prices printed on the tariff sheet), which, far from being fixed in stone, fluctuate widely according to the laws of supply and demand.

SPECIAL BREAKS

Many travel agencies carry
brochures from the major hotel
chains listing special
offers, which are
usually costed on a
minimum two-night
stay. Some are
extraordinarily good
value compared to
the usual tariff. For
most leisure travel
lers or families with
children, this is the
best way to get
value for money out
of London hotels so
that you can spend
time in the city
without breaking
the bank.
    City-break pack-
ages are organized
by specialist
operators, ferry companies
and airlines, and some
privately owned hotels too.
Sometimes the same hotel
may be featured in several
brochures at widely differing
prices and with different
perks. It's worth asking the
hotel directly what special
rates they offer, and checking
their websites too.

1920s Savoy poster

DISABLED TRAVELLERS

Information about wheelchair
access is based largely on
hotels' own assessments,
but travellers with special
needs should always confirm
when booking whether an
establishment is suitable. If
forewarned, many hotels will
go out of their way to help
disabled visitors. The nationwide *Tourism for All* scheme

provides details on accommodation standards and facilities
for elderly visitors or those with
mobility problems. For information on hotels
that meet the three-
tier "National Acces-
sible Standard",
contact **Visit London**
or **Tourism For All**.
A guide book for
people with access
needs, *Open Britain*,
can be obtained
from **RADAR**.

TRAVELLING WITH CHILDREN

London hotels are
no longer the
notorious child-free
zones they used to
be. A large number
now make a
concerted effort to cater for
the needs of people travelling
with children, providing cots,
high-chairs, baby-sitting
services and special meal
arrangements. Always ask
whether the hotel offers
special deals for children –
some have special rates, or
allow children to stay free of
charge if they sleep in their
parents' room.

SELF-CATERING FLATS

Many agencies offer self-
catering accommodation in
flats, usually for stays of a
week or more. Prices,
depending on size and
location, start at about £300
per week. Some luxury
complexes are fully serviced,
so you don't need to cook,
shop or clean. **Bridge Street**

Worldwide has over
550 London apartments in
smart locations. It caters
mainly for corporate and
professional travellers, but its
properties can be rented for
short-term lets whenever they
are available.
    The **Landmark Trust** rents
apartments in historic or
unusual buildings. These
include apartments in
Hampton Court *(see pp254–7)*
and in a pretty 18th-century
terrace in the City: one of
them was the home of the
late poet laureate, Sir John
Betjeman. A handbook of
Landmark Trust properties is
available for a charge.

STAYING IN PRIVATE HOMES

A number of agencies
organize stays in private
homes; several are registered
with Visit London. Credit card
reservations can be made
through Visit London's
telephone booking service
(see box). Several agencies
have minimum stays of
anything up to a week. Prices
depend on location, starting
at around £20 per person per
night. Sometimes you will
enjoy family hospitality, but
this isn't guaranteed, so
enquire when you book.
Deposits may be requested
and cancellation fees
imposed. The **Bed & Breakfast
and Homestay Association
(BBHA)** is an umbrella
organization for several
reputable agencies whose
properties are inspected
regularly. Several BBHA
members are listed in the
Directory *(see box)*.
    Uptown Reservations
arranges upmarket B&B in
interesting, well-located
London homes which have
been inspected for their
welcome, security and comfort.
Prices start at £95 per night
for a double room. It works
in tandem with **Wolsey
Lodges**, a nationwide consor-
tium of distinctive private
homes, often of historic or
architectural interest, offering
individual hospitality and a
good dinner. Wolsey Lodges
lists a couple of charming
London properties.

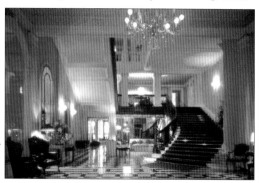

Classical opulence at Claridge's Hotel *(see p286)*

CHAIN HOTELS

Chain hotels are an important feature of the London hotel market. Though they can lack character, they offer some of the best value accommodation in town. Some also offer particular facilities; Novotel, for example, caters for both business guests and families. Other good-value chains include Express by Holiday Inn and easyHotel.

BUDGET ACCOMMODATION

Despite the high cost of many London hotels, budget accommodation does exist, and not only for young travellers.

Dormitory accommodation and youth hostels
These can be booked through the LTB's information centre at Victoria Station for a small fee plus a refundable deposit. Some private hostels near Earl's

City of London Youth Hostel

Court charge little more than £10 a night for a dormitory bed with breakfast. The **London Hostel Association** has a selection of reasonably priced accommodation throughout central London. The **Youth Hostels Association (YHA)** runs seven hostels in London. There is no age limit, though non-members pay a small joining fee and adults also pay

a little more. Of the seven, two are located in the heart of London. The Oxford Street hostel is actually in Noel Street, Soho and the City hostel is located in an atmospheric street near St Paul's Cathedral (*see pp148–51*).

There is an online booking service, the **International Booking Network**, run by the International Youth Hostel Federation, that is the easiest way to book a bed. One of the most popular hostels is Holland House, a Jacobean mansion in Holland Park.

Halls of residence
Many student rooms are available at Easter and from July to September. Some of these are in central locations such as South Kensington and places are sometimes available at short notice. Try **City University**, or, if you need a room in a hurry, **King's College** or **Imperial College** may be able to find you one.

DIRECTORY

RESERVATIONS AND INFORMATION

British Hotel Reservation Centre
13 Grosvenor Gardens
SW1W 0BO.
Tel 020-7592 3055.
www.bhronline.com

Visit London
1 Warwick Row
SW1E 5ER.
Tel 0870-156 6366.
www.visitlondon.com

DISABLED TRAVELLERS

RADAR
Unit 12, City Forum,
250 City Road EC1V 8AF.
Tel 020-7250 3222.
www.radar.org.uk

Tourism For All
c/o Vitalise, Shap Road
Industrial Estate,
Shap Road, Kendal,
Cumbria LA9 6NZ.
Tel 0845-1249971.
www.tourismforall.org.uk

SELF-CATERING AGENCIES

Bridge Street Worldwide
Compass House,
22 Redan Place W2 4SA.
Tel 020-7792 2222.
www.bridgestreet.com

Landmark Trust
Shottesbrooke, Maidenhead, Berks SL6 3SW.
Tel 01628 825925.
www.landmarktrust.org.uk

AGENCIES FOR STAYS IN PRIVATE HOMES

At Home in London
70 Black Lion Lane W6 9BE.
Tel 020-8748 1943.
www.athomeinlondon.co.uk

Bed & Breakfast & Homestay Assoc.
103 Dawes Rd SW6 7DU.
Tel 020-7385 9922.
www.bbha.org.uk

Host & Guest Service
103 Dawes Rd SW6 7DU.
Tel 020-7385 9922.
www.host-guest.co.uk

London Bed and Breakfast Agency
71 Fellows Road NW3 3JY.
Tel 020-7586 2768.
www.londonbb.com

Uptown Reservations
8 Kelso Place W8 5QD.
Tel 020-7937 2001.
www.uptownres.co.uk

Wolsey Lodges
9 Market Place, Hadleigh,
Ipswich, Suffolk, IP7 5DL.
Tel 01473-822058.
www.wolseylodges.com

HOSTEL BOOKING

Hostelling International
Tel 01707-324170.
www.hihostels.com

London Hostels Association
54 Eccleston Sq
SW1V 1PG.
Tel 020-7727 5665.
www.london-hostels.co.uk

Youth Hostels Association
Dimple Rd, Matlock,
Derbyshire DE4 3YH.
Tel 01629-592700.
www.yha.org.uk

BOOKING ADDRESSES FOR RESIDENCE HALLS

City University Accommodation & Conference Service
Northampton Sq
EC1V 0HB.
Tel 020-7040 8037.
www.city.ac.uk/ems

Imperial College Summer Accommodation Centre
58 Princes Gate,
Exhibition Road SW7 2PG.
Tel 020-7594 9507.
www.imperial-accommodationlink.com

King's Conference & Vacation Bureau
King's College London,
Strand Bridge House, 3rd floor, Strand WC2R 1HH.
Tel 020-7848 1700.
www.kcl.ac.uk/kcvb

Choosing a Hotel

These hotels have been selected across a wide price range for their good value, facilities and location; they are listed by area. Starting with west and southwestern districts of London, the guide moves through central parts of the city and on to eastern districts, eventually looking at hotels further outside the city.

PRICE CATEGORIES
For a standard double room per night, inclusive of breakfast, service charges and any additional taxes such as VAT.
£ under £90
££ £90–£140
£££ £140–£200
££££ £200–£250
£££££ over £250

BAYSWATER, PADDINGTON

Prince's Square   £   Map 10 D2
23–25 Prince's Square, W2 **Tel** *020 7229 9876* **Fax** *020 7229 4664* **Rooms** *50*

Behind the grand Victorian façade is a friendly, modern hotel. The refurbished pastel rooms may have standard hotel furnishings, but they are neat and cheerful, and the bathrooms are spotless. There's a handy bar in the lobby and special deals bring the price down considerably. Charge for Wi-Fi use. **www.princessquarehotel.co.uk**

Stylotel   £   Map 11 A2
160–162 Sussex Gardens, W2 **Tel** *020 7723 1026* **Fax** *020 7262 2983* **Rooms** *40*

Offering some of the cheapest rates in central London, Stylotel is true to its name, although the high-tech style may not suit all tastes. Rooms have wooden floors, aluminium walls, light-box bedside tables and futuristic bathrooms. There's a groovy lounge with curved stainless steel bar and blue leather seats. Wi-Fi in public areas (charged). **www.stylotel.com**

Best Western Mornington   ££   Map 10 F2
12 Lancaster Gate, W2 **Tel** *020 7262 7361* **Fax** *020 7706 1028* **Rooms** *66*

A reliable, good-value mid-range hotel just off Hyde Park. Rooms are comfortable and well equipped, enjoyable English breakfasts are served, and there's a cosy bar for sitting and chatting at the end of the day. Discount offers are often available and Wi-Fi use is complimentary. **www.bw-morningtonhotel.co.uk**

Garden Court Hotel   ££   Map 10 D2
30–31 Kensington Gardens Square, W2 **Tel** *020 7229 2553* **Fax** *020 7727 2749* **Rooms** *32*

An antique beefeater guards the lobby of this good-value hotel on a lovely garden square. The hotel celebrated its 50th anniversary in 2004 with a facelift; rooms have tasteful modern wallpaper and wooden furniture. To keep the cost down even further, you can opt for shared facilities. Free Wi-Fi in public areas. **www.gardencourthotel.co.uk**

Pavilion Hotel   ££   Map 11 B1
34–36 Sussex Gardens, W2 **Tel** *020 7262 0905* **Fax** *020 7262 1324* **Rooms** *30*

The conventional Bayswater exterior shields one of London's most special hotels. Each room (some of them very small) has its own extravagant theme decor, from Moroccan-palace in *Casablanca Nights* to 1970s TV in *Honky Tonk Afro*. It's beloved by the rock and fashion world, but rates remain low. Free Wi-Fi in all rooms. **www.pavilionhoteluk.com**

The Delmere   ££   Map 11 A2
130 Sussex Gardens, W2 **Tel** *020 7706 3344* **Fax** *020 7262 1863* **Rooms** *36*

Part of the Best Western chain, the Delmere offers accommodation a stone's throw away from Paddington Station. Rooms are well proportioned and attractively decorated, bathrooms are small yet stylish and there's a pleasant dining room and lounge where you can relax with the day's papers. Free Wi-Fi available. **www.delmerehotels.com**

Vancouver Studios   ££   Map 10 D2
30 Prince's Square, W2 **Tel** *020 7243 1270* **Fax** *020 7221 8678* **Rooms** *47*

These stylishly decorated studios in three 19th-century terraced houses have fully equipped kitchenettes, flatscreen TVs and DVD players. Resident cat Panther presides over the living room with a view onto the secluded garden. Laundry and free Wi-Fi complete the home-from-home package. **www.vancouverstudios.co.uk**

The Royal Park   £££   Map 10 F2
3 Westbourne Terrace, W2 **Tel** *020 7479 6600* **Fax** *020 7479 6601* **Rooms** *48*

This townhouse hotel near Hyde Park has a discreet luxury, which has attracted celebrity guests. Classic, unfussy rooms are furnished with exquisite fabrics, original prints and stone-tiled bathrooms. All the usual gadgetry, plus complimentary welcome drink and evening champagne in the drawing room. Free Wi-Fi in all rooms. **www.theroyalpark.com**

The Hempel   £££££   Map 10 E2
31–35 Craven Hill Gardens, W2 **Tel** *020 7298 9000* **Fax** *020 7402 4666* **Rooms** *50*

Fans of the minimalist aesthetic will be in their element in Anouska Hempel's serene white hotel. Each room, complete with candles and all the requisite gadgetry, including free Wi-Fi, is special. There is a striking geometric landscaped garden and an Italian-Thai fusion restaurant. Conference rooms available. **www.the-hempel.co.uk**

Key to Symbols *see back cover flap*

KENSINGTON, EARL'S COURT

base2stay

25 Courtfield Gardens, SW5 **Tel** *020 7244 2255/0845 262 8000* **Fax** *020 7244 2256* **Rooms** *67*   **Map** *18 E2*

An original hotel with an imaginative combination of sleek boutique hotel-style minimalist design and accessible prices. Rooms are in different sizes, from singles to suites, but all have mini-kitchens and an exceptional range of high-quality electronics (including free Wi-Fi) and other extras. Staff are very helpful. **www.base2stay.com**

Rushmore

11 Trebovir Road, SW5 **Tel** *020 7370 3839* **Fax** *020 7370 0274* **Rooms** *22*   **Map** *17 C2*

Like the nearby Mayflower, the Rushmore is proof that accommodation doesn't have to be expensive to be stylish. Each room in this Victorian townhouse has been designed in a different style; even the bathrooms have been customized to fit in with the mood. Breakfast is served in a chic conservatory. Lower floors have free Wi-Fi. **www.rushmore-hotel.co.uk**

Twenty Nevern Square

20 Nevern Square, SW5 **Tel** *020 7565 9555* **Fax** *020 7565 9444* **Rooms** *20*   **Map** *17 C2*

This townhouse overlooking a private garden square combines unique decor with reasonable rates. Rooms are furnished with gorgeous silks and spectacular beds such as Eastern-carved wooden styles or four-posters. Widescreen TVs, CD players and 24-hour room service are further attractions. Free Wi-Fi throughout. **www.twentynevernsquare.co.uk**

Mayflower Hotel

26–28 Trebovir Road, SW5 **Tel** *020 7370 0991* **Fax** *020 7370 0994* **Rooms** *48*   **Map** *18 D2*

This beautifully furnished, budget boutique hotel is a cut above the rest. The spacious, contemporary rooms have wooden floors and Eastern elements such as elaborately carved beds and rich silks. Marble bathrooms, ceiling fans, CD players and free Wi-Fi are luxurious perks. There are also 35 tasteful apartments nearby. **www.mayflowerhotel.co.uk**

The Gore

190 Queen's Gate, SW7 **Tel** *020 7584 6601* **Fax** *020 7589 8127* **Rooms** *50*   **Map** *10 F5*

The Gore has been in operation for more than 100 years and, while it has been refurbished, it preserves the atmosphere of a bygone age. Rooms feature four-poster beds, antiques, luxurious draperies and opulent fabrics. There's an oak-panelled bar and casual bistro as well. Extra charge for Wi-Fi use. **www.gorehotel.com**

The Milestone Hotel

1 Kensington Court, W8 **Tel** *020 7917 1000* **Fax** *020 7917 1010* **Rooms** *57 + 6 apartments*   **Map** *10 E5*

This plush hotel opposite Kensington Palace features originally designed rooms, from the smart "Savile Row" to the Colonial-style "Safari Suite". Extras include gym and resistance pool, broadband Internet and Penhaligon's toiletries in rooms, 24-hour butler and use of the hotel Bentley. **www.milestonehotel.com**

NOTTING HILL, HOLLAND PARK

New Linden Hotel

59 Leinster Square, W2 **Tel** *020 7221 4321* **Fax** *020 7727 3156* **Rooms** *51*   **Map** *10 D2*

Warm, subtle colour schemes and chic modern design are features of this very stylish, renovated hotel. Rooms combine a fresh, bright feel with sumptuous comforts, and TVs and other equipment (including free Wi-Fi) are state of the art. Breakfasts include plenty of fresh fruit. **www.newlinden.co.uk**

The Main House

6 Colville Road, W11 **Tel** *020 7221 9691* **Rooms** *4*   **Map** *9 B2*

In the heart of Notting Hill, this chic guesthouse features airy suites – one per floor. The decor combines modern elements and antiques. Thoughtful extras include the loan of mobile phones and bicycles, and morning coffee brought to your room on a silver tray. Free Wi-Fi and use of off-site gym. No single-night stays. **www.themainhouse.com**

Guesthouse West

163–165 Westbourne Grove, W11 **Tel** *020 7792 9800* **Fax** *020 7792 9797* **Rooms** *20*   **Map** *9 C2*

Formerly the Westbourne, Guesthouse West is a budget-conscious design hotel in an Edwardian house. Minimalist dark wood and beige rooms boast high-tech entertainment systems and Molton Brown toiletries. Free Wi-Fi is also on offer. Westbourne Grove's bars and boutiques are on the doorstep. **www.guesthousewest.com**

Miller's Residence

111a Westbourne Grove, W2 **Tel** *020 7243 1024* **Fax** *020 7243 1064* **Rooms** *8*   **Map** *10 D2*

Owned by antiques expert Martin Miller and a short stroll from Portobello Road's famous market, this hotel is a bric-a-brac-hunter's fantasy. Rooms are individually furnished with his finds, and free drinks are served in the eccentrically cluttered drawing room, which is candlelit in the evening. Free Wi-Fi available. **www.millershotel.com**

Portobello Hotel

22 Stanley Gardens, W11 **Tel** *020 7727 2777* **Fax** *020 7792 9641* **Rooms** *21*   **Map** *9 B2*

This long-running, popular hotel combines Victorian cosiness with sumptous extravagance in its individually decorated bedrooms, with special features like Moroccan lamps and antique bed-heads. Facilities (including free Wi-Fi) are high-standard. The same owners run Julie's Restaurant next door. Use of nearby health club. **www.portobellohotel.com**

KNIGHTSBRIDGE, BROMPTON, BELGRAVIA

Knightsbridge Green Hotel

159 Knightsbridge, SW1 **Tel** *020 7584 6274* **Fax** *020 7225 1635* **Rooms** *29*   **Map** *11 C5*

A shopaholic's dream, this well-kept hotel is right on Knightsbridge and rates are reasonable for more spending power in Harrods and Harvey Nichols. The tidy, modern rooms (some facing Hyde Park) are regularly upgraded and feature air conditioning, Wi-Fi and satellite TVs. There's also a small business centre on-site. **www.thekghotel.com**

The Rembrandt

11 Thurloe Place, SW7 **Tel** *020 7589 8100* **Fax** *020 7225 3476* **Rooms** *194*   **Map** *19 A1*

This hotel offers contemporary style mixed with original Edwardian features in a great location for visiting the V&A and other museums. After a day exploring the sights, guests can unwind in the swimming pool and spa or relax on the luxurious sofas in the bar. Not all rooms are air conditioned. Wi-Fi in lobby. **www.sarova.com/rembrandt**

The Cadogan

75 Sloane Street, SW1 **Tel** *020 7235 7141* **Fax** *020 7245 0994* **Rooms** *65*   **Map** *19 C1*

Opened in 1888, the Cadogan has welcomed such famous guests as Lillie Langtry and Oscar Wilde. The latter was arrested in room 118. It has a traditional British character, and guests have access to the private Cadogan Place gardens and tennis courts across the road. Free Wi-Fi throughout. **www.cadogan.com**

The Berkeley

Wilton Place, SW1 **Tel** *0808 238 0245* **Fax** *020 7235 4330* **Rooms** *214*   **Map** *12 D5*

Not the best-known of London's luxury hotels, rebuilt in the 1970s, but the Berkeley offers an exceptional range of opulent services (including free Wi-Fi) – with the rooftop pool and spa as a crowning glory. An equally impressive choice of restaurants includes Marcus Wareing at the Berkeley, showcase for one of Britain's finest chefs. **www.the-berkeley.co.uk**

The Capital

22 Basil Street, SW3 **Tel** *020 7589 5171* **Fax** *020 7225 0011* **Rooms** *49*   **Map** *11 C5*

A more intimate variation on the luxury hotel, with just 49 individually designed rooms and suites, all traditionally styled but with superior Wi-Fi and other modern equipment. Service throughout is excellent, and under chef Eric Chavot the Capital restaurant has won two Michelin stars. Good discounts available online. **www.capitalhotel.co.uk**

The Halkin

5 Halkin Street, SW1 **Tel** *020 7333 1000* **Fax** *020 7333 1100* **Rooms** *41*   **Map** *12 D5*

Modern comforts meet Eastern serenity at this gracious luxury hotel. Warm wood, curving lines and creamy bed linen are accented by Southeast Asian art handpicked by the Singaporean owner. Be sure to have a meal at Nahm, it's the only Michelin-starred Thai restaurant outside Thailand. Free Wi-Fi access throughout. **www.halkin.como.bz**

The Knightsbridge

10 Beaufort Gardens, SW3 **Tel** *020 7584 6300* **Fax** *020 7584 6355* **Rooms** *44*   **Map** *19 B1*

With its book-lined library and drawing room full of modern artworks, the Knightsbridge feels like the home of a well travelled intellectual. A bit cheaper than the other Firmdale hotels, this one offers the same lovely, updated English-style bedrooms and faultless attention to detail. Wi-Fi is available at a charge. **www.firmdalehotels.com**

SOUTH KENSINGTON, CHELSEA

Barclay House

21 Barclay Road, SW6 **Tel** *020 7384 3390* **Rooms** *2*   **Map** *17 C5*

Discerning travellers in search of value accommodation enjoy this stylish Victorian townhouse B&B with small, well-arranged double bedrooms, generous breakfasts, welcome cocktails, a spectacular roof terrace and the use of a grand piano. Free Wi-Fi and use of off-site gym facilities. Minimum 3-night stay. **www.barclayhouselondon.com**

easyHotel

14 Lexham Gardens, W8 **Tel** *0870 162 4022* **Fax** *020 7716 1717* **Rooms** *34*   **Map** *18 D1*

Some of the cheapest rates in London for en suite double rooms can be found at the easy group's bright budget hotels. Rooms and service are basic, but clean and well maintained. There are extra charges for using towels and TVs. There are three more easyHotels around London and one at Heathrow. **www.easyhotel.com**

Key to Price Guide *see p282* **Key to Symbols** *see back cover flap*

Aster House
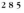 £££

3 Sumner Place, SW7 **Tel** 020 7581 5888 **Fax** 020 7584 4925 **Rooms** 13 — **Map** 19 A2

Three-time winner of the Tourist Board's best B&B award, this friendly hotel in a grand white stucco house has immaculate rooms in a typical English country style. A superior breakfast served in the palm-filled conservatory and a garden complete with pond and ducks attract guests. Free Wi-Fi and access to off-site gym. Minimum 3-night stay. **www.asterhouse.com**

Sydney House
£££

9–11 Sydney Street, SW3 **Tel** 020 7376 7711 **Fax** 020 7376 4233 **Rooms** 21 — **Map** 19 A2

This small hotel is just steps away from the chic shops of Brompton Cross. Airy rooms are furnished with blond wood furniture, Frette linens, contemporary art and thoughtful features such as American wall sockets and water softener in the ultra-modern bathrooms. Free Wi-Fi in rooms. **www.sydneyhousechelsea.com**

The Rockwell
£££

181–183 Cromwell Road, SW5 **Tel** 020 7244 2000 **Fax** 020 7244 2001 **Rooms** 40 — **Map** 18 D2

Housed in a beautifully restored Victorian terrace, The Rockwell is owned by an architect, and it shows in the stunning decor and the glass bridge that links the hotel to its courtyard garden. Other features include 24-hour room service, free Internet access, perfectly fluffy bathrobes and plenty of original English charm. **www.therockwell.com**

myhotel Chelsea
££££

35 Ixworth Place, SW3 **Tel** 020 7225 7500 **Fax** 020 7225 7555 **Rooms** 45 — **Map** 19 B2

Very deliberately hip design – in line with feng shui – and chic luxury are hallmarks of the myhotel group. Their Chelsea hotel has a slightly more traditional look to match the location. High-standard electronics, naturally including free Wi-Fi, are also a feature. The smart mybar restaurant offers varied menus through the day. **www.myhotels.com**

Blakes Hotel
 £££££

33 Roland Gardens, SW7 **Tel** 020 7370 6701 **Fax** 020 7373 0442 **Rooms** 45 — **Map** 18 F2

Blakes is the original "boutique hotel", created by designer Anouska Hempel over two decades ago. Rooms range in style from baronial manor to opulent Oriental and contain pieces collected on her travels. The discreet residential location has made it a favourite celeb hideaway. Only some suites are air conditioned. Wi-Fi is charged. **www.blakeshotels.com**

San Domenico House
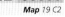 £££££

29–31 Draycott Place, SW3 **Tel** 020 7581 5757 **Fax** 020 7584 1348 **Rooms** 15 — **Map** 19 C2

In the wealthy heart of Chelsea, this intimate boutique hotel offers privacy and opulence, with just 15 rooms and suites decorated with antique furniture and paintings. Hidden away there are modern electronics (including free Wi-Fi) and a gym. Personal service is another trademark. Room service available. **www.sandomenicohouse.com**

VICTORIA, WESTMINSTER, PIMLICO

Dover Hotel
 £

42–44 Belgrave Road, SW1 **Tel** 020 7821 9085 **Fax** 020 7834 6425 **Rooms** 34 — **Map** 20 F2

This well-maintained hotel is terrific value for money. It may not be luxurious once past the grand stucco façade, but the decor is refreshingly modern and every room has satellite TV and pristine en suite shower and WC. It's handy for Victoria Station and Pimlico's many pubs and cafés and it has free Wi-Fi. **www.dover-hotel.co.uk**

Morgan Guest House
 £

120 Ebury Street, SW1 **Tel** 020 7730 2384 **Rooms** 11 — **Map** 20 E2

This comfortable guesthouse in a listed Georgian building offers excellent value for money, especially if you opt for a room without facilities, or one of the spacious family rooms that sleeps four. The decor is light and airy and many rooms contain original fireplaces. There is also a pretty garden and free Wi-Fi. **www.morganhouse.co.uk**

Vandon House
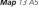 £

1 Vandon Street, SW1 **Tel** 020 7799 6780 **Fax** 020 7799 1464 **Rooms** 32 — **Map** 13 A5

A great location within easy walking distance of Westminster and Buckingham Palace is one reason for the popularity of this budget hotel. Rooms – singles, twins with or without en suite facilities, and family rooms – are simple but good value. Continental breakfast is included. There is a charge for Wi-Fi. **www.vandonhouse.com**

B&B Belgravia
££

64–66 Ebury Street, SW1 **Tel** 020 7259 8570 **Fax** 020 7259 8591 **Rooms** 17 — **Map** 20 E2

This award-winning townhouse B&B set out to revamp the bed and breakfast concept and has succeeded with 17 contemporarily designed bedrooms. It provides outstanding value for money, with free Internet access and Wi-Fi and cooked breakfasts made to order. **www.bb-belgravia.com**

Windermere
 ££

142–144 Warwick Way, SW1 **Tel** 020 7834 5163 **Fax** 020 7630 8831 **Rooms** 20 — **Map** 20 E2

This Victorian house has a long history of hospitality – it was the site of one of the area's earliest B&Bs in 1881. Rooms are spacious with large windows and done in tasteful, traditional chintz, with extras such as satellite TV, free Wi-Fi and safe; all have en suite facilities. The basement restaurant serves evening meals. **www.windermere-hotel.co.uk**

City Inn Westminster 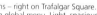   ⓔⓔⓔ

30 John Islip Street, SW1 **Tel** *020 7630 1000* **Fax** *020 7233 7575* **Rooms** *460*   **Map** *21 B2*

There's no great character to this big, modern tower-block hotel near Tate Britain, but the attractions are high-quality services at reasonable rates, especially for online deals. All rooms have computers, free Wi-Fi and other extras, and many have superb views from floor-to-ceiling windows. Rooms are well equipped for disabled guests. **www.cityinn.com**

The Trafalgar   ⓔⓔⓔⓔ

2 Spring Gardens, SW1 **Tel** *020 7870 2900* **Fax** *020 7870 2911* **Rooms** *129*   **Map** *13 B3*

A boutique-style departure for the Hilton group, boasting one of London's best locations – right on Trafalgar Square. There's a roof garden with fabulous views, and the chic Rockwell bar-restaurant offers a global menu. Light, spacious rooms are in luxury-minimalist style, with free Wi-Fi and other fittings. **www.thetrafalgar.com**

41   ⓔⓔⓔⓔⓔ

41 Buckingham Palace Road, SW1 **Tel** *020 7300 0041* **Fax** *020 7300 0141* **Rooms** *30*   **Map** *12 5F*

A boutique hotel with the feel of a private club. Guests are assigned a personal butler for their stay. The classic rooms have a smart, black-and-white colour scheme, state-of-the-art technology (including free Wi-Fi) and marble bathrooms. Some have views of the Royal Mews, where the Queen's horses and carriages are kept. Gym access. **www.41hotel.com**

The Goring   ⓔⓔⓔⓔⓔ

Beeston Place, SW1 **Tel** *020 7396 9000* **Fax** *020 7834 4393* **Rooms** *71*   **Map** *20 E1*

The Goring family have been running this snug luxury hotel since it opened in 1910. It boasts special assets such as a lovely garden and London's most sumptuous family rooms and children's facilities. The style is English traditional but all rooms boast state-of-the-art electronics. Internet access is charged. **www.thegoring.com**

MAYFAIR, ST JAMES'S

Chesterfield 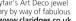   ⓔⓔⓔⓔ

35 Charles Street, W1 **Tel** *020 7491 2622* **Fax** *020 7491 4793* **Rooms** *107*   **Map** *12 E3*

A welcoming luxury hotel near Berkeley Square, the Chesterfield offers a variety of rooms (all with free Wi-Fi), from the understated pinstriped "Savile Row" to the fun-themed "Garden Suite" with trellises and wicker furniture. There's underfloor heating in the marble bathrooms and free use of a nearby health club. **www.chesterfieldmayfair.com**

Brown's Hotel   ⓔⓔⓔⓔ

Albemarle Street, W1 **Tel** *020 7493 6020* **Fax** *020 7493 9381* **Rooms** *117*   **Map** *12 F3*

This historic hotel, composed of 11 Georgian townhouses, has undergone extensive refurbishment, which respects its heritage while introducing contemporary furniture, British art and the latest technology (rooms have broadband; Wi-Fi is payable). There is a bar, English Tea Room and restaurant as well as a health club. **www.brownshotel.com**

Claridges   ⓔⓔⓔⓔⓔ

Brook Street, W1 **Tel** *020 7629 8860* **Fax** *020 7499 2210* **Rooms** *203*   **Map** *12 E2*

Favoured by the European aristocracy in the 19th century (Empress Eugenie wintered here), Mayfair's Art Deco jewel attracts showbusiness, glitterati and corporate guests. Rooms range from Victorian to contemporary by way of fabulous Art Deco suites. Gordon Ramsay's fêted restaurant and a smart bar are further draws. Free Wi-Fi. **www.claridges.co.uk**

Haymarket Hotel   ⓔⓔⓔⓔⓔ

1 Suffolk Place, SW1 **Tel** *020 7470 4000* **Fax** *020 7470 4004* **Rooms** *50*   **Map** *13 A3*

A boutique addition to the West End's luxury hotels, the Haymarket has subtly colourful, very well-equipped rooms and suites designed with panache. Another seductive plus – rare in central London – is a superb indoor pool. The stylish Brumus bar-restaurant serves imaginative Modern European cuisine. Wi-Fi is charged. **www.firmdale.com**

Metropolitan   ⓔⓔⓔⓔ

Old Park Lane, W1 **Tel** *020 7447 1000* **Fax** *020 7447 1100* **Rooms** *150*   **Map** *12 E4*

The Metropolitan redefined the London luxury hotel when it opened in the 1990s with its blond wood, subtle colours and cleanly elegant modern lines. Equally chic are the spa, the Met Bar and the ever-fashionable Nobu Japanese restaurant *(see p302)*. Services and electronics (complimentary Wi-Fi) are naturally first-class. **www.metropolitan.como.bz**

No. 5 Maddox   ⓔⓔⓔⓔⓔ

5 Maddox Street, W1 **Tel** *020 7647 0200* **Fax** *020 7647 0300* **Rooms** *12*   **Map** *12 F2*

Beautiful, contemporary one- to three-bedroom suites, complete with kitchens, hidden in an unmarked townhouse off Regent Street. Many have terraces or balconies. Among the many treats are welcome trays of goodies, linen kimonos, CD and DVD library and in-room holistic treatments. Charge for Wi-Fi and use of off-site gym. **www.no5maddoxst.com**

Stafford   ⓔⓔⓔⓔ

16–18 St James's Place, SW1 **Tel** *020 7493 0111* **Fax** *020 7493 7121* **Rooms** *105*   **Map** *12 F4*

This long-established townhouse hotel near Green Park has won a slew of awards and spends more than £1 million a year keeping up its refined period-style interior. Guests can stay in the main house or the atmospheric restored 17th-century stable yard. The American Bar is a cosy favourite. Free Wi-Fi available. **www.thestaffordhotel.co.uk**

Key to Price Guide *see p282* **Key to Symbols** *see back cover flap*

The Connaught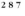

Carlos Place, W1 **Tel** *020 7499 7070* **Fax** *020 7495 3262* **Rooms** *123*   **Map** *12 E3*

One of Mayfair's historic grand hotels, the Connaught has undergone an imaginative renovation, combining its historic features with contemporary gadgets and refined modern design. All guests have a personal butler. The celebrated main restaurant is currently on a high under admired chef Hélène Darroze. **www.the-connaught.co.uk**

The Dorchester

Park Lane, W1 **Tel** *020 7629 8888* **Fax** *020 7409 0114* **Rooms** *250*   **Map** *12 D3*

The epitome of the glamorous luxury hotel, with an outrageously lavish lobby and a star-studded history, the Dorchester has revamped its tasteful floral bedrooms. The Art Deco-style marble baths are probably the deepest in London. For even more pampering, pop down to the fabulous Art Deco spa. **www.thedorchester.com**

The Ritz

150 Piccadilly, W1 **Tel** *020 7493 8181* **Fax** *020 7493 2687* **Rooms** *137*   **Map** *12 F3*

A byword for pampering luxury since it opened in 1906, the Ritz continues to win awards for superior all-round service. Bedrooms and the dazzling dining room are in ornate Louis XVI style, but include every modern extra (Wi-Fi is charged). Afternoon tea at The Ritz is a great London institution and booking is essential. **www.theritzlondon.com**

OXFORD STREET, SOHO

Edward Lear

28–30 Seymour Street, W1 **Tel** *020 7402 5401* **Fax** *020 7706 3766* **Rooms** *31*   **Map** *11 C2*

This characterful small hotel is in the former home of Victorian poet and artist Edward Lear. Rooms are tidy and spacious with satellite TVs. Opt for en suite or shared facilities to keep the cost down. There's a computer with free Internet access (Wi-Fi is also available) and leather seating in the pleasant guests' lounge. **www.edlear.co.uk**

The Leonard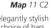

15 Seymour Street, W1 **Tel** *020 7935 2010* **Fax** *020 7935 6700* **Rooms** *48*   **Map** *11 C2*

Rooms at this intimate hotel are seductively comfortable, with traditional decor featuring high-quality materials. Occupying four 18th-century townhouses, it now incorporates free Wi-Fi and other modern musts. As well as standard rooms, the Leonard also has magnificent suites and five fully equipped apartments. **www.theleonard.com**

The Cumberland

Great Cumberland Place, W1 **Tel** *0871 376 9014* **Fax** *0870 333 9281* **Rooms** *1019*   **Map** *11 C2*

This giant hotel near Marble Arch has been transformed into something of a design showcase, with elegantly stylish lounges and rooms fitted with the latest technology and decorated with original artwork. The exceptional choice of bars and dining areas include the hip Carbon bar and chef Gary Rhodes' flagship Rhodes W1 restaurant. **www.guoman.com**

The Sumner

54 Upper Berkeley Street, W1 **Tel** *020 7723 2244* **Fax** *0870 705 8767* **Rooms** *20*   **Map** *11 C1*

Opened in 2006, this boutique hotel has been carefully designed to combine contemporary styling, natural fabrics and state-of-the-art electronics (complimentary Wi-Fi) with the original features of the 1820s building. Each bedroom is different, and the lounges and breakfast room are particularly chic. **www.thesumner.co.uk**

Durrants Hotel

George Street, W1 **Tel** *020 7935 8131* **Fax** *020 7487 3510* **Rooms** *92*   **Map** *12 D1*

Privately owned, the Durrant maintains a cosy, very traditional style, in a row of Georgian townhouses north of Oxford Street. Bedrooms are in English country-house style – but now incorporate Wi-Fi (charged) and other extras – and staff are very welcoming. The George Bar and the restaurant are full of old-world charm. **www.durrantshotel.co.uk**

Hazlitt's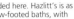

6 Frith Street, W1 **Tel** *020 7434 1771* **Fax** *020 7439 1524* **Rooms** *30*   **Map** *13 A2*

The 19th-century essayist William Hazlitt was just one of the interesting figures to have resided here. Hazlitt's is as close to time travel as you can get: its period rooms feature fireplaces, antique beds and claw-footed baths, with mod cons such as DVD players hidden discreetly away. Free Wi-Fi available, too. **www.hazlittshotel.com**

Radisson Edwardian Hampshire

31–36 Leicester Square, WC2 **Tel** *020 7839 9399* **Fax** *020 7930 8122* **Rooms** *124*   **Map** *11 C2*

Colourful, cinema-lined Leicester Square is a good base if you want to make the most of London's nightlife, as it's well placed for the theatre district, bars, clubs and restaurants. This luxurious Radisson has designer bedrooms with Philippe Starck bathrooms and Bose sound systems in the suites. **www.radissonedwardian.com**

Sanderson

50 Berners Street, W1 **Tel** *020 7300 1400* **Fax** *0207 300 1401* **Rooms** *150*   **Map** *12 F1*

The Sanderson's witty decor – red lips sofa and a framed portrait that seems to hang in mid-air – is like a surreal stage set. Rooms have every comfort (Wi-Fi is charged) and the Suka restaurant and two sophisticated cocktail bars are destinations in their own right. Agua spa offers holistic pampering. **www.sandersonlondon.com**

The Soho Hotel

4 Richmond Mews, W1 **Tel** *020 7559 3000* **Fax** *020 7559 3003* **Rooms** *85 + 6 apartments*   **Map** *13 A2*

Firmdale Hotels' venture combines the light and space of a warehouse-style building with its signature modern English style. Two screening rooms, gym with personal trainer and exclusive Miller Harris products in the granite walk-in showers complete the sophisticated urban experience. Wi-Fi is charged. **www.firmdalehotels.com**

REGENT'S PARK, MARYLEBONE

22 York Street

22 York Street, W1 **Tel** *020 7224 2990* **Fax** *020 7224 1990* **Rooms** *10*   **Map** *3 C5*

This beautiful property is a cut above most B&Bs. Liz and Michael Callis ensure rooms in these two immaculately preserved Georgian houses are spotless and stylishly furnished with antiques and French quilts. A gourmet Continental breakfast is served in the rustic kitchen. Free Wi-Fi access and meeting rooms. **www.22yorkstreet.co.uk**

Hart House Hotel

51 Gloucester Place, W1 **Tel** *020 7935 2288* **Fax** *020 7935 8516* **Rooms** *16*   **Map** *11 C1*

A well-maintained Georgian townhouse hotel with huge windows and high ceilings in some rooms. The dark wood furniture and bold tartan curtains make a refreshing change from frills and florals. The modern tiled bathrooms are spotless. Gloucester Place is a busy road, so you may prefer a back-facing room. Wi-Fi is charged. **www.harthouse.co.uk**

Hotel La Place

17 Nottingham Place, W1 **Tel** *020 7486 2323* **Fax** *020 7486 4335* **Rooms** *20*   **Map** *4 D5*

Located a short walk from Regent's Park, this popular small hotel works hard to keep customers happy with regularly improved facilities and extras such as free Wi-Fi. Spacious bedrooms have opulent traditional decor, and include suites and amply sized family rooms. The pretty bar-restaurant is open all day. **www.hotellaplace.com**

Park Plaza Sherlock Holmes

108 Baker Street, W1 **Tel** *020 7486 6161* **Fax** *020 7958 5211* **Rooms** *119*   **Map** *3 C5*

Though the name hints at a tacky Sherlock Holmes-theme hotel, this large establishment has been given an elegant modern makeover, with light, fresh rooms with delicate colour schemes. The split-level loft suites are especially impressive and the Sherlock Grill restaurant is similarly smart. Wi-Fi is charged. **www.parkplazasherlockholmes.com**

Dorset Square Hotel

39 Dorset Square, NW1 **Tel** *020 7723 7874* **Fax** *020 7724 3328* **Rooms** *37*   **Map** *3 C5*

Regulars prize this award-winning hotel for its character, old-fashioned charm and attention to detail. Bedrooms have been opulently decorated to match the Regency building, creating a romantic feel; hidden behind the period fittings are modern Wi-Fi (charged) and other fittings. The Potting Shed restaurant is in the garden. **www.dorsetsquare.co.uk**

The Marylebone Hotel

47 Welbeck Street, W1 **Tel** *020 7486 6600* **Fax** *020 7486 7492* **Rooms** *256*   **Map** *12 D1*

A classically furnished modern hotel in the heart of Marylebone village, the hotel offers spacious accommodation and great facilities, including its own health club with a swimming pool, whirlpool and sauna, a bar and restaurant. Very cheap seasonal offers are advertised on the website. **www.doylecollection.com**

The Langham, London

1C Portland Place, W1 **Tel** *020 7636 1000* **Fax** *020 7323 2340* **Rooms** *382*   **Map** *12 E1*

The Langham was Europe's first grand hotel when it opened in 1865 and still offers an ultra-luxurious experience behind its sprawling Victorian façade. Rooms achieve a tasteful middle ground between modern and traditional and there are extensive spa facilities including a swimming pool. Near Regent's Park. **www.langhamhotels.com**

BLOOMSBURY, FITZROVIA

Arosfa Bed & Breakfast

83 Gower Street, WC1 **Tel** *020 7636 2115* **Fax** *020 7636 2115* **Rooms** *15*   **Map** *5 A5*

The rooms are plainly furnished, but pristine, in this Georgian townhouse near London University. Every room has a tiny but spotless en suite shower and WC, making this one of the best deals in central London. True to its name, which means "resting place" in Welsh, there's a lounge with books and comfy sofas. Free Wi-Fi, too. **www.arosfalondon.com**

Ashlee House

261–265 Grays Inn Road, WC1 **Tel** *020 7833 9400* **Fax** *020 7833 9677* **Rooms** *34*   **Map** *5 C3*

This Kings' Cross favourite is mainly a backpackers' hostel with dorm-style rooms, but it also has low-cost single and double rooms that are in great demand so they must be booked well ahead. Rooms and common spaces are bright and stylish, and there's an Internet room with Wi-Fi access (charged). **www.ashleehouse.co.uk**

Key to Price Guide *see p282* **Key to Symbols** *see back cover flap*

Hotel Cavendish
75 Gower Street, WC1 **Tel** *020 7636 9079* **Fax** *020 7580 3609* **Rooms** *31*   **Map** 5 A5

This characterful B&B near London University has a fascinating history – DH Lawrence and the Beatles stayed here once. Rooms are simple yet comfortably furnished, and some have original fireplaces. Original artworks brighten up the breakfast room and there's a pretty garden as well. Shared facilities available and free Wi-Fi. **www.hotelcavendish.com**

Euston Square Hotel
152–156 North Gower Street, NW1 **Tel** *020 7388 0099* **Fax** *020 7788 9699* **Rooms** *75*   **Map** 5 A4

An imaginative take on the budget hotel, combining a bit of boutique style with low rates that make it one of London's best bargains. Rooms are small, but bright and smartly designed, with good TVs, Wi-Fi (complimentary) and other extras. At ground level, the FAB bar-restaurant offers an enjoyable global food range. **www.euston-square-hotel.com**

myhotel Bloomsbury
11–13 Bayley Street, W1 **Tel** *020 7667 6000* **Fax** *020 7667 6044* **Rooms** *78*   **Map** 5 A5

East meets West at this stylish contemporary hotel designed according to feng shui principles. The simple, serene rooms have low, Oriental-style beds and Aveda products. On-site facilities include a branch of Yo! Sushi, a buzzy public bar plus guests' library with Internet access and free Wi-Fi, and holistic spa treatments. **www.myhotels.com**

Park Inn London, Russell Square
92 Southampton Row, WC1 **Tel** *020 7242 2828* **Fax** *020 7831 9170* **Rooms** *214*   **Map** 5 C5

The international Park Inn chain has transformed this veteran hotel in the heart of Bloomsbury, giving each room colourful modern decor and high-quality fittings (Wi-Fi is charged) and installing equally fresh bars and restaurants. Facilities are especially good for business guests but bargain rates are a draw for leisure travellers. **www.rezidorparkinn.com**

The Academy
21 Gower Street, WC1 **Tel** *020 7631 4115* **Fax** *020 7636 3442* **Rooms** *49*   **Map** 5 A5

Five Bloomsbury townhouses were linked together to create this discreet boutique hotel, with rooms with full modern fittings (including free Wi-Fi) and soft, often sumptuous traditional decor to maximize comfort. Below there are equally attractive lounges full of cosy sofas, and a garden that's ideal for a drink in summer. **www.theetoncollection.com**

The Montague on the Gardens
15 Montague Street, WC1 **Tel** *020 7637 1001* **Fax** *020 7612 8430* **Rooms** *99*   **Map** 5 B5

This traditional townhouse hotel near the British Museum has high-tech amenities and refurbished bathrooms in its classic, predominantly floral-print rooms and a well-equipped gym with sauna. There are two restaurants, a conservatory and a terrace bar on the secluded gardens. Wi-Fi is charged. **www.montaguehotel.com**

Charlotte Street Hotel
15 Charlotte Street, W1 **Tel** *020 7806 2000* **Fax** *020 7806 2002* **Rooms** *52*   **Map** 13 A1

The ground floor bar is always buzzing with local workers as well as guests in this exquisitely designed hotel in a street full of restaurants. Reflecting the area's history, its decor nods to the Bloomsbury set period with original artworks by Vanessa Bell and others. Weekend films in the screening room and free Wi-Fi. **www.charlottestreethotel.com**

COVENT GARDEN, STRAND, HOLBORN

Citadines London Holborn-Covent Garden
94–99 High Holborn, WC1 **Tel** *020 7395 8800* **Fax** *020 7395 8799* **Rooms** *192*   **Map** 13 C1

The French Citadines *aparthotel* chain has a clever concept. All the well-equipped rooms – single/double studios or larger flats – are full apartments, with kitchens, but maid and other hotel services are offered. Mainly directed at business people, they can be great value for anyone staying more than a few days in London. **www.citadines.com**

Covent Garden Hotel
10 Monmouth Street, WC2 **Tel** *020 7806 1000* **Fax** *020 7806 1100* **Rooms** *58*   **Map** 13 B2

This exquisite hotel's Covent Garden location is one reason why it's popular with thespians. Part of the Firmdale chain, it is decorated in contemporary-English style with antiques and fresh fabrics. Brasserie Max is a popular meeting spot and films are shown in the luxurious screening room at weekends. Wi-Fi is charged. **www.firmdalehotels.com**

One Aldwych
1 Aldwych, WC2 **Tel** *020 7300 1000* **Fax** *020 7300 1001* **Rooms** *105*   **Map** 13 C2

A grand contemporary hotel in former Edwardian newspaper offices. Impressive details include original art and tarazzo-stone bathrooms with heated floors and mini TVs. There's a spacious health club with a swimming pool, several chic restaurants and the buzzing, high-ceilinged Lobby Bar. Free Wi-Fi is available. **www.onealdwych.co.uk**

St Martin's Lane
45 St Martin's Lane, WC2 **Tel** *020 7300 5500* **Fax** *020 7300 5501* **Rooms** *204*   **Map** 13 B2

An outpost of New York-based Morgans Hotel Group, the St Martins has been a flagship of the boutique-hotel wave, with eye-popping design by style guru Philippe Starck. Rooms are in minimalist white, while public spaces are playfully colourful: the Light Bar and Asia de Cuba restaurant are celebrity hot spots. Wi-Fi is charged. **www.stmartinslane.com**

Savoy

Strand, WC2 **Tel** *020 7836 4343* **Fax** *020 7240 6040* **Rooms** *263*   **Map** *13 C2*

This legendary hotel was an afterthought. Richard D'Oyly Carte capitalized on the success of his Savoy Theatre by providing a place to stay. The rest is history. Monet painted the Thames from his window; the dry martini was made popular in the bar. The hotel re-opened in 2010 after a multi-million-pound refurbishment. Free Wi-Fi. **www.fairmont.com/savoy**

SOUTHWARK, LAMBETH

Comfort Inn

87 South Lambeth Road, SW8 **Tel** *020 7735 9494* **Fax** *020 7735 1001* **Rooms** *94*   **Map** *21 5C*

The interior of this modern low-rise chain hotel is surprisingly cool and there are often very cheap offers on the website. Simple, contemporary rooms have en suite power showers and satellite TVs with pay Internet, Wi-Fi and games, while executive suites come with fridge, microwave and Jacuzzi. **www.comfortinnvx.co.uk**

London Bridge Hotel

8–18 London Bridge Street, SE1 **Tel** *020 7855 2200* **Fax** *020 7855 2233* **Rooms** *138*   **Map** *15 B4*

This contemporary, urban hotel near foodies' paradise Borough Market has stylish executive rooms. On-site Malaysian restaurant Georgetown makes a change from the usual bland hotel fare, and guests are given free entry to the adjoining Fitness First health club. Free Wi-Fi available. **www.londonbridgehotel.com**

Southwark Rose Hotel

47 Southwark Bridge Road, SE1 **Tel** *020 7015 1480* **Fax** *020 7015 1481* **Rooms** *84*   **Map** *15 A3*

The name may conjure up images of an old-English inn, but this is a budget version of a modern luxury hotel near Tate Modern and Shakespeare's Globe. Rooms, in a different colour scheme on each floor, are kitted out with modern leather headboards, slick mosaic-tiled bathrooms and Wi-Fi (charged). **www.southwarkrosehotel.co.uk**

Travel Inn London County Hall

Belvedere Road, SE1 **Tel** *0870 238 3300* **Fax** *020 7902 1619* **Rooms** *313*   **Map** *14 D5*

This branch of the budget premier Travel Inn chain is housed in the massive former County Hall on the Thames. The more expensive Marriott, which shares the building, has all the river views, but it's a good-value option next to the London Eye, near Waterloo and the Southbank arts complex. Wi-Fi is available but is charged. **www.premierinn.com**

Novotel London City South

53–61 Southwark Bridge Road, SE1 **Tel** *020 7089 0400* **Fax** *020 7089 0410* **Rooms** *182*   **Map** *15 A3*

Novotel hotels (of which there are nine around London) may not seem to have great character but they have plenty of pluses: attractive modern rooms with many extras (Wi-Fi for an extra charge), enjoyable restaurants, and excellent facilities for families and disabled guests. Frequent online offers ensure good-value prices. **www.novotel.com**

Marriott County Hall

Westminster Bridge Road, SE1 **Tel** *020 7928 5200* **Fax** *020 7928 5300* **Rooms** *200*   **Map** *13 C5*

Housed in the vast former County Hall building on the Thames, this Marriott is on a grand scale, with a magnificent library, gym and spa and one of the largest pools in London. Rooms are in keeping with the period style; some boast four-poster beds and amazing views of Big Ben. There is a charge for Wi-Fi use. **www.marriottcountyhall.com**

CITY, CLERKENWELL

The Hoxton

81 Great Eastern Street, EC2 **Tel** *020 7550 1000* **Fax** *020 7550 1090* **Rooms** *205*   **Map** *7 C4*

Hoxton has been one of London's trendiest areas in the last few years, and it fittingly has the city's hippest hotel, with small but inventively styled rooms with plenty of technology (free Wi-Fi), still at reasonable rates. There's cutting-edge work by local artists in the public areas, and a lively bistro. **www.hoxtonhotels.com**

The Zetter

86–88 Clerkenwell Road, EC1 **Tel** *020 7324 4444* **Fax** *020 7324 4445* **Rooms** *59*   **Map** *6 F4*

In an area known for its loft apartments, this is a loft hotel, in a 19th-century warehouse. Rooms have exposed brick, quirky 1970s furniture, old Penguin books, hot-water bottles and high-tech extras (including Internet access), while vending machines on each floor dispense necessities. Hip Italian restaurant at street level. **www.thezetter.com**

ANdAZ

40 Liverpool Street, EC2 **Tel** *020 7961 1234* **Fax** *020 7961 1235* **Rooms** *267*   **Map** *15 C1*

This magnificent 19th-century railway hotel was formerly the Great Eastern Hotel. It is now a concept hotel with boutique-inspired credentials. There's no check-in desk, the traditional hotel lobby is replaced with a living room and a dedicated team member oversees your stay. **www.london.liverpoolstreet.andaz.com**

Malmaison

Charterhouse Square, EC1 **Tel** *020 7012 3700* **Fax** *020 7012 3702* **Rooms** *97*   *Map 6 F5*

The London outpost of this chic chain is in a red-brick Victorian building on a historic cobbled square; inside a
striking modern, art-filled interior and trendy brasserie. Rooms are spacious and comfortable with upholstered
headboards, CD players, Internet access and French wines. **www.malmaison-london.com**

Rookery

12 Peter's Lane, Cowcross Street, EC1 **Tel** *020 7336 0931* **Fax** *020 7336 0932* **Rooms** *33*   *Map 6 F5*

Occupying six Georgian houses and shops (with faded butchers' and bakers' signs still visible on some), this Dickensian
hideaway retains many original features, such as flagstone floors in the hall and ceiling beams in some of the rooms.
Decorated with antiques throughout, it also offers all the latest technology, including free Wi-Fi. **www.rookeryhotel.com**

FURTHER AFIELD

The Mitre

291 Greenwich High Road, SE10 **Tel** *020 8293 0037* **Fax** *020 8355 6761* **Rooms** *16*   *Map 23 B2*

Bustling pub with rooms close to sights and transport links. The protected 18th-century building was originally a
coffee house, and interior-designed, en suite rooms are traditional in pastel colour schemes. There's a weekday bar
menu and carvery meals at weekends and bank holidays in the pub. Free Wi-Fi available. **www.mitregreenwich.com**

Church Street Hotel

29–33 Camberwell Church Street, SE5 **Tel** *020 7703 5984* **Fax** *020 7358 4110* **Rooms** *30*

A hotel unlike any other in London, decorated by its much-travelled, very friendly Spanish owners with rich Cuban-
Mexican colours and quirky Mexican artefacts, brings a breath of Latin America to unexotic Camberwell. There's a
lovely, atmospheric bar, and generous organic breakfasts. Free Wi-Fi, too. **www.churchstreethotel.com**

Hampstead Village Guesthouse

2 Kemplay Road, NW3 **Tel** *020 7435 8679* **Fax** *020 7794 0254* **Rooms** *9*   *Map 1 B5*

This Victorian home, in the picturesque village and a short walk from the heath, is intriguingly cluttered with antiques and
curios. Breakfast is served in the garden in summer, English weather permitting. Rooms are equipped with a hot-water
bottle and fridge. The rates are cheaper if you forgo en suite facilities. Free Wi-Fi. **www.hampsteadguesthouse.com**

K West

Richmond Way, W14 **Tel** *020 8008 6600* **Fax** *020 8008 6650* **Rooms** *220*

Off the beaten track near BBC HQ, this striking steel and glass hotel is popular with high-profile guests, and often
offers amazingly cheap deals on the website. Sleek rooms are soothingly neutral, there's a cool bar and, best of all,
a luxurious spa with gym, marble Jacuzzi room and E'SPA treatments. There is a charge for Wi-Fi. **www.k-west.co.uk**

Cannizaro House

West Side, Wimbledon Common, SW19 **Tel** *020 8879 1464* **Fax** *020 8879 7338* **Rooms** *46*

This Georgian mansion on the edge of Wimbledon Common is an ideal base for keen tennis fans. Rooms are
decorated in a country-house style; some have four-poster beds and air conditioning. There is a restaurant, cocktail
bar and extensive grounds, where you can play croquet. There is also free Wi-Fi. **www.cannizarohouse.com**

Hilton London Docklands

265 Rotherhithe Street, SE16 **Tel** *020 7231 1001* **Fax** *020 7231 0599* **Rooms** *365*

A modern hotel with great views of Canary Wharf, the Hilton is both family friendly and geared up for business travellers.
Many of the spacious rooms have balconies, there's a fitness centre with a pool and a restaurant on the hotel's terrace overlooking the river. Cheap rates are often available. Internet access and Wi-Fi are charged. **www.hilton.co.uk/docklands**

Novotel Greenwich

173–185 Greenwich High Road, SE10 **Tel** *020 8312 6800* **Fax** *020 8312 6810* **Rooms** *151*   *Map 23 A3*

This modern hotel is conveniently located next to Greenwich station. It is light and airy and has a stylish decor
created from wood, stone and richly coloured furnishings. 24-hour room service is available. There are conference
rooms, computers and Wi-Fi (charged). **www.novotel.com**

The Petersham

Nightingale Lane, Richmond, Surrey, TW10 **Tel** *020 8939 1010* **Fax** *020 8939 1098* **Rooms** *60*

This sprawling Victorian hotel perches on Richmond Hill overlooking the Thames. The elegant rooms are in keeping
with the building's period grandeur, while integrating modern elements; some have spectacular views of the Thames.
Unsurprisingly given its romantic location, it's popular for weddings. Free Wi-Fi available. **www.petershamhotel.co.uk**

Colonnade

2 Warrington Crescent, W9 **Tel** *020 7286 1052* **Fax** *020 7286 1057* **Rooms** *43*

Near the picturesque canals of Little Venice, this hotel in two Victorian mansions has been operating since the 1930s.
Freud stayed here while his house was being redecorated, and JFK paid a visit in the 60s. The interior is grand yet
unintimidating and every luxurious room has a different feel. Wi-Fi is charged. **www.theetoncollection.com**

RESTAURANTS AND PUBS

Hailed as the world's dining capital, London thrives on an extraordinary culinary diversity. From a traditional forte of Indian, Chinese, French and Italian restaurants, eating out in London now enables your palate to take a gastronomic journey around the world, from America to Africa, taking in a pan-European tour, as well as the Middle East, Asia, and the Pacific Rim.

A pre-theatre menu board

CHOOSING YOUR TABLE

The restaurants on pages 296–311 of this guide represent a comprehensive range of styles and prices. They are listed alphabetically within each price category and are spread across the main tourist areas, although some that merit a special trip further afield are also included.

London's café scene has become much more dynamic over the past few years, with good coffee and snacks readily available throughout the day. Good-quality chains have also sprung up all over the capital and include Ask (pizza), Giraffe (for families) and Leon (healthy fast-food). London's pubs have evolved and are now some of the most popular places to eat. "Gastropubs" have become an accepted part of the food scene and offer a wide range of fare. For a selection of mainly informal places to eat and drink, including pubs, see pages 312–19.

LONDON RESTAURANTS

The broadest choice of restaurants can be found in Covent Garden, Piccadilly, Mayfair, Soho and Leicester Square. Knightsbridge, Kensington and Chelsea also offer a good range of restaurants. Central London has few riverside restaurants, but there is a cluster along Chelsea Harbour, in Chelsea, and Butler's Wharf on the south bank of the Thames. While traditional British food can be enjoyed, the style is not so readily available. Chefs such as Fergus Henderson at St

Commissionaire at the Hard Rock Café (see p315)

John are revitalizing British dishes, but the emphasis is on Modern British cooking which combines a variety of culinary influences and techniques from around the world. Home-grown chefs such as Sally Clarke, Alastair Little and Marco Pierre White have been instrumental in helping to elevate restaurant dining over the past two decades.

Alongside great improvements in cuisine, the standard of service has risen, and there has never been so much focus on interior design. This has added to the "diversity" of London's restaurants, which offer anything from classically ornate and romantic decor, to modern and post-modern minimalism. London has long been a paradise for Indian, Chinese, French and Italian food, with more restaurants specializing in regional cuisine. Asian food is increasingly popular, particularly Thai and Japanese, with Soho offering plenty of choice.

Most restaurants provide at least one vegetarian option, and some have a separate vegetarian menu. A growing number of specialist vegetarian restaurants offer more adventurous dishes. Fish and seafood is another speciality, with both traditional and modern-style restaurants.

Great Eastern Dining Room (see p309)

OTHER PLACES TO EAT

Many hotels have excellent restaurants open to non-residents, which in some cases include a menu composed by, or even the actual dishes prepared by, a star chef. These restaurants range from the very formal to the fun and flamboyant, and prices tend to be at the top end of the scale. There are also increasing numbers of pizza, pasta and brasserie chains serving reliable, good-value food across the city.

Among these dramatic improvements are also "gastro-pubs" and wine bars that serve anything from standard staples to Thai curries, accompanied by global wine lists. Otherwise, you can grab a quick snack from one of the many sandwich bars or cafés.

Hakkasan *(see p306)*

TIPS ON EATING OUT

Most London restaurants
serve lunch between noon
and 2:30pm, with dinner from
6:30pm until 11pm, which
usually means that last orders
are taken at 11pm. Ethnic
restaurants may stay open
longer, until midnight or later.
Some restaurants may close for
either lunch or dinner during
the weekend, and it is always
best to check opening times
first. All-day cafés and
brasseries may serve alcohol
without restriction during
licensing hours (11am–11pm).

The traditional British
Sunday lunch appears in many
pubs and restaurants, although
more informal brunches are
increasingly popular. It is
worth checking beforehand,
however, unless traditional
Sunday lunch is what you
particularly want, as even
high-class restaurants may
suspend their normal
menu on Sundays.

Some of the most formal
restaurants insist on a jacket
and tie, or a jacket. Booking
is advisable, especially at
gourmet restaurants and
between Friday and Sunday.

Smoking is banned in all
London pubs and restaurants.

PRICE AND SERVICE

As London is one of the
world's most expensive cities,
restaurant prices can often
seem exorbitant to visitors,
with an average three-course
meal and a few glasses of
house wine, at a medium-

priced central London
restaurant costing around
£25–35 per person. Many
restaurants have set-price
menus which are generally
significantly less expensive
than ordering à la carte and,
in some instances, the price
includes coffee and service.

Similarly, various West End
restaurants serve pre-theatre
set menus (typically from
around 5.30–6pm). Although
geared towards a quick turn-
around, this provides an
opportunity to eat at quality
restaurants at a competitive
price. Lower prices (around
£10–15 a head) apply at
smaller, more modest ethnic
and vegetarian restaurants,
wine bars and pubs, where
the food can nevertheless be
well prepared and offer good
value. However, some of
these establishments will
only accept cash or cheques,
not credit cards.

Before ordering, check the
small print at the bottom of
the menu. Prices will include
Value Added Tax (VAT) and
may add an optional service
charge (between 10 and 15
per cent). Some restaurants
may also impose a cover
charge (£1–£2 a head), or a
minimum charge during the
busiest periods, while some
do not accept certain credit
cards. Beware of the old trick
where service is included in
the bill but staff leave the
"total" box on your credit slip
blank, hoping you will add
another 10 per cent. Expect
different types of service in

different types of restaurant.
This can range from cheerful
and breezy in fast-food joints
to discreet yet attentive in
more expensive venues. At
peak dining times you will
usually have to wait longer
to be served.

St. John *(see p309)*

EATING WITH CHILDREN

Except in Italian restaurants,
fast-food establishments,
branches of Wagamama and a
few other venues such as The
Rainforest Café on Shaftesbury
Avenue (a tropical haven for
young diners), children tend
to be simply tolerated in
London restaurants rather than
warmly welcomed.

However, with the growing
trend for a more informal
style of dining, more and
more restaurants are learning
to become child-friendly,
offering a special children's
menu or smaller portions
and high chairs, while some
provide colouring books
and even put on live
entertainment to keep the
little diners happy. See page
357 for suggested places that
cater for children of a wide
range of ages.

London's top Hungarian restaurant *(see p305)*

The Flavours of London

"Modern European cooking" describes much of what's on offer in London, a reflection of the capital's cosmopolitan nature. However, as competitive restaurateurs vie for customers, they often look to traditional foods, from once-unfashionable beetroot to pig's trotters and offal, while increasing concern about what goes into the growing and rearing of food is also reflected on London menus. Even pub food, once limited to Sunday roasts, the ubiquitous "ploughman's lunch" (cheese or ham with bread and pickles) or sandwiches has been given fresh slant by "gastropubs" and a new breed of sandwich bars offering fresh, top-quality snacks.

Chef and customer at Clerkenwell's St John restaurant

LONDON'S LARDER

Nowhere better exemplifies the city's blossoming love affair with good food than Borough Market *(see p339)*. Its busy stalls of both regional and continental food are a microcosm of what Londoners today like to eat. There is produce from all over Britain – English and Irish cheeses; Scottish beef; Welsh lamb; Devon cider; Suffolk oysters – as well as from the rest of the world. Visitors can snack as they browse, on anything from Cornish scallops to grilled Spanish chorizo.

MODERN BRITISH FOOD

London menus increasingly detail the provenance of ingredients with obvious pride. Ancient or "rare" breeds of cattle are name-checked, such as Gloucester Old Spot pork. Once-overlooked, old-fashioned ingredients like rhubarb and black (blood) pudding are being used in creative new ways. Seasonal and organic produce is also taking more of a centre stage. The new breed of "gastropubs" were among the first to adopt these trends, offering good, imaginative, well-prepared,

Dorstone (Dorset), Waterloo (Berkshire), Blue Stilton, Ashdown (Sussex), Golden Cross (Sussex)

Selection of superb English farmhouse cheeses

TRADITIONAL ENGLISH FOOD

You can still find traditional dishes, such as jugged hare, roast beef or brown Windsor soup, but even fish 'n' chips can be harder to hunt down than tapas, pizza or chicken tikka masala. A "full English breakfast" is a fry-up of sausages, eggs, bacon, tomatoes, mushrooms and bread, perhaps with black (blood) pudding. Baked beans and fried potatoes may be included, as can bubble and squeak (re-fried cabbage and potato). There is an English heritage of heavy "nursery" puddings. These are a favourite of gentlemen's clubs and include such treats as treacle tart, roly-poly (suet and jam) pudding, spotted dick (suet and currants) and fruit crumbles with custard. Teatime may be a thing of the past but some top hotels still offer "cream teas" with scones, cakes and perhaps cucumber sandwiches.

Celery and Stilton soup *The king of English cheeses makes an excellent winter soup when combined with celery.*

Bountiful vegetable stall at south London's Borough Market

chicken tikka masala has been voted the nation's favourite dish (invented here, the legend goes, to satisfy the national passion for gravy by pairing tandoori dry-roasted meat with a mild, creamy sauce), regional Indian food is now to the fore, notably southern cuisine strong on coconut, fish and fruits. The balti is another British take on the food of the subcontinent – named for the bowl-shaped dish in which they are cooked and served, fresh-tasting stews are served alongside vast naan breads for dunking.

In Chinatown, you can enjoy everything from a simple bowl of noodles to gourmet dishes featuring rare ingredients such as razorshell clams and sea urchins.

sensibly-priced food, as well as fine wines and beers, in the relaxed surroundings of the traditional London pub.

Chef Fergus Henderson of St John *(see p308)* is a pioneer of "head-to-toe" eating, espousing anything from ox cheek and tail to entire roast suckling pig.

London's historic seafood favourites, such as cockles and whelks, are increasingly hard to find at present but, as capital of an island nation, the city offers many fine fish restaurants. Concerns about over-fishing and farmed fish means that you are likely to see less cod and haddock and more of such local catch as bream, bass, sole and gurnard, as well as salmon being billed as wild, and scallops as diver-caught.

EASTERN FLAVOURS

Britain has long had a love affair with both Oriental and Indian food, and some of the best examples of each can be found in London. While

A mouthwatering pint of traditional London bitter beer

WHAT TO DRINK

Beers There are two large brewers in London – Young's and Fuller's – and some micro-brewers, too. The main varieties found in Britain are:
Bitter Brewed from malted barley, hops, yeast and water; drunk at room temperature.
Mild ale Sweeter than bitter.
Lager Hundreds of varieties of this pale carbonated beer are available. Served chilled.
Stout Thick, dark, creamy Guinness is the most famous.

Cider English cider has undergone a revival, with producers often featuring single old English apple varieties and using traditional methods.

Dover sole *This is the most tasty flatfish, best served simply grilled with lemon, spinach and new potatoes.*

Roast beef *Horseradish sauce is a traditional accompaniment, as are crisp Yorkshire puddings made of batter.*

Summer pudding *Lightly cooked fruits fill a basin lined with bread, which absorbs the sweet juices.*

Choosing a Restaurant

These restaurants have been selected for their good value or exceptional food and are listed alphabetically within each price category. Starting with west and southwestern districts of London, the guide moves through central parts and on to eastern districts, eventually looking at restaurants further outside the city.

PRICE CATEGORIES
For a three-course meal per person including tax, service, and half a bottle of house wine (unless required to supply your own).
£ under £20
££ £20–£35
£££ £35–£55
££££ £55–£75
£££££ over £75

BAYSWATER, MARYLEBONE

Alounak Kebab
£

44 Westbourne Grove, W2 5SH **Tel** *020 7229 0416*

Map *10 D2*

A typical Iranian restaurant, which means it isn't exactly the same as Persian or any other related cuisine. The food is a little lighter and less rich. The style verges on a bazaar café, simple bare wood tables, with no wine on sale and soft drinks served in the can. The price reflects this simplicity and the presence of so many Iranians proves the authenticity.

Aphrodite Taverna
££

15 Hereford Road, W2 4AB **Tel** *020 7229 2206*

Map *10 D2*

Small and unpretentious, this little tavern tries hard and succeeds. Halloumi, kleftiko, moussaka, baklava and all the Greek greats are delicious and their stuffed vine leaves aren't bathed in vicious brine. If not home-made, they are at least made by someone who cares. Aphrodite excels at starters and is popular with guests from nearby hotels.

Busaba Eathai
££

8–13 Bird Street, W1U 1BU **Tel** *020 7518 8080*

Map *12 D2*

One of a small chain of restaurants by Alan Yau, its communal and casual Thai dining is reasonable, and it meets demand for value and speed of service. As a result, there can be a queue of legendary length after 7pm, so get there early. Tables are shared whatever time you arrive, so not the best choice for a romantic occasion.

Caffe Caldesi
££

118 Marylebone Lane, W1U 2QF **Tel** *020 7935 1144*

Map *12 D1*

This airy Italian bistro with bar offers a frequently changing seasonal menu of classic dishes and a very reasonable all-Italian wine list. The dining space upstairs offers a slightly more formal atmosphere. Tuck into a traditional home-cooked dinner. The café also plays host to La Cucina Caldesi – an Italian cookery school.

Ishtar
££

10–12 Crawford Street, W1U 6AZ **Tel** *020 7224 2446*

Map *3 C5*

Modern Turkish, so no plate throwing and no exotic dancers. You can dine on two levels, including under some romantic cellar arches, and the dishes are familiar but updated. Go for pan-fried sea bass with potatoes and saffron sauce or some well-marinated kebabs. Leave room for some pastries, too!

Queen's Head & Artichoke
££

30–32 Albany Street, NW1 4EA **Tel** *020 7916 6206*

Map *4 E4*

Handily located between Regent's Park and Euston Road, this friendly gastropub is rightly popular. You can eat outside, in the bustling, wood-panelled bar or in a quieter dining room. Fare includes Mediterranean-inspired tapas, steaks, seafood and other dishes, created using high-quality ingredients. There is an excellent wine selection.

Reubens
££

79 Baker Street, W1U 6RG **Tel** *020 7486 0035*

Map *3 C5*

A wonderful dining experience is in store at this Jewish restaurant, with all the Jewish classics on the menu like latkes and salt beef sandwiches. It is, of course, officially kosher and the portions are big and well priced. Takeaways are available from the deli on the ground floor. Closed Saturday.

Tawana
££

3 Westbourne Grove, W2 4UA **Tel** *020 7229 3785*

Map *10 D1*

A restaurant that has been established in the area for many years. A commitment to authentic Thai cuisine means it has a loyal clientele. Ingredients are fresh and the balance of hot and sour is always perfect. Dishes include *tom ka gai* (chicken, lemongrass and coconut milk soup) and red curry with roast duck.

Galvin Bistrot de Luxe
£££

66 Baker Street, W1U 7DJ **Tel** *020 7935 4007*

Map *3 C5*

Brothers Chris and Jeff Galvin run their restaurants with a blend of originality and a thorough French culinary training. The Baker Street restaurant summons up the atmosphere of a traditional Paris bistro, with a menu of flavour-rich, robust but very sophisticated dishes, including wonderful versions of classics like chicken pot roast *landaise*.

Key to Symbols *see back cover flap*

Island Restaurant & Bar

Royal Lancaster Hotel, Lancaster Terrace, W2 2TY **Tel** *020 7551 6070*

Map 10 F2

The north side of Hyde Park is not well supplied with restaurants but inside the Royal Lancaster Hotel there's a bright, attractive contemporary bar-brasserie with friendly, fast-moving staff. Menus feature an enjoyable mix of modern European dishes, from steaks to fresh seafood, and salads and pasta as lighter options.

Royal China Club

40–42 Baker Street, W1U 7AJ **Tel** *020 7486 3898*

Map 12 D1

Much more refined than the standard neighbourhood Chinese, the Royal China serves superior Cantonese food in a beautiful, calm setting. Lunchtime dim sum is exquisite, an irresistible array of little delicacies prepared with great skill. The full menu includes specialities such as razor clams stir-fried with lilies.

Defune

34 George Street, W1U 7DP **Tel** *020 7935 8311*

Map 12 D1

Top-class sushi at a high price, which the experts say is well worth it. A charming minimalist decor is matched by an atmosphere that some find austere but is really just a cool appreciation of the food. This is a decent place and the service is superb. When you're eating raw fish you expect the highest standards and you pay for them.

Locanda Locatelli

8 Seymour Street, W1H 7JZ **Tel** *020 7935 9088*

Map 11 C10

Giorgio Locatelli is a star among London chefs, producing some of the most refined Italian cuisine in the city. The seasonally based menus change frequently, and subtle use of Mediterranean herbs and truffles is a hallmark. The dining room is sleekly elegant and service very smooth. Reservations need to be made well ahead.

Orrery

55 Marylebone High Street, W1U 5RB **Tel** *020 7616 8000*

Map 4 D5

A special-occasion restaurant in the heart of Marylebone village, with elegant contemporary decor, abundant staff, a huge wine list and high prices. On the menu are luxurious modern haute-cuisine dishes featuring first-rate ingredients. In summer, you can also dine on the roof terrace, with lovely views of the old Marylebone churchyard.

Providores & Tapa Room

109 Marylebone High Street, W1U 4RX **Tel** *020 7935 6175*

Map 4 D5

This stylish, much-praised restaurant is almost a showcase for global fusion cooking. Chef Peter Gordon is from New Zealand and his dishes combine Pacific Rim, Mediterranean and many other influences, often using rare, delicate ingredients. As an alternative to the restaurant, you can try equally hip snacks in the Tapa Room alongside.

KENSINGTON, HOLLAND PARK, NOTTING HILL

Bistrot Eleven

11 Abingdon Road, W8 6AH **Tel** *020 7937 0120*

Map 17 C1

Rich colours and striking modern artwork set the tone at this relaxing Kensington bistro, taken over in 2009 by chef Daniel Hillier. The modern European cooking has a fresh style too, with varied salads and tasty dishes like gilthead bream with chickpeas and chorizo. Set-price menus are a great bargain.

Cibo

3 Russell Gardens, W14 8EZ **Tel** *020 7371 6271*

Map 9 A5

You get plenty of bread and olives to pack in while you wait for excellent regional Italian food here. It's been on this site so long it's an institution, while its clever mix of tried and trusted Italian favourites combined with more adventurous dishes never fails to satisfy a young crowd. A good wine list and fixed price lunch complete its appeal.

Utopia

1 Kensington High Street, W8 5NP **Tel** *020 7937 0393*

Map 10 E5

Persian and Greek food par excellence with perfect kebabs grilled to smoky brilliance over a real coal barbecue. Try their tasty, moist pieces of marinated lamb and/or chicken over saffron-scented, buttery rice. Friendly staff are happy to advise on choice of dishes and to stop you from over-ordering, as you may be tempted to do so. Good value, too.

Assaggi

39 Chepstow Place, W2 4TS **Tel** *020 7792 5501*

Map 9 C2

Near to Notting Hill and Bayswater tube station is this small restaurant. The menu is in Italian, but you can guess most dishes and the waiters will explain the rest. It's all smiles from the staff, but then they know you might easily break your bank. Good food, but be careful what you spend.

Geales

2 Farmer Street, W8 7SN **Tel** *020 7727 7528*

Map 9 C3

One of London's classic fish-and-chip cafés, Geales has evolved into a smart upscale fish restaurant, to match its wealthy neighbourhood. Exceptional-quality fish and chips remain the speciality, but you can have fish cooked many other ways. This is a great place for a long lunch, with a fixed-price lunch menu. Good range of wines, too.

Maggie Jones

6 Old Court Place, W8 4PL **Tel** *020 7937 6462*

Map *10 D5*

A quirky ambience and the intimate dining atmosphere make this a peculiarly British dining experience. Huge portions mean no one has left Maggie's hungry for over 45 years now. Service can be eccentric, so just sit back and enjoy. The steak and kidney pie is a must.

Rodizio Rico

111 Westbourne Grove, W2 4UW **Tel** *020 7792 4035*

Map *9 D2*

Brazilian-style eating and great fun. Go for the buffet where you pick up your salad yourself and let the waiters bring you different bits of variously grilled meats at regular intervals. Rodizio is a concept in Brazil, which translates pretty much as "all you can eat". Really not a place for non carnivores, but those who are will never leave hungry.

The Cow

89 Westbourne Park Road, W2 5QH **Tel** *020 7221 5400*

Map *9 C1*

A hub of the Notting Hill social scene, this hugely popular gastropub regularly hosts celebrities among the crowds thronging the bar or climbing the narrow staircase to the dining room. Opulent seafood platters are the big speciality, but steaks also hit the spot. Drinks include a global fine wine collection.

Whits

21 Abingdon Road, W8 6AH **Tel** *020 7938 1122*

Map *17 C1*

A neighbourhood restaurant on a side lane off busy Kensington High Street. Because of its position it does not attract the masses. Serves dishes such as citrus-cured salmon with potted crab brûlée and sourdough bread and duck confit with honey and cumin jus. Food is consistently good and very seasonal, but always very affordable.

Clarke's

124 Kensington Church Street, W8 4BH **Tel** *020 7221 9225*

Map *9 C4*

Sally Clarke learnt her cooking skills in California and pioneered global and Pacific-Rim cuisine in London in the 1980s. Her pretty, tranquil restaurant has stayed true to its style, which now seems more conventional compared to other fusion experiments elsewhere. Superb fresh ingredients are a mainstay, and the breads are delicious.

The Belvedere

Holland Park, off Abbotsbury Road, W8 6LU **Tel** *020 7602 1238*

Map *9 B5*

Once the ballroom of Holland House, the aristocratic mansion around which Holland Park was created, The Belvedere is one of London's most charming restaurants, whether you dine inside or on the garden terrace. Service is very smooth; on the menu are enjoyable versions of mostly French and British dishes, beautifully presented.

SOUTH KENSINGTON, CHELSEA, FULHAM

Bugis Street Brasserie

The Millennium Gloucester Hotel, Ashburn Place, SW7 4LH **Tel** *020 7331 6211*

Map *18 E2*

It's called a brasserie but it's not French food. The Chinese and Singaporean dishes are robust, extremely tasty and come in gigantic portions. Plus, for the area, it's not very expensive. For starters the salt and pepper squid is exceptional. A fixed price menu is available.

Buona Sera at the Jam

289a King's Road, SW3 5EW **Tel** *020 7352 8827*

Map *19 A4*

It can be a Jam by name and nature at this popular Chelsea Italian café: two floors of intimately sized tables have been squeezed into an amazingly snug space, but this all adds to the fun and friendly atmosphere. Fans also enjoy the no-nonsense traditional Italian pasta, pizza and other favourites. Robust wines and beers.

Lots Road Pub & Dining Room

114 Lots Road, SW10 0RJ **Tel** *020 7352 6645*

Map *18 E5*

A smart take on gastropub style: one side of this old pub has been turned into a light, stylish modern dining area, decorated with fresh flowers, but there's still a relaxed bar for sampling the excellent beers. Regulars on the menu include lively salads and gastropub favourites like braised lamb shank and superior-quality burgers.

Pig's Ear

35 Old Church Street, SW3 5BS **Tel** *020 7352 2908*

Map *19 A4*

Affluent Chelsea locals appreciate this traditional-looking pub, with comfy bar and wood-panelled upstairs dining room. The French-influenced menu highlights powerful choices like pork belly and roast cod with olive mash and chicory, and there's a great cheese selection. Try the Pig's Ear bitter, brewed in Gloucestershire.

Racine

239 Brompton Road, SW3 2EP **Tel** *020 7584 4477*

Map *19 B1*

A restaurant that sets out to showcase French cuisine (*racine* also means "root") and succeeds very well. Genuine French food, French waiters, and great atmosphere all combine to keep locals coming back for more. The venison, when in season, is excellent and the menu changes regularly. It includes vegetarian options. The service has improved greatly.

Key to Price Guide *see p296* **Key to Symbols** *see back cover flap*

The Ebury
11 Pimlico Road, SW1W 8NA **Tel** *020 7730 6784* **Map** *20 D2* — £££

This beautifully converted gastropub is a welcome option in this rather upmarket neighbourhood. The high-quality modern British cuisine includes tempting choices for everyone, from bangers and mash to wild mushroom risotto, duck confit and slow-cooked belly of pork. A great place to stop for lunch.

The Painted Heron
112 Cheyne Walk, SW10 0DJ **Tel** *020 7351 5232* **Map** *19 A5* — £££

A nice Indian bistro in a pleasant part of Chelsea. Flavours are fresh with meat and poultry scoring highly for complex spices without overpowering chilli burn. Seafood, like so many Indian restaurants, is not so special although the crabcake starters are very good. It's a good deal classier than many Indian places in every way. Closed Sunday.

Bibendum
Michelin House, 81 Fulham Road, SW3 6RD **Tel** *020 7581 5817* **Map** *19 B2* — ££££

Bibendum's location, in the 1930s former Michelin tyre building, with spectacular Art Deco tiles and stained glass showing Michelin Men riding bicycles, makes any meal here a special occasion. Service is charming and the creative modern cuisine is consistently impressive. Save space for the scrumptious desserts.

Cambio de Tercio
163 Old Brompton Road, SW5 0LJ **Tel** *020 7244 8970* **Map** *18 F2* — ££££

Compact but comfortable, with a vibrant Spanish colour scheme, Cambio is a London showcase for sophisticated modern Spanish cooking. Dishes are refined and very enjoyable, with delectable combinations of flavours, whether in classic dishes (suckling pig) or new creations. There's a superb Spanish wine list, too.

Gordon Ramsay
68 Royal Hospital Road, SW3 4HP **Tel** *020 7352 4441* **Map** *19 C4* — £££££

A tasting menu here costs around £120 per person, but this is probably the best restaurant in London, the UK and, Ramsay might tell you, the world. Everything is perfect from place settings to service. This place deserves all three of its Michelin stars. As a souvenir of London, your meal memories here will last a lifetime. Closed weekends.

L'Etranger
36 Gloucester Road, SW7 4QT **Tel** *020 7584 1118* **Map** *18 E1* — £££££

A gem of a place serving excellent French food with Asian influences in very stylish surroundings. People rave about the caramelized black cod with miso for good reason. But then every dish on this menu is delectable, including the vegetarian options. A massive wine list has been created with passion. And you can dance in the club downstairs.

Tom Aikens
43 Elystan Street, SW3 3NT **Tel** *020 7584 2003* **Map** *19 B2* — £££££

Chef Aikens prepares incredible modern French food at his flagship restaurant, which has been awarded a Michelin star. Dishes are lovingly constructed and beautifully plated with flavours finely balanced with a watchmaker's care. Special lunch and seven-course tasting menus are available, as are vegetarian dishes. Book ahead.

KNIGHTSBRIDGE, BELGRAVIA

Il Convivio
143 Ebury Street, SW1W 9QN **Tel** *020 7730 4099* **Map** *20 E2* — £££

It's a cliché to say that an Italian restaurant is "welcoming" but this one really is. Plus, it has that aroma that makes you feel extra hungry. Couples, groups, children and everyone else cram in to fill up on very good and honest Italian food such as Tuscan black (squid ink) spaghetti with lobster. There are vegetarian dishes too and 150 Italian wines.

La Poule au Pot
231 Ebury Street, SW1W 8UT **Tel** *020 7730 7763* **Map** *20 D2* — £££

Belgravia residents have been calling in at this French bistro for years. There's a pavement terrace in summer while inside it looks like a slice of old France. Menus accordingly stick mainly with French classics – hearty cassoulet, mussels, steak *au poivre*, good cheeses and fruity desserts. The set-price menus are great value.

Mu
Millennium Knightsbridge, 17 Sloane Street, SW1X 9NU **Tel** *020 7201 6330* **Map** *19 C1* — £££

In this location you expect style and at this evening-only restaurant you get it. The food at Mu is hard to categorize. The best way to appreciate it is to go for the tasting menu. Each small dish is assembled with a smart precision. Try seared fillet of red mullet with tomato confit and basil foam or foie gras terrine, braised oxtail and Madeira jelly.

Noura
16 Hobart Place, SW1W 0HH **Tel** *020 7235 9444* **Map** *20 E1* — £££

This is one of three Noura restaurants in London offering award-winning Lebanese cuisine. You can try a little of everything with the hot and cold mezzes, which include plenty of vegetarian options, or order the signature tabbouleh. An extensive wine list offers a good selection of Lebanese wines.

Amaya
Halkin Arcade, 15 Motcomb Street, SW1X 8JT **Tel** *020 7823 1166*   **Map** *12 D5*

A very different Indian restaurant indeed. Spacious, stylish and with the kitchen on honest display. The speciality here is grills and you can see the three stations – tandoori, sigra and tawa – in action all evening. The range of meats and vegetables is brilliant and the presentation and service faultless. Expensive, but worth dining here.

Fifth Floor at Harvey Nichols
Harvey Nichols, Knightsbrige, SW1X 7RJ **Tel** *020 7235 5250*   **Map** *11 C5*

Harvey Nichols has a special place among London's big stores, and its top-floor restaurant too has a special verve. All white, and loved by the fashion crowd, it has wonderfully refined, intricate, delicious modern cuisine. Extravagantly subtle desserts are worth a visit by themselves. À la carte prices are high while the set menus are more accessible.

Nahm
The Halkin, 5 Halkin Street, SW1X 7DJ **Tel** *020 7333 1234*   **Map** *12 D5*

A remarkable Thai restaurant that has a Michelin star so you can arrive with high hopes. The set menu offers not a dull moment. Try the appetizer *ma hor* – minced prawns and chicken simmered in palm sugar with deep fried shallots, garlic and peanuts, served on pineapple and mandarin orange. Not cheap but good, with an extensive wine list.

Zafferano
15 Lowndes Street, SW1X 9EY **Tel** *020 7235 5800*   **Map** *20 D1*

Zafferano has long been recognized as one of the capital's premier Italian restaurants. It's a discreet place, where the emphasis is firmly on the food. Dishes such as rack of lamb with black olives and artichokes and the white truffle tasting menu, in season October to Christmas, allow the quality of the ingredients to shine through.

Foliage
Mandarin Oriental Hyde Park, 66 Knightsbridge, SW1X 7LA **Tel** *020 7235 2000*   **Map** *11 C5*

This fantastic restaurant, designed by Adam Tihany, offers spectacular views of Hyde Park but don't let that distract you from the Michelin-starred menu of modern European dishes. Your four-course set meal is normally five when you include the little tasters in between and the service is faultless. A real jewel.

One 0 One
101 William Street, SW1X 7RN **Tel** *020 7290 7101*   **Map** *11 C5*

Fish and shellfish are the speciality here. Dishes include confit of Norwegian salmon with green pea *velouté* and surf and turf combos like red king crab with roasted Anjou squab pigeon. Meals are reasonably priced considering the quality of the ingredients.

Zuma
5 Raphael Street, SW7 1DL **Tel** *020 7584 1010*   **Map** *11 C5*

Very cool, very trendy and one block opposite Harrods. Celebrities can be spotted here but they come for the great food just like everyone else. Great sashimi, nigiri, sushi and tempura with fancy service and fancy prices. It's definitely an experience, but be prepared to dig deep into your holiday money.

WESTMINSTER, TRAFALGAR SQUARE, VICTORIA

Mekong
46 Churton Street, SW1V 2LP **Tel** *020 7630 9568*   **Map** *20 F2*

This long-standing Vietnamese eatery still fills up on account of its wallet-friendly food. The ground-floor dining area can seem cramped, and the rustic walls painted in clashing pink and green leave something to be desired. But the kitchen delivers some tasty treats. Delightful staff and sought-after alfresco tables add to the experience of it all.

London Showboat – Hispaniola
Victoria Embankment, WC2N 5DJ **Tel** *020 7839 3011*   **Map** *13 C5*

Something different: a four-course English meal and a Thames boat trip combined. As you sail out majestically past London's landmarks you'll be entertained with a cabaret performance of songs from London's top shows. On the way back, the decks are cleared for dancing. Departs at 7pm Wednesday–Sunday.

National Dining Rooms
Sainsbury Wing, National Gallery, Trafalgar Square, WC2N 5DN **Tel** *020 7747 2525*   **Map** *13 B3*

Museum and gallery cafés traditionally tend to be dull and functional, but the National Gallery has improved things with this lively modern brasserie. It's open for breakfast, lunch and dinner, so at different times you can try cakes, teas, steaks, pasta, nicely prepared fish grills or cocktails. There's also a generous children's menu.

The Atrium
4 Millbank, SW1P 3JA **Tel** *020 7233 0032*   **Map** *21 B1*

The name says it all; this is a vast glass-covered space that has a real "wow" factor. The menu changes four times a year, mixing and matching to largely good effect – try seared scallop with pea purée, parma ham and mint oil or braised lamb shank with swede and turnip mash and rosemary jus. Bright and modern in a conservative area.

Key to Price Guide *see p296* **Key to Symbols** *see back cover flap*

Cinnamon Club

30–32 Great Smith Street, SW1P 3BU **Tel** *020 7222 2555*   **Map** *21 B1*

London has hundreds of Indian restaurants, but the Cinnamon Club is not just one of the crowd. It occupies a grand old former library in the heart of Westminster, with an atmosphere of hushed elegance. Under chef Vivek Singh it offers diners very refined, subtle North Indian cuisine, made with the finest ingredients and rare spicings.

MAYFAIR, PICCADILLY, ST JAMES'S

Al Duca

4–5 Duke of York Street, SW1Y 6LA **Tel** *020 7839 3090*   **Map** *13 A3*

Just off Piccadilly, this bright, modern Italian restaurant offers great value in an expensive area, with set-price menus. Classic North Italian dishes are nicely presented, especially grilled fish, pestos and richly flavoured risottos. An excellent wine list and a great range of Italian liqueurs for after your meal. Closed Sun.

Chor Bizarre

16 Albemarle Street, W1S 4HW **Tel** *020 7629 9802*   **Map** *12 F3*

Serving dishes from regional India, this restaurant is always busy. Try the lamb with fenugreek, spinach and ginger and the aubergine with peanut sauce. Waiters can lose interest so keep them on their toes if you don't want to be forgotten. But they are friendly and willing to help you choose from the large menu.

Langan's Brasserie

6 Stratton Street, W1J 8LB **Tel** *020 7491 8822*   **Map** *12 F3*

The original and perhaps still the best Langan's. The eponymous owner went to see the great chef in the sky a while back now, but his style lives on. Service is discreetly attentive and the staff are friendly. The menu changes weekly and includes dishes like soufflé with anchovy sauce.

Momo

25 Heddon Street, W1B 4BH **Tel** *020 7434 4040*   **Map** *12 F2*

Momo has been credited with giving a hip, fashionable appeal to North African food. Classic tagine stews and couscous are infused with fresh flavours of cumin, mint, lemon and coriander, and there are less well known dishes too. The design evokes old Marrakesh with style. Tables are snug, but you might rub elbows with celebrities.

Rasa W1

6 Dering Street, W1S 1AD **Tel** *020 7629 1346*   **Map** *12 E2*

Restaurants of the Rasa chain are among the foremost exponents – in India or abroad – of the distinctive, mainly vegetarian cuisine of Kerala, in South India. As well as some of London's most interesting vegetarian food, branches also have seafood dishes. Seasonings are more subtle than hot, and the flavour-palette is full of delicious surprises. Closed Sun.

The Criterion

224 Piccadilly, W1J 9HP **Tel** *020 7930 0488*   **Map** *13 A3*

A monument of a restaurant, right on Piccadilly Circus. Dating from the 1870s, the giant Criterion has fantastic Arabian-fantasy decor, with a glittering mosaic ceiling, and now has food to match. There are few more impressive places to sit and escape the city outside, enjoying fine wines and succulent, sophisticated Franco-British cuisine.

Wild Honey

12 St George's Street, W1S 2FB **Tel** *020 7758 9160*   **Map** *12 F2*

Oak panelling and striking contemporary art combine to create the look of this elegant modern bistro. Prices are lower than many in the area, but the inventive food is first-rate, and made with the best fresh British and European ingredients. Try Cornish clams with shallots, followed by roast venison with Jerusalem artichokes. Very popular.

Green's Restaurant & Oyster Bar

36 Duke Street, SW1Y 6DF **Tel** *020 7930 4566*   **Map** *12 F3*

Wonderful old-world ambience and extensive champagne list, this is a great establishment. Excellent lobster salads, first-class fish and chips with pea purée and, of course, a nice choice of oysters, most of them down from Scotland that very day. Daily lunch specials include hearty favourites like fish pie. Closed on Sundays from May to September.

Le Caprice

Arlington House, Arlington Street, SW1A 1RJ **Tel** *020 7629 2239*   **Map** *12 F4*

Opened in the 1980s, the Caprice instantly became a media and music-world hangout and still maintains its buzzy feel. Service is famously superb whether or not you're a famous face; fans often come for brasserie standards like superior burgers and grills but there are many other options, and an exceptional vegetarian menu.

The Wolseley

160 Piccadilly, W1J 9EB **Tel** *020 7499 6996*   **Map** *12 F3*

London never had many 19th-century *grands cafés*, but in 2003 this fine Piccadilly building was made into a great modern version of one. The decor is glamorous, with chandeliers hanging from lofty ceilings, and the atmosphere always buzzing. Menus offer plenty of variety, from salads to grills and seafood platters. Also open for breakfast.

Hélène Darroze at the Connaught
 ₤₤₤₤₤
Connaught Hotel, Carlos Place, W1K 2AL **Tel** *020 3147 7200* **Map** *12 E3*

Restaurants in the Connaught have enjoyed an august reputation ever since the hotel opened in the early 1900s. In 2007 it hit a new high with the arrival of renowned French chef Hélène Darroze. Her cooking is endlessly inventive, blending French traditions with rare, intricate spicings. Very expensive, but a real gourmet experience.

Le Gavroche
₤₤₤₤₤
43 Upper Brook Street, W1K 7QR **Tel** *020 7408 0881* **Map** *12 D2*

Brothers Michel and Albert Roux have been synonymous with fine dining in Britain for decades, and the Gavroche is their flagship London restaurant. The head chef is now English, but the restaurant remains true to its traditions of timeless luxury and superb French haute cuisine, with every detail taken care of.

Maze Inside Marriott Hotel
₤₤₤₤₤
10–13 Grosvenor Square, W1K 6JP **Tel** *020 7107 0000* **Map** *12 D2*

Part of the Gordon Ramsey empire, and run by El Bulli veteran Jason Atherton, Maze has been awarded a Michelin star for its highly creative and impeccably presented menus. Dishes such as honey and soy roasted quail, Landes foie gras and spiced pear chutney showcase international influences. Highly recommended tasting menu.

Nobu
 ₤₤₤₤₤
Metropolitan hotel, Old Park Lane, W1K 1LB **Tel** *020 7447 4747* **Map** *12 E4*

London's sleekest, hippest Japanese restaurant was one of the chain's first international ventures. At times it's been more famous for its celebrity diners than its food, but it's also a benchmark for quality: fresh fish and seafood are of supreme quality, and tempura, sashimi and modern Japanese dishes are prepared with immense skill. Closed Sat & Sun lunch.

Umu
₤₤₤₤₤
14–16 Bruton Place, W1J 6L **Tel** *020 7499 8881* **Map** *12 E3*

Seriously expensive (especially the tasting menu) but extremely stylish as well – the futuristic front door will make you gasp. The beautiful interior and impeccable service provided by great staff will also impress. As for the food, this is one of the few places in London where you can find genuine Japanese kaiseki. Vegetarian options available.

Wiltons
 ₤₤₤₤₤
55 Jermyn Street, SW1Y 6LX **Tel** *020 7629 9955* **Map** *13 A3*

A landmark institution, there has been a Wiltons in London since 1742. A quintessential expensive club-dining experience. Whitstable Bay potted shrimps, grilled Dover sole, Scottish lobster thermidor and West Mersey oysters are the main attractions here, but you will also want to bask in the atmosphere and in the attentive service.

SOUTH BANK, SOUTHWARK

Canteen
₤₤
Royal Festival Hall, Belvedere Road, SE1 8XX **Tel** *0845 686 1122* **Map** *14 D4*

Conveniently located for theatregoers, Canteen serves delicious and reasonably priced British dishes in a contemporary setting. Daily specials include roasts and pies, and there's a selection of hearty British puddings such as treacle tart with Jersey cream. Weekend brunch is popular and is well complemented by a Bloody Mary from the cocktail list.

Giraffe
₤₤
Riverside Level 1, Royal Festival Hall, SE1 8XX **Tel** *020 7928 2004* **Map** *14 D3*

Giraffe restaurants form one of London's best something-for-everyone chains. Globetrotting menus have plenty to please kids – burgers, pasta – and grownups – Malay noodles, enchiladas, great bargain salads. Speedy, friendly staff ensure a fun feel. The South Bank branch has a terrace near the river: there are 11 more Giraffes around London.

Kennington Tandoori
 ₤₤
313 Kennington Road, SE11 4QE **Tel** *020 7735 9247* **Map** *22 E3*

One of the best Indian curry houses in London according to many. As it is a short drive from Westminster, many curry-loving Members of Parliament can be found debating policy over a chicken jalfreezi. There are classic dishes and quite a few unique ones with nice innovations such as their own Nilgiri murgh. Reliable food in a calm oasis.

Mar I Terra
 ₤₤
14 Gambia Street, Waterloo, SE1 0XH **Tel** *020 7928 7628* **Map** *14 F4*

Described as a little gem by its fans, this local Spanish restaurant has also been steadily building custom from people living and working miles away. The quality of the ingredients is one of its secrets as is its location off the main drag. This means the diners are discerning gourmets who have come for the food and the cheerful atmosphere.

Tapas Brindisa
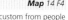 ₤₤
18–20 Southwark Street, SE1 1TJ **Tel** *020 7357 8880* **Map** *15 B4*

Brindisa, based in the adjacent Borough Market, has led the way in importing the finest Spanish foods into the UK – superb Serrano hams, cheeses, piquillo peppers and more. Their tapas bar showcases these delights in a fabulous array, all prepared with as much skill as grand cuisine. Very popular and no booking so come prepared to wait.

Key to Price Guide *see p296* **Key to Symbols** *see back cover flap*

Tate Modern Café2

*Level 2, Tate Modern, Sumner Street, SE1 9TG **Tel** 020 7401 5014*   **Map** 14 F3

The bright, airy café in the Tate Modern (open to non-gallery visitors) is an excellent port of call on the South Bank. Choose between sandwiches, snacks, salads or larger dishes like pan-roast chicken with puy lentils; all are finely presented, with fresh ingredients. On Level 7 there is a smarter, more expensive restaurant, with a superb view.

Tito's Peruvian Restaurant

*4–6 London Bridge Street, SE1 9SG **Tel** 020 7407 7787*   **Map** 15 B4

A favourite lunch spot for City workers, Tito's serves Peruvian staples such as seafood, fish soups and fried *yuca* and rice, and its portions are extremely generous. Try the king prawn *chupe*, which is milky soup with rice, peas and egg, or one of the restaurant's *pisco*-based cocktails.

Troia Bar and Restaurant

*3F Belvedere Road, County Hall, SE1 7GQ **Tel** 020 7633 9309*   **Map** 14 D4

Covering a lot more of Turkey's national dishes than many similar restaurants in London, Troia lets you explore on your own or you can let the set menus do all the hard work. *Kisir*, a cold starter of nuts, bulgar wheat, herbs, and spring onions feels healthy and allows you the space to tuck in to the very hearty main dishes on offer.

Baltic Restaurant & Bar

*74 Blackfriars Road, SE1 8HA **Tel** 020 7928 1111*   **Map** 14 F4

Beetroot vodka-cured salmon? Well that's eastern European for sure. This restaurant exudes charm and is located inside a former coach house, which gives it exciting high ceilings. There's a massive range of vodkas and the food constantly surprises with dishes such as roast guinea fowl kiev with spring greens, chestnuts and cranberries.

Bermondsey Kitchen

*194 Bermondsey Street, SE1 3TQ **Tel** 020 7407 5719*   **Map** 15 D5

A great place for brunch, with dishes such as eggs Florentine. There's a Portuguese flavour to many of the options, with fresh ingredients from nearby Borough Market, and tapas also on the menu, which changes on a daily basis. Global wines and an easygoing atmosphere complete its appeal. The large front windows open in summer.

Cantina del Ponte

*Butlers' Wharf Building, 36C Shad Thames, SE1 2YE **Tel** 020 7403 5403*   **Map** 16 E4

The riverside terrace tables here have one of the best possible views of Tower Bridge, and are understandably in demand. To eat there are all the Italian standards – salads, pizza from a wood-fired oven, pasta with plenty of sea-food – made with perky fresh ingredients, nicely washed down with decent wines. Set lunch menus are great value.

Cantina Vinopolis

*1 Bank End, SE1 9BU **Tel** 020 7940 8333*   **Map** 15 B3

This is next to the massive wine museum *(see p182)* so you know the wine list will be good. The food isn't bad either with a wide choice ranging to suit most tastes. Try the monkfish and sea bass or panfried scallops with herb salad. Can be a little lacking in atmosphere but if you're a wine buff visiting the museum it's an ideal place to lunch.

Delfina Studio Café

*50 Bermondsey Street, SE1 3UD **Tel** 020 7357 0244*   **Map** 15 C4

Don't let the word "café" put you off. A former chocolate factory, it has a light gallery space, charming service, and an interesting, balanced menu. Fish of the day might be from Australia, or you may see springbok. The menu is short but changes every two weeks and is always interesting. There is a good wine list as well. Closed weekends.

Fish!

*Cathedral Street, Borough Market, SE1 9AL **Tel** 020 7407 3803*   **Map** 15 B3

Occupying a prime location in London's foodie mecca Borough Market, this restaurant prepares fine ingredients bought directly from the suppliers on the market floor. It has a strong commitment to sustainable fish, fairly priced. Main courses include classic fish pie and the best of the morning's catch served simply. Daily vegetarian special.

Ozu

*County Hall, Riverside Building, Westminster Bridge Road, SE1 7PB **Tel** 020 7928 7766*   **Map** 14 D5

French owner, whose classic taste in Japanese food has been inspired by the Japanese director Yasujiro Ozu. Simple, contemporary decor and great views over the Thames and Westminster combine with exquisite attention to detail. Ozu serves sushi and sashimi, as well as a full à la carte menu.

The Lobster Pot Restaurant

*3 Kennington Lane, SE11 4RG **Tel** 020 7582 5556*   **Map** 22 F2

A remarkable little restaurant in an unprepossessing location. The French owners set out to recreate Brittany (even down to seagull soundtracks) and succeed brilliantly. The eight-course "surprise" menu is fantastic and the fish is always superbly fresh. Do book in advance, as it's not very big. Vegetarians should call ahead too. Closed Mon & Sun.

Roast

*Floral Hall, Borough Market, Stoney Street, SE1 1TL **Tel** 020 7940 1300*   **Map** 15 B4

The grand Victorian Borough Market is the place to find much of the best meat, fish and fresh produce in London, and Roast, with a sleek modern dining room inside the restored old structure, makes full use of them in its British-inspired menu. It opens early for fabulous breakfasts, and later in the day there are delicious roasts and grills.

The Oxo Tower Restaurant & Brasserie
8th Floor, Oxo Tower Wharf, Barge House Street, SE1 9PH **Tel** 020 7803 3888   **Map** 14 E3

There are plenty of reasonably priced chains along this stretch of the South Bank, all offering river views and easy access to theatres and Tate Modern, but to enjoy a really special evening's dining book a window table at this eighth-floor restaurant. It combines well executed modern European food and slick service with great river views.

SOHO, CHINATOWN

Tokyo Diner
2 Newport Place, WC2H 7JJ **Tel** 020 7287 8777   **Map** 13 B2

This small Japanese eatery boasts an extensive range of dishes, from sushi to curry and soba noodles, at unbeatable prices. The attentive staff will provide complimentary green tea and rice crackers on arrival, but there's no tipping – the menu explains that this is not customary in Japan. Try one of the bento boxes or lunchtime set meals.

Cha Cha Moon
15–21 Ganton Street, W1F 9BN **Tel** 020 7297 9800   **Map** 12 F2

Since it opened in 2008, this popular, canteen-style noodle bar has been regularly winning awards. Owned by Hong Kong-born restaurateur Alan Yau, of Wagamama fame, the menu features an eclectic mix of Chinese, Taiwanese, Singaporean and Malaysian cuisine and includes signature noodle broths with old favourites such as duck or wonton.

Harbour City
46 Gerrard Street, W1D 5QH **Tel** 020 7439 7859   **Map** 13 B2

The pedestrianized centre of Chinatown is home to many restaurants and wonderful grocers. This restaurant doesn't have staff outside trying to lure you in, it relies on regulars. And the food, which is consistently good. The decor is bright, colourful and cheerful.

Jen Café
4–8 Newport Place, WC2H 7JP   **Map** 13 B2

A busy Chinatown café near Leicester Square tube. One corner of the window is usually occupied by a member of staff hand-rolling the house speciality – Beijing dumplings – at an incredible speed. Barbecued meat and rice dishes and noodle soup also feature on the menu. Prices reflect the humble decor. No alcohol and no credit cards.

Masala Zone
9 Marshall Street, W1F 7ER **Tel** 020 7287 9966   **Map** 12 F2

An award-winning restaurant offering exceptional value combined with a healthy delicious meal. Masala Zone features home-style Indian cooking, with dishes ranging from street food to burgers, noodle bowls to thalis. Service is fast and you can order food to go.

New Mayflower
68–70 Shaftesbury Avenue, W1D 6LY **Tel** 020 7734 9207   **Map** 13 A2

This genuine Cantonese restaurant proves Shaftesbury Avenue is not just for theatregoers. Dishes such as bean curd stuffed with shrimp and deep-fried crab are appetizing and fresh. There are vegetarian choices too. Service is efficient and free juicy oranges are given at the end of your meal (a Hong Kong tradition). Open until 4am.

Princi
135 Wardour Street, W1F 0UT **Tel** 020 7478 8888   **Map** 13 A2

Another Alan Yau establishment, this lively café/restaurant in the heart of Soho is a great spot for a quick bite to eat or for a relaxed dinner. Seating is at communal tables or counters, and the menu contains good examples of standard Italian fare: breads, pizzas and pasta.

Andrew Edmunds
46 Lexington Street, W1F 0LW **Tel** 020 7437 5708   **Map** 13 A2

Small and romantically snug, with a secluded conservatory at the back, this feels almost like a country restaurant lost in the middle of Soho. It has gained many fans with its light, creative modern cooking – seen particularly in original, nicely balanced fish and seafood dishes. Be sure to book, as there are only a few tables.

Arbutus
63–64 Frith Street, W1D 3JW **Tel** 020 7734 4545   **Map** 13 A2

The Michelin-starred Arbutus has established itself as a landmark on the London dining scene. The simple, elegant decor offsets the excellent, seasonal cooking perfectly and brings a touch of class to this rowdy street. Menus make the most of top quality British ingredients. Many excellent wines are available in smaller carafes.

Gay Hussar
2 Greek Street, W1D 4NB **Tel** 020 7437 0973   **Map** 13 A1

Once the place of choice for cherry-nosed old journalists to meet and gossip and enjoy (on expenses) second-rate food that reminded them of their private schools. However, now it provides a proper insight into authentic Hungarian cuisine, wines and spirits, and is a charming, cosy restaurant with welcoming staff.

Haozhan

8 Gerrard Street, W1D 5PJ **Tel** 020 7434 3838

Map 13 B2

££££

Haozhan's cool interior continues to entice Chinatown visitors away from standardized sweet-and-sour pork towards more innovative flavours. Prices are reasonable, though the dining experience can feel rushed. The set-lunch deal and fine-wine specials add to Haozhan's appeal. The chef's recommendations are often the best thing on the menu.

L'Escargot

48 Greek Street, W1D 4EF **Tel** 020 7437 2679

Map 13 B2

£££

One of Soho's historic restaurants and a favourite of the media theatrical crowd. It's owned by chef-entrepreneur Marco Pierre White. Menus offer refined modern cuisine such as a lovely tian of crab and avocado, or scallops with tarragon risotto. Choose between the main dining room, or the more luxurious Picasso Room upstairs.

Little Italy

21 Frith Street, W1D 4RN **Tel** 020 7734 4737

Map 13 A2

£££

The name says it all. A busy and vibrant place with a late licence until 4am. A page full of pasta dishes is always a safe bet, but if you feel like splashing out, the main courses are good too. You might miss the unassuming doorway so back up and look again, it's there. Some live music and dancing most nights.

Vasco & Piero's Pavilion

15 Poland Street, W1F 8QE **Tel** 020 7437 8774

Map 13 A2

£££

Most of the dishes on the menu are Italian and the owner's Umbrian heritage ensures that chickpeas and lentils feature frequently. The pasta is made in-house, with the finest quality ingredients and the menu changes twice daily. If you like truffles come visit – in season black or white truffles are imported from Umbria.

Zilli Fish

36–40 Brewer Street, W1F 9TA **Tel** 020 7734 8649

Map 13 A2

£££

Aldo Zilli has brought a new touch to Italian food in London by showcasing Italian fish and seafood cuisine. The style is bright and unfussy: contented diners tuck into platters of tasty grilled squid, spaghetti with lobster or clams, monk-fish in pancetta and more, washed down with well-chilled wines. There are two more Zilli restaurants around Soho.

Quo Vadis

26–29 Dean Street, W1D 3LL **Tel** 020 7437 9585

Map 13 A2

££££

Another Soho restaurant with a long history – it first opened in 1926, but earlier, Karl Marx had lived in the house upstairs. Under its present owners the spacious, elegant dining room presents a fresh, modern British menu, emphasiz-ing superior steaks, but with excellent fish and lighter dishes too. A place with a guaranteed metropolitan buzz.

Veeraswamy

99–101 Regent Street, W1B 4RS **Tel** 020 7734 1401

Map 12 F3

££££

A touch of the old Empire. Slide into London's oldest Indian restaurant (open since 1926) and try some rather unique and genuine Indian cuisine from the "noble houses of India". It is elegant and expensive but the presence of so many people from the subcontinent clearly enjoying themselves speaks for itself.

Corrigan's

28 Upper Grosvenor Street, W1K 7EH **Tel** 020 7499 9943

Map 12 D3

£££££

Irishman Richard Corrigan is not London's best-known chef, but one of its most admired. His Michelin-starred restaurant is intimate and discreet (you ring a bell to be let in) and the creative, robustly flavoured British-Irish based dishes are prepared with immense flair. Service is perfect, and the wine list is renowned. One for a special occasion.

FITZROVIA, BLOOMSBURY

Bam-Bou

1 Percy Street, W1T 1DB **Tel** 020 7323 9130

Map 13 A1

££

The "red" bar upstairs in this Georgian townhouse lures you to a few drinks before you descend to the restaurant proper. Seated at a table with just candlelight playing off dark wood, you feel a million miles from London. This is not your average Southeast Asian restaurant. The food is excellent and the atmosphere relaxed and warm.

Salt Yard

54 Goodge Street, W1T 4NA **Tel** 020 7637 0657

Map 5 A5

££

Given modern London's international flavour, it is no surprise the city has its own take on the traditional Spanish tapas bar. Instead of using only Spanish ingredients, the Salt Yard also uses first-rate Italian and British produce, in small delights like salt cod fritters with orange allioli, or duck and spinach *gnocchetti*. All are hard to resist.

Thai Metro

38 Charlotte Street, W1T 2NN **Tel** 020 7436 4201

Map 5 A5

££

Top-class Thai cuisine that won't break your bank. Go for green curry but be warned, if you aren't hot for chillies you could come out in a sweat. The zingy flavours that characterize Thai food are all here in abundance and if the weather is warm you can enjoy your food in the fresh air. Service is fast, which may not be to everyone's taste.

Elena's L'Etoile
30 Charlotte Street, W1T 2NG **Tel** *020 7636 7189*   **Map** *13 A1*

Another local institution, at lunchtime it fills up with media people from surrounding ad agencies and TV companies. They know what they want and Elena's delivers classic French bistro food under the gaze of celebrity pictures that cover the walls. It's not cheap but you do get what you pay for and that indefinable extra – real atmosphere.

Elysee
13 Percy Street, W1T 1DT **Tel** *020 7636 4804*   **Map** *13 A1*

A legend among London's Greek restaurants, this is a noisy place that's not ideal for romantic couples. That said, it's great fun for a night out with belly dancers, bands and singers all delivering an impressive show. The food does take second billing to the entertainment but it's perfectly good food at a fair price. Roof terrace. Open until 3:30am.

Pescatori
57 Charlotte Street, W1T 4PD **Tel** *020 7580 3289*   **Map** *5 A5*

The cooking always smells great when you pass this place and, because patrons try to sit outside in just about any weather, you get to gaze jealously at their food too. It's easy to go a bit mad and end up with a large bill. Grilled squid is always good and garlicky, while pasta and seafood dishes are consistently tasty. Closed Sat lunch and Sun.

Hakkasan
8 Hanway Place, W1T 1HD **Tel** *020 7927 7000*   **Map** *13 A1*

A very expensive modern Chinese restaurant, but one that has had no problems filling its tables from day one. The basement dining room has a DJ from 9pm each evening. The decor is superbly stylish and the food even more so. It's busy, but if you have the money and love good food you won't leave disappointed. Closed Sunday dinner.

Pied à Terre
34 Charlotte Street, W1T 2NH **Tel** *020 7636 1178*   **Map** *5 A5*

Plush, discreetly elegant decor sets the tone for this celebrated gourmet haven. The haute cusine menus offer all kinds of rare delights, often using rich ingredients as in poached sea bass in a truffle crust. Desserts, such as chestnut mousse in a chocolate pancake, are fabulously seductive, and appetizers and every other detail are superbly done.

COVENT GARDEN, HOLBORN

Belgo Centraal
50 Earlham Street, WC2H 9LJ **Tel** *020 7813 2233*   **Map** *13 B2*

Flagship of a small chain, this remains popular every night. Cool young staff whip up a great variety of mussels dishes, from *moules marinières* to more exotic creations featuring Belgium's famous beers. Meat-eaters are also catered for. Eat at the long refectory tables and enjoy the fun. Very cheap set menu deals available.

Café Mode
57 & 59 Endell Street, WC2H 9AJ **Tel** *020 7240 8085*   **Map** *13 C2*

Always great value and very popular, Café Mode's great salads, pasta and vegetarian dishes, and warm, friendly staff all contribute to a winning formula. Lone diners don't feel out of place and the downstairs Moroccan-themed lounge is a cool retreat from the hustle and bustle of Covent Garden.

Café Pacifico
5 Langley Street, WC2H 9JA **Tel** *020 7379 7728*   **Map** *13 B2*

If you like a lively night, you'll like it here. Occasional Mexican live music, a buzzy atmosphere and, if you're young or young at heart, a few cocktails followed by some filling and reasonably priced food such as burritos will send you singing out into the piazza.

Food for Thought
31 Neal Street, WC2H 9PR **Tel** *020 7836 9072*   **Map** *13 B2*

This relaxed little café has been serving London's vegetarians for decades. The basement dining room is down a narrow staircase: it's packed every lunchtime, but regulars cooperate to make the most of the space. Lasagnes, quiches, salads, fruity desserts and more are full of good flavours. Takeaway options are upstairs.

Kulu Kulu Sushi
51–53 Shelton Street, WC2H 9HE **Tel** *020 7240 5687*   **Map** *13 C2*

Fresh raw fish at a price that's right. Simple decor belies the attention to detail that goes into the creation and presentation of dishes. Salmon sashimi comes recommended by regulars and there's always a line forming at lunchtime as health-conscious office workers choose fish over sandwiches. Closed on Sundays.

Porter's English Restaurant
17 Henrietta Street, WC2E 8QH **Tel** *020 7836 6466*   **Map** *13 C2*

Porter's do warm, hearty, traditional British "grub" with tasty pie dishes such as steak and Guinness, cod, and salm-on and prawn. Desserts are equally large and not for anyone dieting. You'll get a proper fish and chips here too and all served by cheerful staff and at a good price for the location.

Key to Price Guide *see p296* **Key to Symbols** *see back cover flap*

Wahaca

66 Chandos Place, WC2N 4HG **Tel** *020 7240 1883*

Map *13 C3*

A roaring success since it opened in 2007, Wahaca is a great place for a cheap meal in this touristy part of town. The innovative menu, designed by Thomasina Miers who won the television Masterchef title in 2005, brings authentic Mexican flavours to London diners using a mix of imported and British ingredients. Excellent mojitos and tasty desserts.

Bertorelli's

44a Floral Street, WC2E 9DA **Tel** *020 7836 3969*

Map *13 C2*

An Italian institution in Covent Garden, Bertorelli's Roman empire now extends further afield. This is the flagship near the Royal Opera House. You always feel looked after here and the cooking is regional Italian kept simple to bring out the flavours. Good value, too. There is also a café and bar area.

Chez Gérard Opera Terrace

The Market, Covent Garden Piazza, WC2E 8RF **Tel** *020 7379 0666*

Map *13 C2*

The 11 Chez Gérard branches in London all follow the same formula – evoking the classic French brasserie in look and menu. Steak-frites served many different ways is the speciality, but other Gallic classics are on offer too. On the upper level of Covent Garden market, this branch has the bonus of irresistible views from its spacious terrace.

Christopher's The American Grill

18 Wellington Street, WC2E 7DD **Tel** *020 7240 4222*

Map *13 C2*

Rather more formal than you might expect from an American grill, but then this is a superior establishment. And there are plenty of other American favourites to choose from, including delicious prime rib chops, excellent lobsters and New York cheesecake. Good value and unpretentious.

Joe Allen

13 Exeter Street, WC2E 7DT **Tel** *020 7836 0651*

Map *13 C2*

This atmospheric basement has been a favourite with pre-and post-theatre crowds – actors and audiences – for over 30 years, and is often busiest after 11pm. American classics are Joe Allen mainstays – freshly made burgers, crisp Caesar salads – but there are more varied modern dishes too. Service is always on the ball.

Le Deuxieme

65a Long Acre, WC2E 9JD **Tel** *020 7379 0033*

Map *13 C2*

Special pre-theatre meals mean you can enjoy your food confident you'll be on to your coffee in plenty of time before the curtain is raised. A large dining area and a warm team contribute to family-friendly dining. A good choice of dishes with tuna steak being a popular item. The set menu is good value for the area.

Navajo Joe

34 King Street, WC2E 8JD **Tel** *020 7240 4008*

Map *13 B2*

A lively atmosphere, a busy bar and a good mix of spicy food under the umbrella "Pacific Rim street food," make this a popular Covent Garden eatery. Dishes come from South of the Border (down Mexico way) as well as from the heartland so it's hard not to find something to enjoy on the menu. Biggish portions and fairly speedy service.

Sarastro

126 Drury Lane, WC2B 5QG **Tel** *020 7836 0101*

Map *13 C2*

Not any old restaurant: entertainment at this "opera restaurant" includes opera singers – students and professionals – and string quartets. The extravagant decor is just as operatic, with ornate booths covered in velvet, gilt and drapes. To eat, there's a varied Turkish and Mediterranean menu. Don't expect a quiet time, but it's great fun.

The Admiralty

Somerset House, The Strand, WC2R 1LA **Tel** *020 7845 4646*

Map *14 D2*

Neo-Classical Somerset House is one of London's most imposing spaces, around a magnificent courtyard. The Admiralty restaurant is ideal for lunch, with light flooding in through tall windows, and in summer there's a terrace above the river. Enjoyable menus feature lively, French-oriented food, with fine versions of classics like *boeuf bourguignon*.

The Chancery

9 Cursitor Street, EC4A 1LL **Tel** *020 7831 4000*

Map *14 E1*

A little gem of a restaurant tucked away down a side street. Adventurous, modern, and very good cooking in a stylish establishment. Try the terrine of *foie gras*, goose confit and piquant sauce or crisp fillet of sea bass with seared scallops, risotto of herbs and basil oil. It's all very good and well priced. Closed Saturday and Sunday.

The Terrace

Lincoln's Inn Fields, WC2A 3LJ **Tel** *020 7430 1234*

Map *14 D1*

One of London's special oases located in a summer house in the middle of Lincoln's Inn Fields gardens. Chef Patrick Williams combines British and Caribbean cuisine, producing vibrant but subtle original dishes. A delightful place for summer lunch; last orders are taken by 7pm.

White Swan Pub & Dining Room

108 Fetter Lane, EC4A 1ES **Tel** *020 7242 9696*

Map *14 E1*

With so many restaurants to choose from around Covent Garden, there's perhaps been less interest in the "gastro-pub" idea. The bar at the White Swan still looks like a proper pub, but above it is a smart modern dining area, with a sophisticated menu of such enticing options as a smoked trout salad, and delicious roast pork. Good wine list, too.

Indigo

1 Aldwych, WC2B 4RH **Tel** *020 7300 0400*   **Map** *13 C2*

This is a calm, modern and stylish restaurant with an eclectic mixture of dishes beautifully presented and attentively served. Enjoy a drink in the grand bar upstairs before descending in the lift to the plush dining room, where they serve modern European cuisine.

J Sheekey

28–32 St Martin's Court, WC2N 4AL **Tel** *020 7240 2565*   **Map** *13 B2*

Sheekey's fish restaurant first opened near Leicester Square in 1896. It was sadly neglected for years, but since 1998, under the same owners as Le Caprice, its wonderful Victorian interior is again thronged with Theatreland crowds. British fish classics such as a celebrated fish pie are finely done, and the fresh catch-of-the-day fish are superb.

Rules

35 Maiden Lane, WC2E 7LB **Tel** *020 7836 5314*   **Map** *13 C2*

London's oldest restaurant, here since 1798, has retained its fascinating historic decor, and its standards: it remains a temple of fine British cooking. The roast beef is definitive, served with fabulous horseradish sauce. Game is another speciality (freshly brought from Rules' own hunting estate). Service is very smooth. A great institution.

Simpson's-in-the-Strand

100 The Strand, WC2R 0EW **Tel** *020 7836 9112*   **Map** *13 C2*

Simpsons' wood-panelled Grand Divan dining room is a Victorian monument, and a perfect setting for what the restaurant is famous for: true English roast beef, theatrically carved at your table on a silver trolley. Sadly, Simpson's legendary quality and service have been more erratic lately, but eating here is still an event. Also open for breakfast.

The Gaucho Grill

125–126 Chancery Lane, WC2A 1PU **Tel** *020 7242 7727*   **Map** *14 E1*

There are a few Gauchos around London and they remain consistent value. Of course the thing to eat is the steak – big ones, but there's also lobster and hot and cold seafood platters. A large wine list helps wash down your enormous meal and the cocktails aren't bad either. Closed Saturday lunch and Sunday.

Asia de Cuba

4–5 St. Martin's Lane, WC2N 4HX **Tel** *020 7300 5588*   **Map** *13 B2*

Perhaps fusing Cuban and Asian-American food is an experiment too far, but Asia de Cuba seems to be doing well on it. It's not cheap but the portions are massive and the service and attention to detail justify the cost. Calamari salad is popular as are the honey-glazed belly pork ribs. The aptly named "Bay of Pigs" dessert will finish you off!

L'Atelier de Joël Robuchon

13–15 West Street, WC2H 9NE **Tel** *020 7010 8600*   **Map** *13 B2*

Being dubbed France's greatest living chef is no small accolade: having done it all, Joël Robuchon has radically departed from traditional styles in his restaurants. In the Atelier bar, you're encouraged to sample small dishes, almost sushi-style, instead of conventional courses; a luxurious full menu can be had in the dining room above.

Pearl Restaurant & Bar

252 High Holborn, WC1V 7EN **Tel** *020 7829 7000*   **Map** *14 D1*

Go for the multicourse-tasting menu and you won't go wrong. They also score high by offering a very large selection of wines by the glass. The decor is very cool, very Scandinavian using the old high-ceilinged banking hall that it used to be to good effect. The two- and three-course fixed price menus offer good value.

CLERKENWELL, HOXTON, SPITALFIELDS

East is East

230 Commercial Road, E1 2NB **Tel** *020 7702 7222*

A very decent Indian restaurant that doesn't serve Bangladeshi dishes like some do. Of course you are spoiled for choice in this part of London for "an Indian" but this one seems to get top marks every time for its authentic cuisine and friendly service. And it's very low priced, which is always a bonus.

Bengal Cuisine

12 Brick Lane, E1 6RF **Tel** *020 7377 8405*   **Map** *8 E5*

Just about every building in Brick Lane is an Indian restaurant, but the quality varies. It's certainly a lot cleaner and more modern here than some we daren't mention. Very good value and the cook goes easy on the chilli to suit the more Western customers. Staff are happy to advise on dishes if asked. Good Sunday buffet as well.

Cantaloupe

 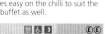

35–42 Charlotte Road, EC2A 3PD **Tel** *020 7613 4411*   **Map** *7 C4*

One of the most hip bar-restaurants in one of London's trendiest districts, with DJs in the bar several nights each week. In such a party venue food can be neglected, but Cantaloupe's kitchen keeps up a high standard: the pan-Lat-in menu is full of fun dishes such as Brazilian stews, Argentinian steaks and Spanish tapas. Great cocktails.

Key to Price Guide *see p296* **Key to Symbols** *see back cover flap*

The Eagle
159 Farringdon Road, EC1R 3AL **Tel** *020 7837 1353* **Map** 6 E4

Credited with being the original "gastropub" and popular with journalists based in offices nearby, The Eagle serves hearty Mediterranean-inspired food from a tiny open kitchen. There's no à la carte menu, just a range of tapas and eight main courses on a chalkboard. Pub-style features include bar service and no reservations. Closed Sunday dinner.

The Real Greek
14–15 Hoxton Market, N1 6HG **Tel** *020 7739 8212* **Map** 7 C3

Join the crowd in Hoxton and take in a massive selection of Greek dishes. They're all very tempting but keep an eye on the prices or you could end up with financial indigestion. The food is home-style cooking so many of the dishes on the menu have never been seen in the UK before. The wine bar serves Greek wines as well. Closed Sundays.

Vinoteca
7 St. John Street, EC1M 4AA **Tel** *020 7253 8786* **Map** 6 F5

This is a relaxed, European-style winebar and shop, serving simply prepared, good food made from high quality ingredients. The constantly evolving wine list is displayed on chalk boards and features a wide variety of wines by the glass. Each of these is paired with one of the dishes on the menu. In summer, tables spill out onto the street.

Acorn House
69 Swinton Street, WC1X 9NT **Tel** *020 7812 1842* **Map** 5 C3

Laid back café by day, grown up restaurant by night, Acorn House takes every care to create a wholly ethical dining experience – the interior was built from 100 per cent recycled materials and the kitchen uses sustainable Fairtrade ingredients to create first class dishes such as char-grilled mackerel fillet with cardamom and ginger. Closed Sunday.

Great Eastern Dining Room
54–56 Great Eastern Street, EC2A 3QR **Tel** *020 7613 4545* **Map** 7 C4

Very tasty and popular, Great Eastern has been a raging success since day one. It serves Pan-Asian food such as phad thai, Singapore noodles, sushi, dim sum and curries. Dim sums are filling and the curries balanced and spicy. And for once, service is impeccable and friendly. DJ sets on Friday and Saturday nights.

Moro
34–36 Exmouth Market, EC1R 4QE **Tel** *020 7833 8336* **Map** 6 E4

A restaurant that has been hugely influential. Inspired by Mediterranean travels, Sam and Samantha Clark create succulent dishes blending Spanish, Portuguese and Moroccan influences, with wonderful fresh ingredients. Instead of a full meal, you can also try equally irresistible tapas at the bar. It's noisy, and very popular, so book well ahead.

The Peasant
240 St John Street, EC1V 4PH **Tel** *020 7336 7726* **Map** 6 F4

This giant old pub, with its own Wat Tyler beer, has been successfully turned into a great gastropub. You can eat snacks in the bar, or larger dishes in the upstairs dining room: British-based dishes are hearty and inventive (smoked pollock with fennel, pheasant and black pudding). Don't leave without trying the delightfully tasty, fresh and fruity desserts.

Smiths of Smithfield
67–77 Charterhouse Street, EC1M 6HJ **Tel** *020 7251 7950* **Map** 6 F5

This lofty, post-industrial converted warehouse answers several needs. On the ground floor is a buzzy bar, with snacks and DJs; above is a wine bar. The middle floor is the main dining space where owner John Torode presents lively dishes using the best British produce. The Top Floor is his pricier fine-dining restaurant, with a great rooftop terrace.

St. John
26 St John Street, EC1M 4AY **Tel** *020 7251 0848* **Map** 6 F5

Here they like to eat the bits of animals you barely hear about so don't bring squeamish eaters. Set in a converted smokehouse near the meat markets, the food is fantastic if you want to try something different like the pigs' tongue with dandelion. Feasting menus for large groups can be booked in advance and include whole roast suckling pig.

CITY OF LONDON

Leon
86 Cannon Street, EC4N 6HT **Tel** *020 7623 9699* **Map** 15 B2

Allegra McEvedy and her team have hit the spot with their bright modern cafés. Eat in or take away and choose from a range of mostly Mediterranean-inspired dishes (with plenty of vegetarian options) such as grilled halloumi, salmon fishcakes, "superfood salads", fresh soups and more. Several branches around the city including a big one at Spitalfields.

The Place Below
St. Mary-le-Bow Church, EC2V 6AU **Tel** *020 7329 0789* **Map** 15 A2

A rare find amongst the chains and power-lunching restaurants of the Square Mile, this relaxed, friendly café serves hearty vegetarian fare such as quiches, salads and sandwiches on home-made bread. Open from breakfast until late lunch, make the most of "off-peak" deals from 11:30am to noon and 1:30 to 2:30pm. Closed weekends.

Haz

9 Cutler Street, E1 7DJ **Tel** *020 7929 7923*   **Map** *16 D1*

Lively, fun, and a little posh too, this is a touch of true Turkey in the city. Go for a mixed *meze* starter. They just keep coming and they're all delicious. Go for the well-marinated meat dishes and kebabs and mop up the juice with the lovely flatbread. The office workers throng into Haz at lunchtime so get here before noon.

Wagamama
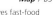

1A Ropemaker Street, EC2Y 9AW **Tel** *020 7588 2688*   **Map** *7 B5*

Popular with suited diners, this City branch of the popular chain of Japanese noodle restaurants serves fast-food noodle and rice dishes to an appreciative crowd. Wagamama's speciality is the ramen noodle bowl, served in soups with delicious topping or teppan fried, offering a nutritionally complete meal.

The Don

The Courtyard, 20 St. Swithin's Lane, EC4N 8AD **Tel** *020 7626 2606*   **Map** *15 B2*

This used to be a wine warehouse so it's no surprise that it has an excellent wine list. It also has very attentive staff, who go out of their way to be helpful. A good sommelier and a range of interesting and unique dishes from a modern European menu make this a very popular restaurant indeed and reservations are pretty much obligatory.

Sauterelle

Royal Exchange, Threadneedle Street, EC3V 3LR **Tel** *020 7618 2483*   **Map** *15 B2*

Location is the great attraction here. Sauterelle occupies a mezzanine level beside the magnificent courtyard of the Neo-Classical Royal Exchange, which, no longer used for trading, is now a luxury shopping mall. The French-based cuisine is rich, inventive and satisfying; the wine list is carefully chosen. A chic hideout in the City.

HAMPSTEAD

Base

71 Hampstead High Street, NW3 1QP **Tel** *020 7431 2224*   **Map** *1 B5*

During the day Base is a gourmet bar offering fresh Mediterranean cuisine and an à la carte menu. In the evening it becomes a fine-dining Mediterranean fusion restaurant, offering sumptuous food with an emphasis on fresh ingredients. The menu changes regularly and is complemented by an extensive wine list. Closed Sunday dinner.

Weng Wah House

240 Haverstock Hill, NW3 2AE **Tel** *020 7794 5123*

Highly regarded by locals for reliably good Chinese food at great prices. Be warned that there is karaoke, which isn't everyone's cup of tea, but it's not too intrusive and can actually be quite fun. Families will feel at home here. The food is actually very tasty so it's worth listening to the amateur Frank Sinatras accompanying it.

The Wells

30 Well Walk, NW3 1BX **Tel** *020 7794 3785*   **Map** *1 B4*

A few steps away from Hampstead Heath, this superior gastropub is a great stop for an indulgent meal after a walk. The bar, with tables outside in summer, has an easy-going pub feel; the delicately decorated upstairs dining rooms are more tranquil, and the menu is both sophisticated and ultra-enjoyable. Plan to take your time, and settle in.

Villa Bianca

1 Perrin's Court, NW3 1QS **Tel** *020 7435 3131*   **Map** *1 B5*

Tucked away from the crowd, this welcoming Italian restaurant seems to make most visitors happy. The charming bow windows invite you in and it has a traditional feel about it. They have set menus, dishes such as beef fillet with truffles and a great wine list. Business lunch served Monday to Friday.

The Gaucho Grill
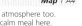

64 Heath Street, NW3 1DN **Tel** *020 7431 8222*   **Map** *1 A4*

Part of a group serving hearty steaks for the larger appetite. A good family place with a lively atmosphere too. Can get a little boisterous when large groups come in, but you can normally have a pleasant calm meal here. On fine days, the outside seating is worth making an effort to secure.

GREENWICH

Greenwich Union

56 Royal Hill, SE10 8RT **Tel** *020 8692 6258*   **Map** *23 B3*

This old pub is now the main outlet for the small Meantime Brewery, so its range of fine beers is unique: as well as their own seven original varieties, there are fine bottled beers from around the world. Wines and spirits are away from the ordinary too, and to eat with all this drink there are generous modern menus. Lunch here is a great bargain.

Key to Price Guide *see p296* **Key to Symbols** *see back cover flap*

Inside

19 Greenwich South Street, SE10 8NW **Tel** *020 8265 5060*   **Map** *23 B3*

Modern European cuisine in a clean minimalist setting and ideally placed to take in a pre-theatre meal. The menu keeps fresh by constantly changing and the staff exudes confidence in their kitchen. Vegetarian options are available. This is a restaurant that could comfortably charge more for your meals, but which so far thankfully doesn't.

Rivington Bar & Grill

178 Greenwich High Road, SE10 8NN **Tel** *020 8293 9270*   **Map** *23 B3*

Back-to-basics British cooking in a comfortable dining room with further tables on a mezzanine floor. The menus feature seasonal British produce. Try potted Morecambe Bay shrimps on toast, followed by whole roast Devon red chicken, or go along for breakfast.

The North Pole

131 Greenwich High Road, SE10 8JA **Tel** *020 8853 3020*   **Map** *23 A3*

One of Greenwich's trendier spots, this old pub now has three distinct spaces. The North Pole bar has snacks, funky decor and a sharp line in cocktails; the much quieter Piano restaurant above has a menu that happily blends Asian and Mediterranean styles. The basement is the South Pole, a club with DJs on weekends and live bands some nights.

The Spread Eagle

1–2 Stockwell Street, SE10 9JN **Tel** *020 8853 2333*   **Map** *23 B2*

Fiercely championed by locals, this place radiates confidence with its innovative French cuisine. Small cosy booths to dine in and a real, roaring fire in winter all conspire to make you want to stay long after the coffee has been cleared away. The food is rich and satisfying and the whole experience is a lot better than the West End, at half the price.

FURTHER AFIELD

Brown's West India Quay

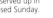

Hertsmere Road, E14 8JJ **Tel** *020 7987 9777*

From its beginnings in Brighton, the Brown's empire has spread out. It's solid British cooking. Sitting amid dark wood café chairs and palms and whirling fans, you get quite a colonial feel. This branch is housed in a sugar warehouse – overlooking the dock at the front there is alfresco dining.

Song Que

134 Kingsland Road, E2 8DY **Tel** *020 7613 3222*

In a large room with plastic tables and chairs, an extensive laminated menu offers all the standard Vietnamese dishes and a few Chinese ones too. For a bargain price, pho – a noodle soup with beef, prawns or pork – is served up in large steaming bowls, accompanied by fresh chillies, beansprouts, Asian basil and lemon wedges. Closed Sunday.

Fig

169 Hemingford Road, N1 1DA **Tel** *020 7609 3009*

A charming neighbourhood restaurant set amongst the Regency terraces and leafy squares of Barnsbury in Islington. Fig has earned a solid reputation with the well-heeled, local clientele for serving sophisticated, seasonal food in an unpretentious environment. The wine list is well balanced and moderately priced. Summer dining under the fig tree.

Manna

4 Erskine Road, NW3 3AJ **Tel** *020 7722 8028*

Manna is a delight for many London vegetarians. In place of the tired meat-free choices served up in many veggie cafés, it has a ground-up approach to vegetarian cooking, producing dishes full of tantalizing flavours like yam and black bean fajitas, or tempura mushrooms. Salads and desserts are invigorating, and it's a very comfortable spot.

Chez Bruce

2 Bellevue Road, Wandsworth Common, SW17 7EG **Tel** *020 8672 0114*

The menu is modern British and after 10 years here, Bruce has got it right. Lots of emphasis on offal, so not a veggie paradise but otherwise a very good restaurant indeed. Great flavour combinations and a sure hand at the stove means it's worth the money.

Morgan M

489 Liverpool Road, N7 8NS **Tel** *020 7609 3560*

A converted old pub in Islington can seem an odd place to find a superb French gourmet restaurant, but this is where chef Morgan Meunier has set up shop. The atmosphere is quiet, calm and formal; menus – great value for this quality – present a gorgeous range of flavours, with every detail outstanding. Reservations are essential.

The River Café

Thames Wharf, Rainville Road W6 9HA **Tel** *020 7386 4200*

This restaurant set on the Thames River rarely disappoints. The River Café's ethos is first-rate seasonal ingredients cooked simply, and the menus change daily. Dishes such as pumpkin soup with mascarpone, pot-roasted pheasant with chardonnay and linguine with crab, combined with friendly staff, make dining here worth every penny.

Light Meals and Snacks

When you want to make the most of the available sightseeing time, it doesn't always make sense to sit down for a lengthy restaurant meal. Or, perhaps you don't have the budget or the appetite for a full-course affair. London has several eateries for every taste and occasion – many of them unmissable institutions – from traditional fish-and-chip and pie-and-mash shops to elegant tearooms and cool cafés.

BREAKFAST

A good breakfast prepares you for a solid day's sight-seeing, with the traditional British breakfast including staples such as bacon and eggs, smoked salmon and grilled kippers. Many hotels *(see pp282–91)* serve traditional breakfasts to non-residents, but to start the day like a 19th-century lord, head for **Simpson's-in-the-Strand**, which on weekdays offers an old-fashioned breakfast menu (as well as classic lunchtime and dinner roasts) in a historic panelled dining room. Porridge, lamb's kidneys, Cumberland sausage and black pudding are just part of the multicourse "10 deadly sins" set breakfast.

Several pubs around Smithfield serve the all-night meat market workers. The most famous of these is the **Cock Tavern**, dishing up good-value fare from 6am onwards. Traditional cafés also fry up artery-clogging working-men's morning meals including egg, sausage, mushrooms and baked beans.

For Continental breakfasts such as pastries and a cappuccino, there are many cafés to choose from. **The Wolseley** serves croissants, brioches and cooked break-fasts in opulent surroundings. Brunch has become increasingly popular in London. The spacious, modern restaurant in the back of popular French grocer/delicatessen, **Villandry**, serves one of the best on Saturday and Sunday. American restaurants such as **Joe Allen** and **Christopher's** also offer brunch, or head for well-heeled Westbourne Grove, where it's a weekend ritual at relaxed eateries such as **202** and **Tom's** delicatessen.

COFFEE AND TEA

For a cappuccino or espresso at any time of day, step into round-the-clock Soho stalwart **Bar Italia**, which also serves a range of pastries and paninis. It's a legendary late-night pitstop, full of colourful characters (but do keep a hand on your bag/wallet). There is no shortage of coffee-bar chains, but one of the best is **Caffè Nero**, which dispenses authentic Italian coffee at reasonable prices across town.

If you're out shopping, many of London's department stores have their own cafés; Harvey Nichols' is one of the most stylish, while Selfridges has a branch of the cool Moroccan tearoom **Momo** among its many eating options. Designer stores such as Emporio Armani, Nicole Farhi and Joseph have trendy cafés – from the outside **202** looks like a chic French-style café, but it showcases Nicole Farhi's fashion and home designs downstairs. **Joe's Café**, surrounded by Joseph's three boutiques at Brompton Cross, is a small yet slick refreshment option; there are a few branches around town. In Portobello Market, quaint tearoom **Still Too Few**, below the antique kitchenalia shop of the same name, serves tea, sandwiches and cakes to bric-a-brac hunters on Saturdays.

Patisseries such as **Maison Bertaux** and **Patisserie Valerie** are a delight, with mouth-watering window displays of French pastries. **Richoux** in Piccadilly is another popular refreshment spot. Smart French bakery/patisserie **Paul** offers delicious tarts and other treats in a Parisian-café atmosphere. The elegantly old-world **The Wolseley** in

Piccadilly has an all-day café menu of sandwiches and salads. If you're strolling in picturesque Little Venice, **Café Laville** commands a spectacular view over Regent's Canal. **Bluebird**, Terence Conran's multi-faceted food centre in the converted 1920s Bluebird motor garage on the King's Road, has a café with tables on its cobbled forecourt as well as a more formal restaurant, bar and market.

No visit to London would be complete without taking afternoon tea. Top hotels such as the **Ritz** and **Brown's** *(see p286)* offer pots of your choice of tea, scones with jam and cream, delicious, thin cucumber sand-wiches and cakes galore. For a relaxed place in beautiful Kensington Gardens, there's nothing to beat **The Orangery**. Its selection of English teas and cakes tastes even better in the elegant surroundings of Sir John Vanbrugh's 18th-century building. Good coffee (and cakes) can also be found at the **Monmouth Coffee House** in Covent Garden. **Fortnum and Mason** *(see p321)* serves both afternoon and high teas. In Kew, the **Maids of Honour** tearoom offers pastries, reputedly enjoyed by Henry VIII. For a more modern experience, **Sketch** offers exquisite contemporary confections in a restyled Georgian room.

TRADITIONAL CAFÉS

These basic greasy spoons all over the city are a London institution, serving up fried breakfasts and such British staples as sausages, pies and grills. They are usually only open until about 5pm; some close earlier. Granddaddy of them all is East End legend **E Pellicci**, with its wonderful Art Deco interior. A vogue for simple British fare has spawned some modern ver-sions of the "caff", including the mini chain **S&M Café** – sausage and mash, before you get any funny ideas.

MUSEUM AND THEATRE CAFÉS

Most museums and galleries have cafés, including the Royal Academy, Tate Modern (with wonderful views over the Thames), the National Portrait Gallery and the British Museum. The National Film Theatre on the South Bank has a buzzing bar/café frequented by film fanatics, while St Martin-in-the-Fields church in Trafalgar Square, famous for its concerts, has a capacious self-service café in its vaulted crypt.

SANDWICH BARS

A leading sandwich chain in London is **Prêt à Manger**, with branches throughout the centre decked out with metalwork features and serving a range of delicious pre-packed sandwiches, salads, cakes and soft drinks. Another popular sandwich chain is **Eat**, which offers a daily changing menu of innovative soups and salads using seasonal ingredients as well as sandwiches made with homemade breads and tortilla wraps. Quality Italian sandwich fillings in focaccia and ciabatta breads can be had at Soho's **Carlton Coffee House**. For a quick bite in Fitzrovia, **Squat & Gobble** does great freshly made doorstep sandwiches, healthy salads and home-cooked dishes, as well as breakfasts.

DELIS

With Londoners becoming more and more interested in high-quality foods from small producers in Britain and abroad, there has been a boom in stylish delis, many of which provide seating so that you can sample their wares on site. **Tom's** is a one-stop deli and café. The chic **Grocer on Warwick Café** offers breakfast and light Oriental-influenced dishes as well as ready-prepared foods to take away, while deli/cheese shop **La Fromagerie** has a large communal table in the back for light bites. Nearby, is the 100-year-old family-run

delicatessen/lunchroom **Paul Rothe & Son**, which serves sandwiches and soups among the shelves of "British and foreign provisions".

DINERS

London is full of American-style fast-food joints, serving burgers, fries, fried chicken, apple pie, milk shakes and cola, particularly around Soho, Leicester Square, Shaftesbury Avenue and Covent Garden. Some time-honoured establishments include family favourite **Maxwell's**, in Covent Garden, the **Hard Rock Café**, and the fun, 1950s-kitsch **Ed's Easy Diner**, but thanks to the continuing vogue for retro burger restaurants, new ones keep popping up. **Hamburger Union**, where you order at the grill before sitting down, is one of the best, while the **Lucky 7** near Notting Hill serves up burgers and breakfasts in a dice-and-cards-themed diner, complete with vinyl-seated booths and blaring rock 'n' roll.

PIZZA AND PASTA

Italian food has now become a staple of the British diet. Street-side stands offer variable quality, while there are well-established chains with several branches, including **Ask**. **Pizza Express** offers thin-crust pizzas that are a step up from the norm. Try the elegant Georgian townhouse outlet on Chelsea's King's Road, or the branch in a converted dairy in Soho where there's also live jazz. **Kettners**, also part of the group, offers casual, inexpensive eating in a legendary old dining room (there's also a champagne bar). The **Carluccio's Caffè** chain, which has a branch with al fresco tables in pedestrianized St Christopher's Place, serves good-quality, freshly made pastas and salads. **Marine Ices** near Camden Market serves great pizza and pasta in addition to its famous ice cream (see Street Food pp314–5). Other reliable pasta chains are **Spaghetti House** and **Café Pasta**. Inexpensive pasta is also served at bustling trattorias such as **Pollo** in Soho.

FOOD IN PUBS

Perhaps the biggest – and most popular – change in the London dining scene in the last 15 years has been the transformation in the food found in pubs. Before the early 1990s, most pubs that provided food at all offered a pretty simple range of salads and sandwiches, put together with no great imagination. The last two decades, though, have seen the rapid rise of the "gastropub", in which the food range is treated with as much care as the beer selection. Grilled steaks, fresh fish or English classics like sausage and mash have been reinvigorated by the use of first-rate, organic ingredients and the menus have become increasingly sophisticated, mixing Mediterranean, Oriental and other global influences.

The neighbourhood gastro-pub has become an essential London institution. Some have separate dining rooms while others have stayed more pub-style, where you order at the bar from a chalked-up menu. All tend to be more relaxed than formal restaurants but they can get busy so book in advance. Among the best are **The Eagle**, **The Engineer**, **The Lansdowne**, **The Queen's Head & Artichoke** and **The Wells** in Hampstead. (See also pp316–9).

FISH AND CHIPS

Fish and chips is typically considered the national dish of Britain, with a "chippy" serving a choice of fish (typically cod or plaice) deep-fried in batter, accompanied by chips (thicker cut than French fries). A range of accompaniments includes bread baps (rolls) for a "chip buttie" (a chip sandwich), mushy peas, pickled eggs or onions. Four of the best places for such fare are the **North Sea Fish Restaurant, Rock & Sole Plaice, Faulkner's** and **Fish Central**. Fish and chips is now considered very "trendy" and is increasingly available on the menu in various smart restaurants and chains such as **Fish!**

BARS AND WINE BARS

The range and quality of London's bars has grown over the past five years. There are numerous wine bars in the centre, such as **Café des Amis du Vin** in Covent Garden (downstairs from its ground-floor brasserie), and the legendary **El Vino**, as well as chains such as **Corney & Barrow** and **Balls Bros**, which also serve good food. The cosy **Tapa Room** on the ground floor of acclaimed **The Providores** restaurant serves globally influenced tapas. Good-value food is also part of the success of such chain bars as **All Bar One**. Capitalizing on young Londoners' habit of spending an entire evening out drinking, many style-conscious, modern bars serve food, such as the sleek **Eagle Bar Diner** off Oxford Street, which has a wide-ranging menu encompassing breakfast, burgers, pasta and grills, and the **Alphabet Bar** in Soho. *(See also pp317–9.)*

BRASSERIES

Now that informal dining is an integral aspect of life in London, brasseries have become part of the landscape. These are based on the classic French blueprint, with its Parisian ambience and decor, serving such favourites as steak frites and seafood platters – a classic example is long-established **La Brasserie** in South Kensington. Among the chains is **Café Rouge**. **Randall & Aubin**

is a buzzy oyster and lobster (plus champagne) bar in a former delicatessen that has retained its period charm and overlooks Soho's lively Brewer Street. Relative newcomer **The Electric Brasserie**, next to Portobello's luxurious art-house cinema of the same name, is a popular update on the traditional model.

JUICE BARS AND ORGANIC CAFÉS

The healthy-diet trend has made juice bars and organic food shops very popular. Longstanding Lebanese favourite **Ranoush Juice** has added outlets to its original Edgware Road location, and chains such as **Crussh** have branches all over London. Organic food chains such as **Planet Organic**, **Fresh & Wild** and its parent company **Whole Foods Market** do a roaring trade in hot and cold fare and freshly squeezed juices alongside their groceries, baked goods and vitamins, with tables on the premises.

NOODLE BARS

Popular chain **Wagamama** still draws queues for its good-value noodles and other Oriental dishes in airy yet basic environs; customers sit at long communal tables. **Dim T Café** serves dim sum and mix-and-match noodles, meat and toppings in a modern café setting. **Taro** is a busy Japanese diner offering cheap sushi, ramen and teriyaki.

STREET FOOD

During summer, many parks have ice-cream vans parked by the entrances, with **Marine Ices** serving some of the town's best ice cream. Hot roasted chestnuts, made on mini-barbecues, are a winter delight found along Oxford Street. Shellfish stalls, selling ready-to-eat potted shrimps, crab, whelks and jellied eels are a feature of many street markets. At Camden Lock and Old Spitalfields Market, you can wander among the stalls choosing from falafel, satay chicken, vegeburgers and honey balls. In the East End, Jewish bakeries such as **Brick Lane Beigel Bake** are open 24 hours a day. Fresh plain bagels as well as ones with a wide range of fillings are available here.

The East End also has the largest number of pie and mash shops, which provide an inexpensive and satisfying "nosh-up" of jellied eels and potatoes, or meat pie with mash and liquor (green parsley sauce). Two classic venues, both on Bethnal Green Road, are **G Kelly** and **S&R Kelly**. Or try **Manze's** on Tower Bridge Road. For the real East End experience, you should drench your food in vinegar and wash it all down with a couple of mugs of strong, hot tea. Modern pie-maker **The Square Pie Company** sells superior pies with gourmet fillings in Old Spitalfields Market and Selfridges.

DIRECTORY

BREAKFAST

202
202 Westbourne
Grove W11.
Map 9 C2.

Christopher's
18 Wellington St WC2.
Map 13 C2.

Cock Tavern
East Poultry Avenue,
Smithfield Market EC1.
Map 6 F5.

Joe Allen
13 Exeter St WC2.
Map 13 C2.

Simpson's-in-the-Strand
100 Strand WC2.
Map 13 C2.

Tom's
226 Westbourne Grove
W11. **Map** 9 B2.

Villandry
170 Great Portland Street
W1. **Map** 4 F5.

The Wolseley
160 Piccadilly W1.
Map 12 F3.

COFFEE AND TEA

Bar Italia
22 Frith St W1.
Map 13 A2.

Bluebird Café
350 King's Rd SW3.
Map 19 A4

Café Laville
Little Venice Parade, 453
Edgware Rd W2.

Emporio Armani Caffè
191 Brompton Rd SW3.
Map 19 B1.

Joe's Café
126 Draycott Ave SW3.
Map 19 B2.

Maids of Honour
288 Kew Rd Richmond,
Surrey.

DIRECTORY

Maison Bertaux
28 Greek St W1.
Map 13 A1.

Monmouth Coffee House
27 Monmouth St WC2.
Map 13 B2.

The Orangery
Kensington Palace, Kensington Gardens W8.
Map 10 D3.

Patisserie Valerie
17 Motcombe St, Belgravia SW1. **Map** 12 D5.

Paul
29 Bedford St WC2.
Map 13 B2.

Richoux
172 Piccadilly W1.
Map 12 F3.

Sketch
9 Conduit St W1.
Map 12 F2.

Still Too Few
300 Westbourne Grove W11. **Map** 9 B2.

TRADITIONAL CAFÉS

E Pellicci
332 Bethnal Green Rd E2.

S&M Café
268 Portobello Rd W11.
Map 9 A1.

MUSEUM AND THEATRE CAFÉS

Café in the Crypt
St Martin-in-the-Fields, Duncannon St WC2.
Map 13 B3.

Film Café
BFI Southbank, South Bank SE1. **Map** 14 D3.

SANDWICH BARS

Carlton Coffee House
41 Broadwick St W1.
Map 13 A2.

Eat
12 Oxo Tower Wharf, Barge House St SE1.
Map 14 E3.

Prêt à Manger
421 Strand WC2.
Map 13 C3.

Squat & Gobble
69 Charlotte Street W1.
Map 5 A5.

DELIS

La Fromagerie
2–4 Moxon St W1.
Map 4 D5.

Grocer on Warwick Café
21 Warwick St W1.
Map 12 F2.

Paul Rothe & Son
35 Marylebone Lane W1.
Map 12 D1.

DINERS

Ed's Easy Diner
12 Moor St W1.
Map 13 B2.

Hamburger Union
4–6 Garrick St WC2.
Map 13 B2.

Hard Rock Café
150 Old Park Lane W1.
Map 12 E4.

Lucky 7
127 Westbourne Park Rd W2. **Map** 9 C1.

Maxwell's
8 James St WC2.
Map 13 C2.

PIZZA AND PASTA

Ask
56–60 Wigmore St W1.
Map 12 D1.

Café Pasta
184 Shaftesbury Avenue WC2.
Map 13 2B.

Carluccio's Caffè
St Christopher's Place W1.
Map 12 E2.
One of several branches.

Kettner's
29 Romilly St W1.
Map 13 A2.

Pizza Express
30 Coptic St WC1.
Map 13 B1.
One of many branches.

Pollo
20 Old Compton St W1.
Map 13 A2.

FISH AND CHIPS

Faulkner's
424–426 Kingsland Rd E8.

Fish!
Borough Mkt SE1.
Map 15 B4.

Fish Central
149–151 Central St EC1.
Map 7 A3.

North Sea Fish Restaurant
7–8 Leigh St WC1.
Map 5 B4.

Rock & Sole Plaice
47 Endell St WC2.
Map 13 B1.

WINE BARS

All Bar One
103 Cannon St EC4.
Map 15 A2.

Alphabet Bar
61 Beak Street W1.
Map 12 F2.

Balls Bros
Hays Galleria Tooley Street SE1. **Map** 15 B3.

Café des Amis du Vin
11–14 Hanover Place WC2. **Map** 13 C2.

Corney & Barrow
19 Broadgate Circle EC2.
Map 7 C5.

Dickens Inn
St Katharine's Dock E1.
Map 16 E3.

Eagle Bar Diner
3–5 Rathbone Place W1.
Map 13 A1.

Providores Tapa Room
109 Marylebone High St W1. **Map** 4 D5.

El Vino
47 Fleet Street EC4.
Map 14 E1.

BRASSERIES

La Brasserie
272 Brompton Rd SW3.
Map 19 B2.

Café Rouge
27 Basil St SW3.
Map 11 C5.

The Electric Brasserie
191 Portobello Rd W11.
Map 9 B2.

Randall & Aubin
16 Brewer St W1.
Map 13 A2.

JUICE BARS AND ORGANIC CAFÉS

Crussh
Unit 1, 1 Curzon Street W1. **Map** 12 E3.

Fluid Juice Bar
208 Fulham Rd SW3.
Map 19 A2.

Fresh & Wild
208–212 Westbourne Grove W11. **Map** 9 B2.

Planet Organic
22 Torrington Place WC1.
Map 5 A5.

Ranoush Juice
43 Edgware Rd W2.
Map 11 C2.

Whole Foods Market
69-75 Brewer St W1
Map 13 A2

NOODLE BARS

Dim T Café
32 Charlotte St W1.
Map 13 A1.

Taro
59–61 Brewer St W1.
Map 13 A2.

Wagamama
101 Wigmore Street W1.
Map 12 D1.

STREET FOOD

Brick Lane Beigel Bake
159 Brick Lane E1.
Map 8 E5.

G Kelly S&R Kelly
Bethnal Green Road E1.
Map 8 D4.

Manze's
87 Tower Bridge Road SE1.
Map 16 D5.

Marine Ices
8 Haverstock Hill NW3.

London Pubs and Bars

Affectionately known as a "pub" as well as "boozer" and "the local", a public house was originally just that – a house in which the public could eat, drink, and even stay the night. Large inns with courtyards, such as The George Inn, were originally stopping points for horse-drawn coach services. Some pubs stand on historic public house sites, for instance the Ship, the Lamb and Flag and the City Barge. However, many of the finest ones date from the emergence of "gin palaces" in the late 1800s, where Londoners took refuge from the misery of their poverty amid lavish interiors, often with stunning mirrors (The Salisbury) and elaborate decorations. Since the 1990s cocktail-bar boom, the traditional pub has been given an image makeover, restoring the British institution's popularity with a fashionable crowd.

RULES AND CONVENTIONS

Visitors to London have long been bemused by early pub closing times, which made a night out a bit tricky – an after-theatre nightcap, for example, was usually out of the question outside of your hotel. In theory, reforms to the licensing laws, which came into effect in 2005, mean pubs can now stay open up to 24 hours, as long as they obtain permission from their local authority, and many extend their hours beyond the 11am–11pm standard. Some may close in the afternoon or early evening and also at weekends. You must be at least 18 to buy or drink alcohol, and at least 14 to enter a pub without an adult. Children can be taken into pubs that serve food, or can use outside areas. Order at the bar and pay when you are served; tips are not customary unless you are served food and drink at a table. "Last orders" are usually called 10 minutes before closing, then "time" is called, and a further 20 minutes is then allowed for finishing up drinks. Since July 2007, smoking has been banned from all pubs and clubs.

BRITISH BEER

The most traditional beers are available in various different strengths and styles, and are flat (not fizzy), and served only lightly cooled. The spectrum of bottled beers goes from "light" ale, through "pale", "brown", "bitter" and the strong "old". A sweeter, lower alcohol alternative is shandy, a classic mixture of draught beer or lager and lemonade. Many traditional methods of brewing and serving beer have been preserved over the years, and there is a great variety of "real ale" in London pubs. Serious beer drinkers should look for "Free Houses", pubs that are not tied to any particular brewery. The main London brewers are Young's (try their strong "Winter Warmer" beer) and Fuller's. The **Orange Brewery** serves a good pint and excellent food, and offers tours of the brewery.

OTHER PUB DRINKS

Cider is another traditional English drink found in every pub. Made from apples, it comes in a range of strengths and degrees of dryness. Blended Scotch whisky and malt whiskies are also staples, together with gin, usually drunk with tonic water. During the winter, mulled wine (warm and spicy) or hot toddies (brandy or whisky with hot water and sugar) may be served. Non-alcoholic drinks are also always available.

HISTORIC PUBS

Many pubs have a fascinating history and decor, whether it is a beamed medieval snug, Victorian fantasy, or an extraordinary Arts-and-Crafts interior, as at the **Black Friar**, a must-see temple to imbibing, featuring bronze bas reliefs, and an intimate, marble-and-mosaic chamber at the back. While many of the "gin palaces" of the 19th century have been revamped or abandoned, there are some notable survivors. At the **Prince Alfred** in Maida Vale the bar is divided by "snobscreens", a feature that enabled the upper set to enjoy a drink without mixing with their servants. The semi-circular **Viaduct Tavern**, opposite the Old Bailey, is a suitably stately setting for distinguished barristers and judges, ablaze with mirrors, chandeliers and etched glass, while the **Princess Louise** retains its magnificent central mahogany bar, complete with original clock, moulded ceiling and vivid wall tiles. Less grand but just as lovingly decorated is the tiny, tiled **Dog & Duck** in Soho – but you may have to battle for a seat or (in warm weather) stand outside with its many devotees.

Many pubs have strong literary associations, such as the **Fitzroy Tavern**, a meeting place for writers and artists in the 1930s and 40s, including Dylan Thomas, George Orwell and Augustus John, **Ye Olde Cheshire Cheese** is associated with Dr Johnson, Charles Dickens frequented the **Trafalgar Tavern**, while Oscar Wilde often went to **The Salisbury**. Samuel Pepys witnessed the Great Fire of London from the **Anchor**, on the river at Bankside. The less literary **Old Bull and Bush** in north London was the subject of a well known old music-hall song, while the 17th-century **Lamb and Flag** – one of central London's few surviving timber-framed buildings down an alleyway – was known as the Bucket of Blood because it was the venue for bare-knuckle prize fights. Some pubs have sinister associations, for example some of Jack the Ripper's victims were found near the **Ten Bells**. Dick

Turpin, the 18th-century highwayman, took refreshment at the **Spaniards Inn** in north London, and the **French House** in Soho was a meeting point for the French Resistance during World War II.

PUB NAMES

Signs have hung outside public houses since 1393, when King Richard II decreed they should replace the usual bush outside the door. As most people were illiterate, names that could easily be illustrated were chosen, such as the Rose & Crown, coats of arms (Freemasons' Arms), historical figures (Princess Louise) or heraldic animals (White Lion).

PUB ENTERTAINMENT

Fringe theatre productions *(see p346)* are staged at the **King's Head**, the **Latchmere**, and at the **Gate Theatre** above the Prince Albert. Some pubs have live music: there is excellent modern jazz at the **Bull's Head** in Barnes and a wide variety of music styles at the popular **Mean Fiddler** *(see pp351–3)*. The diminutive **Golden Eagle**, on a winding backstreet in Marylebone, is a rare central London piano pub with nostalgic singalongs a few nights a week.

OUTDOOR DRINKING

Most pubs with outdoor seating tend to be located slightly outside the city centre. The **Freemason's Arms** for example, near Hampstead Heath, has a very pleasant garden. Some pubs enjoy riverside locations with fine views, from the **Prospect of Whitby** in Wapping and the **Grapes** in Limehouse to the **White Cross** in Richmond.

MICROBREWERIES

Delicious beer is brewed on the premises at microbreweries such as **Mash** where a space-age interior makes you forget that real ale tends to be the domain of older drinkers. This bar is frequented by a young and trendy crowd. Huge orange vats indicate where the actual brewing takes place. The **Bünker Bier Hall Bar and Kitchen** in Covent Garden has three signature beers, and a good atmosphere.

THEMED PUBS AND BARS

Big, brash Irish pubs such as **Filthy McNasty's** and **Waxy O'Connor's** (mocked up like a Catholic church, complete with confessional) attract a young, fun-loving crowd, as does Australian bar chain **Walkabout**. Sports bars are popular as well. The **Sports Café**, near Piccadilly, has three bars, a dance floor – and 120 television sets showing global sporting events on satellite TV. More low-key is "footie" bar **Kick** in Shoreditch (there's a smaller sister establishment, **Café Kick**, in Exmouth Market), which features table-soccer games and organic food in a relaxed setting. Pool players can take their cue at a branch of slick pool-bar chain the **Elbow Room**.

GASTROPUBS

Since the early 1990s, many old pubs have been given gleaming makeovers and kitchens turning out superior fare. Among the first "gastropubs" was the **Eagle**, which offers gourmet dishes from the open kitchen that occupies half of the bar. Many, like **The Lansdowne** and **The Engineer** have dedicated dining rooms as well as laid-back pub rooms where you can eat, drink or do both. TV foodie Roxy Beaujolais serves simple bistro dishes in tiny, quirky old pub the **Seven Stars** near the Royal Courts of Justice. **The Cow** is known for its oysters and Guinness, while the **Chapel**, the **Fire Station** and the **Dusk** are popular with both drinkers and diners. *(See also pp313–15)*

BARS

London's bar scene has been gradually transformed since the mid-1990s; up till then, the choice was limited to either hotel bars, wine bars or pubs *(see pp314–15)*. Propelled by a cocktail revival, as well as the fact that eating and drinking out is now deeply ingrained in daily London life, new bars are opening all the time.

Eagerly sought out by style-conscious connoisseurs, the latest watering holes are now as much a talking point as new restaurants. Soho and Covent Garden are brimming with bars, but to sample the hottest nightspots, head either east or west. In the past decade, Shoreditch has been transformed from no-go area to an evening destination, which is spilling into neighbouring Bethnal Green.

Two of the earliest pioneers – basement lounge **Home** and the no-frills **The Shoreditch Electricity Showrooms** – are still hopping. They've since been joined by, among others, the 1970s-styled warehouse space **T**, which is so vast it will never get too crowded, and, slightly further afield, the gloriously camp **Loungelover**, decorated with crystal chandeliers, vintage handbags and stuffed animals.

Across town in Notting Hill, sip good-value Scorpion Bowls and Zombies in the kitsch tiki-lounge ambience of **Trailer Happiness** or go for classic or more inventive cocktails at the **Lonsdale** with its bronze bubble-studded walls and hazy violet lighting. The area's style bars are in contrast with down-to-earth pubs frequented by the market traders, such as the bustling **Portobello Star**.

If you want to stick to the centre of town, fashionable options include the **Lab Bar**, which serves excellent cocktails, especially Central American drinks such as caprinhas and mojitos, or **Match**, which has a branch in Oxford Circus as well as Clerkenwell. Heading south, the **Fridge Bar** in Brixton has DJs playing decent hip hop and deep house with lots of dancing and drinking.

Many restaurants feature excellent bars. The bar at **Green's Restaurant and Oyster Bar** *(see p301)* is a very special place to go, to drink champagne and eat oysters and lobster in elegant surroundings. **Smiths of Smithfield**, opposite the famous meat market, has a large, industrial-style café/bar at ground level, a sleek cocktail and champagne bar on the next floor, topped by two restaurants upstairs; nearby, **St John** (see p308) has a stylish bar serving excellent wine and bar food. A drink in the bar is the less-expensive way to experience the **Criterion** brasserie's sumptuous, gilded neo-Byzantine decor. Contemporary Chinese restaurant **Hakkasan** (see p305) serves exotic cocktails flavoured with the likes of ginger and lemongrass in its glamorous Oriental-style bar.

SPECIALIST BARS

Aficionados of particular spirits are well served. Modern Russian bar (and restaurant) **Potemkin** has over 130 vodkas in every conceivable flavour, plus imported Russian beers. Scottish restaurant Boisdale's **Macdonald Bar** boasts 170 Scotch malt whiskies (and an impressive selection of Cuban cigars), while the **Rockwell**, an upscale bar in the Trafalgar Hotel, offers London's largest bourbon selection. **Salt** is a slick, modern whisky bar, and **S**, in the basement of a glitzed-up former pub, serves a lengthy martini "library" in

a sexy setting. Mexican bar/restaurant **La Perla** in Covent Garden has an extensive range of tequilas.

CHAIN BARS

They may not be the most exciting places to drink, but London's chain bars are a reliable option. Halfway between a bar and a pub, with large windows and white walls, they are also far more female-friendly than dark, smokey pubs. **All Bar One** is very popular, with chunky wood furniture. **Pitcher & Piano** has sofas and blonde wood surrounds, while the **Slug & Lettuce** chain features paintings on the walls and quiet rooms for talking.

HOTEL BARS

London's hotel bars continue to offer an elegant setting for classic and innovative cocktails, with **The Blue Bar** at the Berkeley Hotel and the **Long Bar** at the Sanderson Hotel prime examples. The **American Bar** at The Savoy, decorated in an Art Deco style, has a pianist, a terrific atmosphere and classic cocktails (try the signature White Lady or the Dry Martini, which the bar introduced to Britain), while another Jazz Age gem, the **Rivoli Bar** at the Ritz, has been resplendently restored. **Claridge's Bar** offers excellent champagne cocktails (among other

concoctions) in a glamorous, contemporary-classic setting. **Trader Vic's** in the Park Lane Hilton offers an exotically tropical setting in which to enjoy an amazing range of rum cocktails. **Pearl Restaurant Bar**, in the Renaissance Chancery Court Hotel, brings sleek, contemporary style to the capacious former banking hall of the Pearl Assurance Building, serving fabulous fruity cocktails and 32 wines by the glass in the glow of striking pearl chandeliers. **Brasserie Max** in the Covent Garden Hotel is always buzzing and is very popular with theatre and film people.

GAY BARS

Old Compton Street in Soho has a well-established gay scene. Tables spill out on to the pavements and there is a lively atmosphere tolerant of all sexual preferences. **Compton's of Soho**, a busy pub, is across the road from the gay bar and eatery **Balans** and close to the well-known gay pub, **The Admiral Duncan**. The **Edge** is a sprawling bar and club over four floors, while **Rupert Street** is a stylishly low-key option for a relaxed drink. The **Candy Bar** is a popular lesbian bar, while, away from the West End, the **Royal Vauxhall Tavern** hosts Duckie's outrageous cabaret and DJs on Saturday nights.

DIRECTORY

DIRECTORY

Salt
82 Seymour St W2.
Map 11 C2.

Slug & Lettuce
19 Hanover St W1.
Map 12 F2.

Trader Vic's
22 Park Lane. **Map** 12 D3.

COVENT GARDEN, STRAND

American Bar
The Savoy, Strand WC2.
Map 13 C2.

Bünker Bier Hall Bar and Kitchen
41 Earlham St WC2.
Map 13 B2.

Lamb and Flag
33 Rose St WC2.
Map 13 B2.

La Perla
28 Maiden Lane WC2.
Map 13 C2.

Rockwell Bar
The Trafalgar 2 Spring Gardens SW1.
Map 13 B3.

The Salisbury
90 St Martin's Lane WC2.
Map 13 B2.

Seven Stars
53–54 Carey St WC2.
Map 14 D1.

Walkabout
11 Henrietta St WC2.
Map 13 C2.

BLOOMSBURY, HOLBORN

Fitzroy Tavern
16 Charlotte St W1.
Map 13 A1.

Princess Louise
208 High Holborn WC1.
Map 13 C1.

Pearl Restaurant Bar
Renaissance Chancery Court Hotel
252 High Holborn WC1.
Map 13 C1.

THE CITY, CLERKENWELL

All Bar One
103 Cannon St EC4.
Map 15 A2.

Balls Brothers
11 Blomfield St EC2.
Map 15 C1.

Black Friar
174 Queen Victoria St EC4.
Map 14 F2.

Corney & Barrow
19 Broadgate Circle EC2.
Map 7 C5.

S
2 Exmouth Market EC1.
Map 6 E4.

Eagle
159 Farringdon Rd EC1.
Map 6 E4.

Elbow Room
97–113 Curtain Rd EC2.
Map 7 C4.

Filthy McNasty's
68 Amwell St EC1.
Map 6 E3.

Home
100–106 Leonard St EC2.
Map 7 C4.

Kick
127 Shoreditch High St E1.
Map 8 D3.

Match
45–47 Clerkenwell Rd EC1.
Map 6 E5.

Loungelover
1 Whitby St E1.
Map 8 D4.

Potemkin
144 Clerkenwell Rd EC1.
Map 6 E5.

Ship Tavern
23 Lime St EC3.
Map 15 C2.

The Shoreditch Electricity Showrooms
39a Hoxton Sq N1.
Map 7 C3.

Smiths of Smithfield
67–77 Charterhouse St EC1.
Map 6 F5.

T
The Tea Building 56 Shoreditch High St E1.
Map 8 D4.

Ten Bells
84 Commercial St E1.
Map 8 D5.

Viaduct Tavern
126 Newgate St EC1.
Map 14 F1.

Ye Olde Cheshire Cheese
145 Fleet St EC4.
Map 14 E1.

SOUTHWARK AND SOUTH BANK

Anchor
34 Park Street SE1.
Map 15 A3.

Fire Station
150 Waterloo Rd SE1.
Map 14 E4.

George Inn
77 Borough High St SE1.
Map 15 B4.

HAMPSTEAD

Freemasons Arms
32 Downshire Hill NW3.
Map 1 C5.

Old Bull and Bush
North End Way NW3.
Map 1 A3.

Spaniards Inn
Spaniards Rd NW3.
Map 1 A3.

KNIGHTSBRIDGE, BELGRAVIA

Blue Bar
Wilton Pl SW1.
Map 12 D5.

Boisdale
15 Eccleston St SW1.
Map 20 E1.

The Lansdowne
90 Gloucester Ave NW1.
Map 4 D1.

PRIMROSE HILL, MARYLEBONE

Chapel
48 Chapel St NW1.
Map 3 B5.

Dusk
79 Marylebone High St W1.
Map 4 D5.

Golden Eagle
59 Marylebone Lane W1.
Map 12 D1.

The Engineer
65 Gloucester Ave NW1.
Map 4 D1.

BAYSWATER, NOTTING HILL

The Cow
89 Westbourne Park Rd W11.
Map 9 B1.

Lonsdale
44–48 Lonsdale Rd W11.
Map 9 B2.

Portobello Star
171 Portobello Rd W11.
Map 9 B2.

Prince Albert
11 Pembridge Rd W11.
Map 9 C3.

Trailer Happiness
177 Portobello Rd W11.
Map 9 B2.

FURTHER AFIELD

Bull's Head
373 Lonsdale Rd SW13.

City Barge
27 Strand-o-t-Green W4.

Fridge Bar
1 Town Hill Parade SW2.

Grapes
76 Narrow St E14.

King's Head
115 Upper St N1.
Map 6 F1.

Latchmere
503 Battersea Pk Rd SW11.

Prince Alfred
5a Formosa St W9.

Prospect of Whitby
57 Wapping Wall E1.

Royal Vauxhall Tavern
372 Kennington Lane SE11.
Map 22 D3.

Trafalgar Tavern
Park Row SE10.

White Cross
Water Lane, Richmond, Surrey.

SHOPS AND MARKETS

L ondon is still one of the most lively shopping cities in the world. Here ultramodern stores sit alongside the old-fashioned emporia presided over by tailcoated staff. You can buy anything here, as long as you're prepared to pay. Luxury goods are expensive, although bargain-hunters will find a wealth of cheap goods in the thriving markets, which simply exude a carnival atmosphere. Explore the famous department stores, which encompass a huge breadth of merchandise, or seek out specialist shops.

Bags from two of the most famous West End shops

In general, you'll find upmarket designer stores around Knightsbridge, Regent Street and Bond Street, while Oxford Street is the frenetic centre for mid-priced labels as well as mainstream department stores. Notting Hill, Islington, Soho and the vicinity of Covent Garden are all rich in small, independent shops. Specialities include clothes from raincoats and traditional tweeds to cutting-edge design and catwalk copies; books and records; toiletries; art and antiques; and craft goods such as jewellery, ceramics and leather.

WHEN TO SHOP

In central London, most shops open from 10am and close between 5.30pm–6pm from Monday to Saturday; many department stores have longer hours. The "late night" shopping until 7 or 8pm is on Thursdays and Fridays in Oxford Street and the rest of the West End, and on Wednesdays in Knightsbridge and Chelsea. Some shops in tourist areas, such as Covent Garden *(see pp110–19)* and the Trocadero, are open until 7pm or later every day and on Sundays. Some street markets *(see pp339–41)* and a number of other shops are usually open on Sundays as well.

HOW TO PAY

Most shops accept all major credit cards, including Master-Card, AmericanExpress, Diners Club, Japanese Credit Bureau and Visa. However, smaller shops and street markets do not. Some of the stores also accept traveller's cheques, especially if they're in sterling; for other currencies the rate of exchange is less favourable than in a bank. You need your passport. Most shops will accept a personal cheque, but only if drawn on a UK account and accompanied by a cheque guarantee card. Debit cards are accepted in many major stores, as are Euros.

RIGHTS AND SERVICES

On a defective purchase, you usually get a refund, if proof of purchase is produced and the goods are returned. This isn't always the case with sales goods, so inspect them carefully. Most large stores, and some small ones, will pack goods up for you and send them anywhere in the world.

VAT EXEMPTION

VAT (Value Added Tax) is a sales tax of 17.5% which is charged on virtually all goods sold in Britain. The exceptions are books, food and children's clothes. VAT is mostly included in the advertised or marked price, although business suppliers, including some stationers and electrical goods shops, often charge separately.

Non-European Union visitors to Britain who stay no longer than three months may claim back VAT. If you plan to do so, carry your passport when shopping. You must complete a form in the store when you buy the goods and then give a copy to Customs while leaving the country. The tax refund may be returned by cheque or attributed to your credit card, but then a service charge will be deducted and most stores have a minimum purchase threshold (often £50 or £75). If you arrange to have your goods shipped directly home from the store, VAT should be deducted before you pay.

Harrods' elaborate Edwardian tiled food halls

TWICE-YEARLY SALES

The traditional sale season is from January to February and June to July, when shops slash their prices and sell off imperfect or unwanted stock. The department stores have some of the best reductions; for the famous **Harrods** (see p211) sale queues start to form outside long before opening.

BEST OF THE DEPARTMENT STORES

The king of London's department stores, by tradition is **Harrods**, with over 300 departments and a staff of 5,000. The spectacular food hall with Edwardian tiles displays fish, cheese, fruit and vegetables. The specialities also include fashions for all ages, china and glass, kitchenware and electronics. **Harvey Nichols** aims to stock the best of everything. Clothes are particularly strong on high fashion, with emphasis on talented British, European as well as American names. There's also an impressive menswear section. The food hall, opened in 1992, is one of London's most stylish.

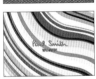

Some well-known names in British clothes design

   Selfridges, on Oxford Street, has a wide choice of labels, a great lingerie department and a section devoted to emerging designers. A melange of high-street concessions on the ground-floor caters to young women. It also has a food hall featuring global delicacies.
   The original **John Lewis** was a draper, and even today his shop has a good selection of fabrics and haberdashery. Its china, glass and household items make John Lewis, and its popular Sloane Square partner, Peter Jones, equally popular with Londoners. **Liberty** (see p109) near Carnaby Street still sells beautiful silks and other Oriental goods, for which it was famed after opening in 1875. Look out for the famous scarf department.

Fortnum and Mason's ground-floor food department is so engrossing that the upper floors of classic fashion and luxury items often remain free of crowds. The food section has everything from Fortnum's tins of biscuits and tea to the lovely wicker hampers.
   The latest addition to the retail scene is **Westfield London**, an impressive, upmarket shopping destination with over 250 retailers, as well as several restaurants.

MARKS AND SPENCER

Marks and Spencer has come a long way since 1882, when the Russian emigré, Michael Marks had a single stall in Leeds' Kirkgate market with the sign, "Don't ask the price – it's a penny!" It now has more than 640 stores worldwide and everything in them is "own label"– Marks and Spencer's underwear in particular is a staple of the British wardrobe. The food department mostly stores convenience foods. The main Oxford Street branches at the Pantheon (near Oxford Circus) and Marble Arch are best for clothes and household goods.

SHOPPING AREAS

As well as offering a wealth of delights for the discerning bargain hunter, London's thriving markets also provide an atmospheric glimpse into the past, with many dating back to Medieval times.
   Soak up the rich colours, aromas and flavours at specialist food stalls, browse quaint antique shops for curios or pick up a retro bargain at one of the many vintage clothes outlets that spill on to the streets. Early risers have a better chance of finding a bargain (see also pp339–41.)

Doorman at Fortnum and Mason

DEPARTMENT STORES

Fortnum and Mason
181 Piccadilly W1. **Map** 12 F3.
Tel 020-7734 8040.

Harrods
87–135 Brompton Rd SW1.
Map 11 C5. *Tel* 020-7730 1234.

Harvey Nichols
109–125 Knightsbridge SW1.
Map 11 C5. *Tel* 020-7235 5000.

John Lewis
300 Oxford St W1. **Map** 12 E1.
Tel 020-7629 7711.

Liberty
210–220 Regent St W1.
Map 12 F2. *Tel* 020-7734 1234.

Selfridges
400 Oxford St W1. **Map** 12 D2.
Tel 0870-837 7377.

Westfield London
http://uk.westfield.com/london

Penhaligon's for scents (see p333)

London's Best: Shopping Streets and Markets

London's best shopping areas range from
the elegance of Knightsbridge, where
porcelain, jewellery and couture clothes
come at the highest prices, to colourful
markets such as Brick Lane, Spitalfields
and Portobello. Meccas for those who
enjoy searching for a bargain, London's
markets also reflect the vibrant street life
engendered by its enterprising multi-
racial community. The city is fertile
ground for specialist shoppers: there are
streets crammed with antique shops,
antiquarian booksellers and art galleries.
Turn to pages 324–38 for more details of
shops, grouped according to category.

Kensington Church Street
*Home to over 60 antique dealers with
one of the largest selections of art and
antiques in London.* (See p215.)

*Regent's Park
and Marylebone*

Portobello Road Market
Over 1,000 stalls sell objets
d'art, *jewellery, medals,
paintings and silverware –
plus fresh fruit and
vegetables.* (See p341.)

*Kensington and
Holland Park*

*South Kensington
and Knightsbridge*

See inset map

*Piccadilly
and St
James's*

Knightsbridge
*Exclusive designer-wear
is on sale here, at
Harrods as well
as smaller stores.*
(See p211.)

Chelsea

King's Road
*Once a centre for
avant-garde fashion
in the 1960s and
1970s, the street is
now home to chain-
stores and designer
shops. There is also
a good antiques
market.* (See p196.)

LONDON'S WEST END SHOPS

Oxford Street is sometimes called London's High
Street and many of the shops that line it are
branches of national or international chains. The big
department stores such as Selfridges and John Lewis
also loom along this street, as do smaller shops selling
clothes and tourist souvenirs. South of Oxford Street,
on Regent Street, Piccadilly and Bond Street, prices
rise and shoppers search for specialized purchases
among the designer clothes and accessories shops,
jewellers and art and antique dealers.

Brick Lane Market
*In this East End
street, everything
from old books to
new trainers is on
sale.* (See p339.)

Bloomsbury
and Fitzrovia

Smithfield and
Spitalfields

Holborn and
the Inns of
Court

Soho
and
Trafalgar
Square

Covent
Garden and
the Strand

The City

RIVER THAMES

South
Bank

Southwark and
Bankside

| 0 kilometres | 1 |
| 0 miles | 0.5 |

Pall Mall and
Westminster

Gabriel's Wharf
*The wharf has been con-
verted into small shops
selling art, jewellery and
crafts.* (See p191.)

Petticoat Lane
*London's most famous
market has leather,
clothes, watches,
jewellery and toys.*
(See p341.)

Charing Cross Road
*Crammed shops selling
old and new books
line this long street.*
(See p330.)

Covent Garden
and Neal Street
*Street enter-
tainers perform
in this lively and
historic market.
The specialist
shops of Neal
Street are nearby.*
(See p115.)

Clothes

London has never been better for clothes shopping, offering a virtually inexhaustible range of styles, price levels and quality, across a far reaching and varied geographical area. Besides the traditional British-style famous the world over, you'll also find international designers, global and home-grown chains and an ever increasing number of independent boutiques catering to every taste. While old-fashioned tailors, shirt-makers and cobblers still thrive, often in their original premises, shops are increasingly design-led. The hugely popular high-street chains have perfected the art of producing good-quality catwalk knock-offs, while a new generation of British design talent has revitalized the fashion scene.

TRADITIONAL CLOTHING

British tailoring and fabrics are world-renowned for their high quality. In Savile Row, you can follow in the sartorial footsteps of Winston Churchill and the Duke of Windsor, among other dapper luminaries, and have a suit made to measure or buy one off the peg. Established in 1806, **Henry Poole** was the first tailor in the Row. At **H Huntsman & Sons**, you can choose from three options – bespoke, custom-made, and ready-to-wear. The bespoke suits are painstakingly hand-stitched on the premises, which partly explains the exorbitant £3,000-plus price tag. In addition to making suits to order, **Gieves & Hawkes** has two ready-to-wear lines.

A new generation of fashion-conscious tailors, known for modern cuts and vibrant fabrics, has joined the distinguished and traditional line-up, including **Ozwald Boateng** and **Richard James**. Jermyn Street is famous for smart shirts. At venerable shops such as **Turnbull & Asser** or the family-run **Harvie & Hudson**, you can either have them custom-made or choose the less expensive standard-sized options. Many manufacturers, including the popular shirt chain **Pink**, now also sell a wide variety of classic women's blouses.

In the past few years, several bastions of classic British style have completely reinvented themselves as fashion labels. **Burberry** is the

best example of this, although it still does a brisk trade in its famous trenchcoats, checked clothing (for children too) and distinctive accessories. **Aquascutum** is also a good choice for classic raincoats, suits and accessories for both sexes, as is **Daks**, which produces high-fashion takes on traditional British looks. **Dunhill** specializes in immaculate, if expensive, menswear and accessories, while at the **Crombie** outlet, you can buy the famous fitted overcoat which came to be known by the company's name. The famous menswear emporium, **Hackett**, caters to a younger, yet still conservative, clientele. Designers **Margaret Howell** and **Nicole Farhi** create updated versions of relaxed British country garments for men and women, such as knitwear, tweeds and sheepskin coats. You can still find a more traditional, smart country look in the Regent Street, Piccadilly or Knightsbridge areas. Waxed Barbour jackets are on sale at Harrods (see p321). **Cordings**, established 1839, is good for country-gent/-lady gear, such as check shirts, moleskin trousers and Covert coats.

While **Liberty** (see p109) now has a good selection of contemporary designers, it still uses its famous patterned prints to make blouses and stylish men's shirts as well as scarves and ties. Floral print "English rose" dresses and feminine blouses can be found

---

SIZE CHART

For Australian sizes follow British and American convention

Children's clothing

British	2–3	4–5	6–7	8–9	10–11	12	14	14+ (years)	
American	2–3	4–5	6–6X	7–8	10–12	14	16 (size)		
Continental	2–3	4–5	6–7	8–9	10–11	12	14	14+ (years)	

Children's shoes

British	7½	8	9	10	11	12	13	1	2
American	7½	8½	9½	10½	11½	12½	13½	1½	2½
Continental	24	25½	27	28	29	30	32	33	34

Women's dresses, coats and skirts

British	6	8	10	12	14	16	18	20
American	4	6	8	10	12	14	16	18
Continental	32	34	36	38	40	42	44	46

Women's blouses and sweaters

British	30	32	34	36	38	40	42
American	6	8	10	12	14	16	18
Continental	34	36	38	40	42	44	46

Women's shoes

British	3	4	5	6	7	8
American	5	6	7	8	9	10
Continental	36	37	38	39	40	41

Men's suits

British	34	36	38	40	42	44	46	48
American	34	36	38	40	42	44	46	48
Continental	44	46	48	50	52	54	56	58

Men's shirts

British	14	15	15½	16	16½	17	17½	18
American	14	15	15½	16	16½	17	17½	18
Continental	36	38	39	41	42	43	44	45

Men's shoes

British	7	7½	8	9	10	11	12
American	7½	8	8½	9½	10½	11	11½
Continental	40	41	42	43	44	45	46

at **Laura Ashley**, although the store has introduced more contemporary looks as well.

MODERN BRITISH DESIGN AND STREET FASHION

London designers are known for their eclectic, irreverent style. Grand dames Vivienne Westwood and Zandra Rhodes have been on the scene since the 1970s – the latter opened the **Fashion and Textile Museum** in south-east London in 2003. It features 3,000 of her own garments as well as examples by other influential fashion figures. Many British designers of international stature have their flagship stores in the capital, including the popular **Paul Smith** and **Stella McCartney**, both of whom showcase their collections in fabulous townhouses. **Matthew Williamson** and the late **Alexander McQueen** also have stand-alone stores. Young home-grown talent such as Alice Temperley, whose feminine frocks are beloved of the London party set, Eley Kishimoto, characterized by bold prints, and avant-garde design duo Boudicca, can be found in most of the capital's boutiques.

Selfridges (see p321) also has an impressive selection of emerging designers. **Dover Street Market**, conceived by Comme des Garçons' Rei Kawakubo, revives the age-old London tradition of the covered clothes market, but in a much more upmarket milieu. Its four minimalist floors showcase a varied array of goods, from glitzy shoes by king of the platform, Terry de Havilland to cool art books and vintage and contemporary designer clothes.

If you want to take home a bit of British design, but can't afford the high prices, it's worth visiting **Debenhams**, which has harnessed the talents of numerous leading designers, including Jasper Conran, Julien Macdonald and Ben De Lisi, to create cheaper collections exclusive to the store. Young designers often start out with a stall on Portobello Road or Old Spitalfields Market (see p341), both

good sources of interesting clothing. There are also a few good designer sale shops: **Paul Smith Sale Shop** and **Browns Labels for Less** are both in central London. While those looking for **Burberry** bargains at its factory outlet will have to travel a bit further afield to the East End.

BOUTIQUES

London is home to an extensive variety of boutiques – hot new shops crop up and, it must be said, close down with dizzying regularity. The mother of them all is **Browns**. Established in the 1970s, it occupies several storefronts in South Molton Street and stocks a wide selection of international labels. But the highest concentration of boutiques is in Notting Hill, near the intersection of Westbourne Grove and Ledbury Road. Because of the numerous cafés in the area, and the relaxed, affluent atmosphere away from the crowded West End shopping districts, it's an extremely pleasant place to browse.

JW Beeton embodies quirky British style, while **Matches**, which also has outposts in Richmond and Wimbledon, dominates Ledbury Road with three separate shops – one for both sexes, another just for women plus one specializing in frocks by Diane von Furstenberg. Like Browns in the West End, **Matches** stocks international designer labels, including Balenciaga, Prada and Chloé, interspersed with a variety of British talent such as Temperley, Bella Freud, Matthew Williamson and Georgina Goodman.

Question Air and **Feathers** also stock designer labels, while **Aimé** specializes in French clothes and homewares. A short walk away in a quiet residential street, celebrity favourite, **The Cross** is a delightfully understated little shop, packed with women's fashion, cute children's clothes and toys, toiletries and varied displays of unusual accessories. **Cross The Road**, located opposite, caters to chic interiors while

The Dispensary in Kensington Park Road is much loved by locals for its Notting Hill style. Primrose Hill, Islington, Soho and the streets radiating off Seven Dials near Covent Garden are also dotted with independent fashion shops. Some, such as **Labour of Love** in Islington, combine clothes with a careful selection of interior items, art books and CDs. **Diverse**, also in Islington, caters for both sexes with a great selection of labels.

CHAIN STORES AND STREET FASHION

In Britain, designer looks are no longer, as they once were, the exclusive preserve of the rich. National fashion chains – or "high-street" stores – have never been better, both in terms of quality and design. Moreover, the cheaper versions of all the latest styles appear in the shops, almost as soon as they have been sashayed down the catwalk. **Oasis** and **Topshop** have both won celebrity fans for their up-to-the-minute, young womenswear. The latter, which proudly claims to be "the world's largest fashion store", is a complete mine of inexpensive clothes and beautiful accessories; there is even an in-store "boutique" with latest collections by hip designers, and a vintage section as well.

Vintage fashion (see p326) has become so popular, many high-street chains either sell it or feature collections which recreate the style.

The upmarket chains, **Jigsaw** and **Whistles** are more expensive with the emphasis on beautiful fabrics and shapes which, while stylish, don't slavishly copy the catwalk. **Jigsaw Junior**, available in larger branches, offers delectable mini versions of its designs for little girls. **Reiss** and **Ted Baker** are more popular with the trend-conscious young men, though they also have good women's collections. More streetwise shops can be found in and around Newburgh Street, behind Carnaby Street. **Cecil Gee** in Covent Garden is among the trail-blazers for men.

VINTAGE FASHION

The city offers a vast hunting ground for the aficionados of vintage style, from market stalls to the exclusive shops showcasing immaculately preserved designerwear. Head east for funky emporia such as **Rokit**, which also has other branches in Camden and Covent Garden, in addition to the huge warehouse, **Beyond Retro**. Grays Antique Market *(see p340)* covers all the bases with the award-winning Vintage Modes, spanning the styles of the past century as well as fashion-conscious Advintage, run by a former department-store personal shopper. Glamorous evening gowns and pin-up lingerie for the girls, flashy Hawaiian shirts and novelty bar accessories for the guys, can be found at Sparkle Moore's gloriously kitsch string of stalls, **The Girl Can't Help It** in Alfies Antique Market, which also houses excellent vintage shop **Persiflage**.

For mint-condition 1930s bias-cut silk slips and 1920s flapper dresses, head to **Annie's Vintage Clothes** in Camden Passage. Those looking for old designer gems should pay a visit to **Appleby** in West London, which is pretty much strong on the 1950s through 80s. Be warned, neither of these ex-cellent shops is cheap, they both charge quite handsomely.

KNITWEAR

From the sought-after Fair Isle jumpers to Aran knits, the traditional British knitwear is famous. The best places for these are in Piccadilly, Regent Street and Knightsbridge. Heritage labels **Pringle** and **Ballantyne** have recently been revitalized with more contemporary shapes and vivid colours. Luxurious, casual label, **Joseph** features modern chunky knits, while **John Smedley** concentrates on more simple designs in fine-gauge wool and sea island cotton. For cashmere, **N Peal**, which has both men's and women's shops at opposite ends of the Burlington Arcade, has a great selection – including a fairly cheaper, fashion-conscious line, npealworks. While the popular chain, **Brora** offers an affordable range of contemporary, Scottish cashmere for the entire family. **Marilyn Moore**, designs hip interpretations of classic knitwear.

UNDERWEAR AND LINGERIE

Marks & Spencer *(see p321)* is the most popular source of reasonably priced basics, it now has several fashionable lingerie lines as well. **Agent Provocateur**, owned by the famous designer, Vivienne Westwood's son and his wife, oozes retro pin-up glamour, from the slightly kinky, pink-uniforms worn by the staff to its nostalgically seductive bra sets. **Myla** sells contemporary lingerie and designer sex toys, that can pass for objets d'art. **Miss Lala's Boudoir** located in Primrose Hill, is an exquisitely feminine shop. Its collection includes, wispy negligées and hand-made, frilled undergarments, mixed in with items of clothing such as kitsch sequinned T-shirts, pretty tutu skirts and some vintage pieces.

CHILDREN'S CLOTHES

You can get traditional hand-smocked dresses and romper suits from Liberty, **Young England** and **Rachel Riley**, which stock smocks, gowns and tweed coats. Burberry's New Bond Street store has a children's section showcasing adorable mini macs, kilts and other items featuring the famous check. **Trotters** offers everything from shoes and clothes to haircuts, while **Their Nibs** sells eclectic designer children's clothing. For the very special, quintessentially English girls' clothes in pretty, patterned vintage fabrics, as seen on Madonna's daughter, visit **Bunny London**, in Harrods and Harvey Nichols until a new London store opens.

SHOES

Some of the most famous names in the footwear industry are based in Britain. If you have a few thousand pounds to spare, you can have a pair custom-made by the Royal Family's shoemaker, **John Lobb**. In the East End, ex-Lobb shoemaker, **Jason Amesbury** creates a bespoke range of footwear for considerably less, but you will still end up paying over £1,500. Ready-made, traditional brogues and Oxfords are the mainstay of **Church's Shoes**, while **Oliver Sweeney** gives classics a contemporary edge. For traditional, bench-made shoes at bargain prices, it's worth travelling further afield to Battersea, and splurge at the **Shipton & Heneage** outlet. It offers an exceptionally wide range of Oxfords, Derbys, loafers and boots crafted in the same Northamptonshire factories as some of the most celebrated names, for considerably lower prices, the out-of-the-way location keeps costs down.

Fans of the Fab Four can step into their idols' shoes; **Anello & Davide** designed the original Beatle Boot and still sells bespoke shoes in a range of materials. **The British Boot Company** in funky Camden has the widest range of Dr Martens, which were originally designed as hard-wearing work boots and appropriated by the rock 'n' rollers. **Jimmy Choo** and **Manolo Blahnik** are certainly, two beloved designers of most fashionable women worldwide. Their sophisticated high heels and cutting-edge designs are much sought-after.

While **Gina** emulates its namesake, Gina Lolobrigida with super-sexy designs, such as jewelled stiletto sandals, **Emma Hope** in Sloane Square is best known for simple, timeless shapes embellished with embroidery or beadwork. Less expensive, yet good quality designs can be found in **Hobbs** or **Pied à Terre**, while **Faith** and **Office** turn out young fashion-led styles, the latter also sells men's shoes. If you are on a look out for something that's a bit different, it's worth visiting London designer, **Georgina Goodman's** shop in the picturesque Shepherd Market, where she showcases her unique ready-to-wear range.

DIRECTORY

TRADITIONAL CLOTHING

Aquascutum
100 Regent St W1.
Map 12 F3.
Tel 020-7675 8200.

Burberry
21–23 New Bond St W1.
Map 12 F2.
Tel 020-7930 3343.

Cordings
19–20 Piccadilly W1.
Map 13 A3.
Tel 020-7734 0830.

Crombie
48 Conduit St W1.
Map 12 F2.
Tel 020-7434 2886.
One of two branches.

Daks
10 Old Bond St W1.
Map 12 F3.
Tel 020-7409 4000.

Dunhill
48 Jermyn St W1.
Map 12 F3.
Tel 0845-458 0779.

Gieves & Hawkes
1 Savile Row W1.
Map 12 E3.
Tel 020-7434 2001.

H Huntsman & Sons
11 Savile Row W1.
Map 12 E3.
Tel 020-7734 7441.

Hackett
87 Jermyn St SW1.
Map 13 A3.
Tel 020-7930 1300.
One of several branches.

Harvie & Hudson
77 Jermyn St SW1.
Map 12 F3.
Tel 020-7930 3949.
One of three branches.

Henry Poole & Co
15 Savile Row W1.
Map 12 F3.
Tel 020-7734 5985.

Jaeger
200–206 Regent St W1.
Map12 F2.
Tel 020-7979 1100.

Laura Ashley
House of Fraser, 318
Oxford St W1. **Map** 12 F1.
Tel 0871-223 1425.
One of several branches.

Liberty
Regent St W1.
Map 12 F2.
Tel 020-7734 1234.

Margaret Howell
34 Wigmore St W1.
Map 12 E1.
Tel 020-7009 9006.

Nicole Farhi
158 New Bond St W1.
Map 12 E2.
Tel 020-7499 8368.
One of several branches.

Ozwald Boateng
12a Savile Row &
9 Vigo St W1.
Map 12 F3.
Tel 020-7437 0620.

Pink
85 Jermyn St SW1.
Map 12 F3.
Tel 020-7930 6364.
One of several branches.

Richard James
29 Savile Row W1.
Map 12 F2.
Tel 020-7434 0605.

Turnbull & Asser
71–72 Jermyn St SW1.
Map 12 F3.
Tel 020-7808 3000.

MODERN BRITISH DESIGN AND STREET FASHION

Alexander McQueen
4–5 Old Bond St W1.
Map 12 F3.
Tel 020-7355 0088.

Browns Labels for Less
50 South Molton St W1.
Map 12 E2.
Tel 020-7514 0052.

Burberry Factory Shop
29–53 Chatham Place E9.
Tel 020-8985 3344.

Debenhams
334–348 Oxford St W1.
Map 12 E2.
Tel 08445-616 161.

Dover Street Market
17–18 Dover Street W1.
Map 12 F3.
Tel 020-7518 0680.

Fashion and Textile Museum
83 Bermondsey St SE1.
Map 15 C4.
Tel 020-7407 8664.

Matthew Williamson
28 Bruton St W1.
Map 12 E3.
Tel 020-7629 6200.

Paul Smith
Westbourne House
120 & 122 Kensington
Park Rd W11.
Map 9 B2.
Tel 020-7727 3553.
One of several branches.

Paul Smith Sale Shop
23 Avery Row W1.
Map 12 E2.
Tel 020-7493 1287.

Stella McCartney
30 Bruton St W1.
Map 12 E3.
Tel 020-7518 3100.

Vivienne Westwood
6 Davies St W1.
Map 12 E2.
Tel 020-7629 3757.

BOUTIQUES

Aimé
32 Ledbury Rd W11.
Map 9 C2.
Tel 020-7221 7070.

Anna
126 Regent's Park Rd
NW1.
Tel 020-7483 0411.

b Store
24a Saville Row W1.
Map 12 F2.
Tel 020-7734 6846.

Browns
23–27 South Molton
St W1.
Map 12 E2.
Tel 020-7514 0016.

The Cross
141 Portland Rd W11.
Map 9 A3.
Tel 020-7727 6760.

Diverse
286 & 294 Upper St,
Islington N1. **Map** 6 F1.
Tel 020-7359 8877.

Feathers
176 Westbourne Grove
W11.
Map 9 C2.
Tel 020-7243 8800.

JW Beeton
48–50 Ledbury Road W11.
Map 9 C2.
Tel 020-7229 8874.

Koh Samui
65–67 Monmouth St
WC2.
Map13 B2.
Tel 020-7240 4280.

Labour of Love
193 Upper St N1.
Map 6 F1.
Tel 020-7354 9333.

Matches
60–64, 83 & 85
Ledbury Rd W11.
Map 9 C2.
Tel 020-7221 0255.

Question Air
229 Westbourne Grove
W11.
Map 9 C2.
Tel 020-7221 8163.

CHAIN STORES AND STREET FASHION

Cecil Gee
36 Long Acre WC2.
Map 13 B2.
Tel 020-7379 0456.

The Dispensary
200 Kensington Park Rd
W11. **Map** 9 B2.
Tel 020-7727 8797.

Hobbs
84–88 King's Rd SW3.
Map 19 C2.
Tel 020-7581 2914.
One of many branches.

Jigsaw
6 Duke of York Sq, Kings
Rd SW3. **Map** 19 C2.
Tel 020-7730 4404.
One of many branches.

Karen Millen
262–264 Regent St W1.
Map 12 F1.
Tel 020-7629 1901.
One of several branches.

DIRECTORY

Oasis
12–14 Argyll St W1.
Map 12 F2.
Tel 020-7434 1799.
One of several branches.

Reiss
Kent House, 14-17 Market Place W1.
Map 12 F1.
Tel 020-7637 9112.
One of several branches.

Ted Baker
9–10 Floral St WC2.
Map 13 C2.
Tel 020-7836 7808.
One of several branches.

Topshop
Oxford Circus W1.
Map 12 F1.
Tel 0844-848 7487.
One of several branches.

Whistles
12–14 St Christopher's Pl W1.
Map 12 D1.
Tel 020-7487 4484.
One of several branches.

VINTAGE FASHION

Annie's Vintage Clothes
12 Camden Passage N1.
Map 6 F1.
Tel 020-7359 0796.

Appleby
95 Westbourne Park Villas W2.
Map 9 C1.
Tel 020-7229 7772.

Beyond Retro
110–112 Cheshire St E2.
Map 8 E4.
Tel 020-7613 3636.

The Girl Can't Help It
Alfies Antiques Market, 13–25 Church Street NW8.
Map 3 A5.
Tel 020-7724 8984.

Persiflage
Alfies Antiques Market, 13–25 Church St NW8.
Map 3 A5.
Tel 020-7724 7366.

Rokit
101 & 107 Brick Lane E1.
Map 8 E4.
Tel 020-7375 3864.
One of three branches.

KNITWEAR

Ballantyne
153a New Bond St W1.
Map 12 F2.
Tel 020-7495 6104.

Brora
81 Marylebone High St W1.
Map 4 D5.
Tel 020-7224 5040.
One of several branches.

John Smedley
24 Brook St W1.
Map 12 E2.
Tel 020-7495 2222.

Joseph
77 Fulham Rd SW3.
Map 19 B2.
Tel 020-7823 9500.
One of several branches.

Marilyn Moore
7 Elgin Crescent W11.
Map 9 B2.
Tel 020-7727 5577.

N Peal
Burlington Arcade, Piccadilly, W1.
Map 12 F3.
Tel 020-7499 6485.

Pringle Scotland
112 New Bond St W1.
Map 12 E2.
Tel 020-7297 4580.

UNDERWEAR AND LINGERIE

Agent Provocateur
6 Broadwick St W1.
Map 13 A2.
Tel 020-7439 0229.
One of several branches.

Miss Lala's Boudoir
148 Gloucester Ave NW1.
Map 4 D1.
Tel 020-7483 1888.

Myla
77 Lonsdale Rd W11.
Map 9 B2.
Tel 020-7221 9222.
One of several branches.

Rigby & Peller
22A Conduit St W1.
Map 12 F2.
Tel 0845 076 5545.

CHILDREN'S CLOTHES

Bunny London
Tel 020-7627 2318.

Rachel Riley
82 Marylebone High St W1. **Map** 4 D5.
Tel 020-7935 7007.
One of two branches.

Their Nibs
214 Kensington Park Road W11. **Map** 9 A1.
Tel 020-7221 4263.

Trotters
34 King's Rd SW3.
Map 19 C2.
Tel 020-7259 6920.

Young England
The Old Imperial Laundry, 71 Warrior Gardens SW11.
Tel 0845-055 9722.

SHOES

Anello & Davide
15 St Alban's Grove, Kensington W8.
Map 10 E5.
Tel 020-7938 2255.

The British Boot Company
5 Kentish Town Rd NW1. **Map** 4 F1.
Tel 020-7485 8505.

Church's Shoes
201 Regent St W1.
Map 12 F2.
Tel 020-7734 2438.

Emma Hope
53 Sloane Sq SW1.
Map 19 C2.
Tel 020-7259 9566.
One of three branches.

Faith
192–194 Oxford St W1.
Map 12 F1.
Tel 020-7580 9561.
One of several branches.

Georgina Goodman
12–14 Shepherd St W1.
Map 12 E4.
Tel 020-7499 8599.

Gina
189 Sloane St SW1.
Map 19 C1.
Tel 020-7235 2932.

Hobbs
47–48 South Molton St W1.
Map 12 E2.
Tel 020-7629 0750.
One of several branches.

Jason Amesbury
32 Elder St E1.
Map 8 D5.
Tel 020-7377 2006.

Jimmy Choo
27 New Bond St W1.
Map 12 F2.
Tel 020-7493 5858.

John Lobb
88 Jermyn St SW1.
Map 12 F3.
Tel 020-7930 8089.

Kate Kuba
22 Duke of York Square, King's Rd SW3.
Map 19 C2.
Tel 020-7259 0011.

Manolo Blahnik
49–51 Old Church St, Kings Road SW3.
Map 19 A4.
Tel 020-7352 8622.

Office
57 Neal St WC2.
Map 13 B1.
Tel 020-7379 1896.
One of several branches.

Oliver Sweeney
66 New Bond St W1.
Map 12 E2.
Tel 020-7355 0387.

Pied à Terre
19 South Molton St W1.
Map 12 E2.
Tel 020-7629 1362.

Shelly's
14–18 Neal St WC2.
Map 13 B2.
Tel 020-7240 3726.
One of several branches.

Shipton & Heneage
117 Queenstown Rd SW8.
Map 20 E5.
Tel 020-7738 8484.

Specialist Shops

London may be famed for the grand department stores such as Harrods, but there are many specialist shops which should also figure on the visitor's itinerary. Some have expertise built up over a century or more, while others are new and fashionable or cater to the whims of eccentric collectors. Whether you are looking for traditional British products and food, high-tech gadgets, or the latest trends in music, London has a wide range of stores to suite everyone's tastes.

FOOD

Britain's reputation for terrible food is proving hard to shake off, but over the past decade, not only has the national cuisine improved immeasurably, London has become one of the culinary capitals of the world. There is an unprecedented interest in local and organic produce as well as delicacies imported from all over Europe. This is reflected in the growing number of food markets, the main one being Borough Market *(see p339)*. Specialities that are well worth sampling, include a variety of chocolates, biscuits, preserves, cheeses and teas *(see pp294–5)*.

The food halls of Fortnum & Mason, Harrods and Harvey Nichols *(see p321)* are good outlets for all of these, but it's also worth visiting the gastronomic gems dotted around town. Of these, **A Gold**, housed in an atmospheric old milliner's shop near Spitalfields Market, specializes in traditional foods from across Britain. Its wares, including cheeses, sausages, jams, baked goods, English wines and mead, are advertised on chalkboards. **Paxton & Whitfield**, a delightful shop dating from 1797, stocks more than 300 cheeses, including baby Stiltons and Cheshire truckles, along with pork pies, biscuits, oils and preserves.

The shelves of tiny **Neal's Yard Dairy** groan with huge British farmhouse cheeses. **Paul Rothe & Son** is a family-run deli that has hardly changed since it opened more than a century ago. Besides selling "British and foreign provisions", such as preserves, old-fashioned sweets and biscuits, the white-coated

proprietors also serve morning toast and sandwiches on proper china. For traditional English chocolates, such as violet or rose creams and after-dinner mints in beautiful gift boxes, head for **Charbonnel et Walker** in Royal Arcade of Old Bond Street. It has been in business for more than 100 years, and holds Royal warrants. True chocoholics will be in their element at **The Chocolate Society's** shop/café, where only the finest pure chocolate is available. Also committed to "real" chocolate, **Rococo** is well-known for its unique blue-and-white Victorian-esque packaging.

DRINKS

Tea, the most British of drinks, comes in all kinds of flavours. Fortnum & Mason's traditional teas come in appealingly refined gift selections. **The Tea House** is packed with myriad varieties from classic to creative (such as "summer pudding"), colourful tourist-oriented tins and teapots. **Postcard Teas** is another specialist retailer of high-quality teas.

The quaint 19th-century **Algerian Coffee Stores** manages to pack over 140 varieties of coffee and 200 teas into its small shop. Family business **HR Higgins**, sells fine coffees and teas from around the world. There are many attractive gift boxes and you can try before you buy in the coffee room downstairs.

For whisky lovers, **The Vintage House** displays the widest array of single malts in England, including some very old bottles. **Berry Bros & Rudd** is one of the oldest wine merchants in the world, still trading in wines, fortified

wines and spirits from its ancient, panelled shop in St James's. In contrast, **Vinopolis** *(see p182)*, Bankside's "wine city", which charges admission, has a vast range of wines to choose from once you been on their interactive world wine tour and enjoyed five tastings. You can continue to imbibe in the restaurant or wine bar.

ONE-OFFS

Sadly, many of London's quirky old specialist shops have closed, but there are still some fascinating anachronisms, as well as interesting newcomers, to be found across the city. A large number of specialist traders operate from stalls in antiques markets such as Alfies and Portobello Road *(see p341)*, where you can find everything from old military medals to commemorative china and vintage luggage. A notable survivor is **James Smith & Sons**, the largest and oldest umbrella shop in Europe. It first opened for business in 1830. Behind its mahogany and glass-panelled façade lies an array of high-quality umbrellas and walking sticks, including the once ubiquitous city gent brolly.

Halcyon Days specializes in little enamelled copper boxes, the delightful products of a revived English 18th-century craft. Top-quality wooden chess sets and boards, including an ornamental design featuring Sherlock Holmes characters, are available at **Chess & Bridge Ltd. VV Rouleaux**, on the other hand, is festooned with every imaginable type of ribbon and flamboyant trimming.

For serious collectors of model-making kits and historic TV character dolls and toys, **Comet Miniatures** has the largest selection in London. **Honeyjam** sells traditional toys and games for all ages. Without a Gameboy in sight, **Benjamin Pollock's Toyshop** does a nifty line in miniature self-assembly paper theatres as well as other traditional toys and antique teddies. **Flower Space** specializes in

1960s and 1970s furniture and classic movie prints.

At **The Bead Shop** in Covent Garden you will find two floors stocked with everything from Swarovski crystals to semi-precious beads and sterling silver. The tasteful erotic boutique **Coco de Mer**, banishes the seedy sex shop cliché with its exquisite hand-made lingerie and aesthetically pleasing sex toys.

James Bond wannabes will love **Spymaster**, which stocks such indispensable items as shark repellent and a bug-detector "pen". Although it's a serious stockist to the military and law-enforcement agencies, amateur sleuths are always welcome to browse.

BOOKS AND MAGAZINES

Bookshops are high among London's specialities. Charing Cross Road *(see p108)* is undoubtedly the focal point for those searching for new, antiquarian and second-hand volumes. Although film buffs won't be able to browse in the shop that inspired the book and film, *84 Charing Cross Road*, they will be consoled by a commemorative plaque marking the site of the now defunct Marks & Co, which bore the celebrated address.

On the strip there are plenty of other antiquarian book-sellers, shelves groaning with dusty finds. **Francis Edwards** here has a good selection covering travel, natural history, naval and military history and art and literature. Many shops offer a book-finding service if the title you want is no longer in print.

Charing Cross Road is famously the home of **Foyles**, known for its massive but notoriously badly organized stock; however, it was given a facelift and is now much easier to navigate. Here, you'll find everything from the latest bestsellers to academic tomes.

London's largest women's interest bookshop, **Silver Moon**, is on the third floor, there's a jazz shop and a cool café *(see below)*, plus an art gallery and real live piranhas

in the children's department. As well as large branches of chains **Waterstone's** and **Blackwell**, many specialist bookshops are based here. A popular one is **Magma**, which is excellent for design subjects and avant-garde illustrated books.

Stanfords *(see p112)*, which stocks maps and guides to cover the globe, is in Long Acre; more travel books can be found at the **Travel Bookshop** in Notting Hill. Nearby is **Books for Cooks**, complete with café and test kitchen.

The beautiful Edwardian **Daunt Books** in Marylebone has a soaring, galleried back room devoted entirely to travel titles and, unusually, related fiction organized by country. Graphic novels and American and European comics are the speciality at **Gosh!** and **Orbital Comics**, while fantasy and science fiction abound at **Forbidden Planet**. For gay writing, visit the pioneering **Gay's The Word**, near Russell Square. The best selection of books on movies is found at the **Cinema Store**.

London's oldest bookshop, **Hatchards** in Piccadilly, is also one of the best, offering a well-organized and extensive choice. **Grant & Cutler** is an unrivalled source of foreign books and videos, while **The Banana Bookshop** in Covent Garden must be London's most endearing remainder shop, artistically decorated with jungle murals.

Cecil Court *(see p101)* is a charming pedestrian alleyway lined with dealers specializing in everything from illustrated children's books to modern first editions. There are also shops selling old prints covering every theme – great for gifts – and especially theatrical memorabilia.

The French Bookshop in South Kensington is stocked full of best-selling French titles. If you are looking for newspapers and magazines from abroad, Borders has an extremely wide selection, to keep you abreast with the latest. **Capital Newsagents** stocks among others,

American, Italian, French, Spanish and Middle Eastern publications. **Gray's Inn News** is also worth a visit for European press. For those with a keen interest in vintage magazines, there are more than 200,000 in the basement of **Vintage Magazines** in Soho, dating from the early 1900s all the way through to the present day. There are also all manner of movie and popular-culture memorabilia and gifts on the ground floor of the shop.

CDS AND RECORDS

As one of the world's greatest centres of recorded music, London has a huge and excellent selection of record shops catering to fans of all musical styles. Stores in the **HMV** chain are a reliable source of mainstream platters from pop to punk to peaceful easy listening, and their Oxford Circus branch stocks a comprehensive range of classical music.

Small specialist shops tend to cater to the more esoteric tastes. **Rough Trade** was at the centre of the emerging punk scene and still sniffs out interesting indie talent today, found in both East and West London. For jazz, check out **Ray's Jazz**, which is now housed in Foyle's bookshop along with a cool café where you can chill out to the vibe.

Even if you're not a collector of rare vinyl, if you happen to be in the area, it's worth having a look at the kitsch Hawaiian hut interior of **Intoxica!**. It offers almost everything, from the 1960s surf pop to funk, punk and independent rock.

Stern's has long been without an equal when it comes to exclusive collection of African music, and has recently broadened its scope to cover all world music.

There is a high concentration of indie vinyl and CD shops in and around Berwick Street. For 12-inch singles, the medium of club and dance music, **Vinyl Junkies** and **Black Market** are certainly two of the most central places to visit.

DIRECTORY

FOODS

A Gold
42 Brushfield St E1.
Map 8 D5.
Tel 020-7247 2487.

Charbonnel et Walker
1 Royal Arcade, 28 Old Bond St W1. **Map** 12 F3.
Tel 020-7491 0939.

The Chocolate Society
36 Elizabeth St SW1.
Map 20 E2.
Tel 020-7259 9222.

Neal's Yard Dairy
17 Short's Gardens WC2.
Map 13 B2.
Tel 020-7240 5700.

Paul Rothe & Son
35 Marylebone Lane W1.
Map 12 E1.
Tel 020-7935 6783.

Paxton & Whitfield
93 Jermyn St SW1.
Map 12 F3.
Tel 020-7930 0259.

Rococo
321 King's Rd SW3.
Map 19 A4.
Tel 020-7352 5857.

DRINKS

Algerian Coffee Stores
52 Old Compton St W1.
Map 13 A2.
Tel 020-7437 2480.

Berry Bros & Rudd
3 St James's St SW1.
Map 12 F4.
Tel 0870-900 4300.

HR Higgins
79 Duke St W1.
Map 12 D2.
Tel 020-7629 3913.

Postcard Teas
9 Dering St W1.
Map 12 E2.
Tel 020-7629 3654.

The Tea House
15A Neal St WC2.
Map 13 B2.
Tel 020-7240 7539.

Vinopolis
1 Bank End SE1.
Map 15 B3.
Tel 0870-241 4040.

The Vintage House
42 Old Compton St W1.
Map 13 A2.
Tel 020-7437 2592.

ONE-OFFS

Benjamin Pollock's Toyshop
44 The Market, Covent Garden Piazza WC2.
Map 13 C2.
Tel 020-7379 7866.

Chess & Bridge Ltd
44 Baker St W1.
Map 12 D1.
Tel 020-7486 8222.

Coco de Mer
23 Monmouth St WC2.
Map 13 B2.
Tel 020-7836 8882.

Comet Miniatures
44–48 Lavender Hill SW11.
Tel 020-7228 3702.

Flower Space
301 Portobello Rd W10.
Map 9 A1.
Tel 020-8968 9966.

Halcyon Days
14 Brook St W1. **Map** 12 E2.*Tel 020-7629 8811.*

Honeyjam
267 Portobello Rd W11.
Map 9 A1.
Tel 020-7243 0449.

James Smith & Son
53 New Oxford St W1.
Map 13 B1.
Tel 020-7836 4731.

Spymaster
3 Portman Square W1. **Map** 12 D1.
Tel 020-7486 3885.

The Bead Shop
21a Tower St WC2.
Map 13 B2.
Tel 020-7240 0931.

VV Rouleaux
102 Marylebone Lane W1.
Map 4 D5.
Tel 020-7224 5179.

BOOKS AND MAGAZINES

The Banana Bookshop
Unit 42 The Market, Covent Garden Piazza WC2.
Map 13 C2.
Tel 020-7836 0561.

Blackwell
100 Charing Cross Rd WC2. **Map** 13 B2.
Tel 020-7292 5100.

Books for Cooks
4 Blenheim Crescent W11.
Map 9 B2.
Tel 020-7221 1992.

Capital Newsagents
48 Old Compton St W1.
Map 13 A2.
Tel 020-7437 2479.

Cinema Store
Unit 4B, Upper St Martin's Lane WC1. **Map** 13 B2.
Tel 020-7379 7838.

Daunt Books
83–84 Marylebone High St W1. **Map** 4 D5.
Tel 020-7224 2295.

Forbidden Planet
179 Shaftesbury Ave W1. **Map** 13 A2.
Tel 020-7420 3666.

Foyles
113–119 Charing Cross Rd WC2. **Map** 13 B1.
Tel 020-7437 5660.

Francis Edwards
13 Great Newport St, Charing Cross Rd WC2.
Map 13 B1.
Tel 020-7379 7669.

The French Bookshop
28 Bute St SW7. **Map** 18 F2. *Tel 020-7581 2840.*

Gay's The Word
66 Marchmont St WC1.
Map 5 B4.
Tel 020-7278 7654.

Gosh!
39 Gt Russell St WC1.
Map 13 B1.
Tel 020-7636 1011.

Gray's Inn News
50 Theobalds Rd WC1.
Map 6 D5.
Tel 020-7405 5241.

Hatchards
187 Piccadilly W1.
Map 12 F3.
Tel 020-7439 9921.

Magma
8 Earlham St WC2.
Map 13 B2.
Tel 020-7240 8498.

Orbital Comics
8 Great Newport St, WC2. **Map** 13 B2.
Tel 020-7240 7672.

Stanfords
12–14 Long Acre WC2.
Map 13 B2.
Tel 020-7836 1321.

Travel Bookshop
13 Blenheim Crescent W11. **Map** 9 B2.
Tel 020-7229 5260.

Waterstone's
421 Oxford St W1.
Map 11 D2.
Tel 020-7495 8507.

Vintage Magazines
39–43 Brewer St W1.
Map 13 A2.
Tel 020-7437 8525.

CDS AND RECORDS

Black Market
25 D'Arblay St W1.
Map 13 A2.
Tel 020-7437 0478.

Fopp
1 Earlham St WC2.
Map 13 B2.
Tel 020-7845 9770.

HMV
150 Oxford St W1.
Map 13 A1.
Tel 020-7631 3423.

Intoxica!
231 Portobello Rd W11.
Map 9 B2.
Tel 020-7229 8010.

Ray's Jazz
(See Foyles).
Tel 020-7437 5660.

Rough Trade West
130 Talbot Rd W11.
Map 9 C1.
Tel 020-7229 8541.

Rough Trade East
91 Brick Lane E1.
Map 8 E5.
Tel 020-7392 7788.

Stern's
74–75 Warren St W1.
Map 4 F4.
Tel 020-7387 5550.

Vinyl Junkies
94 Berwick St W1.
Map 13 A1.
Tel 020-7439 2923.

Gifts and Souvenirs

London is a wonderful place to shop for gifts. It presents an impressive array of original ceramics, jewellery, perfume and glassware, exotic merchandise from around the world including jewellery from India and Africa, stationery from Europe and kitchenware from France and Italy. The elegant, Regency-period Burlington Arcade (see p91), the largest of several covered shopping arcades in the area, is popular for its high-quality clothes, antique and new jewellery, leather goods and other items, many of which are made in the UK. It is also a real boon when the famously unpredictable weather turns nasty.

The shops at big museums, such as the Victoria and Albert (see pp202–5), the Natural History (see pp208–9) and the Science Museum (see pp212–13) often have unusual items to take home as mementoes, while Contemporary Applied Arts and the market in Covent Garden Piazza (see p114) sell a range of British pottery, knitwear, pictures, clothing and other crafts. To buy all your gifts under one roof, go to Liberty (see p109), where beautiful stock from the world over fills every department, and the classic Liberty print features on many goods.

GIFT SHOPS

If the phrase "gift shop" conjures up images of tacky tourist souvenirs, think again. A number of interesting shops bringing together a variety of present-friendly goods under one roof, has sprung up in the capital in recent years. Just off Brick Lane, one-room **Shelf** showcases stationery, prints, ceramics and other objects by local and European artists and designers. It's only open Friday to Sunday; call hours before making a special trip. There are several other quirky, small shops in this street good for gift-hunting, including **Labour & Wait**.

A short walk away, **Story**, in a beautifully preserved 18th-century residential street looks more like a gallery space than a shop. The fascinating mix of wares unites vintage dresses, organic bath products and modern and classic furnishings.

Across town in Notting Hill, **Coco Ribbon** is a girly emporium, kitted out with antique armoires and chandeliers, selling everything from 1950s-influenced embroidered cushions and scented candles to prettily packaged toiletries, hand-made lingerie and Australian designer fashion. The **Design Museum Shop** is a museum gift shop with a difference. It displays post-modern toys, games and innovative – and in some cases surprisingly affordable – accessories for home and office by big design names such as Arne Jacobsen, Tord Boontje and Eames. There are some wonderfully witty items, such as shoe-shaped shoe brushes and a doorstop in the form of a figure holding it open. Boutiques, **Saloon** and **Labour of Love** (see p327) also sell an eclectic range of items.

JEWELLERY

There are styles to suit every taste, from the fine, traditional jewellery found in the exclusive shops of Bond Street to unusual pieces by independent designers in areas like Covent Garden (see pp110–19), Gabriel's Wharf (see p191), and Camden Lock (see p339). Antique jewellery can be found in Hatton Garden and the Silver Vaults (see p141). The Crown Jeweller, **Garrard** in Albemarle Street, has been brought bang up-to-date under creative director Jade Jagger. Be warned, the spectacular creations have pricetags to match. Its former business partner, **Asprey** sells updated classics. While **Butler & Wilson** specializes in reproductions of vintage jewellery and accessories, **Electrum Gallery** next door showcases striking contemporary pieces. **Jess James's** unusual shop design, featuring a tropical fish tank and display cabinets that illuminate as you step in front of them, match the original stock. Popular London design house **Erickson Beamon**, which is also sold in Harrods (see p321), typically features dramatic chokers and earrings dripping with beads. The husband and wife duo, **Wright & Teague** design covetable modern silver and gold charm bracelets and necklaces, among other things.

The **Victoria & Albert shop** sells modern replicas of ancient British designs, as does the shop at the British Museum (see pp126–9). The **Lesley Craze Gallery**, which also deals in other handmade accessories and crafts, sells jewellery by designers from around the globe. Liberty (see p109) stocks a wide range of attractive jewellery as well.

HATS

Traditional men's headgear, from flat caps to trilbies and toppers, can be found at **Edward Bates**. Venerable hatter **Lock & Co**, established in 1672, caters for both men and women, while Swaine Adeney Brigg sells hats for both sexes by well-known name **Herbert Johnson**.

Philip Treacy is Britain's most celebrated milliner and his fabulous creations are on display at his shop on Elizabeth Street and in upmarket department stores. Established name **Stephen Jones** also has some very eye-catching looks, while **Rachel Skinner's** beautifully made, slightly nostalgic designs range from cute cloches to extravagant Ascot confections, which are less expensive than more famous names. **Fred Bare's** funky, affordable designs can be bought from the shop in Columbia Road on Sundays when the weekly flower market is in bloom, or from high-end department stores.

BAGS AND LEATHER GOODS

Traditional British luggage, bags and small leather goods can be found in the streets and arcades off Piccadilly. **Swaine Adeney Brigg** sells umbrellas, hats, classic bridle-leather bags, old-fashioned walking sticks and other accoutrements for the country gent and lady. Well known for its classic, hard-wearing bags and luggage is upmarket **Mulberry**. Established in 1971, its modern interpretations of English country clothes and accessories are sought after by fashion folk as well as anyone who appreciates fine quality.

The ultimate luxury is **Connolly**, a name famous for crafting sleek leather interiors for Rolls-Royce. Its two swish shops sell items that hark back to the golden age of motoring, such as leather driving jackets and shoes, magnificent tool cases and smart luggage, bound diaries and other extravagant home accessories and clothes.

J&M Davidson, owned by an Anglo-French couple, produces beautifully crafted, slightly retro bags, belts and small leather goods, often in unusual colours or skins. The shop in Notting Hill also stocks a line of clothes and interior items. Not far away is **Bill Amberg's** shop, which sells simple, contemporary bags in various types of leather, suede and other skins, plus gloves, wallets, leather boxes and unusual items such as a sheepskin baby "papoose".

Lulu Guinness and **Anya Hindmarch** both bring British wit and eccentricity to their handbags. Guinness's elaborate designs include a bag in the shape of a flowerpot topped with red roses and a circular purse resembling an old fashioned rotary telephone dial and there are also many London-themed items. Hindmarch is famous for personalised, digitally printed photo bags, but also produces classic leather ones. For less expensive but high quality unique bags, try **Radley**.

SCARVES

Ginka by Neisha Crosland is a tiny shop crammed with items bearing the designer's signature colourful, graphic prints; besides scarves there are bags, gloves, hats, clothes and stationery. Of course, Liberty's famous print scarves are perennially popular. Small, stylish **Fenwick** is also known for its accessories department, which includes a wide array of interesting scarves by the likes of Pucci and Missoni, as well as bags, hats and a huge range of hair decorations. The **V&A Museum** shop has a good selection of scarves, including William Morris print silk scarves and stunning replica scarves inspired by V&A collections. N Peal (*see p328*) has an extensive choice of cashmere scarves and shawls.

PERFUMES AND TOILETRIES

Many British perfumeries use recipes that are hundreds of years old. **Floris** and **Penhaligon's**, for example, still manufacture the same flower-based scents and toiletries for men and women that they sold in the 19th century. The same goes for men's specialists **Truefitt & Hill** and **George F Trumper**, where you can buy some wonderful reproductions of antique shaving equipment as well. Chemist and perfumer **DR Harris** has been making its own range of toiletries for over two centuries; it's worth stopping in just to see the old-fashioned shop.

Neal's Yard Remedies employs traditional herbal and floral remedies as bases for its natural, therapeutic products. Former facialist **Jo Malone** uses such delicious aromas as herbs, fruit, even coffee, as well as traditional floral essences in her fragrances, skincare and candles, which come in simple yet sophisticated packaging. If you're looking for an unusual scent, head for **Miller Harris**; young Grasse-trained perfumer Lyn Harris creates fragrances with remarkable depth, which come in boxes decorated with botanical prints. **Scent Systems** is a contender for the smallest shop in the capital, but its fragrances are worn by some of London's biggest names. The tiny shop near Carnaby Street brings together an exclusive selection of marvelously packaged perfumes from Europe and the US, including Mandy Aftel's Pink Lotus, which was specially commissioned for Madonna.

Space NK stocks the best and the most up-to-date collection of beauty products from around the world, along with its popular own-brand range. **The Body Shop** uses recyclable plastic packaging for its affordable natural cosmetics and toiletries, and encourages staff and customers alike to take an interest in environmental issues. **Molton Brown** sells a range of natural cosmetics, body and haircare products in branches throughout London. **The Studio Perfumery** stocks a selection of luxury brand fragrances and beauty products.

STATIONERY

For luxurious writing paper and desk accessories, try the Queen's stationer, **Smythson** of Bond Street. The little bound notebooks and address books embossed with a wide selection of amusing and practical titles, such as "Travel Notes" and "Blondes, Brunettes, Redheads" make great gifts and souvenirs. Fortnum and Mason (*see p321*) does handsome leather-bound diaries, blotters and pencil holders, while Liberty (*see p109*) embellishes desk accessories with its famous Art Nouveau prints. For personal organizers covered in anything from vinyl to iguana skin, try **The Filofax Centre**. **Asprey** also does a chic line of pocket diaries, organizers, key fobs and jewellery boxes in a variety of eye-catching skins.

Tessa Fantoni's attractive, paper-covered photo albums used to be sold at the Conran Shop and Harrods, but nowadays they are only available from her shop in

Clapham, where you will also find an appealing selection of gifts, cards and wrapping paper. Neisha Crosland's striking contemporary prints adorn a wide range of stationery items, including wrapping paper, cards and notebooks, as well as photograph albums.

Shepherd's Bookbinders stocks a range of handmade and decorative papers. Its marbled paper, can make a glorious giftwrap for that very special present. Finally, for greeting cards, pens, gift wrapping paper and general stationery, pop into one of the branches of **Paperchase**.

INTERIORS

Wedgwood still makes the famous pale blue Jasper china that Josiah Wedgwood designed in the 18th century. You can buy this and the Irish Waterford crystal, at **Waterford Wedgwood** on Piccadilly. For a fine variety of original pottery, visit **Contemporary Ceramics**, the gallery of the Craft Potters Association, or go to **Contemporary Applied Arts**. **Mint's** hand-picked selection of unique furniture, home accessories, china and glassware by established names and up-and-coming design talent is a pleasure to browse. Large interior stores,

Heal's and the **Conran Shop** have a great display of stylish, modern accessories for the home. Those with more traditional tastes may prefer **Thomas Goode**, presided over by courteous tail-coated staff, which sells exquisite china, glassware, crystal, linen and gifts, including some antique pieces. The **Nicole Farhi Home** line exudes the same laid-back luxury as her clothes. If you're on a tighter budget, check out **Graham & Green**, which stocks a huge array of attractive items from around the globe, ranging from Moroccan tea glasses to Mongolian cushions and pretty nightwear.

Labour & Wait is a wonderful source of solid, functional British items for home and garden, such as old-fashioned stainless steel kettles, Welsh blankets and Guernsey sweaters. **David Mellor** is famous for his streamlined modern cutlery designs, while **Divertimenti** sells all manner of kitchen equipment and has a pleasant cafe at the back.

Bridgewater Pottery has chunky mugs, crockery and tea towels, which are decorated with traditional motifs and amusing mottoes. The **Irish Linen Company** has everything from lacy hankies and appliquéd guest towels to tea towels and

tablecloths. **Cath Kidston** designs fresh, nostalgic, English-style prints which adorn everything from humble household items to fashion accessories. There's a huge range of pretty, giftable goods such as toiletries, ironing board covers, laundry bags, eiderdowns, clothes for women and children, bags, china and stationery.

Several interiors stores on Upper Street in the affluent Islington offer an impressive cache of gifts. **After Noah** is a big warehouse-like space bursting with vintage and retro-look items which also include, Bakelite rotary telephones, nostalgic toiletries, old metal tins and street signs, classic board games and a huge assortment of children's toys. There is another branch in King's Road and a concession in Harvey Nichols *(see p321)*.

The modern interiors emporium **Aria** has two stores in the same vicinity. One of these concentrates entirely on furniture and housewares by designers such as Alessi and Philippe Starck, while its satellite across the street sells gifts, including stationery, frames, bags and jewellery. Also on the same stretch is the contemporary-design heavyweight **twentytwentyone**.

DIRECTORY

DIRECTORY

Stephen Jones
36 Great Queen St WC2.
Map 13 C1.
Tel 020-7242 0770.

BAGS AND LEATHER GOODS

Anya Hindmarch
15–17 Pont St SW1.
Map 20 D1.
Tel 020-7838 9177.

Bill Amberg
21–22 Chepstow Corner
W2. **Map** 9 C2.
Tel 020-7727 3560.

Connolly
41 Conduit St W1. **Map**
12 F2. *Tel 020-7439 2510.*

J&M Davidson
97 Goldborne Rd W10.
Tel 020-7313 9532.

Lulu Guinness
3 Ellis St SW1. **Map** 19 C2.
Tel 020-7823 4828.

Mulberry
41–42 New Bond St W1.
Map 12 E2.
Tel 020-7491 3900.

Radley
37 Floral St WC2. **Map** 13
B2. *Tel 020-7379 9709.*

Swaine Adeney Brigg
54 St James's St SW1.
Map 12 F3.
Tel 020-7409 7277.

SCARVES

Fenwick
63 New Bond St W1.
Map 12 E2.
Tel 020-7629 9161.

Ginka by Neisha Crosland
137 Fulham Rd SW3.
Map 19 B2.
Tel 020-7589 4866.

V&A Enterprises
Victoria and Albert
Museum, Cromwell Rd
SW7. **Map** 19 A1.
Tel 020-7942 2696.

PERFUMES AND TOILETRIES

The Body Shop
64, 360 & 374, Oxford St
W1. **Map** 12 D2–F1.
Tel 020-7631 0027.

DR Harris
29 St James's St SW1.
Map 12 F3.
Tel 020-7930 3915.

Floris
89 Jermyn St SW1.
Map 13 A3.
Tel 0845-702 3239.

George F Trumper
9 Curzon St W1.
Map 12 E3.
Tel 020-7499 1850.

Jo Malone
23 Brook St W1.
Map 12 E2.
Tel 0870-192 5181.

Molton Brown
58 South Molton St W1.
Map 12 E2.
Tel 020-7499 6474.

Miller Harris
21 Bruton St W1.
Map 12 E3.
Tel 020-7629 7750.

Neal's Yard Remedies
15 Neal's Yard WC2.
Map 13 B1.
Tel 020-7379 7222.

Penhaligon's
41 Wellington St WC2.
Map 13 C2.
Tel 020-7836 2150.

Scent Systems Studio
13 Rugby St WC1.
Map 6 D5.
Tel 0780-943 3153.

Space NK
131 Westbourne Grove
W2.
Map 9 C2.
Tel 020-7727 8002.

The Studio Perfumery
170 Regent's Park Rd
NW1. **Map** 3 C1.
Tel 020-7722 1478.

Truefitt & Hill
71 St James's St SW1.
Map 12 F3.
Tel 020-7493 8496.

STATIONERY

Asprey
167 New Bond St W1.
Map 12 F3.
Tel 0870-905 0767.

The Filofax Centre
21 Conduit St W1.
Map 12 F2.
Tel 020-7499 0457.

Paperchase
213 Tottenham Court Rd
W1.
Map 5 A5.
Tel 020-7467 6200.

Shepherd's Bookbinders
76 Southampton Row
WC1.
Map 5 C5.
Tel 020-7831 1151.

Smythson
40 New Bond St W1.
Map 12 E2.
Tel 020-7629 8558.

Tessa Fantoni
73 Abbeville Rd SW4.
Tel 020-8673 1253.

INTERIORS

After Noah
121 Upper Street N1.
Map 6 F1.
Tel 020-7359 4281.

Aria
Barnsbury Hall,
Barnsbury St N1.
Map 6 F1.
Tel 020-7704 6222.

Bridgewater Pottery
81a Marylebone High St.
Map 4 D5.
Tel 020-7486 6897.
Also: 739 Fulham Road.
Map 17 C5.
Tel 020-7371 5264.

Cath Kidston
51 Marylebone High St
W1.
Map 4 D5.
Tel 020-7935 6555.

Conran Shop
Michelin House, 81
Fulham Rd SW3.
Map 19 A2.
Tel 020-7589 7401.

Contemporary Applied Arts
2 Percy St W1.
Map 13 A1.
Tel 020-7436 2344.

Contemporary Ceramics
Somerset House,
Strand WC2.
Map 14 D2.
Tel 020-7845 4600.

David Mellor
4 Sloane Sq SW1.
Map 20 D2.
Tel 020-7730 4259.

Divertimenti
33–34 Marylebone High St
W1.
Map 4 D5.
Tel 020-7935 0689.

Graham & Green
4 Elgin Crescent W11.
Map 9 B2.
Tel 020-7243 8908.

Heal's
196 Tottenham Court Rd
W1.
Map 5 A5.
Tel 020-7636 1666.

Irish Linen Company
Burlington Arcade W1.
Map 12 F3.
Tel 020-7493 8949.

Mint
2 North Terrace SW3.
Map 19 A1.
Tel 020-7224 4406.

Nicole Farhi Home
17 Clifford St W1.
Map 12 F3.
Tel 020-7494 9051.

Thomas Goode
19 South Audley St W1.
Map 12 D3.
Tel 020-7499 2823.

twentytwentyone
274 Upper St N1.
Map 6 F1.
Tel 020-7288 1996.

Waterford Wedgwood
173–174 Piccadilly W1.
Map 12 F3.
Tel 020-7629 2614.

Art and Antiques

London's art and antique shops are spread across the length and breadth of the capital city. While the more fashionable and more expensive dealers are mainly concentrated in a relatively small area bounded by Mayfair and St James's, other shops and galleries catering to a relatively modest budget are scattered over the rest of the city. Whether your taste is for Old Masters or young modern artists, Boule or Bauhaus, you are bound to find something of beauty in London that is within your financial means.

MAYFAIR

Cork Street is the centre of the British contemporary art world. The huge line-up of galleries offers work in varying degrees of the avant-garde. The biggest name to look out for is **Waddington Galleries**, and if you want to discover the flavour of the month, a stop here is a must. However, purchasing is only for the serious and rich collector. The **Mayor Gallery**, famous for Dada and Surrealism, was the first gallery to open in the street. **Redfern Gallery** shows mainstream modern art while **Flowers Central**, part of a growing modern-gallery chain, has some unusual British pieces. A couple of doors down, **Browse and Darby Gallery** sells 19th- and 20th-century British and French paintings as well as contemporary works.

Also look into Clifford Street, where **Maas Gallery** excels in Victorian masters, and Sackville Street for **Henry Sotheran's** rare books and prints. Walk down Dover Street towards Piccadilly and, on your right you'll see a discreet sign for the **Piccadilly Gallery**, which sells modern British pictures. Although it is tucked away in the building's basement, casual visitors are always welcome.

Nearby, New Bond Street is the centre of the fine antiques trade in London. If it's Turner watercolours or Louis XV furniture you're after, this is the place. A walk up from Piccadilly takes you past the lush portals of **Richard Green** (which also has a gallery in Dover Street) and the **Fine Art Society**, among other extremely smart galleries. For jewellery and objets d'art visit **David Aaron Ancient Art** and **Grays Antique Market**; for silver go to **S J Phillips**; and for 18th-century British furniture and art, try **Mallet Antiques**.

Even if you are not a buyer, these galleries are fascinating places to visit, so don't be afraid to walk in – you can learn more from an hour spent here than you can from weeks of studying text books. Also on New Bond Street are two of the big London auction houses, Bonhams and Sotheby's.

ST. JAMES'S

South of Piccadilly lies a maze of 18th-century streets. This is gentlemen's club country *(see Pall Mall p92)* and the galleries mostly reflect the traditional nature of the area. The centre is Duke Street, home of Old Master dealers, **Johnny van Haeften** and **Derek Johns**. Nearby, on King Street, you will find the main salerooms of **Christie's**, the well-known auction house where Van Goghs and Picassos change hands for millions. On the corner of Bury Street, celebrating past masculine pleasures is the sophisticated **Pullman Gallery**, which specializes in automobile art and collectables, vintage cocktail shakers, racy cigarette cases and other bar accessories.

Walk back up Bury Street past several interesting galleries, including the **Tryon Gallery** for traditional British sporting pictures and fine sculptures. Also duck into Ryder Street to take in **Chris Beetle's** gallery of works by illustrators and caricaturists.

KNIGHTSBRIDGE

If you walk around to the back of **Harrods** *(see p321)*, you'll find the beginning of pretty Walton Street, which is lined with art galleries, traditional interior shops and boutiques. As you would expect in this exclusive area, prices are high. On nearby Brompton Road the **Crane Kalman** gallery shows an enticing variety of contemporary art. Not far away is **Harvey Nichols** *(see p321)*, Knightsbridge's other swish department store. Motcomb Street houses some notable galleries, including the fascinating **Mathaf Gallery**, which features 19th-century British and European paintings of the Arab world.

PIMLICO ROAD

The antique shops that line this road tend to cater predominantly for the pricey requirements of the interior decorator. This is where to come if you are searching for an Italian leather screen or a silver-encrusted ram's skull. Of particular fascination is **Westenholz**. While he doesn't deal in antiques, the Queen's nephew, furniture designer **Viscount Linley** produces some beautiful pieces that could pass as such, as well as contemporary designs. The finely crafted accessories, such as inlaid wooden boxes and frames, make great gifts.

EAST AND WEST

London's East End is a growth area for contemporary art. In addition to the famous **White Cube Gallery** in Hoxton Square and **Flowers East** in Kingsland Road, there is a cluster of art dealers and galleries in **The Tea Building** on nearby Shoreditch High Street. The **Approach Tavern** combines an upstairs gallery with a good pub, frequented by local artists.

On the other side of the river in south east London, **Purdy Hicks**, based in a converted warehouse near Tate Modern, is great for contemporary British painting. Over in Mayfair, **Eyestorm** is a gallery that shows the work of both leading and emerging artists.

The **Oxo Tower Wharf**, in a landmark Thameside building topped by a good restaurant, is a hive of creativity, housing over 30 design and craft studios. You can find everything from handwoven textiles and jewellery to homewares and fashion. Among the highlights are Black + Blum's innovative, affordable interior designs – for example, a lamp in the shape of a reading figure, made up of a lightbulb "holding" a book shade. Bodo Sperlain's delicate modern china and Studio Fusion's striking enamel pieces are also a draw for the visitors.

There are also some very interesting contemporary galleries in the vicinity of Portobello Road and Westbourne Grove. Some of the popular names include, **East West Gallery** for contemporary art, **Themes & Variations**, which combines striking post-war and contemporary furniture and decorative art, and **The State of the Art**, selling works ranging from pop art and graffiti to fine art and photography.

A browse along Kensington Church Street in west London will reveal everything from Arts and Crafts furniture to Staffordshire dogs in a concentration of small antiques emporia.

NORTH

High-profile American dealer Larry Gagosian has been at the forefront of the regeneration of famously sleazy King's Cross by opening his second gallery here, in a capacious former garage. Expect world-class contemporary names as well as lesser-known artists at **Gagosian Gallery**. **Victoria Miro's** massive Victorian warehouse in Islington is a showcase for British as well as young international talent. At its two spaces in the same quiet Marylebone Street, the **Lisson Gallery** often features cutting-edge installations. **Thompson's Gallery** has locations in Marylebone and the City, selling a diverse mix of appealing if somewhat mainstream current British art.

AFFORDABLE ART

For the chance to acquire a work by what could become one of the big names of the future, visit the **Contemporary Art Society**. Its annual ARTFutures market showcases the work of more than 100 artists, their prices run from £100 into the thousands.

Open seven days a week all year round, **Will's Art Warehouse** in Putney sells pieces from £50–£3,000. This friendly gallery offers a wide variety of art to choose from and holds a new exhibition every six weeks. The owner founded the aptly named Affordable Art Fair, which takes place twice a year in Battersea Park.

PHOTOGRAPHY

The largest collection of original photographs for sale in the country is at the **Photographers' Gallery**. **Special Photographers Company** is well known for selling top-quality work by unknown artists as well as some famous photographic names. **Hamiltons Gallery** is worth visiting, especially during its major exhibitions.

Michael Hoppen's new three-floor space in Chelsea shows both vintage and current works. If you want to take home a piece of London's rock n' roll heritage, the **Rock Archive** in Islington, is a great source of limited-edition prints of British music legends such as Paul Weller posing with Pete Townshend or Mick Jagger jamming with Ronnie Wood.

To pick up an interesting work on a budget, head to **55 Max**, where limited-edition framed prints often cost £55. It showcases a range of subjects and styles by young photographers and photojournalists, from moody London cityscapes and abstractions to fashion and celebrity shots.

BRIC-À-BRAC AND COLLECTABLES

For smaller, more affordable pieces, it's worth going to one of the established London markets, such as Portobello Road, Alfies Antique Market, Camden Passage *(see p340)* or Bermondsey *(see p339)*, which is the main antiques market, catering to the trade. Conveniently situated in the city's main shopping district, Grays Antique Markets *(see p340)* have some great specialist dealers, but the prices are a bit higher than elsewhere given the location, while further afield, Greenwich Market *(see p340)* is well worth a rummage and may throw up some bargains. Many high streets out of the centre of town have covered markets of specialist stalls.

Cary Grant's small shop hidden on a side street near Sadlers Wells contains a collector's cache of immaculate post-war ceramics by the modern designers of the day, including the young Terence Conran.

AUCTIONS

If you are confident enough, auctions are a much cheaper way to buy art or antiques, but be sure to read the small print in the catalogue, which usually costs around £15. Bidding is simple – you need to register, take a number, then raise your hand when the lot you want comes up. The auctioneer will see your bid. It's as easy as that, and can be great fun.

The main auction houses in London are **Christie's Fine Art Auctioneers**, **Sotheby's Auctioneers** and **Bonhams**. Don't forget Christie's saleroom in Kensington, and Sotheby's premises in Olympia, which both offer art and antiques for the modest budget. Bonhams' second London saleroom in Knightsbridge holds weekly auctions of affordable antiques and collectables.

DIRECTORY

MAYFAIR

Browse and Darby Gallery
19 Cork St W1.
Map 12 F3.
Tel 020-7734 7984.

David Aaron Ancient Art
22 Berkeley Square W1.
Map 12 E3.
Tel 020-7491 9588.

Fine Art Society
148 New Bond St W1.
Map 12 E2.
Tel 020-7629 5116.

Flowers Central
21 Cork St W1.
Map 12 F3.
Tel 020-7439 7766.

Grays Antique Markets
58 Davies St & 1-7 Davies Mews W1. **Map** 12 E2.
Tel 020-7629 7034.

Henry Sotheran
2–5 Sackville St W1.
Map 12 F3.
Tel 020-7439 6151.

Maas Gallery
15a Clifford St W1.
Map 12 F3.
Tel 020-7734 2302.

Mallet Antiques
141 New Bond St W1.
Map 12 E2.
Tel 020-7499 7411.

Mayor Gallery
22a Cork St W1.
Map 12 F3.
Tel 020-7734 3558.

Piccadilly Gallery
43 Dover St W1.
Map 12 F3.
Tel 020-7629 2875.

Redfern Gallery
20 Cork St W1.
Map 12 F3.
Tel 020-7734 1732.

Richard Green
33 & 147 New Bond St.
Also: 39 Dover St W1.
Map 12 E2.
Tel 020-7493 3939.

S J Phillips
139 New Bond St W1.
Map 12 E2.
Tel 020-7629 6261.

Waddington Galleries
11, 12, 34 Cork St W1.
Map 12 F3.
Tel 020-7851 2200.

ST. JAMES'S

Chris Beetle
8 & 10 Ryder St SW1.
Map 12 F3.
Tel 020-7839 7551.

Derek Johns
12 Duke St SW1.
Map 12 F3.
Tel 020-7839 7671.

Johnny van Haeften
13 Duke St SW1.
Map 12 F3.
Tel 020-7930 3062.

Pullman Gallery
14 King St SW1.
Map 12 F4.
Tel 020-7930 9595.

Tryon Gallery
7 Bury St SW1.
Map 12 F3.
Tel 020-7839 8083.

KNIGHTSBRIDGE

Crane Kalman
178 Brompton Rd SW3.
Map 19 B1.
Tel 020-7584 7566.

Mathaf Gallery
24 Motcomb St SW1.
Map 12 D5.
Tel 020-7235 0010.

PIMLICO ROAD

Viscount Linley
60 Pimlico Rd SW1.
Map 20 D2.
Tel 020-7730 7300.

Westenholz
80–82 Pimlico Rd SW1.
Map 20 D2.
Tel 020-7824 8090.

EAST AND WEST

Approach Tavern
1st Floor, 47
Approach Rd E2.
Tel 020-8983 3878.

East West Gallery
8 Blenheim Cres W11.
Map 8 D4.
Tel 020-7229 7981.

Eyestorm
27 Hill St W1.
Map 12 E3.
Tel 0845-643 2001.

Flowers East
82 Kingsland Rd E2.
Tel 020-7920 7777.

Oxo Tower Wharf
Bargehouse St SE1.
Map 14 E3.
Tel 020-7021 1600.

Purdy Hicks
65 Hopton St SE1.
Map 14 F3.
Tel 020-7401 9229.

The State of the Art
281 Portobello Rd W10.
Map 9 A1. **Tel** 0770 868 932, 0184-428 1812.

The Tea Building
56 Shoreditch High St E1.
Map 8 D4.
Tel 020-7729 2973.

Themes & Variations
231 Westbourne Grove
W11. **Map** 9 B2.
Tel 020-7727 5531.

White Cube Gallery
Hoxton Square N1.
Map 7 C3.
Tel 020-7930 5373.

NORTH

Gagosian Gallery
6–24 Britannia St WC1.
Map 5 C3.
Tel 020-7841 9960.

Lisson Gallery
29 & 52-54 Bell St NW1.
Map 3 B5.
Tel 020-7724 2739.

Thompson's Gallery
76 Marylebone High St W1.
Map 4 D5.
Tel 020-7935 3595.

Victoria Miro
16 Wharf Rd N1.
Map 7 A2.
Tel 020-7336 8109.

AFFORDABLE ART

Contemporary Art Society
11–15 Emerald St WC1.
Map 6 D5.
Tel 020-7831 1243.

Will's Art Warehouse
180 Lower Richmond Rd
SW15.
Tel 020-8246 4840.

PHOTOGRAPHY

Hamiltons Gallery
13 Carlos Place London
W1. **Map** 12 E3.
Tel 020-7499 9493.

55 Max
6 Lonsdale Rd,
Queen's Park NW6.
Tel 020-7625 3774.

Michael Hoppen
3 Jubilee Place SW3.
Map 19 B3.
Tel 020-7352 3649.

Photographers' Gallery
16–18 Ramilies St W1.
Map 12 F1.
Tel 0845-262 1618.

Rock Archive
110 Islington High St N1.
Map 6 F2.
Tel 020-7704 0598.

Special Photographers Company
236 Westbourne Park Rd
W11. **Map** 9 B1.
Tel 020-7221 3489.

BRIC-À-BRAC AND COLLECTABLES

Cary Grant
18 Arlington Way EC1.
Map 6 E3.
Tel 020-7713 1122.

AUCTIONS

Bonhams, W & FC, Auctioneers
Montpelier St SW7.
Map 11 B5.
Tel 020-7393 3900.
Also: 101 New Bond St
W1. **Map** 12 E2.
Tel 020-7447 7447.

Christie's Fine Art Auctioneers
8 King St SW1. **Map** 12 F4.
Tel 020-7839 9060.
Also: 85 Old Brompton
Road SW7. **Map** 18 F2.
Tel 020-7930 6074.

Sotheby's Auctioneers
34–35 New Bond St W1.
Map 12 E2.
Tel 020-7293 5000.
Also: Hammersmith Rd
W14.
Map 17 A1.
Tel 020-7293 5555.

Markets

Even if you're not looking for cut-priced cabbages or a silk sari, it's worth paying a visit to one of London's crowded, colourful markets. Many mix English traditions with those of more recent immigrants, creating an exotic atmosphere and a fascinating patchwork quilt of merchandise. At some, the seasoned cockney hawkers have honed their sales patter to an entertaining art, which reaches fever pitch just before closing time as they advertise ever-plummeting prices. Keep your wits about you and your hand on your purse and join in the fun. For details go to www.visitlondon.com.

Antiquarius

131–141 King's Road SW3.
Map 19 B3. ⊖ *Sloane Sq.*
▦ 19, 22. **Open** *10am–6pm Mon–Sat.*

This former 1920s gentlemen's club and pool hall claims to be London's oldest antique centre, which has been in operation since the 1960s. Behind its smart, green awnings are more or less 100 stalls. The dynamic merchants of the market include specialists in vintage Louis Vuitton luggage, sporting and equestrian antiques, Art Deco furniture, costume and fine jewellery.

Bermondsey Market (New Caledonian Market)

Long Lane and Bermondsey St SE1.
Map 15 C5. ⊖ *London Bridge, Borough.* **Open** *4am–3pm Fri. Starts closing midday. See p182.*

Bermondsey is the gathering point for London's antique traders every Friday. Serious collectors start early and scrutinize the paintings, the silver and the vast array of old jewellery. Browsers might uncover some interesting curiosities but most bargains go before 9am.

Berwick Street Market

Berwick St W1. **Map** 13 A1.
⊖ *Piccadilly Circus, Leicester Sq.*
Open *9am–6pm Mon–Sat. See p108.*

The spirited costermongers of Soho's Berwick Street sell some of the cheapest and most attractive fruit and vegetables in the West End. Spanish black radish, star fruit and Italian plum tomatoes are among the produce you might find here, in addition to the various nuts and sweets. The market is good for fabrics and cheap household goods too, as well as for leather handbags and delicatessen. Separated from Berwick Street by a seedy passageway is the quieter Rupert Street market, where stallholders sell cheap street fashion.

Borough Market

Southwark St SE1. **Map** 14 F3.
⊖ *London Bridge.* **Open** *11am–5pm Thu, noon–6pm Fri, 8am–5pm Sat. See p176.*

On one of London's most ancient trading sites, Borough has for many years been a wholesale market catering to the restaurant and hotel trade. Now open to the public from Thursday to Saturday, the award-winning market has a reputation as London's premier centre for fine foods, selling a vast array of British and international foodstuffs. Among the cornucopia is organic meat, fish and produce, top-quality handmade cheeses, breads, sweets, chocolates, coffees and teas and also soaps. It's a favourite foraging ground for the city's celebrity chefs.

Brick Lane Market

Brick Lane E1. **Map** 8 E5.
⊖ *Shoreditch, Liverpool St, Aldgate East.* **Open** *8am–2pm Sun. See pp170–1.*

This massively popular East End jamboree is at its best around its gloriously frayed edges. Pick through the mish-mash of junk sold on Bethnal Green Road or head east on Cheshire Street, past the new outcrop of fashionable home-design and gift shops, to explore the indoor stalls, packed with tatty furniture and old books. Much of the action takes place in cobbled, Sclater Street and the lots on either side. Here you'll find everything from fresh shellfish and trainers to old power tools and new bicycles. Further south on Brick Lane itself, the trendy boutiques and cafés give way to spice shops and curry restaurants in this centre for London's Bangladeshi community.

Brixton Market

Electric Ave SW9. ⊖ *Brixton.*
Open *8am–6pm Mon, Tue, Thu–Sat; 8am–3pm Wed.*

This market offers a wonderful assortment of Afro-Caribbean food, from goats' meat, pigs' feet and salt fish to plantain, yams and breadfruit. There is an abundance of produce in the large Brixton Village and Market Row arcades, where exotic fish are a highlight. You'll also find Afro-style wigs, strange herbs and potions, traditional African ensembles and fabrics, and children's toys. From record stalls, the bass of raw reggae pounds through this cosmopolitan market like a heartbeat.

Broadway Market

Broadway Market, between Andrews Rd & Westgate St E8. ▦ 394 .
Open *8am–6pm Sat.*

Although this market is a bit tricky to get to because it's not served by the tube, it's worth getting a bus from Islington or walking from Bethnal Green tube. One of London's oldest, Broadway Market had gone into decline until its rebirth as a regular organic farmers' market. On Saturdays the historic street running between London Fields and the Regent's Canal, comes alive with around 40 stalls selling fruit and vegetables, cheeses, baked goods, meats and confectionery. Also lining Broadway Market are some interesting, arty shops, catering to the young creative types who have been colonizing this part of Hackney over the past couple of decades. Black Truffle (No.74), owned by shoemaker Melissa Needham, stocks a range of accessories made by independent designers – both local and international – while textile designer Barley Massey sells her own unusual designs and those of others at Fabrications (No.7). L'Eau à la Bouche (No.49) is a superior deli offering everthing from charcuterie to fruit tarts. There are also a couple of contemporary galleries such as Flaca (No.69) and Seven Seven (No.75–77). When it's time to refuel, duck into the Dove pub (No.24–28) for a Belgian brew.

Camden Lock Market

Chalk Farm Road NW1. ⊖ *Camden Town.* **Open** *9.30am–5.30pm Mon–Fri, 10am–6pm Sat and Sun.*

Camden Lock Market has grown swiftly since its opening in 1974, spreading along Chalk Farm Road and Camden High Street. Crafts, new and second-hand street fashion, wholefoods, books, records and antiques, form the bulk of the goods that a shopper can choose from. Often, thousands of young people come here simply to enjoy the vibrant atmosphere, especially at weekends when Camden Lock is abuzz with activity *(see p246)*.

Camden Passage Market

Camden Passage N1. **Map** 6 F1. 🚇
Angel. **Open** 9am–6pm Wed, Sat.

Camden Passage is a quiet walkway where cafés nestle among
bijou antique shops. Prints, silverware, 19th-century magazines,
jewellery and toys are among the
many collectables that are on show.
Don't miss the tiny shops tucked
away in the atmospherically poky
Pierrepont Arcade; one is precari-
ously stacked with 18th and 19th-
century porcelain; another specializes in antique puzzles and
games. Jubilee Photographica deals
in photographs from the 19th
century onwards. The passage is
also lined with shops – Annie's
Vintage Clothes is known for
pristine 1920s–40s frocks, while
Origin sells classic 20th-century
furniture. There's a specialist
book market on Thursdays.

Chapel Market

Chapel Market N1. **Map** 6 E2.
🚇 Angel. **Open** 9am–3.30pm Tue,
Wed, Fri, Sat; 9am–1pm Thu, Sun.

This is one of London's most
traditional and exuberant street
markets. Weekends are best; the
fruit and vegetables are varied and
cheap, the fish stalls are the finest
in the area, there are also stalls selling European delicacies and
cheeses and a wealth of bargain
household goods and clothes.

Church Street Market

Church St NW8 and Bell St NW1.
Map 3 A5. 🚇 Edgware Rd.
Open 8am–6pm Mon–Sat.

Like many of London's markets,
Church Street reaches a crescendo
at the weekend. On Friday and
Saturday, stalls selling cheap
clothes, household goods, fish,
cheese and antiques join the
everyday fruit and vegetable
stalls. Alfies Antique Market
(No.13–25) houses around 100
dealers selling everything from
jewellery to furniture.
   There is also a cluster of
interesting stand-alone antique
furniture shops, plus the fascinating
Gallery of Antique Costume and
Textiles (No.2), which showcases
immaculate garments dating back
as far as the 17th century.

Columbia Road Market

Columbia Rd E2. **Map** 8 D3.
🚇 Shoreditch, Old St.
Open 8am– 3pm Sun. See p171.

This is the perfect place to come
to buy greenery and blossoms,
or just to enjoy the fragrances
and colours. Cut flowers, plants,
shrubs, seedlings and pots are all

sold at about half their normal
prices on a Sunday morning in this
charming Victorian street. (During
December, as you might expect,
there's a brisk trade in Christmas
trees.) There are also some lovely
shops that keep market hours,
such as Angela Flanders' pretty
perfumerie (No.96), Salon
for vintage jewellery and cufflinks
(No.142) and hip hatter, Fred
Bare (No.118).
   When you're shopped out, take
tea at Treacle (No.160), which
turns out cute retro cupcakes and
classic jam sponge cakes, plus
cups of proper tea to wash them
down. There is also a selection of
vintage and modern china for
sale. People with a sweet tooth
can snack on deep-fried prawns
from hole in the wall, Lee's
Seafoods (No.134).

Earlham Street Market

Earlham St WC2. **Map** 13 B2.
🚇 Covent Garden. **Open**
10am–4pm Mon–Sat.

Situated on a short road just off
Shaftesbury Avenue, this market is
a small affair. Several stalls sell a
range of items from exotic flowers
and secondhand clothes to
fashion jewellery and accessories.

East Street Market

East St SE17. 🚇 Elephant and
Castle. **Open** 8am–5pm Tue–Fri,
8am–6.30pm Sat; 8am–2pm, Sun.

East Street Market's high spot is
Sunday, when more than 250
stalls fill the narrow street and a
small plant and flower market is
set up on Blackwood Street. The
majority of traders sell clothes,
accessories and household goods,
although there is plenty of British
and Afro-Caribbean produce, fish
and other delicacies. Charlie
Chaplin (see p37) was born in this
street and sought inspiration for
his characters in the area.

Gabriel's Wharf and Riverside Walk Markets

56 Upper Ground and Riverside Walk
SE1. **Map** 14 E3. 🚇 Waterloo.
Gabriel's Wharf Open 11am–6pm
Tue–Sun; **Riverside Walk open**
noon–7pm Sat, Sun. See p191.

Little shops filled with ceramics,
paintings and jewellery surround
a bandstand in Gabriel's Wharf
where jazz groups sometimes play
in the summer. A few stalls are set
up around the courtyard, selling
ethnic clothing and handmade
jewellery and pottery. The book
market under Waterloo Bridge
includes a good selection of new
and old Penguin paperbacks.

Grays Antique Markets

58 Davies St & 1–7 Davies Mews W1.
Map 12 E2. 🚇 Bond Street. **Open**
10am–6pm Mon–Fri; 11am–5pm Sat.

Conveniently placed in the West
End, Grays probably isn't the
place to bag a bargain – the
liveried doorman is a tip-off that
this place is posh – but it makes a
pleasant place to browse. There
are some lovely pieces here, from
costume jewellery and fabulous
vintage fashion to enamel boxes
and modern first editions from
Biblion bookseller.

Greenwich Market

College Approach SE10. **Map** 23 B2.
🚊 Greenwich. 🚇 Cutty Sark DLR.
Open 10am–5.30pm Wed–Sun.

At weekends, the area west of
Hotel Ibis accommodates dozens
of trestle tables piled with coins,
medals, banknotes, second-hand
books, Art Deco furniture, assorted
bric-à-brac and vintage clothing.
The covered crafts market
specializes in wooden toys, clothes
made by young designers, hand-
made jewellery and accessories.

Jubilee and Apple Markets

Covent Gdn Piazza WC2.
Map 13 C2. 🚊 Covent Gdn.
Open 9am–5pm daily.

Covent Garden has become the
centre of London streetlife, with
some of the capital's best busking.
Both these markets sell crafts and
designs. The Apple Market, inside
the Piazza where the famous fruit
and vegetable market was housed
(see p114), has knitwear, jewellery
and novelty goods. Jubilee Hall
sells antiques on Monday, crafts at
the weekend, and a large selection
of clothes, handbags, cosmetics
and tacky mementoes in between.
During the first weekend of
November, the Covent Garden
Market is the venue for renowned
food writer, Henrietta Green's
Food Lovers' Fair. During that time
it comes alive with around 100
speciality food producers from all
over Britain. The event also
features cookery demonstrations
and celebrity chefs.

Leadenhall Market

Whittington Ave EC3. **Map** 15 C2.
🚇 Bank, Monument. **Open**
7am–4pm Mon–Fri. See p159.

There has been a marketplace
on this site since medieval times,
but the present spectacular, glass-
roofed structure was built in
1881. Leadenhall Market was
traditionally famous for fish, meat
and poultry, but only fishmonger

HS Linwood & Sons remains. The smart, red and green façades now bear the names of upmarket clothing chains, restaurants, pubs and gift shops. Leadenhall does, however, retain something of its reputation as a centre of fine food. More than a dozen stalls set up shop on the cobblestones beneath this dramatic structure Monday to Friday from 11am to 4pm. Wares include European cheeses, cured meats, baked goods, condiments and other gourmet goods as well.

Leather Lane Market

Leather Lane EC1. **Map** 6 E5.
🚇 *Farringdon, Chancery Lane.*
Open *10.30am–2pm Mon–Fri.*

This ancient street, originally called Leveroun Lane, has played host to a market for over 300 years. The history of the Lane, however, has nothing to do with leather. Stalls here sell cut-price high-street clothes, plus shoes, bags, jewellery and accessories. All are well worth having a browse through.

Marylebone Farmers' Market

Cramer St carpark, behind Marylebone High St W1. **Map** 4 D5.
🚇 *Baker Street, Bond Street.*
Open *10am–2pm Sun.*

In response to Britain's interest in local organic produce, weekly markets have sprung up all over the city. This enables farmers and other producers to sell directly to the public. Marylebone is the largest and most central, offering seasonal fruit and veg, dairy products, fish, meat, breads, preserves and sauces. There is also a line-up of excellent gourmet shops in adjacent Moxon Street, including a renowned rare-breed pork butcher, the Ginger Pig, and La Fromagerie delicatessen with its extensive cheese cave. Other locations include Islington Green and the carpark behind Waterstone's, Notting Hill.

Old Spitalfields Market

Commercial St E1. **Map** 8 E5.
🚇 *Aldgate East, Liverpool Street.*
Open *10am–4pm Mon–Fri,*
9am–5pm Sun. See p170.

The main market is on a Sunday, and is a mecca for those interested in the latest street fashion trends. Many young designers have stalls, and prices are also reasonable. The stalls are of mixed quality, so you have to really search for the gems. The organic food stalls and a selection of cafés make it a good brunch venue any day. A varying number of stalls are open during the week.

Petticoat Lane Market

Middlesex St E1. **Map** 16 D1.
🚇 *Liverpool St, Aldgate, Aldgate East.* **Open** *9am–2pm Sun (Wentworth St 10am–2.30pm Mon–Fri). See p169.*

Probably the most famous of all London's street markets, Petticoat Lane continues to attract many thousands of visitors and locals every Sunday. The prices may not be as cheap as some of those to be found elsewhere, but the sheer volume of leather goods, clothes (the Lane's traditional strong point), watches, cheap jewellery and toys more than make up for that. A variety of fast-food sellers do a brisk trade catering for the bustling crowds that throng the market on a weekend.

Piccadilly Crafts Market

St James's Church, Piccadilly W1.
Map 13 A3. 🚇 *Piccadilly Circus, Green Park.* **Open** *10am–6pm Wed–Sat.*

Many of the markets in the Middle Ages were held in churchyards and Piccadilly Crafts Market is rekindling that ancient tradition. It is aimed mostly at visitors to London rather than locals, and the merchandise on display ranges from tacky T-shirts to wooden toys. All are spread out in the shadow of Wren's beautiful church *(see p90)*.

Portobello Road Market

Portobello Rd W10. **Map** 9 C3.
🚇 *Notting Hill Gate, Ladbroke Grove.* **Open** *antiques and junk: 5.30am–5.30pm Sat. General market: 9am–5pm Mon–Wed, Fri, Sat; 9am–1pm Thu. See p219.*

Portobello Road is really three or four markets rolled into one. The Notting Hill end has more than 1,000 stalls in numerous arcades and on the street, displaying a compendium of objets d'art, jewellery, old medals, paintings and silverware. Most stalls are managed by experts, so bargains are very rare. Further down the gentle hill, antiques give way to fruit and vegetables.

The next transformation comes under the Westway flyover, where young fashion designers sell inexpensive creations alongside second-hand clothes, record and food stalls on Fridays and Saturdays. It's also worth venturing into the covered Portobello Green market, which has an interesting mix of small shops selling everything from avant-garde fashion to kitsch cushions and lingerie. From this point on, the market becomes increasingly shabby.

Ridley Road Market

Ridley Rd E8. 🚆 *Dalston.* **Open** *9am–3pm Mon–Wed. 9am–noon Thu. 9am–5pm Fri, Sat.*

Early last century Ridley Road was a centre of the Jewish community. Since then, Asians, Greeks, Turks and West Indians have also settled in the area and the market is a lively celebration of this cultural mix. Highlights include the 24-hour bagel bakery, shanty-town shacks selling green bananas and reggae records, colourful drapery stalls and cheap fruit and vegetables.

Roman Road Market

Roman Rd, between Parnell Rd and St Stephen's Rd E3. 🚇 *Bethnal Green.*
🚌 *8.* **Open** *10am–3pm Tue & Thu; 9am–4pm Sat. Farmers' market 1st Sat of month.*

This lively market established in the 19th century has a real East End flavour and traditionally sells everything from cheap bedding and fashion to cut-price cleaning products and fruit and veg. Chances are that you'll be treated to some colourful cockney patter from the stallholders trying to drum up custom. Recently, some more unusual vendors have been added to the mix, thus offering a unique variety to please the customers.

When you pay a visit to the Roman Road Market, you may just be tempted to buy some of the handmade jewellery, vintage clothes or antiques being sold at the stalls.

Shepherd's Bush Market

Goldhawk Rd W12.
🚇 *Goldhawk Road, Shepherd's Bush.* **Open** *9am–6pm Mon–Sat.*

A focal point for many of the local ethnic communities, this rambling market contains an impressive volume of eclectic wares.

West Indian food, Afro wigs, Asian spices, exotic fish, rugs and other household goods are just some of the major attractions. There are acres of cheap clothing for every occasion, from floral flannel nighties and men's suits to clubwear and elaborately beaded wedding gowns. Cheap fabric stalls are a highlight of the Shepherd's Bush Market, and there is even an on-site tailor and barber, if you please.

ENTERTAINMENT IN LONDON

Café sign advertising free live music

London has the enormous, multi-layered variety of entertainment that only the great cities of the world can provide, and, as always, the city's historical backdrop adds depth to the experience. While few things could be more contemporary than dancing the night away in style at a famed nightclub such as Café de Paris or Heaven, you could also choose to spend the evening picturing the ghosts of long-dead Hamlets pacing ancient boards in the shadow of one of the living legends that grace the West End theatres today. There's a healthy, innovative fringe theatre scene too, plus world-class ballet and opera in fabled venues such as Sadler's Wells, the Royal Opera House and the Coliseum. In London you'll be able to hear the best music, ranging from classical, jazz and rock to rhythm and blues, while dedicated movie buffs can choose from hundreds of different films each night, both in large, multi-screen complexes and excellent small independent cinemas. Sports fans can watch a game of cricket at Lords, cheer on oarsmen on the Thames or eat strawberries and cream at Wimbledon. Should you be feeling adventurous and sporty yourself, you could try going for a horse ride along Rotten Row in Hyde Park. There are festivals, celebrations and sports to attend, and there's plenty for children to do, too – in fact, there's plenty for everyone to do. Whatever you want, you'll be sure to find it on offer in London; it's just a question of knowing where to look.

Cultural classics: a concert at Kenwood House *(top)*; open-air theatre at Regent's Park *(above left)*; performers at the Coliseum *(above right)*

INFORMATION SOURCES

For details of events in London, check the comprehensive weekly listings and review magazine *Time Out* (published every Tuesday), sold at most newsagents and many bookshops. The commuter newspaper *Metro* (week days) and London's evening newspaper, the *Evening Standard*, are both free and give brief daily listings. The *Independent* has daily listings and also reviews a different arts sector every day, plus a weekly round-up section, "The Information"; the *Guardian* has arts reviews in its G2 section every day and weekly listings in "The Guide" on Saturday. The *Independent, Guardian* and *The Times* all have lists of ticket availability.

Specialized news sheets, brochures and advance listings are distributed free in the foyers of theatres, concert halls, cinemas and arts complexes such as the South Bank and Barbican. Tourist information offices and hotel foyers often have the same publications. Fly posters advertise forthcoming events on billboards everywhere.

The Society of London Theatre (SOLT) publishes an informative free broadsheet every fortnight, available in many theatre foyers. It tends to concentrate on mainstream theatres, but does provide invaluable information about what's on. The National Theatre and the Royal Shakespeare Company also publish free broadsheets detailing future performances, distributed at the theatres.

SOLT's website (www.officiallondontheatre.co.uk) provides full details of current productions. It also has news,

interviews, access
information and online
ticket booking. Many theatres
operate a faxback service
which enables you to see a
seating plan showing the
unsold seats for
any performance.

Line-up from the Royal Ballet, on stage at Covent Garden

BOOKING TICKETS

Some of the more popular
shows and plays in London's
West End – the latest Lloyd
Webber musical for instance –
can be totally booked out for
weeks and even months
ahead and you will find it
impossible to purchase any
tickets. This is not the norm,
though, and most tickets
will be available on the
night, especially if you would
be prepared to queue in
front of the theatre for
returns. However, for a stress-
free holiday it helps to
book tickets in
advance; this will
ensure that you get
the day, time and
seats that you want.
You can book
tickets from the box
office in person, by
telephone, online or
by post. Quite a few
hotels have concierges
or porters who will
give advice on where
to go and arrange
tickets for you.

Palace Theatre
plaque

Box offices are usually
open from about 10am–8pm,
and accept payment by cash,
credit card, traveller's cheque
or else a personal UK cheque

when supported by a cheque
guarantee card. Many venues
will now sell unclaimed or
returned tickets just before
the performance; ask at the
box office for the queuing
times. To reserve seats by
telephone, call the box office
and either pay on arrival or
send payment – seats are
usually held for three
days. Some venues
now have separate
phone numbers for
your credit card
bookings – check
before you call.
Reserve your seat,
and always take
your credit card with
you when you collect
your ticket. Some smaller
venues do not accept
credit cards.

DISABLED VISITORS

Many London venues are old
buildings and were not
originally designed with
disabled visitors in mind, but

a lot of facilities have been
updated, particularly to give
access to those using wheel-
chairs, or for those with
hearing difficulties.

Telephone the box office
prior to your visit to reserve
the special seating places or
equipment, which are often
limited. Special discounts
may be available: for details
and information on facilities
call Artsline (020-7388 2227,
www.artsline.org.uk).

TRANSPORT

Night buses (see p383) are
now the preferred late-night
mode of transport, or phone
for a cab from the venue. If
you find yourself outside the
city centre late at night, do
not rely on being able to
hail a black taxi quickly in
the street. Never take an
unlicensed mini-cab. The
Underground usually runs
until just after midnight, but
check the timetables in the
stations (see pp380–81).

BOOKING AGENCIES

The major
listings
magazines

Tickets are also available from agencies. Try the theatre box office first;
if no seats are available there, find out
the standard prices before going to
an agency. Most, but not all, are reputable. Agencies advertising top show
tickets for "tonight" may really have them,
and they may be a fair price. If you order
by phone, tickets will be posted to you
or sent to the theatre for you to collect.
Commission should be a standard 22%.
Some shows waive the agency fee by
paying the commission themselves; this is
usually advertised, and agencies should then
charge standard box office prices. Always compare prices, try to avoid agencies in bureaux de
change, and do not be tempted to buy from ticket
touts or unofficial Internet sources.

Ticket booth in Leicester Square

London's Theatres

London offers an extraordinary range of theatrical entertainment – this is one of the world's great stages, and, at its best, standards of quality are extremely high. Despite their legendary reputation for reserve, the British are passionate about theatre and London's theatres reflect every nuance of this passion. You can stroll along a street of West End theatres and find a sombre Samuel Beckett, Brecht or Chekhov play showing next door to some absurdly frothy farce like *No Sex Please, We're British!* Amid such diversity there is always something to appeal to everyone.

WEST END THEATRE

There is a distinct glamour to the West End theatres. Perhaps it is the glittering lights of the foyer and the impressively ornate interiors, or maybe it is their hallowed reputations – but whatever it is, the old theatres retain a magic all of their own.

The West End billboards always feature a generous sprinkling of world-famous performers such as Judi Dench, Kenneth Branagh, John Malkovich and Kevin Spacey.

The major commercial theatres cluster along Shaftesbury Avenue and the Haymarket and around Covent Garden and Charing Cross Road. Unlike the national theatres, most West End theatres survive only on profits; they do not receive any state subsidy. They rely on an army of ever-hopeful "angels" (financial backers) and producers to keep the old traditions alive.

Many theatres are historical landmarks, such as the classic **Theatre Royal Drury Lane**, established in 1663 *(see p115)*, and the elegant **Theatre Royal Haymarket** – both superb examples of early 19th-century buildings. Another to note is the **Palace** *(see p108)*, with its terracotta exterior and imposing position right on Cambridge Circus.

NATIONAL THEATRE

The **National Theatre** is based in the Southbank Centre *(see p188)*. Here, the large, open-staged Olivier, the proscenium-staged Lyttelton and the small, flexible Cottesloe offer a range of size and style, making it possible to produce every kind of theatre from large, extravagant works to miniature masterpieces. The complex is also a lively social centre. Enjoy a drink with your friends before your play begins; watch the crowds and the river drift by; wander around the many free art exhibitions; relax during the free early evening concerts in the foyer or browse through the theatre bookshop.

The **Royal Shakespeare Company** is Britain's national theatre company, one of the world's great theatre ensembles, with an unparalleled reputation for its dramatic interpretation of Shakespeare and other leading dramatists. Although its official home since the 19th century has been in Stratford-upon-Avon, the company has maintained a regular London presence since the 1960s. Its London base used to be the Barbican Centre, but now the RSC enjoys regular London seasons in the West End, at the Novello Theatre and other smaller venues. If you want to find out where the RSC is performing in London call their ticket hotline.

NATIONAL THEATRE BOOKING ADDRESSES

National Theatre
(Lyttelton, Cottesloe, Olivier)
South Bank SE1. **Map** 14 D3.
Tel 020-7452 3000.
www.nationaltheatre.org.uk

Royal Shakespeare Company
Tel 01789-403 4444 *(information)*.
Tel 0844-800 1110 *(tickets)*.

PANTOMIME

Should you happen to be visiting London between December and February, one unmissable experience for the whole family is pantomime. "Panto" is an absurd tradition in which major female characters are played by men and male characters by women, and the audience has to participate, shouting encouragement according to a set formula. Whatever adults may think of it, children love the experience.

OPEN AIR THEATRE

A performance of one of Shakespeare's airier creations, such as *A Midsummer Night's Dream*, takes on an atmosphere of pure enchantment among the green vistas of **Regent's Park** *(see p224)*. Lavish opera productions are staged during the summer months in **Holland Park** *(see p218)*. Wear warm clothing, take a blanket and, to be safe, an umbrella. Refreshments are available, or you can take a picnic.

Open-air performances of a different kind can be experienced at **Shakespeare's Globe** on Bankside *(see p177)*. This authentic reproduction of an Elizabethan playhouse, open to the skies – but with protected seating – is open to visitors all year round but only puts on performances in the summer months.

OPEN AIR THEATRE BOOKING ADDRESSES

Holland Park Theatre
Holland Park. **Map** 9 B4.
Tel 020-7361 3570. **Open** Jun–Aug.
www.operahollandpark.com

Open Air Theatre
Inner Circle, Regent's Park NW1.
Map 4 D3. **Open** Jun–Sep.
Tel 0844- 826 4242.
http://openairtheatre.org

Shakespeare's Globe
New Globe Walk SE1. **Map** 15 A3.
Tel 020-7401 9919.
Performances Apr–Oct.
www.shakespeares-globe.org

WEST END THEATRES

Adelphi ⑬
Strand WC2.
Tel 0844-412 4651.

Aldwych ⑱
Aldwych WC2.
Tel 0844-847 2330.

Ambassadors ㉖
West St WC2.
Tel 0844-811 2334.

Apollo ㉜
Shaftesbury Ave W1.
Tel 0844-579 1971.

Cambridge ㉔
Earlham St WC2.
Tel 0844-412 4652.

Comedy ⑧
Panton St SW1.
Tel 0844-871 7612.

Criterion ⑦
Piccadilly Circus W1.
Tel 0870-847 1778.

Dominion ㉓
Tottenham Court Rd.
Tel 0844-847 1775.

Duchess ⑯
Catherine St WC2.
Tel 0844-412 4659.

Duke of York's ③
St Martin's Lane WC2.
Tel 0844-871 7623.

Fortune ⑳
Russell St WC2.
Tel 0844-871 7626.

Garrick ④
Charing Cross Rd WC2.
Tel 0844-579 1974.

Gielgud ㉛
Shaftesbury Ave W1.
Tel 0844-482 5141.

Her Majesty's ⑩
Haymarket SW1.
Tel 0844-482 5158.

Lyceum ⑮
Wellington St WC2.
Tel 0844-844 0005.

Lyric ㉝
Shaftesbury Ave W1.
Tel 0844-412 4661.

New Leicester Square Theatre ⑤
Leicester Pl W1.
Tel 0844-847 2475.

New London ㉑
Drury Lane WC2.
Tel 020-7452 3000.

Noel Coward ①
St Martin's Lane WC2.
Tel 0844-482 5120.

Novello ⑰
Aldwych WC2.
Tel 0844-482 5170.

Palace ㉘
Shaftesbury Ave W1.
Tel 0844-755 0016.

Phoenix ㉗
Charing Cross Rd WC2.
Tel 0844-871 7627.

Piccadilly ㉞
Denman St W1.
Tel 0844-412 6666.

Playhouse ⑫
Northumberland Ave WC2.
Tel 0870-060 6631.

Prince Edward ㉙
Old Compton St W1.
Tel 0844-482 5151.

Prince of Wales ⑥
Coventry St W1.
Tel 0844-482 5115.

Queen's ㉚
Shaftesbury Ave W1.
Tel 0844-482 5160.

Shaftesbury ㉒
Shaftesbury Ave WC2.
Tel 020-7379 5399.

St Martin's ㉕
West St WC2.
Tel 0844-499 1515.

Theatre Royal Drury Lane ⑲
Catherine St WC2.
Tel 0844-412 2955.

Theatre Royal Haymarket ⑨
Haymarket SW1.
Tel 0845-481 1870.

Trafalgar Studios ⑪
Whitehall SW1.
Tel 0844-871 7632.

Vaudeville ⑭
Strand WC2.
Tel 0844-412 4663.

Wyndham's ②
Charing Cross Rd WC2.
Tel 0844-482 5138.

FRINGE THEATRE

London's fringe theatre acts as an outlet for new, adventurous writing and for writers from other cultures and lifestyles – works by Irish writers appear regularly, as do plays by Caribbean and Latin American authors and feminist and gay writers.

The plays are usually staged in tiny theatres based in pubs, such as the **Gate Theatre** above the Prince Albert pub in Notting Hill, the **King's Head** in Islington and the **Latchmere** pub in Battersea, or in warehouses and spare space in larger theatres, such as the **Donmar Warehouse** and the **Lyric**.

Venues like the **Bush Theatre**, the **Almeida** and the **Jerwood Theatre Upstairs** at the Royal Court have earned their reputations for discovering outstanding new works, some of which have subsequently transferred successfully to the West End.

Foreign-language plays are sometimes performed at national cultural institutes; for example you might be able to catch Molière at the **Institut Français** or Brecht at the **Goethe Institute**; check the listings magazines.

For alternative stand-up comedy and cabaret, where you can encounter the sharp edge of satire with its brash, newsy style, try the **Comedy Store**, the birthplace of so-called "alternative" comedy, or the **Hackney Empire**, a former Victorian music hall, completely refurbished in 2003 to its former glory to host a variety of shows.

BUDGET TICKETS

There is a wide range of prices for seats in London theatres. The cheaper West End tickets, for example, can cost under £10, whereas the best seats for musicals hover around £35–50. However, it is usually quite possible to obtain cheaper tickets.

"tkts" (see p345) is the only official discount theatre ticket shop in London, and sells tickets on the day of the performance for a wide range of mainstream shows. Located on the south side of Leicester Square, the booth is open Monday to Saturday (10am–7pm) for matinee and evening shows, and Sunday (noon–3:30pm) for matinees only. Payment is by cash or credit card, and there is a strict limit of up to four tickets per purchase, and a small service charge.

You can sometimes get reduced price seats for matinee performances, press and preview nights – it is always worth checking with the box office to see what they currently have on offer.

CHOOSING SEATS

If you go to the theatre in person, you will be able to see its seating plan and note where you can get a good view at an affordable price. If you book by telephone, you should note the following: stalls are in front of the stage and expensive. The back stalls are slightly cheaper; dress, grand or royal circles are above the stalls and cheaper again; the upper circle or balcony are the cheapest seats but you will have to climb several flights of stairs; the slips are seats that run along the edges of the theatre; boxes are the most expensive option.

It is also wise to bear in mind that some of the cheap seats have a restricted view.

THEATRE-RELATED ACTIVITIES

If you are curious about how the mechanics of the theatre work, you would probably enjoy a back-stage tour. The National Theatre organizes tours (contact the box office – see p344 – for details). The tour includes the Lyttleton, Olivier and Cottesloe auditoria, as well as the workshops and dressing rooms. The Theatre Museum collections at the V&A are worth a visit.

IRATE GHOSTS

Many London theatres are reputed to have ghosts; however, the two most famous spectres haunt the environs of the Garrick and the Duke of York's (see p345). The Garrick is heavily atmospheric and the ghost of Arthur Bourchier, a manager at the turn of the 20th century, is reputed to make fairly regular appearances. He hated critics and many believe he is still trying to frighten them away. The ghost occupying the Duke of York's theatre was Violet Melnotte, an actress manager during the 1890s, who was famed for her extremely fiery temper.

FRINGE THEATRE

Almeida
Almeida St N1.
Tel 020-7359 4404.

Bush Theatre
Shepherds Bush Green
W12.
Tel 020-8743 5050.

Comedy Store
28a Leicester Sq WC2.
Map 13 B3.
Tel 0844-847 1728.

Donmar Warehouse
41 Earlham St WC2.
Map 13 B2.
Tel 0844-871 7624.

Gate Theatre
The Prince Albert Pub,
11 Pembridge Rd W11.
Map 9 C3.
Tel 020-7229 0706.

Goethe Institute
50 Prince's Gate, Exhibition
Rd SW7. **Map** 11 A5.
Tel 020-7596 4000.

Hackney Empire
291 Mare St E8.
Tel 020-8985 2424.

Institut Français
17 Queensberry Pl SW7.
Map 18 F2.
Tel 020-7073 1350.

King's Head
115 Upper St N1.
Map 6 F1.
Tel 020-7226 8561.

Lyric
King St, Hammersmith
W6. **Tel** 0871-221 1729.

Theatre 503
The Latchmere Pub, 503
Battersea Park Rd SW11.
Tel 020-7978 7040.

Royal Court
Sloane Sq SW1.
Map 19 C2.
Tel 020-7565 5000.

Cinemas

If you can't find a movie you like in London, then you don't like movies. The huge choice of British, American, foreign-language, new, classic, popular and special-interest films makes London a major international film centre, with about 250 different films showing at any one time. There are about 50 cinemas in the central district of London alone, many of them ultra-modern multi-screened complexes. The big commercial chains show current smash-hits and a healthy number of independent cinemas offer some inventive programmes drawing on the whole history of film. London's listings magazines carry full details of what's on where.

WEST END CINEMAS

West End is a loose term for the main cinemas in the West End of London which show new releases, such as the **Odeon Leicester Square** and the **Cineworld** Shaftesbury Avenue at the Trocadero, but it also includes the cinemas found in Chelsea, Fulham and Notting Hill. Programmes begin around midday and are then repeated every two or three hours, with the last show around 8.30pm; there are often late-night screenings on Fridays and Saturdays.

West End cinemas are very expensive, but admission is often cheaper for afternoon performances or on Mondays. Reserve your seats well in advance for screenings of the more popular films on Friday and Saturday evenings and Sunday afternoon.

BFI LONDON IMAX

The largest IMAX screen in Britain shows specially created movies accompanied by surround sound. Subjects like spaceflight or the undersea world suit this breathtaking format well, as do animations.

REPERTORY CINEMAS

These cinemas often show foreign-language and slightly more "off-beat" art films and sometimes change programmes daily or even several times each day. Some cinemas show two or three films, often on the same theme, for one entrance charge.

These include the **Prince Charles**, which is situated centrally, close to Leicester Square, the **Everyman** in north London, the ICA in the Mall, the refurbished **Ritzy** in South London and the BFI Southbank.

BFI SOUTHBANK

Formerly known as the National Film Theatre, BFI Southbank is located in the Southbank Centre, near Waterloo Station. It has two cinemas of its own, which together offer a huge and diverse selection of films, both British and international. The BFI Southbank also holds regular screenings of rare and restored films and television programmes. It is absolutely essential for movie buffs to pay a visit.

FOREIGN-LANGUAGE FILMS

These are screened at a number of repertory and independent cinemas, including the **Renoir**, the **Prince Charles**, the **Curzon Soho** in Shaftesbury Avenue, the **Screen** cinemas chain and the **Ciné Lumière**. Films are shown in the original language, with English subtitles.

FILM CERTIFICATES

Children are allowed to go to a cinema unaccompanied by an adult to films which have been awarded either a U (universal) or a PG (parental guidance advised) certificate for viewing. Children must be accompanied by an adult to view a film rated 12A.

With other films, the numbers 12, 15 or 18 quite simply denote the minimum ages allowed for admission to the cinema.

LONDON FILM FESTIVAL

The most important cinema event in Britain is held every November, when over 100 films – some of which will have already won awards abroad – from a number of countries are screened. The BFI Southbank, several of the repertory cinemas and some of the big West End cinemas have special showings of these films. Details are published in the listings magazines. Tickets are quite hard to come by but some "stand-by" tickets will generally be available to the public 30 minutes before a screening.

CINEMA ADDRESSES

BFI London IMAX
Waterloo Rd SE1.
Map 14 D4.
📞 0870-787 2525.

BFI Southbank
Southbank Centre, SE1.
Map 14 D3.
Tel 020-7928 3232.

Ciné Lumière
Institut Français, 17 Queensberry Pl SW7. **Map** 18 F2. **Tel** 020-7073 1350.

Cineworld (at the Trocadero)
Coventry St W1. **Map** 13 A3. 📞 0871-200 2000.

Curzon Soho
93–107 Shaftesbury Ave W1. **Map** 13 B2.
📞 0871-703 3988.

Everyman
Hollybush Vale NW3.
Map 1 A5.
📞 0870-066 4777.

Odeon Leicester Sq
Leicester Sq, WC2. **Map** 13 B2.
📞 0871-224 4007.

Prince Charles
Leicester Pl, WC2.
Map 13 B2.
Tel 020-7494 3654.

Renoir
Brunswick Sq WC1.
Map 5 C4.
📞 020-7837 8402.

Ritzy
Coldharbour Lane SW2.
Tel 0871-704 2065.

Screen Cinemas
96 Baker St NW1
Map 3 C5.
Tel 0870-066 4777.

Opera, Classical and Contemporary Music

Opera has always been tarred with a somewhat elitist reputation in Britain. However, televised concerts and free outdoor concerts in Hyde Park and the Piazza, Covent Garden, have greatly increased its popularity. London is home to five world-class orchestras and a veritable host of smaller music companies and contemporary music ensembles; it also houses three permanent opera companies and numerous smaller opera groups and leads the world with its period orchestras. It is a major centre for the classical recording industry, which helps to support a large community of musicians and singers. Mainstream, obscure, traditional and innovative music are all to be found in profusion. Time Out magazine *(see p342)* has the most comprehensive listings of the classical music on offer around the capital.

Royal Opera House

Floral Street WC2. **Map** 13 C2.
Tel 020-7304 4000. See p115.
www.roh.org.uk

The building, with its elaborate red, white and gold interior, is opulent; it looks, and is, expensive. It is the home of the Royal Opera and the Royal Ballet, but visiting opera and ballet companies also perform here. Many productions are shared with foreign opera houses, so check that you haven't already seen the same production at home. Works are always performed in the original language, but English translations are flashed up above the stage.
  Seats are usually booked well in advance, particularly if major stars such as Placido Domingo or Anna Netrebko are performing. The sound is best in the seats centre of stage, right in the front. Tickets range from about £5 to £200 or more for a world-class star. The cheapest seats tend to go first, although a number of these tickets are reserved for sale on the day. Some of the cheaper seats have extremely restricted views. Standing passes can often be obtained right up to the time of a performance. Standby information is available on the day, and there are often concessions on tickets. It is worthwhile queuing for last-minute returns.

London Coliseum

St Martin's Lane WC2. **Map** 13 B3.
Tel 0871-911 0200 (24 hrs).
See p119. **www**.eno.org

The Coliseum, home of the English National Opera (ENO), underwent renovations from 2000–4. Founded in 1961, the company's hallmarks are performances in English, high musical standards and a permanent ensemble complemented by guest appearances. Productions range from the classic to the adventurous.

They are often praised for their contemporary interpretations. The audiences tend to be younger than at the Royal Opera House, the seats are much cheaper and there is less corporate entertaining. For weekday performances, there are 500 prebookable seats at £10 and under.

Southbank Centre

Southbank Centre SE1. **Map** 14 D4.
Tel 0844-875 0073. See pp186–7.
www.southbankcentre.co.uk

The Southbank Centre includes the **Royal Festival Hall (RFH)**, the **Queen Elizabeth Hall**, the **Purcell Room** and **The Hayward**. There are nightly performances, mostly of classical music, interspersed with opera, jazz, ballet and modern dance seasons, as well as festivals of contemporary and ethnic music. The largest concert hall on the South Bank is the RFH. Built in the 1950s, it is now considered one of the best modernist structures in London. A major renovation was completed in 2007. The RFH is ideal for major orchestras and large-scale choral works. The airy halls outside the auditorium are also used to house exhibitions, a number of cafés, a book and music shop, and the occasional free performance.
  The Purcell Room is comparatively small and tends to host chamber and contemporary music in addition to many debut recitals of young artists. The Queen Elizabeth Hall lies somewhere in between. It stages medium-sized ensembles whose audiences, while too large for the Purcell Room, would not fill the Festival Hall. Jazz and ethnic music are performed here and the innovative and often controversial Opera Factory makes several appearances throughout the year. It performs a range of modern interpretations of the classics, and often commissions

LONDON MUSIC FESTIVALS

The BBC-run Promenade concerts are mostly held at the Royal Albert Hall *(see p349)* between July and September. More than 70 concerts feature soloists, orchestras and conductors from around the world, performing a wide repertoire from much-loved classics to newly commissioned pieces. Every concert is broadcast live both on the radio and online. Tickets are best bought in advance, but 500 standing or 'promming' places are sold on the day, one and a half hours before the performance. The City of London Festival is held annually in June and July, when churches and public buildings in the City host a range of varied musical events. Venues such as the Tower of London *(see p154)* and Goldsmiths' Hall lend a special atmosphere to the events. Many concerts are free. For more details, apply to the information office (020-7583 3585) from May onwards.

new works. The London Philharmonic Orchestra and the Philharmonia are resident at the South Bank. The Royal Philharmonic and the BBC Symphony Orchestra are frequent visitors, along with leading ensembles and soloists such as Angela Gheorghiu, Mitsuko Uchida, Stephen Kovacevich and Anne-Sofie von Mutter. Visiting international musicians cover a wide repertoire of music from the Kronos Quartet to the Vienna Symphony Orchestra. World-class conductors who have played here include Daniel Barenboim, Kurt Masur and Simon Rattle.
  The Academy of St Martin-in-the-Fields, the London Festival Orchestra, Opera Factory, the London Classical Players and the London Mozart Players all have regular seasons. There are also frequent free foyer concerts, and throughout the summer the centre is well worth visiting as musical events take place on the terraces when the weather permits.

Barbican Concert Hall

Silk Street EC2. **Map** 7 A5.
Tel 020-7638 4141. See p165.
www.barbican.org.uk

The Barbican is the home of the London Symphony Orchestra (LSO). Classical concerts are performed by the resident LSO and the BBC Symphony Orchestra, as well as many other visiting orchestras and ensembles, as part of the Barbican's own international concert seasons. The concert hall is also renowned for its performances of contemporary music, including jazz, blues and world music, which attract the top musicians in their field.

Royal Albert Hall

Kensington Gore SW7. **Map** 10 F5.
Tel 020-7589 8212. See p207
www.royalalberthall.com

Each year the Royal Albert Hall hosts over 300 concerts, from ballet to rock, pop, opera and national events. From mid-July to mid-September it is devoted to the Henry Wood Promenade Concerts, the "Proms". Organized by the BBC, the season features the BBC Symphony Orchestra performing modern symphonies and other works as well as classics. Visiting orchestras make up a varied programme. Tickets for the Proms can be bought on the day of performance or booked in advance, but long queues build up early in the day, so experienced Promenaders take cushions to sit on. Tickets sell out weeks ahead for the "Last Night of the Proms", which has become a national institution.

The hall is also open for tours that take you on a journey of its extraordinary history, and give you the chance to experience the workings of this performing arts venue.

Handel House Museum

25 Brook St W1. **Map** 12 E2.
Tel 020-7495 1685. **Open** 10am–6pm Tue–Sat (until 8pm Thu), noon–6pm Sun.
www.handelhouse.org

Located in the finely restored Georgian house where George Frideric Handel lived from 1723 until his death in 1759, the Handel House Museum provides an intimate venue for performances. Thursday night recitals of baroque music on period instruments are held in the panelled rehearsal and performance room, where Handel himself would have entertained his guests. Concert tickets include access to the museum. Check the website for more concerts, lectures and workshops.

OUTDOOR MUSIC

London has many outdoor musical events in summer. At Kenwood House on Hampstead Heath (see p234), a grassy hill leads down to a lake, beyond which is the concert platform. Arrive early as the concerts are popular, particularly if fireworks are to accompany the music. Deck-chairs tend to be booked up early, so most people sit on the grass. Take a sweater and a picnic. Purists beware – people walk around, eat and talk throughout and the music is amplified so it can be a little distorted. You don't get your money back if it rains, as they have never abandoned a performance yet.

Other venues include Marble Hill House in Twickenham (see p252), with practices similar to Kenwood, Crystal Palace Park and Holland Park.

Wigmore Hall

36 Wigmore St W1. **Map** 12 E1.
Tel 020-7935 2141. See p226.
www.wigmore-hall.org.uk

Because of its excellent acoustics the Wigmore Hall is a favourite with visiting artists, and attracts international names such as Andreas Scholl and András Schiff for a wide-ranging programme of events. It presents seven evening concerts a week, BBC Monday lunchtime concerts, and a Sunday morning concert from September to July.

St Martin-in-the-Fields

Trafalgar Sq WC2. **Map** 13 B3.
Tel 020-7766 1100. See p102.
www.smitf.org

This elegant Gibbs church is where the famous Academy of St Martin-in-the-Fields and the famous choir of the same name began life. Orchestras as disparate as the Delmont Ensemble and the London Oriana Choir provide evening concerts. The choice of each programme is partly dictated by the religious year; for example, Bach's *St John Passion* is played at Ascensiontide. Free lunchtime concerts are held on Mondays, Tuesdays and Fridays by young artists.

St John's, Smith Square

Smith Sq SW1. **Map** 21 B1.
Tel 020-7222 1061. See p81.
www.sjss.org.uk

This converted Baroque church has good acoustics and comfortable seating. It hosts varied concerts by groups such as the Academy of Ancient Music, the London Mozart Players, the Monteverdi Choir and Polyphony. The concert period runs from September to mid-July.

Broadgate Arena

3 Broadgate EC2. **Map** 7 C5.
Tel 020-7505 4068. See p169.

This open-air venue in the City offers a summer season of lunch-time concerts, with varied programmes, frequently from up-and-coming musicians.

MUSIC VENUES

Orchestral

Barbican Concert Hall
Broadgate Arena
Queen Elizabeth Hall
Royal Albert Hall
Royal Festival Hall
St Martin-in-the-Fields
St John's, Smith Square

Chamber and Ensemble

Barbican Concert Hall
Broadgate Arena
Handel House Museum
LSO St Luke's
Purcell Room
Royal Festival Hall foyer
St Martin-in-the-Fields
St John's, Smith Square
Wigmore Hall

Soloists and Recitals

Barbican Concert Hall
Handel House Museum
Purcell Room
Royal Albert Hall
St Martin-in-the-Fields
St John's, Smith Square
Wigmore Hall

Children's

Barbican Concert Hall
Royal Festival Hall

Free

Barbican Concert Hall
Royal Festival Hall foyer
Royal National Theatre foyer (see p344)
St Martin-in-the-Fields (lunchtime)

Early Music

Purcell Room
Wigmore Hall

Contemporary Music

Barbican Concert Hall
Southbank Centre

Dance

London-based dance companies present a range of styles from classical ballet to mime, jazz, experimental and ethnic dance. London is also host to visiting comp-anies as diverse as the classic Bolshoi Ballet and the innovative Jaleo Flamenco. Most dance companies (with the exception of the resident ballets) have short seasons that seldom last longer than a fortnight and often less than a week – check the listings magazines for details *(see p342)*. Theatres that regularly feature dance are the **Royal Opera House**, the **London Coliseum, Sadler's Wells** and **The Place Theatre**. There are also performances at the **Southbank Centre** and other arts centres throughout the city.

A purpose-built space in Deptford, south London, the **Bonnie Bird Theatre**, presents a rich and diverse mix of dance, music and physical theatre. Other venues include the **Institute of Contemporary Arts** (ICA) *(see p92)* and the **Chisenhale Dance Space**, a centre for small companies currently regarded as being on the experimental fringes.

BALLET

The **Royal Opera House** *(see p115)* and the **London Coliseum** in St Martin's Lane are by far the best venues for classical ballet, providing the stage for foreign companies when they visit London. The Opera House is home to the Royal Ballet, which usually invites major international guest artists to take up resi-dence. Book well in advance for classics such as *Swan Lake* and *Giselle*. The company also has an unusual repertoire of modern ballet; triple bills provide a mixture of new and old and seats are normally quite readily available.

The English National Ballet holds its summer season at the **London Coliseum**. It has a similar repertoire to the Royal Ballet and stages some very popular productions.

Visiting companies also perform at **Sadler's Wells**, which, although it is London's premier venue for contemporary dance, also hosts a few companies with a classical repertoire.

CONTEMPORARY

A plethora of new and young companies is flourishing in London, each one with a distinctive style. **Sadler's Wells** in Islington, near Angel, has a proud reputation as the host of contemporary dance companies from around the world. There are regular visits from such luminaries of dance as the Nederlands Dance Theatre and the Alvin Ailey Company from New York. The innovative English ensemble, the Rambert Dance Company, have a regular, twice-a-year slot at the theatre – usually in May and November. A stunning modern theatre was built on the historic site of the Sadler's Wells Ballet in 1998. The **Peacock Theatre** (the West End home of Sadler's Wells) also features contemporary dance as part of its programme.

The Place is the home of contemporary and ethnic dance companies and has a year-round programme of performances from these and a number of visiting dancers.

ETHNIC

There is a constant stream of visiting groups coming to perform traditional dance from all over the world. Both **Sadler's Wells** and the **Riverside Studios** are major venues, while classical ethnic dance companies, including Indian and Far Eastern, have seasons at the Southbank Centre, often in the **Queen Elizabeth Hall**. Check the listings magazines for details.

DANCE FESTIVALS

There are two major contemporary dance festivals each year in London, featuring many different companies. Spring Loaded runs from February to April, while Dance Umbrella runs from early October to early November. The listings magazines carry all details.

Other smaller festivals include Almeida Dance, from the end of April to the first week of May at the **Almeida Theatre**, and The Turning World, a festival running in April and May offering dance from all over the world.

DANCE VENUES			
Almeida Theatre Almeida St N1. *Tel* 020-7359 4404.	**ICA** Nash House, Carlton House Terrace, The Mall SW1. **Map** 13 A4. *Tel* 020-7930 3647.	**Peacock Theatre** Portugal St WC2. **Map** 14 D1. *Tel* 0844-412 4322.	**Riverside Studios** Crisp Rd W6. *Tel* 020-8237 1111.
Bonnie Bird Theatre Creekside SE8. **Map** 23 A2. **Tel** 020-8691 8600.		**The Place** 17 Duke's Rd WC1. **Map** 5 B3. *Tel* 020-7121 1100.	**Royal Opera House** Floral St WC2. **Map** 13 C2. *Tel* 020-7304 4000.
Chisenhale Dance Space 64 Chisenhale Rd E3. *Tel* 020-8981 6617.	**London Coliseum** St Martin's Lane WC2. **Map** 13 B3. *Tel* 0870-145 0200.	**Queen Elizabeth Hall** Southbank Centre SE1. **Map** 14 D4. *Tel* 020-7960 4200.	**Sadler's Wells** Rosebery Ave EC1. **Map** 6 E3. *Tel* 0844-412 4300.

Rock, Pop, Jazz, Reggae and World Music

You will find the whole range of popular music being strummed and hummed, howled, growled or synthesized in London. There may be as many as 80 listed concerts on an ordinary weeknight, featuring rock, reggae, soul, folk, country, jazz, Latin and world music. In addition to the gigs, there are music festivals in the summer at parks, pubs, halls and stadiums throughout the capital (see p353). Check the listings magazines and keep your eyes open for publicity posters (see p342).

MAJOR VENUES

The largest venues in London are host to an extraordinary variety of music.

Places where pop idols hope to draw enormous crowds of adoring fans include the **O2 Arena** in Greenwich, the indoor **Wembley Arena**, the **Hammersmith Apollo**, or, if they take themselves seriously, the grand **Royal Albert Hall**.

The **O2 Academy Brixton** and the **Town and Country Club** are next in prominence and size. Each can take well over 1,000 people, and for many Londoners these former cinemas are the capital's best venues, with seating upstairs, large dance-floors downstairs and accessible bars.

ROCK AND POP

Indie music is one of the mainstays of London's live music output. Following the leads of Manchester and Bristol, the capital has a healthy, cross-fertilized rock scene: venues all over town offer Britpop, bratpop, hip-hop, trip-hop and the many other variations on pop which have yet to be labelled for the mass market. The **Union Chapel** in Islington hosts a variety of bands. Kentish Town's **Bull and Gate** is good for goth, and rock is the order of the day at venues such as **The Bullet Bar** and **The Shepherd's Bush Empire** among others.

The **Underworld** in Camden is a famous live venue for up and coming bands as well as big name artists such as Sheryl Crow, Radiohead and The Darkness. The venue is also home to two nightclubs.

London is the home of pub-rock, which is a vibrant blend of rhythm and blues, rock and punk that has been evolving since the 1960s as a genre in which bands frequently develop before finding their real musical identity. Such diverse bands as the Clash, Dr Feelgood and Dire Straits all started as pub rockers. While there's usually no entrance fee to pub gigs, drinks tend to be surcharged.

New bands have a popular showcase at the **Betsey Trotwood** in Clerkenwell most week nights, while **Borderline**, near to Leicester Square, is frequented by record company talent scouts.

The **Barfly** in Chalk Farm delivers a good range of indie acts. **Koko** in Camden is a great intimate venue in a restored theatre dating from 1900. Here you can listen to the finest established artists such as Madonna or Coldplay and live performances from up-and-coming indie bands. Another good venue for stimulating rock bands in North London is **The Relentless Garage** at Highbury Corner.

JAZZ

The number of jazz venues in London continues to grow – both the music and the lifestyle which are romantically imagined to go with it are officially hip once again. **Ronnie Scott's** in the West End is still the pick of the vintage crop, and since the 1950s many of the finest performers in the world have come to play here. The **100 Club** in Oxford Street is another very popular venue for confirmed jazzniks.

Jazz and food have formed a partnership at venues such as the **Palookaville** in Covent Garden, the **Dover Street Wine Bar** and the largely vegetarian **Jazz Café**. Others include the **Pizza Express** on Dean Street and the **Pizza on the Park**, by Hyde Park Corner.

The **Southbank Centre** (see pp186–7) and also the **Barbican** (see p165) feature formal jazz concerts and free jazz in the foyers.

REGGAE

London's large West Indian community has made the city the European reggae capital. At the **Notting Hill Carnival** (see p57), late in August, many top bands perform free.

Reggae has now become integrated with the mainstream rock music scene, and bands appear at most of London's rock venues.

WORLD MUSIC

Musicians from every corner of the globe live in London. "World music" includes African, Latin, South American, anything exotic, and its popularity has sparked a revitalization of British and Irish folk music. **Cecil Sharp House** has regular shows for folk purists, while the **ICA** (see p92) hosts innovative acts. **Cargo** in Shoreditch has an eclectic programme of live music that includes African beats and Latin funk. Hot Latin nights can be found at **Cuba Libre** in Islington, and laid-back vibes pervade the **Notting Hill Arts Club**. For all French Caribbean and African sounds you could check **Le Café de Piaf** inside Waterloo Station; and for the widest selection of African sounds and food in town, try visiting the **Africa Centre** in Covent Garden. The **Barbican Centre**, the **Royal Festival Hall** and the **Queen Elizabeth Hall** at the Southbank Centre all offer plenty of world music.

Clubs

The old cliché that London dies when the pubs shut no longer holds true. Europe has long scoffed at Londoners going to bed at 11pm when the night is only just beginning in Paris, Madrid and Rome, but London has caught on at last and you can revel all night if you want to. The best clubs are not all confined to the city's centre – initial disappointment that your hotel is a half-hour tube-ride from Leicester Square can be offset by the discovery of a trendy club right on your doorstep.

ETIQUETTE

Fashions and club nights change very rapidly and nightspots open and close down all the time. Some of the best club nights are one-nighters – check the listings magazines *(see p.342)*. Be aware that there are sometimes bouncers on the door, enforcing a variety of dress or other appearance codes for a particular club. If you are set on visiting one of these, do some research before you go.

A few clubs require that you arrange membership 48 hours in advance, and you may also find that you have to be introduced by a member. Again, check these details in the listings magazines. Groups of men may not be welcome, so split up and find a woman to go in with; expect to queue to get in. Entrance fees may seem reasonable, but drinks tend to be over-priced.

Opening times are usually 10pm–3am Monday to Saturday, although many clubs stay open until 6am at the weekend and some open on Sunday from about 8pm to midnight.

MAINSTREAM

London offers a broad selection of nightclubs that cater for all musical tastes and budgets.

Most of the more upmarket nightclubs in London, for example **Annabel's**, have a strict members-only policy; they require nominations by current members and have long waiting lists, so unless you mix in privileged circles you are unlikely to get in.

Traditional disco-type clubs which are easier to enter include the **Café de Paris**, where you can dine and boogie the night away. For those with a lust for samba and Latin beats **Guanabara** in Covent Garden is friendly, unpretentious and fun.

Further north, the **Forum** hosts popular club nights, which feature classic soul, funk and rhythm and blues. Similar clubs are **East Village** in Shoreditch and the **Tattershall Castle**, a disco boat moored on the bank of the Thames.

FASHIONABLE VENUES AND CLUB NIGHTS

Over the last few years London has become one of the most innovative and sought-after club capitals in the world. It is now a major stage where trends are set. **Heaven** hosts England's premier "house" night. With its huge dance floor, excellent lasers, sound systems and lightshows it's very popular, so start queuing early. **Punk** in Soho is a trendy spot playing a mixture of sounds (you might even spot a celebrity). The **Ministry of Sound** is a New York-style club that set the pattern for others to follow, hosting some of the world's best-known DJs. If you are feeling energetic, club nights are also run at the **Queen of Hoxton** in Shoreditch. Try **Envy Nightclub** for funky house, electro and old skool, and for die-hard clubbers there's always the music-loving **Fabric**.

As with many clubs, **Bar Rumba** has different themes on different evenings, but if you like your dancing with a dash of spice and a lot of sauce, sashay along to its salsa night with dance classes also available. **Cargo**, the pioneering live/mixed music venue, features some of London's funkiest sounds. **93 Feet East** showcases a variety of live music and club nights from indie and rock to techno beats. Dress in uniform for the "School Disco Night" with 70s, 80s and 90s sounds. It takes place on Saturdays in the **HMV Forum**, but check listings – it moves sometimes.

Disappointingly, there are surprisingly few regular reggae nights. **Soho Lounge** has the best dance reggae on Saturday nights and a tremendous toe-tapping tripartite rhythm riot of ska, classic soul and R n' B sounds on Thursdays.

GAY

London has a number of gay nightclubs. The best-known and most popular is **Heaven**, with its huge dance floor and bar and video lounge under the arches of Charing Cross station. The **Fridge** and the **Queen of Hoxton** host mixed gay nights, and the Fridge holds women-only nights.

TRANSVESTITE

Watch for the occasional "Kinky Gerlinky" night in the listings magazines, an outrageously kitsch collection of drag queens and assorted exotica. In Soho, **Madame Jojo**'s revue is a fabulous whirl of glittering colour and extreme high camp.

CASINOS

To gamble in London you must be a member, or at least the guest of a member, of a licensed gaming club. Most clubs are happy to let you join but membership must be arranged 48 hours in advance. Many will let you in to use facilities other than the gambling tables until about 4am, when most close. Try the excellent restaurants and bars, which are often subject to the usual licensing laws *(see p.318)*. Many clubs also have "hostesses" – beware the cost of their company.

DIRECTORY

MAJOR MUSIC VENUES

Hammersmith Apollo
Queen Caroline St W6.
Tel 020-8563 3800.

HMV Forum
9–17 Highgate Rd NW5.
Tel 020-7284 1001.

O2 Academy Brixton
211 Stockwell Rd SW9.
Tel 020-7771 3000.

Royal Albert Hall
See p203.

Wembley Arena
Empire Way, Wembley,
Middlesex HA9.
*Tel 0844-815 0815
(tickets), 020-8782 5500
(enquiries).*

ROCK AND POP VENUES

Barfly
49 Chalk Farm Rd NW1.
Map 4 F1.
Tel 0844-847 2424.

Betsey Trotwood
56 Farringdon Rd
EC1. **Map** 6 E4.
Tel 020-7253 4285.

Borderline
Orange Yard, Manette St
WC2. **Map** 13 B1.
Tel 020-7734 5547.

Bull and Gate
389 Kentish Town Rd
NW5.
Tel 020-8826 5000.

The Bullet Bar
147 Kentish Town Rd
NW1.
Tel 020-7485 6040.

Envy Nightclub
41–43 Woodfield Rd W9.
Tel 020-7266 3030.

Koko
1a Camden High St NW1.
Map 4 F2.
Tel 0870-432 5527.

The Relentless Garage
20–22 Highbury Corner,
N5. *Tel 020-7619 6720.*

Shepherd's Bush Empire
Shepherd's Bush Green
W12.
Tel 0905-020 3999.

The Underworld
174 Camden High St
NW1.
Map 4 F1.
Tel 020-7482 1932.

Union Chapel
The Vestry, Compton
Ave N1.
Tel 020-7226 1686.

JAZZ VENUES

100 Club
100 Oxford St W1.
Map 13 A1.
Tel 020-7636 0933.

Barbican Hall
See p165.

Dover Street Wine Bar
8–10 Dover St W1.
Map 12 F3.
Tel 020-7629 9813.

Jazz Café
5 Parkway NW1.
Map 4 E1.
Tel 020-7485 6834.

Pizza Express
10 Dean St W1.
Map 13 A1.
Tel 0845-602 7017.

Pizza on the Park
11 Knightsbridge SW1.
Map 12 D5.
Tel 020-7235 7825.

Ronnie Scott's
47 Frith St W1.
Map 13 A2.
Tel 020-7439 0747.
www.ronniescotts.co.uk

Royal Festival Hall
See p348.

Vortex Jazz Club
Dalston Culture House
Gillett St, N16.
Map 8 1D.
*Tel 020-7993 3643 or
020-7254 4097.*

WORLD MUSIC

Africa Centre
38 King St WC2.
Map 13 C2.
Tel 020-7836 1973.

Barbican Centre
See p349.

Cargo
83 Rivington St EC2.
Map 7 C3.
Tel 020-7749 7840.

Cecil Sharp House
2 Regent's Park Rd NW1.
Map 4 D1.
Tel 020-7485 2206.

Cuba Libre
72 Upper St N1.
Map 6 F1.
Tel 020-7354 9998.

ICA
See p350.

Notting Hill Arts Club
21 Notting Hill Gate
W11. **Map** 9 C3.
Tel 020-7460 4459.

Queen Elizabeth Hall
Southbank Centre SE1.
Map 14 D4.
Tel 020-7960 4200.

Royal Festival Hall
See p348.

CLUBS

93 Feet East
150 Brick Lane,
Shoreditch E1.
Map 8 E4.
Tel 020-7770 6006.

Annabel's
44 Berkeley Sq W1.
Map 12 E3.
Tel 020-7629 1096.

Bar Rumba
36 Shaftesbury Ave
WC2. **Map** 6 E2.
Tel 020-7287 6933.

Café de Paris
3 Coventry St W1.
Map 13 A3.
Tel 020-7734 7700.

Cargo
89 Rivington St EC2.
Map 7 C3.
Tel 020-7749 7840.

East Village
89 Great Eastern St EC2.
Map 7 C4.
Tel 020-7739 5173.

Fabric
77a Charterhouse St EC1.
Map 6 F5.
Tel 020-7336 8898.

Fridge
Town Hall Parade,
Brixton Hill SW2.
Tel 020-7326 5100.

Guanabara
Drury Lane WC2.
Map 13 C1.
Tel 020-7242 8600.

Heaven
Under the Arches,
Villiers St WC2.
Map 13 C3.
Tel 020-7930 2020.

Madame Jojo
8–10 Brewer St W1.
Map 13 A2.
Tel 020-7734 3040.

Ministry of Sound
103 Gaunt St SE1.
Tel 0870-060 0010.

Punk
14 Soho St W1.
Map 13 A1.
Tel 0871-223 1242.

Queen of Hoxton
1 Curtain Rd EC2.
Map 7 C3.
Tel 020-7422 0958.

Soho Lounge
69 Dean St W1.
Map 13 A2.
Tel 020-7734 1231.

Tattershall Castle
Victoria Embankment,
SW1.
Map 13 C3.
Tel 020-7839 6548.

Sport

The range of sports on offer in London is quite phenomenal. Should you feel the urge to watch a game of medieval tennis or go scuba-diving in the city centre, you've come to the right place. More likely, you'll just want to watch a football or rugby match, or play a set of tennis in a park. With far more public facilities than most European capitals, London is the place to enjoy cheap, accessible sport. Wembley Stadium, the national stadium for football, is located in north-west London. Several new arenas are also being built in Stratford for the summer Olympics, which London will host in 2012. Events will be held at venues across the city, however.

ATHLETICS

Athletes will find a good choice of running tracks, often with free admission. **Linford Christie Stadium** has good facilities; **Regent's Park** is free; try also **Parliament Hill Fields**. For a sociable jog, meet the Bow Street Runners at **Jubilee Hall** on Tuesdays at 6pm.

CRICKET

Five-day test matches and one-day internationals are played in summer at **Lord's** (see p246) and the **Brit Oval**, near Vauxhall. Tickets for the first four days of tests and for one-day games are hard to get, but you may get in on the last day and see a thrilling finish. When Middlesex and Surrey play county games at these grounds there are always seats.

FOOTBALL (SOCCER)

This is the most popular spectator sport in Britain, its season running from August to May, with matches on weekends and weekday evenings. It is the most common topic of conversation in pubs, where games are often shown live on TV. Premier League and FA Cup games are frequently sold out in advance. London's top clubs include **Arsenal, Chelsea, West Ham** and **Tottenham Hotspur**.

GOLF

There are no golf courses in central London, but a few are scattered around the outskirts. The most accessible public courses are **Hounslow Heath, Chessington** (nine holes, train from Waterloo) and **Richmond Park** (two courses, computerized indoor teaching room). If you didn't pack your clubs, sets can be hired at a reasonable price.

GREYHOUND RACING

At a night "down the dogs", you can follow the races on a screen in the bar, stand by the track or watch from the comfort of the restaurant (book in advance) at **Romford Stadium or Wimbledon Stadium**.

HORSE RACING

High class flat racing in summer and steeplechasing in winter can be seen at **Ascot, Kempton Park** and **Sandown Park**, which are all less than an hour from central London by train. Britain's most famous flat race, the Derby, is run at **Epsom** in June.

HORSE-RIDING

For centuries, fashionable riders have exercised their steeds in Hyde Park; **Ross Nye** will provide you with a horse so that you can follow a long tradition.

ICE-SKATING

Ice-skaters should head for London's best-known rink, **Queens**. The most attractive ice rinks, open only in winter, are in the **Broadgate** complex in the City, and at **Somerset House** (see p117).

RUGBY FOOTBALL

Rugby union, or rugger, is a 15-a-side game, once played only by amateurs, but now a professional sport. International matches are played at **Twickenham Rugby Football Ground**. The season runs from September to April and you can watch "friendly" weekend games at local grounds. Top London teams **Saracens** and **Rosslyn Park** can be seen at their own grounds outside the centre of town.

SQUASH

Squash courts tend to be busy, so try to book at least two days ahead. Many sports centres have squash facilities and will hire out equipment, including **Swiss Cottage Sports Centre** and the **Oasis Sports Centre**.

SWIMMING

Best indoor pools include **Chelsea Sports Centre**, the **Oasis** and **Porchester Baths**; for outdoor swimming, try **Highgate** (separate ponds for men and women), **Hampstead** and the **Oasis**.

TENNIS

There are hundreds of tennis courts in London's public parks, most of them cheap to hire and easily reserved. It can be busy in the summer, so book a court two or three days ahead. You must supply your own racquet and balls. Good public tennis courts include **Holland Park** and **Parliament Hill**.

Tickets for the Centre Court of the **All England Lawn Tennis Club** at Wimbledon are hard to obtain – it is possibly easier to enter the tournament as a player than to obtain tickets for Centre Court; try queueing overnight, or queue for return tickets after lunch on the day – for a bargain price, you can still enjoy a good four hours of tennis (see p57).

TRADITIONAL SPORTS

An old London tradition is the University Boat Race, held in March or April, when teams from Oxford and Cambridge row from Putney to Mortlake (see p56); a newer tradition is the London Marathon, which is run from Greenwich to The Mall at Westminster (see p56) on an April Sunday. You can watch croquet at **Dulwich Croquet Club** and medieval (real) tennis at **Queen's Club**.

WATER SPORTS

There are facilities for a wide variety of water sports at the **Docklands Sailing & Water Sports Centre**. You can choose from sports such as windsurfing, dinghy sailing, powerboating, waterskiing and canoeing. Rowing boats are also available for hire by the hour on the calmer, central London waters of the **Serpentine** in Hyde Park and **Regent's Park Lake**.

WORKING OUT

Most sports centres have gymnasiums, work-out studios and health clubs. If you are a member of the YMCA, you'll be able to use the excellent facilities at the **Central YMCA. Jubilee Hall Clubs** and the **Oasis Sports Centre** both offer a variety of aerobic classes, keep-fit and weight training. For those who have overdone it, the **Chelsea Sports Centre** has a sports injury clinic.

DIRECTORY

London 2012
Tel 020-3 2012 000.
For general enquiries.
www.london2012.com

All England Lawn Tennis and Croquet Club
Church Rd, Wimbledon SW19. *Tel* 020-8946 2244.

Arsenal (Emirates) Stadium
Ashburton Grove N7.
Tel 020-7704 4000.

Ascot Racecourse
Ascot, Berkshire.
Tel 0870-727 1234.

Brit Oval
Kennington Oval SE11.
Map 22 D4.
Tel 08712-461100.

Broadgate Ice Rink
Broadgate Circle EC2.
Map 7 C5.
Tel 020-7505 4120.

Central YMCA
112 Great Russell St WC1.
Map 13 B1.
Tel 020-7343 1844.

Chelsea Football Club
Stamford Bridge SW6.
Tel 0871-984 1955.

Chelsea Sports Centre
Chelsea Manor St SW3.
Map 19 B3.
Tel 020-7352 6985.

Chessington Golf Course
Garrison Lane, Surrey.
Tel 020-8391 0948.

Docklands Sailing & Watersports Centre
235a Westferry Rd, E14.
Tel 020-7537 2626.
www.dswc.org

Dulwich Croquet Club
Giant Arches Rd, Off Burbage Rd SE24.
Tel 020-7928 9834.
www.dulwichcroquet.com

Epsom Racecourse
Epsom Downs, Surrey.
Tel 01372-470047.

Hampstead Ponds
off East Heath Rd NW3.
Map 1 C4.
Tel 020-7482 7073.

Highgate Ponds
Millfield Lane N6. Map 2 E3.
Tel 020-7482 7073.

Holland Park Public Tennis Courts
1 Ilchester Place W8. Map 9 B5. *Tel* 020-7602 2226.

Hounslow Heath Golf Course
Staines Rd, Middlesex TW4.
Tel 020-8570 5271.

Jubilee Hall Clubs
30 The Piazza, Covent Garden WC2. Map 13 C2.
Tel 020-7836 4007.

Kempton Park
Sunbury on Thames, Middx.
Tel 01932 782292.

Linford Christie Stadium
Du Cane Rd W12.
Tel 020-8749 6758.

Lord's Cricket Ground
St John's Wood NW8.
Map 3 A3.
Tel 020-7289 1611.

Oasis Swimming Pool & Sports Centre
32 Endell St WC2.
Map 13 B1.
Tel 020-7831 1804.

Parliament Hill
Highgate Rd NW5.
Map 2 E5.
Tel 020-7485 4491.

Porchester Centre
Queensway W2.
Map 10 D1.
Tel 020-7792 2919.

Queen's Club (Real Tennis)
Palliser Rd W14.
Map 17 A3.
Tel 020-7385 3421.

Queens Ice Skating Club
17 Queensway W2.
Map 10 E2.
Tel 020-7229 0172.

Regent's Park and Lake
Regent's Park NW1.
Map 3 C3.
Tel 020-7486 7905.
Tel 020-7724 4069
(boat hire).

Richmond Park Golf
Roehampton Gate, Priory Lane SW15.
Tel 020-8876 3205.

Romford Stadium
London Road, Essex RM7.
Tel 01708-762 345.

Rosslyn Park Rugby
Priory Lane, Upper Richmond Rd SW15.
Tel 020-8876 1879.

Ross Nye Stables
8 Bathurst Mews W2.
Map 11 A2.
Tel 020-7262 3791.

Sandown Park Racecourse
Esher, Surrey.
Tel 01372 464348.

Saracens Rugby Football Club
5 Vicarage Rd, Watford, Hertfordshire, WD1.
Tel 01727-792 800.

Serpentine
Hyde Park W2. Map 11 B4.
Tel 020-7298 2100 (boat hire).

Somerset House Ice Rink
Strand WC2. Map 14 D2.
Tel 020-7845 4600.

Tottenham Hotspur FC
White Hart Lane, 748 High Rd N17.
Tel 0844-499 5000.

Twickenham Rugby Ground
Whitton Rd, Twickenham, Middlesex.
Tel 0870-405 2000.

West Ham United
Boleyn Ground, Green St, Upton Park E13.
Tel 0870-112 2700.

CHILDREN'S LONDON

London offers children a potential goldmine of fun, excitement and adventure. Each year finds new attractions and sights opening up and older ones being updated.

First-time visitors may want to watch traditional ceremonies *(see pp52–5)* or visit famous buildings *(see p37),* but these are merely the tip of the iceberg. While London's parks, zoos and adventure playgrounds provide outdoor activities there are also loads of workshops, activity centres and museums providing quizzes, hands-on experiments and interactive displays. A day out need not be costly: children under 11 are entitled to free tube, bus and DLR travel provided they are travelling with an adult who has a valid ticket or Oystercard. And most museums are free anyway.

Humpty Dumpty doll

PRACTICAL ADVICE

A little planning is the key to a successful outing. You may want to check the opening hours of the places you plan to visit in advance, by telephone or online via the venue's website. Work out your journey thoroughly using the tube map at the end of this book.

If you are travelling with very young children remember that there are very likely to be queues at the Underground stations or bus stops near popular sights. These will be long during peak hours, so buy your tickets, Travelcard or Oyster card in advance *(see p378).*

Children under 11 can travel free on buses and tubes and child fares operate for all children between the ages of 11 and 15. Children very often enjoy using public transport, especially when it's

Punch and Judy show in the Piazza, Covent Garden

a novelty, so plan your outing carefully using one form of transport for the outward journey and another for the journey home. You can get around London easily by bus, Underground, taxi, train and riverboat *(see pp378–85).*

Visiting all the exhibitions and museums as a family doesn't have

Covent Garden clowns

to be as expensive as it sounds. The majority of London's principal museums have no entry charge. For those where you do have to pay, an annual family season ticket, usually for two adults and up to four children, is available. This often costs only marginally more than the initial visit.

In some cases you can buy a family ticket that covers a group of museums. Being able to visit a sight more than once means that you won't exhaust your children and put them off museums for life by trying to see absolutely everything over one long, tiring day.

If your children want a break from sightseeing, most borough councils provide information on activities for children such as playgroups, theatres, fun-fairs and activity centres in their area. Leaflets are usually available from libraries and leisure centres, as well as local town halls. During the long summer school holidays (July to the beginning of September) there are organized activity programmes all over London.

CHILDREN AND THE LAW

Children under 14 are not allowed into British pubs and wine bars (unless there is a special family room or garden) and only people over 18 can drink or buy any alcohol. In restaurants, the law is a little more relaxed. Those over 16 can drink wine or beer with their meal, but you

EATING OUT WITH CHILDREN

Restaurants are becoming more welcoming of tiny patrons. Italian eateries are often the most friendly, but even the traditional British pub, once resolutely child-free, has relented, with beer gardens and family rooms. As long as your offspring are reasonably well-behaved, most informal restaurants will be happy to serve a family. Some can also provide highchairs and booster cushions, as well as colouring mats to keep children entertained while waiting for their food to arrive. Many will also offer special children's menus with small helpings which will cut the cost of your meal.

Over the weekend some restaurants (such as **Smollensky's** and **Sticky Fingers**) provide live entertainment for children in the form of clowns, face painters and magicians. A number accept bookings for children's parties. It is always worth trying to book in advance (especially for Sunday lunch), so that you don't have to hang around waiting with tired and hungry children.

London has a number of restaurants ideal for older children. Among these are the **Rainforest Café** and the **Hard Rock Café** on Old Park Lane.

For budget eating, try the Café in the Crypt, St Martin-in-the-Fields *(see p102)*.

Coming up for air at Smollensky's

Dine with the elephants at the Rainforest Cafe

USEFUL ADDRESSES

Hard Rock Café
150 Old Park Lane W1. **Map** 12 E4.
Tel 020-7514 1700.

Rainforest Café
20 Shaftesbury Ave W1. **Map** 13 A2.
Tel 020-7434 3111.

Smollensky's
105 Strand WC2.
Map 14 D2. *Tel 020-7497 2101.*

Sticky Fingers
1a Phillimore Gdns, W8. **Map** 9 C5.
Tel 020-7938 5338.

still have to be over 18 to be served spirits. In general, young children are rarely welcome anywhere they might create a nuisance. Some films are classed as unsuitable for children *(see p347)*.

If you want to take your children by car, you must use seat belts wherever they are provided. Babies will need a special child seat. If you are in doubt, ask at any police station.

GETTING THEM OFF YOUR HANDS

Many of London's great museums *(see pp40–43)* and theatres *(see pp344–6)* provide weekend and holiday activities and workshops where you can leave children over a certain age for a few hours or even for a whole day, and the children's theatres are a great way to spend a rainy afternoon. A day at the fair is always a success – try Hampstead fair on summer bank holidays.

London has a great many sports centres *(see pp354–5)*, which usually open daily and often have special clubs and activities to occupy children of every age.

If you want a total break, call **Nannies Unlimited, Sitters, Kensington Nannies**, or **Pippa Pop-Ins**, a nursery school offering full-day childcare.

CHILDMINDING

Kensington Nannies
3 Hornton Place W8.
Map 10 D5. *Tel 020-7937 2333.*
www.kensington-nannies.com

Nannies Unlimited
11 Chelverton Rd, Putney SW15.
Tel 020-8788 9640.

Pippa Pop-Ins
430 Fulham Road SW6 **Map** 18 D5.
Tel 020-7731 1445.
Also at 233 New King's Rd SW6.

Sitters
126 Rickmansworth Rd, Watford
WD18. *Tel 0800-389 0038.*
www.sitters.co.uk

Airborne at the Hampstead fair

Holiday fun at Pippa Pop-Ins

SHOPPING

All children love a visit to **Hamleys** toy shop or Harrods toy department *(see p321)*. **Davenport's Magic Shop** and **The Disney Store** are smaller and more specialized.

Both the **Early Learning Centre** (many branches) and **The Cat and the Fiddle** have good selections of books. Some shops organize readings and signings by children's authors, especially during Children's Book Week, held in October.

USEFUL NUMBERS

The Cat and the Fiddle *Tel 020-8989 8100; Davenport's Magic Shop Tel 020-7836 0408; The Disney Store Tel 020-7491 9136; Early Learning Centre Tel 020-7581 5764; Hamleys Tel 0844-855 2424.*

Bears at Hamleys toy shop

MUSEUMS AND GALLERIES

London has a wealth of museums, exhibitions and galleries; more information on those listed here is to be found on pages 40–43. Most have been updated over the last few years to incorporate some exciting modern display techniques. It's unlikely that you'll have to drag reluctant children around an assortment of lifeless, stuffy exhibits.

The V&A Museum of Childhood *(p248)*, the children's branch of the

V&A in East London, and Pollock's Toy Museum *(p131)* are both especially good for young children.

For older children try one of London's Brass Rubbing Centres: the great Brass Rubbing Centre in the Crypt of St Martin-in-the-Fields *(p102)* or at St James's Church on Piccadilly *(p90)*. Madame Tussauds *(p224)* and Tower Bridge *(p153)* are firm favourites with children.

The British Museum *(pp126–9)* has fabulous treasures from all over the world, and the Horniman Museum *(p250)* has colourful displays from many different cultures. The Science Museum *(pp212–13)*, with over 600 working exhibits, is one of London's best attractions for children – its hands-on galleries in the basement, including the much-loved Launch Pad, will help keep them amused for hours. The interactive displays in the high-tech Wellcome Wing are also entertaining. If you have the stamina, the Natural History Museum *(pp208–9)* next door contains hundreds of amazing objects and animals from the world of nature. Included is a Dinosaur Exhibition. Suits of armour built for knights and monarchs can be seen at the

Shirley Temple doll at Bethnal Green Museum

Tower of London *(pp154–7)*. More up-to-date armoury and weapons, including aircraft and the tools of modern warfare, can be seen at the National Army Museum *(p197)* and the Imperial War Museum *(pp190–91)*. Also worth a visit is the Guards' Museum *(p80)* located on Birdcage Walk. London's colourful past is brought alive at the Museum of London. The superb London Aquarium *(p188)*, on the bank of the Thames, offers close-up encounters with sea life from starfish to sharks.

THE GREAT OUTDOORS

London is fortunate in having many parks and open spaces *(see pp48–51)*. Most local parks contain conventional playgrounds for children, many with modern, safe equipment. Some parks also have One O'Clock Clubs (enclosed areas for children under 5 with activities supervised by play-workers) as well as adventure playgrounds, nature trails, boating ponds and athletic tracks for older children and energetic adults.

Puppets at the Little Angel Theatre, Islington

Playground at Gunnersbury Park

A delightful children's park in Bloomsbury is Coram's Fields *(p125)*, where grassy areas, sand-pits and playgrounds make it perfect for picnics. Kite-flying on Blackheath *(p243)*, Hampstead Heath or Parliament Hill can be fun, as can boating in Regent's Park. A trip to Primrose Hill *(pp266–7)* can be combined with a visit to the Zoo and Regent's Canal *(p227)*. The large parks are one of London's greatest assets for parents who have energetic children.

For a good walk or cycle ride, there are parks all over London. For instance, there's Hyde Park in the city centre; Hampstead Heath up in the north; Wimbledon Common in southwest London; and Gunnersbury Park in west London. Cyclists should be sure to watch out for pedestrians and remember that some paths may be out of bounds.

Battersea Park has a children's zoo and Crystal Palace Park (Penge SE20) has a dinosaur park. Richmond Park has a deer herd. For a relaxing trip, go and feed the ducks in St James's Park.

Tuojiangasaurus skeleton at the Natural History Museum

CHILDREN'S THEATRE

Introducing children to the theatre can be great fun for adults too. Get involved at the **Little Angel Theatre,** or the **Puppet Theatre Barge** in Little Venice. The **Unicorn Theatre** offers the best range of children's theatre and the **Polka Children's Theatre** has some good shows.

USEFUL NUMBERS Little Angel Theatre **Tel** 020-7226 1787. Polka Children's Theatre **Tel** 020-8543 4888. **www**.polkatheatre.com Puppet Theatre Barge Marionette Performers **Tel** 020-7249 6876. **www**.puppet barge.com Unicorn Theatre **Tel** 020-7645 0560. **www**.unicorntheatre.com

Deer in Richmond Park

SIGHTSEEING

For seeing the sights of London you can't beat the top of a double-decker bus *(see pp382–3)*. It's a cheap and easy way of entertaining children, and if they get restless you can always jump off the bus at the next stop. London's colourful ceremonies are detailed on pages 52–5. Children will also enjoy such spectacles as the summer fun-fairs in London's parks, the firework displays throughout London on

Guy Fawkes Night (every 5 November) and the Christmas decorations in Oxford Street and Regent Street and Trafalgar Square's Christmas tree.

BEHIND THE SCENES

Older children in particular will love the opportunity to look "behind the scenes" and see how famous events or institutions are run.

If you have a brood of sports enthusiasts, you should visit Twickenham Rugby Football Ground *(see p355)*, Lord's Cricket Ground *(p246)*, the Wimbledon Lawn Tennis Museum *(p251)*, and Chelsea Football Stadium *(p355)*.

For budding theatre buffs, the Royal National Theatre *(p188)*, the Royal Opera House *(p115)*, Sadler's Wells *(p350)*, and the Theatre Royal Drury Lane *(p115)* all offer tours.

Other good buildings for children to visit include the Tower of London *(pp154–7)*, the Old Bailey law courts *(p147)* and the Houses of Parliament *(pp72–3)*.

If none of the above satisfies the children, the London Fire Brigade (020-7587 4063) offers more unusual guided tours.

Boating lake near Winfield House in Regent's Park

SURVIVAL
GUIDE

PRACTICAL INFORMATION

London has responded well to the demands of modern tourism. The range of facilities on offer to travellers, from ATM machines and medical clinics to boutique hotels and late night transport, continues to expand. Whether you find London an expensive city will depend on the exchange rate between the pound and your own currency. It is known for high hotel prices, but even here there are good mid-range and budget options *(see pp278–81)*. You need not spend a lot on food, if you choose carefully and make the most of the range London has to offer, for the price of a single meal at some West End restaurants you could eat enjoyably for several days *(see pp312–15)*. The following tips will help you make the most of your visit.

Crossing the Millenium Bridge

WHEN TO GO

London's weather is famously changeable, but in general it is chilly from November to February, and warmest from June to August *(see p59)*. It can rain at any time of year, so pack accordingly. Extremes of temperature – whether of cold in winter or heat in summer – are rare, so there is no time of year when London "closes down" and everyone goes on holiday. Events and cultural programmes run throughout the year. Many major concert series and exhibitions take place in winter and spring, but there are plenty of cultural events during the summer too, such as the BBC Proms season of classical concerts, and open-air theatre seasons. In short, there's plenty to see all year round *(see pp56–9)*.

VISAS AND PASSPORTS

Citizens of European Union countries may enter the UK for an unlimited period with a passport or national identity card. Visitors from the United States, Canada, Australia and New Zealand need only a full passport for tourist and business stays of up to six months, but on arrival they must fill in an Immigration Card, which is given out on incoming flights. Citizens of some countries may require a visa; details can be found in the "Visa Services" section of the **UK Border Agency** (UKBA) website. The UK is not signed up to the Schengen open-borders agreement operated by most EU countries. Hence, visitors arriving from France or any other Schengen country must still pass through immigration checks when entering the UK.

The UKBA has a strict points-based visa system under which anyone from any non-EU country (including the USA, Canada, Australia and New Zealand) entering Britain for any purpose other than pure tourism or short business trips (this includes students on short study-abroad programmes) must obtain a visa before travelling. The visa system is complicated and detailed, so check well in advance; details are on the UKBA website.

CUSTOMS INFORMATION

EU residents may carry any amount of goods between EU countries without paying duty, as long as the goods are for their personal use. Customs officers can still question whether large amounts of any item are genuinely for your own use. Examples of amounts usually accepted are: up to 3,200 cigarettes and up to 90 litres of wine. For travellers arriving from outside the EU, stricter allowances apply – for example, 200 cigarettes. Visitors not resident in the EU can reclaim the Value Added Tax (VAT) on many goods when they leave Britain, but note that the items must have been bought from a shop operating the VAT Retail Export Scheme (which should be indicated in the shop window). Ask the retailer for the correct form, which has details on how to obtain your refund; these can also be found on the UKBA website under "Travel and Customs".

TOURIST INFORMATION AND TOURS

Visit London is the city's central tourism service and is a key source of information. The main tourist office is the **Britain and London Visitor Centre** *(see p365)*; there are also Tourist Information Centres in the City (by St Paul's Cathedral), at main rail stations and at several other locations (visitlondon.com has a full list). The centres sell travelcards and **London Pass** *(see p363)* discount cards, provide currency exchange and distribute Visit London's handy free monthly magazine, *London Planner*.

For comprehensive listings information – including art, cinema, music, theatre and nightlife – visit the websites of **LondonNet** and *Time Out*

Signposted directions

Double-decker sightseeing boat on the Thames

London, London's leading listings magazine.

Guided tours are an effective way to explore the city; a trip in an open-topped double-decker bus makes a good introduction. **Original London Sightseeing Tours** and **Big Bus Tours** are the main companies offering hop-on, hop-off services, with tickets valid for 24 or 48 hours. Other tour companies include **London Walks**, which offers over 40 different routes, and **London Duck Tours**, for tours in a World-War-II-era amphibious vehicle. To find a private tour guide to suit your interests, contact the **Association of Professional Tourist Guides**. For river cruises and commuter services, *see page 61*.

Major sights in London are often crowded and queues are likely. Museums and galleries get particularly busy at weekends and on late-opening nights, so try to visit midweek and earlier in the day.

ADMISSION PRICES

Admission to the main collections of London's major public museums and galleries is free, but you will pay to see temporary exhibits. Private museums and other attractions have admission charges; they vary greatly, but for adults most are between £5 and £15. There are often reduced prices for seniors, students and children.

If you aim to do lots of sightseeing, you can cut costs with a **London Pass**, a card that gives you free entry and fast-track admission at many attractions. Cards are valid for 1, 2, 3 or 6 days and can be combined with a bus and Underground travelcard. A London Pass can be bought in advance from visitlondon.com and mailed to your home or collected from a tourist centre.

OPENING HOURS

Opening times for individual sights are listed in the *Area by Area* section of this book. Core visiting times are 10am to 5pm or 6pm daily; last admission is usually 1 hour before closing time. Most of the big museums have at least one late-opening day each week. Opening hours are often shorter on Sundays and public holidays. Some smaller attractions are closed on Mondays.

SOCIAL CUSTOMS AND ETIQUETTE

Londoners are traditionally renowned for queueing – whether for theatre tickets, taxis or takeaways. Things aren't quite as genteel as they used to be, but in general, anyone barging in will still encounter frosty glares.

Casual clothing is accepted in most restaurants, and only a few upscale establishments still require men to wear a jacket and tie.

The religious pattern of London reflects the city's huge ethnic diversity; all of the world's major faiths are represented here.

Smoking is forbidden in all public indoor spaces. Some hotels still designate bedrooms for smokers, but it's best to double check when booking.

TIPPING

It is usual to tip in restaurants, hotels, hairdressers, taxis and minicabs, but not for bar service in pubs. Many restaurants add a service charge – usually 12.5 per cent – to the bill, in which case an extra tip is not necessary. Be wary of places that add a service charge, then encourage you to add a "gratuity" when you pay by credit card. In taxis and cabs, tip around 10 per cent; for hotel porters, £1 is usually sufficient.

TRAVELLERS WITH SPECIAL NEEDS

Access to transport and attractions, and services for wheelchair users and others with mobility problems is continually improving. The Visit London website has a guide to access and services. **Transport for London** (TfL) produces a *Getting around London* guide, which can be downloaded from the TfL or Visit London websites, and is available free from Underground stations. **Artsline** gives information on facilities at cultural events and venues.

Nearly all London buses have wheelchair-access ramps, and all licensed taxis and some minicabs are wheelchair-accessible. The huge task of improving access to the entire Underground network is ongoing. Underground maps show accessible stations. Most museums and theatres have access facilities, but hotels with fully adapted rooms are scarce.

Disabled drivers with a blue badge allowing free parking should note that in four London boroughs – the City, Westminster, Kensington & Chelsea, and Camden – it allows you to park only in designated blue-badge bays.

London bus with ramp for easy wheelchair access

The Natural History Museum, a great day out for the whole family

TRAVELLING WITH CHILDREN

Under Transport for London's "Kids Go Free" scheme, travel is free on buses, the Underground, DLR and trains within London for all children aged under 11 accompanied by an adult (up to four children per adult). Children aged 11–15 can also travel free, with or without an adult, on all buses, and for reduced prices on the Underground and DLR *(see p378)*; also available is a Zip Oyster 11–15 Identity Card, which can be ordered online and collected at a tourist information centre on arrival in London; see the Visit London and Transport for London websites.

Most museums and attractions have reduced prices for children under 11; at several, entry is free for under-5s. Many also offer good-value family tickets. Plenty of restaurants welcome children, and a number of hotels have family rooms; the Novotel chain represents particularly good value for families.

London is a child-friendly city. A huge variety of entertainment and activities are laid on for children, and many museums have special kids' programmes. There are dozens of parks, many of them with playground facilities. The Visit London website's "Family" pages are a useful source of information. *Time Out London's* "Kids" pages are good for current attractions.

SENIOR TRAVELLERS

Older visitors enjoy fewer special benefits than younger ones, but there are reduced admission prices for over-60s at most museums, exhibitions and other attractions. You may be asked to show photo ID. Free travel on public transport is only available to residents.

GAY AND LESBIAN TRAVELLERS

London has a huge and diverse gay scene. Its core is Soho – it even has a (non-official) **LGBT Tourist Office**, which offers advice on everything from the best gay bars to accommodation. It's hard to keep track of everything going on, but the **Pink Paper** and **Gay London** websites, as well as the gay pages of *Time Out London,* are all useful and up-to-date sources of information.

TRAVELLING ON A BUDGET

London can be a very expensive city, but sightseeing costs can be cut with the London Pass *(see p363)*, and remember that admission to London's largest museums is free. To get around town by public transport, always buy a travelcard rather than single tickets; for trips out of town, coach is much cheaper than train, especially when booked in advance. Discounted theatre tickets can be bought at the **tkts** booth in Leicester Square, and many theatres have cheap-ticket nights.

London has plenty of budget restaurants and cafés, and even quite grand restaurants offer accessibly priced lunch menus. As well as dorm-style hostels, there are no-frills budget hotels with private rooms, some ensuite, for under £50 *(see p281)*. There's also a growing trend for spare-room lets and "couch surfing" via the **Crashpadder** website.

Students pay lower admission to many exhibitions, and holders of an **ISIC** (International Student Identity Card) or IYTC (International Youth Travel Card) are eligible for a range of other discounts. A **Hostelling International** card is also handy for lower rates at hostels and other discounts.

ELECTRICITY

The voltage in London is 240V AC, and plugs have three square pins. Visitors will need plug adaptors for appliances, and with any older North American 110V equipment you may also need a current transformer.

CONVERSION CHART

Officially the metric system is used, but imperial measures are still common.

Imperial to metric
1 inch = 2.5 centimetres
1 foot = 30 centimetres
1 mile = 1.6 kilometres
1 ounce = 28 grams
1 pound = 454 grams
1 pint = 0.6 litre
1 gallon = 4.6 litres

Metric to imperial
1 millimetre = 0.04 inch
1 centimetre = 0.4 inch
1 metre = 3 feet 3 inches
1 kilometre = 0.6 mile
1 gram = 0.04 ounce
1 kilogram = 2.2 pounds

International Student Identity Card (ISIC)

TIME

London is on Greenwich Mean Time (GMT) during the winter months, 5 hours ahead of Eastern Standard Time and 10 hours behind Sydney. From late March to late October, clocks are set forward 1 hour to British Summer Time (equivalent to Central European Time). At any time of year you can check the correct time by dialing 123 on a BT landline to contact the 24-hour auto-mated Speaking Clock service (note that there is a charge).

RESPONSIBLE TOURISM

London has set itself ambit-ious targets for improving the urban environment and reducing energy use. **Thames 21**, for example, is an evironmental charity which invol-ves the local com-munity in schemes to help keep the river Thames clean and clear.

The **Green Tourism Business Scheme** awards "Green Tourism" badges to

businesses in the UK that meet the highest environmental standards. These standards ensure that each business is committed to sustainable tourism and dedicated to minimising its damage to the environment. See the website for green accommod-ation details.

Recycling bins, which separate paper and plastic are widely available and many shoppers carry reusable cloth bags to avoid using plastic bags.

Green Tourism badge

DIRECTORY

Personal Security and Health

London is a large city which, like any other, has had its share of urban problems. It has also been a terrorist target, and London life is sometimes disrupted by security alerts. Nearly all of these turn out to be false alarms, but they should always still be taken seriously. Never hesitate to approach one of London's many police constables for assistance – they are trained to help the public with problems.

Mounted police

POLICE

If you are robbed, or are the victim of any other kind of crime, report it to the police as soon as possible. Patrolling police officers are generally fairly easy to find in central London, but if you cannot find one, call or go to the nearest police station – these are listed on the **Metropolitan Police** website; alternatively your hotel should be able to advise. Note that the **City of London Police** is a separate force, with its own website. Police stations are also shown on the Street Finder maps towards the end of this book (pp386–423).

When you report a crime, police will take a statement from you, and you will need to list any lost or stolen items.

WHAT TO BE AWARE OF

It is unlikely that your stay in London will be blighted by crime. Even in run-down parts of town, the risk of having your pocket picked or bag stolen is not particularly great. It is actually more likely to happen in the middle of heaving shopping crowds in areas like Oxford Street or Camden Lock, or perhaps on a packed Underground platform.

As in any big city, the risk of being a victim of street crime can be further reduced by following a few sensible precautions. Make sure your possessions are adequately insured before you travel. Do not carry all your valuables around with you but take only as much cash as you need, and leave the rest in a hotel safe or a locked suitcase. Avoid poorly lit or isolated places like backstreets, parks and unmanned railway stations at night, and don't use ATMs after dark. To be extra careful, try to travel around in a group at night.

In crowds, be aware of anyone standing especially close. Keep bags zipped up; keep a hand on your bag when walking along; and never leave bags unattended in any public place – they may be stolen or considered a security threat. When you sit at a table, especially outdoors, always keep your bag within reach and in sight – preferably on your lap or on the table – and never leave it on the ground or hanging on the back of a chair.

IN AN EMERGENCY

In a serious emergency you can call 999 – or the European emergency number 112 – to summon police, fire or ambulance services. Note that this is only for genuine emergencies, so if you have a lesser problem it is better to contact a police station or hospital directly.

LOST AND STOLEN PROPERTY

Although you should report thefts, or loss of any property, to the police, be warned that it's unlikely that they will be able to recover any of it for you. However, they will give you a copy of your police statement, which you will need to make an insurance claim.

If you lose anything on buses, Underground and DLR trains or in taxis (black cabs), it should eventually reach the **Transport for London Lost Property Office** in Baker Street. You can also enquire about lost items online, through the TfL website (under "Help & Contact" or "Useful Contacts"). It will usually take a few days for items to reach the office, so if you notice the loss the same day, try to enquire about it at the station nearest to where you lost it, or at the nearest police station. Items lost on river boats or in minicabs should be held by the individual companies.

HOSPITALS AND PHARMACIES

All European Union nationals with a European Health Insurance Card (EHIC), as well as citizens of some other countries with special agreements with the UK (Australia and New Zealand among them), can obtain free treatment from the British **National Health Service (NHS)**. Visitors from other non-EU countries should have full medical cover as part of their travel insurance, and if necessary make use of an NHS or private hospital (such as **Medical Express**) on a paying basis. In case of emergency, anyone – EU or non-EU – will be treated free of charge.

If you have an accident or other problem needing medical attention, ask your hotel to recommend a doctor,

Traffic police officer

Typical London police car

London ambulance

London fire engine

or go to the nearest NHS health centre (doctor's surgery) or hospital Accident & Emergency (A&E) department. Not all hospitals have A&E departments, but those that do are listed on the NHS

and Visit London websites, and in local phone books. In many cases the simplest thing may be to call **NHS Direct**, a free advice service that will give you immediate health advice and also direct you to the nearest hospital A&E department.

If you have a dental problem, you can also call NHS Direct for addresses of emergency dentists. Dental treatment through the NHS is not entirely free, so it may make more sense to arrange private treatment (again, hotels should be able to recommend a dentist) and claim on your insurance policy.

Pharmacies (also known as chemists) are plentiful around London, and staff are trained to dispense and advise on a wide range of medications. Some medicines are only available with a

Pharmacy sign

prescription. It is worth noting that prescription drugs are not free even if you are entitled to NHS treatment; if you are not, you will be charged the full price, and so will need to make an insurance claim. The **Boots** company is the largest chain of pharmacies in the UK. Most pharmacies are closed on Sundays, but those listed in the Directory, below, have extended hours.

TRAVEL AND HEALTH INSURANCE

All visitors to London should have a comprehensive travel insurance policy providing adequate cover for all eventualities including potential legal expenses, theft, lost luggage or other property, accidents, cancellations, travel delays and medical cover. Even if you are entitled to use the NHS for medical needs, it can be a good idea to have private medical insurance included too, as a backup, since this may allow you to get quicker treatment with fewer formalities. Your insurance company should provide you with a 24-hour emergency number in case of need.

DIRECTORY

EMERGENCIES

Police, Fire & Ambulance services
Tel 999 or 112.
Calls are free.

POLICE

City of London Police
Tel 020-7601 2222.
www.cityoflondon.
police.uk

Metropolitan Police
Tel 0300-123 1212.
www.met.police.uk

West End Central Police Station
27 Saville Row, W1.
Map 12 F2.
Tel 0300-123 1212.

LOST PROPERTY

Transport for London Lost Property Office
200 Baker St, NW1.
Map 3 C5.
Tel 0845-330-9882.
www.tfl.gov.uk. *Open* 8.30am–4pm Mon-Fri.

HEALTH SERVICES

Medical Express (Private)
117A Harley St, W1.
Tel 0800-9800 700.
www.medicalexpress
clinic.com

NHS
www.nhs.uk
To locate a hospital, look under "Find and choose services".

NHS Direct
Tel 0845-4647.
www.nhsdirect.nhs.uk
(24-hr health information and nurse-led advice).

University College Hospital
Accident and Emergency,
235 Euston Road NW1.
Map 5 A4.
Tel 0845-155 5000.

DENTISTS

24-Hour Emergency Dental Clinic
8F Gilbert Place WC1.
Map 13 B1. *Tel* 020-8123 3132. www.24hour-london-emergencydentist.
co.uk

LATE-OPENING PHARMACIES

Bliss Chemist
5–6 Marble Arch W1.
Map 11 C2. *Tel* 020-7723 6116. *Open* 9am until midnight daily.

Boots the Chemist
44–46 Regent St, W1.
Map 13 A3. *Tel* 020-7734 6126. www.boots.
com *Open* 8am–midnight Mon–Fri, 9am– midnight Sat, noon–6pm Sun.

Superdrug
508–520 Oxford St, W1.
Map 11 C2. *Tel* 020-7629 1649.
www.superdrug.com
Open 7am–11pm Mon–Fri, 8am–10pm Sat, 12:30–6:30pm Sun.

Banking and Local Currency

Visitors to London will find that banks usually offer the best rates of exchange, but care should be taken to check the small-print details relating to commission and other charges before completing any transaction. Privately owned bureaux de change have variable exchange rates and commissions – some, in particular, charge more for changing smaller amounts of money – but they do stay open long after the banks have closed.

Cashpoint machine

BANKS AND BUREAUX DE CHANGE

Banking hours vary. The minimum opening hours for all banks are 9.30am–3.30pm Mon–Fri, but many branches now stay open till 5 or 5.30pm, especially in central London; some also open on Saturdays from about 10am–4pm. All banks are closed on Sundays and public holidays *(see p59)*. The commission charged on currency exchange will vary from bank to bank.

When banks are closed, there are plenty of other facilities for changing cash and traveller's cheques across the city. You will find bureaux

de change at airports, main rail stations, in large stores, and at many other locations. **Chequepoint, Thomas Cook** and **Travelex** are some of the largest companies. The central London (Piccadilly) branch of **Money Corporation** is open 24 hours daily.

CREDIT CARDS AND TRAVELLER'S CHEQUES

Major credit cards such as Visa and MasterCard, and debit cards such as Delta, Maestro and Cirrus, are widely accepted all over London. Fewer businesses accept the American Express card, because of their high charges.

British credit and debit cards operate on a chip-and-PIN security system; you must enter your PIN number into a card reader to validate the purchase. If you have a North American or other card that does not use chip-and-pin technology, your card will have to be swiped in the more traditional way.

It may also be useful to have some currency with you in traveller's cheques, in case you lose your cards. Traveller's cheques cannot be used to pay for goods directly in shops in the UK, but must be

DIRECTORY

BUREAUX DE CHANGE

All have branches across London.

Chequepoint
Tel 0844-445 5055.
www.americanexpress.com

Money Corporation
18 Piccadilly, W1. **Map** 13 A3.
Tel 020-7439 2100.
www.moneycorp.com
Open 24-hrs daily.

Thomas Cook
Tel 0845-246 4353.
www.thomascook.com/money

Travelex
Tel 08702-405 405.
www.thomascook.com/money

LOST CREDIT CARDS

American Express
Tel 01273-696 933.

MasterCard
Tel 0800-964 767.

Visa
Tel 0800-891 725.

exchanged for cash at a bank or bureau de change. US dollar and Euro traveller's cheques are easily exchanged at all banks and change desks. Again, check the latest commission rates and conditions before cashing your cheques.

ATMS

There are ATM cash machines (also known as cashpoints), from which you can obtain cash with any of the major credit or debit cards, at all bank branches, many post offices and many other locations such as stations. The cards accepted by each ATM are indicated on the machine, which usually gives instructions in several languages. Given the high commission rates sometimes charged by banks and bureaux de change for exchanging traveller's cheques, the most economical, as well as most convenient, way to get cash can be to withdraw it from an ATM with a debit card.

MAIN HIGH STREET BANKS

These are some of the high-street banks found all over London. Many will also offer currency-exchange facilities, but proof of identity may be required.

Royal Bank of Scotland logo

National Westminster logo

HSBC logo

Barclays Bank logo

Lloyds TSB logo

Avoid using the independent ATMs found in some small shops, as they often carry expensive extra charges There is also a certain risk of crime at some ATMs. Avoid using any in dark streets at night, and don't use an ATM if any part of it looks damaged or as if it has been tampered with, especially the card slot. Be aware of anyone standing close to you when using an ATM, and shield the numbered keypad with your hand as you enter your PIN.

CURRENCY

Britain's currency is the pound sterling (£), which is divided into 100 pence (p). Since there are no exchange controls in Britain, there is no limit to how much cash you may import or export. Many large stores in London accept payments in US dollars and Euros, but often at a poor exchange rate.

English bank notes of all denominations always feature the Queen's head on one side

Bank Notes
English notes used in the UK are £5, £10, £20 and £50. Scotland has its own notes which, despite being legal tender throughout the UK, are not always accepted.

£50 note

£20 note

£10 note

£5 note

Coins of the Realm
Coins in circulation are £2, £1, 50p, 20p, 10p, 5p, 2p and 1p (they are shown here slightly smaller than actual size). They all have the Queen's head on the other side.

2 pounds (£2)

1 pound (£1)

50 pence (50p)

20 pence (20p)

10 pence (10p)

5 pence (5p)

2 pence (2p)

1 pence (1p)

Communication and Media

British Telecom logo

The telecommunications systems in Britain are efficient and inexpensive. Most static landline phones and public phoneboxes are operated by British Telecom (BT), and there are many other mobile phone operators and Internet service providers. Charges on BT lines depend on when, where and for how long you talk. National calls are most expensive from 9am to 1pm on weekdays. A cheap rate applies before 8am or after 6pm on weekdays, and all day at weekends. Cheap times for overseas calls vary, but tend to be at weekends and in the evening.

INTERNATIONAL AND LOCAL TELEPHONE CALLS

All London landline telephone numbers have 11 digits and begin with the code 020. Phone numbers in central London continue with 7, and in outer London with 8, although some business numbers continue with 3. If you are calling from another London number you do not need to dial the 020, but only the remaining eight digits. Every other part of Britain has its own area code, beginning with 01 or 02.

Whenever possible, avoid making calls from hotels – above all, long-distance – as most add hefty surcharges, and some even charge for free-phone lines. There are several special-rate numbers within the UK. Phone numbers beginning 03 are low-cost numbers used mostly by public bodies, such as the police. All 0800 or 0808 numbers are free to call from UK landlines (but not from mobile phones). 0844, 0845, 0870 and 0871 numbers are reduced-rate lines that are used by many companies and organizations for information services. Numbers beginning 09 are premium-rate and so particularly expensive.

To call Britain from abroad, dial 00 44, but then omit the initial zero from the UK area code. So to call the London number 020 7123 4567 from abroad, you would dial 00 44 20 7123 4567. To call abroad from London, dial 00 and then the usual country code (for example, Australia: 61; USA and Canada: 1).

MOBILE PHONES

All UK mobile phone numbers begin with 07. Calling a mobile from a landline is considerably more expensive than calling another landline. There is a very high level of mobile ownership in London and signal coverage is good all over the city. UK mobiles use the European-standard 900 and 1900 MHz frequencies, so mobiles from other European countries work easily here so long as they have their roaming facility enabled. North American and Asian cell phones will not operate here unless they have a tri- or quad-band facility (which is increasingly standard on current phones). Before using a mobile while travelling, always check with your own service provider on the current level of roaming charges, which can be high. Many companies offer "packages" of foreign calls to cut costs.

If you anticipate using the phone a great deal, it may well be more economical to buy a cheap "pay-as-you-go" British mobile (a basic phone can cost as little as £10, or less) from one of the main local providers such as **O2**, **Orange**, **T-Mobile** or **Vodafone**, all of which have shops all over the city.

PUBLIC TELEPHONES

You will find a **BT** phonebox on many streets in central London, and in every railway station. Some are the old-style red ones, others are much more modern in appearance; but whichever type, they generally have the same technology inside. Some have multimedia terminals allowing Internet and email access. You can pay with coins, or by credit or debit card. Payphones accept 10p, 20p, 50p, £1 and £2 coins; some also accept Euro coins (50c, €1 and €2). The minimum call cost is 40p for the first 20 minutes to a UK landline; and 10p for each 10 minutes after that. For a short call, use 10p or 20p pieces, as payphones only return unused coins. For credit-card calls, the minimum charge is £1.20.

Old BT phonebox

Modern BT phonebox

USEFUL DIALLING CODES

- The area code for London is 020.
- Phone numbers in central London start with 7 or 3, and in outer areas with 8. The 020 prefix must be used if dialling from outside these two areas.
- British Telecom directory enquiries is 118 500.
- If you have any problems contacting a number, call the operator on 100.
- To make an international call, dial 00 followed by the country code (USA and Canada: 1; Australia: 61; New Zealand: 64), the area code and the number. The international operator number is 155 (freephone).
- A phonecard needs at least £2 credit for an international call.
- **In an emergency, dial 999 or 112. All emergency calls are free.**

INTERNET AND EMAIL

Internet access is very easy to find in London. Public libraries, tourist information centres and some other public buildings have free terminals. Internet cafés are common in every part of the city, and rates per hour are often very low.

Many hotels and a growing number of budget B&Bs and hostels offer Wi-Fi access. Some hotels charge, but this is increasingly rare. There are also many free Wi-Fi hotspots across London, in public libraries, arts centres, cafés, restaurants and pubs.

POSTAL SERVICES

Standard post in the UK is handled by the **Royal Mail**. There are main post offices providing all postal services in every London district, as well as many smaller sub-post offices attached to news-agents and other small shops – these can handle all normal mail. Main post offices are usually open from 9am to 5.30pm Monday to Friday, and to 12.30pm on Saturday. **Trafalgar Square Post Office** has extended hours: 8am–8pm Monday to Saturday. Post offices also exchange money and handle international money transfers.

Post within the UK can be sent by first- or second-class mail. First-class costs a little more and is quicker. Stamps can be bought from post offices or any shop with a "Stamps sold here" sign. Newsagents usually sell them, but may only have UK first- and second-class stamps, so for international mail you may need to find a Post Office.

Old-style pillar box

Hotels nearly always sell stamps, and larger ones may have mail boxes. Public post boxes come in different shapes and sizes – some are sunk into walls – but are always red, and can

Newsagent stocking a range of international newspapers

be found throughout the city. There are several collections a day (Mon–Sat); collection times are indicated on the box.

International letters and cards sent from London take about three days to reach European destinations, and four to six days to North America, Japan or Australasia. A competitively priced Airsure service is available for express deliveries (2–4 days worldwide), as well as a much slower but cheaper surface mail option.

NEWSPAPERS AND MAGAZINES

London's main local paper is the *Evening Standard*, distributed free in the centre of town from noon on week-days. *Time Out London* magazine, published each Thursday, is London's most comprehensive listings guide.

A range of international newspapers and magazines, including *USA Today*, *International Herald Tribune* and major European papers, is on sale at many newsstands and newsagents around central London. For more specialist foreign press, one of the best places to go is Old Compton Street in Soho, where newsagents regularly carry an extraordinary global variety.

TV AND RADIO

Five TV channels are available throughout the UK via a traditional analogue signal: two run by the publicly-owned BBC; and the independent ITV,

Channel 4 and 5. In addition, many hotels also have digital or satellite systems. Extra chan-nels available include BBC3 (youth-oriented), BBC4 (arts-oriented), various movie, shop-ping and music channels, and CNN. If you want to be able to view a wide range of US and other international channels (such as ESPN), ask whether a hotel has Sky Plus or an enhanced Freeview package.

The BBC also has a large number of radio stations, of which Radios 1 (97–99 FM) and 2 (88–91 FM) focus on pop music of different kinds, Radio 3 (90.2 FM) on classical and jazz, Radio 4 (92–96 FM) on speech and drama, and Radio 5 (909/693 AM) on news and sport. BBC London (94.9 FM) is good for keeping up with local issues and interests. A shuffle around the dial will present a huge number of other music and talk stations.

DIRECTORY

TELEPHONE SERVICES

British Telecom (BT)
Tel 150 or 0800-800 150.
www.bt.com

O2
Tel 0844-202 0202.
www.o2.co.uk

Orange
Tel 07973-100 150.
www.orange.co.uk

T-Mobile
Tel 0800-956 2208.
www.t-mobile.co.uk

Vodafone
Tel 0808-0044 423.
www.vodafone.co.uk

POSTAL SERVICES

Royal Mail
Tel 0845-7740 740.
www.royalmail.com

Trafalgar Square PO
24 William IV St, WC2. **Map** 13
B3. *Tel* 020-7930 9580.

NEWSPAPERS & MAGAZINES

Evening Standard
www.thisislondon.co.uk

Time Out
www.timeout.com/london

GETTING TO LONDON

London is one of Europe's central hubs for international air and rail travel. By air, travellers face a bewildering choice of carriers from Europe, North America, Australasia, the Far East and every other part of the globe. Stiff competition on some routes, especially from major European countries and North America, means that low-fare deals can often be found, so it's always worth shopping around. Since 1995, the Channel Tunnel has provided an efficient high-speed train link – Eurostar – between France and Belgium and the UK, as well as a fast, weatherproof Channel crossing for drivers. Eurostar trains depart from St Pancras International Station in London's King's Cross. Many European cruises sail from or finish at ports not far from London, such as Southampton, Dover or Tilbury, and there are efficient passenger and car ferry services from Europe, using large ferries and faster jetfoils and catamarans, across the North Sea and the English Channel.

Station concourse at St Pancras International

ARRIVING BY RAIL

Eurostar runs frequent daily trains to London from Paris, Brussels and Lille, where the Paris and Brussels lines meet. Non-stop trains from Paris (Gare du Nord) take 2 hours 15 minutes; from Brussels, 1 hour 50 minutes. Some trains also stop at Calais before entering the Channel Tunnel on the French side, and at Ashford and Ebbsfleet on the English. If you travel by train from any other part of Europe and want to connect with Eurostar, it's best to do so at Lille, as you change trains in the same station – quicker and far easier than doing so in Paris. Check-in on Eurostar is only 30 minutes before departure, so it's generally far quicker than flying.

Eurostar trains arrive in London at St Pancras International, on the northern edge of central London, next to King's Cross Underground station. The station is a junction of six Underground lines, so is well connected with every part of the city. Eurostar fares vary a good deal according to flexibility and the time of day you travel (early morning trains are often the cheapest), so check current rates on the website when booking. Information and bookings for connecting trains from other parts of Europe can be found on the **Rail Europe** website.

London has eight mainline rail stations at which trains from different parts of Britain terminate: Paddington serves the West Country, Wales and the South Midlands; Liverpool Street serves East Anglia and Essex; King's Cross, St Pancras and Euston cover northern Britain; and Charing Cross, Victoria and Waterloo cover southern England, and also the main Channel ferry ports.

The current UK railway system is complicated and can be confusing. Lines are run by several different companies, but they are coordinated by **National Rail**, which operates a joint information service.

Fare structures are especially complex: tickets can be very expensive or surprisingly cheap, depending on whether you grasp how the system operates. Going to a station the same day you want to travel and buying a ticket over the counter is always the most expensive way to travel. Whenever possible book trains in advance and check alternative fares, bearing in mind that the best fares may only be available online. The National Rail website has a useful "cheapest fare finder" feature, which then links you to the relevant company site to make the booking. Also helpful is **Trainline**, an independent booking agency which often has discounted tickets. Tickets booked online can usually be collected at the station.

Fares on suburban rail services around London are less complex, so there is no need to book ahead. Rail lines within London accept the Oyster Card (see p378).

Rail information point at a London station, for help and advice

Cross-channel ferry heading to Calais

ARRIVING BY COACH

International and national coach services from every part of Europe and the UK arrive in London at Victoria Coach Station on Buckingham Palace Road, about 5 minutes' walk from Victoria rail and Underground stations, and with several local bus stops outside. If you're planning to travel to any UK destinations outside of the London area, it's slower but nearly always cheaper to do it by coach than by train, with fares as low as £1 on some London–Oxford services (although some train companies try to offer lower fares on the same routes).

National Express operates the most extensive UK coach network, with around 1,000 destinations covered, and is also associated with Eurolines international coach services. **Megabus** has especially low fares to many UK destinations, and also discount train offers. **Green Line** runs buses between London and the surrounding counties, and has a service to Luton Airport (*see p377*).

ARRIVING BY SEA AND TUNNEL

The **Eurotunnel** shuttle – the other train service using the Channel Tunnel – is a drive-on, drive-off service for cars between Calais and Folkestone, where the Tunnel connects with the M20 motorway to London. There are usually four shuttles per hour, with a journey time of about 35 minutes.

If you prefer to brave the elements, there are still plenty of ferry services between southeast England and Continental ports. Harwich in Essex has ferries from Esbjerg in Denmark, with **DFDS**; and from Hook of Holland in the Netherlands, with **Stena Line**. Dover is the busiest port, with frequent services from France: from Dunkerque with **Norfolk Line**; from Calais with **P&O Ferries** and **Seafrance**; and from Boulogne with **LD Lines**. Newhaven–Dieppe ferries are operated by **LD/Transmanche**.

There are also several routes in the western Channel, which take longer, but may leave you better located for visiting the west of England: to Portsmouth from Caen, Cherbourg and St Malo with **Brittany Ferries**, or from Le Havre with LD Lines; to Poole from Cherbourg with Brittany Ferries; or to Poole or Weymouth from St Malo and the Channel Islands with **Condor Ferries**.

Crossing times to Dover are around 1 hour 15 minutes; in the western Channel it takes more like 5-6 hours, although in summer, fast jetfoils and catamarans cut this to 2–3 hours.

There are also ferry services from Spain: from Santander to Plymouth or Portsmouth with Brittany Ferries; and from Bilbao to Portsmouth with P&O. Crossings take around 24 hours, on comfortable "mini-cruise-ships".

Driving time from Dover or the Channel Tunnel to central London is usually around 2 hours; from Portsmouth, 2½–3 hours. If you bring a car to London, always try to arrange a place to stay with free parking, otherwise this can become extremely expensive.

DIRECTORY

RAIL SERVICES

Eurostar
London St Pancras International.
Tel 08432-186 186.
www.eurostar.com

National Rail
Tel 0845-748 4950.
www.nationalrail.co.uk

Rail Europe
Tel 1-800-622 8600 (USA),
08448-484 064 (UK).
www.raileurope.com

Trainline
Tel 0871-244 1545.
www.thetrainline.com

COACH SERVICES

Green Line
Tel 0844-801 7261.
www.greenline.co.uk

Megabus
Tel 0900-160 0900.
http://megabus.com/uk

National Express
Tel 08717-818 181.
www.nationalexpress.com

TUNNEL AND FERRIES

Brittany Ferries
Tel 0871-244 0744.
www.brittany-ferries.com

Condor Ferries
Tel 01202-207 216.
www.condorferries.co.uk

DFDS Seaways
Tel 0871-522 9955.
www.dfdsseaways.co.uk

Eurotunnel
Tel 08443-353 535.
www.eurotunnel.com

LD Lines/Transmanche Ferries
Tel 0844-576 8836.
www.ldlines.co.uk

Norfolk Line
Tel 0844-847 5042.
www.norfolkline.com

P&O Ferries
Tel 0871-664 5645.
www.poferries.com

Seafrance
Tel 0871-423 7119.
www.seafrance.com

Stena Line
Tel 0844-770 7070.
www.stenaline.co.uk

Arriving by Air

London's two main airports, Heathrow and Gatwick, are augmented by smaller facilities at Luton, Stansted and London City *(see pp376–7)*. Check which airport you will land at, and plan your journey from there. All the airports have train or coach links; Heathrow is also connected to central London by Underground. Because the airports are so far apart from each other, travelling between them is best avoided. Further details can be found online.

Access to the Underground in the arrival terminal at Heathrow

British Airways passenger jet at Heathrow airport

AIRLINES AND FARES

Heathrow and Gatwick have long-haul connections with every part of the world, on scores of airlines. The main United States airlines offering scheduled flights to London include **Delta**, **United**, **American Airlines** and **US Airways**, while from Canada there are frequent services with **Air Canada**. **British Airways** and **Virgin Atlantic** also fly from many North American cities. The flight time from New York is about 6½ hours; from Los Angeles, about 10 hours. The choice of carriers from Australasia and Asia is enormous too: **Qantas**, **Air New Zealand** and British Airways may be the obvious first choices, but operators such as **Singapore Airlines** and **Emirates** offer interesting alternatives.

All the main carrier airlines, such as British Airways, Air France, **Iberia** and **Lufthansa**, offer frequent European connections, mostly to Heathrow or Gatwick, but they now carry less traffic than the low-cost airlines. **Ryanair** has budget flights to all of Europe, Ireland and the UK, mostly from Stansted, while **easyJet** runs almost as extensive a European and British network from Stansted, Luton and Gatwick.

Very few airlines now offer reduced prices for children. Low-cost flights can normally

be booked only through each airline's own website. Note that low-cost airlines regularly add "extra" charges on top of the fare – such as one for checking in luggage. Ryanair in particular, charges £40 if you cannot download and print your own boarding card, and need one issued by ground staff at the airport.

SECURITY

Security is tighter than ever at London airports. Allow at least two hours to check in and get through security before your flight, especially – because of its size – at Heathrow. Allow ample time also (2 hours again) to catch low-cost flights if you are checking in a bag, since in the interests of keeping costs down there are not many check-in staff, so lines move slowly.

HEATHROW (LHR)

Heathrow in west London is one of the world's busiest airports. It has five terminals, so it's important to know which one your flight will arrive at or depart from. Terminals 1, 2 and 3, the oldest, share an Underground station and Heathrow Central rail station; Terminal 4 has its own Underground station; Terminal 5, which opened in 2008, has Underground and rail stations. A free shuttle bus runs between the Terminals. Most British Airways flights use Terminal 5; most other long-haul airlines use Terminals 3 or 4. There are shops and other facilities in every terminal.

There are several ways into London from Heathrow. The fastest rail service is the **Heathrow Express**, with trains every 15 minutes from around 5am to 11.30pm daily to Paddington station on the west side of central London. Journey time is about 15 minutes, and trains also stop at Terminal 5. To get to Terminals 1, 2 and 3, take the shuttle bus from Terminal 4. Fares are quite high, at around £18 single, £32 return (slightly less if you buy online).

Heathrow Terminal 5, used exclusively by British Airways

Heathrow Connect trains run on the same lines but with several stops, and take 25–30 minutes to reach Paddington. Fares are around £8 single.

The Underground (tube) offers a much cheaper way of getting into London, but is also much slower. Trains run frequently, calling at all Heathrow Terminals from around 5am to midnight Monday to Saturday; 5.50am–11.30pm Sunday. Unlike the Heathrow Express, the tube runs right into the city centre; allow about 45 minutes to get to Leicester Square. As on all London public transport, it's cheaper with an Oyster Card (see p378); the adult fare from Heathrow into the city centre is around £4.20.

National Express and other companies run a number of bus routes from Heathrow to Oxford, London, other London airports and other destinations. The main bus station is at Terminals 1, 2 and 3, but buses also stop at 4 and 5. A taxi to central London costs about £40. Driving time is from 30 minutes to 1 hour. It's worth noting that local minicab companies offer much cheaper rates (see p385).

LONDON CITY AIRPORT (LCY)

London City is the closest airport to central London, in the Docklands business area just east of London's financial district (the City). Unlike the low-cost airports, it was created primarily for business travellers, so flights are quite expensive. It offers flights to many European destinations, and a luxury service to New York.

London City has its own station on the Docklands Light Railway (DLR), which connects with the Underground network at Tower Hill and Bank. An Express Shuttle Bus runs

London City Airport, within sight of the city's Docklands area

every 30 minutes to Canary Wharf, for £7 single fare. A taxi to the City will cost about £20 and should take about 30 minutes; to the West End £30, taking around 45 minutes.

LONDON AIRPORTS

Luton
Luton Airport
Stevenage
45km
Stansted Airport
A120
A10
A1(M)
A41
A5
A120
Welwyn Garden City
Harlow
A41
M1
30km
M11
Chelmsford
Lea
High Wycombe
M40
Watford
M25
Enfield
15km
Roding
A12
Brentwood
Thames
Harrow
LONDON
Tottenham Hale
Romford
Basildon
Kings Cross
Slough
Paddington
Liverpool Street
London City Airport
A13
Thames
M4
Victoria
Canning Town
London Bridge
Heathrow Airport
Clapham Junction
Dartford
Gravesend
Bracknell
M25
Kingston upon Thames
Beckenham
15km
Bromley
M2
M3
Croydon
Wey
Woking
Sutton
Epsom
A3
A23
M25
M20
Maidstone
A24
30km
A21
Tonbridge

KEY

🚉 Railway station
🔵 Underground station
✈ Airport
═ Motorway
— 'A' road

Medway
A23
Gatwick Airport
Royal Tunbridge Wells
A22
Crawley
45km

GATWICK (LGW)

Gatwick airport lies due south of central London, and handles long-haul, European and low-cost flights. There are two terminals – North and South – so as at Heathrow, you need to be clear on which you need. The train station and main bus stops are at the South Terminal, from where there is a free shuttle train to the North. Allow around 20 minutes to transfer between terminals. There are banks, shops, cafés and other facilities at both.

There is a choice of three rail services from Gatwick into London, all from the same station. The **Gatwick Express** is the fastest, with trains every 15 minutes to Victoria Station. It runs from around 4.30am to midnight daily and takes about 30 minutes (a little longer on Sundays), but it isn't cheap; the fare is around £17 single, £29 return. Tickets can be bought online. **First Capital Connect** runs around four trains per hour over the same period to St Pancras International via several stops including East Croydon and London Bridge. Journey time is about an hour, and single fare around £9. **Southern Railway** has several trains each hour to London Victoria, with a journey time of 30–50 minutes and a single fare of around £11.

Entrance to Stansted's spacious modern passenger terminal

National Express and other companies run buses from the South Terminal to Heathrow and many towns in southern England (including central London), and **easyBus** runs frequently from the North Terminal to Fulham Broadway Underground in London. Buses are not limited to easyJet passengers, and fares begin at £2. A taxi into central London will set you back around £90, and can take 1–2 hours. As at Heathrow, minicab companies offer better rates to Gatwick.

STANSTED (STN)

Around 40 miles northeast of London, Stansted is the airport in southeast England most popular with the low-cost airlines, and so has a huge number of flights to destinations in every part of Europe.

The rail link into London is the **Stansted Express** train, which runs every 15 minutes from around 6am to 12.30am, with variations at weekends. Trains run to Liverpool Street, on the east side of central London, with a stop at Tottenham Hale (where you can transfer to the Victoria Underground line). Trains from Liverpool Street to Stansted run from approximately 4.40am to 11.30pm daily. The full journey takes 45 minutes. Adult fares to Liverpool Street are £19 single, £28.70 return (cheaper online). **National Express East Anglia** trains also run roughly once an hour to London Stratford station in East London's Olympic Park, with several stops, taking 1 hour for a fare of about £17.

Several bus services run from Stansted to London. National Express runs to Victoria Coach Station (£10.50) and many other destinations around the region, but easy-Bus is again the cheapest,

Gatwick's free monorail service linking the two terminals

AIRPORT	FROM CITY CENTRE	AVERAGE JOURNEY TIME	AVERAGE TAXI FARE
London City	10 km (6 miles)	Tube and DLR: 40 minutes	£20
Heathrow	23 km (14 miles)	Rail: 15 minutes Tube: 45 minutes	£40
Gatwick	45 km (28 miles)	Rail: 30 minutes Bus: 70 minutes	£90
Luton	51 km (32 miles)	Rail: 35 minutes Bus: 70 minutes	£60
Stansted	55 km (34 miles)	Rail: 45 minutes Bus: 75 minutes	£90

with tickets to Baker Street Underground station from £2. A taxi to central London can take 1 hour 30 minutes and cost £90–100.

LUTON (LTN)

Luton airport lies northwest of London near the M1 motorway, and is used almost exclusively by charter flights and low-cost airlines, especially easyJet. A shuttle bus connects the terminal with Luton Airport Parkway train station (about a 5-minute drive), from around 5am to midnight daily. First Capital Connect has about four trains each hour to London St Pancras – a journey of around 25–40 minutes for an adult single fare of £13.50. **East Midlands Trains** operate on the same route, and are a little cheaper, at £11.90. Green Line buses (route 757) run every

15 minutes almost 24 hours daily between the airport and London Victoria Coach station, with adult fares around £11 (*see p373*); easyBus has frequent services to Victoria via Baker Street, with tickets from £2. National Express runs from Luton to Heathrow, Gatwick, Stansted and other destinations. A taxi into London will cost around £60, and take about 45 minutes.

AIRPORT HOTELS

Given the long check-in times at the main airports, it can be a good idea – or even necessary – to stay nearby the night before departure, especially if you have an early-morning flight. There is a large number of hotels in the vicinity of Heathrow and Gatwick; many of these frequently have discount offers. All of them provide shuttle buses to the

Relaxing bar of the popular Sheraton Skyline hotel

airport terminals – in budget hotels this may be charged extra. The **Premier Inn**, **Travelodge** and **Holiday Inn** chains have cheap, functional, rooms close to the airports. A selection of airport hotels is listed below, but there are many more to choose from.

DIRECTORY

MAJOR AIRLINES

Air Canada
www.aircanada.com

Air New Zealand
www.airnewzealand.com

American Airlines
www.aa.com

British Airways
www.britishairways.com

Delta Airlines
www.delta.com

easyJet
www.easyjet.com

Emirates
www.emirates.com

Iberia
www.iberia.com

Lufthansa
www.lufthansa.com

Qantas
www.qantas.com.au

Ryanair
www.ryanair.com

Singapore Airlines
www.singaporeair.com

United Airlines
www.united.com

US Airways
www.usairways.com

Virgin Atlantic
www.virgin-atlantic.com

Travel Websites
www.bestfares.com
www.cheapflights.com
www.ebookers.com
www.expedia.com
www.flights.com
www.orbitz.com
www.priceline.com
www.travelnow.com
www.travelocity.com

AIRPORT INFORMATION

Gatwick
Tel 0844-335 1802.
www.gatwickairport.com

Heathrow
Tel 0844-335 1801.
www.heathrowairport.com

London City Airport
Tel 020-7646 0088.
www.londoncityairport.com

Luton
Tel 01582-405 100.
www.london-luton.co.uk

Stansted
Tel 0844–335 1803.
www.stanstedairport.com

AIRPORT TRANSPORT

easyBus
www.easybus.co.uk

East Midlands Trains
Tel 0845-712 5678.
www.eastmidland trains.co.uk

First Capital Connect
Tel 0845-7-484 950.
www.firstcapitalconnect.co.uk

Gatwick Express
Tel 0845-850 1530.
www.gatwickexpress.com

Heathrow Connect
Tel 0845-678 6975.
www.heathrowconnect.com

Heathrow Express
Tel 0845-600 1515.
www.heathrowexpress.com

National Express East Anglia
Tel 0845-600 7245.
www.nationalexpress eastanglia.com

Southern Railway
Tel 0845-127 2920.
www.southernrailway.com

Stansted Express
Tel 0845-850 0150.
www.stanstedexpress.com

HOTELS

Holiday Inn London Heathrow Ariel
Tel 0871-942 9040.
www.ichotelsgroup.com

Premier Inn Heathrow (Bath Road)
Tel 0870-607 5075.
www.premierinn.com

Sofitel London Gatwick
Tel 01293-567 070.
www.sofitel.com

Travelodge Gatwick Airport
Tel 0871-984 6031.
www.travelodge.co.uk

GETTING AROUND LONDON

"Heritage" bus

London has one of the busiest and most extensive public transport systems in Europe; it also has all the problems of overcrowding to match. A programme is under-way to upgrade the Underground (tube) train system, and new services are due to be introduced in time for the Olympic Games in 2012. Within London and its suburbs, most of the public transport systems – the Underground, city buses, overground rail lines, river buses – are coordinated by Transport for London (TfL), which operates a common ticketing system centred on the Oyster Card, a "smartcard" that is rapidly replacing the need for paper tickets.

GREEN TRAVEL

Travelling around London by foot, tube, bus, train or river bus is more energy-efficient than taking your own vehicle or a taxi. The Congestion Charge helps to discourage driving in the city centre (see p379). London has improved conditions for cyclists, and this can be the fastest way to get around the city – **Transport for London's** website has a dedicated cycling page. Many of London's black cabs now run on alternative fuels. There are several "green" minicab companies that use hybrid or alternative-fuel vehicles, such as **Gogreencar** and **Climatecars**.

THE TRANSPORT SYSTEM

The Underground railway – or "tube", as Londoners call it – is generally the fastest, most convenient way to get around the city. The Docklands business district and some other areas of east London and Green-wich are served by the Dock-lands Light Railway (DLR), which connects with the tube network principally at Bank, Tower Hill, Canary Wharf and Stratford. Tube and DLR lines do not run to every part of the city, however; in particular, large parts of south London are reliant on overground rail connections. Bus routes cover every part of London. There are also several riverbus boat services (see p61).

Avoid travelling on public transport during morning and evening "rush hour" – 7–10am and 4–7pm Monday to Friday – if at all possible.

For detailed information on every aspect of transport in London, ring Transport for London information or check the TfL website, which has an invaluable "Journey Planner" feature. TfL also has several Travel Information Centres, at Heathrow and Piccadilly Circus Underground stations and Euston, King's Cross, Liverpool Street and Victoria mainline stations, which provide free maps and other information.

OYSTER CARDS & TRAVELCARDS

London's public transport is relatively expensive compared to that of many European cities, but if you use one of the multi-journey cards available to visitors you will cut your costs considerably. For tube, DLR and local train fares, London is divided into six main fare zones radiating out from Zone 1 in the centre (on buses, there is a flat fare for each trip, no matter how far you travel). If you aim to pack all your sightseeing into one or two days, the best ticket to get will be a one-day off-peak Travelcard, which gives unlimited travel on all systems after 9.30am on weekdays (or any time on Saturday and Sunday) within your chosen zones for a flat fee (currently £5.60 for an adult card for Zones 1 and 2, which covers most of the main sights in London).

BAKER STREET

A London Underground sign outside a station

If you expect to travel more freely, it will be better to get a pay-as-you-go Oyster Card, which you can charge up with as much credit as you wish. Whenever you use public transport, you "touch in" with your card on a yellow Oyster Card reader, and the corresponding amount is deducted. On Underground, DLR and overground trains you must also remember to "touch out" at the station where you finish your journey, or you will be charged the maximum fare for the line.

Travelcards and Oyster Cards can be bought at tube and local rail stations, Travel Information Centres and hundreds of small shops that have the TfL "Ticket Stop" sticker in the window. You can also obtain them before arriving in London, on Eurostar, Gatwick Express or Stansted Express trains, or online, with advance delivery to 63 countries, through the Visit London and TfL websites.

Travel is free on all buses for under-16s; the Underground and DLR are free for under-11s, and have reduced fares for 11–15-year-olds. A one-day Travelcard for 11–15s costs only £2 for main fare zones, 1 to 6. Details of all current fares and tickets can be found on www.tfl.gov.uk.

Pre-paid Oyster card being placed on a card reader

A pedestrian zebra crossing

WALKING

Once you get used to traffic driving on the left, London can be enjoyably explored on foot, but take care crossing the road. There are two types of pedestrian crossing in London: striped "zebra" crossings, marked by beacons; and push-button crossings at traffic lights. Traffic should stop if you wait at a zebra crossing, but at push-button crossings, cars will not stop until they have a red light. Look out for instructions printed on the road, which tell you from which direction you can expect traffic to appear.

DRIVING IN LONDON

For visitors, driving is usually the worst way of getting around town. Traffic moves at an average of 11 mph (18 kmh) for much of the day, parking is scarce and expensive, and in the city centre there is the added cost of the Congestion Charge – an £8-a-day fee for private vehicles entering the central charging zone (roughly: the City, the West End, Notting Hill and Kensington in the west; and south as far as Kennington) between 7am and 6pm Monday to Friday. If you are determined to drive, remember always to drive on the left.

All the well-known car-rental firms are represented in London. Renting a car in advance through a site such as **Auto Europe**, or as an add-on with your flight, will get the best rates. To drive right out of London from the centre takes about 1 hour in any direction; if you want to tour the countryside, it can be less tiring to take a train to a city like Oxford and rent there.

PARKING

Parking is prohibited at all times wherever the street is marked with red or there are double yellow lines by the kerb. If there is a single yellow line, parking is normally allowed from 6.30pm–8am Monday to Saturday and all day Sunday, but exact hours vary, so always check the signs along each street. Where there is no line at all, parking is free at all times, but this is rare in central London. Note that rental car drivers are still liable for parking fines.

CYCLING

The TfL "Cycling" page is an invaluable source of information on cycling around the city. TfL also publishes several free local cycle guides, available online or from Travel Information Centres. Cycle routes – sometimes even separate cycle lanes – are signposted around the city.

There are many cycle hire companies. **Go Pedal!** and the **London Bicycle Tour Company** both deliver and collect bikes to and from your location. With your rented bike you should be given a helmet, lock and other accessories.

A cycle path in one of London's parks

DIRECTORY

TRANSPORT FOR LONDON

Tel *0843 222 1234* (info), *0845 900 1234* (Congestion Charge).
www.tfl.gov.uk

GREEN TRAVEL

Climatecars
Tel *020 7350 5960.*
www.climatecars.com

Gogreencar
Tel *020 7502 3670.*
www.gogreencar.co.uk

DRIVING

Auto Europe
Tel *1-888-223 5555 (USA), 0800-358 1229 (UK).*
www.autoeurope.com

Europecar
Tel *0871-384 9847 (UK).*
www.europecar.com

Hertz Rent a Car
Tel *1-800-654 3001 (USA), 0870-841 5161 (UK).*
www.hertz.com

PARKING

National Car Parks
Tel 0845-050 7080.
www.ncp.co.uk

CYCLING

Go Pedal!
Tel *07850-796320.*
www.gopedal.co.uk

London Bicycle Tour Company
Tel *020-7928 6838.*
www.londonbicycle.com

London Cycling Campaign
Tel *020-7234 9310.*
www.lcc.org.uk

Travelling by Underground

The Underground system, known as the "tube" to Londoners, has some 270 stations, each identified by the Underground logo. Trains run every day except Christmas Day, from about 5.30am till midnight Monday to Thursday; 5.30am till 1am on Friday and Saturday; and 6.30am to 11.30pm on Sunday. Exact times of first and last trains are posted at stations and on the Transport for London website: www.tfl.gov.uk. The Docklands Light Railway (DLR), with some 40 stations in east and southeast London, connects with the tube and also runs to London City Airport. For schedules and all other information, call 0843-222 1234 or check the TfL website.

London Underground train

PLANNING YOUR JOURNEY

There are 12 tube lines, all named and colour-coded (red for Central, blue for Victoria, and so on), which intersect at various stations. Some lines, like the Jubilee, have a single branch; others, like the Northern, have more than one, so it's important to check the digital boards on the platform and the destination on the front of the train. The Circle Line is a continuous loop around central London. Maps of the entire Tube system *(see inside back cover)* are posted at every

station. Note that the tube map is topological, not geographical; it isn't to scale, nor can it be relied upon for directions. From it, you can work out where to change lines to travel to any station on the system. All eight of London's mainline rail stations *(see p372)* have associated Tube stations. Due to the ongoing tube improvement programme, services are sometimes suspended, usually at weekends. When this happens, a replacement bus service is always provided. Check for line closures before travelling.

HOW TO READ THE JOURNEY PLANNER MAPS
(see inside back cover)

Station for changing between lines or to British Rail train

Double circle, meaning two stations are linked

Station serving two lines

BUYING A TICKET

All tube and DLR stations fall within one of six main fare zones *(see p378)*. The zones you travel through determine the cost of your journey. Unless you plan on making very few journeys by tube, it will usually be best to travel with a multi-journey Travelcard or an Oyster Card *(see p378)*. However, you can also buy single or return tickets from ticket offices and ticket machines. All Underground and DLR stations have touch-screen machines that give step-by-step instructions in a variety of languages. They accept coins, notes and credit and debit cards, and you can also use them to top up your credit on an Oyster Card. To check on current fares, select the ticket type you need, choose the station you wish to travel to, and the fare will be displayed on screen.

TUBE ARCHITECTURE

The Underground's reputation for exciting architecture was established in the 1930s. In 1999 the Jubilee Line Extension opened to great acclaim, with six imposing and elegant new stations designed by a group of top architects including Will Alsop (North Greenwich), Norman Foster (Canary Wharf) and Matthew Hopkins (Westminster). A similarly light, spacious style has been adopted in the impressive tube, DLR, bus and mainline rail hub at Stratford, which will be the gateway to the Olympic Park.

Concourse at Canary Wharf Station, Jubilee Line

MAKING A JOURNEY BY UNDERGROUND

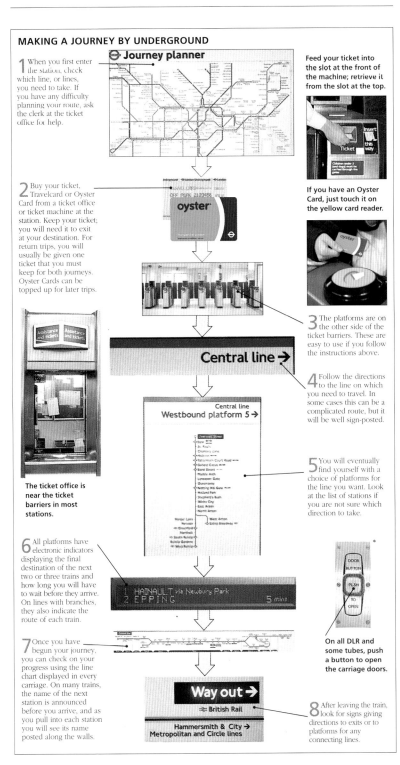

1 When you first enter the station, check which line, or lines, you need to take. If you have any difficulty planning your route, ask the clerk at the ticket office for help.

Journey planner

Feed your ticket into the slot at the front of the machine; retrieve it from the slot at the top.

2 Buy your ticket, Travelcard or Oyster Card from a ticket office or ticket machine at the station. Keep your ticket; you will need it to exit at your destination. For return trips, you will usually be given one ticket that you must keep for both journeys. Oyster Cards can be topped up for later trips.

oyster

If you have an Oyster Card, just touch it on the yellow card reader.

The ticket office is near the ticket barriers in most stations.

3 The platforms are on the other side of the ticket barriers. These are easy to use if you follow the instructions above.

Central line →

4 Follow the directions to the line on which you need to travel. In some cases this can be a complicated route, but it will be well sign-posted.

Central line
Westbound platform 5 →

5 You will eventually find yourself with a choice of platforms for the line you want. Look at the list of stations if you are not sure which direction to take.

6 All platforms have electronic indicators displaying the final destination of the next two or three trains and how long you will have to wait before they arrive. On lines with branches, they also indicate the route of each train.

1 HAINAULT via Newbury Park
2 EPPING   5 mins

DOOR
BUTTON
PUSH
TO
OPEN

On all DLR and some tubes, push a button to open the carriage doors.

7 Once you have begun your journey, you can check on your progress using the line chart displayed in every carriage. On many trains, the name of the next station is announced before you arrive, and as you pull into each station you will see its name posted along the walls.

Way out →
⇌ British Rail

Hammersmith & City →
Metropolitan and Circle lines

8 After leaving the train, look for signs giving directions to exits or to platforms for any connecting lines.

Travelling by Bus and Boat

Distinctive logo used on London bus stops

The red double-decker bus is one of London's most recognizable symbols, but the design of London buses has changed a great deal over the years. The old, classic open-backed Routemaster buses have been withdrawn (with the exception of two "heritage" routes), and in their place there are modern, square-sided double-deckers, single-deckers for less busy routes and very long, articulated, single-decker "bendy buses" that "bend" around corners. Travelling by bus is an enjoyable, easy way to see London, especially in the middle of the day, and much cheaper than going by tube or DLR if you have an Oyster Card. On the minus side, bus journeys can be slow, especially during rush hour (7–10am and 4–7pm Monday to Friday).

FINDING THE RIGHT BUS

Bus maps showing all the main routes are available free from Travel Information Centres, or can be downloaded from the Visit London and Transport for London websites. All London bus stops have bus route signs displaying the routes that run from that stop, with lists of their main destinations. On streets that are used by several bus routes – notably Oxford Street in the West End – routes are "bunched together" at different stops

Bus Stops
If you are boarding a bus at a yellow stop (below), you must buy a ticket at the adjacent machine before boarding. At some stops, called request stops, the driver will not halt unless asked. If you want to board, raise your arm as the bus approaches the stop; when you want to get off, ring the bell once before your stop.

near each other, so make sure you find the right one. Stops also have local area maps showing which of the adjacent bus stops, identified by a letter, you need for buses to a particular area. If in doubt, check with the bus driver when boarding.

USING LONDON'S BUSES

Buses halt at stops marked with the London bus logo. Some stops are "request"

stops, where drivers will not stop unless they are waved down by a passenger. Destinations are displayed clearly on the front of the bus, and on many buses the next upcoming stop is indicated on electronic information boards, or announced by an automatic voice system. However, if you are unsure which stop you need, ask the driver to alert you, and stay on the lower deck.

Board buses at the front, so that you can touch in your Oyster Card on the yellow Oyster reader by the driver's cab, show your Travelcard or buy a single ticket. In central London, single tickets cannot be bought on board the bus, but must be bought in advance from ticket machines at the bus stop, and then shown to the driver. Fares are the same for each bus trip no matter how far you travel, at £2 for a single ticket or £1.20 with an Oyster Card – so the Oyster saving is considerable. Note that inspectors check regularly whether passengers have valid tickets or passes.

USEFUL BUS ROUTES

Several of London's bus routes are particularly convenient for the capital's main sights and shops. If you arm yourself with an Oyster Card or Travelcard and are in no particular hurry, sightseeing or shopping by bus can be great fun. The cost of a journey by public transport is far less than any of the charges levied by tour operators, although you won't have the commentary that tour companies give you as you pass sights *(see p362–3)*.

There are also some sights or areas in London that are either hard to get to by Underground, or can be reached much more directly by bus. Buses run regularly from the city centre to, for instance, the Albert Hall *(see p207)* and Chelsea *(see pp192–7)*.

Marble Arch ⊖

Hyde Park Corner ⊖

Knightsbridge ⊖

Harrods

Sloane Square ⊖

Natural History Museum

South Kensington ⊖

Victoria and Albert Museum

BUS STOP
Parliament Square
towards
Elephant & Castle
| 12 | 53 | 159 |
| 453 | N155 | N159 |
N381
Buy tickets before boarding on all routes

Thames Clipper boat on the river heading towards Waterloo Bridge

NIGHT BUSES

Some main bus routes run 24 hours daily. Night bus services (indicated by the letter "N" added before the route number) also run on many popular routes from 11pm until 6am, generally 3–4 times per hour up to 2–3am, but often only once an hour after that. Many night bus routes originate in or pass through Trafalgar Square, then run out into the suburbs. In the centre they are often very crowded, especially at weekends, but empty out quickly as they move further out. Plan your journey carefully; London is so big that even if you board a bus going in the right direction, you can still be a long walk from your accommodation. As always, be aware of your personal security when travelling at night.

RIVERBOATS

Some of London's most spectacular views can only be seen from the River Thames. River trips have also been integrated into London's general transport service. **Thames Clippers** has a riverbus service with catamarans running every 20 minutes from 6am to 1am daily in both directions, on a route between Waterloo and Woolwich, via the London Eye, Tower Bridge, Greenwich and other stops at the various river piers. They also operate the **Tate Boat**, a direct boat between the Tate Britain and Tate Modern museums (every 40 minutes in each direction, 10am to 5pm), as well as special services for events at the O2 Arena. Oyster Cards can be used on board, and Travelcard holders get discounted tickets. For all details check with Thames Clippers or www.tfl.gov.uk.

DIRECTORY

RIVERBOAT SERVICES

Tate Boat
Tel 020-7887 8888.
www.tate.org.uk/tatetotate

Thames Clippers
Tel 020-7001 2222.
www.thamesclippers.com

For more information on river cruises see "Cruise Highlights" on p61.

Travelling by Rail

Railway sign

London's local and suburban train lines (also known as the "overground") are used by hundreds of thousands of commuters every day. For visitors, rail services are most useful for trips to the outskirts of London and areas of the city without nearby Underground connections (especially in south London). If you are planning to travel outside of the capital, always try to book rail tickets in advance, and check to see what alternative fares are available; for more on rail tickets see p372.

USEFUL ROUTES

Two of the most popular rail lines for visitors to London are those from Charing Cross (via London Bridge) and, on weekdays, Cannon Street to Greenwich *(see pp237–43)*; and Waterloo to Hampton Court *(see pp254–7)*. A First Capital Connect line runs right through London, north to south, from Luton via St Pancras International to Gatwick. The North London line makes a loop around north London all the way from the East End to Kew *(see pp260–61)* and Richmond.

USING THE TRAINS

London has eight main railway terminuses serving different parts of Britain. Each terminus is also the start-point for local and suburban lines that cover the whole of southeast England. There are over one hundred smaller London stations. Rail services travel overground and vary between trains that stop at every station, faster suburban trains, and express trains that run non-stop to major destinations. Some train doors will open automatically; others at the touch of a button.

RAIL TICKETS

Travelcards and Oyster Cards are valid on nearly all overground rail services that fall entirely within the London area (defined as Transport for London fare zones 1–6, plus three more suburban zones), so using one or the other will generally be much more economical, and a lot quicker, than buying individual tickets. Be aware, though, that on most overground trains, peak travel times include the evening rush hour (4–7pm Monday–Friday) as well as the morning one (before 9.30am), so with an Oyster you will be charged more during these times. Many small stations do not have staffed ticket counters, just machines.

Return tickets for rail travel

DAY TRIPS

Southern England has a lot to offer visitors besides London. By rail or by bus *(see p373)*, getting out of the city is fast and easy. For details of sights contact Visit Britain (www.visitbritain.com; 020-8846 9000). National Rail (0845-748 4950) has details of all rail services.

Boating on the River Thames at Windsor Castle

Audley End
Village with a stunning Jacobean mansion nearby.
🚆 *from Liverpool Street.*
40 miles (64 km); 1 hr.

Bath
Beautiful Georgian city, with Roman baths, which has escaped redevelopment.
🚆 *from Paddington.*
107 miles (172 km); 1 hr 25 mins.

Brighton
Lively and attractive seaside resort. See the Royal Pavilion.
🚆 *from Victoria. 53 miles (85 km); 1 hr.*

Cambridge
University city with fine art gallery and ancient colleges.
🚆 *from Liverpool Street or King's Cross. 54 miles (86 km); 1 hr.*

Canterbury
Its cathedral is one of England's oldest and greatest sights.
🚆 *from Victoria.*
62 miles (100 km); 1 hr 25 mins.

Hatfield House
Elizabethan palace with remarkable contents.
🚆 *from King's Cross or Moorgate to Hatfield station.*
21 miles (33 km); 20 mins.

Oxford
Like Cambridge, famous for its ancient university.
🚆 *from Paddington.*
56 miles (90 km); 1 hr.

St Albans
Cathedral and Roman theatre.
🚆 *from King's Cross or Moorgate.*
25 miles (40 km); 30 mins.

Salisbury
Famous for its cathedral, and close to Stonehenge.
🚆 *from Waterloo.*
84 miles (135 km); 1 hr 40 mins.

Windsor
Riverside town with Britain's grandest royal castle.
🚆 *from Paddington, change Slough.*
20 miles (32km); approx. 30 mins.

Travelling by Taxi

London's well-known black cabs are as much of an institution as its red buses. Black cabs (some of which, it should be pointed out, are not actually black – you will often see blue, green, red or even white cabs) are the only cabs licensed to pick up passengers who hail a cab on the street, and their drivers have to take a stringent test on their knowledge of London and its traffic routes before they are awarded a licence. Minicabs, which by law must be booked in advance, not hailed, are a cheaper alternative for specific journeys.

London taxi rank

FINDING A CAB

Licensed London taxis, or "black cabs", are large, distinctive vehicles – of which there are now several models – whose yellow "Taxi" sign is lit up whenever the taxi is free. You can hail them on the street, phone for them, or find them at taxi ranks, especially at airports, main rail stations and major hotels. Raise your arm and wave purposefully. If a cab stops, it must take you anywhere within a radius of 6 miles (9.6 km), as long as it

is in the Metropolitan Police district, which includes most of the Greater London area and Heathrow Airport.

TAXI FARES

All black cabs have meters that start ticking at around £2.20 as soon as the driver accepts your custom. The fare then increases by the minute, or for each 311 m (340 yds) travelled. There are also three tariff time bands: the cheapest is 6am–8pm Monday–Friday; the next-most expensive, 8–10pm Monday–Friday and 6–10pm Saturday–Sunday; the most expensive, 10pm–6am nightly. The meter must be clearly visible in the vehicle. It is usual to tip taxi and minicab drivers. If you lose anything in a licensed taxi, contact Transport for London's lost property office *(see p367).* You will need the driver's cab licence number, displayed in the back of the taxi.

MINICABS

Licensed minicabs are badged with a blue-and-white Transport for London sticker, usually on the back window. Do not use the unlicensed cabs that sometimes cruise for business in the street. Transport for London's Cabwise service is a good way of finding a safe cab: text "CAB" to 60835 and you will be sent phone numbers for one black cab office and two reliable minicab companies in the area. If your mobile is international, text your location (street name and postal district) to 00-44-7797 800 000 to access the same service (international charges will apply).

DIRECTORY

Complaints (Public Carriage Office)
Tel 0845-300 7000.
www.tfl.gov.uk

Computer Cabs
Tel 020-7908 0000.
www.computercab.co.uk

Dial-a-Minicab
Tel 0800-019 6768.
www.dialaminicab.com

Lady Minicabs (women-only drivers)
Tel 020-7272 3300.
www.ladyminicabs.com

Radio Taxis
Tel 020-7272 0272.
www.radiotaxis.co.uk

The light, when lit, shows the cab is available.

The meter displays your fare as it increases, and surcharges for extra passengers, luggage or unsocial hours. Fares are the same in all licensed black cabs.

Fare   Surcharges

Licensed Taxi Cabs
London's cabs are a safe way of travelling around the city. They can carry a maximum of five passengers, are all accessible for wheelchair users and have ample luggage space.

STREET FINDER

he map references given with all sights, hotels, restaurants, shops and entertainment venues described in this book refer to the maps in this section only (*see* How Map References Work *opposite*). A complete index of street names and all the places of interest marked on the maps can be found on the following pages.

The key map shows the area of London covered by the *Street Finder*, with the postal codes of all the various districts. The maps include the sightseeing areas (which are colour-coded), as well as the whole of central London with all the districts important for hotels, restaurants, pubs and entertainment venues.

Postal districts are labelled and outlined in orange.

KEY

-- Postal district boundary

HOW THE MAP REFERENCES WORK

The first figure tells you which Street Finder map to turn to.

Wesley's Chapel-Leysian Mission ⓬

49 City Rd EC1. **Map 7 B4**
Tel 020-7253 2262. 🔵 *Old St.*
House open 10am–4pm Mon–Sat,
12.30–1.45pm Sun. 🚫 *not house.* ✝
9.45am (not 1st Sun of month), 11am
Sun, 12.45pm Thu. 📷 *groups book*
ahead. 🖥 **www**.wesleyschapel.org.uk

A letter and number give the grid reference. Letters go across the map's top and bottom; figures on its sides.

The map continues on map 15 of the Street Finder.

KEY TO STREET FINDER

▦	Major sight
▥	Other sight
☐	Other building
🔵	Underground station
🚆	Railway station
🚌	Coach station
⛴	River boat pier
ℹ	Tourist information office
✚	Hospital with casualty unit
🅿	Police station
⛪	Church
✡	Synagogue
⊠	Post office
	Railway line
	Motorway
	Pedestrian street
◄130	House number (main street)

SCALE OF MAP PAGES

0 metres — 200
0 yards — 200

1:12,000

Street Finder Index

Each place name is followed by its postal district and then by its Street Finder reference

Each place name is followed by its postal district and then by its Street Finder reference

Each place name is followed by its postal district and then by its Street Finder reference

Rheidol Terr N1	7 A1
Richard's Pl SW3	19 B2
Richborne Terr SW8	22 D5
Richmond Terr SW1	13 B4
Rick La SW5	18 D3
Rickett St SW6	17 C4
Ridgmount Gdns WC1	5 A5
Ridgmount St WC1	5 A5
Riding House St W1	12 F1
Riley Rd SE1	16 D5
Ring, The W2	11 A3
Risinghill St N1	6 D2
Rita Rd SW8	21 C5
Ritz Hotel SW1	12 F3
River St EC1	6 E3
Rivington St EC2	7 C3
Roan St SE10	23 A2
Robert St NW1	4 F3
Robert Adam St W1	12 D1
Roberta St E2	8 F3
Robin Gro N6	2 F2
Rochester Row SW1	21 A2
Roderick Rd NW3	2 E5
Rodmarton St W1	11 C1
Rodmere St SE10	24 E1
Rodney St N1	6 D2
Roger St WC1	6 D4
Roland Gdns SW7	18 F3
Roland Way SW7	18 F3
Romilly St W1	13 A2
Romney Clo NW11	1 A1
Romney Rd SE10	23 B2
Romney St SW1	21 B1
Rona Rd NW3	2 E5
Rood La EC3	15 C2
Ropemaker St EC2	7 B5
Roper's Garden SW3	19 A4
Rosaline Rd SW6	17 A5
Rosary Gdns SW7	18 E2
Rosaville Rd SW6	17 B5
Rose Alley SE1	15 A3
Rose St WC2	13 B2
Rose Theatre SE1	15 A3
Rosebery Ave EC1	6 E4
Rosemoor St SW3	19 B2
Rosewood Gdns SE13	23 A5
Rosmead Rd W11	9 A2
Rosslyn Hill NW3	1 C5
Rossmore Rd NW1	3 B4
Rotary St SE1	14 F5
Rotten Row SW7	11 A4
Roupell St SE1	14 E4
Rowallan Rd SW6	17 A5
Royal Academy of Arts W1	12 F3
Royal Academy of Music NW1	4 D4
Royal Albert Hall SW7	10 F5
Royal Ave SW3	19 C3
Royal College of Art SW7	10 F5
Royal College of Music SW7	10 F5
Royal College St NW1	5 A1
Royal Courts of Justice WC2	14 D2
Royal Exchange EC4	15 C2
Royal Festival Hall SE1	14 D4
Royal Free Hospital NW3	2 D5
Royal Hill SE10	23 B3
Royal Hospital Cemetery SE10	24 F1
Royal Hospital Rd SW3	19 C3
Royal Hospital Rd SW3	20 D3
Royal Mint St E1	16 E2
Royal Ms SW1	12 E5
Royal Naval College (Old) SE10	23 C2
Royal Opera House WC2	13 C2

Royal Parade SE3	24 E5
Royal Rd SE17	22 F4
Royal St SE1	14 D5
Rudall Cres NW3	1 B5
Rumbold Rd SW6	18 E5
Rupert St W1	13 A2
Rushton St N1	7 B2
Rushworth St SE1	14 F4
Russell Gdns W14	9 A5
Russell Gdns Ms W14	9 A5
Russell Rd W14	17 A1
Russell Sq WC1	5 B5
Russell St WC2	13 C2
Russett Way SE13	23 A5
Ruston Ms W11	9 A1
Rutherford St SW1	21 A2
Ruthin Rd SE3	24 F2
Rutland Gdns SW7	11 B5
Rutland Gate SW7	11 B5
Ryculf Sq SE3	24 F5
Ryder St SW1	12 F4
Rylston Rd SW6	17 B4

S

Saatchi Gallery SW3	19 C2
St Agnes Pl SE11	22 E4
St Alban's Rd NW5	2 F3
St Alban's St SW1	13 A3
St Alfege Passage SE10	23 B2
St Andrew's EC4	14 E1
St Andrew's Gdns WC1	6 D4
St Andrew's Pl NW1	4 E4
St Andrews St EC4	14 E1
St Anne's Clo N6	2 F3
St Ann's St SW1	21 B1
St Ann's Terr NW8	3 A2
St Austell Rd SE13	23 B5
St Barnabas St SW1	20 D2
St Bartholomew's Hospital EC1	14 F1
St Bartholomew's-the-Great E1	6 F5
St Botolph Church EC1	15 A1
St Botolph St EC3	16 D1
St Bride St EC4	14 E1
St Bride's EC4	14 F2
St Chad's Pl WC1	5 C3
St Chad's St WC1	5 C3
St Clement Danes WC2	14 D2
St Crispin Clo NW3	2 D5
St Cross St EC1	6 E5
St Edmund's Terr NW8	3 B1
St Ethelreda's EC1	6 E5
St George's Bloomsbury WC1	13 B1
St George's Cathedral SE1	14 E5
St George's Circus SE1	14 F5
St George's Dri SW1	20 F2
St George's Fields W2	11 B2
St George's Gdn W1	12 D3
St George's Gdns WC1	5 C4
St George's Rd SE1	22 F1
St George's Sq SW1	21 A3
St German's Pl SE3	24 F4
St Giles EC2	7 A5
St Giles, Cripplegate High St WC2	13 B1
St Helen's Bishopsgate EC3	15 C1
St James's Church SW1	13 A3
St James's Palace SW1	12 F4
St James's Park SW1	13 A4
St James's Pk Lake SW1	13 A4
St James's Pl SW1	12 F4
St James's Rd SE16	16 F5
St James's Sq SW1	13 A3
St James's St SW1	12 F3

St John St EC1	6 E2
St John's SE1	14 E4
St John's Gdns SW1	21 B1
St John's High St NW8	3 A2
St John's La EC1	6 F5
St John's Pk SE3	24 F3
St John's Smith Sq SW1	21 B1
St John's Sq EC1	6 F4
St John's Wood Church Gdns NW8	3 A3
St John's Wood High St NW8	3 A2
St John's Wood Rd NW8	3 A3
St John's Wood Terr NW8	3 A2
St Katherines Dock E1	16 E3
St Katherines Pier E1	16 E3
St Katharine's Way E1	16 E3
St Lawrence Terr W10	9 A1
St Leonard's Terr SW3	19 C3
St Loo Ave SW3	19 B4
St Luke's Ms W11	9 B1
St Luke's Rd W11	9 B1
St Luke's St SW3	19 B3
St Magnus the Martyr EC3	15 C3
St Margaret Pattens EC3	15 C2
St Margaret's Church SW1	13 B5
St Margaret St SW1	13 B5
St Mark St E1	16 E2
St Mark's Cres NW1	4 D1
St Mark's Rd W11	9 A2
St Martin's La WC2	13 B2
St Martin's Le Grand EC1	15 A1
St Martin's Pl WC2	13 B3
St Martin's St WC2	13 B3
St Martin-in-the-Fields WC2	13 B3
St Mary Abbots Terr W14	17 B1
St Mary at Hill EC3	15 C2
St Mary Axe EC3	15 C1
St Mary's Hospital W2	11 A1
St Mary Le Strand WC2	14 D2
St Mary's Path N1	6 F1
St Mary's Wlk SE11	22 E2
St Mary-le-Bow EC4	15 A2
St Marylebone Parish Church W1	4 D5
St Matthew's Row E2	8 E4
St Michael's St W2	11 A1
St Olaf's Rd SW6	17 A5
St Oswald's Pl SE11	22 D3
St Pancras Church WC1	5 B3
St Pancras Way NW1	5 A1
St Paul St N1	7 A1
St Paul's Cathedral EC4	15 A2
St Paul's Church WC2	13 C2
St Paul's Churchyard EC4	15 A2
St Peter's Clo E2	8 F2
St Peter's St N1	6 F1
St Petersburgh Pl W2	7 A2
	10 D3
St Stephen Walbrook EC4	15 B2
St Stephen's Gdns W2	9 C1
St Stephen's Terr SW8	21 C5
St Swithin's La EC4	15 B2
St Thomas St SE1	15 B4
St Thomas' Hospital SE1	13 C5
St Thomas' Way SW6	17 B5

Sackville St W1	12 F3
Saffron Hill EC1	6 E5
Sail St SE11	22 D1
Salamanca St SE1, SE11	21 C2
Sale Pl W2	11 A1
Salem Rd W2	10 D2
Salisbury Ct EC4	14 E2
Salisbury St NW8	3 A4
Sampson St E1	16 F4
Sancroft St SE11	22 D2
Sandwich St WC1	5 B3
Sandys Row E1	8 D5
Sans Wlk EC1	6 E4
Saunders Ness Rd E14	23 B1
Savernake Rd NW3	2 E5
Savile Row W1	12 F2
Savona St SW8	20 F5
Savoy Chapel WC2	13 C2
Savoy Hill WC2	13 C3
Savoy Pl WC2	13 C3
Savoy Row WC2	13 C3
Savoy St WC2	13 C2
Savoy, The WC2	13 C2
Scala St W1	5 A5
Scarborough St E1	16 E2
Scarsdale Vlls W8	17 C1
	18 D1
Science Museum SW7	18 F1
	19 A1
Sclater St E1	8 E4
Scott Lidgett Cres SE16	16 F5
Scott St E1	8 F4
Scovell Cresent SE1	15 A5
Scrutton St EC2	7 C4
Seagrave Rd SW6	17 C4
	18 D4
Sebastian St EC1	6 F3
Sedlescombe Rd SW6	17 C4
Seething La EC3	16 D2
Selby St E1	8 F4
Selfridge's W1	12 D2
Selwood Pl SW7	18 F3
Selwood Terr SW7	18 F3
Semley Pl SW1	20 E2
Serle St WC2	14 D1
Serpentine Gallery W2	11 A4
Serpentine Rd W2	11 C4
	12 D4
Serpentine, The W2	11 B4
Settles St E1	16 F1
Seven Dials WC2	13 B2
Seville St SW1	11 C5
Seward St EC1	7 A4
Seymour Ms W1	12 D1
Seymour Pl W1	3 B5
	11 B1
Seymour St W1,W2	11 C2
Seymour Wlk SW10	18 E4
Shad Thames SE1	16 E4
Shaftesbury Ave W1	13 A2
Shaftesbury Ave WC2	13 B1
Shaftesbury St N1	7 B2
Shafto Ms SW1	19 C1
Shafts Ct EC3	15 C1
Shakespeare's Globe SE1	15 A3
Shalcomb St SW10	18 F4
Sharsted St SE17	22 F3
Shawfield St SW3	19 B3
Sheffield Ter W8	9 C4
Sheldon Ave N6	2 D1
Sheldrake Pl W8	9 C5
Shelton St WC2	13 B2
Shenfield St N1	8 D2
Shepherd Mkt W1	12 E4
Shepherd St W1	12 E4
Shepherdess Wlk N1	7 A2
Shepherd's Wlk NW3	1 B5
Shepperton Rd N1	7 B1
Sherbourne La EC4	15 B2
Sherbrooke Rd SW6	18 D5

Each place name is followed by its postal district and then by its Street Finder reference

D | **E** | **F** | **2**

SHELDON AVE
STORMONT ROAD
BISHOPSWOOD RD
LANE
HAMPSTEAD
HAMPSTEAD LANE
BISHOPSWOOD ROAD
HIGHGATE CLOSE

1

FITZROY PARK
THE GROVE
NORTH GROVE
HIGHGATE WEST HILL
NORTH ROAD
HIGHGATE HIGH STREET
SOUTH GROVE
SWAIN'S
BISHAM GARDENS

MILLFIELD LANE
FITZROY PARK
THE HEXAGON
HIGHFIELDS GREEN
HIGHGATE WEST HILL

HIGHGATE CEMETERY

LANE

2

MILLFIELD
LANE
MERTON LANE
WEST HILL PK
WEST HILL PARK
HOLLY LODGE GARDENS
HIGHGATE WEST HILL
ROBIN GROVE
HILLWAY
OAKESHOTT
AVENUE

Highgate
MILLFIELD LANE
MILLFIELD PLACE
MAKEPEACE
AVENUE
LANGBOURNE
HILLWAY
AVENUE
BROMWICH AVENUE

3

Ponds
WEST HILL COURT
ST ANNE'S CLOSE
SWAIN'S LANE
ST ALBAN'S ROAD
HIGHGATE
COUTT'S CRESCENT

PARLIAMENT

HILL

HIGHGATE ROAD
CROFTDOWN ROAD
WOODSOME ROAD
GROVE TERRACE

4

SOUTH HILL PARK GARDENS
SOUTH HILL PARK
PARLIAMENT HILL
TANZA ROAD
THE OLD ORCHARD
NASSINGTON ROAD
LISSENDEN GARDENS
GLENHURST AVENUE
GORDON HOUSE ROAD

Hampstead Heath
ST CRISPIN CLOSE
SOUTH END CLOSE
AGINCOURT ROAD
CONSTANTINE ROAD
MACKESON ROAD
LISBURNE ROAD
CRESSY ROAD
RODERICK ROAD
SHIRLOCK ROAD
COURTHOPE ROAD
ESTELLE ROAD
SAVERNAKE ROAD
RONA ROAD
Gospel Oak
OAK VILLAGE
OAK
KILN PLACE

5

FLEET ROAD
Royal Free Hospital
MANSFIELD ROAD
ELAINE GROVE
LAMBLE STREET

D | **E** | **F**

General Index

Acknowledgments

Dorling Kindersley would like to thank the following people whose help and assistance contributed to the preparation of this book.

Main Contributor

Michael Leapman was born in London in 1938 and has been a journalist since he was 20. He has worked for most British national newspapers and writes about travel and other subjects for several publications, among them *The Independent, Independent on Sunday, The Economist* and *Country Life*. He has written ten books, including *London's River* (1991) and the award-winning *Companion Guide to New York* (1983, revised 1991). In 1989 he edited the acclaimed *Book of London.*

Contributors

James Aufenast, Yvonne Deutch, Guy Dimond, George Foster, Iain Gale, Fiona Holman, Phil Harriss, Lindsay Hunt, Christopher Middleton, Steven Parissien, Christopher Pick, Bazyli Solowij, Matthew Tanner, Mark Wareham, Jude Welton, Ian Wisniewski.

DORLING KINDERSLEY wishes to thank the following editors and researchers at Webster's International Publishers: Sandy Carr, Matthew Barrell, Siobhan Bremner, Serena Cross, Annie Galpin, Miriam Lloyd, Ava-Lee Tanner.

Additional Photography

Max Alexander, Peter Anderson, Stephen Bere, June Buck, Peter Chadwick, Michael Dent, Philip Dowell, Mike Dunning, Philip Enticknap, Andreas Einsiedel, Rhiannon Furbear, Steve Gorton, Christi Graham, Alison Harris, Peter Hayman, Stephen Hayward, Roger Hilton, Sean Hunter, Ed Ironside, Colin Keates, Dave King, Bob Langrish, Neil Lukas, Neil Mersh, Nick Nichols, Robert O'Dea, Ian O'Leary, Vincent Oliver, John Parker, Tim Ridley, Ellen Root, Rough Guides/Viktor Borg, Kim Sayer, Chris Stevens, James Stevenson, James Strachan, Doug Traverso, David Ward, Mathew Ward, Steven Wooster, Nick Wright.

Additional Illustrations

Ann Child, Gary Cross, Tim Hayward, Arghya Jyoti Hore, Fiona M Macpherson, Janos Marffy, David More, Chris D Orr, Richard Phipps, Michelle Ross, John Woodcock.

Cartography

Andrew Heritage, James Mills-Hicks, Chez Picthall, John Plumer (DK Cartography). Advanced Illustration (Cheshire), Contour Publishing (Derby), Euromap Ltd (Berkshire). Street Finder maps: ERA Maptec Ltd (Dublin) adapted with permission from original survey and mapping from Shobunsha (Japan).

Cartographic Research

James Anderson, Roger Bullen, Tony Chambers, Ruth Duxbury, Jason Gough, Ailsa Heritage, Jayne Parsons, Donna Rispoli, Jill Tinsley, Andrew Thompson, Iorwerth Watkins.

Design and Editorial

MANAGING EDITOR Douglas Amrine
MANAGING ART EDITOR Geoff Manders
SENIOR EDITOR Georgina Matthews
EDITORIAL DIRECTOR David Lamb
ART DIRECTOR Anne-Marie Bulat
PRODUCTION CONTROLLER Hilary Stephens
PICTURE RESEARCH Ellen Root, Rhiannon Furbear
DTP EDITOR Siri Lowe
REVISIONS Keith Addison, Elizabeth Atherton, Sam Atkinson, Lydia Baillie, Chris Barstow, Oliver Bennett, Julie Bowles, Chloe Carleton, Michelle Clark, Carey Combe, Vanessa Courtier, Lorna Damms, Hannah Dolan, Jessica Doyle, Nicola Erdpresser, Jane Ewart, Simon Farbrother, Gadi Farfour, Fay Franklin, Simon Hall, Marcus Hardy, Sasha Heseltine, Paul Hines, Phil Hunt, Stephanie Jackson, Gail Jones, Laura Jones, Nancy Jones, Stephen Knowlden, Priya Kukadia, Esther Labi, Michelle de Larrabeiti, Chris Lascelles, Jude Ledger, Jeanette Leung, Carly Madden, Hayley Maher, Ferdie McDonald, Alison McGill, Caroline Mead, Jane Middleton, Rebecca Milner, Sonal Modha, Fiona Morgan, Catherine Palmi, Louise Parsons, Marianne Petrou, Andrea Powell, Leigh Priest, Rada Radojicic, Mani Ramaswamy, Nick Rider, Liz Rowe, Simon Ryder, Sadie Smith, Susannah Steel, Kathryn Steve, Anna Streiffert, Rachel Symons, Andrew Szudek, Hugh Thompson, Diana Vowles, Matthew Walder, Andy Wilkinson.

Special Assistance

Christine Brandt at Kew Gardens, Sheila Brown at The Bank of England, John Cattermole at London Buses Northern, the DK picture department, especially Jenny Rayner, Pippa Grimes at the V&A, Emma Healy at the V&A Museum of Childhood, Alan Hills at the British Museum, Emma Hutton and Cooling Brown Partnership, Gavin Morgan at the Museum of London, Clare Murphy at Historic Royal Palaces, Ali Naqei at the Science Museum, Patrizio Semproni, Caroline Shaw at the Natural History Museum, Gary Smith at National Rail, Monica Thurnauer at Tate, Simon Wilson at Tate, Alastair Wardle.

Photographic Reference

The London Aerial Photo Library, and P and P F James.

Photography Permissions

DORLING KINDERSLEY would like to thank all the museums, galleries, churches and other sights that allowed us to photograph at their establishments.

Picture Credits

t = top; tl = top left; tc = top centre; tr = top right; cla = centre left above; ca = centre above; cra = centre right above; cl = centre left; c = centre; cr = centre right; clb = centre left below; cb = centre below; crb = centre right below; bl = bottom left; b = bottom; bc = bottom centre; br = bottom right.

Works of art have been reproduced with the permission of the following copyright holders: *Three Studies for Figures at the Base of the Crucifixion*, (1944, detail), Francis Bacon © Estate of Francis Bacon/DACS, London 2006 83b; *The Bath*, 1925, Pierre Bonnard © ADAGP, Paris and DACS, London 2006 181b; *Maman*, 2000 © Louise Bourgeois/VAGA, New York/DACS, London 2006 181cr; Fish 1926, Constantin Brancusi © ADAGP, Paris and DACS, London 2008 178tr; *After Lunch*, 1975 © Patrick Caulfield. All rights Reserved, DACS 2006 180t; *Spatial Concept "Waiting"*, 1960, © Fondazione Lucio Fontana, 179cr; *Lobster Telephone*, 1936 © Salvador Dali, Gala-Salvador Dali Foundation/DACS 2006 41cr; *The First Marriage (A Marriage of Styles I)* 1962 Oil on Canvas 72 x 60" David Hockney 85t; Bust of *Lawrence of Arabia* © The Family of Eric H. Kennington, RA 151bl; *Skydiver VI* 1964 Oil on canvas support 2032 x 1467mm © Gerald Laing; *Whaam!* 1963, Roy Lichtenstein © The Estate of Roy Lichtenstein/DACS, London 2008 178cla; Mario Merz 178la; *The Snail*, 1953, Henri Matisse © Succession H. Matisse/DACS, London 2008 179tl; The works by Henry Moore illustrated on the following pages have been reproduced by kind permission of the Henry Moore Foundation: 45c, 85c, 266cb. *Soft Drainpipe – Blue (Cool) version*, 1967 © Claes Oldenburg 179c; *Summertime: Number 9A*, 1948, Jackson Pollock © ARS, New York and DACS, London 2006 181; *Quattro Stagioni* 1993–4, © Cy Twombly 178cl.

The Publishers are grateful to the following individuals, companies and picture libraries for permission to reproduce their photographs: ALAMY IMAGES: Martyn Goddard 367tl; Robert Harding World Imagery 100clb; BJANKA KADIC: 364tl; THE ALBERMARLE CONNECTION: 91t; ARCAID: Richard Bryant, Architect Foster and Partners 126t; Richard Bryant 249cr; ARCBLUE: Peter Durant 189cl; THE ART ARCHIVE: 21bl, 28c, 28bc, 29bl, 30br, 31cra, 31clb, 35tc, 35cr, 188b, 188bl; British Library, London 20cr; Imperial War Museum, London 32bc; Museum of London 17b, 29br, 30bl; Science Museum, London 29cla; Stoke Museum Staffordshire Polytechnic 25bl, 27cl, 35bc; Victoria and Albert Museum, London 22c, 23bc, 27tr; AXIOM: James Morris 164tl.

GOVERNOR AND COMPANY OF THE BANK OF ENGLAND: 145tr; BRIDGEMAN ART LIBRARY: London: 23t, 30t; British Library, London 16, 21tr, (detail) 23br, 26cb, (detail) 34tl, 34bl; Courtesy of the Institute of Directors, London 31cla; Guildhall Art Gallery, Corporation of London (detail) 28t; Guildhall Library, Corporation of London 26br, 76c; ML Holmes Jamestown – Yorktown Educational Trust, VA (detail) 19bc; Master and Fellows, Magdalene College, Cambridge (detail) 25clb; Marylebone Cricket Club, London 246c; William Morris Gallery, Walthamstow 21tl, 249tl; Museum of London 24–5; O'Shea Gallery, London

(detail) 24cl; Royal Holloway & Bedford New College 157bl; Russell Cotes Art Gallery and Museum, Bournemouth 38tr; Thyssen-Bornemisza Collection, Lugano Casta 257b; Westminster Abbey, London (detail) 34bc; White House, Bond Street, London 30cb. BRITISH AIRWAYS: Adrian Meredith Photography: 372t, 374tl; reproduced with permission of the BRITISH LIBRARY BOARD: 125b; © THE BRITISH MUSEUM: 18t, 18ca, 19tl, 40t, 91c, 126–7 all pics, 128–9 all pics; BRITTANY FERRIES: 373tl; BT GROUP PLC: 370tl.

CAMERA PRESS, London: P. Abbey - LNS 73cb; Cecil Beaton 79tl; HRH Prince Andrew 95bl; Allan Warren 33cb; COLLECTIONS: Oliver Benn 60b; John Miller 163bl; COLORIFIC!: Steve Benbow 55t; David Levenson 66–7; CONRAN RESTAURANTS 293cl, 322bc; CORBIS: 259t; Bruce Burkhardt 289c; Tim Graham 3br, 95bl; Angelo Hornak 61c, 183b; London Aerial Photo Library 189bl, 189t; Kim Sayer 2br; Patrick Ward 61t; Courtesy of the CORPORATION OF LONDON: 55c, 146t; COURTAULD INSTITUTE, London: 41c, 117b; CUTTY SARK TRUST: 238cla.

COPYRIGHT: Dean & Chapter of Westminster 78bl, 79tr; DEWYNTERS LTD.: 117t; Courtesy of the GOVERNORS AND THE DIRECTORS DULWICH PICTURE GALLERY: 43bl, 250bl.

FRANCIS EDWARDS: 323clb; ENGLISH HERITAGE: 252b, 258b; Jonathon Bailey 241clb; ENGLISH LIFE PUBLICATIONS LTD: 252b; PHILIP ENTICKNAP: 255tr; MARY EVANS PICTURE LIBRARY: 18bl, 18br, 19bl, 19br, 22bl, 24bl, 26t, 27bc, 27br, 29t, 29cb, 29bc, 32bl, 34br, 35tl, 35cl, 35bl, 35br, 38tl, 39bl, 72cb, 72b, 90b, 112b, 114b, 135t, 139t, 155bl, 159t, 162ca, 174ca, 177l, 207b, 216t, 226b.

Courtesy of FAN MUSEUM (Helene Alexander Collection) 243b; FREUD MUSEUM, LONDON: 246t. GATWICK EXPRESS: 375t; GORE HOTEL, London: 279b; GEFFRYE MUSEUM, London: 248tl; GETTY IMAGES: 33br; GREEN TOURISM BUSINESS SCHEME: 365tr; GREENWICH INC: 238bc; GREENWICHMARKET.NET: 238cl.

ROBERT HARDING PICTURE LIBRARY: 33ca, 42c, 52ca, 169tl, 343t, 367cl, 384b; Philip Craven 210t; Nigel Francis 376tr; Sylvain Gradadam 289tl; Brian Hawkes 23clb; Michael Jenner 23cra, 242t; 58t, 227t; Mark Mawson 113tl; Nick Wood 63bl; HARRODS (printed by kind permission of Mohamed al Fayed): 320b; HAYES-DAVIDSON (computer generated images): 174bl; HAYWARD GALLERY: Richard Haughton 273tl; Reproduced with permission of HER MAJESTY'S STATIONERY OFFICE (Crown Copyright): 156 all pics; JOHN HESELTINE: 51tr, 63br, 98, 124b, 132, 172, 220; FRIENDS OF HIGHGATE CEMETERY: 244, 246b; HISTORIC ROYAL PALACES (Crown Copyright): 5ca, 7t, 37tc, 154cla, 254–255 all except 254br, 256–7 all except 257b; THE HORNIMAN MUSEUM, London: 256br; HOVERSPEED LTD: 377b; HULTON GETTY: 26bl, 124tl, 135cr, 232t. THE IMAGE BANK, London: Gio

Barto 55b; Derek Berwin 33t, 272t; Romilly Lockyer 12bl, 13br, 72t, 94br; Leo Mason 56t; Terry Williams 139b; Courtesy of ISIC, UK: 370t; iStockphoto.com: Alan Crawford 374br, peterspiro 379. Peter Jackson Collection: 26–7; Jewish Museum, London: 247tl.

Leighton House: 216b; Little Angel Marionette Theatre: 359tl; London Ambulance Service: Tim Saunders 367cla; London Aquarium 3c, 188c, 188r; London City Airport: 375tr; London Dungeon: 183t; London Palladium: 103; London Regional Transport: 380t; London Transport Museum: 30ca, 380–81 all maps and tickets.

Madame Tussauds: 222c, 224t; Mansell Collection: 21br, 22t, 22br, 23bl, 24t, 24cl, 25br, 29ca, 34tr; Metropolitan Police Service: 365t; Rob Moore: 115t; Museum of London: 15crb, 18cb, 19tr, 19cb, 20t, 23crb, 41tc, 166–7.

National Express Ltd: 376; Reproduced by courtesy of the Trustees, The National gallery, London: (detail) 37c, 104–5 all except 104t, 106–7 all except 107t; National Portrait Gallery, London: 4t, 41tl, 101cb, 102br; National Postal Museum, London: 28bl; By permission of the Keeper of the National Railway Museum, York: 30–31; National Trust Photographic Library: Wendy Aldiss 25ca; John Bethell 252t, 253t; Michael Boys 38b; Natural History Museum, London: John Downs 12clb, 209t, 209cr; Derek Adams 208b, 208cl; New Shakespeare Theatre co: 342bl.

Pa Photos Ltd: 33cr; Palace Theatre Archive: 108t; Peretti Communications: Chris Gascoigne & Lifschutz Davidson 292cr; Pictor International, London: 60cl, 174br; Pictures Colour Library: 54br; Pippa Pop-ins Children's Nursery, London: 357b; Pitzhanger Manor Museum: 258c; Popperfoto: 31tl, 31crb, 32tl, 32tr, 32c, 35tr, 39br; The Portobello Hotel: 279tr; Post House Heathrow: Tim Young 377t; Press Association Ltd: 31bl, 31br; Public Record Office (Crown Copyright): 20b.

Bill Rafferty: 342br; Rainforest cafe: 357cl; RBS Group: 366c, 366cb; Rex Features Ltd: 53tl; Peter Brooker 53tr; Andrew Laenen 54c; Jonathon Player 288cla; The Ritz, London: 91b; Royal Academy of Arts, London: 90tr; The Board of Trustees of The Royal Armouries: 41tr, 155tl, 157t, 157br; Royal Botanic Gardens, Kew: Andrew McRob 48cl, 56b, 260–61 all pics except 260t & 260br; Royal Collection, St James's Palace © HM The Queen: 8–9, 53b, 88t, 93t, 94–5 all pics except 94br & 95bl, 96t, 254br; Royal College of Music, London: 200c, 206c.

St Paul's Cathedral: Sampson Lloyd 148cl, 150cla, 151tr. The Savoy Group: 116cr, 274t, 274b; Science Museum, London: 212–13 all pics; Science Photo Library: Maptec International Ltd 12b; Society of London Theatre/tkts: 343br; Somerset House: Peter Durant/arcblue.com 117tr; Spencer House Ltd: 88b; Southbank Press Office: 186bl; Stephen Cummiskey 186cla; Graeme Duddridge 272cla; STA Travel Group: 364cb; Syndication International: 33bl, 37tr, 52cb, 53c, 58bl, 59t, 136; Library of Congress 27bl.

Tate London 2001: 12br, 41cr, 43br, 82–3 all pics, 84–5 all pics, 178–9 all pics, 180–81 all pics; 273br. Transport for London: 364br, 378br; 382bl, 383tl; Courtesy of the Board of Trustees of The Victoria and Albert Museum: 12cl, 37br, 40b, 201cl; 202–3 all pics, purchased with the assistance of the NACF and the Goldsmith's Company 203cra, 204–5 all pics, 254b, 358t; View Pictures: Dennis Gilbert 380br. The Waldorf, London: 272b; By kind permission of the trustees of The Wallace Collection, London: 40ca, 226cl; Philip Way Photography: 64lb, 150clb, 177b; Courtesy of the Trustees of the Wedgwood Museum, Barlaston, Stoke-on-Trent, Staffs, England: 28br; Vivienne Westwood: Patrick Fetherstonhaugh 33br; The Wimbledon Lawn Tennis Museum: Micky White 251t; Photo © Woodmansterne: Jeremy Marks 37tl, 149t; Gregory Wrona 267r. Youth Hostel Association: 277; Zefa: 12t, 52b, 342c; Bob Croxford 57t; Clive Sawyer 57b. Zwemmer Media: David Bennett 323bl. Front Endpaper: All special photography except John Heseltine: Left page tr, Right page tr.

Jacket: Front – Photolibrary: Flirt Collection/Paul Hardy. Back – Alamy Images: David Pearson cla, AWA Images: Travel Pix Collection bl, Dorling Kindersley: Rough Guides/Victor Borg clb, Matthew Ward tl. Spine –Photolibrary: Flirt Collection/Paul Hardy t.
Map Cover – Photolibrary: Flirt Collection/Paul Hardy.
All other images © Dorling Kindersley
For further information see www.DKimages.com

SPECIAL EDITIONS OF DK TRAVEL GUIDES

DK Travel Guides can be purchased in bulk quantities at discounted prices for use in promotions or as premiums. We are also able to offer special editions and personalized jackets, corporate imprints, and excerpts from all of our books, tailored specifically to meet your own needs.

To find out more, please contact:
(in the United States) **SpecialSales@dk.com**
(in the UK) **TravelSpecialSales@uk.dk.com**
(in Canada) DK Special Sales at **general@tourmaline.ca**
(in Australia)
business.development@pearson.com.au

The London Underground

MAYOR OF LONDON

Website
tfl.gov.uk

24 hour travel information
0843 222 1234*

Improvement works may affect y